Also by Madhur Jaffrey

An Invitation to Indian Cooking (1973)

THIS IS A BORZOI BOOK
PUBLISHED IN NEW YORK
BY ALFRED A. KNOPF, INC.

Madhur Jaffrey's
World-of-the-East
Vegetarian Cooking

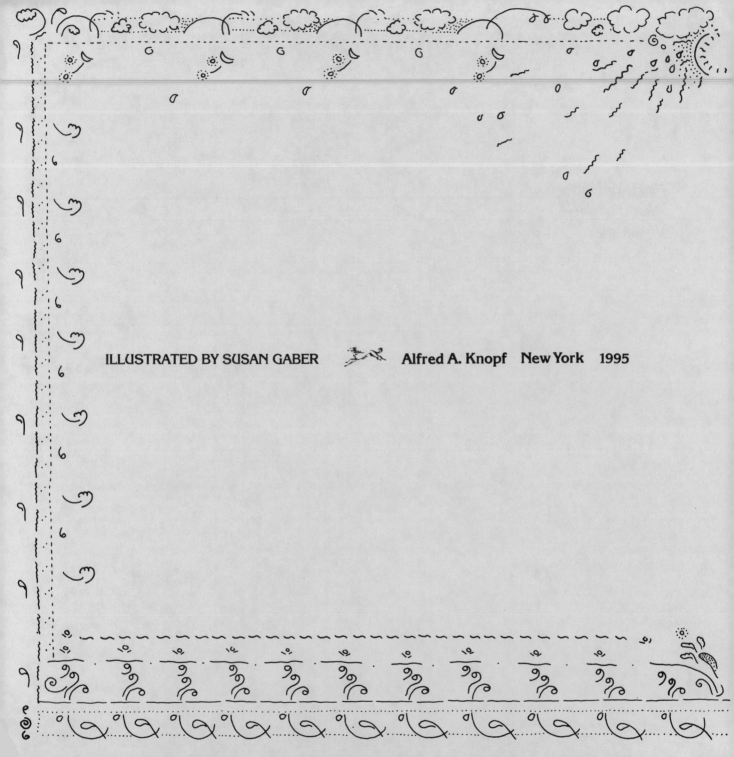

ILLUSTRATED BY SUSAN GABER   Alfred A. Knopf   New York   1995

Madhur Jaffrey's
World-of-the-East
Vegetarian Cooking

This is a Borzoi Book
Published by Alfred A. Knopf, Inc.

Copyright © 1981 Madhur Jaffrey
Illustrations Copyright © 1981 by Susan Gaber
All rights reserved under International and Pan-American
Copyright Conventions. Published in the United States by
Alfred A. Knopf, Inc., New York, and simultaneously in
Canada by Random House of Canada Limited, Toronto.
Distributed by Random House, Inc., New York.

Library of Congress Cataloging in Publication Data
Jaffrey, Madhur.
Madhur Jaffrey's World-of-the-East vegetarian
cookbook.
Includes index.
1. Cookery, Oriental.   I. Title.   II. Title:
World-of-the-East vegetarian cookbook.
TX724.5.A1J33   641.5'636   81-47517
ISBN 0-394-40271-5   AACR2
ISBN 0-394-74867-0

Manufactured in the United States of America
Published November 27, 1981
Reprinted Ten Times
Twelfth Printing, October 1995

To
the Hearty Eaters—
Sanford,
Zia, Meera, and Sakina
with
all my love

CONTENTS

ACKNOWLEDGMENTS

I would like to gratefully acknowledge the help given to me by the following—Devi Mangaldas, Neela Patel, Mrs. Patel, Pallavi Shah, Tatie Wawo-Runtu, Audrey Chan, Anne Loke, the management and staff of the Tawaraya Inn, Yien-koo King, the departments of tourism for Korea, Hong Kong, Japan, Thailand, Philippines, and Singapore, Sudha Doshi, Snighda Mukerji, Vijay Bhatt, Terb Xoomsai, Taw Kritakara, Mrs. Kalaya, the entire Roxas family, Glenda Barretto, Doreen Fernandez, Gary Jenanyan, Sandra Cahill, Mrs. Chawdhry, Usha Ismail, Maribel Lin and Ahtong, Mrs. Han, Jyothi Baswan, Jhab, Ismail, Zakiya Kurrien, Alun, Juji, Maya, Asha, K, Chub and Judith.

INTRODUCTION

Over the past decade, as my vegetarian friends and I have sat around nibbling on radishes smeared with sweet butter or dining more elegantly on asparagus soufflés, we have been elated at the thought of vegetarianism finally coming of age in this country. But with this elation, many vegetarian cooks have also expressed an awareness of the limitations of their repertoire.

I have lived in America for more than twenty years now. I grew up, however, in India where a majority of the population is vegetarian and where delicious vegetarian dishes are to be found under every proverbial bush. I found myself thinking back to the sweet-and-sour stuffed eggplants I had eaten in a royal Hyderabadi household, the crisp-soft split-pea and rice pancakes that are sold in every South Indian coffee shop, and the hot, spicy chickpeas offered as a Sunday treat by our Punjabi neighbor.

My thoughts jumped beyond India to other Asian countries that I have explored over the years. In Bali, I have sat barefoot on the verandah of a seaside villa and dined on the most magnificent greens that had been cooked very simply with a mound of shallots and a touch of garlic. In Korea, I have climbed the seemingly endless steps of a Buddhist temple to partake of a vegetarian feast that included mung-bean noodles, stir-fried with julienned zucchini, mushrooms, carrots, and cabbage. When our children were quite little, we all shared a Kuwaiti breakfast at which we were served, among other things, pita breads and freshly made yogurt cheese dressed with olive oil and paprika.

And what about *falafel*—the chickpea patties we consumed in Israel?

I decided then that I would go again to many of the Asian countries that I already knew to ferret out as many treasures as possible. I would taste them on their home grounds, bring them back and then try to recreate them in my New York kitchen.

As I began collecting my recipes, I was amazed to find that in Asia the most ordinary vegetables can be cooked in hundreds of different ways. I love vegetables. This probably dates back to my very early childhood and a time when my father grew just about everything from potatoes to eggplant on several acres that stretched out on one side of our house. It was a yearly ritual—poring over the seed catalogues, waiting for the seeds to arrive from Calcutta, and then waiting for the first seedlings to show themselves. Until I was twelve, I had never eaten a store-bought vegetable. I plucked the tomatoes straight off the vines and ate them with salt and pepper that I carried around with me for the purpose; I helped dig up the tiny new potatoes that we would sauté with cumin seeds; I cut the upstanding white heads of cauliflower that would later be cooked with potatoes, fennel, and fenugreek seeds; and I pulled up the beets that would be stewed with tomatoes.

Over the years, my passion for vegetables has stayed with me. I can get quite excited in Hong Kong when I am served a dish of crisp asparagus that is tinged with sesame oil or in Japan over a dish of cabbage seasoned with *umeboshi* plums.

The recipes for all these dishes are, of course, in this book.

If vegetables flesh out vegetarian meals and provide much of the minerals and vitamins, it is judicious combinations of dried beans, grains, and dairy products that provide much of the protein.

Nutritionists today are telling us that if we combine beans (such as soy or mung) with grains (such as wheat or rice) and a dairy product (such as yogurt) at the same meal, our protein needs for that meal are pretty much taken care of. Well, that is just what the vegetarians of India and China have been doing for over a thousand years. While an Indian might eat a cumin-flavored mung-bean dish with whole-wheat griddle breads and wash them both down with buttermilk, a Chinese might be dining on bean curd spiced up with garlic, scallions, and red pepper, some rice, and perhaps a Hot-and-Sour Soup which has egg in it. Indians make the most scrumptious pancakes out of bean batters, many of which they eat for breakfast so they may go to work well fortified. Another nourishing breakfast dish from South India is called Uppama. It is a kind of spicy pilaf, made out of semolina and filled with diced vegetables. It starts the day on a very perky note.

Spices and seasonings will do that. Perk things up, that is. They can also transform the same food so it tastes different from day to day. Potatoes taste one way when cooked with sesame seeds, another when stewed with soy sauce, and quite different when fried with mustard and cumin seeds.

Apart from giving variety to our foods, spices and seasonings in Asia have clearly defined (but not scientifically proven) attributes that are supposed to help the body in specific functions. Ginger, asafetida, and turmeric are all considered digestives and are therefore thrown into pots of beans or split peas to fight off their hard-to-digest stubbornness. Mint does the same thing. It also kills germs. Asafetida is also considered a nerve tonic. Cumin and green cardamom are cooling, so they are put into summer drinks. Clove and cinnamon are warming, so they are put into hot winter teas. Ginger teas are offered to those with a cold, while raw garlic is swallowed by thousands suffering from circulatory ailments and jangled nerves. Red chilies, in small doses, have an antiseptic action. Black pepper livens the appetite and acts as a tonic for new mothers . . . and so on. Asian herbalists have practiced their art for thousands of years and a lot of what Asians eat has a firm basis in their ancient herbalogy.

I have given a lot of attention to condiments, dips, chutneys, relishes, and pickles, most of which may either be prepared in advance, or may be put together very quickly at the last minute. One of the exciting aspects of Asian food is that at every home-cooked meal, you get what amounts to a multiple-choice meal. Let us say that you are serving that exquisite Chinese bread with scallions, Yow Bing. For one bite, you could dip it into my Chinese Dipping Sauce. For the next bite you might have it with Bean Curd with a Deliciously Spicy Sauce and a third bite might be with Hot-and-Sour Soup and the fourth with Ginger Quick-Pickled in Soy Sauce. Each bite will taste different, with the dips and relishes adding as much to the meal as the so-called main dishes. A dish of cauliflower may be sweetened, soured, or spiced, according to what relish we eat it with. Every meal becomes more of an adventure this way and every dish gets imbued with the possibilities of many added tastes.

How should meals be put together from this

book? Should you try to stick to dishes from one country at a time or is it all right to "mix and match"? Part of the fun of being an American cook is that you may, indeed, put together anything that strikes your fancy. A Korean soup served with a Japanese bean-curd dish and a Chinese stir-fried vegetable sounds wonderful to me. The Indian casserole of aromatic *basmati* rice, nutty *chana dal* (a split pea), and fresh dill would, I think, be quite happy sitting beside a Greek salad that has lettuce, feta cheese, and tomatoes in it. A Persian *kookoo* (egg pie) could easily be eaten with an Indian rice dish and an American carrot salad.

Most foods from Lebanon, Armenia, Israel, and Syria are so lightly seasoned with herbs quite recognizable in the West that there should be no trouble at all in incorporating them into Western meals. Foods from the Philippines, especially their dried beans and vegetables, are so close to Spanish food that you could easily pick up, say, Green Beans with Onion, Garlic, and Tomato, and serve it with scrambled eggs and French bread.

Use your judgment and put together what *you* think goes together. At the end of the book, I have a whole lot of menus, some traditional ones, others pleasant international mixes that also happen to make nutritional sense. Use them as a guide if you feel the need.

No special utensils are absolutely necessary for Asian cooking. It helps to have a wok but, for most recipes, a heavy skillet could be substituted. The grinding of spices, very important in Asia, is done on different types of grinding stones. These stones are heavy and unwieldy, particularly if you are not used to them. I find that an electric coffee grinder (or other spice grinder) works beautifully for dry ingredients, from sesame seeds to mustard seeds. For wet ingredients, a food processor or blender is essential. A great many Asian foods are steamed. Here again, you may buy cheap aluminum or bamboo steamers and set them up in a wok or on top of a large pot. Or else you can balance colanders on top of pots and improvise. Nonstick skillets seem to be *made* for Persian egg *kookoos* and for Indian pancakes. I find that they are useful utensils to have around and take the worry out of cooking tricky dishes.

Whether you are a confirmed vegetarian or a partial one, I think you will find much here to tempt you. As well as exciting new dishes to serve at mealtime, there are new ideas for snacks, treats for your children's lunchbox (or your own), cooling drinks, and cocktail nibbles. I hope this book will open up another world for you and that you will have as much fun with the recipes as I did.

Madhur Jaffrey's
World-of-the-East
Vegetarian Cooking

Vegetables

Once, when I had just finished a lecture in Springfield, Illinois, I was approached by a lady whose daughter had become a vegetarian. "What *do* vegetarians eat?" this lady asked me with a big, sad sigh; "lots of boiled vegetables, I suppose." Then she began listing "frozen broccoli, frozen beans . . ." feeling sorrier and sorrier for her daughter as she went along.

This chapter is part of my answer to that worried mother. Nobody needs to be sorry for anyone eating *these* vegetables. Some of the vegetables here are stir-fried and seasoned with ginger and Chinese *shaohsing* wine (dry sherry makes a good substitute), others are smothered with a spicy yogurt sauce, and still others are dipped in a chickpea flour batter and deep fried. All the vegetable dishes are different—and there are more than a hundred of them. The chapter starts with Stir-fried Asparagus, Flavored with Sesame Oil, a dish from Hong Kong, and moves slowly (and alphabetically) toward Zucchini "Meatballs," cooked in Indian style. After that follow recipes for mixed vegetables and batter-fried vegetables.

You will find some of the commonest vegetables here, cooked in uncommon ways: green beans, for example, are cooked with garlic and red pepper; cabbage is cooked with tomatoes in mustard oil; peas are cooked with fresh ginger; and potatoes are cooked with garlic and sesame seeds. There are a great many recipes for eggplant. From Japan, I have a recipe in which eggplant slices are smeared with fermented bean paste—*miso*—and then broiled. From a royal Indian household, I have sneaked out a recipe for tiny eggplants stuffed with a hot, sweet, and sour paste that includes sesame seeds and tamarind. And from Turkey I have a recipe for fried eggplant slices served with a garlic-flavored yogurt sauce.

I have many recipes for potatoes as well. I love potatoes. If properly cooked, they can be so very good. From Nepal, I have a cold potato salad with a sesame seed, lemon, oil, and green chili dressing. Then from western India I have a stew that combines potatoes, tomatoes, and fresh coconut. I can taste it even as I am writing about it. It is wonderful. In Bali, I was served one of the tastiest hot, sweet, and sour dishes of shoestring potatoes. You will find that in this chapter as well.

There are some recipes here where the main vegetable might be unfamiliar to you. For example, there are a few dishes using lotus roots, bitter melon, kohlrabi, long beans, and a kind of cabbage that is called *choy sum* in Cantonese. Unless you live in a large metropolitan area or in a town with Oriental grocery stores, you may not have access to these vegetables. On the other hand, you may be able to grow them at home. Lotus root tastes a bit like artichoke heart, only it is crunchier in its texture. Bitter melon is a squash. It *is* bitter. Asians like its taste and also believe that it helps cleanse the blood. Kohlrabi tastes like broccoli stems, and is excellent both raw and cooked. Long beans (sometimes called asparagus beans) are about a foot long. They taste like regular green beans, only their flavor is a bit more intense. *Choy sum* tastes like a cross between tender collard greens and cabbage. Once you discover this vegetable, you will not want to give it up.

There is a recipe for collard greens as well. It comes from Kashmir, India's most northern state. The greens are cooked very simply in mustard oil with a touch of asafetida. Even the liquid left at the bottom of the pot is irresistible. Kashmiris usually mop it up with their rice.

The use of different oils can make such a difference to a dish. In China and Korea, a dash of sesame oil is often dribbled over stir-fried vegetables. This enriches them, just as a dollop of butter might, and gives them a nutty flavor as well. In some parts of India, vegetables are cooked in mustard oil. This fiery, pungent oil turns sweet and docile when it is heated. It envelops vegetables in a gentle warmth.

Each Asian country has its own way of adding seasonings to vegetables. In China, one of the techniques used is to keep a mixture of soy sauce, wine, sugar, cornstarch, and stock handy, which is poured over the vegetables once they have been stir-fried. Then they are seasoned and a sauce is created, all in one step. In Indonesia, shallots, garlic, red peppers, and salt are first pounded into a paste. This paste is fried before vegetables are added. In India, hot oil is "seasoned" first with whole spices, such as cumin seeds, fennel seeds, and mustard seeds. The oil, now perfumed with the smell of fried spices, proceeds to perfume any vegetables that are sautéed in it. Hundreds of such techniques are used throughout the length and breadth of Asia. You will find quite a few of them in this chapter.

It goes without saying that you should always use vegetables that are fresh, crisp, and in their prime. If the tomatoes you buy have no color, leave them unrefrigerated until they turn red. I rarely use frozen vegetables. Peas and okra might well be the exceptions. But then, I do live in an area where good vegetables are constantly available. Buy whatever seems freshest in your grocery stores. Beets, carrots, broccoli, and beans can all be cooked in such interesting ways. Whenever you begin to wonder what new thing you could do with some ordinary vegetable—such as cabbage—consult this chapter as well as the index to this book.

STIR-FRIED ASPARAGUS FLAVORED WITH SESAME OIL

HONG KONG

(serves 4–6)

2 ½ pounds fresh green asparagus (about 5 cups trimmed)
3 tablespoons vegetable oil
½ teaspoon salt
1 ½ tablespoons sesame oil

Trim away the woody bottom section of the asparagus and wash it. Peel the lower 2 to 3 inches of each spear with a potato peeler. Cut each spear into 1-inch lengths. Put the spears into a bowl of cold water for half an hour. (This is not essential but it crisps up the asparagus nicely.) Drain.

Heat the vegetable oil in a 10- to 12-inch skillet over a medium-high flame. When hot, put in the drained asparagus. Stir and fry for about 30 to 40 seconds. The asparagus should be coated with oil. Add the salt and stir. Add ¼ cup water and bring to a fast simmer. Cover, turn heat to medium-low, and cook gently for 2 to 4 minutes or until asparagus is cooked through but still crisp and bright green. (This will vary according to the thickness of the asparagus.) Remove lid. Turn heat to high and quickly boil away any extra water, if there is any, stirring asparagus gently all the time. Add the sesame oil. Mix gently and turn off heat. Serve at once.

Yien-koo's GREEN BEANS WITH GARLIC AND RED PEPPER

CHINA

(serves 6)

1 ½ pounds fresh green beans
2 cups vegetable oil
6 to 8 cloves garlic, peeled and minced
1 dried hot red pepper, coarsely crumbled
1 tablespoon Chinese thin soy sauce
¼ teaspoon salt
¼ teaspoon sugar

Trim the beans and cut them into 1 ½-inch lengths. Make sure that the beans are quite dry. If necessary, rub them with a dish towel.

Heat the oil in a wok over a medium-high flame. When smoking hot, put in all the beans and turn the heat to high. Fry the beans, stirring now and then, for 1 to 2 minutes or until the skins just begin to crinkle but the beans are still crisp and bright green. Take out all the beans with a slotted spoon and put them in a colander that is resting in a large bowl. Turn off the heat under the wok.

Remove all but 4 tablespoons oil from the wok. Alternatively, you could use a fresh 10- to 12-inch skillet and spoon 4 tablespoons of oil into it. Heat on a medium flame. When hot, put in the garlic and the red pepper. Stir and fry until the garlic turns a light to medium brown color. Put in the beans and stir once. Now put in the soy sauce, salt, and sugar. Stir again to mix. Serve immediately.

For information about ingredients and basic techniques that may be unfamiliar, see General Information, pages 418–36.

GREEN BEANS WITH SESAME PASTE AND GARLIC

INDIA

(serves 6–8)

2½ pounds fresh green beans
1   tablespoon plus ½ to ¾ teaspoon salt
6   tablespoons vegetable oil
2   teaspoons black mustard seeds
8 to 9 medium-sized cloves of garlic, peeled and very finely minced
A 1-inch cube of fresh ginger, peeled and finely grated
3   tablespoons ground roasted sesame seeds
4   tablespoons well chopped fresh Chinese parsley
⅛   teaspoon freshly ground black pepper
¹⁄₁₆ teaspoon cayenne pepper
1   tablespoon lemon juice

Trim the beans and cut them into 1-inch pieces. Put about 4 quarts of water in a 5-quart pot. Add 1 tablespoon salt and bring to a rolling boil. Put the beans in and boil over high heat 4 to 5 minutes or until they are tender but still crisp. Empty the beans into a colander and run cold water over them to fix the bright green color. Drain.

Shortly before you sit down to eat, heat the oil in a 10- to 12-inch skillet over a medium flame. When the oil is very hot, put in the mustard seeds. As soon as the mustard seeds begin to pop (this will take just a few seconds), add the garlic and stir. As soon as the garlic browns lightly, add the ginger and stir once. Now put in the drained beans, the ground roasted sesame seeds, Chinese parsley, black pepper, cayenne pepper, lemon juice, and ½ to ¾ teaspoon salt. Turn heat to low and mix well. Taste for seasonings. When the beans are heated through, turn off the heat and serve.

Sandra's

GREEN BEANS WITH ONION, GARLIC, AND TOMATO

PHILIPPINES

The Philippines have been influenced by the Chinese, the Portuguese, and the Spanish, to say nothing of the Americans. This simple but delicious recipe from that country hints at Mediterranean roots.

(serves 6)

1½ pounds fresh green beans
2   medium-sized onions, peeled
2   medium-sized cloves of garlic, peeled
1   pound red-ripe tomatoes (or 7 to 8 canned Italian plum tomatoes)
4   tablespoons vegetable oil
1½ to 2 teaspoons salt
Freshly ground black pepper

Trim the beans and cut them into 1-inch pieces. Cut the onions in half, lengthwise, and then cut them crosswise into fine slices. Mince the garlic very fine. Drop the tomatoes into boiling water for 15 seconds. Remove with a slotted spoon, rinse in cold water, and peel. Chop tomatoes into ½-inch dice. (If you are using canned tomatoes, drain and chop them.)

Heat the oil in an 8- to 9-inch-wide pot over a medium-low flame. When hot, put in the minced garlic and stir-fry for about 30 seconds. Add the onions. Stir-fry for another 2 to 3 minutes or until onions begin to turn translucent. (Do not let the onions take on any color.) Now put in the tomatoes, beans, salt (start with 1½ teaspoons), some freshly ground black pepper, and ½ cup water. Bring to a boil. Cover, lower heat and simmer gently 15 to 20 minutes or until beans are cooked.

For information about ingredients and basic techniques that may be unfamiliar, see General Information, pages 418–36.

GREEN BEANS WITH FRESH COCONUT AND SESAME SEEDS

INDIA

(serves 4)

½ cup freshly grated coconut
¼ cup finely minced Chinese (or other) parsley
A generous pinch of crushed asafetida
½ to 1 fresh hot green chili, minced
½ teaspoon plus 1 tablespoon salt
1 pound fresh green beans, trimmed and cut into
    1-inch lengths
6 tablespoons *ghee* or vegetable oil
2 tablespoons sesame seeds
1 tablespoon whole black mustard seeds
⅛ to ¼ teaspoon cayenne pepper (optional)

Combine the coconut, Chinese parsley, asafetida, green chili, and ¼ teaspoon salt in a bowl. Rub mixture well with your hands. Set aside.

Add 1 tablespoon salt to 2½ quarts of water and bring to a boil in a large pot. Add the cut beans. Boil rapidly for 3 to 4 minutes or until beans are tender but still bright green and crisp. Drain in a colander and refresh by moving the colander under cold running water. Set aside.

Heat *ghee* or oil in a 10- to 12-inch-wide sauté pan or heavy pot over a medium flame. When hot, put in the sesame and mustard seeds. As soon as the mustard seeds begin to pop (this will happen within a few seconds), add the cayenne pepper. Stir once and add the beans. Sauté the beans over medium-low heat for 1 to 2 minutes or until they are heated through and well coated with the seeds. Add ¼ teaspoon salt and stir. Now add the coconut-parsley mixture, stir once, and remove from heat. Serve immediately.

Remove lid. Turn up heat and reduce liquid in the pot by about three-quarters. Stir the beans gently a few times as you do so. Taste for salt.

GREEN BEANS WITH SOY SAUCE

JAPAN

(serves 6)

1½ pounds fresh green beans
2 tablespoons Japanese soy sauce
2 tablespoons *mirin*
¼ teaspoon salt
¼ teaspoon sugar
1 tablespoon lemon juice
1/16 teaspoon 7-spice seasoning

Trim the beans and cut into 2-inch lengths. In a 5-quart pot, bring about 3¾ quarts water to a boil. Add the beans and bring to a second boil. Boil rapidly 4 to 5 minutes or until beans are just tender but still crunchy. Drain immediately in colander. Run cold water over the beans to fix their bright green color. Drain well. Put beans in a bowl. Add the soy sauce, *mirin*, salt, sugar, lemon juice, and the 7-spice seasoning. Toss well.

GREEN BEANS AND PEAS WITH GINGER

INDIA

Here is a quick and delicious way to prepare a combination of green beans and peas. You could substitute carrots, peeled and diced into ¼-inch cubes, for any one of the green vegetables. I find it very interesting that this dish, cooked in the western region of India, should be so similar to another dish, Peas with Ginger (see page 47), cooked thousands of miles away in Japan. These beans are also excellent cold and may be served as a "salad" course at a Western meal.

(serves 4)

2   tablespoons vegetable oil
½   teaspoon salt
1   pound fresh green beans, trimmed and cut into ¼-inch rounds
1½ cups shelled peas, fresh or frozen
1   teaspoon sugar
3   tablespoons minced Chinese parsley
1   tablespoon finely grated fresh ginger
½   fresh hot green chili, minced (optional)

Put 1 cup water, the oil, and salt in a 10-inch skillet or sauté pan. Bring to a boil. Add the cut beans (there should be about 2 cups) and peas—if using frozen, thaw quickly by running hot water over them. Bring to a boil again. Cover, and simmer on a medium-low flame for about 5 minutes or until vegetables are cooked. Arrange your heat so that there are 2 to 3 tablespoons of water left at the bottom of the skillet at the end of this cooking period. Now add the sugar, the Chinese parsley, the ginger, and green chili. Cook for about half a minute on a medium flame with the cover off,

stirring as you do so. You should boil away the remaining water. Serve immediately.

It is best to make this dish just before you eat it, but if you do want to make it ahead of time, leave a tablespoon or so of water in the skillet to enable you to reheat it. And do not cover it after the initial 5-minute cooking period or the vegetables will discolor. You could serve this dish with almost any Indian meal. Leftovers, once they have completely cooled, may be refrigerated in a closed plastic container.

Zakiya's

GREEN BEANS COOKED WITH MUSTARD SEEDS AND RED PEPPER

INDIA

(serves 6)

1½ pounds fresh green beans*
5   tablespoons vegetable oil
A pinch of ground asafetida
1   teaspoon whole black mustard seeds
1   teaspoon whole cumin seeds
2   teaspoons *urad dal*
1 to 2 whole dried hot red peppers
⅛ to ¼ teaspoon cayenne pepper
1¼ to 1½ teaspoons salt
¼   cup freshly grated coconut

*NOTE: Long beans found in Chinese and Indian grocery stores may be used instead.

For information about ingredients and basic techniques that may be unfamiliar, see General Information, pages 418–36.

Trim the beans and cut them into ¼-inch rounds. Put them in a bowl, add 6 cups of water, and let the beans "refresh" for 20 minutes. Drain.

Heat the oil in a 10-inch skillet or sauté pan over a medium flame. When hot, put in first the asafetida, then, a second later, the mustard seeds, cumin seeds, and *urad dal*. Stir once and put in the red peppers and cayenne pepper. Stir once again and put in the drained beans and salt. Turn heat down a bit and mix beans with the spices. Now cover, turn heat to low and simmer gently 6 to 7 minutes. Remove cover and turn heat up a bit. Stir and sauté beans 3 to 4 minutes or until *all* liquid has evaporated. The beans should have a *very* dry look. Add the coconut, stir, and turn off heat.

GREEN BELL PEPPERS COOKED WITH CHICKPEA FLOUR

INDIA

In this dish, tiny lumps of cooked chickpea flour cling to diced, sautéed green peppers just as bits of bread stuffing might cling to pieces of onion or celery. The use of chickpea flour makes the dish a bit more substantial and a bit more nutritious.

(serves 4–6)

⅓ cup chickpea flour
3 large green bell peppers
5 tablespoons vegetable oil
⅛ teaspoon ground asafetida
¹⁄₁₆ to ⅛ teaspoon cayenne pepper
1 teaspoon whole black mustard seeds
1 teaspoon salt
1 tablespoon finely minced Chinese parsley
¹⁄₁₆ teaspoon freshly ground black pepper

Sift the chickpea flour. Place the flour in a small, heavy, preferably cast-iron skillet, and roast it on a medium flame, stirring constantly, until it turns a few shades darker. A good way to check if it is done is to taste a pinch of it. It should not taste raw. It will also have developed a "roasted" aroma. Empty the chickpea flour in a bowl and set it aside.

Cut peppers in half, then core and seed them. Chop into ¼- to ⅓-inch dice.

Heat the oil in an 8-inch (preferably nonstick) skillet or sauté pan over a medium flame. When it is hot, put in first the asafetida and then, a second later, the cayenne pepper. Stir once. Add the mustard seeds. As soon as the mustard seeds begin to pop, put in the diced peppers. Stir and sauté them over a medium-high flame for about 5 minutes or until they are just cooked. Now turn heat to medium and put in the salt, the Chinese parsley, the black pepper, and the roasted chickpea flour. Stir a few times. Gradually add ⅓ cup water, stirring gently and scraping off all the chickpea flour that clings to the bottom of the pan. Cook for 2 minutes, stirring and scraping the bottom. Turn down the heat if the chickpea flour seems to be catching. Now turn off the heat. Let the pan sit for a minute. Stir and scrape the bottom once again.

STEWED BEETS WITH TOMATOES

INDIA

Because this is a "wet" dish, it's best to serve it in small, individual bowls, such as Indian *katoris*.

(serves 6)

1½ pounds red-ripe tomatoes
2 pounds beets (weight without leaves)
3 tablespoons vegetable oil
1/16 teaspoon ground asafetida
1 teaspoon whole cumin seeds
1 whole dried hot red pepper
1 teaspoon ground turmeric
1 teaspoon salt

Drop the tomatoes into boiling water for 15 seconds. Then peel, mince, and put them in a bowl.

Peel the beets and cut them into ¾-inch dice.

Heat the oil in a 3½-quart stainless-steel pot over a medium-high flame. When hot, put in the asafetida. Two seconds later, put in the cumin and the red pepper. Stir once and add the turmeric. Stir once again and put in the tomatoes. Cover the pot immediately and keep it covered until all the loud sizzling noises subside. Add the beets and the salt. Bring to a simmer. Cover, lower heat and simmer gently for 1 hour or until beets are tender.

STIR-FRIED BITTER MELON

INDIA

Bitter melon is eaten all across southern and eastern Asia and is credited with preventing everything from cancer to cholesterol-related diseases. Bitter foods, Asians believe, cleanse the blood. Whether such theories would survive scientific scrutiny, I cannot say. I grew up with bitter melons and love their taste. But I know that it is not easy for most Americans to eat them. So I am providing just three simple recipes: this one from India and the one that follows from the Philippines, and Pinakbet (see page 30), also from the Philippines.

(serves 6)

1¼ pounds bitter melons
2 tablespoons plus ¾ teaspoon salt
3 medium-sized onions
5 tablespoons vegetable oil
2½ teaspoons *panchphoran*
⅛ to ¼ teaspoon cayenne pepper

Trim away the two pointed ends of the bitter melons and then cut them in half lengthwise. Remove the pale, seeded section with a grapefruit spoon and discard it. Now cut the outer shells crosswise, at a slight diagonal, into ¼-inch-wide strips. Prepare a solution of 2 tablespoons salt and 4 cups water in a bowl. Put in the bitter-melon strips and soak for 2 hours. Drain. Rinse the strips under a faucet. Drain and pat dry.

Peel the onions, cut in half lengthwise, then slice into fine half rings.

Heat the oil in a 9-inch skillet over a medium flame. When hot, put in the *panchphoran*. Stir and

---

For information about ingredients and basic techniques that may be unfamiliar, see General Information, pages 418–36.

cook for 10 seconds. Put in the onions. Stir and fry for 2 minutes. Add the bitter-melon strips, the ¾ teaspoon salt, and the cayenne. Stir and fry for 10 to 12 minutes or until the bitter melon is tender. If the onion pieces and parts of the bitter melon turn a bit brown, that is all for the good.

Mrs. Roxas'
BITTER MELON WITH EGGS
PHILIPPINES

Please read the opening remarks in the preceding recipe. For those unfamiliar with the taste of bitter melons, this dish may well serve as the best introduction. The bitter taste of this unusual vegetable does not go away here—its aficionados would have a fit if it did—but it is modified somewhat by the tomatoes, onions, and eggs.

(serves 4–6)

½ pound bitter melon (1 large or 2 small)
1 tablespoon plus ⅛ teaspoon salt
1 scallion
2 medium-sized onions
4 tablespoons vegetable oil
6 cloves of garlic, peeled and minced
3 small tomatoes, peeled and chopped
3 large eggs, lightly beaten

Trim away the two pointed ends of the bitter melons and cut them in half lengthwise. Remove the

pale, seeded section with a grapefruit spoon and discard it. Cut the darker green outer shells crosswise, at a slight diagonal, into ¼-inch-wide strips. Prepare a solution of 2 cups water and 1 tablespoon salt in a bowl. Put the bitter-melon strips into this bowl and set aside for 2 hours.

Drain the bitter melon and rinse the strips under running water. Drain again and pat dry.

Cut the scallion into 2-inch lengths and then cut each section lengthwise into thin strips. Peel the onions and cut them in half lengthwise; then slice them into fine half rings.

Heat the oil in a well-seasoned or nonstick 8-inch-wide skillet over a medium flame. When hot, put in the garlic. Stir and fry until the garlic pieces start to brown. Add the onions. Stir and fry for about 2 minutes. Add the tomatoes. Stir and fry another 2 minutes. Now put in the bitter melon. Turn down the heat. Stir occasionally and fry for about 10 minutes or until bitter melon is tender. Stir in the beaten eggs and the ⅛ teaspoon salt. Stir and cook as you would scrambled eggs until the eggs have reached a consistency you like. Take off the heat, quickly fold in the scallion strips, and serve.

BRUSSELS SPROUTS STIR-FRIED WITH DRIED CHINESE MUSHROOMS

CHINA

(serves 4)

8 large Chinese dried black mushrooms
¾ pound Brussels sprouts, trimmed and washed
3 tablespoons peanut oil
1 teaspoon finely minced garlic
3 tablespoons *shaohsing* wine or dry sherry
½ teaspoon salt
¾ teaspoon sugar

Soak the mushrooms (if you have small ones, use more than 8) in ½ cup water for 1 hour.

Remove mushrooms from their soaking liquid. (Do not discard this liquid. Save 3 tablespoons of it in such a way that you leave the grit behind. Put the 3 tablespoons in a small cup.) Cut off the coarse stems. Now cut the mushroom caps into 4 quarters. (If the mushrooms are small, cut the caps in half.)

Quarter the Brussels sprouts lengthwise. Very small sprouts may be cut in half.

Heat the oil in a wok over medium-high heat. When hot, put in the minced garlic. Stir and fry for 4 to 5 seconds or until garlic turns a light brown. Quickly add the mushrooms and Brussels sprouts. Stir-fry for about 20 seconds. Now add the wine, salt, and sugar and stir-fry another 20 seconds. Add the 3 reserved tablespoons of the mushroom-soaking liquid and cover the wok immediately. Turn heat to low and simmer 5 minutes or until sprouts are just cooked.

CABBAGE WITH CARROT AND SCALLIONS

CHINA

This dish is generally eaten hot; however, it is very good cold, too. If you want to have it that way, spread it out on a platter as soon as it is cooked and let it cool off. Then put it into a covered container and refrigerate.

(serves 6)

1¾ pounds cabbage (½ medium-sized head)
1 carrot
3 scallions
¼ cup vegetable oil
2 quarter-sized slices of fresh ginger, lightly mashed
1¼ teaspoons salt
2 tablespoons *shaohsing* wine or dry sherry

Remove the coarse outer leaves of the cabbage as well as its hard core. Now cut the cabbage evenly into long, ⅛-inch-wide strips.

Peel the carrot and cut it crosswise, at a slight diagonal, into ⅛-inch-thick ovals. Cut the ovals, a few at a time, into ⅛-inch-wide julienne strips.

Cut the scallions into 2½-inch lengths. With a sharp pointed knife, cut these sections *lengthwise* into thin strips.

Heat the oil in a wok or large skillet over a medium flame. When hot, put in the ginger. Stir and fry for about 20 seconds. Put in all the vegetables and the salt. Stir and fry for about 3 minutes. Add the wine, cover, and cook for about 4 minutes or until the cabbage is tender enough to eat but still retains some of its crispness. Uncover, turn heat to high. Stir and cook for 1 minute. Remove ginger before serving.

For information about ingredients and basic techniques that may be unfamiliar, see General Information, pages 418–36.

CABBAGE SEASONED WITH UMEBOSHI PLUMS

JAPAN

Umeboshi plums, small and exceedingly sour, come pickled in salt. The Japanese often eat them, one per person, for breakfast just as Americans drink orange juice, which is the way I had them for the first time in Japan. But the same plums can also be used as a seasoning, and that is how I have used them in this recipe. They add a wonderful tartness to the dish. *Umeboshi* plums are available in most health-food and Japanese stores.

(serves 4)

½ medium-sized head of cabbage
About 4 *umeboshi* plums (to make 2½ teaspoons
    pulp)
2½ tablespoons vegetable oil
¼ to ½ teaspoon salt
¼ teaspoon sugar

Core the cabbage and cut
it into long, thin slivers.
Remove the pits from the
plums. Pound the flesh in a
Japanese *suribachi* or mortar
until you have a paste.
   Heat the oil in a skillet over a
medium flame. Put in the cabbage and salt.
Stir and fry for 3 to 4 minutes or until the cabbage
has wilted and is just cooked. Add the sugar and
plum paste. Stir and mix.

SHREDDED CABBAGE WITH MUSTARD SEEDS AND FRESH COCONUT

INDIA

In this quick-cooking recipe from Bengal, the cabbage stays green and crunchy. It is flavored very delicately with the mustard oil in which it is cooked, and with mustard seeds, bay leaves, and freshly grated coconut.

(serves 6)

6 tablespoons mustard oil
1 teaspoon whole black mustard seeds
2 bay leaves
3 to 3½ pounds cabbage, cored and finely shred-
    ded (1 medium-sized head)
¾ to 1 teaspoon salt
½ teaspoon sugar
1 fresh hot green chili, cut into fine, long strips
⅓ cup freshly grated coconut

Heat the oil in a heavy, wide, casserole-type pot over a medium-high flame. When hot, put in the mustard seeds and bay leaves. As soon as the bay leaves darken a bit and the mustard seeds begin to pop (this just takes a few seconds), put in the shredded cabbage. Turn heat to medium. Stir and cook for about 5 minutes. Add the salt, sugar, and the green chili strips. Stir and cook another 3 to 5 minutes. Cabbage should be bright green and slightly wilted, though still crunchy. Turn off heat. Sprinkle with coconut, mix well, and serve.

CABBAGE WITH YOGURT

INDIA

Here, as in many South Indian foods, a dried split pea—*urad dal*—is used as a seasoning. The dish is served warm, although I like it cold as well.

(serves 4)

1¾ pounds cabbage (½ medium-sized head)
¼ cup vegetable oil
3 tablespoons whole black mustard seeds
2 teaspoons *urad dal*, picked over
⅛ to ¼ teaspoon cayenne pepper
2 teaspoons ground coriander
1 medium-sized onion, peeled, cut in half lengthwise, then into ¼-inch half rings
1½ teaspoons salt
⅓ to ½ cup freshly grated coconut
1 cup plain yogurt

Remove the coarse outer leaves of the cabbage as well as its hard core. Now cut the cabbage evenly into ⅛-inch-wide strips.

Heat the oil in a wok or a large sauté pan over a medium flame. When hot, put in the mustard seeds and *urad dal*. As soon as the mustard seeds begin to pop—this just takes a few seconds—put in the cayenne and the coriander. Stir once and quickly put in the cabbage and onion. Stir for 1 minute. Add the salt. Stir to mix. Cover, lower heat and cook about 5 to 8 minutes or until cabbage is just tender. Add the coconut and mix. Keep warm.

Put the yogurt in the top of a double boiler and beat until creamy. Heat. Stir continuously in one direction as it warms through. Do *not* let it get hot.

Put the cabbage into a warmed serving bowl. Add the yogurt and fold it in.

For information about ingredients and basic techniques that may be unfamiliar, see General Information, pages 418–36.

Sheila's

CABBAGE AND TOMATOES COOKED IN MUSTARD OIL

INDIA

(serves 4–6)

1 pound cabbage (½ small head)
5 small Italian plum or 2 medium-sized tomatoes, peeled
6 tablespoons mustard oil
A generous pinch of ground asafetida
1 teaspoon ground cumin seeds
½ teaspoon whole black (or other) cumin seeds
1 to 1½ teaspoons salt
⅛ to ¼ teaspoon cayenne pepper

Core the cabbage and cut the leaves into 1-inch squares.

Cut the tomatoes into ¼-inch dice.

Heat the oil in a deep 9- to 10-inch skillet or sauté pan over a medium-high flame. When hot, put in the asafetida. One second later, put in the tomatoes. Stir and fry for about 1 minute and then put in the ground cumin, black cumin, salt, and cayenne. Stir for another minute. Put in the cabbage and stir to mix. Cover, turn heat to low, and let the cabbage cook 12 to 15 minutes until it is just done.

CABBAGE WITH MISO

JAPAN

(serves 4–6)

4 cups finely shredded cabbage
1½ tablespoons red *miso*
1 tablespoon rice vinegar
½ teaspoon salt
½ teaspoon sugar
⅛ teaspoon 7-spice seasoning

Bring 3 quarts of water to a boil in a 4-quart pot. Drop in the cabbage and boil for a minute. Drain in a colander, squeezing all the water out of the cabbage. Put cabbage in a bowl. Add the *miso*, vinegar, salt, and sugar. Mix well.

Either make small mounds and serve in individual Oriental dishes or make a large mound in the center of a single large serving bowl. Dust with the 7-spice seasoning. Serve warm, either as a first course or as a salad.

CARROTS IN BATTER

KOREA

This is a quick, wonderful way to cook carrot slices. It makes them delicately crunchy on the outside while keeping them sweet and tender inside. The dish should be eaten as soon as it is made. Have all the ingredients ready. The frying takes just a few minutes and can be done right at the end. The cooked carrots are usually eaten with a dipping sauce. Incidentally, you may cook sweet potatoes the same way.

(serves 2–4)

2 medium-sized carrots
¼ cup unbleached, all-purpose white flour
1 large egg
⅛ teaspoon salt
Vegetable oil for shallow frying
Dipping sauce: Any one of the five Korean Dipping
 Sauces on pages 358 to 359

Peel the carrots. Cut them crosswise at a slight diagonal so that you get ovals that are ⅓-inch thick. (If you are not frying the carrots immediately, put them into a plastic bag and refrigerate them.)

Spread the flour out on a plate.

Break the egg into a shallow bowl. Add the salt and beat it.

Put ¼ inch oil in an 8-inch skillet and heat over a medium-low flame until it reaches a temperature of 350° to 375° F.

Dip the carrot pieces in the flour so that they are well coated on all sides. Now, working fairly quickly, dip one carrot piece at a time into the beaten egg and then put it into the oil. Make sure that all the carrot pieces lie in a single layer in the skillet. Fry until the slices turn golden brown on one side. Turn them over and fry the second side until it, too, is golden brown. Remove the carrot slices with a slotted spoon, drain briefly on paper towels, and serve immediately.

CARROTS WITH RAISINS AND DATES

IRAN

(serves 4)

5   medium-sized carrots
1   medium-sized onion, peeled
4   tablespoons unsalted butter
¼   cup raisins
¼   cup pitted dates, cut into ¼-inch-thick slivers
⅓ to ½ teaspoon salt
¼   teaspoon sugar

Peel the carrots and slice, slightly diagonally, into ¼-inch-thick ovals.

Cut the onion in half lengthwise, and then cut the halves crosswise into ¼-inch-thick half rings.

Melt the butter in an 8-inch skillet over a medium-low flame. Turn the heat to medium and put in the carrots, onion, raisins, and dates. Stir and fry gently for 5 minutes. Add the salt and sugar. Stir and fry for another 4 to 5 minutes or until carrots are just tender and onion is soft.

CARROTS COOKED IN DASHI

JAPAN

(serves 2–4)

2   medium-sized carrots
½   cup *dashi* (see page 291)
½   teaspoon salt
2   teaspoons sugar

Peel the carrots and cut them into ¼-inch-thick slices. Put the carrots and *dashi* into a small pot and bring to a simmer. Cover, lower heat and simmer gently for 4 to 5 minutes or until the carrots are just tender. Remove cover, add salt and sugar, and turn the heat up a bit. Cook until almost all the liquid has been absorbed. (The little remaining liquid may be used to reheat the carrots, if necessary.)

CAULIFLOWER IN A CASHEW AND SESAME SEED SAUCE

INDIA

(serves 6)

2¾ to 3 pounds cauliflower (1 medium-sized head)
½   cup freshly grated coconut
2   tablespoons sesame seeds
5   tablespoons vegetable oil
½   cup raw cashews
1   fresh hot green chili, sliced into rounds, or ⅛ to ¼ teaspoon cayenne pepper
1   teaspoon black mustard seeds
1   teaspoon salt
1   teaspoon sugar
1   tablespoon lemon juice

Cut cauliflower flowerets in such a way that no piece is longer than 1½ inches and no wider at the head than ¾ inch. Longer stems, if tender, may be peeled and sliced into rounds.

Put the coconut into a small heated cast-iron skillet over a medium flame. Dry-roast the coconut, stirring frequently until lightly browned, then empty into a bowl.

For information about ingredients and basic techniques that may be unfamiliar, see General Information, pages 418–36.

Put sesame seeds into the same skillet and roast, shaking the skillet frequently over a medium flame, until sesame seeds are lightly browned. Empty into bowl with coconut.

Heat 1 tablespoon oil in the same skillet over a medium flame. Add the cashews. Fry, stirring, until cashews turn a light brown. Remove with a slotted spoon and put them with the coconut and sesame seeds. Turn off heat.

Empty contents of bowl into the container of an electric blender or a food processor. Add ⅔ cup water and the sliced green chili. Blend until you have a smooth paste.

Heat 4 tablespoons of oil in a large, heavy skillet over a medium-high flame. When very hot, add the mustard seeds. As soon as they begin to pop (this will happen almost immediately), put in the cauliflower. Stir the cauliflower around on medium heat for 3 to 4 minutes: some of the flowerets should pick up a few brown specks. Now add the paste from the blender, 1¼ cups water, the salt, sugar, and lemon juice. Stir to mix. Bring to a boil. Cover. Lower heat and simmer gently about 10 to 15 minutes or until cauliflower is cooked through but still a bit crisp. Stir now and then during the cooking.

CAULIFLOWER WITH ALMONDS AND LIMA BEANS

CHINA

(serves 4)

1¾ pounds cauliflower (1 smallish head)
1 cup shelled large lima beans, fresh or frozen
1½ teaspoons cornstarch
1 tablespoon *shaohsing* wine or dry sherry
2 teaspoons sesame oil
¼ cup vegetable oil
½ cup whole blanched almonds
2 cloves garlic, peeled and mashed lightly
2 quarter-sized slices of fresh ginger,
    lightly mashed
1¼ teaspoons salt

Cut the cauliflower into very slim flowerets that are about 2 inches long, 1 inch wide at the head, and ¼-inch thick. You should end up with about 4 heaping cups. Leave them to soak in a bowl of cold water for half an hour. (This crisps them up nicely.) Bring 4 cups of water in a pot to a rapid boil, then drop in the lima beans. Boil rapidly for about 5 minutes or until the beans are just barely tender. Drain.

Mix together the cornstarch, wine, sesame oil, and 2 tablespoons water in a cup. Heat the oil in a wok or skillet over medium heat. When it is hot, put in the almonds. Stir and fry until the almonds are golden brown. Remove them with a slotted spoon and leave to drain on paper towels. Put the garlic and ginger into the same oil. Stir and fry for about 10 seconds. Add the cauliflower, lima beans, and salt. Stir and fry for 2 minutes. Add 2 tablespoons water and cover immediately. Cook for about 2 minutes or until the cauliflower is crisply tender. Remove the cover. Turn the heat to medium-low, give the ingredients in the cup a stir, and add them to the wok. Stir and cook for about 30 seconds. Add the almonds and stir once. Empty into a warm serving dish and remove the garlic and ginger pieces.

CAULIFLOWER AND POTATOES COOKED WITH FENUGREEK AND FENNEL SEEDS
INDIA

This North Indian dish, supplemented with stuffed Parathas and Sour Lime Pickle (see pages 275 and 368), is put into small, brass "tiffin-carriers" and taken as lunch by thousands of school children and office workers. Rolled in the same *parathas*, it may be taken on picnics or long car journeys.

(serves 6)

2 pounds cauliflower (1 smallish head)
2 medium-sized boiling potatoes (about ¾ pound)
6 tablespoons vegetable oil
¼ teaspoon whole fenugreek seeds
1 teaspoon whole fennel seeds
1 teaspoon whole cumin seeds
1 to 2 whole dried hot red peppers
¾ teaspoon ground turmeric
1 teaspoon ground coriander seeds
1 to 1¼ teaspoons salt
⅛ teaspoon freshly ground black pepper
1 teaspoon *garam masala*

Discard leaves and coarse stem of cauliflower. Break head into 2-inch-long flowerets. Now cut each floweret lengthwise into very slim flowerets, with the heads never wider than ½ inch. Soak in cold water for half an hour.

Peel the potatoes. Cut them into dice, about ½ × ½ × ⅓ inch. Soak in a bowl of cold water for half an hour.

Drain cauliflower and potatoes and dry them in a dish towel. Heat oil in a large 12- to 14-inch skillet over high heat. When the oil is smoking, scatter in the fenugreek seeds, the fennel seeds, the cumin seeds, and the red peppers. Stir once and quickly add the cauliflower and the potatoes. Stir again and turn the heat to medium. Sprinkle the turmeric, coriander, salt, and pepper over the vegetables and sauté them for about 8 to 10 minutes. Now add ¼ cup water and cover immediately. Turn heat to very low and steam vegetables gently about 7 to 10 minutes or until vegetables are tender. Sprinkle the *garam masala* over the vegetables, stir once, and serve.

CAULIFLOWER STEAMED WITH WHOLE SPICES
INDIA

This Indian dish is both tasty and very easy to make.

(serves 6)

3 pounds cauliflower (1 medium-sized head)
4 to 5 tablespoons vegetable oil
1 teaspoon whole cumin seeds

For information about ingredients and basic techniques that may be unfamiliar, see General Information, pages 418–36.

1   teaspoon whole coriander seeds
1   teaspoon *kalonji*
1   dried hot red pepper
1   medium-sized onion, peeled and minced
7 to 8 cloves garlic, peeled and minced
2   teaspoons ground coriander seeds
2   teaspoons ground cumin seeds
½   teaspoon ground turmeric
1   teaspoon salt
¼   teaspoon cayenne pepper (optional)

Break the cauliflower into small flowerets about 1 inch long and ¾ inch wide at the flower.

Heat enough oil to line a 10- to 12-inch skillet or sauté pan over a medium-high flame. When very hot, add the whole cumin and whole coriander seeds as well as the *kalonji*. As soon as the seeds begin to sizzle (this just takes a few seconds), put in the red pepper. It will brown immediately on one side. Quickly turn it over to brown on the other side. Lower heat to medium and put in the minced onion and garlic. Stir and fry for about 5 minutes or until onion-garlic mixture is lightly browned.

Add the cauliflower, ground coriander, ground cumin, turmeric, salt, and cayenne pepper. Stir to mix. Now put in ¼ cup water and bring to a simmer. Cover with a tight-fitting lid and steam cauliflower on very low heat 10 to 15 minutes or until tender but still slightly crunchy. Stir every 3 to 4 minutes, replacing the lid each time. If any extra liquid is left, it should be boiled away so cauliflower has a "dry" look.

CAULIFLOWER WITH ZUCCHINI
INDIAN STYLE

(serves 4)

1   pound cauliflower (½ smallish head)
2   medium-sized zucchini (about 1 pound)
2½ teaspoons salt
4   tablespoons vegetable oil
1½ teaspoons peeled, finely minced fresh ginger
3 to 5 medium-sized cloves of garlic, peeled and finely minced
¼   teaspoon minced fresh hot green chili
1/16 teaspoon freshly ground black pepper

Cut up the cauliflower into flowerets as described for Cauliflower and Potatoes ... (see opposite page). You should have 4 cups.

Wash and trim the zucchini. Cut them in half lengthwise. Remove the seeded area with the help of a grapefruit spoon. Sprinkle zucchini shells with a little salt (less than ¼ teaspoon) and set aside for half an hour. Drain and wipe well. Cut the shells crosswise into ¼-inch-wide sections.

Bring 3 quarts of water to a boil in a 4- to 5-quart pot. Add 1½ teaspoons salt and the cauliflower. As soon as the water comes to a boil again, turn off the heat. Drain the cauliflower in a colander. (If not eating immediately, the cauliflower should be refreshed under cold running water and set aside.)

Heat the oil in a large 10- to 12-inch, heavy skillet over a medium flame. When hot, put in the ginger, garlic, and green chili. Fry, stirring, until the garlic is lightly browned. Add zucchini and cauliflower. Stir and fry on medium-low heat for 7 to 10 minutes or until vegetables are cooked through but still a bit crunchy. Add about ½ teaspoon salt and the black pepper. Stir a few times and serve.

Tatie Wawo-Runtu's
TUMIS SAWI
(Choy Sum with Shallots)
INDONESIA

For a note on *choy sum*, a Chinese vegetable of the cabbage family, see General Information. Here is a simple and scrumptious way to cook it which requires a fair amount of shallots, a little garlic, and some fresh hot red pepper. If you cannot find these peppers, use slivers of fresh, sweet red pepper or bottled pimientos to give splashes of red to the greens and use hot green chilies to provide as much "hotness" as you like. Mrs. Wawo-Runtu makes this dish with a combination of *kang kung* (swamp cabbage) and *choy sum*, but since the former is less easily available, I have left it out. It is usually served with rice to sop up all the delicious juices.

(serves 4–6)

1¼ pounds *choy sum*
5   ounces shallots, peeled
2   cloves garlic, peeled
1 to 2 fresh hot
      red peppers
¼ cup vegetable
      oil
1   teaspoon salt

Wash the *choy sum* thoroughly. Cut the leafy section crosswise into 2-inch-wide pieces and cut the stalks into 3-inch-long segments. Peel the coarser lower stems. Now cut all the stems lengthwise into ⅛- to ¼-inch strips.

Cut the shallots into halves, lengthwise. Cut each half lengthwise into strips that are about ⅛-inch thick. (You should have about 1 cup of *cut* shallots.)

Cut the cloves of garlic into halves, lengthwise. Now cut each half lengthwise into strips that are about ⅛-inch thick.

Cut the red peppers crosswise into ⅛-inch-wide rings.

Heat the oil in a wok or heavy skillet over a medium-high flame. When hot, put in the shallots and garlic. Stir and fry for 2 minutes. Add the red peppers and salt. Stir to mix. Add the cut greens. Stir again to mix. Add ½ cup water. Cover and cook for 5 minutes.

For information about ingredients and basic techniques that may be unfamiliar, see General Information, pages 418–36.

Sheila's
HAAK
(Collard Greens)
INDIA

Kashmiris who come to America yearn for one of their state's most popular dishes, *haak*. They suffer deep depression until an existing Kashmiri grapevine informs them that their beloved vegetable is, indeed, available under the name of collard greens! In their own mountainous homeland, Kashmiris eat *haak* all through the year. In the summer and early fall, they pluck the leaves right off the stalks and cook them very simply in mustard oil with a touch of asafetida. The asafetida has traditionally come from their neighbor, Afghanistan. As the chill of winter sets in with a staying determination, *haak* is dried in plaited wreaths to preserve it for the long snowy winter months.

The very large, coarser leaves will not do for this dish. Kashmiris like to keep their leaves whole, stem and all, so only the younger, more tender greens should be used. If you have no access to the tender variety, use whatever collards you find, discard the very coarse leaves and then cut up the larger ones. This dish *is* hot—it is cooked with both red peppers and green chilies—and very delicious. You could, if you like, leave out the peppers and chilies. It will still be delicious. Kashmiris tend to put baking soda in this dish to keep the leaves green. I have omitted it as I am told it kills the vitamins.

(serves 4–6)

1¾ pounds tender collard greens
½ cup mustard oil
¼ teaspoon ground asafetida

1¼ teaspoons salt or more to taste
1 to 5 whole dried hot red peppers
1 to 5 whole fresh hot green chilies

Trim away the coarse lower stems of the greens. Separate each leaf and wash it well. Keep the leaves whole.

Heat the oil in an 8- to 9-inch-wide, 4-quart pot over a medium flame. When hot, put in the asafetida. Let it sizzle for 5 seconds. Put in the greens and cover the pot immediately. Uncover the pot after 10 seconds and stir the greens. Add the salt. Stir and sauté the greens for a minute. Now add the red peppers, the green chilies, and 3½ cups of water. Bring to a boil. Cover, lower heat and simmer gently for 1 hour or until greens are tender. There should be about ¾ cup liquid left at the bottom of the pot. If there is more, boil it away. Check the salt. Serve in a warm bowl with plain rice as an accompaniment.

Usha's
CORN WITH COCONUT MILK
INDIA

This dish, from India's upper western coast, is a thick corn stew that is normally made with young maize cobs, each cut into 3 to 4 sections. As I cannot find maize in New York, I make the dish with sweet corn scraped off the cob. You may use frozen corn, if you wish. Defrost it quickly in boiling water and drain it well.

(serves 6–8)

2   cups coconut, freshly grated
4   cups uncooked corn, scraped from the cob
6   tablespoons vegetable oil
3   medium-sized onions, peeled, cut in half length-
      wise, then cut into very fine half rings
2   cloves garlic, peeled and mashed to a pulp
1½ teaspoons ground cumin seeds
¼   teaspoon ground turmeric
⅛ to ¼ teaspoon cayenne pepper
1   teaspoon salt
1   teaspoon sugar

Make thick coconut milk (also called the first coconut milk) using 2 cups grated coconut and 1 cup boiling water. See page 423 for directions. Set this milk aside. Now make a second coconut milk using the remaining coconut "grounds" and another cup of boiling water, as directed on the same page. Keep this second milk separate from the first.

Combine the corn and the second coconut milk in a 2-quart flameproof casserole, bring to a boil, and cook for 1 minute on medium-high heat. Turn off the heat.

Heat the oil in a 7- to 8-inch skillet over a medium-high flame. Put in the sliced onions. Stir and fry them for about 10 minutes or until they are a rich brown color (do not burn them) and crisp. Remove with a slotted spoon and spread them out on a paper towel. Turn the heat off under the skillet and let the oil in it cool slightly.

Preheat oven to 350° F.

Combine the garlic, cumin, turmeric, cayenne, and ¼ cup water in a small cup. Mix it well. Heat the oil in the skillet again, this time on medium heat. When hot, put in the spice paste. Stir and fry for about 1 minute or until the oil separates from the spices. Now stir and fry for another 30 seconds. Empty the contents of the skillet into the pot with the corn. Add the first thick coconut milk, salt, fried onions and sugar. Stir, and bring to a boil. Cover well and place the pot in the oven. Bake for 45 minutes.

EGGPLANT SLICES WITH WHITE MISO
JAPAN

There is a slightly sweet, delicate white *miso* that is used in Kyoto for this elegant and tasty eggplant recipe. If you cannot find it in your local market, substitute the more readily available pale yellow *miso*. Taste the *miso* for sweetness; add a teaspoon of honey to it if you like.

For information about ingredients and basic techniques that may be unfamiliar, see General Information, pages 418–36.

(serves 2–4)

¾- to 1-pound eggplant
5 to 6 tablespoons vegetable oil
About 4 tablespoons sweet white or pale yellow
 miso
¼ teaspoon white poppy seeds

Wash the eggplant and wipe it dry. Trim away the stalk and sepal area. Cut eggplant into about 8 ½-inch-thick round slices. Heat 5 tablespoons of oil in a large skillet over a medium flame. When hot, put in as many slices as the skillet will hold easily in one layer. Brown lightly, cooking slices 3 to 4 minutes on each side. When all the eggplant slices have been browned (you may need to add more oil to the skillet), lay them out in a single layer on a broiling tray.

Preheat broiler.

Just as you would put jam on toast, smear the upper surface of each eggplant slice with about 1½ teaspoons of the white *miso*. Use the flat side of a wet knife to smooth out the *miso*. Use the cutting edge of a wet knife to make a pretty ½-inch-wide diamond or grid pattern on the surface of the *miso*. Dust lightly with poppy seeds and place under the broiler for about 2 minutes or until the *miso* gets some brown spots on it. Serve immediately.

SWEET-AND-SOUR EGGPLANT
INDIA

Though normally served hot, this eggplant dish may also be served cold at a buffet or picnic.

(serves 6)

2 pounds eggplant
2 teaspoons salt
1 medium-sized onion
Vegetable oil for shallow frying
1 tablespoon *panchphoran*
2 teaspoons ground *amchoor* or lemon juice
2½ teaspoons sugar
⅛ to ¼ teaspoon cayenne pepper
1 tablespoon roasted and lightly crushed sesame
 seeds

Cut off the stem ends of the eggplants and quarter them lengthwise. Cut the quarters crosswise into ½-inch-thick slices and put in a sieve set over a bowl. Sprinkle with the salt and mix well. Set aside for 30 to 45 minutes. Pat dry.

Peel the onion, slice it in half lengthwise, then cut into ¼-inch slices.

Heat ⅓ inch oil in a 9-inch-wide skillet over a medium-high flame. When hot, put in as many slices of the eggplant as the skillet will hold in a single layer. Fry for about 3 minutes on each side or until eggplant slices turn a medium reddish-brown color. Remove with a slotted spatula and set aside. Do all the eggplant this way.

Pour off all but 3 tablespoons of the oil in the skillet and turn heat to medium. Put in the *panchphoran*. Within a second or two, the spices will begin to sizzle and pop. As soon as that happens, put in the sliced onion. Stir and fry until the onion just starts to turn brown at the edges. Now put in the fried eggplant, *amchoor*, sugar, cayenne, and sesame seeds. Stir gently and cook for 1 minute.

EGGPLANT "FANS" IN BATTER

PHILIPPINES

You can only make this dish with small Italian eggplants that are about 4 inches in length. The eggplant skins are first charred—either over a flame or under the broiler—and then they are peeled off. The flesh, now smelling slightly "smoked" and still attached to stems and sepals, is fanned out and flattened, then dipped in beaten egg and fried. Filipinos eat the eggplants hot and crisp with a vinegar-based dipping sauce (see page 357).

(serves 4)

4   small Italian eggplants,
    with stems and sepals attached
Vegetable oil for shallow frying
1   large egg
¼   teaspoon salt

Prick the eggplants very lightly with a fork— about two jabs to a side—and place two each

directly over the low flames of two gas burners. As one side gets charred, turn each eggplant a bit, using the stem end to do this. Char the entire surface of the eggplants this way, not forgetting their tips. If you have an electric stove, preheat the broiler. Arrange eggplants on a baking tray and place under the broiler. As each side gets charred, turn the eggplants a bit. Char all the skins this way.

Peel the eggplants. Rinse them off quickly to rid them of little pieces of charred skin and then pat them dry. Flatten out the eggplant flesh, fanning it out as you do so; it must still stay attached to the stem and green sepals.

Heat ¼ inch oil in an 8-inch skillet over a medium-low flame to about 350° to 375° F.

Meanwhile, beat the egg in a shallow bowl, add about ⅛ teaspoon salt, and beat again to mix. Sprinkle about ⅛ teaspoon salt on both sides of each eggplant.

Dip the eggplants, one at a time, into the beaten egg and then place them gently in the skillet. Fry 4 to 5 minutes on each side or until the eggplants are reddish-brown and crisp on the outside. Remove the eggplants from the skillet with a slotted spatula and leave to drain briefly on paper towels.

For information about ingredients and basic techniques that may be unfamiliar, see General Information, pages 418–36.

CUBED EGGPLANT COOKED WITH ONIONS

INDIA

Fennel and fenugreek seeds go particularly well with eggplant, as you will see in this simple North Indian recipe. It is usually served hot, but it is also fine at room temperature or cold.

(serves 6)

3   pounds eggplant (about 2 largish eggplants)
2   teaspoons salt
5   tablespoons vegetable oil
1   teaspoon whole fennel seeds
½   teaspoon whole fenugreek seeds
2   medium-sized onions, peeled and very coarsely
     chopped
1   teaspoon ground coriander
1   teaspoon ground cumin
1   teaspoon ground *amchoor* or lemon juice
$\frac{1}{16}$ to ⅛ teaspoon cayenne pepper

Peel eggplants and cut into 1-inch cubes. Put cubes in a bowl. Sprinkle with salt. Rub well and set aside for 1 hour. Squeeze out as much liquid as possible from the eggplant cubes and pat them dry with paper towels. Set aside.

Heat oil in a large 12- to 14-inch heavy skillet over a medium flame. When hot, put in the fennel and fenugreek seeds. As soon as they turn a few shades darker (this takes just a few seconds), put in the onions and eggplant cubes. Stir and fry the eggplants and onions for 20 minutes, lowering the heat a bit if necessary (the eggplant should not burn). Add the coriander, cumin, *amchoor*, and cayenne. Stir and fry another minute. Now add 1 cup water, cover, lower heat, and simmer gently about 15 minutes or until eggplant is completely cooked. Stir a few times as the eggplant simmers. Check salt and *amchoor* (you may wish to add a bit more) and serve.

CREAMED EGGPLANT

INDIA

(serves 6)

2¾ to 3 pounds eggplant
     (3 medium-sized eggplants)
5   tablespoons vegetable oil
½   teaspoon whole fennel seeds
¼   teaspoon whole fenugreek seeds
2   medium-sized onions, peeled and chopped
8   cloves garlic, peeled and minced
6   tablespoons tomato sauce
2   teaspoons finely grated fresh ginger
1   teaspoon salt
⅛   teaspoon cayenne pepper, or more
½   teaspoon freshly ground black pepper
½   teaspoon ground roasted cumin seeds
3   tablespoons heavy cream
2   tablespoons very finely minced Chinese
     (or other) parsley

Preheat broiler.

Prick the eggplants with a fork (about 2 to 3 jabs to a side) and lay them down on a baking tray lined with aluminum foil. Put the tray under the broiler. When the skin gets charred on one side, give the eggplants a quarter turn. Roast this side and turn a little bit again. Continue to do this until the entire eggplant skin is charred and the pulp of the vegetable is soft and mushy.

Peel away the charred skin under cold running water and chop up the softened eggplants. Heat the oil in an 8-inch skillet (preferably a nonstick skillet) over a medium flame. When hot, put in the fennel seeds and the fenugreek seeds. Five seconds later, put in the onions and garlic. Fry, stirring for 5 to 7 minutes, or until the onions are a golden brown. Now add the tomato sauce, a tablespoon at a time, and keep frying another 2 to 3 minutes. Put in the chopped eggplant, ginger, and salt. Turn heat to medium-low and sauté the eggplant for 10 to 15 minutes. Add cayenne, black pepper, cumin, cream, and parsley. Cook for another minute to heat the cream.

Heat the oil in an 8- to 10-inch skillet over a medium-high flame. When hot, put in the mustard seeds. As soon as the mustard seeds begin to pop (this just takes a few seconds), put in the potatoes and eggplant. Stir once. Now put in the coriander, cumin, turmeric, cayenne, and salt. Stir and fry for a minute. Add 3 tablespoons water, cover immediately with a tight-fitting lid, turn heat to low and simmer gently 10 to 15 minutes or until potatoes are tender. Stir every now and then. If the vegetables seem to catch at the bottom of the skillet, add another tablespoon of water.

You may garnish this dish with a tablespoon of minced Chinese parsley.

EGGPLANT WITH TOMATOES
IRAN

You could serve this dish with Rice with Fresh Herbs and Baby Lima Beans (see page 142) and a yogurt relish.

(serves 6)

2 pounds eggplant
2½ teaspoons salt
Vegetable oil for shallow frying
6 scallions
3 medium-sized tomatoes, peeled and chopped
½ cup chopped fresh parsley
⅛ teaspoon freshly ground black pepper

Cut off the stem ends of the eggplants and quarter them lengthwise. Cut the quarters crosswise into

Neela's
EGGPLANT AND POTATO
INDIA

(serves 4)

4 tablespoons vegetable oil
½ teaspoon whole black mustard seeds
1 cup peeled, diced boiling potatoes (½-inch cubes)
1 cup diced eggplant (½-inch cubes)
1½ teaspoons ground coriander seeds
1 teaspoon ground cumin seeds
¼ teaspoon ground turmeric
⅛ to ¼ teaspoon cayenne pepper
½ teaspoon salt
1 tablespoon Chinese parsley (optional)

For information about ingredients and basic techniques that may be unfamiliar, see General Information, pages 418–36.

½-inch-thick slices and put them in a sieve set over a bowl. Sprinkle with 2 teaspoons of the salt and mix well. Set aside for 30 to 45 minutes. Pat dry.

Heat ⅓ inch oil in a 9-inch-wide skillet over a medium-high flame. When hot, put in as many slices of eggplant as the skillet will hold in a single layer. Fry for about 3 minutes on each side or until eggplant slices turn a medium reddish-brown color. Remove with a slotted spoon and place in a colander to drain. Prepare all the eggplant this way.

Cut the scallions into ⅓-inch rounds, using all of the green sections.

Pour off all the oil in the skillet. Put the fried eggplant, the tomatoes, scallions, parsley, pepper, and some of the remaining salt into the skillet. (Put in only ⅓ teaspoon salt first; add the rest if you need it.) Cover and bring to a simmer. Lower heat and simmer gently for 10 minutes.

Maya's
EGGPLANT COOKED WITH CRUSHED MUSTARD SEEDS AND YOGURT

INDIA

This quick-cooking dish from eastern India uses three ingredients that are very typical of Bengali cooking—mustard oil, *panchphoran*, and crushed black mustard seeds.

(serves 4)

1 to 1½ pounds eggplant
1½ tablespoons whole black mustard seeds
⅛ teaspoon cayenne pepper
7 tablespoons mustard oil
1 tablespoon *panchphoran*
1½ teaspoons salt
1 cup yogurt
⅛ teaspoon freshly ground black pepper
⅛ teaspoon freshly ground cardamom seeds

Discard the stem end of the eggplant and dice eggplant into 1-inch cubes.

Grind the mustard seeds lightly in a coffee grinder (see page 430) and then empty into a bowl. Add the cayenne and 1 cup water. Mix and set aside. Heat the oil in a 12-inch skillet or sauté pan over a medium-high flame. When hot, put in the *panchphoran*. Stir the spices once. Immediately put in the mustard-seed mixture, the cubed eggplant, and 1 teaspoon of the salt. Keep stirring and cooking over a medium-high flame until most of the liquid is absorbed. Add another cup of water, cover, and turn heat to low. Simmer gently for about 15 minutes or until eggplant pieces are quite tender. Remove cover and turn up heat to boil off about half the liquid.

Just before serving, beat the yogurt and ½ teaspoon salt with a fork until it becomes a smooth paste and pour the yogurt over the eggplant. Heat through but do not bring to a boil. Sprinkle black pepper and ground cardamom over the eggplant, stir, and serve at once.

Sheila's

KHATTE BAIGAN
(Sour Eggplants)
INDIA

Probably because Kashmir is tucked away in the upper reaches of India's northernmost Himalayan mountains, its inhabitants tend to use more dried, powdered ginger than any of the southern states. The other spices in the recipe are asafetida, powdered fennel seed, cumin, cayenne, and, for souring, tamarind. These seasonings, when mixed together, make up the very special "Kashmiri taste" that I happen to love so much.

I use small Italian eggplants for this dish. If you cannot get them, use regular eggplants, cut in half lengthwise and then cut crosswise into ¼-inch-thick slices.

(serves 4–5)

1 pound small Italian eggplants
Vegetable oil for shallow frying
2 teaspoons whole fennel seeds
¾ teaspoon dry, powdered ginger
1 teaspoon ground cumin seeds
¼ teaspoon whole black cumin seeds, or regular cumin seeds
¼ teaspoon ground turmeric
⅛ to ¼ teaspoon cayenne pepper
A generous pinch of ground asafetida
1 tablespoon tamarind paste
½ teaspoon salt, or to taste

Cut off the sepals from the eggplants but keep the stems. Cut eggplants lengthwise into ¼-inch-thick slices.

Heat ¼ inch oil in a 9-inch

skillet over a medium-high flame. When hot, put in as many slices as the skillet will hold in a single layer and fry them until they are a reddish-brown color on both sides. On the pieces that have it, the skin side should be cooked very briefly as it tends to get tough. Remove the eggplant slices with a slotted spoon and keep on a plate lined with paper towels. Do all the eggplant slices this way. Turn off the heat. Remove most of the oil (save it for another dish). You will only need 3 tablespoons in the skillet.

Put the fennel seeds in a coffee grinder reserved for spices and grind until you have a powder. Put this powder, as well as the ginger, ground cumin, whole black cumin, turmeric, and cayenne in a small cup.

Heat the 3 tablespoons of oil in the skillet over a medium flame. When hot, put in the asafetida. A second later, add all the spices in the cup plus 2 tablespoons of water. Stir for 20 seconds and then put in another ¼ cup of water. Stir for another 10 seconds. Lower heat and add the tamarind, salt (you will probably need a bit more than ½ teaspoon), and another cup water. Mix. Put in the slices of eggplant and bring to a simmer. Spoon the sauce over the eggplant slices, cover, lower heat, and simmer gently for 5 minutes.

For information about ingredients and basic techniques that may be unfamiliar, see General Information, pages 418–36.

SPICY EGGPLANT WITH ONION

CHINA

Here is one of those Chinese dishes that can be reheated and hence may be made ahead of time. Plain rice should be served on the side.

(serves 4)

1 pound eggplant
1½ to 2 teaspoons chili paste with soy bean and garlic
5 teaspoons Chinese thin soy sauce
2 teaspoons sugar
1 cup vegetable oil
2 cloves garlic, peeled and minced
1 large onion, peeled and cut into ¾-inch cubes

Cut the eggplant into 1½-inch cubes.

Mix the chili paste, soy sauce, sugar, and ½ cup water in a cup.

Heat ½ cup of the oil in a wok over a medium flame. When hot, put in the eggplant. Stir and fry for about 4 to 5 minutes. The eggplant will absorb all the oil. Add the remaining ½ cup of oil by pouring it around the edges of the wok and letting it slither downward toward the vegetable. Stir and fry for another 5 minutes or until the eggplant has browned lightly and is tender enough to eat. Remove eggplant with a slotted spoon and place in a sieve set over a bowl.

Remove all but ¼ cup oil from the wok. Add the garlic. Stir and fry for 15 seconds. Put in the onion. Stir and fry until the pieces turn soft, about 3 to 4 minutes. Turn the heat down a bit if onion starts to brown. Separate the onion layers as you cook. Put the eggplant into the wok. Stir the mix-ture in the cup and pour it over the eggplant. Cook on medium heat, stirring as you do so, until all the liquid is absorbed. Remove eggplant with a slotted spoon, leaving all the oil behind in the wok.

Alun's
PATLICAN
(Fried Eggplant with a Yogurt Sauce)
TURKEY

This is a delicate, melt-in-the-mouth dish that tastes best if eaten as soon as the eggplant is fried. Although it is not traditional, I have removed the eggplant skin at the suggestion of my husband because it tends to get quite tough when fried. I often serve 2 or 3 slices per person as an appetizer, each slice dotted with a dollop of the yogurt.

(serves 2–4)

1 ¾-pound eggplant
1 teaspoon salt
1 tablespoon lemon juice
Olive oil for shallow frying
Yogurt prepared as in the recipe for Yogurt with Garlic in a Turkish style (see page 217)

Peel the eggplant and cut it into ½-inch-thick slices. Lay the slices out flat on a board. Sprinkle with ½ teaspoon salt and 1½ teaspoons lemon juice. Rub this in. Turn the slices over and repeat with another ½ teaspoon salt and the remaining lemon juice.

Put the salted slices in a bowl and leave for 30 minutes.

Heat ¼ inch olive oil in an 8- to 10-inch skillet over a medium flame. When hot, put in as many slices as the skillet will hold in a single layer. Fry about 2 to 3 minutes on each side or until eggplant turns a rich reddish-brown. Remove with a slotted spoon and arrange on a serving plate. Do all the slices this way. Serve the yogurt as a sauce.

PINAKBET
(Mixed Vegetable Stew with Eggplant and Long Beans)
PHILIPPINES

This popular Filipino stew, eaten in the president's palace as well as in the poorest of homes, consists of eggplant, long beans (also called asparagus beans, the kind that are about a foot long and are found in Indian and Chinese grocery stores), okra, fresh lima beans, and bitter melon, all stewed quickly with onions, garlic, and tomatoes. In the Philippines, a salty fish paste provides the final flavoring, but I have left that out and substituted a little soy sauce instead. The Filipinos use the slim, 6-inch-long, pinkish-purple eggplants that are found in many Oriental grocery stores. On the West Coast, I have heard them referred to as "Japanese" eggplants. If you cannot find them, use slim, white eggplants, or small Italian eggplants. If none of the above can be found, use the familiar-sized oval eggplant cut into 1-inch-thick and 2½-inch-long "fingers." They may disintegrate a bit but the taste of the dish will not be greatly changed. You may easily substitute regular green beans for the long beans, frozen whole okra for the fresh, and frozen large lima beans for the fresh kind. If you cannot find bitter melon, leave it out, though that would really be a pity. That slight bitterness gives *pinakbet* its special kick.

(serves 6)

About ½ of a 6-ounce bitter melon
¾ pound slim eggplants
1¼ to 1½ teaspoons salt
8 to 10 whole fresh or frozen okra*
16 long beans or 5 ounces green beans
¼ cup vegetable oil
4   quarter-sized slices of fresh ginger
2   cloves garlic, peeled and cut into slivers
1   medium-sized onion, peeled and chopped
1¼ pounds red-ripe tomatoes, chopped
4   teaspoons Japanese soy sauce
1½ cups fresh or frozen lima beans*

*NOTE: If the okra or lima beans are frozen, leave at room temperature until you can separate them.

Cut the half bitter melon in half lengthwise, and remove all the seeds. Cut the halves into strips that are about 2 inches long and ½ inch wide. Sprinkle the strips with ¼ teaspoon salt and then stand them up in a bowl for 20 to 30 minutes. Rinse off the strips.

Trim away the stem end of the eggplants and cut

For information about ingredients and basic techniques that may be unfamiliar, see General Information, pages 418–36.

Tatie Wawo-Runtu's
SAJUR LODEH
(Eggplant and Long Beans Stewed in Coconut Milk)
INDONESIA

them into 2- to 3-inch lengths. You should now have tubelike pieces. The Filipinos cut gashes at both ends of the tubes this way: Hold the tube so it is standing on one end. Make a lengthwise cut down the center but stop when you reach about midway. Stand the tube on its other end. Give the tube a quarter turn and make another lengthwise cut down the center, again stopping about midway. Your gashes should resemble a cross, with one side of the cross at one end of the tube and the other at the other end. The two gashes should never meet.

Trim away the okra caps and points. If the okra is fresh, cut gashes on it just as you did for the eggplant.

Trim away the ends of the long beans and cut them into 3-inch lengths.

Heat the oil in a 4-quart pot over a medium-high flame. When hot, put in the ginger, garlic, and onion. Stir and fry for about 2 minutes. Add the tomatoes. Stir and cook for 4 to 5 minutes or until tomatoes have softened. Turn the heat down a bit, if necessary. Add 2 cups water, the soy sauce, 1 teaspoon salt, the bitter melon, eggplant, okra, long beans, and lima beans. Stir. Cook for 15 to 20 minutes on medium to medium-low heat. You should keep the pot at a vigorous simmer. Stir the vegetables gently throughout the cooking period (the Filipinos prefer to shake the pot and toss the vegetables every now and then). The liquid should reduce and become thick and all the vegetables should be tender. Check the salt. Add more if you need it. Remove the pieces of ginger.

Some of the best food in all of Bali is to be found at the Wawo-Runtus' home and at their charming Tanjung Sari restaurant, both located on fashionable Sanur Beach. This particular dish is traditionally cooked with tiny pieces of meat and is seasoned with pounded dried shrimp. One of the Wawo-Runtu daughters is a vegetarian and the version of *sajur lodeh* that I was served is one that the family has adapted for her.

The eggplants that Tatie used were ovals of a pale green color, a variety that I have never seen in the United States. Use Italian eggplants or the slim, pinkish-purple eggplants sold in Chinese and Indian grocery stores.

(serves 6)

¾ pound eggplants (see note above)
¾ pound long beans or fresh green beans
2 fresh hot red chilies
1 fresh hot green chili
¼ cup vegetable oil
1 clove garlic, peeled and slivered
4 ounces shallots, peeled and slivered (a heaping ½ cup)
A silver-dollar-sized piece of fresh galanga root, lightly crushed, or ½ teaspoon dried, ground galanga root
6 to 7 dried *daun salaam* leaves
3 cups fresh coconut milk
1½ teaspoons salt
1 teaspoon sugar

Trim away the stem end of the eggplants and cut them into 1-inch, cubelike chunks. Trim away the ends of the long beans and cut them into 2-inch lengths.

Cut the chilies into strips, or just leave them whole if they are small.

Heat the vegetable oil in a 4-quart pot over a medium-high flame. When hot, put in the red chilies, green chili, garlic, shallots, and galanga. Stir and fry for about 3 minutes or until the mixture is lightly browned. Add the *daun salaam* and stir once or twice. Now put in the coconut milk and turn the heat down to medium. Slowly bring the milk to a boil, stirring all the time so it does not curdle. Now add the eggplant, long beans, salt, and sugar. Continue to cook over a medium to medium-low heat, stirring gently so as not to break up the vegetables. The liquid should keep bubbling and the coconut milk should reduce a bit.Cook 8 to 12 minutes or until vegetables are just tender.

BAGHARA BAIGAN
(Eggplant Cooked in the Hyderabadi Style)
INDIA

When there were still maharajas and princes in India, Hyderabad, in the south, was the seat of successive, semi-independent Nizams, reputed to be among the richest men in the world. The Nizams, and the ruling aristocracy of Arab, Persian, and Central Asian ancestry, were Moslems but the people over whom they ruled were Hindus. The cuisine of the affluent reflected these divergent influences. The use of coconut, tamarind, jaggery, and

mustard seeds was typical of the vegetarian Hindus. These seasonings are incorporated into this superb, festive dish in which small and tender eggplants are partially quartered, stuffed with a hot, sour, sweet, and salty mixture and then cooked slowly. A final *baghar*, or addition of hot oil flavored with spices, finishes off the dish—and also gives it its name.

I use small, 3- to 4-inch, purple eggplants. On those occasions when I have been able to get small, white eggplants, I have preferred to use them, as their skin tends to be softer and they cook in barely 15 minutes. If you have a garden and are planning for a future season, keep these white eggplants in mind. (Whenever I have been able to buy them it has been from Chinese grocery stores.) If you want to serve this dish cold, use oil instead of *ghee* for the final garnish.

(serves 6)

2   pounds small, 3- to 4-inch-long eggplants (if unavailable, use the slightly larger 5- to 6-inch-long, slim eggplants)
1   tablespoon plus 1½ teaspoons kosher salt
2   tablespoons sesame seeds
2   tablespoons desiccated, unsweetened coconut
1   dried hot red pepper
1½ tablespoons ground coriander seeds
2   teaspoons whole cumin seeds
8   tablespoons vegetable oil
2   medium-sized onions, peeled and minced
5   cloves garlic, peeled and minced
¼   teaspoon ground turmeric
2 to 3 tablespoons tamarind paste
1   tablespoon shredded jaggery (*gur*)
2   tablespoons *ghee* or vegetable oil
1½ tablespoons black mustard seeds
½   fresh hot green chili, seeded and cut into 1-inch slivers

---

For information about ingredients and basic techniques that may be unfamiliar, see General Information, pages 418–36.

Wash the eggplants and wipe them. Do not remove any of the green portion (i.e., the stems and sepals). Quarter the eggplants lengthwise in such a way that the sections remain attached for at least ½ inch at the stem end. Rub the 1 tablespoon salt into all the cut sections and leave the eggplants, stems up, standing in a bowl for 45 minutes to an hour.

Meanwhile, heat a small cast-iron skillet over a medium flame. Put in the sesame seeds, coconut, dried red pepper, coriander, and whole cumin seeds. Dry-roast, stirring constantly for 2 to 3 minutes, or until seasonings have turned a few shades darker and give out a delicious roasted aroma. Remove from heat and empty spices into a small bowl. When the spices have cooled a bit, put them into a coffee grinder reserved for spices. Grind and set aside.

Squeeze out as much moisture as possible from the eggplants and wipe them off.

Heat the 8 tablespoons oil in a skillet or sauté pan large enough to hold the eggplants in a single layer. Put in the minced onions and garlic. Fry over a medium flame until reddish-brown at the edges. Take the skillet off the heat and add the turmeric, the ground spices from the coffee grinder, the tamarind paste (put in 2 tablespoons first and add more later if you think you need it), the jaggery, and 1½ teaspoons salt. Return to the fire, keeping the heat very low. Mix all the ingredients in the skillet and cook, stirring, for 1 minute. Add just enough water to the spice mixture to make a thick but not dry paste (about ½ cup). Keep stirring and

cooking until jaggery has melted completely. This mixture will be the stuffing for the eggplants. Taste it for balance of sweet, sour, hot, and salty flavors. Make adjustments, if necessary. Turn off the heat.

Empty the stuffing into a small bowl. Spread a portion of the stuffing in between the cut sections of each eggplant and then lay the eggplants in the same skillet you had used earlier for cooking the spice mixture. The eggplants should lie in a single layer. Any leftover stuffing may be sprinkled over the top.

Add ¾ cup water to the skillet and bring to a simmer. Cover with a tight-fitting lid, turn heat to low, and cook gently for 40 to 60 minutes or until eggplants are quite tender. (Very young eggplants may cook faster.) Using tongs to pick up the eggplants by their stem ends, turn them over at least 4 to 5 times during this cooking period. Stir the sauce by sliding a spatula under the eggplants and spoon some of the sauce over them. If they seem to be catching at the bottom, add 1 tablespoon of hot water. Replace the lid every time you stir or turn the eggplants.

When the eggplants are tender, heat the *ghee* in a small skillet or a very small pot over a medium flame. When hot, put in the mustard seeds and the green chili. When the mustard seeds begin to pop—this just takes a few seconds—pour the *ghee* and spices over the cooked eggplants.

To serve, lay the eggplants out in a single layer, all stems pointing in the same direction, on a warmed platter. Spoon some of the thick sauce over them but leave behind all the fat.

HIJIKI WITH SHIITAKE MUSHROOMS

JAPAN

Hijiki is a black, twinelike, dried sea vegetable, rich in calcium, that is sold in all health-food and Japanese stores. It is exceedingly tasty and combines well with a variety of vegetables. Because dried *hijiki* is fairly stiff, it is difficult to measure accurately. Just stuff it into a measuring cup and aim for an approximate amount. This dish may be eaten warm or at room temperature.

(serves 4)

¼ cup *hijiki*
8 dried *shiitake* mushrooms*
3 tablespoons vegetable oil
½ cup well-drained,
   julienned bamboo shoots
1 carrot, peeled and cut
   into julienne strips
5 tablespoons *dashi*
   (see page 291)
½ teaspoon salt
2 teaspoons sugar
1 tablespoon *mirin*
1 tablespoon Japanese soy sauce

*NOTE: Mushrooms used to make *dashi* may be reused for this dish.

Rinse off the *hijiki* quickly under cold running water. Put it to soak in 4 cups of warm water for 30 minutes. Lift the *hijiki* out of the water, leaving all the grit behind, then rinse it off again.

Rinse off the mushrooms quickly and leave to soak in 3 cups warm water for 30 minutes. Drain

the mushrooms and remove the hard stems. Cut the mushroom caps into ⅛-inch-thick strips.

Heat the oil in a skillet over a medium flame. When hot, put in the *hijiki*, mushrooms, bamboo shoots, and carrot. Sauté for 1 minute. Add the *dashi*, salt, sugar, *mirin*, and soy sauce. Bring to a simmer. Cover, lower heat and simmer gently for 10 minutes. Remove cover, turn up the flame a bit and boil off most of the liquid, stirring gently as you do so. This last step should take just a few seconds.

HIJIKI WITH SWEET POTATOES

JAPAN

Read about *hijiki* in the introduction to the preceding recipe. Here, if you like, you can substitute seeded zucchini strips or long cabbage shreds for the sweet potatoes. You would have to adjust the cooking times and seasonings slightly. This dish is good both warm and at room temperature. You might like to include it on a vegetable platter with Snowpeas Cooked in Dashi (see page 58), and Cabbage Cooked with Bean Curd (see page 172).

For information about ingredients and basic techniques that may be unfamiliar, see General Information, pages 418–36.

KOHLRABI WITH CHINESE BLACK MUSHROOMS

CHINA

(serves 4)

¼ cup *hijiki*
1 medium-sized sweet potato (about 10 ounces)
4 tablespoons vegetable oil
5 tablespoons *dashi* (see page 291)
½ teaspoon salt
3 to 4 teaspoons sugar
1 tablespoon *mirin*
1 tablespoon Japanese soy sauce
1 tablespoon roasted sesame seeds

Rinse off the *hijiki* quickly under cold running water. Put it to soak in 4 cups of warm water for 30 minutes. Lift the *hijiki* out of the water, leaving all the grit behind. Rinse it off again.

Peel the sweet potato and cut it crosswise at a slight diagonal into ¼-inch-thick slices. Now cut these slices into ¼-inch-thick strips.

Heat the oil in a skillet over medium heat. Add the sweet potatoes. Stir and fry for about 2 minutes. Add the *hijiki*. Stir and fry for another half minute. Add the *dashi*, salt, sugar, *mirin*, and soy sauce. Bring to a simmer. Cover, lower heat and simmer 4 minutes. Uncover, turn the heat up a bit and boil away most of the liquid, stirring gently as you do so. This last step should only take you a few seconds. Sprinkle the sesame seeds over the top.

Kohlrabi, a turnip-shaped vegetable of the cabbage family, is delicious eaten both raw and cooked. If you wish to eat it raw, just peel and slice it; then eat with a sprinkling of salt and pepper or put into salads. If you wish to eat it cooked, cut it into chunks and throw it into stews and soups. Here is a simple way to stir-fry it, Chinese style, with dried black mushrooms. If you cannot get kohlrabi, use broccoli stems. The taste is similar.

(serves 4–6)

10 large Chinese dried black mushrooms
1½ pounds kohlrabi (about 4 good-sized kohlrabi)
2 scallions
1 teaspoon cornstarch
1 tablespoon *shaohsing* wine or dry sherry
1 teaspoon sesame oil
¼ teaspoon salt
⅛ teaspoon freshly ground white pepper
¼ teaspoon sugar
3 tablespoons vegetable oil
2 quarter-sized slices of fresh ginger, lightly mashed
1 teaspoon salt

Soak the mushrooms in 1 cup boiling water for 30 minutes.

Take the mushrooms out of their soaking liquid. Strain the liquid. You will need 7 tablespoons of this strained liquid later in the recipe. Cut off and

Sheila's
LOTUS ROOT AND TOMATOES COOKED WITH FENNEL AND DRIED GINGER
INDIA

discard the hard mushroom stems. Cut the caps into ⅛-inch-thick strips.

Peel the kohlrabi, making sure you remove the tough, fibrous root ends of the vegetable. Slice into ⅛-inch-thick rounds and then cut the rounds into ⅛-inch-wide strips.

Cut the scallions into 2-inch-long segments. Cut these segments, lengthwise, into fine strips.

Mix together in a cup the cornstarch, wine, sesame oil, salt, pepper, and sugar with 3 tablespoons of mushroom water. Place near your cooking area. Have the remaining ¼ cup strained mushroom liquid at hand as well.

Heat the oil in a wok or heavy skillet over a medium flame. Do not let the oil get too hot. Put in the ginger. Stir around for 10 seconds. Now put in the mushrooms, kohlrabi, and scallions. Stir and cook for a minute. Add the 1 teaspoon salt and stir once. Add the ¼ cup mushroom liquid, cover and cook for a minute. Uncover and turn heat to medium-low. Give the ingredients in the cup a stir and pour them over the vegetables. Cover and cook another minute. Lift cover and stir once. Turn off heat and serve immediately.

Have you ever wandered through a Chinese grocery store and stared with curiosity at lotus roots, which look like stiffened link sausages or brown sugar cane, and wondered what on earth you could do with them if you took them home? Lotus roots—they are a rhizome, really—are scrumptious in stews, mixed vegetable dishes, and, if they are young and tender, in soups and salads. First you have to scrape them as you would a new potato, or else peel them with a potato peeler and then slice them crosswise—often at a slight diagonal—into ⅛- to 1/16-inch-thick slices. Lotus roots are harder than potatoes and full of the most prettily arranged holes. They take about as long to cook as beets—about 1 to 1½ hours—but you can do them in a pressure cooker in about 20 minutes. Very young lotus roots take less time to cook. When the roots are done, they do not become soft like a potato. Instead, they retain a nice crunchiness.

This dish is a Kashmiri "stew" of sliced lotus roots and fresh tomatoes. It is not hot. It is not really spicy. It *is* very good. Kashmir's lakes are filled with lotus flowers— and therefore lotus roots. This dish is a fine example of that northern state's "home-style" cooking.

For information about ingredients and basic techniques that may be unfamiliar, see General Information, pages 418–36.

LOTUS ROOT WITH SOY SAUCE DRESSING

KOREA/JAPAN/HONG KONG

(serves 6)

2½ teaspoons whole fennel seeds
1¼ pounds lotus roots
¾ cup mustard oil or other vegetable oil
½ teaspoon ground asafetida
1½ teaspoons freshly roasted whole cumin seeds
1¼ pounds red-ripe tomatoes, peeled and cut into
    ½-inch dice
2 teaspoons salt or to taste
½ teaspoon ground dried ginger

Grind the fennel seeds in a coffee grinder or other spice grinder.

Divide the lotus roots into links. Trim away the ends of each link. Now scrape the lotus-root skin. Cut the links, crosswise and at a slight diagonal, into ⅛- to 1/16-inch-thick slices. Leave the slices in a bowl of water until you are ready to start cooking. Drain.

Use a pressure cooker, if you have one. Otherwise any 8-inch-wide, 3- to 4-quart-capacity pot will do. Heat the oil in the pot over a medium-high flame. When it is hot, put in the asafetida and let sizzle for 5 seconds. Add the sliced lotus root and the roasted cumin seeds. Stir and fry for 2 to 3 minutes. Now add the tomatoes, salt, fennel, and ginger. If you are using a pressure cooker, cover and bring it up to 15 pounds pressure. Cook for 20 minutes. Relieve the pressure by putting the pot under cold running water. If you are using a regular pot, bring its contents to a boil, cover, lower heat, and simmer gently for 1½ hours or until lotus root is tender. Check the salt. Serve with rice to sop up the delicious sauce.

Lotus roots have the taste of artichoke hearts, a firm, crunchy texture, and make spectacularly pretty slices. Here is the saladlike version that I ate, with slight variations, in Korea, Hong Kong, and Japan, served warm or at room temperature or cold.

(serves 2–4)

5 ounces lotus roots
5 teaspoons Japanese soy sauce
1 tablespoon Japanese rice vinegar
1 teaspoon sugar
2 teaspoons sesame oil
2 teaspoons roasted sesame seeds

Separate the lotus-root links. Scrape off the skin with a knife or else peel it with a potato peeler. Cut into ⅛- to 1/16-inch-thick slices. These slices could be rounds or, if you cut at a slight diagonal, ovals. Keep the slices in a bowl of water until you are ready to cook them.

Arrange a pot for steaming. You could have boiling water in a wok and then set a bamboo steamer just above the water, or you could place a perforated steaming trivet inside a large pot, making sure that the boiling water in the pot stays below the body of the trivet.

Drain the lotus-root slices and put them inside the perforated steaming utensil. (Some people like to line bamboo steamers with cheesecloth, lettuce leaves, or bamboo leaves first.) Cover and steam for about an hour. Remember that younger lotus roots will cook faster. Remove the lotus-root slices and place in a bowl. Mix all the remaining ingredients and pour over the lotus root. Stir to mix.

MUSHROOMS COOKED IN ALUMINUM FOIL

KOREA

I was served these simply prepared mushrooms in many of Korea's older, traditional restaurants. The mushrooms, wrapped inside an aluminum foil packet, are cooked over direct heat—either a gas burner or live charcoal—so that all the aroma, flavor, and juices get trapped inside. The foil is then opened with noticeable flourish at the table. These mushrooms are not seasoned. They are either eaten plain as a contrast to other hot and garlicky Korean specialties, or else with a dipping sauce.

(serves 2–4)

6   ounces mushrooms
Any one of the five Korean Dipping Sauces on
    pages 358–9

Wipe the mushrooms lightly with a damp cloth. Cut into ¼-inch-thick slices that include the stem.

Cut a piece of aluminum foil, about 20 x 12 inches. Put the mushrooms in the center of it. Cover first with the long ends and then with the short ends until you have a neat package.

You may now cook over a charcoal fire or over a gas burner. Set your grill about 4 inches above the charcoal. If you use gas, turn a burner on to low. Lay the package over the grill or the burner. As soon as steam begins to escape from the packet—a matter of 5 to 7 minutes—the mushrooms are done.

Eat the mushrooms as soon as they are done, dipping them in one of the above sauces.

Asha's
MUSHROOMS WITH ONION, GARLIC, AND GINGER

INDIA

This is really my mother's recipe which I have acquired via my sister-in-law. It is very simple—and good.

(serves 4)

¾ pound medium-sized mushrooms
A 1-inch cube of fresh ginger, peeled and finely
    grated
6   cloves garlic, mashed to a pulp or grated
4   tablespoons vegetable oil
1   medium-sized onion, peeled and very finely
    minced
¼ teaspoon ground turmeric
⅛ teaspoon cayenne pepper, or more to taste
½ to ¾ teaspoon salt

Wipe off the mushrooms with a damp cloth and then halve them.

Combine the ginger and garlic in a small cup with 3 tablespoons water.

Heat the oil in a 7-inch-wide pot over a medium-high flame. When hot, put in the minced onion and fry, stirring, for about 2 minutes or until onion is a golden-brown color. Add the ginger-garlic paste. Keep stirring and frying for another 2 minutes. If the water evaporates, sprinkle a little more in (about 2 teaspoons). Now add the turmeric and cayenne. Stir for a second. Add the mushrooms, ½ teaspoon salt, and ½ cup water. Stir, and bring to a simmer. Cover, lower heat, and simmer gently for 10 minutes. Check the salt. You may wish to add a bit more. Stir. Serve with an Indian bread or a rice dish.

For information about ingredients and basic techniques that may be unfamiliar, see General Information, pages 418–36.

SAUCED MUSHROOMS WITH SESAME SEEDS

INDIA

This dish was, traditionally, made by North Indians with the seasonal and very delicate monsoon mushrooms that begin to sprout out of the damp earth around July and completely disappear by mid-September. Today, with regular white-cap mushrooms available all year round, many well-heeled Delhi residents assuage their palates with the hardier, farm-grown variety.

(serves 6)

30 medium-sized, well-formed mushrooms
    (1¼ to 1½ pounds)
1 large or 2 small onions, peeled and coarsely chopped
4 to 6 cloves garlic, peeled and coarsely chopped
A ½-inch cube of fresh ginger, peeled and coarsely chopped
5 tablespoons vegetable oil
3 tablespoons tomato sauce
2 teaspoons ground coriander
1 teaspoon ground cumin
½ teaspoon salt
Freshly ground black pepper to taste
⅛ teaspoon cayenne pepper, or to taste
1 tablespoon lemon juice
1 tablespoon roasted sesame seeds

Cut off the mushroom stems so they are level with the caps. Reserve the stalks for making stock. Wipe mushrooms with a damp cloth.

Put the chopped onions, garlic, and ginger into the container of an electric blender or food processor along with ¼ cup water. Blend until you have a smooth paste.

Heat the oil in a 10-inch-wide pot, sauté pan, or deep skillet over a medium flame. When hot, pour in the paste from the blender (keep face averted). Stir and fry for 8 to 10 minutes or until paste is a golden-brown color. Lower the flame and add the tomato sauce, the coriander, cumin, salt, black pepper, and cayenne. Fry, stirring, for 1 minute. Now put in the mushroom caps, lemon juice, and ⅔ cup water. Mix well and bring to a boil. Cover, lower heat, and simmer gently for 15 minutes. Stir every now and then during this cooking period.

Neatly arrange 5 mushrooms in the center of each of 6 small, shallow bowls. Spoon a little sauce over each serving. Then sprinkle the roasted sesame seeds on top of the mushroom caps.

Audrey Chan's
THREE AUNTIES AND THREE GRANDMOTHERS
(Three Kinds of Mushrooms and Three Kinds of Vegetables)
SINGAPORE

I love this dish. It is fairly easy to make, especially if you have access to the Chinese green, *choy sum*, which I have seen only in Chinese grocery stores. Its stalks and leaves are a rich green color and sometimes there are a few yellow flowers as well. If you cannot find it and if you like broccoli rabe, use that as a substitute. It will, of course, add its own unique sharpness to the dish, a sharpness that *choy sum* does not have.

(serves 4–6)

10 medium-sized Chinese dried black mushrooms
¾ pound *choy sum*
1 teaspoon cornstarch
⅛ to ¼ teaspoon freshly ground white pepper
1 teaspoon salt
5 tablespoons vegetable oil
2 cloves garlic, peeled and minced
2 shallots, peeled and minced
1 teaspoon sesame oil
½ cup canned button mushrooms, drained
½ cup canned straw mushrooms, drained
6 canned ears of baby corn, drained, cut in half lengthwise
3 freshwater (or canned) chestnuts, peeled and sliced into ⅛-inch-thick rounds

Soak the dried mushrooms in 1 cup hot water. Remove them after 1 hour, saving the liquid. Cut off and discard the coarse stems. Cut each cap in half and set aside. Strain the mushroom liquid and set aside.

Trim away the coarse, woody section of the *choy sum* stems, if there are any. (Sometimes the lower stems can just be peeled.) Otherwise leave the stems attached, just as you bought them. Wash the *choy sum* and stack it neatly into a bundle so it looks very much like the bundle you bought, with all the stalks facing the same direction.

Combine the mushroom liquid, cornstarch, white pepper, and salt. Mix thoroughly and set aside.

Heat 3 tablespoons oil in a large wok over a medium-high flame. When hot, put in half of the garlic and half of the shallots. Stir and fry for about 30 seconds. Then put in about 5 cups of water. Cover, and bring the water to a boil. Remove the cover and put in the bundle of greens, all stalks facing the same direction. The greens should be almost completely submerged; if they are not, add some more boiling water. The stalks must stay

---

For information about ingredients and basic techniques that may be unfamiliar, see General Information, pages 418–36.

underwater as they need to cook more thoroughly. Boil the greens rapidly for about a minute, turning them over occasionally with tongs or chopsticks so that those on the top get a chance to go to the bottom. By this time, the stalks should be just tender. Turn off the heat. Lift the *choy sum* out of the water and put it, still in a bundle, on a cutting board. Cut it into 3-inch lengths. Put the *choy sum* on a long, warmed platter, re-forming the original bundle shape, with all the stalks on one side, the leaves on the other. Keep the platter in a warm place.

Work quickly now. Rinse off the wok and dry it. Heat 2 tablespoons of vegetable oil and the 1 teaspoon of sesame oil in the wok over a medium-high flame. When hot, put in the remaining garlic and shallots. Stir them around for 10 seconds. Add the soaked, drained black mushrooms. Stir and fry them for about 30 seconds. Push them to one side and put in the button and straw mushrooms. Stir and fry them for about 30 seconds and push them to one side as well. Put in the baby corn and water chestnuts. Stir and fry them for a second. Mix up all the vegetables. Cover and cook for 1 minute. Uncover and turn the heat down to medium low. Stir the cornstarch mixture and add it to the vegetables. Stir to mix. Cover again for 30 seconds. Uncover and give a final stir.

Quickly spread the mushroom-chestnut-corn mixture over the *choy sum*. Pour the sauce in the wok evenly over all the vegetables. Serve immediately with plain rice.

SWEET AND SALTY DRIED SHIITAKE MUSHROOMS
JAPAN

(serves 4 at a Japanese meal)

½ ounce or about 6 to 7 medium-sized dried
   shiitake mushrooms
2 tablespoons Japanese soy sauce
2 tablespoons sugar

Rinse the mushrooms quickly under cold running water and then soak in 1 cup boiling water for ½ hour.

Remove the mushrooms from their soaking liquid (save the liquid for soups) and cut away the coarse stems. Slice the mushroom caps into ⅛-inch-thick slices.

Put the mushroom caps, soy sauce, and sugar in a small pot and bring to a simmer. Cook on low heat for about 4 minutes. A little liquid should remain.

STIR-FRIED TREE EAR FUNGUS AND SUMMER OYSTER MUSHROOMS

HONG KONG

The Chinese believe very firmly in the curative powers of various varieties of fungi, with the expensive silver ear fungus often displayed in glass cases at Hong Kong restaurants as if it were priceless porcelain. Tree ear fungus is a cheaper variety, but still credited with preventing heart disease.

Because canned vegetables can sometimes taste quite "tinny," I boil them briefly in vegetable stock to rid them of this unpleasant flavor. (I have done so with the summer oyster mushrooms.)

(serves 4–6)

¼ cup tree ear fungus
1   10-ounce can of summer oyster mushrooms
10 medium-sized fresh mushrooms
2   cups Delicious Stock . . . (see page 292)
1   teaspoon cornstarch
1   tablespoon *shaohsing* wine or dry sherry
1   teaspoon sesame oil
1   teaspoon Chinese thin soy sauce
½ teaspoon sugar
¼ cup vegetable oil
1   clove garlic, peeled and minced
½ teaspoon salt, or to taste
1   scallion, cut into ⅛-inch-thick rounds

Rinse the tree ear fungus and soak in 2 cups boiling water for ½ hour. Remove them from the soaking liquid and rinse. Feel for the hard "eyes" and cut them out.

Drain the summer oyster mushrooms. The sizes of the pieces may vary, so make sure that none is longer than 1½ inches or wider than ½ inch.

Wipe off the regular mushrooms and cut them into ¼-inch-thick slices.

Combine the tree ear fungus and oyster mushrooms in a 1½-quart pot. Add the stock and bring to a boil. Cover, turn heat to low and simmer for 3 minutes. Uncover and allow to cool for at least 1 hour. Drain, reserving 3 tablespoons of the broth. (The rest of the broth may be saved for another dish.)

Combine the cornstarch, wine, 3 tablespoons of broth, sesame oil, soy sauce, and sugar in a small cup. Mix until smooth and set aside.

Heat the oil in a wok or heavy skillet over a medium-high flame. When hot, put in the garlic. Stir and fry for 15 seconds. Add the sliced regular mushrooms. Stir and fry for 1 minute. Now put in the tree ear fungus, the summer oyster mushrooms, and the salt. Stir and fry for 2 minutes. Turn heat to medium-low. Stir the ingredients in the cup and pour them over the contents of the wok. Add the scallion. Cover and cook for 1 minute.

Remove cover and stir again.

Serve immediately
with plain rice.

For information about ingredients and basic techniques that may be unfamiliar, see General Information, pages 418–36.

MOREL MUSHROOMS WITH PEAS

INDIA

Morels grow in the northern state of Kashmir. They are dried and shipped to the rest of the country. For more on the subject, see the introduction to Kashmir-Style Gucchi Pullao, page 146.

(serves 4)

½ ounce dried or 12 fresh
    morel mushrooms
A 1-inch cube of fresh
    ginger, peeled
4 cloves garlic, peeled
3 tablespoons vegetable oil
    or *ghee*
1 teaspoon ground coriander seeds
2 teaspoons ground cumin seeds
¼ teaspoon ground turmeric
⅛ teaspoon cayenne pepper
6 ounces tomatoes (1 large or 2 small), peeled
    and minced
2 cups fresh shelled or defrosted frozen peas
1½ teaspoons salt
¼ teaspoon *garam masala*

Rinse off the dried morels quickly and then leave them to soak in 1½ cups water for 20 to 30 minutes or until they are quite tender; if you are using fresh, there is no need, of course, to soak them. Drain, saving the soaking liquid as you do so. Strain the soaking liquid through a clean piece of cloth and set it aside. Cut each mushroom in half lengthwise.

    Put the ginger and garlic into the container of a food processor or blender. Add ¼ cup water and blend until you have a smooth paste. Heat the oil in a 2½- to 3-quart pot over medium heat. When hot, put in the paste from the food processor (keep face averted). Stir and fry for 1 minute. Add the coriander, cumin, turmeric, and cayenne. Stir and fry for another minute. Put in the minced tomato. Stir and fry for about 3 minutes, gently mashing the pieces of tomato with the back of your stirring spoon. You should end up with a relatively smooth paste. Now put in the morels, their strained soaking liquid (or 1½ cups water, if you are using fresh morels), the peas, and the salt. Bring to a simmer. Cover, lower heat and simmer gently for 10 minutes. Add the *garam masala*. Stir to mix.

MUSTARD GREENS
OR BROCCOLI RABE, COOKED IN THE PUNJABI STYLE

INDIA

Cold winter days in India's northwestern state of Punjab are almost synonymous with soft, buttery mustard greens (*sarson da sag*) eaten with flat cornmeal breads (*makki di roti*).

(serves 4–6)

1   pound mustard greens or broccoli rabe
½   pound spinach
A ½-inch cube of fresh ginger, peeled
½   fresh hot green chili
9   tablespoons unsalted butter
2½   tablespoons cornmeal
1   teaspoon salt

Trim and wash the greens. Chop them coarsely and place in a large pot. Add 1 cup water and bring to a boil. Cover, turn heat to medium-low, and cook for about 15 minutes or until greens are tender.

Put the ginger and green chili into the container of an electric blender or food processor and mince them. (If your machine cannot manage this, mince the green chili by hand and grate the ginger.) Remove the cooked greens with a slotted spoon and put them into the machine container with the ginger and chili. Do not worry about squeezing out all the liquid from the greens; you will need the small amount that clings to them. Blend the greens with the ginger and green chili until you have a smooth paste. Depending upon your machine, you may need to do this in two batches.

In a heavy 2½-quart pot, heat 6 tablespoons of the butter over a medium-low flame. Add the cornmeal and cook for about 2 minutes, stirring all the time. Do not allow it to turn brown. Turn the heat down, if necessary. Add ¼ cup water and keep stirring for another half a minute. Now put in the puréed greens and the salt. Cook on medium-low heat, stirring often, for about 10 minutes. Serve the greens in a warm dish topped with 3 tablespoons of butter, accompanied by any Indian bread.

WHOLE OKRA

INDIA

(serves 6)

1½   pounds fresh, tender okra
6   tablespoons vegetable oil
2   medium-sized onions, peeled and minced
6   cloves garlic, peeled and minced
½   teaspoon ground turmeric
1¼ to 1½ teaspoons salt
⅛   teaspoon freshly ground black pepper
1/16 to ⅛ teaspoon cayenne pepper (optional)

Wash okra and trim it. (To trim whole okra, cut off a small section at the tip. The stem end looks prettiest if trimmed in a conical shape.)

Heat oil in a 10- to 12-inch skillet over a medium flame. Add the onions and garlic and fry, stirring frequently, for 5 minutes. Add okra and fry for another 5 minutes. Now put in the turmeric, salt, black pepper, cayenne, and ¼ cup water. Stir well

For information about ingredients and basic techniques that may be unfamiliar, see General Information, pages 418–36.

to mix. Cover tightly, lower heat, and steam gently for about 15 to 20 minutes or until okra is tender. (Larger pods will take a bit longer to cook through.)

Stir very gently every 5 minutes, replacing the lid each time. If any extra liquid remains in the skillet, it should be boiled away so okra has a "dry" look.

Usha's
SWEET-AND-SOUR OKRA WITH CHICKPEAS
INDIA

This is a wonderful dish and a great family favorite. Not only is it fairly simple to make, but it can be made a day in advance. In fact, the flavor seems to improve if it sits overnight in the refrigerator. The original recipe called for only okra. You can make it that way, if you like—it is scrumptious. I added the chickpeas to improve the food value of the dish and because I think that the combination of okra and chickpeas, drenched in a sweet and sour tamarind sauce, is quite felicitous. This is an easy dish to prepare in advance.

I make it with fresh okra, but you could use a package of frozen, cut okra if fresh is unavailable. Defrost first. Remember that fresh okra should always be washed and wiped off *before* it is cut.

(serves 4–6)

¾ pound fresh okra
4 tablespoons vegetable oil
1 teaspoon whole black mustard seeds
6 to 7 fresh or 9 to 10 dried curry leaves
8 cloves garlic, peeled and minced
1 teaspoon ground cumin seeds
2 teaspoons ground coriander seeds
½ teaspoon ground turmeric
⅛ teaspoon cayenne pepper, or more to taste
1 cup drained chickpeas, canned or home-cooked, (see page 83)
½ teaspoon salt
2 tablespoons tamarind paste
1 tablespoon sugar

Wash the okra and dry it off. Trim it at the ends. The top looks best if trimmed—almost peeled—in a cone shape. Now cut the okra crosswise into ½-inch pieces.

Heat the oil in an 8- to 9-inch skillet over a medium flame. When hot, put in the mustard seeds and the curry leaves. A few seconds later, put in the garlic. Stir and fry until the garlic pieces turn brown at the edges. Now put in the okra, cumin, coriander, turmeric, and cayenne. Stir and cook for 1 minute. Add 1 cup water. Bring to a simmer, cover, turn heat to low, and cook gently for 10 minutes or until okra is almost done. Now add the chickpeas, salt, tamarind paste, and sugar. Mix gently. Bring to a simmer again. Cover and cook on low heat another 5 minutes. Stir.

OKRA FRIED WITH ONION AND GREEN CHILI

INDIA

If you wish to double the recipe, double the okra, onion, green chili, and salt. Use a 12-inch skillet with a good ½ inch of oil in it. The cooking time should remain about the same.

(serves 2 as a vegetable, more as a topping for rice or in yogurt)

6   ounces fresh okra
1   small onion
Vegetable oil for shallow frying
½   fresh hot green chili, minced
⅛   teaspoon salt

Wash the okra and pat it as dry as possible. Trim the okra at both ends and cut into ⅛-inch rounds.

Peel the onion. Cut it in half lengthwise and then cut into very fine half circles. Heat ⅓ inch oil in a 8- to 9-inch skillet over a medium flame. When the oil is smoking, put in the okra, onion, and green chili. Turn heat to medium-high. Stir and fry for about 10 minutes or until okra is crisp and onion is a medium-brown color and also crisp. Remove with a slotted spoon and put on a plate lined with a paper towel. Sprinkle salt over okra, mix, and serve hot.

OKRA WITH TOMATOES

KUWAIT
                                        (serves 6)

1½ pounds fresh (or frozen) tender okra
6   tablespoons olive oil
4   cloves garlic, peeled and minced
2   medium-sized onions, peeled and cut into ¾-inch dice
2   medium-sized tomatoes, peeled and coarsely chopped
1   teaspoon ground coriander
1½ teaspoons salt, or to taste
⅛   teaspoon freshly ground black pepper
1   tablespoon lemon juice

Wash the okra and trim it. (To trim the okra, cut off a small section at the tip. The stem end looks prettiest if trimmed in a conical shape.)

Heat the oil in a 10- to 12-inch skillet over a medium flame. Put in the garlic and onions. Stir and fry until onions turn translucent, turning the heat down if necessary. Put in the okra. Stir and fry for another minute. Now put in all the remaining ingredients plus ½ cup water and bring to a simmer. Cover, turn heat to low, and cook gently for 15 to 20 minutes or until okra is tender. (Larger pods will take a bit longer to cook through.)

Serve either hot or cold.

For information about ingredients and basic techniques that may be unfamiliar, see General Information, pages 418–36.

PEAS WITH GINGER

JAPAN

(serves 4)

1 cup *dashi* (see page 291)
½ teaspoon sugar
½ teaspoon *mirin*
1 teaspoon Japanese soy sauce
¼ teaspoon salt
2 cups shelled peas
2 teaspoons finely grated fresh ginger

Combine the *dashi*, sugar, *mirin*, soy sauce, and salt in a small (1½-quart) pot. Add the peas and bring to a boil. Cover, lower heat, and simmer about 5 minutes or until the peas are tender. Drain but do not discard the liquid.

Divide the peas into four portions, put each portion in the center of a small bowl and add 1 tablespoon of the cooking liquid. Now arrange a small cone of grated ginger—½ teaspoon to a serving—on top of each pile of peas. Before eating, each diner uses his chopsticks to mix the ginger with the peas.

PEAS WITH PARSLEY AND COCONUT

INDIA

This Gujarati dish is normally made with fresh peas and fresh Chinese parsley. Once, when those two ingredients were unavailable, I came up with this variation.

(serves 6)

1 cup freshly grated coconut
1 cup finely chopped parsley, firmly packed
1 fresh hot green chili, minced
¾ to 1 teaspoon salt
2 teaspoons sugar
3 tablespoons sesame seeds, dry roasted and coarsely ground
⅛ teaspoon freshly ground black pepper
3 10-ounce packages frozen peas
4 tablespoons unsalted butter

In a bowl, mix together the coconut, parsley, green chili, salt, sugar, sesame seeds, and black pepper. Rub with your hands to mix thoroughly.

Bring 2 cups of water to a boil in a heavy saucepan. Add the peas. Bring to a boil again. Cover and cook 2 minutes. Empty the peas into a colander and drain away the water. Melt the butter in the same saucepan over a low flame. Add the peas and stir them around in the butter. Add the coconut-parsley mixture and mix gently. Cover the saucepan and steam the peas on very low heat for about 2 to 3 minutes. Stir once or twice as the peas steam.

Zakiya's
POTATOES AND ONIONS
INDIA

This dish, while it can be eaten as part of any Indian meal, forms the traditional "stuffing" for *dosas* (see page 267). The *dosa*, a kind of pancake or bread made with rice and *urad dal*, is put on a plate, some of this potato-onion mixture is placed on top of it, and the *dosa* is folded over once. The stuffed *dosa* is then called a *Masala Dosa* and serves the same function as a sandwich does in America.

(serves 4–6 as a vegetable dish and will stuff 8 dosas)

4   medium-sized boiling potatoes (1 pound)
A   ¾-inch cube fresh ginger, peeled and cut into 3 to 4 pieces
1   fresh hot green chili, or more to taste, cut into 2 to 3 pieces
¼   cup vegetable oil
A   generous pinch of ground asafetida
1   teaspoon whole black mustard seeds
2   medium-sized onions, peeled and coarsely chopped
¼   teaspoon ground turmeric
1   teaspoon salt

Boil the potatoes until tender. Let them cool, then peel and cut them into ¾-inch dice.

Put the ginger and green chili into the container of a food processor or blender along with ¼ cup of water and blend until you have a somewhat grainy paste. Set aside.

Heat the oil in an 8- to 9-inch skillet over a medium flame. When hot, put in the asafetida first and then, a second later, the mustard seeds. As soon as the mustard seeds begin to pop (this takes just a few seconds), put in the onions. Turn the heat down slightly and sauté the onions for about 5 minutes or until they turn translucent. (Do not let them brown.) Now add the paste from the food processor as well as the turmeric. Stir and cook for 1 minute. Put in the potatoes, 1 cup water, and the salt. Cover, and cook on medium-low heat for about 5 minutes. Lift cover and, using a slotted spoon, break the potato pieces into smaller ⅓- to ½-inch cubes. Cover again and cook on very low heat for another 3 to 4 minutes. The "sauce" for the potato dish should now be very thick. Serve either as is or stuff *Masala Dosa* according to directions on page 267.

Usha's
POTATOES AND TOMATOES COOKED WITH FRESH COCONUT
INDIA

I love this dish with an irrational passion. Irrational, because the basic ingredient, the very humble potato, does not go through some glamorous transformation. It does not, for example, turn into anything resembling the many-petaled Pommes Anna. Nor is it mashed and squeezed into soft, dainty patterns. No, here the humble potato stays the humble potato and is cooked, very simply, with rather prosaic ingredients—garlic, tomatoes, cumin, turmeric, and coconut. But the dish is utterly delicious, especially when eaten with Indian breads.

I am not sure what region of India is responsible for this tasty marvel. I got this recipe from a friend whose parents, from the western Kutch region,

---

For information about ingredients and basic techniques that may be unfamiliar, see General Information, pages 418–36.

often cooked it. She suspects the dish is Kutchi, but is not sure. It is a kind of thick, earthy potato stew.

NOTE: Do not use an aluminum pot for this dish.

(serves 6)

3   medium-sized boiling potatoes
    (about 1¼ pounds)
4   tablespoons vegetable oil
6   cloves garlic, peeled and minced
1   whole dried hot red pepper
1   teaspoon whole cumin seeds
1½ cups freshly grated coconut
½   teaspoon ground turmeric
2   teaspoons ground cumin seeds
1¼ pounds fresh, red-ripe tomatoes, peeled and
    diced into ½-inch pieces, or a 16- to 20-ounce
    can of Italian tomatoes
2   teaspoons salt
2   teaspoons sugar
1   teaspoon red wine vinegar

Peel the potatoes, then cut into ¾-inch dice and put into a bowl of cold water.

Heat the oil in a heavy, 3-quart pot over a medium-high flame. When hot, put in the minced garlic. Stir for about 5 seconds. Now put in the red pepper and the cumin seeds. Stir for another 3 seconds. The garlic should brown lightly, the red pepper should darken, and the cumin seeds should sizzle. Lower the heat to medium, put in the grated coconut and stir it around for 10 to 15 seconds.

Drain the potatoes. Add them as well as the turmeric, ground cumin, tomatoes (including any juice that may have accumulated or the juice in the can), the salt, and 1½ cups of water. Bring to a boil. Cover, turn heat to low, and simmer for about

45 minutes or until potatoes are tender. Stir gently every 7 to 8 minutes during this cooking period.

Put in the sugar and vinegar. Stir again and cook, uncovered, for 1 minute.

POTATOES WITH CHICKPEAS
MIDDLE EAST

(serves 6)

6   tablespoons olive oil
3   cloves garlic, peeled and minced
2   medium-sized onions, peeled and
    coarsely chopped
3   medium-sized tomatoes, peeled and chopped
4   medium-sized potatoes, freshly boiled, peeled,
    and cut into ¾-inch dice
1½ cups drained, cooked chickpeas (see page 83)
1½ to 2 teaspoons salt, or to taste
⅛   teaspoon freshly ground black pepper
1½ tablespoons lemon juice

Heat the oil in a 10-inch skillet over a medium flame. When hot, put in the garlic and onions. Stir and fry until onions are translucent, turning the heat down if necessary. Add the chopped tomatoes. Stir and cook for 1 minute. Add all the remaining ingredients plus 1 cup water. Bring to a boil. Cover. Lower heat and simmer gently for 20 minutes.

POTATO STEW

CHINA

This is one of those Chinese vegetable dishes that is not stir-fried. There are many hearty stews cooked all over China, though such dishes are rarely served in the Chinese restaurants of this country. Here is one such dish. The vegetables do not retain any of their crispness or their color. They turn quite soft from the slower cooking and quite dark from the soy sauce. Nonetheless, they are very tasty.

This dish may be cooked ahead of time and reheated. If you wish to do that, leave about 1 inch of sauce at the bottom; this way you can do the boiling down and the reheating simultaneously.

(serves 4–6)

¼ cup vegetable oil

2 cloves garlic, peeled and lightly crushed

2 quarter-sized slices of fresh ginger, lightly crushed

¾ pound boiling potatoes, peeled and cut roughly into 1½-inch cubes

½ pound green beans, trimmed and cut into 2-inch lengths

2 carrots, peeled and cut crosswise into 1½-inch-long segments

6 ounces mushrooms (if possible, with approximately 1½-inch caps)

¼ cup Chinese dark soy sauce

4 teaspoons sugar

2 tablespoons *shaohsing* wine or dry sherry

Heat the oil in an 8-inch-wide, heavy-bottomed pot over a medium-high flame. When hot, put in the garlic and ginger. Stir and fry for 15 seconds. Add the potatoes, beans, and carrots. Stir and fry for 1 minute. Add the mushrooms. Stir and fry for

another minute. Now put in 2 cups water, the soy sauce, sugar, and wine. Bring to a boil. Cover, lower heat, and simmer for about 20 minutes or until potatoes are just tender. Remove cover and turn heat to high. Boil away most of the liquid. You should have about ⅛ inch of sauce left at the bottom of the pot. Stir the vegetables gently as you boil the liquid down. Remove the ginger and garlic, if you like.

Pallavi's

ALOO ACHAAR
(Potato Salad)

NEPAL

Eaten frequently as a snack, this potato salad comes from the kingdom of Nepal on India's northern frontier. Its dressing is made with ground sesame seeds, sesame oil, lemon juice, and hot green chilies. The chilies provide the "hotness" and lots of vitamin C. If you do not like hot foods, regular green pepper can be substituted for the hot chili. Asafetida is also used in this recipe, chiefly because of its digestive powers. Even though *Aloo achaar* can be eaten an hour or two after it's made, it tastes best when the dressing has been allowed to be absorbed for 12 hours; it keeps well in the refrigerator for 3 to 4 days.

(serves 4–6)

4 medium-sized waxy boiling potatoes

4 tablespoons ground roasted sesame seeds

For information about ingredients and basic techniques that may be unfamiliar, see General Information, pages 418–36.

"DRY" POTATOES COOKED WITH MUSTARD SEEDS
INDIA

3 tablespoons or more lemon juice
1 teaspoon salt
1 to 4 fresh hot green chilies, very finely minced, or 2 tablespoons minced green pepper
4 tablespoons sesame oil
2 teaspoons vegetable oil
A pinch of ground asafetida
8 to 10 whole fenugreek seeds
3 tablespoons minced Chinese (or other) parsley

Put the potatoes to boil.

Combine the ground sesame seeds, lemon juice, salt, and green chilies in a stainless-steel or nonmetallic bowl. Add the 4 tablespoons of sesame oil a few drops at a time, and beat in with a thin wire whisk or a fork.

Heat the vegetable oil in a metal ladle (hold the ladle over the heat) or a small butter warmer. When very hot, put in the asafetida and the fenugreek seeds. As soon as the fenugreek seeds begin to darken (this takes just a few seconds), pour the oil and spices into the dressing. Mix well. Add the minced Chinese parsley and mix again. Check seasonings.

When the potatoes are cooked, drain and peel them while they are still hot. If necessary, hold them with a fork to do so. Dice the hot potatoes into ¾-inch cubes. Put the diced potatoes into the bowl with the dressing and mix gently. Adjust seasonings, if necessary. Let cool, cover, and refrigerate if not eating within the next couple of hours. This salad may be eaten cold or at room temperature.

Traditionally, this dish is made in a *karhai* (wok), but a skillet will work very well also.

(serves 4)

4 medium-sized boiling potatoes, the waxier the better (1½ pounds)
6 tablespoons vegetable oil
1/16 teaspoon ground asafetida
1 tablespoon whole black mustard seeds
¼ teaspoon ground turmeric
¾ to 1 teaspoon salt
1/16 to 1/8 teaspoon cayenne pepper

Peel the potatoes and dice them into ¾-inch pieces. Put the diced potatoes into a bowl of water and drain them just before you start to cook.

Heat the oil in a 10- to 12-inch skillet over a medium-high flame. As soon as the oil is hot, put in the asafetida. A second after that, put in the mustard seeds. Half a second after that, put in the turmeric. Now quickly put in the drained potatoes. Stir and fry for ½ minute. Cover the potatoes and turn flame to low. Cook, covered, for about half an hour or until potatoes are cooked through but retain their shape. Stir gently every 5 to 7 minutes, replacing the cover each time. When the potatoes are done, sprinkle the salt and cayenne over them. Stir again to mix.

DUM ALOO
(Moghlai Potatoes in a Thick Brown Sauce)
INDIA

When the Moghuls ruled India, not too many vegetables were eaten in their grand courts. They ate salads—raw cucumber, tomatoes, and radishes—as well as cooked spinach. And they ate potatoes. The potatoes were often cooked as if they were meat, in thick, dark sauces. A cooking technique that the formerly nomadic Moghuls had picked up during their sojourn in areas like modern Uzbekistan, Kazakhstan, Iran, and Afghanistan, was something they referred to as *dum*. It was a form of covered baking—of letting foods cook in their own steam—without using ovens of any kind. After a food had been browned, it was put into a heavy pot along with fried onions, spices, and herbs, and then covered with a heavy lid. A long, snakelike roll of dough was wrapped around the outer edges of the lid to seal the pot completely. The pot was placed over very low heat—often just smoldering ashes—and extra live coals were piled on top of the lid. The food, getting gentle heat from above and below, "baked" slowly.

Even though what you see below is the classical recipe for *Dum Aloo*, I cook the dish entirely on top of the stove, without any live coals on the lid!

(serves 4–6)

12 smallish potatoes (about 1½ pounds)
1½ tablespoons plus 1 teaspoon kosher salt
8 to 10 blanched almonds (½ ounce)
2 tablespoons white poppy seeds
2 large black cardamom pods
2 teaspoons ground coriander seeds

1½ teaspoons whole cumin seeds
4 cloves garlic, peeled and chopped
A 1-inch cube fresh ginger, peeled and chopped
8 tablespoons vegetable oil
1 medium-sized onion, peeled and minced
5 whole cardamom pods, very lightly crushed
¼ teaspoon ground turmeric
⅛ teaspoon cayenne pepper
8 ounces (1 cup) plain yogurt
1 teaspoon *garam masala*

Peel the potatoes and prick them well with a fork. Soak them for 1 hour in a bowl with 4 cups water and 1½ tablespoons salt.

Meanwhile, put the almonds, white poppy seeds, black cardamom, ground coriander, and 1 teaspoon of the whole cumin seeds in a small cast-iron skillet and dry-roast them, stirring frequently, until the almonds turn golden in spots. Put all the roasted ingredients into the container of a clean coffee grinder and grind as finely as possible. Leave in grinder container.

Put the garlic and ginger, along with ⅓ cup water, into the container of an electric blender or food processor. Blend until you have a smooth paste. Leave in blender container.

When the potatoes have soaked for an hour, drain and wipe them well. Heat oil in a heavy, 10-inch-wide pot, sauté pan, or deep skillet over a medium flame. Put in the potatoes and fry them, stirring, until they turn a golden brown on all sides. Remove with a slotted spoon and set aside on a plate.

For information about ingredients and basic techniques that may be unfamiliar, see General Information, pages 418–36.

(serves 6)

Add the remaining ½ teaspoon whole cumin seeds to the oil in the pot and stir once. Now put in the minced onion. Fry, stirring, until the onion turns a light brown. Add the crushed cardamom pods, the turmeric, and the cayenne. Fry and stir for a few seconds. Next, put in the garlic and ginger paste from the blender, the nut and spice mixture from the coffee grinder, and 1 teaspoon salt. Stir and fry the mixture. Whenever it seems to dry up and begins to get ready to catch at the bottom, add a tablespoon of yogurt. Keep stirring and frying, adding yogurt whenever necessary, until all the yogurt is used up. (It is important that the yogurt fry and assimilate slowly with the sauce. This can only happen if a little yogurt is added at a time.)

Add *garam masala* and ½ cup water. Mix well. Put in the browned potatoes and mix gently. Cover the pot tightly with aluminum foil, making sure you crimp and seal the edges, and then with its own lid. Turn heat to very low and cook gently for about 30 minutes or until potatoes are cooked through. Stir gently a few times while the potatoes are cooking, always replacing the foil and the lid. The potatoes should have a very thick sauce clinging to them when they are done.

DICED POTATOES WITH SPINACH
INDIA

All over North India, potatoes are cooked with greens. Fenugreek greens are preferred, but spinach makes a good alternative.

5 medium-sized waxy boiling potatoes (about 2 pounds)
1 tablespoon plus 1 teaspoon salt
1 pound fresh or 1 package frozen leaf spinach
6 tablespoons vegetable oil or *ghee*
½ teaspoon whole black mustard seeds
1 large onion (3 to 3½ ounces), peeled and chopped
2 cloves garlic, peeled and minced
1 teaspoon *garam masala*
1/16 to ⅛ teaspoon cayenne pepper (optional)

Bring 2½ quarts of water to a boil. Peel potatoes and dice into ¾-inch cubes, then add to boiling water with 1 tablespoon salt. Bring to a boil again. Cover, turn heat to low and cook potatoes until they are just tender—about 6 minutes. Do not overcook. Drain. Spread potatoes out and leave to cool.

If using fresh spinach, wash carefully and drop into large kettle of boiling water to wilt. Drain. Squeeze out as much liquid as possible from spinach and chop fine. If using frozen leaf spinach, cook according to instructions. Drain, squeeze out liquid, and chop. Set aside.

Heat oil in a heavy, 12-inch, preferably nonstick skillet over a medium-high flame. When very hot, put in the mustard seeds. As soon as the seeds begin to pop (this just takes a few seconds), add the onion and the garlic. Turn heat to medium and fry for 3 to 4 minutes. Onions should turn very lightly brown at the edges. Now put in the chopped spinach and keep stirring and frying for another 10 minutes.

Add the cooked potatoes, 1 teaspoon salt, the *garam masala*, and the cayenne pepper. Stir and mix gently until potatoes are heated through.

POTATOES WITH WHOLE SPICES AND SESAME SEEDS

INDIA

Here is another scrumptious (and easy) dish in which the potatoes are first boiled, allowed to cool, diced, and then shallow-fried with cumin, fenugreek, and mustard seeds, as well as lots of sesame seeds. As the potatoes brown lightly, the spices form a delicious "crust" around them.

(serves 6)

8 to 9 medium-sized boiling potatoes (2 pounds)
2   teaspoons whole cumin seeds
¼ teaspoon whole fenugreek seeds
2   teaspoons whole black mustard seeds
6   tablespoons vegetable oil
⅛ teaspoon ground asafetida
1 to 3 dried hot red peppers
2   tablespoons sesame seeds
¼ teaspoon ground turmeric
2   teaspoons salt
Freshly ground black pepper to taste
2   teaspoons ground *amchoor*

Boil the potatoes in their jackets. Drain and allow them to cool for 3 to 4 hours. Peel the potatoes and then dice them into approximately ¾-inch cubes.

Combine the cumin, fenugreek, and mustard seeds in a small cup and arrange all the ingredients near the stove in the order in which they go into the skillet.

Heat the oil in a large 12- to 14-inch heavy skillet over a medium flame. When very hot, put in the spices in this order: First put in the ground asafetida and let it sizzle for 3 seconds; then put in the combined cumin, fenugreek, and black mustard seeds and let them sizzle another 5 seconds; put in the red peppers and stir the spices around for 3 seconds; put in the sesame seeds and stir spices another 5 seconds; now add the turmeric, stir once, and put in the diced potatoes.

Turn heat up to medium-high. Stir and fry the potatoes for 5 minutes. Add the salt, pepper, and the *amchoor*. Stir and fry for another 5 minutes. The potatoes should get a few light-brown spots on them.

Tatie Wawo-Runtu's

SAMBAL GORENG KENTANG KERING
(Spicy "Shoestring" Potatoes)

INDONESIA

It is hard enough for me to keep my hands off "shoestring" potatoes when they are freshly made and seasoned very simply with salt and pepper. Indonesians go a step further and add a fried paste of fried red peppers, shallots, and garlic to them as well. The result is quite irresistible.

(serves 4–6)

4   ounces shallots,
      peeled and coarsely
      chopped to make
      a heaping ½ cup
2   cloves garlic, peeled
4   fresh or dried
      hot red chilies, seeded

For information about ingredients and basic techniques that may be unfamiliar, see General Information, pages 418–36.

1   pound boiling potatoes
Vegetable oil for deep frying
1   teaspoon salt

Put the shallots, garlic, and red peppers into the container of a food processor or blender. Add 3 tablespoons water and blend until you have a smooth paste.

Peel the potatoes and cut them into ⅛-inch-thick slices. You may use a mandolin, food processor, or knife to do this. Stack about five slices together at a time and cut them into "shoestrings," about ⅛-inch thick. (You should either fry the potatoes as soon as you have finished cutting them or else leave them to soak in water and then pat them dry whenever you are ready for the frying.)

Line a sieve with paper towels and place it over a bowl. Keep another plate or bowl nearby. Heat oil for deep frying, preferably in a wok, over a medium flame. You should have about 2½ inches of oil in the center of the wok and aim for a temperature of about 350° to 375° F. When the oil is hot, put in just enough of the potatoes to make a ⅓-inch-thick layer on top of the oil. Stir and fry until the potatoes are golden and crisp, adjusting the heat if necessary. Remove the potatoes with a slotted spoon and leave them to drain in the sieve. Fry a second batch the same way. Just before you remove this second batch from the wok, take the first batch out of the sieve and put it on the plate nearby. Change the paper towel in the sieve. Now you are ready to take the second batch out of the wok and let it drain in the empty sieve. Do all the potatoes this way.

Turn the heat off from under the wok and let the oil cool slightly. Remove all but ¼ cup oil from the wok. Heat the oil again over a medium-low flame.

When hot, put in the paste from the food processor. Stir and fry for 10 to 12 minutes or until the paste is fairly dry. Add the potatoes and salt. Stir gently to mix.

POTATOES COOKED WITH GARLIC AND SESAME SEEDS
INDIA

For this Gujarati recipe, I prefer using boiling potatoes, no wider than 2 inches in diameter. The waxier the potato, the better this dish will taste and look.

(serves 4–6)

2   pounds medium-sized boiling potatoes
5   tablespoons vegetable oil
1   tablespoon sesame seeds
3   good-sized cloves garlic, peeled and slivered
½   teaspoon ground turmeric
⅛   teaspoon ground asafetida
1   teaspoon salt
⅛   teaspoon cayenne pepper (optional)

Peel the potatoes and cut into fingers ("French fries"), ⅓- to ½-inch thick. Put fingers into a bowl of cold water for half an hour or more. Drain and wipe dry.

Heat the oil in an 8- to 9-inch skillet over a medium flame. When it is hot, put in the potatoes and cook them, turning once or twice, for 8 to 10 minutes. The potatoes should be partially cooked and not browned. Remove potatoes with a slotted spoon to a plate and set aside.

Put the sesame seeds into the same skillet. Stir once. Now add the slivers of garlic, continuing to stir and fry over a medium flame. When the garlic begins to turn brown, put in the turmeric and asafetida. Stir once. Now quickly add the half-cooked potatoes, salt, and cayenne. Stir again. Cover. Turn heat to low and cook gently until potatoes are done. Stir frequently.

Mrs. Chawdhry's
FRIED POTATOES
PAKISTAN

Mrs. Chawdhry is a wonderful cook who has taught me a great deal about northwestern Indian foods. She lives in Delhi now but her original home was in Multan which, since the Partition of 1947, has been part of Pakistan. As the northwestern section of the Indo-Pakistan subcontinent is close to Afghanistan and Iran, it has always been the region most influenced by the cooking style of its northern neighbors. This potato recipe uses a Multani spice combination that has dried pomegranate seeds in it. The pomegranate, used with great frequency in Persian foods, as well as the very Indian dried green mango powder *(amchoor)*, add a tartness to this dish that is most pleasing. I love this potato dish so much that I can have it at almost any time of the day—with fried eggs and grilled tomato halves for breakfast, with a cup of steaming tea in the late afternoon, and with almost any Indian lunch or dinner.

(serves 4)

8   small, smooth, boiling potatoes (¾ to 1 pound)
4   tablespoons vegetable oil
¼   teaspoon black (or other) cumin seeds
¼   teaspoon turmeric
¼   teaspoon or more salt
¹⁄₁₆ teaspoon cayenne pepper (optional)
¼   teaspoon Multani *garam marsala*
¼   teaspoon ground *amchoor*
A   generous pinch black salt (optional)

Boil the potatoes in their jackets. Either refrigerate overnight or allow the potatoes to cool for several hours, then peel and cut into quarters lengthwise.

Heat the oil in a heavy skillet or wok over a medium flame. When smoking, put in the cumin seeds. They will begin to sizzle immediately. Quickly put in the turmeric, stir once, and add the potatoes. Gently stir and fry the potatoes until they are golden brown on all sides. Remove potatoes with a slotted spoon and place on a warm plate lined with paper towels. Mix the salt, cayenne, *garam masala*, *amchoor*, and black salt, making sure that there are no *amchoor* lumps. Arrange the potatoes on a warm serving dish in a single layer and sprinkle with the dry spice mixture. Serve immediately.

For information about ingredients and basic techniques that may be unfamiliar, see General Information, pages 418–36.

YELLOW PUMPKIN COOKED WITH SOY SAUCE

JAPAN

This is an utterly delicious way of preparing fall pumpkins. The vegetable cooks quickly and holds its shape. The Japanese use a green-skinned pumpkin for this recipe. They leave the cubes unpeeled, and often etch patterns, like the veins of leaves, on the skin. Many Japanese vegetable stores sell already cubed and "etched" pumpkin pieces to grateful housewives—Japanese stores in Japan, that is.

At formal Japanese meals just one or two pumpkin cubes (without their liquid) are served to each person. The pumpkin generally shares a plate with other vegetables.

(serves 4)

A 1-pound section of yellow pumpkin
½ cup sugar
1   tablespoon soy sauce
½ teaspoon salt

Peel the pumpkin and cut into approximately ¾-inch cubes. Put 4 cups water, the sugar, and the pumpkin cubes into a pot and bring to a boil. Cover, lower heat, and simmer about 5 minutes or until pumpkin is barely tender. Remove pumpkin with slotted spoon. Boil down the sweet cooking liquid until you have about 1½ cups left. Add soy sauce and salt. Put the pumpkin back into the pot and simmer, uncovered, another minute. Let pumpkin cool in the liquid. Reheat before serving.

FRESH SOY BEANS, STEAMED

CHINA

Fresh soy beans, still green and in their pods, are available in America chiefly around the farmlands where they are grown. They are harder to find in large cities, unless, of course, those cities have Chinese grocery stores. And they are only available in season. But if you ever see a vegetable that resembles a hairy pea pod, ask if it is a soy bean and do buy it. Soy beans are excellent—and quite addictive—when steamed. The Chinese steam them for 15 to 20 minutes, often throwing a star anise into the steaming water for its special aroma, and then sit around with a bowlful between them, peeling the pods and eating the beans as a snack.

(serves 4)

1   star anise (optional)
1   pound fresh green soy beans in their pods

Set up a steaming apparatus. You could place a bamboo steamer on top of a wok that has water in it or else place a steaming trivet inside a pot. Throw the star anise into the water and bring it to a boil. Remember that the water should stay just below the level of the perforated steamer. Once the water is boiling, put in the soy beans. Cover your bamboo steamer or pot and steam for 15 to 20 minutes or until beans are tender. Remove from heat.

Serve the beans in a bowl. Then just peel and eat them. They may be eaten hot, warm, or cold.

SNOWPEAS COOKED IN DASHI

JAPAN

(serves 4)

5 ½ ounces snowpeas
1   teaspoon salt
¼ cup *dashi* (see page 291)
1   teaspoon sugar
2   teaspoons Japanese soy sauce

String the snowpeas by bending their little stems backward and then dragging them along the spines of the peas. Put the peas in a bowl. Add ½ teaspoon salt and toss. Set aside for 10 minutes. Rinse off the peas.

Put the *dashi*, remaining ½ teaspoon salt, and sugar into a pot. Bring to a simmer. Add the peas and simmer so the liquid is always bubbling, for 1 minute. Stir the peas as you do this. Remove the peas with a slotted spoon and spread out on a plate to cool.

Add the soy sauce to the liquid in the pot. Stir and boil down for a few seconds. You should have about 2 tablespoons of liquid left. Let this liquid cool off. Then pour it over the peas.

OSHITASHI
(Spinach with Roasted Sesame Seeds)

JAPAN

This simple spinach dish is also served in Korea, where it is called *sigumchi namul*.

(serves 4)

10 ounces to 1 pound spinach, well washed and
    trimmed
1 ½ tablespoons soy sauce
1 ½ tablespoons *mirin*
1   tablespoon sesame seeds, roasted and lightly
    crushed

Fill a 4- to 5-quart pot three-quarters full of water and bring to a rolling boil. Drop the spinach into it. Push the spinach down, if necessary. Cook the spinach 2 to 3 minutes or until it has wilted completely. Drain spinach in a colander. Run some cold water over the spinach to cool it off and fix its bright-green color. Squeeze all the water out of the spinach and put it into a bowl. Add the soy sauce, *mirin*, and crushed sesame seeds. Mix well. Divide into four portions. Make hillocklike piles of each portion. Place the hillocks in the center of four small Japanese or Chinese dishes. Serve at room temperature.

For information about ingredients and basic techniques that may be unfamiliar, see General Information, pages 418–36.

Tatie Wawo-Runtu's

SPINACH WITH SHALLOTS

INDONESIA

(serves 4)

2 pounds spinach, trimmed and washed
½ to 1 fresh hot red pepper or green chili
¼ cup vegetable oil
4 ounces shallots, peeled and slivered to make a
    heaping ½ cup
About ¾ teaspoon salt, or to taste
1 teaspoon sugar

Cut the spinach crosswise into 2-inch-wide strips.

Cut the hot pepper crosswise into ⅛-inch-thick rings.

Heat the oil in a wok or a large, heavy skillet over a medium-high flame. Add the shallots. Stir and fry for about 2 minutes. Put in the red pepper, salt, and sugar. Stir to mix. Add the spinach, stirring to mix. Add ½ cup water, cover, and cook for 5 minutes on the medium-high flame. Remove cover. Stir and mix again.

Yien-Koo's

SPINACH WITH FERMENTED BEAN CURD

CHINA

Fermented bean curd, best compared to a strong, ripe, soft cheese like Camembert, has quite a powerful taste and aroma. It gives its own very special flavor to foods that are cooked with it. As it is fairly salty, it seasons the foods at the same time. The bottled fermented bean curd that I have seen in New York comes in approximately ½-inch cubes. My favorite is the winy Red Bean Curd.

(serves 3–4)

1 teaspoon salt
1¼ teaspoons sugar
1 pound fresh spinach, trimmed and washed
3 cubes of fermented bean curd
½ teaspoon sesame oil
3 tablespoons vegetable oil
3 quarter-sized slices of fresh ginger, very lightly
    mashed

Bring 4 quarts of water to a boil in a large pot. Add the salt, sugar, and the spinach. Bring the water to a boil again. Let the spinach boil for 1 minute or until it is tender. Drain and rinse under cold water. Press out as much liquid from the leaves as possible. Separate the leaves so they are not all entangled.

In a small bowl, mash the fermented bean curd. Slowly add 2 teaspoons of water so you have a thick paste. Add the sesame oil and mix it in.

Heat the vegetable oil in a wok over a medium-high flame. When hot, put in the ginger slices and stir them around for 15 to 20 seconds, pressing them against the sides of the wok. Remove the ginger with a slotted spoon and discard it. Put the spinach in the wok. Stir and fry it for about 1 minute. Pour the bean-curd mixture over the spinach. Stir to mix and serve at once.

SPINACH WITH SCALLIONS, COOKED IN THE MOGHLAI STYLE

INDIA

(serves 6)

3 pounds spinach, trimmed and washed
8 tablespoons *ghee* or vegetable oil
6 scallions, trimmed, white and pale green sections finely minced
2 teaspoons fresh ginger, finely grated
1 teaspoon minced fresh hot green chili
1 ½ teaspoons salt
½ teaspoon sugar
½ teaspoon *garam masala*

Fill a large 4- to 5-quart pot three-quarters full with water and bring to a boil. Put the spinach, a few handfuls at a time, into the water, just long enough to wilt it. Remove each batch with a pair of tongs and place in a colander. Do all the spinach this way.

Squeeze as much water as possible out of the spinach and chop it fine.

Heat *ghee* or oil in a wide, heavy pot over a medium flame. Put in the scallions and sauté for 2 to 3 minutes. Scallions should not brown but they should wilt slightly. Now add the ginger and green chili. Sauté another minute or two. Scallions should be quite translucent. If they start browning, turn down the heat. Add spinach, salt, and sugar. Sauté on low heat, stirring frequently, for 20 minutes. Sprinkle with *garam masala* and mix.

Mrs. Sinha's
SPINACH COOKED IN A BIHARI STYLE

INDIA

The Indian state of Bihar lies south of Nepal and just west of Bengal. Like their Bengali neighbors, Biharis cook many vegetables in mustard oil. This dish, traditionally made with mixed greens that include *chana* greens, mustard greens, and spinach, resembles an Italian pesto, though it is much thicker in consistency. In place of olive oil, mustard oil is used and, apart from the taste of the greens themselves, the other strong flavors include raw garlic, raw ginger, green chilies, and Chinese parsley. It is eaten for breakfast at room temperature, accompanied by *pooris* and hot tea.

For those who might recoil at the very thought of raw garlic so early in the morning, let me repeat here that Indians consider this seasoning to be much more than a mere culinary boon. They view it as medicinal manna, the cure-all for circulatory ailments. Hundreds of thousands in India swallow a crushed clove of garlic every morning in the same way that Americans swallow vitamin and iron pills.

The mustard oil used in this dish is not cooked. Hence it has the lovely nose-tingling pungency that is characteristic of the raw oil (see General Information).

(serves 4–6)

1 ½ pounds fresh spinach, washed
½ teaspoon finely grated fresh ginger
½ teaspoon finely mashed garlic (use a mortar or a grater)
½ teaspoon very finely minced fresh hot green chili
½ teaspoon salt

For information about ingredients and basic techniques that may be unfamiliar, see General Information, pages 418–36.

2 tablespoons very finely minced fresh Chinese
   parsley
2 tablespoons mustard oil

Bring 4 quarts of water to a rolling boil in a large
pot. Put in the spinach and cook it on high heat for
1 to 2 minutes or until it is wilted. Drain it, rinse
under running water, and then squeeze out as much
liquid as you can easily.

Put the spinach in the container of a food processor or blender. Add 2 tablespoons of water and
blend until spinach is smooth. You should have a
fairly thick paste.

Take the spinach out and put it in a serving
bowl.

Mix the ginger, garlic, green chili, salt, Chinese
parsley, and oil in a cup just as you would a
dressing. Pour the mixture over the spinach and
mix it in thoroughly.

YELLOW SQUASH WITH ONIONS, TOMATO, AND CUMIN

INDIA

This popular North Indian dish is normally made
with the pale green, bowling-pin-shaped squash
available in America only in Indian and Chinese
grocery stores. If you can manage to find it, peel it
first and then proceed with the recipe. Otherwise
yellow squash makes a good substitute.

(serves 6)

2 medium-sized onions
3 largish yellow squash (about 2½ pounds)

4 tablespoons vegetable oil
1 teaspoon whole cumin seeds
1 large tomato (about ½ pound), peeled
   and chopped
About 1½ teaspoons salt
1/16 teaspoon freshly ground black pepper
1½ tablespoons lemon juice
1/16 to 1/8 teaspoon cayenne pepper (optional)
4 tablespoons minced Chinese (or other) parsley

Peel the onions, cut in half lengthwise, then slice
into fine half rings.

Trim the ends off the squash, then quarter them
lengthwise. Cut away the seeded section and then
cut crosswise into ½- to ¾-inch sections.

Heat the oil in a large skillet over a medium
flame. When hot, put in the whole cumin seeds. As
soon as they turn a few shades darker (this takes
just a few seconds) put in the onions. Turn heat to
medium and sauté onions for about 2 minutes.
Add the tomatoes and stir for a few seconds. Now
cover, lower heat, and let onions and tomatoes
cook for 10 minutes. Lift cover and gently mash
down the tomato pieces. Add the squash and 1¼
teaspoons salt (add the other ¼ teaspoon salt toward
the end if you think you need it). Stir and fry for
another 2 minutes on medium heat.

Add 2 tablespoons water, cover immediately
with a well-fitting lid, turn heat down and steam
gently for 15 to 20 minutes or until squash is
tender but still retains some of its crispness. (Younger
squash will cook much faster.) Lift cover, and add
black pepper, lemon juice, cayenne pepper, and
minced parsley. Mix and taste for salt-sour balance. Cover and steam for another minute. Serve
either hot or cold on a bed of lettuce leaves as a
salad.

STUFFED YELLOW SQUASH

HONG KONG

Here is a wonderful dish to make when you are entertaining. It consists of a dome made out of squash shells, stuffed with a mixture of peas, bamboo shoots, carrots, mushrooms, and bean-curd skin. The dome sits in the center of a platter topped with white fungus and surrounded by stir-fried broccoli.

There are several steps to the dish but since many of them can be done ahead of time, it is fairly easy to assemble quickly at the last minute. If you are going to eat the stuffed squash in the evening, make the necessary vegetable stock (you need about 1½ cups in all) a day in advance and refrigerate it. Do all the chopping of the vegetables and the soaking of the fungus on the morning of the same day. In the late afternoon, soak the bean-curd skin, steam the squash and line a bowl with its outer shell. Stir-fry the stuffing and fill the squash with it. Blanch the broccoli and rinse it off under cold water. Mix the sauce that will go over the squash. When you get ready to eat, steam the stuffed squash to reheat it (10 minutes) and stir-fry the broccoli and white fungus (about 2 minutes).

(serves 4–6)

A scant ¼ cup white or silver ear fungus
8 sheets of dried bean-curd skin
2 yellow squash (about 1¼ pounds)

SAUCE FOR THE STUFFING
1 tablespoon cornstarch
¼ cup Vegetable Stock (see page 292)
2 teaspoons Chinese thin soy sauce

1 teaspoon sesame oil
¼ teaspoon salt
⅛ teaspoon freshly ground white pepper

STUFFING
3 tablespoons vegetable oil
3 cloves garlic, peeled and minced
2 quarter-sized slices of fresh ginger, minced
1 cup finely sliced scallions
1 cup mushrooms, cut into ¼-inch dice
1 cup fresh shelled or defrosted frozen peas
1 cup bamboo shoots cut into ¼-inch dice
1 cup peeled carrots cut into ¼-inch dice
¼ cup Vegetable Stock (see page 292)
2 cups broccoli flowerets, about ¾ inch at the head and 1½ to 2 inches long

SAUCE TO POUR OVER THE SQUASH DOME
2 teaspoons cornstarch
1 cup Vegetable Stock (see page 292)
2 teaspoons Chinese thin soy sauce
1 teaspoon sesame oil
⅛ teaspoon freshly ground white pepper
¼ teaspoon salt

3 tablespoons vegetable oil
3 cloves ginger, peeled and minced
¼ teaspoon salt

Soak the fungus in 3 cups water for 15 minutes, then drain.

Rinse the dried bean curd under hot water, then soak it in hot water for 10 minutes and drain.

Meanwhile put the 2 whole squash in a steamer and steam them for about 20 to 30 minutes or until they are tender but not mushy. Rinse them

---

For information about ingredients and basic techniques that may be unfamiliar, see General Information, pages 418–36.

1

under cold water. Trim the ends of the squash and cut them in half lengthwise.

1. Using a spoon, scoop out the seeded section in each half in such a way that it stays in one unbroken piece. Keep these seeded sections on a plate.

2. Lay the squash shells skin side down in a single layer in a shallow, wide bowl so that they overlap very slightly. (You will eventually overturn these shells to form the dome, so neatness is important.) Press down on the shells very lightly near their ends so that they lie flat against the contours of the bowl.

Rinse the soaked and drained white fungus. Feel with your fingers for the hard knots and cut them off.

2

Cut four of the rectangles of bean-curd skin into ½-inch squares. Leave the other four as they are.

Mix together in a cup the sauce for the stuffing and keep it beside you on the stove.

Prepare the stuffing.

Heat 3 tablespoons of oil in a wok over a medium-high flame. When it is hot, put in the minced garlic and the minced ginger. Stir for about 5 seconds. Put in the scallions and stir for about 10 seconds. Add the mushrooms. Stir-fry for about 30 seconds. Now put in the peas, bamboo shoots, carrots, and squares of bean-curd skin. Stir and fry the vegetables for about 4 minutes. Add the ¼ cup stock, cover and cook for 1 minute. Stir the reserved stuffing sauce and pour it over the vegetables. Stir and cook the vegetables for 30 seconds. Turn off the heat.

3

3. Spoon the vegetables into the squash shell cavities. Spread them out evenly and pat them down lightly. Lay the strips of the seeded squash in rows to cover the vegetables. Lay the rectangles of bean-curd skin in rows over the seeded squash sections but at right angles to them. The squash is now ready for a final steaming. Rinse off the wok and dry it.

Bring 8 cups of water to a boil. Drop in the broccoli flowerets. Bring to a boil again. Boil rapidly for 30 seconds. Drain the broccoli in a colander and rinse it under cold running water. Leave the broccoli to drain.

About 15 minutes before you are to eat, put a round platter—about 10 inches in diameter—in a warming oven. (Just take the chill off.)

Put the bowl with the stuffed squash in a steamer and steam for 10 minutes or until the vegetables have heated through. (If you are not using a domed Chinese bamboo steamer, cover the vegetables lightly with a piece of foil before you steam them.)

Lift the bowl out of the steamer and drain away any liquid that may have accumulated around the squash. 4. Put the platter over the bowl. 5. Invert the bowl over the platter so the stuffed squash looks like a dome sitting in the center of the platter. Keep the platter in a warm place.

Mix together ingredients for the sauce that is to be poured over the squash dome and keep it beside you near the stove.

Heat 3 tablespoons of oil in the clean wok over a medium-high flame. When it is hot, put in the remaining minced garlic. Stir it around for 10 seconds. Put in the broccoli and stir-fry it for about 30 seconds. Sprinkle ¼ teaspoon salt over the broccoli and stir to mix. Remove broccoli with a slotted spoon and quickly arrange it around the squash dome. Put the fungus into the wok. Stir-fry it for about 30 seconds. Stir the sauce that you have near the stove and pour it over the fungus. Stir the fungus around for 10 seconds in the sauce. Remove the fungus with a slotted spoon and put it on top of the squash dome. 6. Pour the sauce in the wok over the dome so as not to disturb the fungus. Serve immediately.

For information about ingredients and basic techniques that may be unfamiliar, see General Information, pages 418–36.

Sheila's
TOMATOES COOKED IN THE BENGALI STYLE
INDIA

(serves 4–6)

This dish of what might be described as stewed tomatoes is very similar to the two dishes that follow—Tomatoes Cooked in the Gujarati Style and Tomatoes Cooked in the Delhi Style. I have included all three because they show how regional Indian foods can, at times, be interrelated and yet quite different in their final flavors. The Bengali tomatoes are accented with mustard oil—a Bengali favorite—and by the typically Bengali spice combination, *panchphoran* (see General Information), containing whole cumin, mustard, fennel, *kalonji*, and fenugreek seeds. The Gujaratis prefer using peanut oil, and instead of the Bengali 5-spice combination, they use only cumin and mustard seeds as well as asafetida. They also add grated ginger when the dish is cooked to give a nice pungency. In Delhi, mustard seeds are rarely used for cooking; they *are* used for pickling, however. So the tomatoes there are cooked with cumin and asafetida as well as with sautéed onions. Sweetening, so frequently added to both Bengali and Gujarati foods, is entirely omitted in Delhi.

While fresh, red-ripe tomatoes are best for this recipe, canned tomatoes, with some can juices included, may be substituted. If too much can juice is added, it will make the dish very watery. If the canned tomatoes are large, cut them into ¾-inch pieces. Plum tomatoes should be cut in half, while sliced tomatoes may be left the way they are.

2 pounds red-ripe tomatoes
3 tablespoons mustard oil
1½ teaspoons *panchphoran*
1 dried hot red pepper, or 1 fresh hot green chili
1 teaspoon salt
¹⁄₁₆ teaspoon freshly ground black pepper
1½ teaspoons crumbled palm sugar,
    crumbled jaggery, or dark brown sugar

Heat 4 quarts of water in a large pot. When it is boiling, drop in the tomatoes. Remove tomatoes after 15 seconds. Peel the tomatoes and dice them into ¾-inch pieces.

Heat the oil in a heavy stainless-steel or porcelain-lined pot over a medium-high flame. When hot, put in the *panchphoran*. As soon as the mustard seeds pop (this takes just a few seconds), put in the red pepper or green chili. Stir once. Now add the cut-up tomatoes and immediately cover the pot. (This keeps the aromatic fumes inside the pot.) Turn heat to medium. When tomatoes stop making noises from inside the pot, take off the lid and add the salt, black pepper, and palm sugar, jaggery, or brown sugar. Cover again, turn heat to low, and simmer 7 to 10 minutes (less, if you prefer) or until tomatoes are just cooked through.

TOMATOES COOKED IN THE DELHI STYLE

INDIA

See introduction to Tomatoes Cooked in the Bengali Style, page 65.

(serves 4–6)

2   pounds red-ripe tomatoes
4   tablespoons vegetable oil
A pinch of crushed asafetida
1½ teaspoons whole cumin seeds
1   whole dried hot red pepper
1   medium-sized onion, peeled
    and coarsely chopped
1   teaspoon salt
1/16 to 1/8 teaspoon freshly ground black pepper

Heat 4 quarts of water in a large pot. When it is boiling, drop in the tomatoes. Remove the tomatoes after 15 minutes. Peel the tomatoes and dice them into ¾-inch pieces.

Heat the oil in a heavy stainless-steel or porcelain-lined pot over a medium-high flame. When hot, put in the asafetida and, a few seconds later, the cumin seeds. As soon as the cumin seeds sizzle and turn a shade darker, put in the red pepper. It will swell and darken almost immediately. Now put in the onion and turn the heat to medium-low. Stir and sauté the onion until it turns translucent. Do not let it brown. Add the tomatoes, salt, and black pepper. Bring to a boil. Cover, turn heat to low, and simmer gently 7 to 10 minutes or until tomatoes are just cooked through.

TOMATOES COOKED IN THE GUJARATI STYLE

INDIA

This dish from western India should be made in the summer months when tomatoes are in season. During the rest of the year, canned tomatoes (with can juices) may be used, though they will not taste quite as good. (See introduction to preceding recipe.)

(serves 4–6)

2   pounds red-ripe tomatoes
3   tablespoons vegetable oil
A pinch of crushed asafetida
½ teaspoon whole cumin seeds
1   teaspoon whole black mustard seeds
1   whole dried hot red pepper
1   teaspoon salt
1/16 teaspoon freshly ground black pepper
1   teaspoon peeled, finely grated fresh ginger
1½ teaspoons chopped-up jaggery or brown sugar
1   tablespoon chickpea flour

In a large pot, heat about 4 quarts of water. When it is boiling, drop in the tomatoes. Remove the tomatoes after 15 seconds with a slotted spoon. Peel the tomatoes and dice them into ¾-inch pieces.

Heat the oil in a heavy stainless-steel or porcelain-lined pot over a medium-high flame. When smoking hot, put in the asafetida. Two seconds later, put in the cumin and mustard seeds. As soon as the mustard seeds begin to pop (this takes just a few seconds), put in the red pepper. A few seconds later (the pepper should swell and darken), put in the cut-up tomatoes and immediately cover the pot (this keeps all the aromatic fumes

---

For information about ingredients and basic techniques that may be unfamiliar, see General Information, pages 418–36.

inside the pot). Turn heat to medium. When the tomatoes stop making noises from inside the pot, take off the lid and add the salt, black pepper, ginger, and jaggery. Stir. Cover again, turn heat to low, and simmer gently 7 to 10 minutes or until tomatoes are just cooked through. Slowly mix chickpea flour with 2 tablespoons water to make a smooth paste. Add to the tomatoes, stirring, and let simmer for another minute.

TOMATOES STUFFED WITH POTATOES AND PEAS

INDIA

My mother often made stuffed tomatoes for us. Generally, the tomatoes were stuffed with the same potato and pea combination that was used to make *samosas*. You could, if you like, stuff the tomatoes with Devi's Sprouted Mung Beans Cooked with Mustard Seeds (see page 102).

(serves 6)

6 firm, flat-bottomed, medium-large tomatoes
¼ teaspoon salt
Freshly ground black pepper
The potato-and-pea stuffing for Samosas (see page 327)

Preheat oven to 400° F.
  Wash and wipe the tomatoes. With a sharp, pointed knife, cut a cone-shaped cap at the stem end of the tomato, pull it out, and discard it. Keep this opening in the tomato as small as possible, just allowing yourself enough room to be able to go

inside the tomato with a grapefruit spoon to scoop out all the pulp and the seeds. As you do this, be careful not to pierce or otherwise damage the shell of the tomato. Sprinkle the inside of the tomato shells with a little salt and pepper and drain the tomatoes by turning them upside down for 10 minutes. Then stuff them with the potato-pea mixture. (Do not overstuff or the tomatoes will crack open.) Let the stuffing protrude a little from the opening in the tomatoes and cover with small caps made out of aluminum foil. Place the tomatoes on a baking tray and bake in oven 10 to 15 minutes or until they are just cooked through. Serve immediately.

TURNIPS COOKED IN DASHI

JAPAN

(serves 4 at a Japanese meal)

2 good-sized turnips (about ¾ pound), peeled and quartered
1½ cups *dashi* (see page 291)
1 tablespoon Japanese soy sauce
1 tablespoon sugar
⅛ teaspoon salt

Combine all ingredients in a small pot. Bring to a boil. Cover and simmer about 20 minutes on medium-low heat or until turnips are tender. Uncover and allow the turnips to cool in the liquid, turning the pieces around every now and then so they color evenly. Serve at room temperature or reheat in the same liquid.

WAKATAKE
(Wakame Seaweed and Bamboo Shoots)
JAPAN

(serves 4)

5   6-inch-long strips of dried *wakame* seaweed
½ cup bamboo shoots, sliced into pieces 1½ inches
    long x ½-inch wide x ¹⁄₁₆-inch thick
1   cup *dashi* (see page 291)
2   teaspoons Japanese soy sauce
1   teaspoon *mirin*
1   teaspoon sugar

Soak the seaweed in 4 cups water for 10 minutes, then drain. Cut away the coarse spines of the seaweed and then cut the leaves into 1½ x ½-inch pieces.

Combine the seaweed, bamboo shoots, *dashi*, soy sauce, *mirin*, and sugar in a small pot. Bring to a simmer. Simmer uncovered, over a medium-low flame, for about 20 minutes. There should be some concentrated liquid left at the bottom of the pot.

WATER CHESTNUTS, PLAIN AND BOILED

Water chestnuts grow underwater in the mud and there are several varieties that are eaten all over East, Southeast, and South Asia. The Indian version is triangular. It has several hornlike protrusions and is a green or deep red color. This is not available anywhere in America. But the dark, purplish-black Chinese water chestnut *is* available in Chinese grocery stores and should be pounced upon whenever the opportunity presents itself.

I am referring, of course, to fresh water chestnuts. The canned ones just do not compare. For me, fresh water chestnuts, raw or boiled, Indian or Chinese (the two varieties are fairly similar in taste), are a treat and once I start eating them, I find it impossible to stop. If you have never eaten fresh water chestnuts and if you find yourself in the neighborhood of a Chinatown, or a Chinese grocery store that carries them, here is what I suggest you do.

Buy a dozen chestnuts. When you come home, rinse them under running water to wash off the mud. Peel one (just as you would a potato) with a paring knife. Rinse it again and eat it. The chestnut has the texture of a raw potato but is deliciously sweet. Now take about 4 of the chestnuts and put them in a small, 1½-quart pot. Put enough water in the pot so it is 1 inch above the tops of the chestnuts. Bring the water to a boil. Cover, lower the heat, and simmer gently for 15 minutes. Peel with a paring knife (you can wait for them to cool), and eat them. See which you prefer, the raw chestnuts or the boiled ones. Eat the remaining chestnuts according to your preference.

In Asia, raw and boiled chestnuts are sold at outdoor festivals and sports events in the same manner as popcorn and hot dogs are sold. In India, water chestnuts are available only during the monsoon season. We buy 1 or 2 pounds at a time. If they are tender and sweet, we just peel and eat them. If they have matured a bit, we boil them. Once boiled, the chestnuts are either eaten plain or

For information about ingredients and basic techniques that may be unfamiliar, see General Information, pages 418–36.

else they are sliced, along with boiled potatoes, bananas, and cucumber, and made into a hot, spicy, and sour "salad," which is eaten as a snack. If bought in the bazaars of Delhi, this "salad" is served on leaves and eaten with toothpicks.

ZUCCHINI STUFFED WITH SMOKED EGGPLANT

INDIAN STYLE

(serves 4)

1 medium-sized eggplant (about 1 pound)
4 medium-sized zucchini (about 1½ to 2 pounds)
About 1⅓ teaspoons salt
6 medium-sized cloves garlic
6 tablespoons vegetable oil
1 2-ounce onion, peeled and finely chopped
½ teaspoon peeled, grated, fresh ginger
½ to 1 fresh hot green chili, minced
4 canned plum tomatoes, chopped,
    plus 2 tablespoons liquid from the can
1/16 teaspoon freshly ground black pepper
½ tablespoon lemon juice
3 tablespoons Parmesan cheese, freshly grated
    (optional)

Line a gas burner with foil to protect it from eggplant juice. Turn flame to medium-low. Place eggplant directly over the flame and let it get charred on one side. Keep turning the eggplant until the entire skin looks burnt and the vegetable turns limp and soft. (If you have an electric range, prick the eggplant with a fork and place it under the broiler. Turn it as its skin chars.) Peel away the charred skin under cold, running water. Chop the eggplant pulp.

Scrub zucchini and trim ends. Cut each zucchini in half lengthwise. Using a grapefruit spoon, scrape away all the seeded area, leaving boat-shaped shells. Sprinkle shells with a little salt (about ⅓ teaspoon) and set aside for half an hour.

Peel the cloves of garlic. Mince 4 of them.

Heat 3 tablespoons oil in a skillet over a medium flame. When hot, put in the minced garlic and stir for about 10 seconds. Now put in the onion and sauté for about 5 minutes or until the onion looks translucent and just begins to brown at the edges. Add the eggplant pulp, the ginger, green chili, the tomatoes and liquid, ¾ teaspoon salt, and the black pepper. Stir and sauté for 2 to 3 minutes. Add the lemon juice, stir and taste for salt. Cover, turn heat to low, and simmer gently for about 15 minutes, stirring every now and then.

Preheat broiler.

Drain all the liquid from the zucchini and pat the shells dry. In one large 10- to 12-inch skillet (you could use two smaller skillets), heat 3 tablespoons oil over a medium flame. When hot, put in the 2 remaining whole cloves of garlic. Stir them around until they brown and then discard them. Put the zucchini, cut side down, into this garlic-flavored oil. As soon as the cut edges turn a light brown, turn zucchini boats over and let the green skin turn a light brown. Cover the skillet. Turn heat to low and let the zucchini steam in its own juices for about 5 minutes or until tender but still slightly crunchy. Remove and place on a broiling tray.

Divide the eggplant mixture into eight portions and fill the zucchini boats with it. Sprinkle the Parmesan cheese on top and place under broiler until lightly browned.

ZUCCHINI STIR-FRIED WITH GARLIC

CHINA

(serves 4–6)

1½ pounds small (about 6 inches) zucchini
About 2¼ teaspoons salt
3 tablespoons vegetable oil
4 cloves garlic, peeled and minced
¼ teaspoon sugar
1 tablespoon *shaohsing* wine or dry sherry

Trim away the zucchini ends. Do not peel. Cut each zucchini *lengthwise* into ¼-inch-thick slices. Lay each slice down on a cutting board and, with a sharp pointed knife, cut it into ¼-inch-wide strips. These strips may now be cut so they are about 2½ inches in length. Put the strips in a bowl. Add 2 teaspoons of the salt and mix well. Set aside for 15 minutes. Drain and pat as dry as possible in a dish towel.

Heat the oil in a wok or skillet over medium-high heat. When hot, put in the garlic. Stir and fry for a few seconds until the garlic has browned lightly. Put in the zucchini. Stir and fry for about 3 minutes or until the zucchini has just cooked through but still retains some crispness. Add the sugar and stir quickly. Add the *shaohsing* by pouring it around the edges of the wok and letting it slither down toward the zucchini. Stir again and serve immediately. Or if you wish to eat it cold, spread it out on a large plate as soon as it is cooked and let it cool off. Then put it in a covered container and refrigerate it.

ZUCCHINI STUFFED WITH FRESH COCONUT AND CHINESE PARSLEY

INDIA

(serves 6)

1 cup freshly grated coconut
½ cup chopped Chinese parsley, firmly packed
1 fresh hot green chili, minced
1 teaspoon salt
⅛ teaspoon ground asafetida
6 medium-sized zucchini (about 2½ pounds)
5 tablespoons vegetable oil
⅛ teaspoon freshly ground black pepper
2 tablespoons lemon juice
1 teaspoon sugar

Combine the coconut, parsley, green chili, ¾ teaspoon salt, and asafetida in a bowl. Rub the mixture well with your hands.

Wash and trim the zucchini. Cut each zucchini into 4 1½-inch-long chunks. Sit the chunks on one of their cut ends and make two deep slits, like a cross, going an inch down their lengths. The zucchini chunks will seem quartered at the top but will remain whole at the bottom. Now gently pry apart the cut sections and stuff with the coconut mixture.

Pour the oil as well as ½ cup water into a large, 12- to 14-inch skillet. (Two smaller skillets may be used.) Carefully place all the zucchini, stuffed side down, in the skillet. If there is any stuffing left over, sprinkle that, as well as ¼ teaspoon salt, the black pepper, lemon juice, and sugar on top. Bring to a simmer, cover tightly, lower heat and simmer gently for about 5 to 6 minutes. Using two spoons, turn the zucchini pieces over gently so their quartered, stuffed sections are on top. If cooking liquid has evaporated, add a little more hot water.

For information about ingredients and basic techniques that may be unfamiliar, see General Information, pages 418–36.

Cover again and cook another 7 to 10 minutes. The zucchini should be cooked through but retain some of its crispness. There should be no liquid left in the skillet. Serve immediately.

ZUCCHINI "MEATBALLS"
INDIA

An exquisitely elegant dish, it consists of tender "meatballs" made out of grated zucchini, bathed in a creamy, spicy sauce. In India, a long green squash, shaped rather like a bowling pin, is used for this dish. If you can find such a squash in Chinese or Indian grocery stores, do use it. It needs to be peeled and seeded before it is grated. If you cannot find it, zucchini makes an excellent substitute.

(Makes 16 "meatballs" and serves 4–6 people)

FOR THE "MEATBALLS"
3 medium-sized zucchini (about 1 to 1¼ pounds)
½ teaspoon salt
About 1 fresh hot green chili, minced
3 tablespoons finely minced onion
½ teaspoon peeled and very finely grated fresh ginger
2 tablespoons finely minced Chinese parsley
⅓ cup chickpea flour
Vegetable oil for deep frying

FOR THE SAUCE
5 tablespoons vegetable oil from deep frying
2 medium-sized onions, peeled and very finely minced
¼ teaspoon ground turmeric
1/16 teaspoon cayenne pepper
1 teaspoon ground cumin seeds
2 teaspoons ground coriander seeds
½ pound tomatoes (about 2 tomatoes), peeled and finely minced
1 cup heavy cream
½ teaspoon *garam masala*
½ teaspoon ground roasted cumin seeds
¼ to ⅓ teaspoon salt

Wash, trim, and grate the zucchini. Put it into a bowl and sprinkle it with the ½ teaspoon salt. Set it aside for half an hour.

Squeeze as much liquid as possible out of the zucchini by pressing handfuls of it between your two palms. Save this zucchini liquid for the sauce. Dry off the bowl and put the zucchini back in it. Add the minced chili (you may want to use more than 1 chili, depending on your taste), the 3 tablespoons minced onion, the grated ginger, and the Chinese parsley. Sift the chickpea flour over this vegetable mixture. Mix well and form 16 neat balls.

In a skillet, wok, or other utensil for deep frying, heat about 1½ inches of oil over a medium flame (a wok should have 1½ inches at its center). When hot, put in 5 to 6 of the balls, or as many as the utensil will hold easily in one layer. Fry for about 1½ minutes, or until the balls turn a rich, reddish-brown color. Turn the balls every now and then as they fry. Remove them with a slotted spoon when they are done and leave to drain on a plate lined with paper towels. Do all the "meatballs" this way.

To make the sauce, remove 5 tablespoons of the oil used in deep frying and put this in a 10-inch skillet or sauté pan. Heat the oil over a medium flame. When hot, put in the minced onions. Stir and fry for 7 to 8 minutes or until the onions begin to turn brown at the edges. Take the pan off the fire for a couple of seconds and add the turmeric, cayenne, ground cumin, and ground coriander. Stir once and put the pan back on the fire. Stir for another 5 seconds and then add the minced tomatoes. Stir and fry on medium heat for 5 minutes. Add the zucchini juice. (You need 1 cup; if you have less, add some water.) Bring to a boil. Cover, lower heat and let the sauce simmer gently for 15 minutes. (This much of the recipe may be prepared several hours ahead of time.) Add the cream, *garam masala*, ground roasted cumin, and the ¼ to ⅓ teaspoon salt. Mix well, bring to a simmer and cook for 1 minute. Now put in the "meatballs." Spoon the sauce over them. Cover, and simmer very gently for 6 to 7 minutes. Spoon the sauce over the "meatballs" a few times during this cooking period.

These "meatballs" turn very soft when cooked in the sauce, so handle them gently and serve immediately.

For information about ingredients and basic techniques that may be unfamiliar, see General Information, pages 418–36.

AVIYAL
(Mixed Vegetables)
INDIA

This mixed vegetable dish from southwestern India is generally made with odd vegetables left over in the vegetable bin. The vegetables are cut or diced (never too small), cooked (by blanching, boiling, or steaming), and then folded in with what might be called a "dressing" that includes fresh coconut, mustard seeds, green chilies, Chinese parsley, and yogurt. I have used potatoes, green beans, carrots, and peas here but you could add lima beans, sliced white radishes, diced turnips, diced green pepper, and diced winter melon. (The last gives a wonderful flavor to the dish.)

(serves 4–6)

1   medium-sized boiling potato
¾ pound green beans, trimmed and cut into 1-inch lengths
2   carrots, peeled and cut into ½-inch pieces (about 2 cups)
1   cup shelled fresh or defrosted frozen peas
1 to 2 fresh hot green chilies, minced
1   cup grated fresh coconut
1½ tablespoons vegetable oil
A generous pinch of ground asafetida
½ teaspoon whole black mustard seeds
1   teaspoon whole cumin seeds
2   tablespoons *urad dal*
1¾ cups plain yogurt
2   teaspoons salt, or to taste
2   tablespoons minced fresh Chinese parsley

Cover the potato with water in a small pot and bring the water to a boil. Cover pot, turn heat to

PECEL
(Vegetable Salad with a Spicy Peanut Sauce)
INDONESIA

low and allow potato to cook. Do not allow it to get mushy.

While potato boils, combine beans, carrots, and peas in another small pot. Add 1 cup water and bring to a boil. Cover, lower heat, and cook for about 4 to 5 minutes or until vegetables are just tender (but still crunchy) and the water is almost all absorbed. You may have to adjust the heat to achieve this.

Drain the cooked potato. Peel and dice it into ⅔-inch cubes. Combine all the vegetables in a wide, heavy 3- to 4-quart pot or sauté pan. Sprinkle the green chilies and coconut over the vegetables. Do not mix yet.

Heat the oil in a small, heavy skillet or very small butter-warmer type pot over a medium flame. When hot, put in the asafetida and, a few seconds later, the mustard and cumin seeds. As soon as the mustard seeds begin to pop (this takes just a few seconds), put in the *urad dal*. Stir and fry until the *dal* turns a light reddish-brown. Empty contents of the small skillet over the cooked vegetables.

Empty the yogurt into a bowl and mix with a fork or thin whisk until it is creamy. Add the salt to it and mix again. Pour this yogurt over the vegetables and mix gently. Heat the vegetable pot over a low flame. Remove from heat before *aviyal* comes to a boil.

Serve hot, warm, at room temperature, or even cold, sprinkled with the Chinese parsley.

Among Indonesia's saladlike dishes in which a combination of raw, blanched, boiled, and fried foods are served with different peanut sauces, *pecel* (pronounced "pechel") is perhaps the easiest to make. This recipe, which comes from Betty's Restaurant in Denpasar, Bali, uses pounded shrimp in the sauce. I have substituted soy sauce for the shrimp. The sweetening in the sauce is provided by *gula Bali*, a palm sugar. You can generally find palm sugar in Southeast Asian grocery stores, but if it isn't available, use light brown sugar.

The different items, neatly arranged on my plate in Denpasar, were bean curd, *tempeh*, potatoes, eggs, greens, cabbage, and mung-bean sprouts. Here is how you should prepare them, with the amounts being left to your discretion:

BEAN CURD—Sauté the bean curd according to the recipe on page 175. You may sprinkle the bean-curd pieces very lightly with salt before sautéing them.

TEMPEH—See recipe for Fried, Preseasoned Tempeh, page 109.

POTATOES—Use new or boiling potatoes. Boil potatoes in their jackets. Let them cool without refrigerating them. Peel and either cut into ¼-inch-thick slices or else into ½-inch cubes.

EGGS—Hard-boil the eggs and let them cool. Peel and quarter lengthwise.

GREENS—Indonesians use swamp cabbage for this dish but you may use the more readily available spinach instead. Trim and wash fresh spinach, making sure all the leaves are separated. Drop the leaves into boiling water to which you have added a little salt and a little sugar. Bring the water to a second boil. Boil rapidly for 2 minutes. Drain and rinse under cold water. Squeeze out any extra moisture and loosen the wad of leaves.

CABBAGE—Shred the cabbage. You may use it raw or else drop it into lightly salted boiling water for 1 minute. Drain and rinse under cold water. Drain again.

MUNG-BEAN SPROUTS—Rinse them well. Break off their threadlike tails if you feel up to it. You may use them raw or else drop them into boiling water and boil rapidly for 15 seconds. Drain and rinse under cold water. Gently squeeze out all extra moisture and fluff up again.

To serve, arrange small amounts of each item on individual plates. Offer Spicy Peanut Sambal on the side (see page 363), about 2 tablespoons per person, either in small, shallow, individual bowls or saucers.

YUM TAVOY
(Salad of Cooked Mixed Vegetables)
THAILAND/BURMA

This very aromatic dish could contain almost any combination of vegetables—carrots, cabbage, cauliflower, turnips, green bell peppers, eggplant, any of them may be used. As it happens, I use a firm, green squash shaped rather like a fat baseball bat (called *hu lu* in Chinese grocery stores and *doodhi* in Indian ones), long beans, and that lovely green, *choy sum* (see General Information), all of which I buy in New York's Chinatown. You could, if you like, use eggplant instead of the squash, regular

beans instead of the long beans, and throw in some cabbage or cauliflower if you cannot find *choy sum*. The vegetables are first cooked in coconut milk and then seasoned with a Thai curry paste, ground peanuts, and tamarind pulp. It is the curry paste that provides the aroma. It contains, among other things, lemon grass, galanga root, and the peel of the kaffir lime.

(serves 6)

2 to 3 whole dried red peppers, seeded
2 teaspoons dried, sliced lemon grass
2 quarter-sized rounds of dried galanga root
A 2-inch × 1-inch (roughly) piece of dried kaffir lime peel
12 to 14 ounces of eggplant or firm green squash (see note above)
¼ pound long or regular green beans
¼ pound *choy sum* or cauliflower
2½ cups fresh or canned unsweetened coconut milk
1½ teaspoons salt
1 teaspoon sugar
2 tablespoons chopped, peeled shallots
2 cloves garlic, peeled
4 slim roots from fresh Chinese parsley, washed
1½ tablespoons ground roasted or fried unsalted peanuts
3 tablespoons tamarind paste
1 teaspoon bright-red sweet paprika
2 teaspoons roasted sesame seeds

Put the red peppers, lemon grass, galanga root, and kaffir lime peel into the container of an electric coffee grinder or other spice grinder. Grind until you have a powder.

Cut the eggplant into 1½-inch cubes. If you are using the squash, peel it with a potato peeler and cut it into 1½-inch chunks. Trim the beans and cut into 2-inch lengths. Cut the *choy sum* leaves crosswise into 2-inch strips. The *choy sum* stalks can be cut into 2-inch lengths. If you are using cauliflower, break it into flowerets that are about 1½ inches across at the head.

Remove ½ cup of the top coconut cream (see General Information) and set it aside.

Combine the cut vegetables, 2 cups of the remaining coconut milk, ½ teaspoon salt, and ½ teaspoon sugar in a 3½-quart pot and bring to a boil over a medium-high flame. Cover and cook on medium-high heat for about 10 minutes or until the vegetables are tender. Turn off heat and remove cover.

Put the shallots, garlic, and Chinese parsley roots into the container of a food processor or blender. Add ¼ cup of liquid from the vegetable pot and blend until you have a smooth paste.

Put this paste, the ½ cup coconut cream, and the spices you have just ground into a small, heavy pot. Bring to a simmer over medium heat. Keep stirring and cooking until all the liquid evaporates and the paste begins to fry a little in the oil released by the coconut cream. Turn the heat down a bit when this begins to happen. You should end up with a blob of paste.

Add this fried curry paste, the ground peanuts, tamarind paste, paprika, 1 teaspoon salt, and ½ teaspoon sugar to the cooked vegetables. Stir and bring to a simmer. Simmer for 1 minute. Sprinkle sesame seeds over the top.

TEMPURA

JAPAN

It is said that batter-fried foods like tempura were introduced into Japan in the sixteenth century by the Portuguese. Whatever the origin, the Japanese have done to this dish what they did to the Buddhist tea-drinking ceremony, which came from China, and floral designs for cotton prints, which came from India—they have made it totally Japanese.

The word "tempura" translates as a woman in a gossamer-thin dress giving tantalizing glimpses of her barely hidden physical beauty. The actual dish contains beauties of another sort—fish, asparagus, eggplant slices, lotus-root slices, sweet pepper slices, green beans, onion slices, quail eggs, etc.—are dipped in a very light batter, deep fried, drained, and then served with a dipping sauce containing, among other things, soy sauce and grated white radish. In my own travels through Japan, I was never served bean-curd tempura in a tempura meal, but I usually include it in order to make the dish more nutritious. You may, if you like, smear the bean-curd pieces with a little *miso*—red, if you like a salty taste, white or yellow if you like a sweeter taste—before you dip them in the batter.

In Japan, there are "bars," counters really, that specialize in serving just tempura. Diners sit on stools while the chef behind the counter dips foods in batter and deep fries them. The vegetables are not all fried at once. Very small batches go into the wok. One batch may consist of green beans, another of sweet potatoes, another of eggplant, and so on. As soon as the chef finishes cooking a batch, he hands it over to the diners, dividing it up among several plates. All batter-fried foods get soggy as they sit, so diners eat them as soon as they get them. This is very hard to manage in a home kitchen unless you, as chef, choose to stay at the stove and feed your guests a batch at a time. There are ways around this. You could serve tempura only to small groups of people. You could also divide the frying duties with a friend, spouse, or child so that the eating and frying can go on continuously.

In a tempura, the fried vegetables remain light and crunchy. To achieve this, care has to be taken in several areas. Cut the vegetables evenly. All eggplant slices should be of the same thickness, as should all onion slices, and so on. You may put more than one kind of vegetable into the oil at the same time, but make sure—and here you have to use your judgment—that all the vegetables you put in require about the same cooking time.

The batter is also important. Recipes vary throughout Japan with some combining flour with a whole egg, others with just the yolk, and some with no egg at all. Tempura batter should not be well blended; it is left fairly lumpy and therein lies its success. I will give two recipes for the batter. Try both and see which you eventually prefer. Both are good. Many chefs sprinkle a little flour on the vegetables before dipping them in the batter, which makes the batter adhere a bit better. For this same reason, I like to wet hard-boiled quail eggs and *then* flour them lightly before dipping them in batter. Some tempuramakers specialize in building up the batter so it extends far beyond the extremities of the slice of vegetable. This is done by dribbling extra batter along the length and width of the slice of vegetable while it is frying.

I use peanut oil for frying but you may use salad oil or any mild vegetable oil. The temperature of the oil should be between 350° and 375° F. If the oil is smoking, it is too hot. As soon as the vegetables have fried, they should be drained. In Japan, this is done by removing them from the hot oil with a skimmer and then placing them on slightly elevated, coarse mesh trays. At some tempura bars, the "plates" for tempura consist of baskets lined with paper towels or trays with an elevated napkin-lined mesh section to hold the fried food.

Clean the oil of all batter particles between each batch. Fine mesh skimmers are best, but a finely slotted spoon will do. In Japan these batter particles are not thrown away. After being rinsed quickly to remove extra oil, they are dropped into clear broths and make a good soup!

The dipping sauce for tempura varies. The base is generally soy sauce thinned out with Japanese Stock (see page 291). To this can be added finely grated white radish, finely grated horseradish, or finely grated ginger. At one tempura bar in Kyoto, I was offered plain salt and lemon juice as dips as well.

(serves 4)

BATTER NUMBER I
1 egg yolk, from a large egg
1 cup plus 1 tablespoon ice-cold water
1 cup all-purpose unbleached white
   flour, sifted

BATTER NUMBER II
1 large egg
1 cup ice-cold water
1 cup all-purpose unbleached
   white flour, sifted with
½ teaspoon baking soda

For information about ingredients and basic techniques that may be unfamiliar, see General Information, pages 418–36.

TEMPURA INGREDIENTS

½ pound medium or hard bean curd, cut into 1½ × 2 × ½-inch pieces

8 even-sized green beans

8 asparagus spears

8 ¼-inch-thick slices of peeled onion

8 fresh or canned quail eggs (if fresh, boil them for 5 minutes and then peel)

Vegetable oil for deep frying

8 ¼-inch-thick slices of peeled sweet potato, cut crosswise

8 ½-inch-wide slices of green pepper, cut lengthwise

8 ¼-inch-thick slices of small eggplant, cut crosswise

About 2 extra tablespoons all-purpose unbleached white flour

Tilt a chopping board and lay some paper towels on it. Place the pieces of bean curd on the towel. Cover with another piece of towel and pat down lightly. Let the bean curd drain for 2 hours. Change the paper towels when they get soaked.

Trim the green beans and cut them in half lengthwise. Lay 4 halves alongside each other and thread a toothpick through their centers. Do this with all the bean halves so you end up with four "tooth-picked" servings of beans.

Trim away the woody section of the asparagus. Peel the lower three-quarters of the remaining spear with a potato peeler.

Put a toothpick through each slice of onion to hold the rings together.

Put a toothpick crosswise through the middle of each egg.

Make a batter using one of the two suggested recipes. Put the egg or egg yolk in a bowl and beat until smooth. Slowly add the ice water, beating as you do so. Now put in all the flour (or flour and baking soda) all at once. Beat four or five times to mix. Do not overmix. The batter should be lumpy. Set the batter aside for 10 minutes while you heat the oil for deep frying. You may use a wok or a deep skillet or an electric deep-frying pot. You need medium heat, about 350° to 375° F.

When the oil is hot, dip the beans in the batter to coat them lightly. Let any extra batter on the beans drip back into the bowl. Now put the beans into the oil and deep fry, turning once or twice, for 2 to 3 minutes or until the batter has turned golden and crisp. Remove the beans from the oil and drain on a wire mesh rack or on paper towels. Clear the oil of any batter drippings with a skimmer. Dip the sweet potato slices in the batter and cook them the same way as the beans. Follow these with the green peppers and the onion slices. Make sure you drain each batch thoroughly. Dust the eggplant slices very lightly with flour. Then dip them in the batter and fry. Drain. Do the same with the asparagus spears. Sprinkle a little water on the quail eggs, dust lightly with flour, dip in the batter and fry. Drain. Give the bean-curd pieces a final pat with a paper towel. (You may smear a little *miso* on them at this stage.) Dust lightly with flour, dip in batter and fry. Drain. Serve as soon after it is made as possible. With it, offer Tempura Dipping Sauce (see page 357), as well as tiny individual bowls of salt and lemon juice for those who might like a choice.

UKOY
(Vegetable Fritters)
PHILIPPINES

This street snack is made with grated pumpkin (a special, small pumpkin is used), and bean sprouts, with a shrimp embedded in the center. I have removed the shrimp and the result is still very good. *Ukoy* is eaten with a simple dipping sauce containing vinegar, garlic, and salt.

(makes 22–24 fritters)

THE BATTER
1   cup all-purpose unbleached white flour
¼ teaspoon baking soda
1½ teaspoons salt
½ teaspoon freshly ground black pepper
1   large egg
1   cup cold Vegetable Stock (see page 292) or cold
     water

Vegetable oil for shallow frying
2   cups peeled and coarsely grated butternut squash
1   cup mung-bean sprouts, washed,
     drained thoroughly, patted as dry as possible
3   scallions, cut into 2-inch pieces and then cut
     lengthwise into fine strips

Make the batter by sifting the flour, baking soda, salt, and pepper together in a large bowl. Beat the egg in a separate smaller bowl and slowly add the stock to it. Then slowly add the egg-stock mixture to the flour mixture, beating as you do so.

Heat ½ inch oil in a skillet over a medium flame. The ideal temperature for frying the fritters is between 350° and 375° F.

Put the grated squash, bean sprouts, and scallions into the batter and mix. Remove heaping tablespoons of the fritter mixture and drop gently into the skillet. Fry for about 3 minutes on each side or until fritters are a nice medium-brown color. If the fritters begin to brown too fast, turn the heat down. Remove fritters with a slotted spoon and drain on paper towels or on a wire mesh rack. Do all fritters this way, putting only as many in the oil as the skillet will hold easily.

Serve hot, with small, individual bowls of Filipino Dipping Sauce (see page 357).

VEGETABLE PAKORIS
(Vegetable Fritters)
INDIA

This is the Indian version of Japan's tempura and Italy's *fritto misto*. Almost any vegetable, whole or sliced depending on its size, may be dipped in a chickpea-flour batter and fried until it is crisp on the outside. I like the batter to be quite thin, though some people prefer a more solid encasement. As no egg is used in the batter, these fritters would be particularly good for vegetarians who do not eat any animal products.

Almost any fresh vegetable may be used to make these *pakoris*—flowerets of cauliflower, slices of eggplant, slices of peeled potato or sweet potato, onion rings, green beans, slices of green pepper, and even fiery hot red peppers. Although *pakoris* may be eaten with just a sprinkling of salt, they are generally served with some sort of sour chutney

---

For information about ingredients and basic techniques that may be unfamiliar, see General Information, pages 418–36.

which might be tamarind-based, mint-and-Chinese-parsley-based, or it could even be tomato-based. It is nearly always sour and hot. These days, though, this "chutney" could be tomato ketchup!

Pakoris should be eaten while they are hot and crisp or else they turn soggy. They are a snack food in India and are often served with tea, coffee, or soft drinks.

(serves 4–6)

THE BATTER
1½ cups chickpea flour
¾ teaspoon salt
½ teaspoon baking soda
¼ teaspoon ground turmeric
½ teaspoon ground cumin
¾ teaspoon ground coriander
¾ teaspoon whole ajwain seeds or whole cumin
    seeds
¼ teaspoon freshly ground black pepper
¼ teaspoon cayenne pepper

Vegetable oil for deep frying
1 medium-sized potato,
    peeled and cut into ⅛-inch-thick rounds
1 medium-sized onion,
    peeled and cut into ⅛-inch-thick rounds
½ medium-sized sweet potato, peeled and cut into
    ⅛-inch-thick rounds
16 cauliflower flowerets, about 2 inches long, 1½
    x ½ inch at the head
16 green beans, trimmed at the ends
4 hot Italian peppers (optional)

Sift the chickpea flour, salt, and baking soda together into a bowl. Add all the other spices for the batter. Very slowly and gradually pour in 1¼ cups water, beating with a fork or a wooden spoon as you do so. You should have a smooth batter.

Heat the oil in a wok or other utensil for deep frying over a medium flame. The temperature of the oil should be between 350° and 375° F.

Put the potato slices into the batter. Lift out a handful with your fingers and let any extra batter drip back into the bowl. Now put these slices into the hot oil, as many as the wok will hold in a single layer. Fry slowly, about 7 minutes on each side. When the outside is golden brown and crisp, remove fritters with a slotted spoon and leave to drain on a mesh rack or on paper towels.

Separate the onion rings, put them in the batter, and fry them the same way as the potatoes. Do all the vegetables this way, dipping them in the batter, frying them, and then draining them. The hot peppers may be left whole. Ideally, as each batch is fried, it should be eaten. With the *pakoris*, you could serve one or all of these chutneys: Tamarind-Mint Chutney, Hot and Spicy Hyderabadi Tomato Chutney, and Fresh Chinese Parsley and Mint Chutney (see pages 363-64).

Beans and Dried Peas

Next to eggs, it is beans and peas, when combined with grains and a milk product at the same meal, that provide vegetarians with their best source of usable protein. Beans are also a cheap source of protein which the Asian world has depended upon for more than a thousand years.

In this country, beans are used in relatively few ways. Northerners are familiar with Boston baked beans. They may have also had beans in a soup or a salad. Southerners, somewhat better informed on the subject, cook a variety of beans with ham hocks and then eat them with rice. It is only in Asia that the full range of bean dishes, from appetizers and snacks to desserts, has been fully explored.

In India, for example, I could have *dosas* for breakfast. These are crisp-soft bean-and-rice pancakes which are usually washed down in the mornings with coffee or glasses of buttermilk. For lunch, I might have Chana Dal with Cucumber and some whole-wheat griddle breads. *Dals* are split peas and India has dozens of varieties, each one with its own very distinct taste. At teatime, I might have *dhoklas*, savory cakes made out of mung beans and quite encrusted with mustard and sesame seeds. After dinner, I might well munch on a fudge made with chickpea flour. In the course of this one day, no bean dish would have looked or tasted like another.

In eastern Asia, although many beans are eaten, it is the soy bean that wins out as being the most versatile, with mung beans coming a close second. Red beans are used chiefly for desserts. Soy beans may be boiled, fried, made into soy milk, bean curd, soy sauces, fermented cheeses, and thick pastes. Mung beans may be made into vermicelli, sprouted, or cooked in stews. If you are looking for a hearty bean stew that is also easy to make, try Mongo, a Filipino dish of whole mung beans, greens, tomatoes, onion, and garlic. Eaten with a squeeze of lime juice, this combination is most satisfying.

If some bean dishes are hearty, others have unsurpassable elegance. Take the Persian dish, Frozen Lima Beans, Braised with Swiss Chard and Dill. Persians are light-handed with their spices but most generous with fresh herbs. Here dill flecks the dish and flavors it most gently.

Beans seem to have changed miraculously over the years so that they no longer take hours to cook. It is quite a mystery to me why lentils cook in less than half an hour. This simple, quick-cooking legume may be puréed into soups, cooked with vegetables such as spinach, and made into Middle Eastern salads with the addition of lemon juice, olive oil, garlic, and parsley. Even the tougher beans, such as navy or *azuki*, do not necessarily have to be soaked overnight. I much prefer the method whereby they are cooked for 2 minutes, left for 1 hour, and then cooked again until tender. Older beans will take longer to cook than those which have been recently harvested and dried.

All beans need to be picked over carefully and washed in several changes of water before they are cooked.

CHANA DAL WITH CUCUMBER

INDIA

Chana dal has a warm, sweet taste which makes it good both when cooked alone and when combined with vegetables. In Bengal as well as in Delhi, *chana dal* is often cooked with a long, green squash shaped somewhat like a long bowling pin. The squash is peeled, seeded, cut into 1-inch sections and added to the *dal* toward the end of the cooking time. It is hard to find this squash in the New York area. I have seen it occasionally in Indian and Chinese grocery stores as well as in a few health-food stores. If you can find it, do use it. If not, cucumbers make a good substitute.

(serves 4–6)

1   cup *chana dal*
½ teaspoon ground turmeric
2   cloves garlic, peeled
2   quarter-sized slices of fresh ginger
1   cucumber
¾ teaspoon salt
½ teaspoon *garam masala*
About ⅛ teaspoon cayenne pepper
1   tablespoon vegetable oil
½ teaspoon whole cumin seeds
2   tablespoons *ghee* or unsalted butter

Pick over the *dal* and wash it in several changes of water. Drain. Put it in a 2- to 3-quart pot along with 4½ cups of water. Bring to a boil. Remove the scum. Add the turmeric, garlic, and ginger and turn heat to very low. Cover the pot in such a way that the lid is just slightly ajar. (This prevents the *dal* from boiling over.) Cook gently for about 1½

hours or until *dal* is quite tender. Stir every 10 minutes during the last hour of cooking. If the *dal* sticks to the bottom, stir more frequently.

While the *dal* is cooking, peel the cucumber and cut it in half lengthwise. Scoop out all the seeds with a teaspoon or a grapefruit spoon. Now cut the two cucumber halves crosswise into 1-inch-long segments.

When the *dal* is tender, add the cucumber, salt, *garam masala*, and cayenne pepper. Stir, and bring to a simmer. Cover and cook on very low heat for 5 to 10 minutes or until cucumber is tender but still a bit crisp. Turn off heat and uncover.

Heat the oil in a small skillet or other very small butter-warmer-type pot over a medium flame. When hot, put in the cumin seeds. As soon as they sizzle and turn a shade darker (this takes just a few seconds), pour the hot oil with cumin seeds over the *chana dal* and cover the pot immediately. Reheat the *dal* before serving and mix in the *ghee* or butter.

For information about ingredients and basic techniques that may be unfamiliar, see General Information, pages 418–36.

On Cooking Dried Chickpeas

Pick over 1 cup of dried chickpeas and wash them in several changes of water. Drain them. Put the chickpeas and ⅛ teaspoon baking soda in 5 cups of water and soak for 12 hours. Now put the chickpeas and their soaking liquid into a heavy pot and bring to a boil. Cover, lower heat, and let the chickpeas simmer for 45 minutes. Add 1 teaspoon salt and simmer for at least another 15 minutes. Taste a chickpea. If it is still hard, continue the cooking. The cooking time generally varies with the freshness of the chickpeas. Older and therefore harder peas take longer to cook. Sometimes my chickpeas have been done in 1 hour, at other times I have cooked them for 3 hours. Another way of cooking the chickpeas is by using a pressure cooker. After the chickpeas have soaked, put them and their soaking liquid into a pressure cooker. Add 1 teaspoon salt. Cover and bring up the pressure to 15 pounds. Let the chickpeas cook for 30 minutes and then let the pressure drop by itself.

Depending upon your recipe, the chickpeas may now be drained. Save the liquid for soups. If any of your chickpea recipes call for water, you may substitute this liquid.

One cup of dried chickpeas will yield about 3 cups of cooked, drained chickpeas.

You may, at times, substitute canned chickpeas for the home-cooked kind. A 20-ounce can of chickpeas generally yields about 2¼ cups of drained chickpeas.

CHICKPEA SALAD

INDIA

Served as a snack throughout India, this is the simplest version of the Indian chickpea salad.

(serves 4–6)

2 20-ounce cans chickpeas, or 4½ cups home-cooked chickpeas (see opposite column) and their cooking liquid
6 scallions, trimmed and finely sliced halfway up their green sections
2 tablespoons lemon juice
¾ to 1 teaspoon salt
¼ teaspoon freshly ground black pepper
2 tablespoons minced Chinese (or other) parsley
1 fresh hot green chili, minced, or green pepper, minced
¼ teaspoon cayenne pepper

Pour contents of chickpea cans or home-cooked chickpeas into a saucepan. Bring to a boil. Drain, discarding liquid.

In a serving bowl, combine chickpeas with all the other ingredients. Mix well and set aside, unrefrigerated, for 1 hour. Mix again. Serve cold or at room temperature.

CHICKPEA AND GREEN BEAN SALAD

NORTH INDIAN STYLE

This is a salad that I have made up. I find that the use of *garam masala* and grated ginger in the dressing gives a very interesting piquancy.

(serves 6)

2   cups cooked chickpeas (see page 83) or 2 cups, canned chickpeas

DRESSING FOR THE CHICKPEAS
½ cup vegetable oil
¼ cup wine vinegar
¼ to ⅓ teaspoon salt
1   teaspoon *garam masala*
2   cloves garlic, peeled and crushed to a pulp
¹⁄₁₆ to ⅛ teaspoon cayenne pepper

DRESSING FOR GREEN BEANS
¼ cup vegetable oil
2   tablespoons lemon juice
½ teaspoon salt
½ teaspoon *garam masala*
2   tablespoons finely minced onions
1   teaspoon finely grated fresh ginger

½ pound fresh green beans
½ teaspoon salt

Heat the chickpeas in their own liquid and drain. Empty them into a bowl. Beat together all the ingredients for the chickpea dressing and pour it over them while they are still hot. Mix well and adjust seasonings. Cool, cover, and set aside.

Combine all the ingredients for the dressing to go on the green beans. Wash and trim the green beans and cut them into ¾-inch-long pieces. Bring 6 cups of water to a boil and add ½ teaspoon salt to it. When the water is boiling rapidly, put in the cut beans. Keep boiling on high heat for 3 to 4 minutes or until beans are just cooked through. Drain the beans thoroughly. Shake them about in the colander or sieve used for draining until they look very dry. Put beans in a bowl (not the same one as the chickpeas). Pour their dressing over them and let them sit for 5 minutes. Combine the two salads and mix well. (I usually let the chickpeas sit in their dressing for 2 to 5 hours before proceeding with the cooking of the green beans. This gives the chickpeas time to absorb their dressing properly. However, if you are rushed, you may cook the green beans as soon as you are through with making the chickpea salad.) Serve at room temperature or cold in individual portions on small salad plates.

CHICKPEAS WITH GARLIC, TOMATOES, AND GREEN CHILIES

INDIA

To serve: This dish may be served with almost any Indian meal, accompanied by a green vegetable, a yogurt relish and a bread. When my daughters' friends drop in at odd hours, hungry of course, I

For information about ingredients and basic techniques that may be unfamiliar, see General Information, pages 418–36.

often put out a bowl of these chickpeas, some pita bread, and a quick cucumber and yogurt combination.

(serves 8)

18 to 24 cloves garlic, peeled
4 tablespoons vegetable oil
2 teaspoons whole cumin seeds
2 cups tomato sauce, canned or homemade (see page 361)
3 20-ounce cans of drained chickpeas or 6½ cups boiled, drained chickpeas (see page 83)
6 medium-sized potatoes, boiled, peeled, and cut into ¾-inch cubes
1½ to 2 teaspoons salt
5 fresh hot green chilies
2 teaspoons ground cumin seeds
1 teaspoon ground *amchoor* or lemon juice
⅛ teaspoon cayenne pepper

Put the garlic into the container of a food processor or blender. Add ¼ cup water and blend until you have a smooth paste.

Heat the oil in a 10-inch-wide, heavy pot over a medium-high flame. When hot, put in the cumin seeds. A few seconds later, put in the garlic paste. Fry for about 2 minutes, stirring all the time. Add the tomato sauce. Keep stirring and cook for another minute. Add the drained chickpeas, diced potatoes, 2 cups water, salt, green chilies, ground cumin, *amchoor*, and cayenne. Stir gently and bring to a simmer. Cover, turn heat to low, and simmer gently for 20 minutes.

CHICKPEA AND TOMATO STEW

MIDDLE EAST

(serves 4–6)

6 medium-sized tomatoes
½ cup olive oil
2 medium-sized onions, peeled and chopped
4 cloves garlic, peeled and minced
2 cups boiled, drained chickpeas (see page 83) or drained canned chickpeas
½ cup very finely chopped fresh parsley
½ teaspoon dried thyme
1 teaspoon salt, or to taste

Drop the tomatoes into boiling water for 15 seconds. Remove with a slotted spoon and peel. Mince the tomatoes.

Heat the oil in a 7- to 8-inch-wide pan over a medium flame. Put in the onions and garlic. Stir and fry for 3 to 4 minutes or until onions are soft. Put in the tomatoes. Stir and cook them for 3 to 4 minutes or until they are soft and pastelike. Add the chickpeas, parsley, thyme, salt, and 1 cup water. Bring to a boil. Cover, lower heat and simmer gently for 10 to 15 minutes.

VERY SPICY, DELICIOUS CHICKPEAS

INDIA

This is my mother's recipe for chickpeas. It is wonderfully tart and hot. My mother's family, still living in the narrow lanes of an Old Delhi built in the seventeenth century, tended to eat very spicy foods. My father's side of the family, which had moved in the 1920s into a more westernized section of town built outside the Old City walls, ate a calmer, less fiery cuisine. As a child, I loved both styles of food but because my father and his very "proper" ways smacked of Establishment, I would often sneak off with my mother to eat spicy bazaar food served on leaves of dubious cleanliness in the narrow lanes of Old Delhi.

This chickpea dish is still sold in Delhi's bazaars by hawking vendors. The chickpeas used are the dried variety that have to be soaked overnight and then boiled until tender.

The paprika that I have used is a substitute for the Kashmiri red pepper, which gives a red color—but no heat—to the dishes in which it is used.

These spicy chickpeas can easily be made up to two days ahead of time. In fact, their flavor improves if they are left, refrigerated, for 24 hours.

(serves 4–6)

5   tablespoons vegetable oil
2   medium-sized onions, peeled and minced
8   cloves garlic, peeled and minced
1   tablespoon ground coriander seeds
2   teaspoons ground cumin seeds
¼ to ½ teaspoon ground cayenne pepper
1   teaspoon ground turmeric

6   tablespoons finely chopped, skinned, fresh or canned red-ripe tomatoes
2   20-ounce cans chickpeas, drained, or 4¼ cups home-cooked chickpeas (see page 83)
2   teaspoons ground roasted cumin seeds
1   tablespoon ground *amchoor*
2   teaspoons sweet paprika
1   teaspoon *garam masala*
½ teaspoon salt (or to taste)
1   tablespoon or more lemon juice
1   fresh hot green chili, minced (use more or less as desired)
2   teaspoons very finely grated fresh ginger

Heat the oil in a wide pot over a medium flame. When hot, put in the minced onions and garlic. Stir and fry until the mixture is a rich medium-brown shade. Turn heat to medium-low and add the coriander, cumin (*not* the roasted cumin), cayenne, and turmeric. Stir for a few seconds. Now put in the finely chopped tomatoes. Stir and fry until the tomatoes are well amalgamated with the spice mixture and brown lightly. Add the drained chickpeas and 1 cup water. Stir. Add the ground roasted cumin, *amchoor*, paprika, *garam masala*, salt, and lemon juice. Stir again. Cover, turn heat to low, and simmer for 10 minutes. Remove cover and add the minced green chili and grated ginger. Stir and cook, uncovered, for another 30 seconds.

For information about ingredients and basic techniques that may be unfamiliar, see General Information, pages 418–36.

FALAFEL
(Chickpea Patties)
MIDDLE EAST

Falafel, made out of dried peas or beans, are a popular snack throughout the Middle East. Beans are soaked, ground, and seasoned with onions and parsley. They are then formed into balls or patties and deep fried.

(makes about 18 patties)

1 cup dried chickpeas, soaked in 5 cups water for 24 hours
1 teaspoon baking soda
1 teaspoon salt
½ cup very finely minced onion
2 tablespoons very finely minced parsley
1 teaspoon ground roasted cumin seeds
1 teaspoon ground coriander
2 cloves garlic, peeled and mashed to a pulp
A little freshly ground black pepper
1 tablespoon lemon juice
⅛ teaspoon cayenne pepper
Oil for deep frying

Drain the chickpeas and put them into the container of a food processor or blender. Add the baking soda and salt. Turn the machine on and blend until you have the texture of coarse bread crumbs or fine bulgar wheat. You should *not* have a paste.

Empty the chickpeas into a bowl. Add the onion, parsley, cumin, coriander, garlic, black pepper, lemon juice, and cayenne. Mix gently with a fork. Do not pat down. This mixture should be loose and crumbly.

Put 2 inches of oil in a wok or other utensil for deep frying and set to heat on a medium-low flame. You need a temperature of 350° to 375° F. While the oil heats, form the first batch of patties. Using a very light touch, form patties that are about 2¼ inches in diameter, about ¾-inch thick in the center and less so at the edges. Do not pat down or try to be too neat. The patties should just about hold together. Put as many patties into the hot oil as the utensil will hold in a single layer. Fry about 4 minutes or until the patties are reddish-brown on both sides. Turn at least once during the frying process. When the patties are done, remove them with a slotted spoon and drain on paper towels. Do all patties this way.

Serve hot, with Tahini Dipping Sauce. You may also tear open an edge of a pita bread, stuff in two falafel and some shredded lettuce and sliced tomatoes, and then douse the stuffing with 2 tablespoons of Tahini Dipping Sauce to make a Middle Eastern sandwich.

Usha's Mother's
BESAN
(A Savory Chickpea Flour "Quiche")
INDIA

This dish resembles a quiche only in as much as it is like a set custard that can be cut and served in sections. There the similarity ends. If you have eaten a *socca* in Nice and can imagine something similar made out of chickpea flour but much thicker, then you have the Kutchi dish called *besan*.

To make it, a mixture of chickpea flour, spices, and water is cooked in a pot very much as you would *choux* pastry—with constant stirring. As the mixture thickens, it begins to leave the sides of the pot. It is then poured into a cake tin and allowed to set. Chinese parsley, minced green chilies, and shredded fresh coconut are sprinkled over it as garnishes. Once it has cooled completely, it is cut into squares and served as a snack or with a meal.

(serves 6–8)

2½ cups chickpea flour, sifted
3 to 4 cloves of garlic, peeled and mashed to a pulp
½ teaspoon finely grated fresh ginger
1½ teaspoons ground cumin seeds
½ teaspoon ground turmeric
½ to 1 teaspoon cayenne pepper
1 medium-sized onion
5 tablespoons vegetable oil
5 to 6 dried or fresh curry leaves
2 teaspoons salt
1 tablespoon lemon juice
1 tablespoon minced fresh Chinese parsley
1 to 2 fresh hot green chilies, minced
¼ cup grated fresh coconut

Put the sifted chickpea flour in a bowl. Slowly add 4¼ cups water, a few tablespoons at a time. Stir as you do so, breaking up all lumps with the back of a wooden spoon. (If the batter still has lumps in it, put it through a strainer.)

Combine the garlic, ginger, cumin, turmeric, and cayenne, according to your taste, in a small cup. Add ¼ cup water and mix well. Set aside.

Peel and cut the onion in half lengthwise, then slice into fine half rings.

Heat the oil in a heavy, well-seasoned (or non-stick) 2- to 2½-quart pot over a medium flame. When hot, put in the curry leaves and then, a few seconds later, the sliced onions. Stir and fry the onions for 2 to 3 minutes. Do not let them brown. Add the spices in the small cup. Stir and fry them for about 1 minute. Now put in the chickpea-flour mixture and bring it to a boil, stirring all the time. Turn the heat to medium-low. Keep stirring vigorously with a wooden spoon until mixture seems to leave the sides of the pot. This should take about 20 minutes. Add the salt and lemon juice. Stir to mix. Taste the chickpea-flour mixture. It should have a cooked taste. (In other words, it should not taste raw.) Empty the mixture into a 9 × 9 × 1½-inch cake tin. Smooth over the top with a spatula. Sprinkle the Chinese parsley, green chilies—as much as you like—and coconut over the top and allow to cool. Cut into 1½-inch squares.

You may have this dish as a snack at teatime or you may serve it as a part of an Indian meal.

For information about ingredients and basic techniques that may be unfamiliar, see General Information, pages 418–36.

Fava Beans

These large, meaty beans are used in the cooking of both West and East Asia. In the Middle East, they are often seasoned with herbs like dill and thyme and used to make cold salads and soothing main dishes; in China they can be stir-fried with vegetables or braised with seasonings to make hearty accompaniments for rice.

Fava beans are available in several forms. There are the fresh beans, hidden inside large green pods, that appear seasonally in specialty markets. To prepare these for cooking, you first have to open the pods and extract the beans. The beans themselves are also clothed in their own "seed coats" or skins, which are hard and tasteless. Unless the beans are very young and tender, these skins need to be removed. Here is the best way to go about this: Boil the beans for about 10 minutes in lightly salted water. By this time they should be quite tender inside their coats. The best way to check this is to bite into one. The coat will still be coarse but the bean inside should be tender. Drain and let them cool under running water. Now they are ready to be peeled. (Two pounds of pods yield about 2 to 2½ cups of beans.) If I am not in too much of a hurry, I refrigerate the beans in a plastic container for a few hours before I peel them. This way the beans inside get a bit firmer and there are fewer breakages while peeling. Once the beans are peeled, their skins can be discarded and the beans folded into hot butter or oil, either alone or with other vegetables. Fresh fava beans taste a bit like fresh lima beans.

Then there are dried fava beans which are available all year round at Chinese, Greek, and Middle Eastern stores. They come without their pods, of course, but you can get them both with and without their skins. They taste somewhat like chestnuts after they have been cooked. I generally buy the beans with the seed coats on them because they are easier to find. I boil them for 2 minutes and then let them sit in the hot water for 1 hour. Then I boil them for another 30 to 45 minutes or until they are just tender. I cool them off under running water before I peel away the skins. The beans can then be put into salads or puréed and put into scrambled eggs. One cup of dried fava beans with skins yields about 2 cups of cooked, skinned beans.

Middle Eastern stores also sell canned fava beans that have been peeled and cooked. You could, if you like, use these in salads and main dishes.

FRESH FAVA BEANS WITH THYME
MIDDLE EAST

You may cook fresh or frozen lima beans in the same manner. If you use frozen lima beans, cook them according to package instructions and drain them. Then sauté them in the olive oil with the thyme. Fresh lima beans should be simmered until just tender before they are sautéed. You will not, of course, need to peel them.

(serves 4–6)

3 cups shelled fresh fava beans (see page 89)
1 teaspoon salt
6 tablespoons olive oil
½ teaspoon dried thyme

Put the beans, 2 cups water, and ½ teaspoon salt in a pot and bring to a boil. Cover, lower heat and simmer for 10 minutes or until beans are tender. Drain the beans and cool them under running water. Now peel away and discard their outer skins.

Heat the oil in an 8-inch skillet over a medium flame. Put in the skinned beans, the thyme, and the remaining ½ teaspoon salt. Stir and sauté for 2 minutes.

FRESH FAVA BEANS WITH STRAW MUSHROOMS
CHINA

Here the fava beans are served in their skins, but the skins are not to be eaten. The Chinese like to pinch them with their teeth (or their fingers) so the tender inner bean pops into the mouth.

(serves 4)

1 cup shelled fresh fava beans (see page 89)
1 20-ounce can of straw mushrooms
1 tablespoon Chinese *shaohsing* wine
  or dry sherry

2 tablespoons vegetable oil
1 tablespoon sesame oil
½ teaspoon salt
1½ teaspoons sugar
1 star anise

Make a small cut in the outer shell of each bean with the point of a knife.

Combine the fava beans, the entire contents of the can of mushrooms, wine, the two oils, salt, sugar, and the star anise in a pot and bring to a boil. Cover. Cook on medium heat for about 10 minutes or until beans are tender. There should be just 2 to 3 tablespoons liquid left at the bottom of the pot. If there is more, boil it away. Remove the star anise.

DRIED FAVA BEAN AND GREEN BELL PEPPER SALAD
MIDDLE EAST

(serves 4–6)

1 cup dried fava beans with skins (see page 89)
1 small green bell pepper (enough to make about 1 cup when cut)
½ cup finely chopped fresh parsley

THE DRESSING
5 tablespoons olive oil
4 tablespoons lemon juice
¾ teaspoon salt
⅛ teaspoon freshly ground black pepper
1 clove garlic, peeled and mashed to a pulp

For information about ingredients and basic techniques that may be unfamiliar, see General Information, pages 418–36.

Combine the beans and 5 cups water in a pot. Bring to a boil. Cover, lower heat and simmer 2 minutes. Turn off the heat and let the pot sit, covered, for 1 hour. Bring the beans to a boil again. Cover, lower heat and simmer for 30 to 50 minutes or until beans are just tender. Drain and cool under running water. Peel the beans and discard their skins.

Remove the seeded section of the green pepper and cut into ¼-inch dice. Put the peeled beans, green pepper, and parsley in a bowl. Beat all the ingredients for the dressing together and pour over the contents of the bowl. Stir gently to mix.

LOBIO
(Red Kidney Bean Salad with a Walnut Dressing)
CAUCASUS

When my husband and I were in the Soviet Union, we found that the food we liked the most came from areas that lie to the east and west of the Caspian Sea. We had *lobio* for the first time at the Aragvi restaurant in Moscow, where it is served as one of the appetizers, along with flat bread and pickled vegetables.

I use canned red kidney beans for this recipe. If you wish to use the dried variety, here is how you go about it: Pick over 1 cup of beans. Then wash and drain them. Put the beans in a pot along with 6 cups water and bring to a boil. Lower heat and simmer, uncovered, for 2 minutes. Turn the heat off and let the beans sit, uncovered, for 1 hour. Bring the beans to a boil again. Cover, and simmer on low heat for 45 minutes. Add 1½ teaspoons salt

and simmer, covered, for another 15 minutes. Drain, but reserve some of the liquid for the dressing.

(serves 4)

1 1-pound can of red kidney beans
1 clove garlic, peeled
½ cup shelled walnuts
1 tablespoon plus 1 teaspoon red wine vinegar
2 tablespoons vegetable or olive or walnut oil
⅛ teaspoon salt
⅛ teaspoon freshly ground black pepper
1/16 to ⅛ teaspoon cayenne pepper
1 tablespoon finely sliced scallion
2 tablespoons minced fresh Chinese parsley

Drain the beans and put them in a small bowl. *Save the liquid.*

You need a food processor or blender to make the dressing. (If you have neither, pound the garlic and walnuts in a mortar. Add the vinegar, salt, pepper, and cayenne. Mix. Slowly add the oil, beating well with a fork.) Start your machine and put in the garlic. When it is minced, put in the walnuts. When they have turned crumblike, add the vinegar. Slowly add 4 tablespoons of the reserved bean liquid. Blend until you have a paste. You may have to stop the machine and scrape down a few times. Now add the oil in a steady stream and then the salt, pepper, and cayenne. Blend until you have a smooth dressing.

Pour the dressing over the beans. Add half the scallion and half the Chinese parsley. Mix and taste for seasonings. You may cover and chill the salad until you are ready to eat; it improves if allowed to sit around for a few hours. Just before you are ready to eat, put the salad on a clean serving dish and sprinkle the remaining scallion and Chinese parsley over the top.

RED BEANS COOKED WITH GARLIC AND GINGER

INDIA

(serves 4–6)

1   cup small red *azuki* beans
2   whole cloves garlic, peeled
2   quarter-sized slices of fresh ginger
1   whole dried hot red pepper
1   tablespoon lime or lemon juice
¾ to 1 teaspoon salt
⅓ teaspoon *garam masala*
½ cup heavy cream
3   tablespoons *ghee* or vegetable oil
½ teaspoon very finely minced garlic
½ teaspoon very finely minced fresh ginger
¼ teaspoon cayenne pepper

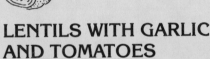

Put the beans and 5 cups water into a heavy 2½-quart pot and bring to a boil. Turn heat to low and simmer for 2 minutes. Turn the heat off and let the beans sit, uncovered, for 1 hour. Add the whole garlic cloves, the slices of ginger, and the whole red pepper. Bring to a boil. Cover in such a way as to leave the lid very slightly ajar, lower heat and simmer gently for 1 hour. Mash the cloves of garlic against the sides of the pot. Remove and discard the ginger slices and the whole red pepper. Now take 1½ cups of the beans and liquid as well as ½ cup of just the beans (removed with a slotted spoon) and put them into the container of a food processor or blender. Blend until smooth. Pour this paste back into the pot with the beans. Add the lime juice, salt, *garam masala*, and cream. Stir and taste. Leave the beans uncovered on a low flame.

Heat the *ghee* in a small skillet or a very small pot over a medium flame. When hot, put in the minced garlic and ginger. Stir for a few seconds. The garlic should brown slightly. Add the cayenne, stir once, and pour this *ghee*-spice mixture over the beans. Cover immediately and turn the heat off under the beans.

LENTILS WITH GARLIC AND TOMATOES

MIDDLE EAST

(serves 4)

4   tablespoons olive or other vegetable oil
5   cloves garlic, peeled and minced
½ pound tomatoes (1 large or 2 smaller ones), peeled and minced
1   cup dried lentils, picked over, washed, and drained
¾ to 1 teaspoon salt
1   tablespoon lemon juice

Heat the oil in a heavy, wide, 2½-quart pot over a medium flame. When hot, put in the garlic. Stir and fry until the garlic browns lightly. Put in the tomatoes. Stir and cook about 5 minutes or until tomatoes turn into a paste. Put in the lentils and 2½ cups water. Bring to a boil. Cover, lower heat and simmer gently for ½ hour. Add the salt and lemon juice. Stir to mix.

For information about ingredients and basic techniques that may be unfamiliar, see General Information, pages 418–36.

LENTIL SALAD

MIDDLE EAST

This salad may be stored in the refrigerator for several days. It is excellent to take on picnics.

(serves 8)

1 pound (about 3 cups) dried lentils
1 teaspoon ground cumin seeds
2½ teaspoons salt
4 scallions
4 to 4½ tablespoons lemon juice
⅛ to ¼ teaspoon freshly ground black pepper
½ cup olive oil
1 cup minced parsley, well-packed

In a 3- to 4-quart pot, combine the lentils with 5½ cups of water. Add the cumin, 1 teaspoon salt and bring to a boil. Cover, and simmer gently for 25 minutes. Remove cover and let the lentils cool a bit. Slice the scallions in very fine rounds halfway up their green sections. When lukewarm, add the remaining salt, the lemon juice, the black pepper, oil, parsley, and scallions.

Stir and cool. Serve at room temperature or cold.

LENTILS WITH SPINACH

MIDDLE EAST

(serves 6)

1¼ pounds fresh or frozen leaf spinach
1 medium-sized onion, peeled
5 tablespoons vegetable oil
2 cloves garlic, peeled and minced
1 cup dried lentils, picked over, washed, and drained
1½ to 1¾ teaspoons salt
1 teaspoon ground cumin seeds
⅛ teaspoon freshly ground black pepper

Separate the fresh spinach leaves and wash well. Do not discard the pinkish roots. Wash them as well. (They will taste very good when cooked.) Bunch up a few leaves at a time and cut them crosswise into ½-inch-wide strips. Cut each root into 2 to 3 pieces. If using frozen spinach, cook according to directions, drain and chop coarsely.

Cut the onion in half lengthwise, and then cut the halves into fine half rings.

Heat the oil in a heavy, wide, casserole-type pot over a medium flame. When hot, put in the onion and garlic. Stir and sauté for 2 minutes. Now put in the lentils and 3 cups of water. Bring to a boil. Cover, lower heat and simmer about 25 minutes or until lentils are just tender. Add the spinach leaves and roots, salt, and cumin. Stir to mix and bring to a simmer. Cover and simmer another 10 to 15 minutes or until spinach is tender and well mixed into the lentils. Stir gently a few times during this period. Put in the black pepper and mix again. This dish may easily be made ahead of time and reheated.

CANDIED DRIED LIMA BEANS

JAPAN

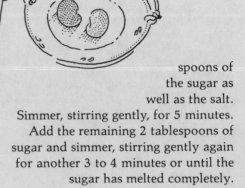

The Japanese candy various large, kidney-shaped beans and then serve them, sometimes in solitary splendor, arranged prettily on a plate that holds small servings of other foods as well. The sweet beans contrast beautifully with other salty and sour foods and, especially when there are just two or three of them, show off their exquisite shape as if Elsa Peretti had designed them for Tiffany.

Candied beans may be simmered in soy sauce, which gives them a dark brown color, or, if they are white to begin with, they can be left with their natural color.

Serve these at any meal where you might have candied sweet potatoes.

(serves 4–6)

1 cup dried, large lima beans
4 tablespoons sugar
½ teaspoon salt

Pick over the beans, then wash and drain them. Put them with 4 cups water into a heavy, 2½-quart pot and bring to a boil. Cover, lower heat and simmer gently for 2 minutes. Turn off the heat and let the pot sit, covered, for 1 hour. Uncover and bring to a boil again. Cover, lower heat and simmer gently for 30 to 40 minutes or until beans are tender but still retain their shape and some firmness. (Older beans might take longer to cook.) Drain the beans but save ¼ cup of their liquid. (The rest of the liquid may be used for soups.) Now put the beans and the ¼ cup of liquid back into the pot and place the pot over a low flame. Add 2 table-spoons of the sugar as well as the salt. Simmer, stirring gently, for 5 minutes. Add the remaining 2 tablespoons of sugar and simmer, stirring gently again for another 3 to 4 minutes or until the sugar has melted completely.

FROZEN LIMA BEANS BRAISED WITH SWISS CHARD AND DILL

IRAN

This is a delicate and delightfully simple dish. If you cannot find Swiss chard, you could substitute romaine lettuce or any other mild-flavored, tender green.

(serves 4–6)

1 10-ounce package frozen Fordhook lima beans
1 head Swiss chard (4 well-packed cups), cut
5 tablespoons unsalted butter
1 medium-sized onion, peeled and cut into ½-inch dice
½ cup fresh, chopped dill, well-packed, or 1½ teaspoons dried
½ teaspoon salt

For information about ingredients and basic techniques that may be unfamiliar, see General Information, pages 418–36.

Defrost the lima beans slightly under warm running water, enough to separate them.

Separate the Swiss chard leaves and wash them well. Lay them side by side and cut them, crosswise, at ½-inch intervals all the way from the leafy sections to the bottom of the stems.

Heat the butter in a heavy, wide, casserole-type pot over a medium flame. When the butter has melted and is frothing, put in the onion. Stir and sauté for 1 minute. Add the lima beans. Stir and sauté another minute. Put in the Swiss chard and the dill. Stir and sauté 2 to 3 minutes. Add the salt and ¼ cup water. Bring to a simmer. Cover tightly, lower heat and simmer gently for about 15 minutes or until chard is cooked.

Devi's
LIMA BEANS WITH RAISINS
INDIA

This delicious dish is made by my friend, Devi Mangaldas of Ahmedabad. Gujarati food ranks among the best vegetarian food in the world and Devi's is cooked and presented with a special delicacy. Sometimes the food—like this dish—is very simple and easy to make. At other times, when she cooks the lightest rice-flour pancakes between two almond leaves, it tends to get fairly tricky—though not impossible—to master.

The chief spice in this dish is *ajwain* (see General Information), which looks like celery seed and tastes, as one of my students once said, like a cross between anise and black pepper. Raisins complement the lima beans beautifully. It may seem like a very unusual combination, but it is a very tasty one.

It is best to use the medium-sized dried green or white lima beans for this dish. You do have to soak them for 20 hours but they hold their shape and have a nice bite to them.

(serves 3–4)

1 cup medium-sized dried green or white lima beans
3 tablespoons vegetable oil
1 teaspoon whole *ajwain* seeds
¼ teaspoon ground turmeric
⅛ teaspoon cayenne pepper, or to taste
½ teaspoon salt
2 to 4 tablespoons golden raisins
2 teaspoons sugar
1 tablespoon lemon juice

Pick over the lima beans and wash them. Put them in a bowl and cover them with 3 cups of water. Leave to soak for 20 hours. Drain.

Heat the oil in a heavy, 2- to 3-quart pot over a medium-high flame. When hot, put in the *ajwain* seeds and stir once. Now put in the drained lima beans and turn the heat to medium-low. Add the turmeric, cayenne to taste, salt, raisins, sugar, and lemon juice. Stir to mix. Add ¾ cup water and bring to a simmer. Cover tightly and simmer very gently for 30 minutes. Check the beans after every 10 minutes. If the water evaporates, add a tablespoon of hot water whenever needed. There should be no liquid left when the lima beans have finished cooking.

MUNG OR MASOOR DAL

INDIA

These two basic split peas are North Indian staples and are cooked in pretty much the same way. The cooking time and amount of water can vary slightly according to the age of the dal. Masoor dal is salmon-colored when uncooked and is sold as red lentils or Egyptian lentils in some health-food stores.

There are many variations of the final flavoring that is provided in this recipe by the asafetida, cumin, and red peppers. You might like to try them at some time or other. Into the 2 tablespoons of hot oil, you may put: (1) 2 teaspoons whole black mustard seeds, 1 bay leaf, ½ teaspoon finely grated fresh ginger, and 3 fresh hot green chilies; (2) 1 teaspoon *kalonji*, 1 bay leaf, ½ teaspoon finely grated fresh ginger, and 3 fresh hot green chilies; (3) 1 teaspoon ground cumin, 1 teaspoon ground coriander, ½ teaspoon finely grated fresh ginger, and ⅛ to ¼ teaspoon cayenne pepper; or (4) 1 tablespoon minced onion, ½ teaspoon minced garlic. Let them fry a bit and then add 1 teaspoon ground cumin, and ⅛ to ¼ teaspoon cayenne pepper.

(serves 4–6)

1 cup mung or *masoor dal*
1 quarter-sized slice of fresh ginger
¾ teaspoon ground turmeric
1 teaspoon salt
2 tablespoons vegetable oil or *ghee*
A pinch of ground asafetida
1 teaspoon whole cumin seeds
2 whole, hot dried red peppers

Pick over the *dal* and wash in several changes of water. Drain, then put with 4 cups of water into a heavy, 2½-quart pot. Bring to a boil and skim away all the surface scum. Add the ginger and turmeric. Turn the heat to low and cover in such a way as to leave the lid just very slightly ajar (or else the *dal* will boil over). Cook for 1 to 1½ hours or until *dal* is no longer grainy. When done, a thick purée settles at the bottom and a thin *dal* "water" rises to the top. You should stir the *dal* a few times during the last 15 minutes of the cooking time and turn the heat to very low if necessary in order to avoid sticking. Add the salt and mix it in. Keep the *dal* covered and hot.

Heat the oil in a small skillet or a very small pot over a medium flame. When hot, put in first the asafetida, then, a second later, the cumin and, when the seeds start to sizzle, the red peppers. Turn the red peppers over so all sides turn dark and crisp. This entire step should take about 10 seconds. Quickly pour the oil and all the spices into the hot *dal*. Cover the *dal* immediately and let it absorb the flavorings for at least 1 minute before serving.

For information about ingredients and basic techniques that may be unfamiliar, see General Information, pages 418–36.

Maya's
ROASTED MUNG DAL
INDIA

Here the *dal* is cooked almost exactly as in the preceding recipe, with this one difference—it is roasted lightly before it is cooked in water. To do this, pick over the *dal* but do not wash it. Rub it in a dishcloth to get rid of loose dust. Then put it into a 6- to 7-inch cast-iron skillet or heavy wok over a medium-low flame. Stir and roast the *dal* until it turns light brown in spots. Remove it from the fire. *Now* wash it in several changes of water and proceed with the recipe.

Finish off the *dal* with either the first or second suggestion in the introduction opposite.

MONGO
(Mung Beans with Spinach and Tomatoes)
PHILIPPINES

This earthy dish consists of cooked mung beans added to a medley of sautéed vegetables—garlic, onion, and tomatoes. Then, during the final minutes of cooking, the very nutritious *malunggay* leaves, rich in vitamin A, or bitter-melon leaves are thrown into the pot. Just before eating, the dish is further perked up with the juice of the *kalamansi* lime and a little olive oil. I have substituted spinach for the Filipino greens. Instead of the *kalamansi* lime, ordinary lime or lemon may be used.

(serves 4–6)

1   cup whole mung beans
5   tablespoons vegetable oil
7   cloves garlic, peeled and lightly mashed
2   medium-sized onions, peeled and chopped
¾   pound red-ripe tomatoes, peeled and chopped
½   pound tender spinach leaves, well washed and
       separated
1   teaspoon salt
1   tablespoon lime juice
1   lime, cut into wedges
¼   cup fruity olive oil (optional)

Clean and pick over the beans. Wash in several changes of water. Drain. Put the beans and 5 cups water into a 2-quart pot and bring to a boil. Cover, lower heat and simmer for 2 minutes. Turn off the heat and let the pot sit, covered, for 1 hour. Bring the beans to a boil again. Turn heat to low and simmer gently for 1½ hours or until the beans are tender and slightly mushy. Stir gently during the last half hour of cooking to prevent sticking.

Heat 5 tablespoons vegetable oil in an 8-inch-wide sauté pan over a medium flame. When hot, put in the garlic. Stir and fry until the garlic turns a pale brown color. Add the onions. Stir and sauté them until they turn translucent. Add the tomatoes. Stir and fry for 5 to 6 minutes or until tomatoes just start to catch. Add the cooked mung beans and bring to a simmer. Simmer, stirring now and then, for 5 minutes. Now put in the spinach leaves, salt, and the 1 tablespoon lime juice. Stir and bring to a simmer. Simmer, stirring occasionally, for about 5 minutes or until spinach is cooked.

Pass the lime wedges and olive oil on the side and serve with rice.

"DRY" MUNG DAL

INDIA

As opposed to the more "soupy" *dal* dishes, here each grain stands, plump and firm, all by itself. To achieve this, the split peas are first soaked for 3 hours and then cooked, simply and quickly, in a small quantity of water. The cooking time is only about 15 minutes. For a quick lunch, I often stuff whole-wheat pita halves with this *dal* along with some sliced ripe tomatoes and lettuce.

(serves 4)

1 cup mung *dal*
3 tablespoons vegetable oil
A generous pinch of crushed asafetida
1½ teaspoons whole cumin seeds
½ teaspoon ground turmeric
⅛ teaspoon cayenne pepper
½ teaspoon salt
3 tablespoons *ghee* or unsalted butter

Pick over the *dal* and wash it in several changes of water. Drain. Put *dal* in a bowl. Add 2 cups water and soak *dal* for 3 to 4 hours. Drain.

Heat the oil in a heavy, 2- to 3-quart pot over a medium-high flame. When hot, put in the asafetida and, 2 seconds later, the whole cumin seeds. As soon as the cumin seeds turn a shade darker (this just takes a few seconds), put in the *dal*, turmeric, cayenne, and salt. Turn heat to medium-low and stir to mix. Now put in 1 cup water and bring to a simmer. Cover tightly, turn heat to very, very low and cook gently for about 15 minutes. The *dal* should be tender enough to eat but each grain should be quite separate. Put in the *ghee* or butter, stir, and serve at once.

HOW TO SPROUT YOUR OWN MUNG BEANS FOR CHINESE, JAPANESE, AND OTHER FAR EASTERN AND SOUTHEAST ASIAN DISHES

Wherever there are Chinese grocery stores, you should be able to buy fresh mung-bean sprouts by the pound. The sprouts, which look like 3-inch tails attached to small whitish heads, are not only used in rice, noodle, and vegetable dishes, but are excellent to put in salads along with more mundane things like raw mushrooms, lettuce, and cucumber. If you cannot buy any fresh sprouts in your neighborhood, make them at home. They are not difficult to make, though they do take 3 to 4 days to reach the correct length.

In America, most people are familiar only with the Oriental type of bean sprout which is more tail than bean. Just to avoid any confusion, there is another mung-bean sprout that I will be referring to in this book and that is the Indian version. In India, we let the mung beans sprout, but just barely. Just the tiniest shoots are allowed to emerge

For information about ingredients and basic techniques that may be unfamiliar, see General Information, pages 418–36.

before the beans are gobbled up. I will describe these sprouts later in the recipes that require them.

Health-food stores today carry dry mung beans and, very often, an array of gadgets in which you can do your sprouting. If you happen to have such a gadget, by all means use it. But there is no need at all to go and buy one, because the equipment that you already have in your home can be made to work just as well.

(makes about 6 cups)

½ cup whole mung beans*

*NOTE: A pound of fresh, crisp mung-bean sprouts is equivalent to about 4 cups. A pound of wilted, waterlogged sprouts, however, may fit into 2 cups.

Pick over the mung beans and discard any broken ones. Rinse in lukewarm water. Put the beans in a bowl and pour 3 cups of lukewarm water over them. Cover the bowl and let the beans soak for 8 hours.

Rinse the beans in lukewarm water again and put them in a plastic bag that has been punched all over with holes (you can do this with a fork). Put the bag in a colander or sieve. Leave the mouth of the bag open. Cover this opening with a doubled or tripled well-dampened dishcloth. Now put the sieve or colander in a large bowl (if it is a sieve, it should be balanced on a bowl) and then place the bowl in a dark and, if possible, humid place with the ideal temperature ranging between 70° and 75° F. Some people use the area under their sinks. Every 4 hours, take out the bowl. Put the sieve or colander under a faucet and let lukewarm water pour through the dish towel, over the beans, out through the holes in the plastic bag, and, finally, out through the sieve or colander. Place the sieve or colander back in the bowl (some dripping will continue) and put the bowl back in the selected dark place for another 4 hours. Never disturb the beans. Continue to do this for 3 to 4 days or until the sprouts are 2 to 3 inches long. (This is the ideal method for sprouting. However, since I do not believe in losing sleep over bean sprouts, I give the beans a good soaking before I retire and another when I get up in the morning. As a result, not all my sprouts are perfect. Some actually look a bit stunted. That does not bother me. My sprouts are still crunchier and less waterlogged than 90 percent of the sprouts that can be bought in New York's grocery stores.)

Now put the sprouts in a very large bowl or basin and fill it with water. "Rinse" the sprouts by rubbing them gently with your hands. This should make the green skin of the bean slip off. Tilt the basin to get rid of the skins. Those that do not float away should be picked off. Drain the sprouts. Put the sprouts in a container, fill the container with water, and refrigerate until needed. Do not cover the sprouts. If you change the water in this container every day, the sprouts should stay looking healthy for at least 3 days.

SOY-BEAN SPROUTS

There are many ways to make these sprouts. You could follow the method used for mung-bean sprouts and continue the sprouting process for about 6 days until you have sprouts of the right size. You must remember to water and drain the soy beans at least 3 to 4 times a day or they will go bad, which can happen easily if you are at all negligent. The easier method is to buy a dark sprouting jar with a mesh lid that is available in most health-food and even some gardening stores. Here is the jar method.

(makes about 3 cups)

½ cup dried soy beans*

Pick over the beans and remove any cracked or broken ones. Rinse the beans in several changes of water. Drain. Soak the beans in 5 cups of water for 12 hours. Drain. Rinse gently and drain again. Put the beans in the jar and put on its mesh lid. Place the jar on its side in a warm, draft-free, dark place. I use my empty oven *without* the pilot light turned on. Now for the next 6 days or so, remove the jar from its warm place at least 4 times a day. Without tilting it about unduly, fill it with water and then pour *all* the water out. Put the jar back in its warm place. Keep doing this until the sprouts are about 3 inches long. Empty the contents of the sprouting jar into a bowl of water. The soy-bean skins will float to the top. Pour them out. Put the sprouts in a bowl of water and refrigerate until you need them. They should last at least 4 to 5 days. Change the water every day.

*NOTE: The tail-like, rooty ends of the sprouts are usually snipped off before they are cooked.

For information about ingredients and basic techniques that may be unfamiliar, see General Information, pages 418–36.

STIR-FRIED MUNG-BEAN SPROUTS, CARROTS, AND CABBAGE

CHINA

(serves 4)

3 scallions
½ pound cabbage (¼ small to medium-sized head)
2 carrots
3 cups mung-bean sprouts
1 to 2 fresh hot green chilies
4 tablespoons vegetable oil
2 cloves garlic, peeled and very lightly mashed
3 quarter-sized slices of fresh ginger
1 tablespoon Chinese *shaohsing* wine
   or dry sherry
½ teaspoon salt, or to taste
½ teaspoon sugar
1 tablespoon sesame oil

Prepare the vegetables: Cut the scallions into 3-inch-long sections and then cut lengthwise into thin strips. Remove the core from the cabbage, then shred the leaves into fine, long strips (you will have about 2 well-packed cups). Peel the carrots, trim them, and cut into fine julienne strips—about 1½ cups. Rinse the bean sprouts, drain and pat dry. Cut the chilies into fine, long shreds.

Heat the oil in a large wok over a high flame. When hot, put in the garlic and ginger. Stir them around for about 15 seconds, pressing the pieces against the sides of the wok. Put in the scallions and stir once. Now put in the cabbage, carrots, mung-bean sprouts, and green chilies. Stir and fry for about 1½ minutes. Add the wine by pouring it around the sides of the wok. Stir once. Add the salt, sugar, and sesame oil. Stir for 3 to 4 seconds. Remove the ginger slices and serve at once.

Yien-Koo's
SALAD OF MUNG-BEAN SPROUTS AND EGG STRANDS

CHINA

(serves 4)

3 large eggs
1 tablespoon Chinese *shaohsing* wine or dry
   sherry
⅛ plus ¼ teaspoon salt
4 teaspoons vegetable oil
4 cups mung-bean sprouts, rinsed and drained
1 tablespoon distilled white cider vinegar
1 tablespoon Chinese thin soy sauce
1 tablespoon sesame oil
½ teaspoon sugar

Beat the eggs well (but not to a froth) in a large bowl. Add the *shaohsing* wine, 2 tablespoons water, and ⅛ teaspoon salt. Beat lightly to mix.

Brush a 7- to 8-inch, nonstick skillet with 1 teaspoon oil and let it heat on a low flame. Pour in a quarter of the beaten eggs—just enough to barely cover the bottom of the skillet. You will have to tilt the skillet around in order to let the egg mixture flow evenly to the edges. Let the mixture set until firm. This may take 6 to 7 minutes. Ease a plastic spatula under the egg crepe and remove it. Put it on a plate and let it cool. Make four crepes this way, letting each cool on separate plates. Roll up each crepe and then cut it crosswise into fine, ¼-inch-wide strands.

Heat 4 cups of water in a large pot. When boiling furiously, drop in the bean sprouts. Bring to a boil again. Turn off the heat immediately and drain the sprouts. Rinse the sprouts under cold water and leave to drain for 15 minutes. Pat dry.

Put egg strands and sprouts in a serving bowl. Add the vinegar, soy sauce, ¼ teaspoon salt, sesame oil, and sugar. Toss to mix and taste for seasonings.

Devi's
SPROUTED MUNG BEANS COOKED WITH MUSTARD SEEDS
INDIA

Indians eat sprouted mung beans, too, but these are sprouted quite differently from the ones in East and Southeast Asia. We barely allow our sprouts to emerge from the beans before we eat them. The result of this is that even though Indian mung-bean sprouts are easy to digest, they are much more substantial.

In the Indian state of Gujarat, these beans are often served for breakfast, along with Soft Yogurt, Cheese with Chinese Parsley and Scallions Gujarati Style (see page 235), a fresh mint chutney, and kakra, a crisp bread resembling Scandinavian wheat wafers.

(serves 6)

2 cups whole mung beans, picked over and washed
4 tablespoons vegetable oil
2 teaspoons black mustard seeds

5 to 6 medium-sized cloves of garlic, peeled and minced
½ teaspoon ground turmeric
About ⅛ to ¼ teaspoon ground cayenne pepper
1¾ to 2 teaspoons salt
⅛ to ¼ teaspoon freshly ground black pepper
2 to 3 tablespoons lemon juice

Soak beans in 7 cups of water. Cover and leave for 12 hours. Drain. Line a bowl with a wet dish towel in such a way that you leave enough of the towel on one side to cover the beans. Put the beans inside the towel-lined bowl. Cover them with the overhanging towel section. Now cover the bowl loosely with any lid that will not press down on the beans. Leave in a dark place (like an oven) for another 12 hours. The beans will just begin to sprout.

Heat the oil in a heavy saucepan over a medium-

For information about ingredients and basic techniques that may be unfamiliar, see General Information, pages 418–36.

high flame. When very hot, put in the mustard seeds and turn the heat down to medium. As the mustard seeds pop (this will happen almost immediately), put in the minced garlic and stir until garlic browns lightly. Now add the turmeric, cayenne, and, a few seconds later, the sprouted beans. Stir. Add the salt and ⅓ cup water. Bring to a boil.

Cover tightly. Turn heat to low and cook gently for 15 to 20 minutes or until beans are tender. Stir a few times during the cooking. If the water evaporates, add a tablespoon of hot water.

Add the black pepper and lemon juice. Mix well. Taste for balance of hot, sour, and salty seasonings. This dish may be made ahead of time and reheated.

SPROUTED MUNG BEANS WITH SPINACH

INDIA

Here is another Indian dish using barely sprouted mung beans. This time they are combined with spinach and Chinese parsley. While this dish may be served hot at breakfast, lunch, or dinner, it is also quite wonderful when served cold at picnics and buffet-style parties.

(serves 8)

1 pound fresh spinach, trimmed and well washed (or 1 package frozen chopped spinach, cooked and drained)
5 tablespoons vegetable oil
1 tablespoon whole black mustard seeds
1 tablespoon whole cumin seeds
2 teaspoons coarsely grated fresh ginger
9 to 10 medium-sized cloves garlic, peeled and minced
1 fresh hot green chili, or more to taste, minced
2 cups whole mung beans, semi-sprouted (according to directions in preceding recipe)
4 tablespoons minced Chinese parsley
2 teaspoons salt
2 teaspoons ground cumin seeds

2 teaspoons ground coriander seeds
1 teaspoon *garam masala*
2 tablespoons lemon juice, or more to taste

In a large pot, bring about 3½ quarts of water to a boil. Drop in the spinach and let it cook 2 to 3 minutes or until it is completely wilted. Drain, squeeze out as much liquid as you can, and then mince the spinach. Set aside.

Heat the oil in a wide, 3½- to 4-quart pot over a medium flame. When very hot, put in the black mustard seeds and the whole cumin seeds. As soon as the seeds begin to pop and sizzle (this takes just a few seconds), put in the ginger, garlic, and green chili. Stir and fry for about 1 minute or until garlic pieces turn a light brown. Now add the sprouted beans, the minced spinach, the Chinese parsley, the salt, and 1 cup of water. Bring to a boil. Cover tightly and simmer gently for 10 minutes.

Remove the cover and add the ground cumin seeds, the ground coriander seeds, the *garam masala*, and the lemon juice. Stir to mix. Cover and simmer another 5 minutes.

Devi's
SALAD OF SPROUTED MUNG BEANS
INDIA

This cool, green and white, lemony salad is a Gujarati favorite. Celery, considered foreign and therefore exotic in India, is not one of its normal ingredients. However, my friend Devi Mangaldas does grow it in her Ahmedabad home and often adds it, most imaginatively, to a host of Indian foods—like this salad. The salad also contains onions, green peppers, and Chinese parsley, all chopped very small so the pieces are of the same size as the beans themselves.

For this recipe, the whole mung beans are sprouted somewhat differently from the method used in the two preceding recipes.

The beans soak for *48* hours and are then left to sprout for 12 to 16 hours. These sprouts are meant to be eaten raw.

Here is how you make Indian-style bean sprouts for raw salads: Soak 1 cup mung beans in 6 cups of water. Cover and leave for 48 hours, making sure to change the water every 12 hours. Drain. Line a bowl with a wet dish towel in such a way that you leave enough of the towel on one side to cover the beans. Put the beans inside the towel-lined bowl. Cover with the overhanging towel section. Now cover the bowl loosely with any lid that will not press down on the beans. Leave in a dark place (like a cool oven) for 12 to 16 hours.

The beans should just begin to sprout. One cup of mung beans will make about 5 cups of Indian-style sprouts. If you are not going to eat the sprouts immediately, rinse them and put them in an uncovered bowl filled with water. Refrigerate for up to 36 hours.

(serves 6–8)

5 cups Indian-style (see above) mung-bean sprouts, washed and drained
2 sticks (about 1½ cups) celery, very finely chopped
1 medium-sized green pepper, seeded and very finely chopped
1 medium-sized onion, peeled and very finely chopped
1 well-packed cup washed, dried, and finely chopped Chinese (or other) parsley
3 cloves garlic, peeled and very finely minced
1 fresh hot green chili, very finely minced
1½ teaspoons salt
¼ teaspoon finely ground black pepper
3½ tablespoons (or more) lemon juice

Combine all the ingredients. Toss well and check the seasonings. Serve at room temperature or cold.

For information about ingredients and basic techniques that may be unfamiliar, see General Information, pages 418–36.

SOY-BEAN AND MUNG-BEAN SPROUTS SEASONED WITH SESAME OIL

KOREA

This simple, refreshing dish may be served in place of a salad.

(serves 4–6)

4   cups soy-bean sprouts
4   cups mung-bean sprouts
¼   cup Japanese soy sauce
2   tablespoons sesame oil
1   tablespoon sugar
¼   teaspoon salt
2   teaspoons roasted and lightly crushed sesame
    seeds

Bring 12 cups of water to a boil in a 4-quart pot. Put in the soy-bean sprouts and boil rapidly for 10 minutes. Add the mung-bean sprouts and boil another 2 minutes. Drain thoroughly, squeezing out as much of the water as possible.

Put the sprouts in a bowl. Add all the other ingredients and mix well. Taste for seasonings.

NAVY BEAN SALAD

MIDDLE EAST

(serves 4–6)

1   cup dried navy beans, picked over, washed, and
    drained
5   tablespoons olive oil
3   tablespoons lemon juice
¾   teaspoon salt
½   well-packed cup finely chopped fresh parsley
2   scallions, cut into fine rounds including green
⅛   teaspoon freshly ground black pepper

Put the beans and 4 cups water in a heavy 2½-quart pot. Bring to a boil. Cover, lower heat and simmer 2 minutes. Turn off the heat and let the pot sit, covered, for 1 hour. Uncover, and bring to a boil again. Cover, lower heat, and simmer gently for 40 minutes or until beans are tender but still retain their shape. (Older beans will take longer to cook.) Beat the oil, lemon juice, and salt together, then add to the beans while they are still hot. Add all the other ingredients and mix well. Adjust seasonings, if necessary.

Tatie Wawo-Runtu's
KACANG ASIN
(Salted Peanuts with Garlic)
INDONESIA

These peanuts may be added to Sambal Goreng Tempeh Kering (see page 109). If you wish to do that, double all the ingredients for the spicy paste in that recipe and then fold in the peanuts when you put in the *tempeh*. You may, of course, just serve these peanuts as a nice, crisp snack.

(makes 1 cup)

1 cup raw, shelled, and skinned peanuts
2 teaspoons salt
6 tablespoons vegetable oil
8 cloves garlic, peeled and cut into slivers

Soak the peanuts in 3 cups water for 8 hours or overnight. Drain. Combine the salt and 1 cup water in a bowl. Put the peanuts into it and let them soak for 1 hour. Drain and pat dry.

Heat the oil in an 8-inch skillet over a medium flame. Put in the peanuts. Stir and fry for 3 to 4 minutes or until peanuts just begin to lose their white color. Put in the garlic. Stir and fry another minute or until peanuts are golden. Remove with a slotted spoon and drain on paper towels.

Mrs. Bannerji's
SPINACH WITH RAW PEANUTS
INDIA

Raw peanuts are used in many regions of India to make a host of delicious foods, not the least of which is this simple and tasty dish from Bengal in which peanuts (the Bengalis call them *cheena badaam* or the "almonds of China") are cooked with spinach. As many Southerners in the United States already know, raw peanuts, once cooked, do not taste like peanuts at all (rather, not like roasted peanuts) but more like peas and beans—they are a legume, after all—and like a heavenly cross between chestnuts and water chestnuts.

Peanuts are a concentrated food. Pound for pound, they have more proteins, minerals, and vitamins than beef liver. They do tend to be high in fat, but this is vegetable fat which the body needs. Peanut dishes make an excellent substitute for meat dishes. For vegans who do not eat dairy products, peanut and soy-bean dishes are well worth exploring.

It is best to get raw, shelled peanuts for the recipe that follows. They are available in health-food, Chinese, and Indian grocery stores. If you can get raw peanuts that are skinned, so much the better. Otherwise the reddish skins have to be removed after the soaking period. This dish was prepared with ½-inch-long nuts. Peanuts come in various sizes and you may prefer to use another size.

(serves 3–4)

1 cup raw, shelled peanuts
3 tablespoons vegetable oil
⅛ teaspoon whole fenugreek seeds

For information about ingredients and basic techniques that may be unfamiliar, see General Information, pages 418–36.

Anne Lokes'
PEANUTS WITH LONG GREEN BEANS
SINGAPORE CHINESE

¾ pound fresh spinach, trimmed, washed, and finely chopped

1 tablespoon finely chopped jaggery or dark molasses or dark brown sugar

½ to 1 fresh hot green chili, minced

¼ teaspoon salt

¼ cup plus 2 tablespoons freshly grated coconut

Put the peanuts in a bowl. Add 2 cups of water and soak for 3 to 4 hours. Drain and remove the reddish skins if the peanuts are of the unskinned variety.

Heat the oil in a wide, heavy, 3- to 4-quart pot over a medium flame. When hot, put in the fenugreek seeds. As soon as the seeds begin to sizzle and turn a shade darker (this takes just a few seconds), add the spinach (with the water from washing still clinging to the leaves), the drained peanuts, jaggery, green chili, and salt. Stir for about 30 seconds. Cover, turn heat to low, and simmer gently for 20 minutes. Remove cover. Turn heat to medium and dry off excess liquid if there is any. The dish should have a fairly dry look. Just before serving, add ¼ cup grated coconut and stir once. Remove from heat. Spoon spinach and peanuts into a warm serving dish. Sprinkle with the remaining 2 tablespoons of grated coconut.

Long green beans, the kind that are slim and about a foot long, are available in Indian, Chinese, and other Oriental grocery stores. If you cannot find them, regular green beans may be substituted. Another ingredient normally used in this dish is Chinese preserved radish. Instead, I substitute any one of the following Japanese pickles: White Radish Preserve (see page 378); Cabbage Tsukemono (see page 373); Quick-Salted White Radish Pickle (see page 375); or Shoyu Daikon (see page 375). Each gives a slightly different flavor to the dish and all are good.

(serves 4)

½ pound long green beans

6 shallots, peeled

Preserves or pickles (see note above), about ⅓ cup

3 tablespoons vegetable oil

1 cup fried, unsalted peanuts (see page 322)

1 teaspoon salt

1/16 to ⅛ teaspoon freshly ground white pepper

Trim the ends of the beans and cut them crosswise at ¼-inch intervals.

Cut the shallots into slim slivers.

Cut the pickles or preserves into pieces that are the same size as the cut beans.

Heat the oil in a wok or a heavy skillet over a medium flame. Put in the shallots. Stir and fry for 1 minute. Put in the beans. Stir and fry for 2 minutes. Put in the peanuts, salt, and pepper. Stir and fry for another 2 to 3 minutes. Add 2 tablespoons of water and cover immediately for 30 seconds. Remove cover and add the pickles or preserves. Stir and fry for about 10 seconds.

Tempeh

Many Americans already know of *tempeh*, that flat, whitish cake made with cultured soy beans that is now available in the refrigerated sections of most health-food stores. I was introduced to it a few years ago on a trip to Indonesia. My hostess had cooked Sambal Goreng Tempeh Kering for me. I found myself biting into deliciously spicy "matchsticks" without having any idea what they were made from. All I could identify was a nutty, almost meatlike taste.

Tempeh, I found out, is an ancient Indonesian product (now also found in Singapore and Malaysia) which has almost as much usable protein as chicken. A 4-ounce serving has about 230 calories. It has no saturated fats and is one of the few vegetable products that contains vitamin B12. *Tempeh* is also rich in roughage and is easy to digest. It almost seems to be a perfect food.

While the *tempeh* available in health-food stores at the moment is made from the nutritious soy bean, in Indonesia it is sometimes made from seeds, grains, and other beans as well. Soy-bean *tempeh* is not hard to make, though it does require a warm 85° to 95° F temperature.

The soy beans are first hulled and split. Then they are boiled for 1 hour, after which they are drained and dried off a bit. At this stage a culture is introduced and the beans are packed into lightly perforated plastic bags. The bags need to be flattened out so thinnish, even cakes can form. This takes about a day. A cotton-candylike film miraculously covers the beans and binds them together. This is *tempeh*. It can now be sliced and fried, or cut into cubes and put into stews for about 10 minutes. As *tempeh* is now fairly easily available, I am not providing a recipe. If you wish to make it at home, write to Farm Foods, 156 Drakes Lane, Summertown, TN 38483 (Telephone (615) 964-3584 or -3574). They will send you a starter kit that includes the hulled, split soy beans and the starter spores, as well as instructions.

FRIED TEMPEH
INDONESIA

Fried *tempeh* may be eaten with just a sprinkling of salt. After frying, *tempeh* turns nicely crisp, rather like French fries, and may be served with a dipping sauce. This sauce could be a hot Indonesian *sambal*, a spicy Indian chutney, a Japanese or Korean dipping sauce, or even tomato ketchup.

(serves 2–6)

8 ounces *tempeh*
1 cup vegetable oil
½ teaspoon salt

Cut the *tempeh* into pieces that are approximately 1 x ½ x ¼ inch.

Heat the oil in an 8-inch skillet over a medium flame. When hot, drop in half the *tempeh* pieces.

For information about ingredients and basic techniques that may be unfamiliar, see General Information, pages 418–36.

Stir and fry for 5 to 6 minutes or until the *tempeh* turns golden brown—the same color as French fries. Remove them with a slotted spoon and drain on paper towels. Sprinkle this batch with ¼ teaspoon salt. Fry a second batch exactly the same way. Drain on paper towels and sprinkle with the remaining ¼ teaspoon salt.

Tatie Wawo-Runtu's
FRIED, PRESEASONED TEMPEH
INDONESIA

Uncooked *tempeh* absorbs seasonings like a sponge. So what the Indonesians frequently do is to dip *tempeh* pieces in what could be called a marinade— the marinating period is usually less than a minute— before they proceed with the frying.

(serves 2–6)

8 ounces *tempeh*
1 teaspoon salt
2 to 3 cloves garlic, peeled and mashed to a pulp
1½ teaspoons ground coriander seeds
1 cup vegetable oil

Cut the *tempeh* into "sticks" that are about 2½ x ½ x ¼ inch.

In a bowl, mix together the salt, garlic, coriander, and ½ cup water.

Set the oil to heat in an 8-inch skillet over a medium flame. Meanwhile, put half the *tempeh* sticks into the bowl with the seasonings and stir them about to coat them. Remove the *tempeh* from the bowl, shaking off excess moisture as you do so, and put them into the heated oil. Stir and fry for 5 to 6 minutes or until *tempeh* is golden to reddish-brown and crisp. Remove with a slotted spoon and drain on paper towels. Do a second batch exactly the same way.

Tatie Wawo-Runtu's
SAMBAL GORENG TEMPEH KERING
(Sweet and Sour Tempeh)
INDONESIA

This may well be my favorite *tempeh* recipe. The first time I cooked it, my husband made off with the entire bowlful, muttering something about how well it would go with beer. Here *tempeh* "matchsticks" are fried until crisp, just as they are in the first *tempeh* recipe, then folded into a thick paste that is hot, sour, sweet, and salty at the same time. This *tempeh* may be eaten as a snack or used as a topping for rice. Sometimes fried, seasoned peanuts (see Kacang Asin, page 106) are added to the *tempeh* "matchsticks" before they are enveloped in their spicy paste, making the dish even more nutritious.

(serves 4–6)

4 ounces shallots, peeled and coarsely chopped (a heaping ½ cup)
2 cloves garlic, peeled
4 dried hot red chilies, seeded
1 quarter-sized slice of dry galanga root, shredded by hand
8 ounces *tempeh* (see page 108)
1 cup vegetable oil
3 *daun salaam* leaves, if available
4 teaspoons tamarind paste
1 teaspoon salt
2 teaspoons palm sugar or light brown sugar

Put the shallots, garlic, red chilies, and galanga root into the container of a food processor or blender together with 3 tablespoons of water. Blend until smooth.

Cut the *tempeh* into "matchsticks" that are 1½ x ¼ x ¼ inch.

Heat the oil in an 8-inch skillet over a medium flame. When hot, put in half the *tempeh* pieces. Stir and fry for 5 to 6 minutes or until the *tempeh* turns a golden to reddish-brown and is crisp. Remove move *tempeh* with a slotted spoon and drain on paper towels. Fry a second batch exactly the same way.

Remove all but ¼ cup of oil from the skillet. Put in the *salaam* leaves and stir for a second. Put in the paste from the food processor as well as the tamarind paste. Stir and fry on medium heat for 7 to 8 minutes or until the paste has a dryish look. Add the salt and palm sugar. Stir to mix. Add the fried *tempeh*. Stir gently to mix. Remove the *salaam* leaves. Serve immediately.

TEMPEH COOKED IN COCONUT MILK

INDONESIA

(serves 4)

6 ounces *tempeh* (see page 108)
3 tablespoons vegetable oil
½ cup slivered, peeled shallots
1 clove garlic, minced
1 fresh hot green chili, seeded and cut into thin diagonal rings
2 *daun salaam* leaves
1 quarter-sized slice of dried galanga root
1½ cups coconut milk
¾ teaspoon salt

Cut the *tempeh* into ½-inch cubes.

Heat the oil in an 8-inch skillet over a medium flame. Put in the shallots, garlic, and green chili. Stir and fry for 2 minutes. Put in the *salaam* leaves and galanga root. Stir for another minute. Now put in the coconut milk, salt, and *tempeh* pieces. Bring to a simmer. Cover, lower heat and simmer gently for 10 minutes. Remove *salaam* leaves and galanga root and serve with plain rice.

OILY TOOVAR DAL WITH CLOVES

INDIA

Oily *toovar dal* (*dal* rubbed with oil to preserve it from infestation) is used with great frequency in Gujarat and needs to be washed very well before it is cooked. It has a dark, earthy taste and cloves help bring a spicy sparkle to it.

(serves 4–6)

1 cup oily *toovar dal*
½ teaspoon ground turmeric
¾ teaspoon salt
½ teaspoon sugar
⅛ teaspoon cayenne pepper, more or less to taste
2 tablespoons vegetable oil
8 whole cloves
A 2-inch stick of cinnamon
3 tablespoons *ghee* or unsalted butter

Pick over the *dal* and wash it in several changes of water. Drain. Put *dal* in a heavy 2- to 3-quart pot along with 5 cups of water. Bring to a boil. Remove scum and add the turmeric. Turn heat to very low and cover in such a way that the lid is left very slightly ajar. (This prevents the *dal* from boiling over.) Cook for 1½ hours or until *dal* is very tender. Stir every 10 minutes during the last half hour of cooking. The *dal* should be like a thick soup. Add the salt, sugar, and cayenne. Stir, and turn off heat.

Heat oil in a small skillet or a very small butter-warmer type pot over a medium flame. When hot, put in the whole cloves and cinnamon. When the cloves swell (this takes just a few seconds), pour the oil with spices into the pot with the *dal*. Cover pot immediately.

Reheat the *dal* before serving and stir in the *ghee* or butter. This *dal* is usually served with plain rice.

OILY TOOVAR DAL WITH GREEN BEANS AND TOMATOES

INDIA

Oily *toovar dal* (see preceding recipe) may be cooked with almost any vegetable, making a thick "stew" that can then be eaten with rice or bread.

(serves 6)

1½ cups oily *toovar dal*, picked over, washed, and drained
½ teaspoon ground turmeric
2 quarter-sized slices of fresh ginger
3 tablespoons chopped fresh Chinese parsley
½ pound green beans, trimmed and cut in half
7 cherry tomatoes, peeled
1¼ teaspoons salt
1 teaspoon jaggery or brown sugar
⅛ to ¼ teaspoon cayenne pepper
2 tablespoons lemon juice
3 tablespoons vegetable oil
⅛ teaspoon whole fenugreek seeds
2 teaspoons whole black mustard seeds
½ teaspoon whole cumin seeds
2 whole hot dried red peppers
2 tablespoons unsalted butter or *ghee*

In a heavy 3-quart pot, combine the *dal*, turmeric, ginger, Chinese parsley, and 4 cups of water. Bring to a boil. Cover partially (just leave the lid slightly ajar) and simmer on a low flame for about 45 minutes. Stir a few times during the last 10 minutes. Add the green beans, cherry tomatoes, salt, brown sugar, cayenne pepper, lemon juice, and another cup of water. Stir well and bring to a boil. Cover, lower heat, and simmer for 15 to 20 minutes or until the green beans are tender. Turn off the heat and leave *dal* covered.

Heat the oil in a small skillet or a small pot over a medium flame. When hot, put in the fenugreek seeds, mustard seeds, cumin seeds, and red peppers. The spices will begin to sizzle and pop in seconds. When they do, lift the cover of the pot with the *dal* and empty the contents of the skillet—oil and spices—into it. Replace cover immediately.

Just before serving, heat the *dal* and ladle into a warm serving dish. Cut the butter into 4 to 6 pats and place on top of the hot *dal*. If using *ghee*, spoon it over the hot *dal*.

Neela's
SAMBAR
(South Indian Dal with Vegetables)
INDIA

This South Indian *dal* may be cooked in combination with almost any vegetable. Carrots, long beans (found in Chinese and Indian grocery stores), regular green beans, eggplant, squash, and cauliflower should be sliced or diced and then lightly steamed before being added to the cooked *dal*. Vegetables like okra, onions, radish (white or red), and kohlrabi should be sliced and lightly sautéed in oil or *ghee* before being mixed in with the cooked *dal*. Some South Indians like to boil their vegetables quickly in water to which they have added salt and some tamarind paste. This water is then mixed in with the *dal*, along with the vegetables.

Traditionally, *sambar* is made very, very hot with fistfuls of dried hot red peppers. I have used ground cayenne pepper, which you can adjust to your own taste. Also, in South India, this *dal* is cooked with enough water to make it thin and souplike. It is served in individual bowls and eaten with boiled or steamed rice.

Since most Americans are not used to eating souplike dishes with their hands, I often serve *sambar* in a Western manner. I take warmed soup plates (the shallow, old-fashioned kind) and place a healthy scoop of rice or an *idli* in its center. I then pour the *sambar* carefully around the scoop of rice, letting the top of the scoop rise like an island in the center. As cutlery, I offer a soup spoon. I serve *papadum* (see page 431) on the side and have buttermilk, Indian style (see page 348), as a beverage.

For information about ingredients and basic techniques that may be unfamiliar, see General Information, pages 418–36.

(serves 4–6)

¾ cup *toovar (arhar) dal*
2½ tablespoons *ghee* or vegetable oil
A generous pinch of ground asafetida
1 tablespoon whole coriander seeds
1½ teaspoons whole cumin seeds
1 teaspoon whole fenugreek seeds
2 whole cloves
10 to 12 black peppercorns
A ¾-inch piece of stick cinnamon
¼ to ½ teaspoon cayenne pepper
2 to 3 tablespoons freshly grated coconut, roasted
½ teaspoon whole black mustard seeds
1 medium-sized onion, halved and thickly sliced
6 radishes, trimmed and thickly sliced
1 medium-sized tomato, peeled and diced
½ teaspoon ground turmeric
1 to 2 tablespoons tamarind paste
¾ to 1 teaspoon salt
¼ teaspoon sugar
1 fresh hot green chili, minced
1 teaspoon finely grated fresh ginger
2 tablespoons minced Chinese parsley

Clean and wash the *dal*. Drain. Add 4 cups water and bring to a boil. Turn heat to low, cover in such a way as to leave the lid slightly ajar, and simmer gently until the *dal* is quite tender, about 1½ hours. Stir every now and then during the last 10 minutes of the cooking.

Heat 1 tablespoon of the *ghee* in a small, heavy skillet or a very small pot over a medium flame. When hot, put in the asafetida and, a few seconds later, the coriander, cumin, fenugreek, cloves, peppercorns, and cinnamon. As soon as the spices turn a few shades darker (this takes just a few seconds), put in the cayenne pepper. Stir once and remove from heat.

Put contents of small skillet immediately into the container of an electric blender. Add the roasted grated coconut and ¼ cup water. Blend until you have a smooth paste. Set aside.

In a 2- to 3-quart pot, heat the remaining 1½ tablespoons of *ghee* over a medium flame. When hot, put in the mustard seeds. As soon as the seeds begin to pop (this just takes a few seconds), lower the heat and put in the sliced onion and sliced radishes. Sauté for 3 to 4 minutes. Do not allow any browning. Now add the paste from the blender and stir for a few seconds. Put in the cooked *dal*, the diced tomato, turmeric, the tamarind paste (put in 1 tablespoon of the paste first, adding more later if you think you want it), salt, and sugar. Add more water, if necessary, to get a thin, souplike consistency. Stir well, check for seasoning, and bring to a boil. Cover partially, lower heat, and simmer gently for about 10 minutes.

Add the green chili, ginger, and Chinese parsley. Simmer, uncovered, for another 2 minutes.

Rice and Other Grains

Rice originated in Asia. Emotionally and nutritionally, Asians have depended upon it ever since for their sustenance. For many Asians, a meal without rice is quite inconceivable, and an invitation to dinner often translates as an invitation to "eat rice."

There is something about this soothing, ingratiating grain that is quite addictive. While it has character, fragrance, and texture, it does not obtrude. It seduces without ever having to exert itself.

But it has to be cooked well first. That is the reason I have devoted quite a few pages to basic methods of cooking long-grain rice, Japanese rice, glutinous rice, brown rice, and Persian-style rice.

It is not hard to cook rice. First, see that you have a heavy pot with an even distribution of heat and a good, tight-fitting lid. Heavy aluminum pots, Cuisinart pots, Revere Ware pots all work very well. If you do not have a tight-fitting lid, put a sheet of aluminum foil, well crimped at the edges, between the top of the pot and the lid. The reason for this is that if you are going to cook in a minimum amount of water—as you should—very little steam should be allowed to escape. A tight lid will hold it in, and the rice will actually cook in steam.

What is the correct proportion of rice to water? Disregard the directions on top of rice packages. They suggest far more water than rice ever needs. Instead, follow the recipes in this chapter carefully, as the amount of water will vary depending upon the type of rice and whether it has been washed and soaked. For long-grain Carolina rice, you certainly do not need more than 1½ cups of liquid for every cup of rice. If the rice has been soaked, you can even use 1⅓ cups of liquid. Brown rice is an exception. For that you should use 2 cups of water for every cup of rice. The texture of brown rice improves considerably if you soak it first. Japanese rice requires the least amount of water—1¼ cups for every cup of rice.

Rice is such an amenable grain. It can be elevated to an almost hallowed position when it is served in laquer bowls—plain, unadorned, and in the shape of oval rolls—at the start of the very formal Japanese meals that precede a tea ceremony. It seems equally comfortable combined with millet by a Korean peasant, or brightened with saffron and orange rind for a Persian banquet, or stir-fried with eggs and scallions for a Chinese snack. You can season it with any herb or spice, cook it with any vegetable or bean, eat it as a gruel, make Japanese-style sandwiches—or *sushi*—with it, and even use it to make a variety of meal-in-a-pot dishes.

Rice with Fresh Herbs and Baby Lima Beans is one such meal-in-a-pot dish. Here long-grain rice is cooked in a Persian style with lots of butter, a heap of fresh Chinese parsley, parsley, dill, scallion tops, and the conveniently frozen baby lima beans. You could serve this dish all by itself—just as you would pasta—with perhaps a cooling glass of buttermilk to wash it down.

There is another kind of meal-in-itself rice dish which, although not prepared in a single pot, is served as if it had been and actually consists of separately cooked foods arranged prettily over rice.

My favorite among such dishes is the Korean Bibimbab. A fried egg sits triumphantly over a mound of rice. Radiating down from it are different stir-fried vegetables such as zucchini, bean sprouts, and spinach. A generous dollop of very hot bean sauce is put in a lettuce-leaf cup and also set on the rice. All that is needed then are a pair of chopsticks and an icy cold bottle of beer!

There are other grains besides rice in this chapter—bulgar wheat, which may be cooked in ways very similar to rice; millet and barley, which may be added to rice; and semolina, which is used in South India to make a kind of vegetarian pilaf called Uppama.

SOME GENERAL NOTES ON RICE

Plain, milled rice may be cooked with great ease in an electric rice-cooker. These cookers are now used all over Japan, even in some of the most traditional inns. When all my stove burners are in use, I, too, use the cooker for plain rice. On the whole, you can follow the directions suggested by the manufacturer. But do not put in the amount of water he suggests. Follow my general guidelines and consult specific recipes for different types of plain rice.

Should you wash rice? Asians always do, mainly to get rid of dust and to wash off extra starch left from the milling process. Washing and soaking prevent rice grains from splitting and from sticking to each other. American rices are generally enriched with vitamins after milling. These vitamins are mixed with a little starch and then added to the rice. When you wash rice, you get rid of this unnecessary starch—and also the vitamins. If you feel you need the vitamins, do not wash American packaged rices such as Carolina. But rices from all other countries *must* be picked over and washed in several changes of water.

HOW TO SERVE RICE

When long-grain rice has finished cooking, it tends to sit in the pot as one large lump. To serve it, place a warmed platter nearby. Now ease a slotted metal spoon gently into the rice. Put whatever your spoon collects onto the platter. Break up this "lump" by pressing gently with the back of the same slotted spoon.

GARNISHES FOR RICE

Rice may be served the way it comes out of the pot or it may be garnished. Asian garnishes are not just decorative. They contribute new flavors and textures as well as nutritional value to the rice. Here is a list of some of these garnishes: 1. roasted sesame seeds (see General Information); 2. toasted *nori* (see page 431), cut into shreds, plus roasted sesame seeds; 3. crushed, fried, or roasted peanuts; 4. washed and drained bean sprouts; sliced shallots, fried until brown and crisp; sprigs of mint and fresh Chinese parsley; 5. sliced scallions and egg strands (see page 206); 6. crisply fried onions (see page 360); 7. chopped parsley and pats of butter; 8. finely chopped dill and sliced scallions.

LEFTOVERS

We always make extra plain rice in our house. Whatever is left can be refrigerated and then fried the next day with scallions and egg. If you wish to heat leftover rice, break up all lumps gently and put the rice in a skillet. Sprinkle some water over the top, cover, and heat slowly over a low flame.

PLAIN BOILED RICE

This is the simplest method of cooking rice. If the rice being used is American packaged rice, it requires no picking over and no washing. And it requires no soaking. The use of butter and salt is optional. If you are cooking a Chinese meal, for example, both should be omitted. This rice may also be made in an electric rice-cooker; put in all the ingredients, cover, and switch on. Depending upon the type of cooker used, the rice should be ready about 10 to 15 minutes after its red light switches off.

(serves 4–6)

2 cups long-grain rice
1 tablespoon unsalted butter (optional)
1 teaspoon salt (optional)

Combine the rice, butter, salt, and 3 cups water in a heavy-bottomed, 1½- to 2½ quart pot that has a tight-fitting lid. Bring to a boil. Cover, turn the flame as low as it will go and cook for 25 minutes. (If you are using an electric range, set a second burner on "simmer." Once the rice comes to a boil, cover it and shift it to the second burner. Let the rice cook for 5 minutes and then switch this second burner to "warm." Cook another 20 minutes.) Let the rice rest, covered and undisturbed, for another 5 to 10 minutes.

To serve, ease a slotted spoon gently into the rice. Lift some of it out and put it on a warmed platter or bowl. Gently press down on this rice with the back of the slotted spoon to separate the grains. Remove as much rice from the pot as needed, breaking up all "lumps" the same way.

PLAIN BAKED RICE I

This is a fairly foolproof method of making light, fluffy rice. Rice is first thrown into plenty of boiling water and cooked rather like pasta. It is not cooked completely, though, but left *al dente*, with a slim, hard core still running down its center. Then the rice is drained and put in a slow oven to dry off and finish cooking.

(serves 4–6)

1 tablespoon salt (optional)
2 cups long-grain rice
3 to 4 tablespoons unsalted butter (optional)

Preheat oven to 325° F.
Put about 13 cups water and the salt into a 4-quart pot and bring to a boil. Meanwhile wash the rice in several changes of water and drain it.

When the water is at a rolling boil, put in the rice. Keep stirring until the water comes to a boil for a second time. Boil rapidly for about 7 minutes. The rice grains should be almost done but should retain a slim, hard core down their center. The way to check this is to remove a grain and press it between the first finger and the thumb. You should be able to both see and feel the hard core. Now drain the rice and quickly empty it into a 2- to 3-quart ovenproof pot that has a tight-fitting lid. Add the optional butter, cover, and place in the oven for 25 minutes.

Before serving, mix the butter, if you have used it, evenly into the rice with a slotted spoon.

For information about ingredients and basic techniques that may be unfamiliar, see General Information, pages 418–36.

PLAIN BAKED RICE II

This method of cooking rice, used with slight variations in China, North India, and the Middle East, does not leave the rice light and fluffy. Instead, each grain stays whole, firm, and unsplit. For many North Indian and Middle Eastern meals, the soaked, drained rice is sautéed in 3 to 4 tablespoons of oil or butter before the final liquid is added.

(serves 4–6)

2 cups long-grain rice
1 teaspoon salt (optional)

Wash the rice in several changes of water and drain it. Put it in a bowl, add 5 cups of water and let the rice soak for 30 minutes. Drain it thoroughly and let the rice sit in a strainer set over a bowl for 10 minutes.

   Preheat oven to 325° F.

   Put the drained rice, 2⅔ cups water, and the salt in a heavy, 1½- to 2½-quart pot that is both flameproof and ovenproof and has a tight-fitting lid. Bring to a boil. Turn heat to medium and cook, stirring gently, until all the liquid has evaporated. You may have to turn the heat down slightly during the end of this period. Cover the pot tightly and place in the oven for 25 minutes.

   This rice may be eaten with almost any kind of meal. Japanese rice, though, is perhaps better suited to Japanese and Korean foods.

PLAIN BASMATI RICE
INDIA

Basmati rice is more aromatic and much more delicate than Carolina rice and requires less water. The texture and aroma of *basmati* rice make it somewhat inappropriate for South Indian meals and for foods from Southeast and East Asia, but it may be eaten with almost all Western, Middle Eastern, and North Indian meals. You may omit the sautéing step, if you so prefer. Just combine the soaked, drained rice, salt, and 2½ cups of water in a pot and cook as in the recipe for Plain Boiled Rice (see page 117).

(serves 4–6)

2 cups *basmati* rice, picked over
2 tablespoons unsalted butter (optional)
¾ teaspoon salt (optional)

Wash the rice in several changes of water and drain it. Put it in a bowl, add 5 cups of water and let it soak for 30 minutes. Drain it thoroughly and let it sit in a strainer set over a bowl for 10 minutes.

   Melt the butter in a heavy, 2- to 3-quart pot that has a tight-fitting lid. Add the drained rice. Stir and cook over medium heat, making sure you are gentle and do not break up the grains of rice. Once all the grains are properly coated with butter—this will take about a minute or so—add 2½ cups of water and the salt. Bring to a boil. Cover, turn heat to very low and cook for 20 minutes. Turn off the flame. Let the pot sit, covered and in a warm place, for another 10 minutes.

For information about ingredients and basic techniques that may be unfamiliar, see General Information, pages 418–36.

KATEH
(Plain Boiled Rice with a Crust)
IRAN

It is the pride of Persian housewives, rich and poor, to provide rice that has crusted at the bottom and sides of the pot so that it can be inverted onto a plate like an upside-down cake. Pieces of the crisp crust are always offered to honored guests first. Making the crust is both easy and infuriatingly confounding at the same time. The method, in theory, is simplicity itself — just follow the basic directions for making Plain Boiled Rice (see page 117) and then turn up the heat slightly and let the rice cook for another half hour or so. But to get an evenly golden crust and to get it to come off the sides of the pot require some experimenting with different pots and different temperatures. Here are some hints that will help you to get a perfect *tahdig* or crust the very first time you try it:

Use a heavy pot that has an even distribution of heat. Tin-lined copper and heavy cast-aluminum pots both work very well.

Tight-fitting lids are a great help.

Do not use a very large pot for a small amount of rice. I cook 2 cups of rice in a 1½-quart pot.

For the last half hour or so of cooking, find a temperature that is just slightly higher than "low." I call that "medium-low." It is the temperature at which water would keep up a very active simmer. You will have to work this out on your own stove.

(serves 4–6)

2   cups long-grain rice
1   teaspoon salt
2   tablespoons melted unsalted butter (optional)

Put the rice, salt, and 3 cups water in a heavy, 1½- to 2-quart pot that has a tight-fitting lid and bring to a boil. Cover, turn heat to very low and cook for 25 minutes. Now turn the heat up to medium-low and continue to cook for 35 minutes.

While the rice is cooking, fill the sink or a large bowl with enough water so that it will come three-quarters of the way up the sides of the rice pot. When the rice has finished cooking, lift the pot off the stove and immediately put it in the water for 3 minutes. If the water warms up before the 3 minutes are over, change it. Remove the lid and dribble in the butter. Now turn the pot upside down over a warm plate. The "cake" of rice should just slip out. If it does not, try tapping the back of the pot or try to ease the rice out with a narrow spatula.

If you have a perfect "cake," it can be cut in wedges. If you just have a bottom crust that you have to pry out separately, lay it neatly over the rice. Serve each person some of the soft rice and at least one piece of the crust.

PLAIN BROWN LONG-GRAIN RICE

Brown rice is generally not eaten in Asia except by a few who follow the macrobiotic diet in Japan. However, it is more nutritious than milled and polished rices and should, therefore, be included in all our diets—at least some of the time.

That is all very well. But what if you like the taste of cooked brown rice but cannot abide its gloppy texture? I am afraid I had that problem for a while. Of course, I was either eating it in restaurants or following recipes worked out by people who were basically not rice-eaters. One day I brought a large bag of brown rice home and decided to keep cooking it until I came up with a texture that pleased me. Well, here is the result. I prefer the taste of long-grain brown rice, but you could use the short-grain variety as well. Once you have followed this basic method, you could easily substitute brown rice for the milled, polished rices in this chapter.

(serves 4)

1½ cups long-grain brown rice
¾ teaspoon salt (optional)
2 tablespoons unsalted butter (optional)

Wash the rice in several changes of water. Drain thoroughly. Put in a bowl, add 3 cups water and leave to soak for 1 hour.

Put the rice and its soaking liquid in a heavy, 2-quart pot that has a tight-fitting lid. Add the salt and bring to a boil. Cover, turn heat to very low and cook for 35 minutes. Turn the heat off and let the rice sit, covered and undisturbed, for 10 minutes. Put in the butter and mix gently with a fork.

For information about ingredients and basic techniques that may be unfamiliar, see General Information, pages 418–36.

BROWN RICE WITH SPINACH
NORTH INDIAN STYLE

(serves 6)

1½ cups long-grain brown rice
1½ pounds fresh spinach*
4 tablespoons vegetable oil
1 medium-sized onion, peeled and chopped
1 teaspoon ground cumin seeds
1 teaspoon ground coriander seeds
½ teaspoon ground mace
1 teaspoon salt

*NOTE: Frozen spinach may be used as an alternative; cook it according to instructions, squeeze out all the liquid and then chop it.

Put the rice in a bowl and wash in several changes of water. Drain. Soak the rice in 3 cups water for 1 hour.

While the rice is soaking, separate the spinach leaves and wash them. Do not discard the roots. They taste very good when they are cooked.

Bring 3 quarts of water to a rolling boil in a 4-quart pot. Drop in the spinach. Bring to a boil again and let the spinach cook on high heat for 2 minutes. Drain. Rinse spinach under running water to cool off. Squeeze out all the moisture from the spinach and then chop it, roots and all.

Heat the oil in a heavy, 2¾-quart pot over a medium flame. When hot, put in the onion. Stir and fry until onion pieces turn slightly brown at the edges. Put in the spinach. Stir and fry the spinach for 20 minutes, turning the heat down a bit as the moisture in the spinach reduces. Add the rice and its soaking liquid, the cumin, coriander, mace, and salt. Bring to a boil. Cover with a tight-fitting lid, turn heat to very, very low and cook for 35 minutes. Turn off heat. Remove the lid and immediately cover the pot of rice with a dish towel. Place the lid over the towel. Let the pot sit this way for 15 to 20 minutes in a warm place so that the extra moisture may be absorbed.

GLUTINOUS RICE

Also known as "sweet" rice and "sticky" rice, this short-grain, opaque variety of rice is very popular in East and Southeast Asia. It is put into soups, used in stuffings, topped with coconut cream to accompany fresh fruit, and made into all manner of snacks and desserts. In some parts of Asia, like northern Thailand, it is preferred to other types of rice and is eaten, plain and ungarnished, just as long-grain rice might be. Once glutinous rice is cooked, it turns shiny and translucent. It is somewhat sticky but that is the very quality which endears it to its enthusiasts.

As with other types of rice, there are several methods of cooking glutinous rice. These methods include cooking it in a double boiler and steaming it. I love glutinous rice. If you have never eaten it, make a point of buying some and cooking it.

PLAIN GLUTINOUS RICE COOKED IN A DOUBLE BOILER

This is an excellent rice to take on picnics, as it does not harden the way all other rices do. It is also considered to be the ideal rice to eat with sweet, luscious tropical fruit such as mangoes (see page 387 for recipe).

(serves 4)

1½ cups glutinous rice

Put the rice in a bowl and wash it well in several changes of water. Drain. Cover the rice with 6 cups of water and leave to soak for 6 to 8 hours. (Alternatively, you may soak the rice in hot water for 1 to 2 hours.) Drain the rice and wash it again in fresh water. Drain again.

Get your double boiler ready by putting a sufficient quantity of water in the lower portion and bringing it to a boil. Put the rice in the top portion of the double boiler. Add enough water to it so it comes to half an inch above the top of the rice. Set the top of the double boiler over the lower portion. When the water with the rice begins to simmer, cover the pot and cook the rice on medium heat for 25 minutes.

AZUKI MESHI
(Glutinous Rice Cooked with Azuki Beans)
JAPAN

If you are one of those people who, like me, has a partiality for glutinous rice, you will love this simple dish. If you do not like glutinous rice, substitute plain Japanese rice or a long-grain rice. You could also make this dish with brown rice. Soak it for just 1 hour in water (hot water is not needed) and use 1½ cups of the bean liquid instead of the 1 cup plus 2 tablespoons. Cook for 35 minutes.

Azuki meshi consists of rice and beans, perked up with a little salt, some *sake*, and roasted sesame seeds. I can make a meal of just this, some Japanese pickles, and green tea. You could, and I have done this, serve *azuki meshi* with a Greek salad containing lettuce, tomatoes, olives, and broken-up pieces of feta cheese in an olive oil and lemon dressing.

(serves 4–6)

¾ cup glutinous rice
¾ cup *azuki* beans
¾ teaspoon salt
1 tablespoon *sake*
2 tablespoons roasted sesame seeds

Wash the glutinous rice in several changes of water. Drain. Now soak the rice in 2 cups of hot water for 2 hours. Drain.

Pick over the beans. Put them in a heavy pot and add 4 cups of water. Bring to a boil. Lower heat and simmer, uncovered, for 2 minutes. Turn off the heat and let the pot sit, uncovered, for 1 hour. Bring the beans to a boil again. Cover, lower heat and simmer gently for 30 minutes. Add ½

teaspoon salt and simmer, covered, for another 30 minutes. Drain the beans but *save the liquid.*

Put the drained rice in a heavy, 2½-quart pot. Add the salt, 1 cup plus 2 tablespoons of the bean liquid, as well as the drained beans. Bring to a boil. Cover with a tight-fitting lid and cook on very, very low heat for 20 minutes. Dribble the *sake* over the rice and beans, cover, and continue cooking for another 5 minutes.

Sprinkle sesame seeds over the top before serving.

PLAIN JAPANESE RICE

If you are preparing a Japanese meal, you could, of course, eat plain American rice with it. But you would be losing the real texture of Japanese food. The plump, short-grain, slightly sticky rice that the Japanese eat is an essential component of their cuisine. Rice—Japanese rice—is so interwoven with the tastes and aesthetics of all Japanese food that it might be jarring to replace it, especially in an all-Japanese meal, with fluffy, long-grain rice or, for that matter, with heavy brown rice.

But since the purpose of this book is not to be dogmatic, rather to open up a reservoir of good vegetarian food, perhaps it is best if you decide for

---

For information about ingredients and basic techniques that may be unfamiliar, see General Information, pages 418–36.

yourself which rice you wish to have. If you get yourself familiar with cooking and eating Japanese rice, you will, at least, be making a considered choice.

Japanese rice is sold in Japanese grocery stores. If you do not have such a store in your area, check the mail-order sources at the end of this book. There are several brands available. The one I seem to have at the moment is Tanakaya Kokuho Rose. The rice comes in large sacks and then is usually put into 5-pound bags by the grocery stores.

Traditionally, Japanese rice was always cooked in iron cauldrons that had curved bottoms and heavy, wooden lids. Grains that got caught at the bottom and were slightly burned were either formed into balls and eaten with pickles and soy sauce, or else they were put into a bowl, boiling water was poured over them, and diners were served this burned rice "tea" at the conclusion of their repast. Today, most homes use electric rice-cookers that perform beautifully. Even very old and traditional establishments like the three-hundred-year-old Tawaraya Inn in Kyoto has shifted to a cauldron-sized electric rice-cooker. But once the rice is cooked, tradition reasserts itself here. The shiny, slightly sticky grains are removed with a dampened wooden paddle (dampened so the rice will not stick to it) and stored in a large, lidded, wooden tub. The wood, being a poor conductor of heat, does not allow the warmth to escape; so the rice stays hot for several hours. Whenever any rice is needed, it is put into smaller wooden containers and then carried up to the private rooms of the inn's guests.

The Japanese rice-cooker almost duplicates the Japanese method of cooking rice. (It must be remembered that rice-cookers will cook any plain rice very well.)

(makes about 6 cups and serves about 6)

2 cups Japanese rice

Put the rice in a bowl and wash it in several changes of water, rubbing the rice gently as you do so. Keep washing until the water is no longer milky. Drain the rice in a sieve. Put the sieve over an empty bowl and let the rice drain for 1 hour.

Put the rice in a heavy, 2½-quart pot that has a well-fitting lid. Add 2½ cups water, cover, and bring the water to a boil over a medium flame. When steam begins to escape from under the lid, turn the heat to *very* low and cook for 20 minutes. Turn the heat to high for 3 seconds and then turn it off. Let the pot sit, covered and undisturbed, for another 15 minutes. Do not lift the lid at any stage.

Use a dampened wooden paddle, if you have one, to serve as much of the rice as needed in individual bowls or in a covered wooden or lacquer container.

Leftover rice should be allowed to cool. Then separate the grains with a chopstick, put in a closed container, and store in the refrigerator. The rice can then be reheated with a little water—about 1 tablespoon per cup.

SUSHI RICE

JAPAN

Sushi rice is freshly cooked Japanese rice, seasoned or "pickled" with a mixture of vinegar, sugar, and salt and then cooled off quickly to room temperature with a fan. This rice is used to make different types of *sushi*: There is *nigirir-zushi*, small rice ovals that for vegetarians may be topped with wheels of *datemake* (rolled omelette); there is *norimake-zushi*, in which the seasoned rice, together with ingredients like strips of cucumber or pickles are rolled inside paper-thin, crisp black laver (*nori*) to make what may be called closed sandwiches; there is *chirashi-zushi* in which the rice is piled into a bowl and topped with all manner of edibles that could include shredded eggs, blanched peas, pickles, fried bean curd, blanched and seasoned spinach, and seasoned mushrooms; and there is *inari-zushi* or *sushi* rice stuffed into fried bean-curd bags. You will find recipes for *norimake-zushi* and *chirashi-zushi* directly following; *nigiri-zushi* may be found in the chapter on eggs-(see page 202), and *inari-zushi* in the bean-curd chapter (see page 179). Nearly all *sushi* dishes are served with pickled and sliced ginger, *amazu shoga*, available in Japanese grocery stores.

(makes about 6 cups)

4   tablespoons rice wine vinegar
4   tablespoons sugar
½   teaspoon salt
6   cups freshly cooked Plain Japanese Rice (see page 122)

Mix the rice, wine vinegar, sugar, and salt together thoroughly in a cup.

As soon as the rice has completed its cooking, including its resting period, empty it out onto a large platter or baking tray.
1. Pour the seasonings in the cup over it.
2. Now fan the rice with one hand (you could use

For information about ingredients and basic techniques that may be unfamiliar, see General Information, pages 418–36.

a magazine for this) while you mix it with a dampened wooden paddle or spoon. Continue to do this until the rice has reached room temperature. Put the rice in a covered pot or bowl to prevent it from drying out. Do not refrigerate. The rice will hold for a few hours, though the fresher the rice the better.

NORIMAKE-ZUSHI
(Sushi Rice Rolled in Dark Laver)
JAPAN

The dark laver (*asakusa nori*) used to make this comes in thin, crisp sheets that are usually about 7 inches by 8 inches in size. Sometimes they are packaged in cellophane, at other times in elegant tins. *Nori* sheets need to be toasted before being used. The sheets may be used whole to make thickish rolls or they may be cut in half to make more slender rolls. The rolling is best donè with the help of a special mat called a *sudare*, though a dishcloth may be used as a substitute. Embedded in the rice down the center of the roll could be anything from cucumber lengths to seasoned spinach and simmered mushrooms. The roll is then sliced crosswise into wheels and served with pickled ginger (*amazu shoga*) and soy sauce for dipping.

(serves 4–6)

4   medium-sized dried *shiitake* mushrooms
3   tablespoons Japanese soy sauce
2   tablespoons plus ½ teaspoon sugar
1   tablespoon *mirin*
1   large egg
Salt
½ teaspoon vegetable oil
1   cucumber, preferably pickling Kirbies
3   sheets of *asakusa nori*
About 3 cups Sushi Rice (see page 124)
2   teaspoons roasted sesame seeds
About ¼ teaspoon *wasabi* (see page 360)
½ teaspoon paste from pitted and mashed *umeboshi* plums
6   tablespoons finely sliced *amazu shoga*

Soak the mushrooms in 1½ cups hot water for ½ hour. Lift them out of the water and cut off the hard stems. (Save the water for soups.) Cut the caps crosswise into ¼-inch-thick strips. Put the strips as well as the soy sauce, 2 tablespoons sugar, and *mirin* into a small pot. Bring to a simmer. Turn heat down and simmer for about 5 minutes. You should have a little syrupy liquid left. Set aside.

Put the egg, ½ teaspoon sugar, and a pinch of salt in a bowl. Beat well but not to a froth. Brush a 7-inch nonstick skillet with the oil and heat over a medium flame. Pour in the egg mixture. Tilt the skillet around in order to spread it to the edges. Cook until set. Ease a spatula under the pancake and turn it over. Cook until the second side is set. Remove to a plate and let it cool. Roll up as soon as it has reached room temperature and cut crosswise at ½-inch intervals. Cover loosely and set aside.

If you have a regular cucumber, peel it, cut it in half lengthwise, and seed it. If you are using a pickling cucumber, you do not have to peel it. Just trim the ends. Now cut whichever cucumber you are using into 3½-inch-long by ¼-inch-wide by ¼-inch-thick strips.

1. Toast the *nori*: Hold a sheet between your fingers or with a pair of tongs and wave it systematically, going from one end to the other, directly over a medium-low flame. As each area gets done, it will turn somewhat lighter in color. The *nori* should be about an inch away from the flame. Cut each roasted sheet in half so you have two pieces, each about 7 inches by 4 inches.

2. Lay the *sudare* mat in front of you. (Use a clean dish towel as a substitute.) Place a piece of *nori* on it so its long side is parallel to but about half an inch away from the end of the mat nearest you. Dip your hand in water and remove some rice—about half a cup—and spread it on the *nori*, leaving ½-inch borders on the near end and the far end. The rice layer should be about ½ inch thick.

3. Now make a long, horizontal indentation, rather like a shallow trench, running along the center of the rice. Remove half the mushroom slices from their syrupy liquid and lay them in the trench.

4. Now begin rolling the *sudare* mat tightly away from you, keeping the mushrooms in place with your index fingers, if necessary. Your first roll should take you just past the mushrooms. When the edge of the *sudare* touches the rice, press down slightly to firm up the roll.

5. Keep rolling, this time making sure that the mat stays on top of the roll and does not get rolled *into* it. When the roll is finished, put it on a cutting board and, 6. using a very sharp, slightly dampened knife, cut it crosswise into six equal parts. Do a second roll with the remaining mushrooms.

Make two more rolls with the eggs in exactly the same way. Just sprinkle 1 teaspoon of the sesame seeds over the eggs before rolling.

For the cucumber rolls, spread half of the *wasabi* and half of the *umeboshi* plum paste in each trench before laying the cucumber pieces down. Put about 6 strips of cucumber in each roll and dot each lot with ½ teaspoon sesame seeds. Roll and cut them in the same way as the others.

Serve the *sushi* pieces cut side up with small servings of soy sauce and *amazu shoga*.

For information about ingredients and basic techniques that may be unfamiliar, see General Information, pages 418–36.

CHIRASHI-ZUSHI
(Sushi Rice with Vegetable Topping)

JAPAN

This dish is really a meal in itself.

(serves 5–6)

2 cups freshly made Sushi Rice (see page 124)
2 tablespoons finely sliced *amazu shoga*
Peas with Ginger (see page 47, but do not add the
    ginger)
Egg Strands (see page 206)
Cabbage with Miso (see page 15)
Lotus Root with Soy Sauce Dressing (see page 37)
Sweet and Salty Dried Shiitake Mushrooms (see
    page 41)
Carrots cooked in Dashi (see page 291)
1 tablespoon roasted sesame seeds

Using a dampened wooden paddle or spoon, empty
the Sushi Rice into a large bowl. Add the *amazu
shoga* and the peas and mix gently. Put this rice on
a large serving platter or in individual bowls. Scatter the egg strands over the rice. Drain all the
vegetables of extra liquid and arrange them prettily over the top. You could either make neat piles
of the vegetables or else scatter the cabbage over
the eggs, arrange the mushroom caps in the center,
and ring them with the lotus-root slices and carrots. Sprinkle the sesame seeds over the top.

*For information about ingredients and basic techniques that
may be unfamiliar, see General Information, pages 418–36.*

PERSIAN-STYLE STEAMED RICE

IRAN

Kateh (see page 119) is the rice Persians might eat
with their everyday meals. For special occasions,
they steam their rice in such a way that each grain
comes out looking elegant and refined. First they
soak their rice in salty water overnight. They then
parboil it in more salty water to which a little
vinegar has been added. These steps, they say,
preserve the strength, whiteness, and separateness
of each grain. The rice is then left to steam slowly
in butter, with a cloth covering the underside of
the lid so that it may catch the steam as it con-
denses and not allow it to fall back on the rice.
This last step is done on top of the stove in Iran.
The heat is adjusted to allow the very prized crust
to form at the bottom. If you do not want the
crust, the steaming can be done in the oven. Here
is a recipe for the oven method—Persian-style
steamed rice without the crust.

(serves 6)

2 cups long-grain rice (use Persian Domsiah rice
    if possible, otherwise Indian or Pakistani *basmati*
    rice can be used)
5 tablespoons salt
1 tablespoon any white vinegar
6 tablespoons melted unsalted butter

Pick over the rice and wash it in several changes of
water. Drain. Put rice in a bowl. Add 5 cups of
water and 2½ tablespoons of salt. Stir and leave to
soak overnight or for at least 8 hours. Drain rice in
a sieve. Place sieve under running water and wash
rice again. Drain thoroughly.

Preheat oven to 325° F.

Bring 3¾ quarts of water to a boil in a large pot. Add 2½ tablespoons salt as well as the vinegar. Pour the drained rice into the boiling water in a steady stream. Stir the rice and let it boil rapidly for exactly 6 minutes after the water comes to a boil again. Turn off heat and drain the rice by emptying it into a sieve. Wash the rice again, this time under running lukewarm water. Drain.

Pour 4 tablespoons of the melted butter plus a tablespoon of water into a 9-inch-wide, heavy, casserole-type pot and place the pot on a low flame. Put the rice on top of the melted butter. Pour the remaining 2 tablespoons of melted butter over the rice. Now cover the pot with a doubled piece of paper towel, just slightly larger than the circumference of the pot. Put a piece of aluminum foil, larger than the paper towel, over the paper towel. Attach the paper towel to the foil with 4 straight pins. Crimp the edges of the foil to seal the pot. Now cover the pot with its own lid and place in the oven for 30 minutes.

Mix the rice gently and offer it with almost any American, European, Middle Eastern, or North Indian meal.

STEAMED RICE WITH LENTILS

IRAN

(serves 6)

To make this dish, follow the directions in the preceding recipe. After the rice has finished soaking overnight and the oven has been lit, drop ½ cup lentils into rapidly boiling, salted water (about 1½ teaspoons salt in 2 quarts of water) and boil for 7 to 8 minutes or until lentils are somewhat soft but not fully cooked. Drain. Proceed to parboil the rice. Drain the rice and wash it. Mix it with the drained lentils and then proceed with the recipe.

This dish would be good with Okra with Tomatoes (see page 46) and Yogurt with Fresh Mint, Raisins, and Walnuts (see page 218).

RICE PORRIDGE OR CONGEE

Rice porridges, eaten from Japan to Persia as break-fasts, snacks, and lunches, are considered warming and soothing, as well as a stabilizing influence on the stomach and digestive tract. The English word "congee" is derived from the Indian "*kanji*" (mean-ing "boilings'), a Tamil word for the water in which rice is boiled. ("They gave him to drink the water squeezed out of rice with pepper and cumin," a marveling Portuguese wrote in India in 1563.) In India today, *kanji* refers both to this "rice water" that is drained off when rice is cooked like pasta (see Plain Baked Rice I, page 117) and to the thick gruel made by boiling a little rice with a lot of water.

This thick gruel, or rice porridge, is made in pretty much the same way all over Asia with minor local variations. In China, the congee may be made out of ordinary raw rice (short-grain rice is con-sidered good enough for gruel), or with burned rice (the rice that "catches" and sticks to the bottom of the pot), or with a combination of short-grain and glutinous rice. Vegetables like *bok choy* or *choy sum* may be cut up and thrown in to add extra flavor. The unsalted congee is then served with a choice of flavorings. When I had this porridge in Hong Kong, it was called *chuk*—the "u" pronounced as in "put"—and the seasonings in the center of the table included finely sliced scallions, finely shredded ginger, fresh Chinese parsley, sesame oil, hot sauces (commercial red and green chili sauces), thin soy sauce, vinegar, boiled salted eggs, thousand-year eggs, pickled turnips, and fermented bean curd. Each person put in a favored combination.

In the Philippines, the same rice porridge took on quite a different form. It was flavored with hot chocolate—something that the early Spaniards had brought over from the New World—and called *chumpurado*.

In India, the flavorings added to porridge range from salt, *ghee*, black pepper, and cumin to more elaborate hot and salty pickles. In Gujarat, *ghains* is made by combining rice porridge with beaten yogurt and a little fresh ginger. It is served hot and is considered a good standby for days when one is feeling a little under the weather. Another gruel from India includes both rice and split peas. It is called *khichri* (the English turned this word into "kedgeree") and has been known since ancient times as a nourishing meal-in-a-bowl. It is always served seasoned with *ghee*, salt, and pepper, although other spices and vegetables may be added to the basic dish. My mother always added greens and sliced onions and then called the porridge *saag vali khichri*. It might be noted here that there are actu-ally two types of *khichri* in India—the porridge or wet *khichri* and a dry, puffy, grainy form some-times known as *khili hui khichri* or the "*khichri* that has bloomed."

If you want to eat congee in the Indian style, salt it first. Then add lots of freshly ground pepper and *ghee* or butter. If you like, this *ghee* can be heated, some whole cumin seeds can be popped in it, and the *ghee*-cumin poured over the congee and mixed in. You can also serve Indian-style vegetables, sauced and unsauced, on the side.

Feel free to make your own congee combina-

For information about ingredients and basic techniques that may be unfamiliar, see General Information, pages 418–36.

tions. If you want it sweet, try adding unsalted butter, cream, and brown sugar.

NOTE: Rice gruels should be made in heavy pots with an even distribution of heat.

PLAIN UNSEASONED CONGEE

makes 4 cups)

½ cup long-grain or short-grain rice, or a mixture of ¼ cup short-grain and ¼ cup glutinous rice if you are going to use Chinese seasonings

If the rice is American and "enriched," do not wash it. Otherwise, wash and drain the rice. Put the rice and 5¾ cups of water into a heavy, 3½- to 4-quart pot and slowly bring to a boil. Stir now and then as the water comes to a boil. Turn heat to medium and let the rice cook for 10 minutes. Stir once or twice during this period. Now cover, leaving the lid very slightly ajar, and cook on very low heat for 1¼ hours.

Congee may be made ahead of time and reheated. It tends to get thick and gummy as it sits. Thin it out with a little boiling water and then reheat, stirring frequently, over a low flame. For serving suggestions, see preceding note as well as the recipes that follow.

CONGEE WITH CHINESE CABBAGE AND SCALLIONS

CHINA

This congee is deliberately undersalted so you can season it as you wish later. As seasonings, you might offer finely grated ginger, finely sliced scallions, Chinese parsley, thin Chinese soy sauce, white vinegar, sesame oil (use just a little), fermented bean curd, pickles (both salty and sour varieties bought from Chinese grocery stores), commercial hot chili sauces, boiled and salted ducks' eggs, salt, and white pepper. People can sprinkle whatever and however much they wish. I often reheat leftover stir-fried Chinese vegetables from the day before and stir them into the congee.

(serves 6–8)

½ cup long-grain or short-grain rice, or half-and-half combination of short-grain and glutinous rice
¾ pound Chinese cabbage or *bok choy*, washed and cut into ¼-inch-wide strips, including leaves
3 scallions, finely sliced, including green
1 teaspoon salt

If the rice is American and "enriched," do not wash it. Otherwise, wash and drain it. Combine rice with 5¾ cups water and slowly bring to a boil in a 3½-quart pot. Stir occasionally as rice comes to a boil, making sure that no grains are sticking to the bottom. Turn heat to medium and cook for 10 minutes, stirring once or twice during this period. Add the cabbage, scallions, and salt. Stir and bring to a simmer. Cover, lower heat, and cook very gently for 1¼ hours.

Devi's
GHAINS
(Congee with Yogurt)
INDIA

(makes about 2 cups)

1   cup plain yogurt
2   teaspoons vegetable oil or *ghee*
⅓   teaspoon whole cumin seeds
¼   teaspoon salt, or to taste
1/16 teaspoon freshly ground black pepper, or to taste
¼   teaspoon finely grated fresh ginger
⅛ to ¼ teaspoon very finely minced fresh hot green
      chilies
1   cup Plain Unseasoned Congee (see page 131)

Put the yogurt in a small bowl. Beat gently with a fork or a whisk until the yogurt is creamy and smooth.

Heat the oil in a small 1½-quart pot over a medium flame. When the oil is hot, put in the cumin seeds and remove the pot from the flame. Pour oil and cumin seeds over the yogurt and stir it in immediately. Now put the yogurt into the same pot in which you heated the oil. Add the salt, pepper, ginger, green chilies, and prepared congee. Heat slowly over a medium flame, stirring constantly in one direction. *Do not bring to a boil.* As soon as the *ghains* is heated through, turn off the heat.

Put the *ghains* in small bowls and serve hot for breakfast or as a light lunch. You may also serve this dish cold, with some finely diced cucumber thrown into it at the last minute. You will probably have to adjust your salt if you add the cucumber. Eat the *ghains* with a spoon.

GEELI KHICHRI
("Wet" Khichri)
INDIA

See note on Rice Porridge or Congee, page 131. You could also make this *khichri* with other *dals*, or with the yellow split peas that are available in American supermarkets. Because *khichri* is wet, serve it in small individual bowls and spoon accompanying vegetables, pickles, and chutney over as you eat it.

(makes about 1 quart and serves 6–8)

⅓   cup mung *dal*, picked over, washed, and drained
½   cup long-grain or short-grain rice, washed and
      drained
2   quarter-sized slices of fresh ginger
1¼ teaspoons salt, or to taste
1/16 to ⅛ teaspoon freshly ground black pepper
3   tablespoons *ghee* or vegetable oil
½   teaspoon whole cumin seeds

Put the *dal*, rice, ginger slices, and 7 cups water in a heavy 2½- to 3-quart pot over medium heat and bring to a boil. Stir once, cover, turn heat to low and cook for about 1½ hours or until you have a porridgelike consistency. Stir every 6 to 7 minutes during the last 40 minutes of the cooking to make sure that the *khichri* is not sticking to the bottom of the pot. Remove and discard the ginger slices. Add the salt and pepper. Stir to mix.

Khichri may be made up to this stage several hours ahead of time. Whenever you are getting ready to serve, reheat it over a low flame, stirring all the time, or reheat it in a double boiler. Sometimes adding a little water and thinning it out slightly helps in the reheating process. Put the *ghee*

For information about ingredients and basic techniques that may be unfamiliar, see General Information, pages 418–36.

in a small skillet or in a small pot and heat it over a medium flame. When hot, put in the cumin seeds and let them sizzle for a few seconds. Now pour the hot *ghee* and cumin seeds over the *khichri* and cover the *khichri* pot immediately. One minute later, uncover, and mix.

SAAG VALI KHICHRI
(Porridge of Rice, Mung Beans, and Spinach)
INDIA

I have never had this dish in any house but ours. Perhaps it was my mother's invention. On the other hand, it could be thousands of years old, as most *khichris* date back to antiquity. In India, one is never too sure about these things.

(serves 6–8)

½ cup whole mung beans, picked over, washed, and drained
½ cup long-grain rice, white or brown, washed and drained
1 quarter-sized slice of fresh ginger
1 pound fresh spinach, well washed, with the leaves separated
1½ teaspoons salt, or to taste
4 tablespoons vegetable oil or *ghee*
¹⁄₁₆ teaspoon ground asafetida
1 teaspoon whole cumin seeds
1 small onion, peeled, cut in half lengthwise, then sliced into fine half rounds
1 teaspoon ground cumin seeds
2 teaspoons ground coriander seeds
¹⁄₁₆ teaspoon cayenne pepper
Freshly ground black pepper to taste
(Extra optional seasonings: lemon juice, to taste; a pat of butter per serving; 1 teaspoon minced Chinese parsley per serving)

Put the mung beans in a heavy 3½-quart pot. Add 5½ cups water and bring to a boil over a medium-high flame. Cover, lower heat, and simmer 2 minutes. Turn off the heat and let the pot sit, covered, for 1 hour. Bring the water to a boil again. Add the rice and the ginger and bring to a simmer. Cover, turn heat to low, and cook gently for 1 hour. Stir occasionally during this period. Now add the spinach and salt. Bring to a simmer. Cover and cook gently for ½ hour, stirring now and then to avoid sticking. Add a little hot water if the porridge seems too thick.

Heat the oil in a 6- to 7-inch skillet over a medium flame. When hot, put in the asafetida. Two seconds later, put in the whole cumin seeds. Five seconds later, put in the onion. Stir and fry until the onion begins to turn brown at the edges. Add the ground cumin, coriander, and cayenne. Stir and fry for 1 minute. Empty the contents of the skillet into the rice and bean pot. Stir. Cover and cook for 5 more minutes. Discard the piece of ginger. Sprinkle with freshly ground black pepper. Serve in individual bowls with some or all of the optional seasonings.

GUINATAAN WITH RICE AND MUNG BEANS
(Rice Porridge with Mung Beans)
PHILIPPINES

Here is a Filipino version of the Asian rice porridge, this time flavored with mung beans—not the ordinary whole or split beans, but beans that have been roasted slightly and crushed. The roasting gives the porridge a nutty, smoky taste; the crushing allows the beans to cook much faster than they would ordinarily. Instead of the porridge being cooked in water, it is cooked in coconut milk. In the Philippines it is always sweetened and served with a dollop of coconut cream on the top. It is eaten hot or cold, generally at snack-time. You could, if you like, eat it unsweetened, seasoning it as you might a Chinese congee or an Indian *khichri* (see pages 131–3).

(serves 6)

2 cups freshly grated coconut
2 tablespoons whole mung beans
½ cup glutinous rice
¼ teaspoon salt, or to taste
3½ tablespoons brown or palm sugar, or to taste, or honey

Put the grated coconut into the container of a blender or food processor and start the machine. Slowly add 4 cups of hot water. (If your machine will not hold so much, you could do this in two batches.) Run the machine for 1 minute. Turn it off. Balance a sieve in a bowl and line it with a triple layer of cheesecloth or a man's handkerchief. Pour the contents of the blender or food processor into the lined sieve. Draw up the four corners of the straining cloth and squeeze out as much coco-

nut milk as you can. Pour the milk into a clear glass measuring cup or jug and let it sit for 1 hour. The coconut cream will rise to the top. You will be able to see it through the clear glass. Spoon off half a cup of this cream and set it aside. You should have 4 cups of coconut milk left. If you do not, add enough water to make 4 cups.

Pick over the mung beans and put them in a small cast-iron skillet over a medium flame. Keep shaking the skillet and dry-roast the beans until they turn a brown color and give off a nutty, roasted smell. Take the beans off the fire and put them between two sheets of waxed paper. Now crush them lightly with a pestle or a rolling pin. Each bean should break up into 2 to 4 pieces. The skins will come off the beans and may be just blown away.

Wash the rice in several changes of water and drain. Combine the crushed mung beans, rice, and 4 cups coconut milk in a heavy 1½-quart pot. Place over a medium flame and bring to a boil. Cover, turn heat to low, and simmer gently for 1¼ hours. Stir now and then during this period, making sure that the rice does not stick to the bottom of the pot.

Add the salt and, if you like, as much of the sugar as suits your taste. Mix well.

This dish may be eaten hot or cold, with some coconut cream spooned over the top.

For information about ingredients and basic techniques that may be unfamiliar, see General Information, pages 418–36.

KONGNAMUL BAB
(Rice with Soy-Bean Sprouts)

KOREA

I like this dish very much—the rice gets soft and shiny while the soy sprouts retain a nice crunch. Serve it with Simple Korean Sauce, page 359.

(serves 4–6)

2 cups Japanese rice
4 cups soy-bean sprouts, with the threadlike ends of their tails picked off

Put the rice in a bowl and wash in several changes of water. Drain. Add 6 cups water and leave to soak for ½ hour. Drain.

Bring 8 cups of water to a boil in a 3½-quart pot. Add the soy-bean sprouts and boil rapidly for 2 minutes. Drain thoroughly.

Put the rice at the bottom of a heavy 2½-quart pot. Lay the drained soy-bean sprouts over the rice. Add 2½ cups water and cover with a tight-fitting lid. Bring to a boil over a medium-high flame. When the steam begins to escape from under the lid, turn the heat down to very, very low and cook for 20 minutes. Turn the flame up to medium for 10 seconds. Now turn it off. Let the pot sit, covered and undisturbed, for 15 minutes.

HONSIK BAB
(Rice with Barley)

KOREA

The Koreans cook their rice with all kinds of grains and beans in order to make it more nutritious. Here it is combined with pressed barley, a skinned, quick-cooking variety, that takes just as long to get tender as the rice does.

(serves 4–6)

2 cups Japanese rice
½ cup pressed barley

Combine the rice and barley in a bowl. Wash in several changes of water. Drain. Add 6 cups of water and let the mixture soak for ½ hour. Drain well.

Put the drained grains and 2½ cups water in a heavy 1¾-quart pot. Cover with a tight-fitting lid and bring to a boil over a medium-high flame. When steam begins to escape from under the lid, turn heat down to very, very low and cook, undisturbed, for 20 minutes. Turn the heat up to medium for 10 seconds and then turn it off. Let the pot sit, covered, for 10 minutes.

RICE WITH BEAN SPROUTS, SPINACH, AND LAVER
KOREA

I had this dish for the first time at the Jang Won restaurant in Seoul. As I sat across from my host at a low lacquered table, almost twenty dishes drifted in. This was not a vegetarian restaurant but there was enough here to please the palate of the most finicky vegetarian: raw peeled fall chestnuts (how sweet and wonderful they are in this crunchy form); tender bean curd in a hot-water bath, to be eaten with a spicy dipping sauce; fried carrot slices, all encased in an egg and flour batter; cabbage, radish, and garlic pickles; sweetened walnuts and pine nuts; crisp, lacy seaweed; mountain mushrooms, wrapped in foil and grilled; a "salad" of fresh ginseng, green peppers, cucumbers, and tomatoes; and this delicious rice dish—all followed by fresh fruit and quince tea.

NOTE: This rice dish is not salted and is generally eaten with a spicy sauce, such as Spicy Korean Sauce, page 359.

(serves 4–6)

2   cups Japanese rice
½ pound soy-bean or mung-bean sprouts (about 2 cups)
½ pound spinach, well washed
1½ sheets *nori**
    (approximately 7 × 8 inches)
1   carrot
3   tablespoons Japanese soy sauce
2   teaspoons sesame oil

*NOTE: Dried laver will be found as *nori* in Japanese stores, *kim* in Korean ones.

2   scallions, cut into fine rounds including green
1   clove garlic, minced
2   teaspoons roasted sesame seeds
½ teaspoon sugar

Wash the rice in several changes of water. Drain it. Put the rice in a bowl, add 6 cups water and let the rice soak for ½ hour. Empty the rice into a sieve and let it drain for 15 minutes.

While the rice is soaking, prepare all the other ingredients. Break off the wispy, threadlike ends of the sprouts (if you feel up to it). Wash them well and drain them. Cut the spinach crosswise into ¼-inch-wide strips. Cut up the roots, too; they taste very good.

Heat a large pot of water. When it comes to a rolling boil, drop in the sprouts and the spinach. Bring to a second boil and boil rapidly for 1 minute. Drain, squeezing out as much liquid as you can.

With a pair of scissors, cut the *nori* into thin strips, about 3 inches long and ¼-inch wide.

Peel the carrot, cut it first into three sections and then into julienne strips.

Combine the bean sprouts, spinach, *nori*, and carrot in a bowl. Add the soy sauce, sesame oil, scallions, garlic, sesame seeds, and sugar. Mix and set aside for 15 minutes.

Put the drained rice and seasoned vegetables in a heavy 3-quart pot. Mix gently. Add 2½ cups water, cover with a tight-fitting lid and bring to a boil over a medium flame. When steam escapes from under the lid, turn the heat to very, very low.

For information about ingredients and basic techniques that may be unfamiliar, see General Information, pages 418–36.

Cook for 20 minutes. Turn the heat off and let the pot sit for 10 minutes in a warm place. Do not uncover the pot during this period.

RICE WITH MILLET
KOREA

Korean stores sell hulled versions of both plain and glutinous millet, which are often cooked in conjunction with rice. This gives the rice added nutritional value as well as an extra texture. Serve with Simple Korean Sauce (see page 359) and other vegetables.

(serves 4–6)

2 cups Japanese rice
½ cup hulled plain or glutinous millet

Put the rice and millet in a bowl. Wash in several changes of water. Drain. Add 6 cups of water and leave to soak for ½ hour. Drain thoroughly.

Combine the drained grains and 2½ cups water in a heavy 2-quart pot. Cover with a tight-fitting lid and bring to a boil over a medium-high flame. When steam begins to escape from under the lid, turn the flame down to very, very low and cook for 20 minutes. Turn the flame up to medium for 10 seconds and then turn it off. Let the rice sit, covered and undisturbed, for 15 minutes.

RICE WITH SPINACH
AFGHANISTAN

This rice dish, some beans, yogurt, and a chutney or relish would make a nice, simple meal.

(serves 4–6)

2 cups long-grain rice
1 tablespoon salt
1½ pounds fresh or 2 packages frozen spinach, washed and trimmed
6 tablespoons vegetable oil
2 medium-sized onions, peeled and chopped

Wash the rice in several changes of water and drain it. Put in a bowl, add 5 cups of water and leave to soak for 30 minutes. Drain again.

Put about 4 quarts of water in a 5-quart pot. Add 2 teaspoons salt and bring to a boil. Put a little fresh spinach at a time into the boiling water. As soon as it wilts, lift it out with a slotted spoon and place it in a colander to drain. Do all the spinach this way. Rinse under cold running water and then squeeze out as much moisture as possible. Mince the spinach. If using frozen spinach, cook according to package instructions, drain, and squeeze out moisture.

Heat the oil in a wide, heavy 3-quart pot that has a well-fitting lid. Put in the onions. Stir and sauté over medium heat until they turn soft. Put in the spinach. Stir and sauté for about 25 minutes, turning the heat down if necessary. The spinach should turn dark and rather dry. Add the rice and the remaining 1 teaspoon salt. Continue sautéing for another 5 to 7 minutes, being careful not to break the grains of rice. Add 2⅔ cups water and bring to a boil. Cover, turn heat to very low and cook for 25 minutes. Take the pot off the flame. Remove the lid and quickly cover the pot with a clean dish towel. Put the lid on, over the dish towel. Let the rice sit, undisturbed and in a warm place, for 10 to 15 minutes.

BIBIMBAB
(Korean Rice with Egg and Vegetable Topping)
KOREA

This is Korea's answer to Japan's Chirashi-Zushi — lots of good things arranged neatly on top of rice, this time with a fried egg in the center and some spicy, *kochu chang*-based sauce just beside (or at times under) the egg. I have used the Chinese dish Zucchini Stir-Fried with Garlic as one of the toppings as it is quite similar to a Korean dish. This is really a meal-in-a-bowl and makes a fine lunch or dinner.

(serves 6)

6 cups freshly cooked Plain Japanese Rice (see page 122)
6 fried eggs
Oshitashi (see page 58)
Soy-Bean and Mung-Bean Sprouts Seasoned with Sesame Oil (see page 105), drained
Korean-Style Cucumber Salad (see page 318), drained
Zucchini Stir-fried with Garlic (see page 70), drained
6 crisp, smaller inner leaves Boston (or other) lettuce
4 tablespoons *kochu chang*
2 teaspoons sugar
2 teaspoons sesame oil
1 teaspoon lightly crushed, roasted sesame seeds

Divide up the rice among six bowls that are about 8 inches in diameter at the top and about 2½ inches in height, heaping it in the center in the shape of a mound. (Old-fashioned soup plates may be used.) Put a fried egg on top of each mound of rice. Radiating down from it, in somewhat triangular segments, arrange the Oshitashi, Soy-Bean and Mung-Bean Sprouts Seasoned with Sesame Oil, Korean-Style Cucumber Salad, and the Zucchini Stir-fried with Garlic. Leave a little room for the lettuce leaf "cups." Mix the *kochu chang*, sugar, sesame oil, and sesame seeds and put a dollop in each "cup."

For information about ingredients and basic techniques that may be unfamiliar, see General Information, pages 418–36.

RICE WITH GARLIC

PHILIPPINES

(serves 4–6)

2 cups long-grain rice
5 tablespoons vegetable oil
6 cloves garlic, lightly mashed and peeled
1 teaspoon salt

Wash the rice in several changes of water. Drain. Soak rice in 6 cups water for ½ hour. Drain thoroughly.

Heat the oil in a heavy 2-quart pot over a medium flame. When hot, put in the pieces of garlic. Stir and fry until the garlic pieces turn a medium-brown color. Add the rice and the salt. Stir and fry another minute. Add 2¾ cups water and bring to a boil. Cover tightly, turn heat to very, very low and cook gently for 25 minutes.

RICE WITH TOMATOES

PHILIPPINES

Spain ruled the Philippines for three hundred years, right until the end of the last century. During this period, hundreds of Spanish recipes were absorbed into the Filipino repertoire, some with slight Asian amendments, others almost in their pure European forms. This recipe seems to have altered very little in its new tropical habitat.

(serves 4–6)

2 cups long-grain rice
5 tablespoons vegetable oil (you may use olive oil)
8 cloves garlic, peeled and minced
1 medium-sized onion, peeled and chopped
2 medium-sized tomatoes, peeled and chopped
1 teaspoon salt

Wash the rice in several changes of water. Drain. Soak rice in 6 cups of water for ½ hour. Drain.

Heat the oil in a heavy 2-quart pot over a medium flame. When hot, put in the garlic. Stir and fry until the garlic turns a medium brown. Put in the onion. Stir and fry until onion turns translucent. Add the tomatoes. Stir and fry until tomatoes begin to brown lightly. Add the rice. Stir and sauté for a minute. Add the salt and 2¾ cups water. Bring to a boil. Cover tightly, turn heat to very, very low and cook gently for 25 minutes.

RICE WITH SAUTÉED ONIONS AND MUSHROOMS

INDIA

(serves 4–6)

2 cups long-grain rice
4 tablespoons vegetable oil
½ teaspoon cumin seeds
1 medium-sized onion, peeled and minced
4 medium-sized mushrooms, wiped off and minced
1 teaspoon salt

Wash the rice in several changes of water and leave to drain.

Heat the oil in a heavy 2- to 3-quart pot that has a tight-fitting lid, over a medium flame. When hot, put in the cumin seeds. Stir and fry for a few seconds. Put in the onion and sauté for a few minutes or until the onion turns soft. Add the mushrooms and sauté for another 2 to 3 minutes. Put in the drained rice and salt. Keep sautéing gently for another 3 to 4 minutes. Add 2¾ cups water and bring to a boil. Cover, turn heat to very low and cook for 25 minutes.

RICE WITH COCONUT MILK

ALL SOUTH AND SOUTHEAST ASIA

(serves 4–6)

There are versions of this dish throughout coastal and southern India, Sri Lanka and eastward, all the way to the Philippines. For the simplest version, follow directions for Plain Boiled Rice (see page 117), leave out the butter, include the salt, and substitute coconut milk (see General Information)

for the water. If you want a Thai-Malayasian-Indonesian flavor, you could add the lower third of a bruised stalk of lemon grass to the rice. If fresh lemon grass is unavailable, 2 teaspoons of sliced and dried lemon grass tied up in a cheesecloth bundle would work just as well. Remove the lemon grass before you serve the rice.

Mrs. Wawo-Runtu's

NASI KUNING
(Yellow Turmeric Rice Cooked with Coconut Milk)

INDONESIA

This is one of those delicately flavored, decidedly festive Indonesian dishes that is served exquisitely garnished with red peppers, green peppers, cucumber slices, as well as sundry *sambals* and side dishes, some of which are first ensconced in banana-leaf cups and then embedded in the rice. Apart from its good taste, this dish can be quite a visual delight as well.

In Indonesia, it is fresh turmeric that is used to tint the rice yellow. Fresh turmeric looks a bit like fresh ginger only it is more slender and bright yellow inside. It is unavailable in New York, though I am told that there are occasional deliveries to the West Coast. If you can find some, use a piece that is 1 inch long and about ½ inch thick. You will need to peel and then grate it to a fine pulp. Put

---

For information about ingredients and basic techniques that may be unfamiliar, see General Information, pages 418–36.

it in a strainer and then pour the coconut milk through it.

This rice dish is basically cooked in the upper half of a steamer. I set a small-holed colander over a pot of boiling water and then cover the colander with a lid. You could also use a large sieve set over boiling water or else use the more conventional aluminum or bamboo steamer. If your steamer has very large holes, cover them with a layer of cheese-cloth.

(serves 6)

2   cups long-grain rice
2   cups coconut milk, fresh or canned
2   *daun salaam* leaves
5   inches fresh lemon grass, lightly crushed, or 2
     teaspoons dried, tied up in a cheesecloth bundle
¾   teaspoon ground turmeric powder
1   teaspoon salt

For the garnishes, you could use:

4 to 5 inches of unwaxed cucumber—score the skin with a fork, creating ridges that run length-wise, and then cut the cucumber crosswise into thin slices

5 fresh hot green or green and red chilies—slice the chilies lengthwise at ⅛-inch intervals, starting half an inch below the stem and going straight down all the way to near the tip area; seed and leave in ice water for 1 hour

A few sprigs of mint

Wash the rice in several changes of water and drain. Put in a bowl, add 5 cups water and leave to soak overnight. Drain again.

Set up your steaming apparatus and bring the water in the lower container to a boil. (The water should never touch the rice.) Put the rice in the upper container. Make a few vertical "steam holes" with a chopstick. Now cover the upper container and steam the rice for 10 minutes.

While the rice is steaming, put the coconut milk in a 2-quart pot and add the *salaam* leaves, lemon grass, turmeric, and salt. Stir and bring to a boil. Turn heat to low and simmer 2 to 3 minutes.

Empty the rice into the hot coconut milk. Stir it gently and bring to a boil. Cover, turn the heat off and let the rice sit, undisturbed, for 15 minutes. By this time all the liquid will have been absorbed. Mix gently.

Put the rice back in the steamer. Make fresh "steam holes" with a chopstick and cover. Steam over medium heat for 30 minutes.

Remove the *salaam* leaves and the lemon grass. Put the rice on a platter and arrange garnishes around it.

RICE WITH FRESH HERBS AND BABY LIMA BEANS

IRAN

This is a scrumptious, meal-in-itself rice dish, fragrant with the aroma of fresh herbs. I first had it at the Tavooz Restaurant in New York City and have eaten many variations of it since then. You could make it with fresh fava beans, black-eyed peas, lentils, peas, and vary the herbs to suit your taste. You can eat this dish as a main course, just like a pasta dish.

(serves 4–6)

2   cups long-grain rice
5   tablespoons plus ¼ teaspoon salt
1   10-ounce package frozen baby lima beans
6   tablespoons melted unsalted butter   .
½   cup minced fresh Chinese parsley, firmly packed
½   cup minced fresh parsley, firmly packed
½   cup minced fresh dill, firmly packed
½   cup very finely sliced scallion tops (green only)

Pick over the rice and wash it in several changes of water. Drain. Put the rice in a bowl. Add 5 cups of water and 2½ tablespoons of salt. Stir and leave to soak overnight or for at least 8 hours.

Cook baby lima beans according to package instructions but undercook them so they are still firm. (My package suggested a cooking time of 15 minutes, so I cooked the lima beans for 8 minutes only. Also, I added ¼ teaspoon salt to the cooking liquid, even though the beans were "lightly salted" already.) Drain the lima beans and set them aside.

Preheat the oven to 325° F. Drain the rice in a sieve. Place the sieve under running water and wash the rice. Drain.

Bring 3¾ quarts of water to a boil in a large pot. Add 2½ tablespoons salt. Pour the drained rice into the boiling water in a steady stream. Stir the rice and let the water come to a boil again. Boil rice rapidly for exactly 5 minutes. Turn off heat and drain the rice by pouring it into a sieve. Wash the rice again, this time under running lukewarm water. Drain.

Pour 4 tablespoons of the melted butter plus a tablespoon of water into a 9-inch-wide, heavy, casserole-type pot and place the pot on a low flame. Put half the rice over the butter, spreading it out over the bottom of the pot. Spread the lima beans over the rice. Spread the herbs and scallion tops, mixed together, over the lima beans. Spread the remaining rice over the herbs. Pour the remaining 2 tablespoons of melted butter over the rice. Now cover the pot with a doubled piece of paper towel, just slightly larger than the circumference of the pot. Put a piece of aluminum foil, larger than the paper towel, over the paper towel. Attach the paper towel to the foil with 4 straight pins. Crimp the edges of the foil to seal the pot. Now cover the pot with its own lid and place in the oven for 30 minutes. Take the pot out of the oven and uncover. Stir the rice gently to mix all the ingredients. Put all the covers back on and put rice back in the oven for another 20 to 30 minutes or until rice is cooked through.

For information about ingredients and basic techniques that may be unfamiliar, see General Information, pages 418–36.

RICE WITH PANEER AND PEAS

INDIA

(serves 6)

2   cups long-grain rice
Paneer made according to the recipe on page 238
1¼ teaspoons salt
6   tablespoons vegetable oil
3   bay leaves
A 1-inch stick of cinnamon
5   whole cardamom pods
1   cup shelled fresh peas (frozen, defrosted peas
    may be substituted)
1   teaspoon sugar
1   fresh hot green chili, sliced into fine half rings
1   teaspoon ground cumin seeds

Wash the rice in several changes of water and drain. Put in a bowl, add 5 cups water and leave to soak for 30 minutes. Drain again.

Cut the *paneer* into ½-inch cubes and sprinkle ¼ teaspoon salt over them. Mix gently.

Heat the oil in a seasoned cast-iron or nonstick skillet over a medium flame. When hot, put in the *paneer* cubes and fry until golden on two sides. This will happen rather quickly. Remove with a slotted spoon and set aside on a plate.

Pour the oil from the skillet into a heavy, wide, 2½- to 3-quart pot that has a tight-fitting lid. Heat it again over a medium flame. When hot, put in the bay leaves, cinnamon, and cardamom. Stir once. Now put in the drained rice, peas, 1 teaspoon salt, sugar, green chili, and cumin seeds. Stir and fry for 5 minutes, turning the heat down a bit if the rice begins to stick. Add 2⅔ cups water and bring to a boil. Cover, turn heat to very low and cook for 25 minutes. Take off the lid and quickly put in the

paneer pieces. Cook for another 2 to 3 minutes. Turn off the heat and let the pot sit, covered and undisturbed, for 10 minutes.

The bay leaves, cinnamon, and cardamom are not to be eaten. You might remove them from the serving platter or else warn those eating not to bite on them. Mix the rice gently so that the *paneer* and peas are evenly distributed. With this rice, you could have almost any Indian, Persian, or Indonesian dishes.

BASMATI RICE COOKED WITH CHANA DAL AND DILL
(Khili Hui Khichri)

INDIA

I have used the Indian long-grain *basmati* rice for this recipe but you could use any long-grain rice (like Carolina). Again, I have used the Indian *chana dal*, but you could substitute yellow split peas. The rice, bean, dill, and stock combination makes this an extremely nourishing dish.

(serves 6)

⅓ cup *chana dal*, picked over and washed
2   cups *basmati* rice, picked over and washed
3   tablespoons vegetable oil
½ teaspoon *garam masala*
1   teaspoon salt
4   tablespoons fresh chopped dill
3   cups Delicious Stock . . . (see page 292)

Soak the *dal* in 2 cups hot water for 3 hours.

Soak the rice in 5 cups of water for 1 hour.

Drain the *dal* and the rice.

Heat the oil in a heavy pot (with a tight-fitting lid) over a medium flame. When hot, add the drained *dal* and rice. Stir and fry for 2 to 3 minutes or until all grains are coated with oil. Add the *garam masala*, salt, and dill. Stir and fry for another minute or so. Now put in the stock and bring to a boil. Cover, turn heat to very, very low, and cook gently for 25 minutes. Turn off the heat and let the pot sit in a warm place, covered, for 15 minutes.

Mrs. Patel's

EK HANDI NA DAL CHAVAL
(Rice and Dal, Cooked in One Pot)
INDIA

Here is one of those "casserole" dishes from Gujarat that is a complete meal in itself. It contains rice, *toovar dal*, potatoes, onions, as well as the delicate spicing provided by *garam masala*. The name of the dish translates as "rice and beans (and therefore a meal) cooked in one pot."

There are several stages to making this dish. The *dal*, rice, and potatoes have to be partially cooked first. They are then layered and baked.

(serves 4 as a main dish,
6–8 as part of a larger meal)

1   cup *toovar dal*, oily or plain
¼   teaspoon ground turmeric
2   tablespoons salt
1   quarter-sized slice of fresh ginger

½   cup vegetable oil
2   medium-sized boiling potatoes (about ½ pound), peeled and cut into ¾-inch dice
A 1½-inch stick of cinnamon
5   whole cardamom pods
3   bay leaves
3   medium-sized onions, peeled, cut in half lengthwise, then sliced into very fine half rings
1   teaspoon *garam masala*
2   cups long-grain rice
Garnish: hard-boiled eggs (optional)

Pick over the *toovar dal*, wash and drain it, and then soak it in 3 cups water for 1 hour. Put the *toovar dal* in a 1½-quart pot along with 2 cups water, the turmeric, 1 teaspoon salt, and the slice of ginger. Bring to a boil. Cover, lower heat and simmer for 10 minutes. Drain (the liquid may be saved for soup) and set aside.

Heat the oil in a 9-inch-wide, heavy, casserole-type pot over a medium flame. When hot, put in the potatoes. Fry them, stirring, about 8 to 10 minutes, or until they turn golden on all sides. Remove with a slotted spoon and put on a plate. (Do not turn off heat under pot.) Sprinkle potatoes with ¼ teaspoon salt and set aside.

Put the cinnamon, cardamom, and bay leaves into the remaining oil in the casserole dish. Stir them once and immediately put in the sliced onions. Turn the heat up slightly. Fry the onions, stirring, until medium brown. Add ¼ teaspoon salt and the *garam masala*. Stir once and turn off the heat.

Preheat oven to 325° F.

Bring 3¾ quarts of water to a boil in a large pot. Add 1½ tablespoons of salt to it. When the water is at a rolling boil, pour in the rice in a steady stream. Stir. Let the water come to a boil again and

---

For information about ingredients and basic techniques that may be unfamiliar, see General Information, pages 418–36.

then boil vigorously for 7 minutes. Turn off the heat and drain the rice.

Put a thin layer of rice over the fried onions at the bottom of the casserole. Now put in all the potatoes, in one layer. Add another thin layer of rice. Follow that with a layer of *toovar dal*, using up all the *dal.* End with a final thin layer of rice. Cover the pot with aluminum foil, crimping the edges to seal the pot. Now cover the pot with its own lid. Bake in the oven for 35 to 40 minutes.

To serve, stir the contents of the casserole dish gently and turn out onto a large, warmed platter. Garnish, if you like, with quartered hard-boiled eggs.

VANGI BHAT
(Rice and Eggplant Cooked in the Maharashtrian Style)
INDIA

Even though this dish belongs to the vegetarian Maharashtrians of western India, it can be found, with slight variations, in many regions of South India as well. The rice and eggplant are cooked separately first. They are then combined and seasoned, very much as a rice salad might be. *Vangi bhat* is tangy, spicy, and smells enticingly of roasted coconut.

(serves 6)

2　cups long-grain rice
2½ teaspoons salt
1　medium-sized eggplant (about 1 pound)
1　teaspoon plus 7 tablespoons vegetable oil
2　tablespoons whole coriander seeds
2　teaspoons *chana dal*
A generous pinch of ground asafetida
½ whole hot dried red pepper
A ¾-inch stick of cinnamon
3　tablespoons desiccated, unsweetened coconut
2　tablespoons lemon juice
¼ teaspoon turmeric

Put the rice, 3 cups water, and 1 teaspoon salt in a 1½-quart pot with a tight-fitting lid. Bring to a boil. Cover, turn heat to very, very low, and cook gently for 25 minutes. Turn off heat and let rice sit, covered, for another 10 to 15 minutes. (You may make your rice in an electric rice-cooker instead. Use the same proportions of rice, water, and salt.)

Peel eggplant and dice into ½- to ¾-inch cubes. Place in a bowl and sprinkle with 1 teaspoon salt. Mix well and set aside for half an hour.

Heat 1 tablespoon oil in a small cast-iron skillet over a medium flame. When hot, put in the coriander seeds, *chana dal*, asafetida, red pepper, and cinnamon. Keep stirring. When spices darken by a few shades, remove them with a slotted spoon and place them on a plate lined with a paper towel.

Put the desiccated coconut in the same skillet. Fry, stirring all the time (there will be hardly any oil in the skillet, but that is all right), until the coconut turns a fairly uniform golden-brown color. Remove coconut and place on the paper towel, next to the spices.

Heat 5 tablespoons of oil in a 9- to 10-inch skillet over a medium flame. When hot, add the eggplant. Stir and fry for 5 to 8 minutes or until eggplant is cooked through. Remove with a slotted spoon and keep warm.

Put spices and coconut into an electric coffee

grinder and grind as finely as possible. Leave in coffee grinder.

Combine the lemon juice, about ½ teaspoon salt (you may use a bit less), the turmeric, and 2 tablespoons water in a very small pot (you could use a butter warmer). Bring to a boil. Turn heat to very low and simmer very gently for 3 minutes. Turn off heat.

Spread the freshly cooked rice out on a warmed serving platter. Dribble 2 tablespoons of oil on the rice and mix well, breaking up all lumps as you do so. When the rice is no longer steaming (it should still be warm to the touch), add the eggplant, the coconut-spice mixture, and the lemon-turmeric mixture. Mix well and serve warm or at room temperature. If it is to be served a few hours later, it should be cooled quickly (you may fan it), and then stored, *un*refrigerated, in a tightly closed container (a plastic bag will do).

KASHMIRI-STYLE GUCCHI PULLAO
(Pilaf with Morel Mushrooms)
INDIA

When I was growing up in India, we had this *pullao* about once every three weeks and always for a Sunday lunch. Dried morels came all the way from the northern state of Kashmir and were, as my mother often told us, worth their weight in gold. Naturally, there were never too many of them in a *pullao*. I hid my morels under a mound of rice or under a lettuce leaf. When the meal was almost over, I would suddenly "discover" my treas-

ure with great glee. I ate the morels very, very slowly, savoring each bite for as long as possible.

If you are lucky enough to have access to fresh morels—they generally make their appearance in the spring—use them instead of the dried ones in this recipe. You will not have a "soaking liquid," but water or any of the stocks listed in this book could be used instead.

(serves 4–6)

2 cups *basmati* rice
½ ounce dried morels (10 to 12 mushrooms)
3 tablespoons unsalted butter
1 small onion, peeled, cut in half lengthwise, then sliced into fine half rounds
1 teaspoon salt

Pick over the rice and wash it in several changes of water. Drain. Put in a bowl. Add 6 cups fresh water and leave to soak for half an hour. Drain.

Rinse off the morels and soak them in 1½ cups of boiling water for 15 to 20 minutes or until they are soft. Remove mushrooms from their soaking liquid (reserve this liquid) and rinse them again. Now cut each mushroom in half lengthwise.

Strain the soaking liquid through a clean handkerchief. Add enough water to it to make 2⅔ cups.

Heat the butter in a heavy 2-quart pot over a medium flame. When hot, put in the onion. Sauté until it turns translucent. Add the morels and sauté them for 1 minute. Add the rice and the salt. Stir and sauté the rice for a couple of minutes. Lower the heat a bit if the rice starts to stick. Now add the morel soaking liquid and bring to a boil. Cover tightly, turn heat to very, very low, and cook, undisturbed, for 25 minutes.

For information about ingredients and basic techniques that may be unfamiliar, see General Information, pages 418–36.

VEGETABLE PULLAO

INDIA

(serves 6–8)

1   cup whole mung beans, picked over and washed
2   cups long-grain rice
4½ tablespoons vegetable oil
1   teaspoon whole black mustard seeds
1   medium-sized onion, peeled and finely chopped
4   medium-sized cloves garlic, peeled and finely minced
1   teaspoon peeled, finely minced fresh ginger
⅓   pound string beans, trimmed and cut into ¼-inch-long pieces
¼   pound medium-sized mushrooms, diced into ¼-inch pieces
2   teaspoons *garam masala*
1½ teaspoons ground coriander
2½ teaspoons salt
2   tablespoons finely minced Chinese (or other) parsley

Put mung beans in a bowl with 3 cups of water. Cover lightly and set aside for 12 hours. Drain beans and wrap in a very damp dish towel. Put the wrapped bundle in a bowl. Put this bowl in a dark place (like an unused oven) for 24 hours.

Wash rice well and soak in 4 cups of water for half an hour. Drain well.

Preheat oven to 325° F.

Heat oil in a wide, heavy, 4- to 5-quart ovenproof pot over a medium-high flame. When hot, put in the mustard seeds. As soon as the mustard seeds begin to pop (this takes just a few seconds), put in the onion. Stir and fry for about 5 minutes or until onion turns brown at the edges. Add the garlic and ginger. Fry, stirring, for about 1 minute. Turn heat to medium-low and add the mung beans, rice, string beans, mushrooms, *garam masala*, ground coriander, and salt. Stir and sauté for about 10 minutes or until rice turns translucent and vegetables are well coated with oil. Add 4 cups hot water and the minced parsley. Turn heat to a medium-high flame and cook, stirring, for about 5 minutes or until most of the water is absorbed. (There will be an inch or so of water at the bottom.) Cover the pot first with aluminum foil, crimping and sealing the edges, and then with its own lid. Place in heated oven for half an hour. Fluff up with a fork and serve.

SPICED RICE WITH CASHEWS

INDIA

This dish can be found, with interesting local variations, all over India. It is not hot, just lightly, fragrantly spiced.

(serves 6)

2   cups long-grain rice or Indian *basmati* rice
4   tablespoons vegetable oil
2   tablespoons raw cashews, split in half lengthwise
1   medium-sized onion, peeled, cut in half lengthwise, then sliced into paper-thin half rings
1   clove garlic, peeled and minced
1   teaspoon peeled, grated fresh ginger
½   teaspoon minced fresh hot green chili or ⅛ teaspoon cayenne pepper
¾   teaspoon *garam masala*
1   teaspoon salt
3   cups hot Vegetable Stock (see page 292)

Place rice in a bowl. Add water to cover. Rub the rice grains with your hands. Drain the water. Add more water and repeat the process four or five times until the rice is well washed (the water should not be milky). Cover the rice with 4½ cups of fresh water and leave to soak for half an hour. Drain, and leave rice in a strainer.

Preheat oven to 325° F.

This rice dish cooks on top of the stove and in the oven, so it is more convenient to use a heavy, flame- and ovenproof, 2-quart sauté pan. Heat the oil over medium heat. Put in the split cashews. Fry for a few seconds, stirring all the time, until cashews turn a golden brown. Remove with slotted spoon and leave on paper towel to drain.

Put the onion slices into the same oil. Fry them for 2 to 3 minutes or until they turn brown at the edges. Add the drained rice, the garlic, ginger, green chili, *garam masala*, and salt. Turn the heat to medium-low. Stir and fry the rice for 7 to 8 minutes or until the rice is translucent and well coated with the oil.

Add the heated stock. Keep stirring and cooking on a medium-low flame for another 5 to 6 minutes. When the top of the rice begins to look dry (there will still be a little liquid left at the bottom of the pot), cover with a well-fitting lid (or aluminum foil plus a looser-fitting lid) and place in the oven 20 to 25 minutes or until rice is cooked through. Remove rice pan from the oven and leave, covered, in a warm place for 10 minutes. (If kept covered and in a warm place, this rice will retain its heat for a good half hour.)

Remove rice gently with a slotted spoon, and place on warmed serving platter. Break up all lumps with the back of the slotted spoon. Garnish with the cashews and serve immediately.

SPICED RICE WITH NUTS AND RAISINS

INDIA

This is a superb North Indian rice dish for parties. If you can find the fine-grain *basmati* rice, use it here. If not, an American long-grain rice (like

---

For information about ingredients and basic techniques that may be unfamiliar, see General Information, pages 418–36.

Carolina) will do almost as well. You may garnish this dish with any nuts and dried fruit that you like. I have chosen almonds and raisins because they are traditional; peanuts, cashews, and sesame seeds because they are so nutritious.

(serves 8)

3   cups long-grain rice
10 tablespoons vegetable oil
1½ tablespoons blanched, slivered almonds
2   tablespoons raw shelled peanuts
2   tablespoons raw cashews, split in half lengthwise
¼ cup golden raisins
1   onion, peeled, cut in half lengthwise, then sliced into very fine half rings
1   clove garlic, peeled and minced
A ¾-inch piece of fresh ginger, peeled and finely grated
½ to 1 fresh hot green chili, minced
1   teaspoon *garam masala*
1¾ teaspoons salt
2   tablespoons roasted sesame seeds

Wash the rice well and leave to soak in a bowl filled with 5 cups of water for half an hour. Drain and leave rice in a strainer.

Preheat oven to 325° F.

Line a plate with paper towels and keep beside the stove.

Heat oil over medium heat in a wide, heavy, ovenproof pot. (I use a 10-inch-wide, flame- and ovenproof sauté pan.) When hot, put in the almonds. Stir and fry until almonds turn golden.

Remove with a slotted spoon and place on a paper-towel-lined plate. Put the peanuts into the same oil, stirring and frying them until they are golden. Remove them with a slotted spoon and place them beside the almonds. Now fry the cashews in the same way. When they are golden, spread them out near the peanuts. Finally, put in the raisins. Within a second, they will puff up. Remove them immediately and spread them out beside the cashews.

Remove all but 5 tablespoons of the oil from the pot (you can reuse it for some other dish). Put the onion slices into the oil and fry them for 2 to 3 minutes or until they turn brown in spots. Add the drained rice, the garlic, ginger, green chili, *garam masala*, and salt. Turn the heat to medium-low and fry the rice, stirring constantly, for 7 to 8 minutes or until all the grains are well coated with oil.

Add 4¼ cups of water and bring to a boil. Turn heat to medium-low, stirring and cooking the rice for about 5 minutes or until most of the liquid has evaporated. (There will be a little liquid left at the bottom of the pot.) Now cover the rice first with aluminum foil, crimping the edges to seal the pot, and then with its own lid. Place pot in the center of the oven for 20 to 25 minutes or until rice is cooked through.

This dish will stay hot if left covered in a warm spot for at least half an hour. Just before you sit down to eat, spoon the rice out onto a warm platter with a fork or the side edge of a slotted spoon. Break up any lumps and garnish rice with the nuts, raisins, and roasted sesame seeds.

FRIED RICE WITH EGG AND VEGETABLES

CHINA

(serves 6)

6 tablespoons vegetable oil
4 medium-sized mushrooms, cut into ¹⁄₁₆-inch slices
1½ cups very finely sliced Chinese cabbage or *bok choy*
1⅛ teaspoons salt
6 cups cooked, unsalted, long-grain rice, gently crumbled so it is free of lumps*
1 large egg
2 cups mung-bean sprouts, washed and drained (see page 98)
¾ cup very finely sliced scallions (including green)
¼ cup Chinese chives cut into 1-inch lengths

*NOTE: Use cooked rice that has been steamed, boiled, or baked and cooled 4 to 5 hours or, better, refrigerated overnight.

Heat 2 tablespoons oil in a wok over a medium-high flame. When hot, put in the mushrooms. Stir and fry them for about 30 seconds. Remove mushrooms with a slotted spoon and place on a plate.

Put the Chinese cabbage into the same oil. Stir and fry it for 1 minute. Remove and put on plate with the mushrooms. Sprinkle mushrooms and cabbage with ⅛ teaspoon salt.

Put 4 tablespoons of oil into the wok and heat it on the same medium flame. When hot, put in the rice and stir it once. Make a hole in the center of the rice and break an egg into the hole. Stir the egg, first in its hole and then, when it sets a bit, mix it up with the rice. Stir and fry the rice for another minute. Now add the bean sprouts. Stir and fry for another 5 minutes. Add the scallions, chives, the mushrooms, and cabbage. Stir once and sprinkle in 1 teaspoon salt. Stir and fry for another minute.

THAI FRIED RICE

THAILAND

It is not so much the ingredients in this dish that make it different from Chinese fried rice as the sauce it is eaten with. The main ingredient in this sauce is fermented bean curd, strong cheesy cubes that are available bottled in most Chinese grocery stores, which sell many types of fermented bean curd. The type used here consists of cubes that are doused in a red, winy liquid and are bottled as Red Bean Curd or Nam Yee. At Thai grocery stores, ask for red *tao hoo yee*.

(serves 6)

FOR THE RICE
5 tablespoons vegetable oil
4 to 5 cloves garlic, peeled and minced
¾ cup peeled and finely slivered shallots
4 quarter-sized slices of fresh ginger, cut into fine slivers
1 fresh hot green chili, seeded and cut into fine slivers
6 cups cooked, unsalted, cold Plain Boiled Rice (see page 117)
1 cup mung-bean sprouts, washed and drained
1 large egg
1½ teaspoons salt, or to taste
2 tablespoons minced fresh Chinese parsley

FOR THE SAUCE
Enough mashed Red Bean Curd to make 6 tablespoons
1 tablespoon peeled, very finely grated fresh ginger

For information about ingredients and basic techniques that may be unfamiliar, see General Information, pages 418–36.

2 tablespoons very finely minced fresh hot
   green chilies
2 tablespoons very finely minced peeled shallots
½ cup fresh lime or lemon juice

OPTIONAL GARNISHES
6 sprigs fresh mint
12 cucumber sticks, 3 inches long
   ⅓-inch thick and ⅓-inch wide

Put the oil in a wok or a heavy skillet and heat
over a medium flame. When hot, put in the garlic.
Stir and cook for 1 minute. Add the shallots. Stir
and fry for another 2 minutes. Add the ginger and
the chili. Stir and fry another minute. Put in the
cooked rice and mung-bean sprouts. Stir and fry
for 2 minutes. Make a hole in the center of the rice
and break the egg into it. Stir the egg, first in its
hole and then, when it sets a bit, mix it up with the
rice. Add the salt. Stir and fry the rice for 10
minutes or until it has heated through properly.
Stir in the minced Chinese parsley.

Mix all the ingredients for the sauce and put
them in a bowl.

To serve, make a mound of
the rice in a large platter. Garnish with the mint and
cucumber. Pass
along the sauce
on the side.

SWEET RICE
WITH ORANGE RIND
IRAN

Here is a simplified, vegetarian version of the Persian
Shirin Polo or Sweet Pilaf. It would be perfect for
festive days—Thanksgiving, Christmas, or a wedding. It is sweet but not cloyingly so and goes very
well with savory foods.

(serves 8)

2 cups long-grain rice
2 medium-sized carrots
4 tablespoons unsalted butter
The peel from 1 orange
1 cup sugar
½ cup slivered, blanched almonds
½ teaspoon leaf saffron or ¼ teaspoon yellow liquid food coloring
1 to 2 tablespoons golden raisins
¾ teaspoon salt

Wash the rice in several changes of water and
drain. Put in a bowl, add 5 cups water and leave to
soak for 1 hour. Drain and set aside in a sieve set
over a bowl.

Meanwhile, peel the carrot and cut it into ⅛-inch-
thick diagonal slices. Cut the slices lengthwise into
⅛-inch-thick julienne strips.

Melt the butter in a wide, flame- and ovenproof,
3-quart pot with a tight-fitting lid over a medium
flame. Put in the carrots. Stir and fry for about 5
minutes or until carrots are lightly browned. Turn
off the heat. Remove the carrots with a slotted
spoon and set aside. Leave the remaining butter in
the pot and set that aside as well.

Cut the orange peel into 2-inch-long by ⅛-inch-wide julienne strips. Put them in a pot with 4 cups water and bring to a rolling boil. Immediately invert the pot into a colander set in the sink. Rinse the peel under cold water. Now put the peel and 4 cups fresh water back into the same pot and repeat the entire blanching process, rinsing the peel for a second time at the end of it.

In a heavy saucepan, combine the orange peel, sugar, almonds, saffron or food coloring, and ½ cup water. Bring to a boil. Turn heat down and simmer gently for about 30 minutes, stirring frequently. Add the carrots and raisins. Simmer another 5 minutes or so. The peel mixture should be thick and syrupy, rather like melted jam; be careful to not let it burn. Leave this mixture in a warm place.

Preheat oven to 325° F.

Put the pot with the butter back on the stove and heat it over a medium flame. Put in the drained rice. Stir and fry it for 4 to 5 minutes, turning the heat down slightly if it begins to catch. Add 2⅔ cups water and the salt. Stir gently and cook until almost all the water has evaporated. Quickly spread the peel mixture over the rice, cover tightly and place in the oven for 25 minutes.

Stir the rice gently to mix it before spooning it out onto a warm serving platter.

ZARDA PULLAO
(Sweet Saffron Rice)
INDIA/IRAN

Not very far from the house where I grew up in Delhi is a large seventeenth-century mosque, Jama Masjid, that was built by the same bejeweled potentate, Shah Jahan, who built the Taj Mahal to entomb his beloved wife. The mosque is built on a natural hill, a fact somehow hidden by the rows of steps that lead down from it on three sides. Near these steps and in the shadows of a graciously proportioned dome and minarets are rows of somewhat shabby stalls that pass as restaurants. They may be shabby and of dubious cleanliness but, as all Delhiwalas know, they serve some of the best Muslim food in town. Among the dishes that are openly displayed here are platters of yellow, glistening sweet saffron rice. The price of saffron being what it is, yellow food coloring is now often substituted. But the sweet festive rice still tastes wonderful, either eaten plain or as a foil for hot, spicy foods.

I do use some saffron in my rice to give it the rich aroma. But I, too, have started using some yellow coloring to provide the right, traditional color. You may leave it out, if you so wish.

(serves 4)

½ teaspoon leaf saffron, roasted and crumbled (see page 432)
1 tablespoon warm milk
1 cup long-grain rice
4 tablespoons *ghee* or unsalted butter
2 tablespoons unsalted, shelled pistachios
4 whole cardamom pods
A 1-inch stick of cinnamon

For information about ingredients and basic techniques that may be unfamiliar, see General Information, pages 418–36.

¼ teaspoon liquid yellow food coloring
⅓ teaspoon salt
5 to 7 tablespoons sugar, depending on sweetness
   desired
1 tablespoon golden raisins (optional)

Crumble the saffron into the warm milk and set aside for 2 hours.

Wash the rice in several changes of water and drain. Put the rice in a bowl, add 4 cups water, and leave to soak for 30 minutes. Drain thoroughly.

Preheat oven to 325° F.

Heat the *ghee* in a wide, heavy, flame- and ovenproof pot with a tight-fitting lid over a medium flame. When hot, put in the pistachios. Stir and fry for about 5 seconds or until the pistachios have picked up a faintly brownish tint. Remove the pistachios with a slotted spoon and set aside. Put the cardamom and cinnamon into the same *ghee*. Stir and fry for half a minute. Now put in the drained rice. Stir and fry gently for about 3 minutes, turning the heat down a bit if the rice begins to catch. Add 1⅓ cups water, the yellow food coloring, and salt. Turn the heat back to medium. Gently stir and cook until all the water is absorbed. Put in the saffron milk, sugar, and raisins. Stir to mix, cover and place in the oven for 25 minutes.

To serve, turn the rice into a warmed bowl, removing the cardamom and cinnamon, then sprinkle the pistachios over the rice.

BULGAR WHEAT
(also called Cracked Wheat, Bulghur or Burghul)

This is wheat that has been cooked, dried, and cracked. It is used in the Caucasus region of Asian Russia and in parts of the Middle East to make soups, salads, stuffings, and pilafs. To make pilaf, it is cooked very much like rice, though it does require much less water than rice does. To make soup, bulgar can be thrown into the broth, again, very much like rice. Allowance must be made for it to expand and absorb liquid. For salads, it does not need to be cooked at all. A soaking—½ to 1½ hours—is all that is required. After that the grains of cracked wheat are squeezed to discard excess liquid and then mixed with a traditional Middle Eastern dressing that includes olive oil and lemon juice.

Bulgar wheat may be bought in different-sized grains. The finer grains which require no cooking are used for salads. The medium-sized and coarse grains are used for pilafs and stuffings. The taste and texture of the grains do not vary with the size. Cracked wheat is always nutty in taste and firmer than rice in its texture.

BULGAR WHEAT WITH SCALLIONS AND MUSHROOMS

MIDDLE EAST

(serves 6)

4 tablespoons vegetable oil
2 scallions, trimmed and sliced in fine half rings (including green)
6 medium-sized mushrooms, wiped with a damp cloth and sliced
2 cups medium- or coarse-grained bulgar wheat
1¼ teaspoons salt

Heat the oil in a heavy 1½- to 2-quart pot over a medium flame. Put in the scallions and sauté them for 30 seconds. Now add the mushrooms and sauté for another minute. Add the bulgar wheat and the salt. Stir and sauté for another minute or until the grains of wheat are coated with oil. Now add 2½ cups water and bring to a boil. Cover, turn heat to very low and simmer gently for 25 minutes. Turn off heat. Put a dish towel between the lid and the pot, covering quickly so as not to dissipate the heat. Leave in a warm place for another 20 minutes. The wheat will puff up and not turn soggy.

PILAF OF BULGAR WHEAT AND RED LENTILS

MIDDLE EAST

Red lentils, *masoor dal* (that is what it is called in Indian stores), and Egyptian lentils are one and the same thing—a salmon-colored, hulled and split legume that turns a yellowish color when cooked. We often have this pilaf for brunch with some goat cheese, sliced red-ripe tomatoes dressed with olive oil and lemon juice, and some olives.

(serves 4–6)

½ cup *masoor dal* (red lentils)
4 tablespoons olive oil or any vegetable oil
1 medium-sized onion, peeled and finely chopped
2 cloves garlic, peeled and minced
1 cup medium- or coarse-grained bulgar wheat
2 tablespoons minced fresh parsley
1 teaspoon salt
Freshly ground black pepper

Pick over the lentils and wash in several changes of water. Put in a bowl, add 2 cups water, and leave to soak for 6 hours. Drain.

Heat the oil in a heavy 2- to 3-quart pot with a tight-fitting lid over a medium flame. Put in the onion and garlic. Stir and fry for about 2 minutes or until onion is soft. Add the bulgar wheat and lentils. Stir and cook another 3 minutes or until wheat is lightly browned. Add the parsley, salt, and 1½ cups water. Bring to a simmer. Cover, turn heat to very low and cook for 35 minutes. Turn off the heat. Let the pot sit, covered and undisturbed, for 20 minutes. Add the black pepper and mix.

For information about ingredients and basic techniques that may be unfamiliar, see General Information, pages 418–36.

BULGAR WHEAT WITH CHICKPEAS AND TOMATOES

SYRIA

This is a very tasty way to cook cracked wheat and makes a dish that is almost a complete meal in itself.

(serves 4–6)

4   tablespoons vegetable oil
1   medium-sized onion, peeled and finely chopped
2   medium-sized tomatoes, peeled and minced
1   cup cooked, drained chickpeas, canned or home-made (see page 83)
½   teaspoon plus ¾ teaspoon salt
2   tablespoons minced fresh parsley
1   cup medium- or coarse-grained bulgar wheat
Freshly ground black pepper

Heat the oil in a heavy 2- to 3-quart pot with a tight-fitting lid over a medium flame. Put in the onion. Stir and sauté for 2 minutes or until onion is soft. Add the tomatoes. Stir and cook for 3 to 4 minutes or until tomatoes are pastelike. Add the chickpeas, ½ teaspoon salt, and parsley. Cook for about 10 minutes on lowish heat, stirring gently as you do so. Now put in the bulgar wheat, 1 cup water, and the ¾ teaspoon salt. Stir and bring to a simmer. Cover, turn heat to very low and cook for 35 minutes. Turn off the flame. Remove the lid and quickly cover the pot with a dish towel. Put the lid back on over the dish towel. Let the pot sit in a warm place for 20 minutes. Put in the black pepper and stir the wheat gently.

Amal's
TABOULEH
(Bulgar Wheat and Parsley Salad)

LEBANON

When I first came to this country, I took on a job as a guide at the United Nations in order to support myself. This "support" turned out to be more than just financial. Every evening, we guides found ourselves gathering at each other's homes to have heated, informative discussions on international affairs, and to eat superb food. It was Amal, a Palestinian refugee from Beirut, who introduced me to *tabouleh*. I saw a mound of it on her dining table and could not even begin to guess what it was. It looked speckled—brown, green, and red—was meant to be eaten with scoops of lettuce, and was a sort of salad but not quite. I fell in love with its grainy texture and tart taste then and have continued to make it ever since.

(serves 6)

¾   cup fine-grained bulgar wheat
2   medium-sized tomatoes, peeled
4   tablespoons very finely minced onions
2   cups very finely chopped parsley, loosely packed
3   tablespoons lemon juice
1   teaspoon salt
2   tablespoons olive oil
Crisp inner leaves from a head of romaine lettuce

Soak the bulgar wheat in 4 cups of water for 45 minutes.

Cut the tomatoes in half crosswise. Cup one half at a time in your hand, cut side down, and gently squeeze out and discard the seeds. Core the tomato halves and cut them into ¼-inch dice. Put them in a bowl and set aside for 45 minutes.

Line a colander with a clean dish towel. When the bulgar wheat has finished soaking, empty it, with its soaking liquid, into the towel-lined colander. Draw the dish towel together so it closes over the bulgar. Now squeeze out as much liquid as you can. Empty the bulgar into a bowl.

Water will have collected in the bowl of tomatoes. Drain the diced tomatoes, squeezing them very gently.

Now add the tomatoes, onion, parsley, lemon juice, salt, and oil to the bulgar and mix well. Taste and adjust seasonings if you need to.

To serve, heap *tabouleh* neatly in the center of a large platter, patting it down into a clean mound. Cut or break the lettuce leaves into 2½- to 3-inch lengths and arrange them around the *tabouleh* to be used as scoops.

HOW TO COOK WHOLE, HULLED MILLET

Millet has been cooked in Asia since antiquity. When properly prepared, it has a nutty flavor and a firm, grainy but fluffy texture. If it tastes like Russian kasha, it is with good reason. One of the grains that kasha is made from is millet. It is a good replacement for rice at almost any kind of meal.

(serves 6)

1½ cups whole, hulled millet
¾ teaspoon salt
2 tablespoons butter (optional)

Heat a 7-inch cast-iron skillet over a medium flame. Put in the millet and stir to toast it. The millet is done when it emits a roasted aroma and when some of the seeds begin to turn a light-brown color. A few of the seeds might actually burst open like popcorn.

Put the millet into a heavy, 1½- to 2-quart pot. Add 2¾ cups water and the salt. Bring to a boil. Cover tightly, turn heat to very, very low and cook for 30 minutes. Have some boiling water ready. Add ¼ cup hot water to the millet, stir quickly with a fork, cover, and keep cooking on very, very low heat for another 10 minutes. Turn off the flame and let the pot sit, covered and undisturbed, for 15 minutes. Add the butter, mix gently and serve.

For information about ingredients and basic techniques that may be unfamiliar, see General Information, pages 418–36.

WHOLE, HULLED MILLET COOKED WITH CARROTS AND ONION

I often make a large Greek salad with lettuce, radishes, cucumbers, tomatoes, pickled hot peppers, and feta cheese and then, instead of bread, serve this millet on the side. Again, serve this as you might serve a rice dish.

(serves 6)

1½ cups hulled millet
3 tablespoons unsalted butter or vegetable oil
1 carrot, peeled and julienned in 1½-inch strips
1 medium-sized onion, peeled, cut in half lengthwise, and sliced into fine half rings
A 2-inch stick of cinnamon
5 whole cloves
2 tablespoons raisins
¾ teaspoon salt

Roast millet as suggested in preceding recipe and set aside.

In a heavy 1¾- to 2-quart pot, melt the butter over a medium flame. Add the carrot, onion, cinnamon, and cloves. Stir and sauté for about 5 minutes or until the onion is translucent. Add the raisins. Stir and sauté another 5 minutes or until onion just begins to turn brown at the edges. Add the roasted millet, salt, and 2¾ cups water. Bring to a boil. Cover tightly, turn heat to very, very low and cook for 30 minutes.

Have some boiling water ready. Pour in ¼ cup boiling water over the millet, stir quickly with a fork, cover again and continue to cook on the same low heat for another 10 minutes. Turn the heat off and let the pot sit, covered and undisturbed, for another 15 minutes.

Remove the cinnamon stick and the cloves before serving.

WHOLE, HULLED MILLET COOKED WITH YELLOW SPLIT PEAS

NORTH INDIAN STYLE

(serves 4)

⅓ cup yellow split peas
1 cup whole, hulled millet
3 tablespoons vegetable oil
½ teaspoon whole cumin seeds
1 small onion, peeled, cut in half lengthwise, and
   sliced into very fine half rings
1 clove garlic, peeled and minced
½ teaspoon ground turmeric
½ teaspoon ground cumin seeds
1 teaspoon ground coriander seeds
⅛ teaspoon cayenne pepper
¾ teaspoon salt

Soak the split peas in 2 cups water for 5 hours. Drain.

Roast millet as suggested on opposite page and set aside.

Heat the oil in a heavy 1¾- to 2-quart pot over a medium-high flame. When hot, put in the whole cumin seeds. Five seconds later, put in the onion and garlic. Stir and fry for a few minutes until the edges of the onion begin to turn brown. Put in the millet, split peas, turmeric, ground cumin, coriander, cayenne, and salt. Turn the heat to medium. Stir and sauté for about 2 minutes. Add 2 cups water and bring to a boil. Cover, turn heat to very, very low and cook for 30 minutes.

Have some boiling water ready. Pour in about 2 tablespoons of this water over the millet, stir quickly with a fork, cover, and cook for another 10 minutes. Turn the heat off and let the pot sit, covered and undisturbed, for 15 minutes.

ZAKIYA'S
UPPAMA
(Savory South Indian Cereal)
INDIA

Uppama is made out of semolina (or cream of wheat) and resembles a very fine-grained bulgar wheat pilaf that has been highly spiced and loaded with vegetables. It is generally served at breakfast with a coconut chutney on the side but it could easily be served at lunch or dinner as well. Although it is not traditional, you could use *uppama* to stuff vegetables like tomatoes, eggplant, green peppers, and even okra.

(serves 4)

6   tablespoons vegetable oil
A generous pinch of ground asafetida
½ teaspoon whole black mustard seeds
1   whole dried hot red pepper
1   teaspoon *chana dal*
2   teaspoons *urad dal*
½ medium-sized onion, peeled and minced
1   cup finely shredded cabbage, firmly packed
1   small potato (about 2 ounces), peeled and cut into ¼-inch dice
2   tablespoons shelled fresh or defrosted frozen peas
1   fresh hot green chili, minced
½ teaspoon finely grated fresh ginger
¾ teaspoon salt
1   cup cream of wheat*
1   tablespoon finely minced Chinese parsley

*NOTE: Use the kind that takes 15 minutes to cook.

For information about ingredients and basic techniques that may be unfamiliar, see General Information, pages 418–36.

Put some water to boil. You will need approximately 1¼ cups in about 10 minutes from the time you start the cooking.

Heat the oil in an 8- to 10-inch skillet over a medium flame. When hot, put in, in quick succession, first the asafetida, then the mustard seeds, then the red pepper, *chana dal*, and *urad dal*. When the *dals* turn a reddish color, put in the onion, cabbage, potato, peas, green chili, and ginger. Stir and fry on medium-high heat for about 2 minutes. Cover, turn heat to low, and let the vegetables cook through. This should take about 5 to 6 minutes. Check to see if the potatoes are done. Add the salt and mix. Turn heat to medium and put in the cream of wheat. Stir and fry for about 5 minutes but do not let it brown. Turn heat to low.

Slowly add boiling water, about 2 tablespoons at a time, to the cream of wheat, stirring until it is absorbed before adding any more. Add all the 1¼ cups boiling water this way, taking at least 5 minutes to do so. (You may make your *uppama* a little wetter by adding a few more tablespoons of water. I like mine fairly dry.)

Keep stirring and cooking on low heat for another 10 minutes. Each grain should have puffed up by now and should have shed its dry, whitish look. Serve, garnished with the Chinese parsley.

Soy Milk, Bean Curd, and Wheat Gluten

What an amazing product bean curd really is. It is high in protein—9 to 10 ounces provide most average people with about a third of their daily protein requirements—very low in saturated fats, easy to digest, low in calories, and cheap! It lends itself to being cooked with almost all other foods. If you are in a rush, you could make a quick sauce with minced Chinese parsley and toss it over cubes of bean curd; you could crumble and add it to lightly sautéed cabbage; or you could cook it along with dainty broccoli spears. It accepts hot-and-sour sauces, sweet-and-sour sauces, and peanut-filled sauces with equal equanimity. It even allows itself to be puréed and become a salad dressing.

These dishes are, of course, made with the plain white bean curd that has become a fairly common sight in our health-food stores and even in some of our grocery stores. But there are, as well, several other products, all closely related to the white bean curd, that are eaten throughout East Asia.

First of all, there is soy milk. Once soy beans have been soaked, puréed, and strained, they produce a thick, cream-colored liquid. This is soy milk, which must be boiled before it is drunk. It may be sweetened, or else seasoned with drops of soy sauce, sesame oil, and scallions. It is a very common sight in East Asian markets to see whole families drinking this seasoned soy milk from soup bowls in the early hours of the morning. I have sat on wooden benches in Singapore, Bangkok, Hong Kong, and Seoul and done it myself. Soy milk is served steaming hot and is an excellent breakfast food.

When soy milk cooks at a very low temperature, a skin forms on top of it. If this is done systematically in shallow, rectangular trays, then neat, rectangular sheets form, one after another, and are lifted out and then hung up to dry. Chinese grocery stores call this bean-curd skin or dried bean curd. In Japanese stores, it is called *yuba*. The difference in taste between bean curd and bean-curd skin would be about the same as between milk and cream. Bean-curd skin is richer and creamier. Because it is available here only in its dried form, it needs to be reconstituted by being soaked in water.

Soy milk may be converted into bean curd with the help of a coagulant. In Japan's best bean-curd shops, natural *nigari* is put into hot soy milk, which makes it curdle. The soft, satiny curds are quickly scooped up and emptied into rectangular wooden boxes that are riddled with holes. A weight is placed on top to help firm up and shape the curds. What soon emerges is a quivering block of bean curd which is then quickly cut into smaller blocks. These are lowered into cold water to await sale. (The whey from the curds is not wasted. It is used, rather like soapy water, to clean utensils and mop up the floor.)

Some of the bean curd is cut into thick slices and left to drain on cheesecloth-covered slats. After a few hours, it is fried to make what the Japanese call *age*—fried bean curd, and *aburage*—fried bean-curd pillowcases meant for stuffing. Fried bean curd holds its shape very well when cooked with other foods. It also has a firmer, meatlike texture. *Aburage* is used to make one of Japan's most amusing (and delicious) foods—*inari-zushi*—little pouches filled with pickled rice and tied with ribbons of dehydrated gourd.

It is not hard to make good, sweet-tasting bean curd at home. But it is hard to make excellent bean curd at home unless one invests in proper equipment and then buys the freshest, best quality soy beans, preferably in bulk. Many health-food stores carry all the equipment in a kit form. My own suggestion would be that you go out and buy bean curd, if you have access to it. This way you will be guaranteed excellent quality at a low price. However, if you cannot get bean curd or suspect its freshness, use my recipe which requires no special containers other than a colander and a round steaming trivet that can fit snugly somewhere down the colander. Of course, the shape of my bean curd is somewhat untraditional—round instead of rectangular—but it has a fresh, sweet taste and a medium-firm texture. You may use this bean curd for all my recipes, even those calling for soft bean curd.

If you are buying bean curd, you will notice that it is sold as "soft," "medium" (or "regular"), and "hard." Get whatever the recipe calls for.

There are some types of bean curd mentioned in this book that are fairly hard to make at home. These should be purchased from Oriental stores. Among them are the cheeselike, fermented bean-curd cubes, the hard, brownish, pressed bean curd and the fried bean-curd pillowcases or *aburage*. For more on all three of them and on where they can be purchased, consult General Information at the back of the book.

WHEAT GLUTEN

Meatlike in its chewy texture and very rich in protein, wheat gluten is used primarily in China and Japan to add nutritional value to all manner of dishes. In this country, too, it is not entirely unknown. But it is more disguised and appears in canned versions of mock vegetarian fish and meat dishes.

Once you start making wheat gluten at home, I am sure you will get as excited about it as I am. It lends itself to the cooking of every nationality. You will find some traditional gluten recipes here, such as Fried Wheat Gluten with Broccoli, Carrot, and Mushrooms from China, and Japan's delectable Stew of Baked Wheat Gluten, Potato, Turnip, Carrot, and Cabbage Rolls. But I have gone a step further and concocted some really delicious Indian-style dishes, such as Shredded Wheat Gluten and Cabbage with Fennel Seeds, just to show you how inventive we can all be with this new food.

Most wheat flour has some gluten in it. To extract it and get more concentrated protein, the flour has to be made into a dough and then washed repeatedly to get rid of all the starch. Naturally, it helps to start with a flour that has a high content of gluten to begin with, so it is best to buy "gluten flour" from a health-food store.

Once the gluten has been extracted—it sits in a big, spongy lump—it needs to be precooked before being used in a dish. It is usually broken up into pieces and then fried, boiled, or steamed. I have discovered that it can also be baked with excellent results. Gluten, already spongy before precooking, expands and turns even spongier and lighter as it cooks. This helps it to absorb the flavors of other foods it is eventually combined with, a very important factor for a protein that has little taste of its own. Because frying and baking allow gluten to expand to its maximum and also give it a nice crust, I really prefer these methods of precooking to boiling and steaming.

Precooked wheat-gluten balls may be cut into any shape you like—they may be minced, cut into strips, and cut into halves—and then added to whatever you happen to be making, providing the dish has at least some moisture for the gluten to absorb. Wheat gluten cooks well in soups, braised dishes, and stews. If, for example, you like to braise celery in stock and butter, try braising it with the addition of quartered gluten balls. You will be "inventing" a wonderful dish. If you wish to use gluten in a stir-fried dish, it is a good idea to cook it for 15 minutes in stock or lightly seasoned water first.

It is also a good idea to "wash" the fried gluten balls in a little boiling water to rid them of extra oil.

You can buy ready-made fried gluten balls at Chinese grocery stores but I must confess that I prefer the ones I make myself at home. Once you decide to make the balls, do make a large batch— about forty. You can then keep some in the refrigerator, where they will last for several days, and freeze the rest. Gluten balls freeze beautifully. They may be defrosted very fast by simply throwing them into stock or lightly seasoned boiling water and boiling for a few minutes.

SOY MILK

Soy milk "soups," generally savory but sometimes sweet, are drunk throughout many parts of East and Southeast Asia for breakfast. Early in the morning, vendors can be seen busily ladling out steaming portions of this nutritious meal-in-a-bowl. The version I liked best consisted of thick milk, seasoned with some soy sauce and scallions and containing large rounds of a crullerlike bread. Sometimes this soy milk had been set, just barely, so it was like a delicate custard. At other times it had been sweetened with palm sugar. All versions were very good.

(makes about 3½ cups)

1 cup dried soy beans

Pick over the beans and wash them in several changes of water. Drain. Soak the beans in 4 cups of water for 10 hours.

Drain the beans and wash them again in several changes of water. Drain. Measure the beans. You probably have 2⅔ cups. Put them in a blender. Add an equal amount—that is, 2⅔ cups—warm water and blend for several minutes until you have a very smooth purée.

Line a colander with an open 16 × 16-inch muslin bag or an open pillowcase. (Use an old, clean one.) Set the colander in a large bowl.

Bring 1 cup of water to a boil in a heavy, 4-quart pot. As soon as it is boiling, pour in the purée from the blender. Bring to a boil again and immediately turn off the heat. Pour the liquid into the open bag in the colander. Close the bag. Using the bottom of a jar or a potato masher, press out as much milk as

you can. As the liquid cools a bit, it will become easier to handle. Squeeze out whatever milk is left in the grounds. Open up the bag and let the grounds cool off some more for a couple of minutes. Pour ¾ cup warm water over them and squeeze out some more milk. You do not need the grounds anymore.

Wash out the pot and pour the soy milk into it. Bring to a boil. As soon as the milk begins to rise, turn the heat to low and simmer gently for 10 minutes or until the raw bean taste has disappeared.

You may serve this milk plain, lightly sweetened with sugar, brown or white, or you could pour it into soup bowls and offer sliced scallions, vinegar and Chinese soy sauce as seasonings. Only a few drops of the vinegar and soy sauce should be used.

MAKING YOUR OWN BEAN CURD

(makes about 1 pound, 6 ounces of "medium-hard" bean curd)

1¾ pounds dried soy beans
About 2½ teaspoons natural *nigari* flakes

Pick over the soy beans and then wash them in several changes of water. Drain. Soak the soy beans in 6 cups of water for 10 hours. Drain and wash them in several changes of water again. Drain.

You should have about 4½ cups of soy beans and you need to purée them with 4½ cups of warm water. This is best done in two batches in an electric blender or food processor. 1. Blend 2¼ cups of beans at a time with 2¼ cups warm water.

For information about ingredients and basic techniques that may be unfamiliar, see General Information, pages 418–36.

Blend for several minutes or until you have a smooth purée. You should now have about 9 cups of purée.

2. Line a colander with an open 16 x 16-inch muslin bag or an open pillowcase (use an old, clean one). Place the colander in a large bowl. Bring 9 cups of water to a boil in a large pot. Immediately pour in all the soy-bean purée and stir. Now pour this liquid into the open muslin bag. Close the muslin bag over the liquid and, 3. using the bottom of a jar, press out as much soy milk as you can. As the liquid cools off a bit, it will become easier to handle. Squeeze out whatever milk is left in the grounds.

Clean out your large pot and pour the strained soy milk into it. (The grounds are not needed anymore.) Bring this milk to a boil but watch it closely. As soon as it begins to rise, turn down the heat and simmer 10 minutes.

While the milk simmers, take 1½ teaspoons

of the *nigari* and dissolve it in 5 tablespoons of warm water.

Set the colander in your sink. Inside it, place a trivet used for steaming. It should have small holes, be round, and fit somewhere in your colander. My trivet is about 6½ inches in diameter and fits about two-thirds of the way down my colander. Spread a 16 x 16-inch piece of doubled cheesecloth over the trivet and let it hang over the edges of the colander.

When the soy milk has simmered for 10 minutes, take it off the flame. Stir the *nigari* solution once and, 4. using a circular arm motion, pour it into the soy milk. Stir very gently and cover the pot for 10 minutes. Curds should have formed and separated from a thin, greenish, watery whey. Sometimes this does not happen or does not happen completely. A few curds form and the whey remains milky. If that happens, repeat the process. Bring the milk to another boil, remove from the flame and pour in a solution of 1 teaspoon *nigari* and 2 tablespoons water. Stir gently and cover. Wait another 10 minutes. The curds should have formed.

5. Pour the curds and whey into the colander in the sink. 6. Cover the curds with the overhanging cheesecloth and put a 1- to 1½-pound weight that is about the same circumference as the top of the bean curd on top of it. I happen to have a pot with just the right weight and circumference

that fits snugly over the top of the bean curd. You could cut out a piece of wood, lay it over the bean curd, and then put the required weight on the center of it. Let the weight sit for 15 minutes.

Fill a large bowl or pot with 5 inches of water. 7. Lift up the cake of bean curd gently from the colander, cheesecloth and all, and slide it into the water. Remove the cheesecloth, gently and carefully, while the bean-curd cake is submerged.

You may now eat the bean curd immediately, using it up in one of the many recipes in this book, or you could refrigerate it in its water bath for about four days. Change the water every day.

To make the bean curd "hard," instead of pressing it for 15 minutes, press it for 2 hours and increase the weight to 3 pounds.

5

6

7

For information about ingredients and basic techniques that may be unfamiliar, see General Information, pages 418–36.

UDOFU
(Simmering Bean Curd with Seasonings)
JAPAN

Sometimes spelled *yudofu* (and pronounced "you-doe-foo"), this simple, elegant, and light dish tastes just as good as the bean curd used to make it. Use the freshest bean curd possible, whether homemade or store-bought. Ideally, the bean curd should be soft, though you could, in a pinch, use medium bean curd as well. In Japan, where the best foods are seasonal, this dish is served during the cold winter months in a spectacular wood and bamboo container that holds the bean curd in a hot broth, some dipping sauce, and some charcoal to keep the dish piping hot, all in separate compartments. Because bean-curd cubes retain heat for a long time, *udofu* is even served out-of-doors on the most chilling of days.

(serves 6)

4 scallions
½ pound white radish
1 sheet of *nori*, approximately 7 x 8 inches
1 cup Japanese soy sauce
7 tablespoons *mirin*
A piece of *kombu*, about 5 inches square, wiped lightly with a damp cloth and cut into two sections
6 dried *shiitake* mushrooms, soaked in 1 cup hot water for 20 minutes
6 fresh, soft or medium bean-curd cakes, about 4 ounces each, cut into 1-inch cubes
Sprinklings of 7-spice seasoning

Cut the scallions into very, very fine rounds halfway up their green sections. Soak them in ice water for half an hour. Drain and pat dry.

Peel the radish and grate it over the smallest holes of your grater. The radish should be closer to pulp than shreds.

Toast the *nori* by holding the sheet over a medium-low flame and moving it back and forth for a few seconds. Now crumble the *nori*, not into powder but into small, roughly ⅛- to ¼-inch squares.

Combine the soy sauce and *mirin* in a small pot and bring to a boil. Turn off the heat immediately and keep warm.

In a large pot, bring 3¾ quarts of water to a boil. Throw in the two pieces of *kombu*. Cut off the mushroom stems and put the mushroom caps as well as the mushroom soaking liquid (strain it if it is gritty) into the pot. Boil for 1 minute. Add the bean-curd cubes and bring to a boil again. Turn heat to low and simmer for 5 minutes.

To serve, transfer the bean curd and liquid to one or two chafing dishes placed in the center of your dining table. If you do not have chafing dishes, use an electric skillet turned to "warm" or a flat-bottomed serving dish set on a hot tray. Place a pretty slotted spoon or small Japanese skimmer near the dish of bean curd. Pour the heated sauce into warmed toy teapots or into small warmed bowls. Provide spoons to go with the bowls. Give each person small dishes containing crumbled *nori*, sliced scallions, and mounds of grated radish sprinkled on top with the 7-spice seasoning.

Each person should have a bowl to eat from and chopsticks to eat with. Once the bean curd is lifted out of the broth with the skimmer, it should first be seasoned with the heated sauce and then with a combination of the other seasonings. Diners should do this in their own individual bowls. The liquid in the serving dish as well as the pieces of *kombu* are not for consumption.

BEAN CURD WITH WATERCRESS

SINGAPORE CHINESE

In this dish, the watercress is minced and used as a kind of dressing for the bean curd. As both red and green hot chilies are added to the dressing, the sauce is as pretty as it is fiery. Fresh hot red chilies are hard to find in New York, so I have substituted fresh sweet red pepper. If you do not want to make this dish hot, use a few slices of green bell pepper instead of the hot green chili.

(serves 2–4)

1   large bunch (about 5 ounces) watercress
½ to 1 fresh hot green chili
4   ⅛-inch-thick slices sweet red pepper
½ teaspoon salt
½ pound medium bean curd
1¼ cups Delicious Stock . . . (see page 292)
½ teaspoon cornstarch
2   teaspoons Chinese thin soy sauce
1   teaspoon sesame oil
¼ teaspoon sugar
2   tablespoons vegetable oil
2   cloves garlic, peeled and very lightly mashed
2   quarter-sized slices of fresh ginger, peeled and very lightly mashed
1   teaspoon roasted sesame seeds

Mince the watercress, stalks and all, and put in a bowl. Mince the green chili, removing seeds if you so desire. Mince the slices of red pepper somewhat more coarsely than the watercress and the green chili. Sprinkle ½ teaspoon salt over the vegetables. Mix well and set aside for 20 to 30 minutes.

Put the bean curd in a small pot. Pour 1 cup of the stock over it. Bring to a gentle simmer over a lowish flame. Now turn the heat to very low and let the bean curd sit in this barely simmering broth for 10 minutes. Turn off the flame and let the pot sit in a warm place.

Put the cornstarch in a small cup. Slowly add ¼ cup stock and mix. Add the soy sauce, sesame oil, and sugar. Mix again.

Heat the vegetable oil in a wok over a medium flame. When hot, add the garlic and ginger. Stir and fry the garlic, pressing down upon it with the back of a slotted spoon every now and then. When it turns dark, remove with the slotted spoon and discard. Put the watercress mixture into the wok. Stir and fry for about 1 minute or until the watercress has wilted. Turn the heat to low. Give the cornstarch mixture a quick stir and pour it over the vegetables. Stir and cook for another 30 seconds or until the sauce has thickened slightly. Turn off the heat.

Carefully lift the bean curd out of the liquid and put on a serving dish. (You do not need the liquid anymore.) Cut into ¾- to 1-inch cubes. Pour the vegetable dressing over the bean curd. Sprinkle the sesame seeds over the top and serve.

For information about ingredients and basic techniques that may be unfamiliar, see General Information, pages 418–36.

KOREAN-STYLE BEAN CURD IN A HOT-WATER BATH
KOREA

Heated bean curd is so very warming when the cold winds of fall and winter start to blow. In Korea, it is served with a spicy sauce.

(serves 4–6)

3 cakes soft or medium bean curd (about 4 ounces each)

In a wide pan, bring about 12 cups of water to a boil. Turn the heat down to medium. Add the bean-curd cakes in a single layer and bring to a simmer. Lower heat and simmer gently for 5 minutes. Now remove the cakes with a spatula and place them in a serving dish deep enough so the cakes can be almost submerged in water. Pour in enough of the heating water so it comes about three-quarters of the way up the sides of the cakes.

Serve immediately with Spicy Korean Sauce (see page 359). (For 6 people, you should double the sauce recipe. You could, if you like, divide the sauce up in small, individual saucers.) The purpose of the hot water is to keep the bean curd hot. It should not be drunk. Break off pieces of the bean curd with your chopsticks and dip it into your sauce before eating it.

HIYA-YAKKO
(Chilled Bean Curd)
JAPAN

Japanese cuisine, perhaps more than any other in the world, emphasizes the seasons. Just as *udofu* (see recipe, page 167) is served in the chilly winter months, *hiya-yakko* is served during the sultry summer. The dish itself is simple enough—cold bean curd surrounded by tiny dishes containing soy sauce, grated ginger (or grated white radish), and sliced scallions. For this dish to be good at all, the bean curd has to be absolutely fresh and soft. Once you have that, and you chill the bean curd appropriately, the dish is glorious.

(serves 4)

4 cakes fresh, soft or medium bean curd
  (about 16 ounces in all)
3 scallions
4 teaspoons peeled and finely grated fresh ginger
½ cup Japanese soy sauce

Cut the bean curd into 1-inch cubes. Put the bean curd gently into a large bowl and cover with ice water. You may even put some ice cubes in the bowl. Chill in the refrigerator for an hour or longer.

Cut the scallions into very, very fine rounds, halfway up their green sections. Soak the sliced scallions in 1 cup of ice water for half an hour. Drain and pat dry.

Just before serving, put 4 or 5 ice cubes in four individual bowls. Drain the bean-curd cubes and divide them up among the bowls, laying them on top of or beside the ice cubes.

Each diner needs three small, shallow, saucerlike dishes, one containing a quarter of the sliced scallions, another 1 teaspoon of the ginger made into a tiny mound, and the third, 2 tablespoons of soy sauce.

To serve, each diner has the bowl of bean curd in front of him and the three small dishes with the seasonings arranged on one side. He can now mix his dipping sauce as he pleases, adding as much of the ginger and scallions to the soy sauce as he desires. Or he can keep the seasonings unmixed, and pick up a little ginger and scallions when wanted. The bean-curd cube is picked up with chopsticks, dipped into the soy sauce—seasoned with the ginger and scallions or unseasoned—and then eaten.

Hsu Hung Ying's
BEAN CURD WITH CHINESE PARSLEY
TAIWAN

This refreshing and simple dish is served frequently by the Chinese family that a daughter of mine is staying with in Taipei. It calls for fresh hot red chilies, just as the preceding recipe does. Again, I have substituted strips of fresh sweet red pepper for the color and used Italian hot peppers for the actual fire. The heat of this dish will depend upon the hotness of the peppers. If you prefer the bean curd to be less hot, use just one hot pepper and increase the sweet red pepper.

(serves 2–4)

2 hot Italian peppers
½ smallish sweet red pepper
1 teaspoon cornstarch
2 tablespoons vegetable oil
¼ teaspoon salt
½ pound medium bean curd, cut into ¾-inch cubes

1 tablespoon Chinese thin soy sauce
½ cup finely chopped fresh Chinese parsley, very firmly packed

Cut the hot and sweet peppers into very thin, 1½-inch-long strips.

Mix the cornstarch with ¼ cup water in a small cup.

Heat the oil in a wok over a medium flame. When hot, put in the pepper strips and the salt. Stir and fry for 30 seconds. Put in the cubes of bean curd. Stir gently to mix. Turn heat to low. Dribble the soy sauce over the bean curd. Give the cornstarch mixture a quick stir and pour it over the bean curd. Scatter the parsley over the top. Turn the heat up very slightly and cook until the sauce thickens slightly. Stir very gently during this time. Serve hot.

For information about ingredients and basic techniques that may be unfamiliar, see General Information, pages 418–36.

BEAN CURD WITH BROCCOLI

HONG KONG

You will probably need about half a bunch of broccoli for this dish. Cut the broccoli into small, slim flowerets, peeling the stem wherever it looks too coarse. Each piece should be no more than 1½ inches long. Sometimes I soak the broccoli in cold water for half an hour before cooking it in order to make it extra crisp. If you use some of the thicker parts of the stem too, just peel them and cut into somewhat coarse julienne strips.

(serves 4)

1½ teaspoons cornstarch
¾ cup Delicious Stock . . . (see page 292)
1 tablespoon *shaohsing* wine or dry sherry
2 teaspoons Chinese thin soy sauce
1 tablespoon sesame oil
1 scallion
4 tablespoons vegetable oil
2 quarter-sized slices of fresh ginger, peeled and cut into strips
2 cloves garlic, peeled and cut into thin strips
2 heaping cups broccoli flowerets and stems (see above)
½ teaspoon salt
½ pound medium bean curd, cut into 1 × ½-inch pieces

Put the cornstarch in a cup. Slowly add ¼ cup stock and mix. Add the wine, soy sauce, and sesame oil. Mix again.

Cut the scallion into 1½-inch lengths and then cut each piece lengthwise into strips.

Heat the vegetable oil in a wok over medium heat. When hot, put in the ginger and garlic. Stir and fry for 10 seconds. Put in the broccoli and scallion. Stir and fry for a minute. Add ½ cup stock and the salt. Bring to a simmer. Cover and cook on medium-low heat for a minute or until broccoli is tender-crisp. Remove the broccoli with a slotted spoon and keep in a bowl. Turn heat to low and put in the bean curd. Let it heat through in the small amount of remaining liquid. Give the cornstarch mixture a quick stir and pour it over the bean curd. Mix very gently. Put the broccoli back into the wok. Stir gently to mix. Serve as soon as the sauce is thick and everything is heated through.

CABBAGE COOKED WITH BEAN CURD

JAPAN

One very cold winter day, when I was scouring Kyoto for vegetarian dishes, I walked into a tiny macrobiotics shop on the outskirts of the city. There I was offered warming tea and, as we talked, told of many simple dishes that are not a part of Japan's haute cuisine but are, nonetheless, very tasty and nourishing. This is one of those dishes.

(serves 3–4)

3 large *shiitake* mushrooms
2 cakes medium or hard bean curd
   (about 8 ounces.)
1 pound cabbage — ½ small-sized cabbage
3 tablespoons vegetable oil
½ teaspoon salt
2 teaspoons Japanese soy sauce
1 teaspoon *mirin*

Soak mushrooms in ¾ cup hot water for ½ hour.

Put the bean curd on a tilted, paper-towel-lined board and leave to drain for 20 minutes.

Cut the cabbage half in two, lengthwise. Remove core. Slice cabbage into long shreds, ¼-inch wide.

Remove mushrooms from their soaking liquid. (Save soaking liquid to make *dashi* or other soup.) Cut off and discard coarse stems. Slice the caps into ¼-inch-wide strips.

Heat the oil in an 8-inch skillet over a medium-high flame. When hot, put in the cabbage and mushrooms. Stir and fry for about 1 minute or until cabbage wilts. Now turn heat down to medium. Crumble the bean curd and add it to the skillet. Add the salt, soy sauce, and *mirin* as well. Stir and fry for another 4–5 minutes.

BEAN CURD WITH A DELICIOUSLY SPICY SAUCE

CHINA

If I was *forced* to pick my favorite bean-curd recipe—*forced*, mind you, since I do not normally make such commitments—I might pick this dish. From start to finish, it takes me about 10 minutes to prepare, as I always have vegetable stock sitting in my refrigerator or freezer.

You may make this dish with any fresh bean curd—soft, medium, or hard. Each will give its own very different texture to the dish.

(serves 4)

THE SAUCE
2 teaspoons cornstarch
½ cup Vegetable Stock (see page 292)
1 teaspoon chili paste with soy bean
2 tablespoons Chinese thin soy sauce
1 tablespoon sesame oil
½ teaspoon salt
½ teaspoon sugar

2 tablespoons vegetable oil
3 cloves garlic, peeled and minced
1 teaspoon very finely minced fresh ginger
3 scallions, very finely sliced into rounds, including three-quarters of the green
1 pound bean curd, cut into 1-inch cubes

Prepare the sauce. Put the cornstarch in a small bowl. Slowly add the vegetable stock, mixing as you do so. Now add the chili paste, soy sauce, sesame oil, salt, and sugar. Mix again. Set the sauce aside.

Heat the vegetable oil in a wok over a medium-

For information about ingredients and basic techniques that may be unfamiliar, see General Information, pages 418–36.

high flame. When hot, put in the garlic and ginger. Stir and fry for 10 seconds. Add the scallions. Stir and fry for 5 seconds. Put in the bean curd. Stir and fry for 1 minute. Turn heat to low. Stir the sauce and pour it over the bean curd. Mix gently and bring to a simmer. Let the sauce thicken, stirring gently every now and then as it does so.

CARROTS AND BEANS WITH A BEAN-CURD DRESSING

JAPAN

For this dish, you can use soft, regular, or hard bean curd.

(serves 6–8)

2   bean-curd cakes (8 ounces)
¾   pound green beans
¾   pound (about 4) carrots
4   tablespoons roasted and ground sesame seeds
1   tablespoon sugar
1   tablespoon *mirin*
1   teaspoon salt
1   teaspoon soy sauce
2   tablespoons *dashi* (see page 291) or water

Put the bean-curd cakes into a small pot and cover with water (about 3 cups). Bring to a boil. Lower heat and simmer very gently for 10 minutes. Drain.

Meanwhile, prepare the vegetables: Trim and French-cut the beans into 2-inch-long diagonal strips. Trim, peel, and cut carrots into very fine, 2-inch-long julienne strips.

Put the drained bean curd, the roasted and ground sesame seeds, sugar, *mirin*, salt, soy sauce, and *dashi* into the container of a food processor or blender. Blend until you have a paste. Set aside.

Bring two pots, each containing about 3 quarts of water, to a boil. When boiling, drop the "Frenched" beans into one pot and the julienned carrots into the other. Drain the carrots after 2 to 3 minutes. They should be cooked through but still crunchy. Drain the beans after about 4 minutes. They should be cooked through but still have a bite to them.

Put the carrots and beans in a bowl. Add the dressing and mix well. Serve hot, warm, or at room temperature.

BEAN CURD, MUSHROOMS, AND PEANUTS IN HOISIN SAUCE
CHINESE STYLE

Stir the hoisin sauce before pouring it out for this recipe.

(serves 4–6)

½ cup hoisin sauce
1 tablespoon Chinese thin soy sauce
1 tablespoon *shaohsing* wine or dry sherry
1 teaspoon sesame oil
Salt
Freshly ground black pepper
½ pound medium bean curd
¼ pound fresh mushrooms
1 clove garlic, peeled
2 quarter-sized slices of fresh ginger
4 tablespoons vegetable oil
¾ cup bamboo shoots, cut into ¾-inch dice
3 tablespoons roasted or fried, unsalted peanuts
2 tablespoons finely sliced scallions

Mix together the hoisin sauce, soy sauce, wine, sesame oil, ½ teaspoon salt, black pepper, and ½ cup water in a bowl.

Cut the bean curd into ¾-inch dice.

Wipe off the mushrooms and, depending upon their size, halve or quarter them so that they are about the same size as the bean curd.

Cut the clove of garlic into fine slivers.

Cut the slices of ginger into slivers.

Heat a wok over a medium flame. Put in 2 tablespoons of oil and half of the garlic and ginger. Stir for 5 seconds. Put in the mushrooms. Stir-fry for 30 seconds. Sprinkle about ⅛ teaspoon salt over the mushrooms. Stir once and then remove them and keep in a bowl. Wipe out the wok.

Add 2 more tablespoons of oil to the wok. Put in the remaining garlic and ginger. Stir for 5 seconds. Put in the bamboo shoots and stir-fry for 30 seconds. Put in the hoisin sauce mixture and bring to a simmer. Put in the bean curd and bring to a simmer again. Turn down the heat and simmer very gently for 5 minutes, stirring now and then. Put back the mushrooms and add the peanuts as well. Stir. Heat through and empty into serving dish. Garnish with the scallions.

SAUTÉED BEAN CURD
KOREA

(serves 6)

4 4-ounce cakes of medium bean curd
3 tablespoons vegetable oil

Cut the bean curd into rectangles that are roughly 1½ × ¾ × ¾ inch. Pat dry.

Heat the oil in a 9-inch nonstick or other well-seasoned skillet over a medium-high flame. When hot, put in half the bean curd. Cook for about 3 minutes on one side, or until that side turns a golden color. Turn over and cook the opposite side for about 3 minutes or less or until it, too, is golden. Remove with a slotted spatula and keep on a warmed platter. Do a second batch just as you did the first.

Serve hot, with Korean Dipping Sauce Number 2 (see page 358).

For information about ingredients and basic techniques that may be unfamiliar, see General Information, pages 418–36.

TOFU DENGAKU
(Toasted Bean Curd with a Miso Topping)
JAPAN

Among the very popular winter dishes in Japan is bean curd that is toasted directly over a charcoal fire and then smeared with what looks like a *miso* jam. The toasting is done by the same method used for marshmallows. Small rectangles of bean curd are pierced with skewers and then held up over the fire. The skewers have to be very light and supportive—the Japanese use dainty, double-pronged bamboo skewers—or else the bean curd would fall off them. Also, the bean curd itself has to be made fairly firm by pressing it under a weight before it can be expected to hold its shape.

If you can find forked *dengaku* skewers, toast the bean curd on both sides over a direct flame, either charcoal or gas. If you cannot find the skewers, follow my method of cooking the bean curd on a hot cast-iron griddle or skillet.

(serves 4)

12 ounces medium or hard bean curd
6 to 7 spinach leaves
6 tablespoons white *miso*
2 tablespoons *sake*
2 tablespoons *mirin*
1 tablespoon sugar
¼ cup *dashi* (see page 291) or water
1 teaspoon roasted sesame seeds

Wrap the bean-curd cakes in a dish towel and put a ½-pound weight—such as a plate or a baking tray with a small jar—on top. Let the bean curd sit this way for 1 to 1½ hours, depending upon whether it is hard or medium to begin with. Change the dish towel whenever it gets soaking wet.

Drop the spinach leaves into 3 cups of boiling water and boil rapidly for a minute. Drain and rinse under cold water. Mince.

Combine the *miso*, *sake*, *mirin*, sugar, and *dashi*. Mix to form a smooth paste. Pour this paste into a small, heavy pot or a small, heavy skillet (I use a well-seasoned, 5-inch, cast-iron skillet) and set over a medium-low flame. When the mixture begins to bubble, turn the flame to low. Stir and cook the mixture until it is as thick as applesauce. Remove from the fire and cool. Add the spinach and the sesame seeds. Mix.

Cut the bean curd into rectangles that are no bigger than 2½ × 1 × ¾ inch.

Heat a cast-iron skillet or griddle over a medium flame until it is very hot. Lay the bean-curd pieces in it. Cook each side 2 to 3 minutes or until lightly browned, turning the pieces over carefully with a spatula.

Now smear one side of each piece generously with the *miso* paste. Serve this way or place under a broiler, *miso* side up, until a few dark spots develop. Serve hot.

FRIED BEAN-CURD CUBES

MOST OF EAST ASIA

Fried bean curd develops a nice chewy crust and is used in many meatless dishes throughout East Asia. This recipe will make cubes of fried bean curd. It will not make *aburage*, the fried bean-curd pillow-cases used for Japanese stuffed bean-curd recipes.

Cakes of medium bean curd
Vegetable oil for deep frying

Spread out a dish towel or a paper towel on a slightly tilted board. Lay one or more cakes of bean curd on it in a single layer. Fold the towel over the bean curd. Now put a weight—about ½ pound—on top of the cakes. (If you are frying more than one cake, you could put a baking tray over the towel and then put a small jar on the tray.) Press the bean curd this way for about 1½ hours, changing the towel whenever it gets soaking wet.

Heat oil for deep frying in a wok over a medium flame. Cut the bean curd into 1-inch cubes. When the oil is hot, put in as many bean-curd cubes as the wok will hold in a single layer. Fry, stirring now and then, until cubes are a golden color—about 7 minutes. Remove with a slotted spoon and drain on paper towels.

NOTE: To remove some of the grease from fried bean curd and in order to soften their crusts some-what, the cubes are often dunked in boiling water. This also makes them more porous and more capa-ble of absorbing other flavors.

Yien-Koo's

SOY-BEAN SPROUTS SAUTÉED WITH FRIED BEAN CURD

CHINA

(serves 4–6)

½ pound fried bean-curd cubes (see preceding recipe) or ½ pound store-bought fried bean-curd cubes
4 tablespoons vegetable oil
2 to 3 quarter-sized slices of fresh ginger
1¼ pounds (4 well-packed cups) soy-bean sprouts, thread-like ends removed, washed, and drained
3 tablespoons preserved snow cabbage
¼ teaspoon salt
¼ teaspoon sugar
1 tablespoon Chinese thin soy sauce

Pour 8 cups of boiling water over the bean-curd cubes. Dunk them a few times in the water to remove extra oil. Take the cubes out of the water and squeeze them gently to remove extra water. Quarter each cube diagonally to form small trian-gles.

Heat the oil in a wok over a medium-high flame. When hot, put in the ginger slices. Stir them around for 5 to 6 seconds, pressing them occasionally against the sides of the wok. Turn heat to medium and put in the soy-bean sprouts. Stir the sprouts for 2 to 3 minutes. Now put in the fried bean curd and the preserved snow cabbage. Stir-fry another 2 minutes. Add the salt, sugar, and soy sauce. Stir to mix.

Remove the ginger slices and serve hot or cold. I find that this dish makes an excellent lunch if taken to work in a plastic container.

For information about ingredients and basic techniques that may be unfamiliar, see General Information, pages 418–36.

FRIED BEAN CURD WITH A SWEET-AND-SOUR SAUCE

CHINA

(serves 4–6)

THE SAUCE

1½ teaspoons cornstarch
3 tablespoons plus ¾ cup Delicious Stock . . . (see page 292)
3 tablespoons distilled white vinegar
3 tablespoons sugar
1 tablespoon tomato ketchup
2 tablespoons Chinese thin soy sauce
½ teaspoon salt
⅛ to ¼ teaspoon cayenne pepper
Freshly ground black pepper
1 tablespoon vegetable oil
1 clove garlic, peeled
1 quarter-sized slice of fresh ginger

1 carrot
½ small, fresh sweet red pepper
½ medium-sized green bell pepper
2 scallions
¾ pound bean curd, cut into 1-inch cubes and fried (see page 176)
2½ teaspoons salt
2 tablespoons vegetable oil

Mix the cornstarch with 3 tablespoons of the stock in a small cup.

Combine the ¾ cup stock, vinegar, sugar, ketchup, soy sauce, ½ teaspoon salt, cayenne pepper, and black pepper in a bowl.

Heat the 1 tablespoon oil in a small pot over a medium flame. When hot, put in the garlic and ginger. Stir. As soon as the garlic browns, take the pot off the flame and pour the vinegar mixture from the bowl into it. Put the pot back on the fire and bring to a boil. Turn heat to low and simmer very gently for 4 minutes. Give the cornstarch mixture a quick stir and add that to the pot. Stir and cook gently until the sauce thickens. Check seasonings and add more salt if you think you need it. Remove the garlic and ginger.

Peel the carrot and cut into ¹⁄₁₆-inch-thick diagonal slices. Cut a few slices at a time into very thin strips.

Cut the red and green pepper into very thin strips.

Cut the scallions into 1½-inch lengths. Cut each section lengthwise into very thin strips.

Put the cubes of fried bean curd in a bowl. Add 2 teaspoons salt to 6 cups of water and bring to a boil. Pour this boiling water over the bean curd. Dunk the bean-curd cubes a few times and then leave them in the water.

Heat the 2 tablespoons of oil in a wok over a medium-high flame. Put in ½ teaspoon salt and the carrot, red and green pepper, and scallions. Stir-fry for 30 seconds. Turn off the heat.

Heat the prepared sauce over a low flame. Take the bean curd out of the hot water. Squeeze gently to get rid of extra moisture and put the cubes on a serving platter. Spread the vegetables over the bean curd. Pour the sauce over the vegetables.

Ichehara Takao's
FRIED BEAN-CURD CAKES WITH A MUSTARD SURPRISE
JAPAN

This dish is quite scrumptious—and very easy to make. You need whole cakes of bean curd for it. The size does not really matter as long as they are not much larger than 3 × 3 × 1½ inch. If you are using homemade bean curd, cut it to form such cakes.

(serves 4)

4   medium bean-curd cakes
4   scallions
2   tablespoons plus 2 teaspoons
    Japanese soy sauce
2   tablespoons plus 2 teaspoons *mirin*
¼   cup *dashi* (see page 291)
1   teaspoon English-type dry mustard
4   cut pieces of *nori*, each about 1½ inches square
Vegetable oil for deep frying

Lay two of the bean-curd cakes side by side on a dish towel toward one end of it. Cover over with the longer remaining portion of dish towel. Lay the two other cakes of bean curd on top of the first two pieces. The towel will, of course, be between the two layers. Fold the towel again over this second layer. Now place a baking tray over the top of the towel and put a ½-pound weight in the tray. Press the bean curd this way for 2 hours, changing the towel and moving the top layer to the bottom every time the dish towel gets soaked.

Cut the scallions into very fine rounds. Put the rounds into ice water and refrigerate for 1 hour or longer. Drain and pat dry.

Mix the soy sauce, *mirin*, and *dashi*.

Mix the mustard with 1 teaspoon hot water so you have a paste.

Scoop out a hole, about ¾ inch in diameter and of about the same depth, in the center of one of the larger sides in each cake of bean curd. If possible, remove the scooped-out section in one single conical piece. Now put a quarter of the mustard in the center of each piece of *nori*. Turn up the corners of the nori to cup the mustard and stuff these cups into the holes in the bean curd. Cover these holes with the conical pieces of bean curd that you scooped out. A little protruding *nori* is to be expected.

Heat oil for deep frying in a wok over a medium flame. When hot, put in as many cakes, mustard side up, as the wok will hold in a single layer. Fry for about 5 to 7 minutes or until a nice golden-red color. Every now and then, push the cakes into the oil or else baste them with the hot oil. Remove the cakes with slotted spoons and drain on paper towels.

Divide the soy-sauce mixture among four saucer-shaped shallow bowls. Put the fried bean-curd cakes in the center of each bowl, right on top of the sauce. Top each cake with a mound of scallions. Serve hot, warm, or even at room temperature. As each mouthful of bean curd is eaten, it should be dipped in the sauce.

For information about ingredients and basic techniques that may be unfamiliar, see General Information, pages 418–36.

INARI-ZUSHI
("Bags" of Fried Bean Curd, Stuffed with Sushi Rice)

JAPAN

It is easiest to make this dish with store-bought fried, thin bean curd, sold in Japanese and Korean stores as *aburage* or *abura-age*. If you can buy the fresh "pillowcases" that are about 6 × 3 inches and fairly flat, do use them. Your second choice should be the "dry pack" *aburage* that is unseasoned and comes in a can. Your third choice should be the seasoned, prepared *aburage* that is also canned and comes all ready to be stuffed.

Once it is stuffed, *inari-zushi* resembles old-fashioned money pouches. These pouches are, visually, at their most charming when tied with a "ribbon" made out of *kampyo*, or gourd strips. The entire pouch is, of course, edible and is a most popular picnic food. The Japanese often carry their picnic foods in wooden boxes, but for us, box-shaped plastic containers that could hold the bags in a single layer would work equally well. As with all Sushi Rice dishes, these stuffed bean-curd bags should not be refrigerated. They will keep well enough if left in a cool spot for a day. *Inari-zushi* makes for a very amusing—and tasty—appetizer. Pickled ginger slices, *amazu shoga*, available in Japanese stores, should be served on the side.

(makes 6 bags)

3 *aburage* pieces (about 6 × 3 inches, or
   6 pieces 3 inches square)
1 cup *dashi* (see page 291) or water
¼ cup plus 1 teaspoon Japanese soy sauce
2 tablespoons *mirin*
3 tablespoons plus 1 teaspoon sugar
36 inches of *kampyo*

1½ cups freshly made Sushi Rice (page 124)
1 tablespoon roasted sesame seeds, lightly crushed

If you have the larger *aburage* pieces, cut them into halves so you end up with six squares. If you have the smaller pieces, cut a thin strip off one end of each square so the "bags" can open. Put the *aburage* in a bowl and pour about 5 cups of boiling water over it. This will remove some of the oil. Drain and squeeze gently to remove extra moisture.

Combine the *dashi*, soy sauce, *mirin*, and sugar in a small pot. Stir and bring to a simmer. Put in the *aburage* pieces and the *kampyo*. Cover partially and simmer for about 8 minutes, spooning the liquid over the bean curd every now and then. Uncover and let the bean curd and *kampyo* cool in the liquid.

Mix the Sushi Rice and the sesame seeds. Using dampened hands, divide the rice into six parts and form into balls. Gently pry open the bean-curd bags one at a time and stuff each with a ball of rice. Cut the *kampyo* into six 6-inch lengths and tie each bag just above the area where the rice is. Arrange the bags in a single layer in a plastic bag or box and close. Leave in a cool place until ready to serve.

PRESSED BEAN CURD WITH CABBAGE

CHINA

(serves 4)

1 cake (about 3 ounces) pressed, seasoned bean
   curd
½ pound cabbage (about ½ a medium-sized head)
1 to 2 fresh hot green chilies (optional)
4 dried black Chinese mushrooms, soaked in hot
   water for ½ hour
3 scallions
4 tablespoons vegetable oil
3 quarter-sized slices fresh ginger,
   lightly mashed
3 cloves garlic, peeled and minced
2 tablespoons Chinese *shaohsing* wine or dry
   sherry
1 tablespoon Chinese thin soy sauce
⅓ to ½ teaspoon salt
½ teaspoon sugar
2 teaspoons sesame oil

Cut the pressed bean curd into fine julienne strips.
   Core the cabbage and cut into fine, long shreds.
   Cut the green chilies into fine, long strips.
   Drain the mushrooms (save the liquid for soups),
remove the coarse stems, and then cut the caps
into ⅛-inch-thick slices.
   Cut the scallions into 3 pieces each. Now cut
each piece lengthwise into thin strips.
   Heat 1 tablespoon oil in a wok over medium-
high heat. Put in the pressed bean curd. Stir and
fry for about 10 seconds. Remove with a slotted
spoon and place in a bowl.
   Add the remaining 3 tablespoons oil to the wok.
Put in the ginger slices. Stir and fry them for about

20 seconds, pressing them against the sides of the
wok. Add the garlic, stirring and frying for another
15 seconds until the garlic turns a bit brown. Now
put in the green chilies, mushrooms, and scallions.
Stir and fry for about 30 seconds. Put in the cabbage. Stir and fry for 1 minute. Add the wine by
pouring it around the side of the wok, then stir.
Add the soy sauce, salt, sugar, and sesame oil. Stir
and fry for another minute or until the cabbage
has just wilted. Add the bean curd. Stir again.

*For information about ingredients and basic techniques that
may be unfamiliar, see General Information, pages 418–36.*

Yien-Koo's
SALAD OF PRESSED BEAN CURD, MUNG-BEAN SPROUTS, AND AGAR-AGAR
CHINA

This is a simple, easy-to-make, and very tasty salad. A word about the agar-agar. It is available in several forms in Oriental stores—powdered, in small cakes, as well as in vermicellilike strands. It is the strands that you require for this dish. Nothing else will do. As all Chinese and Japanese grocery stores carry this type of agar-agar, it should not be hard to find.

You need about a third of an ounce of agar-agar. Some Japanese stores sell packets that have 0.35 ounces in them. That amount is just right for this dish. I have mostly seen 1-ounce packets in the Chinese grocery stores. Use one-third of such a Chinese packet.

Uncooked soaked agar-agar is a very interesting salad ingredient. It is unflavored, clear, and bouncy. While it picks up the taste of the seasonings, it contributes its own hard jellylike texture to the salads in which it is used.

All the ingredients for this dish can be assembled ahead of time, covered, and then refrigerated. The seasonings, though, should be added only at the last minute or the salad ends up becoming too watery.

(serves 4)

⅓ ounce agar-agar strands
1 cake (about 3 ounces) pressed, seasoned bean curd
4 cups mung-bean sprouts, rinsed and drained
1 tablespoon distilled white vinegar
1 tablespoon Chinese thin soy sauce
1 tablespoon sesame oil
¾ teaspoon salt
1¼ teaspoons sugar

Cut the agar-agar strands into 3-inch pieces with a pair of scissors, then soak them in 2 cups of cold water for half an hour. Drain and pat dry.

Cut the pressed bean curd into fine, julienne strips.

Bring 4 cups of water to a boil in a large pot. When boiling furiously, drop in the mung-bean sprouts. Bring to a boil again. Turn the heat off immediately and drain the sprouts. Rinse the sprouts under cold water and leave to drain for 15 minutes.

Combine the drained agar-agar, the julienned pressed bean curd, and the drained sprouts in a serving bowl. Cover and refrigerate until ready to eat. You may do this a couple of hours ahead of time. Just before serving, add the vinegar, soy sauce, sesame oil, salt, and sugar. Toss to mix.

1

2

3

4

5

HOW TO MAKE FRIED AND BAKED WHEAT-GLUTEN BALLS

I find it useful to make some fried and some baked balls at the same time.

(makes 40 fried balls or 80 smaller baked ones)

1 pound gluten flour (about 3¾ cups)
Vegetable oil for deep frying and/or greasing baking dish

Put the flour in a large bowl. Slowly add about 1½ cups (or a bit more) water and bring the flour together to make an unsticky ball of medium firmness. 1. Knead for 10 to 12 minutes until the dough is smooth. Leave the dough in a bowl, covered with some aluminum foil, for 1 hour. Knead the dough briefly again. Form a ball and put the dough back in the bowl. Now cover the ball of dough with cold water from the faucet and leave overnight.

2. Begin to wash the dough: Treat the dough like a piece of sponge and squeeze it under the water. Keep doing this until the water turns exceedingly milky from the starch. Throw this starchy water away and cover the dough with fresh cold water. You will be throwing away several batches of water as each turns milky until you are left with just gluten, at which point the water remains almost clear. Place this ball of gluten on a tilted board and let it drain for 15 minutes.

FOR FRYING THE BALLS Set up a platter lined with paper towels. Pour oil into a wok for deep frying and heat over a lowish flame. You should aim for a temperature around 325° F.

3. Break the dough into 1-inch balls, working each in your hand so it is as round as possible.
4. Drop four balls into the wok at a slight distance from each other. Baste the balls gently but constantly with the hot oil as you fry them. The frying should take at least 4 minutes. The balls should expand to at least twice their size and turn a reddish color on the outside. If they brown too fast, they will not expand properly. Adjust the heat if that happens.
5. Remove the balls with a slotted spoon and leave to drain on the platter. The balls will collapse as they cool.

FOR BAKING THE BALLS Preheat oven to 375° F.

Grease a cookie sheet lightly with oil. Break the dough into ½-inch balls and lay as many as will fit on the cookie sheet, about 2½ inches apart. Bake for 15 to 20 minutes or until they are quite puffed up and lightly browned.

When fried or baked gluten balls have cooled, they should be packed in plastic bags or plastic containers and either refrigerated or frozen. They should last in the refrigerator for at least 3 days. To defrost frozen balls, just throw them into boiling water or boiling stock and cook for a few minutes.

Baked balls are particularly suited to light stews and soups. Fried balls are better in heartier stews and in stir-fried dishes.

STEW OF BAKED WHEAT GLUTEN, POTATO, TURNIP, CARROT, AND CABBAGE ROLLS

JAPAN

This is one of the many one-pot Japanese dishes that is cooked and served in the same casserole-type utensil. This utensil is sometimes an iron kettle, quaint and old-fashioned; at other times it is a ceramic masterpiece, made out of hard clay. You may use a humbler and less quaint piece of Corningware or else use a nice porcelained pot and then bring it to the table. Such stews are very popular in the wintertime.

(serves 2–4)

4   baked wheat-gluten balls (see page 183)
1   medium-sized potato
1   medium-sized turnip
3   cups Delicious Stock . . . (see page 292)
1½ medium-sized carrots
Salt
3   large, unbroken outer leaves from a Chinese cabbage
15 fresh spinach leaves
Japanese soy sauce
2   teaspoons dry, English-type mustard

Cut each ball of wheat gluten into 2 pieces. Peel the potato and turnip and dice each into about 6 pieces. Put the gluten, potato, turnip, and stock into a casserole-type pot that is wider than its height. Bring to a boil. Cover, turn heat to low and simmer gently for 20 minutes.

Meanwhile, peel the carrots and cut them into ¾-inch-long chunks. Bring about 12 cups of water to a rolling boil in a large pot. Put about 2 teaspoons salt into it. Now put in the cabbage leaves and bring to a boil again. Cook for a couple of minutes or until the leaves wilt. Throw in the spinach leaves and let them wilt, too. Drain the leaves and rinse under cold running water. Gently squeeze some of the moisture out of the leaves. You do not have to be too thorough. 1. Lay one cabbage leaf in front of you with its root end to your left. Lay another cabbage leaf directly over it but with its root end to your right. Lay the third cabbage leaf over the second, with its root end to your left. 2. Lay the spinach leaves lengthwise along the center of the top cabbage leaf. 3. Roll the cabbage leaves lengthwise away from you. Make a tight roll. The spinach will be in the center. 4. Squeeze each of the smaller rolls gently to firm up the shape and get rid of extra water. 5. Cut the roll crosswise at 1-inch intervals.

Once the stew has cooked for 20 minutes, season it very lightly with about ⅛ teaspoon salt or less, leaving it slightly undersalted. 6. Carefully place the cabbage rolls, cut side up, inside the pot, all bunched together in a single layer in one area. Make room for the carrots somewhere near the cabbage rolls and keep the pieces near each other. Bring to a simmer. Cover and simmer on low heat for another 5 to 10 minutes or until carrots are just tender.

Serve hot, with shallow bowls containing extra soy sauce, salt, and a mustard paste made by mixing the 2 teaspoons dry mustard with 2 teaspoons hot water. The stew should be seasoned at the table to your taste.

For information about ingredients and basic techniques that may be unfamiliar, see General Information, pages 418–36.

1

2

3

4

5

6

FRIED WHEAT GLUTEN
WITH BROCCOLI, CARROT, AND MUSHROOMS
CHINA

(serves 4–6)

FOR THE GLUTEN BALLS
4   fried wheat-gluten balls (see page 183)
¾   teaspoon salt
1   teaspoon Chinese thin soy sauce
1   teaspoon sugar

FOR THE SAUCE
¼   cup Delicious Stock . . . (see page 292) or gluten
      cooking water
1   teaspoon cornstarch
1   teaspoon sesame oil
1   tablespoon Chinese thin soy sauce
½   teaspoon sugar

About ½ bunch broccoli (enough to have 2 heaping
      cups when cut)
1   carrot
4   medium-sized mushrooms
2   tablespoons vegetable oil
¾   teaspoon salt
2   cloves garlic, peeled and very lightly crushed
¼   cup Delicious Stock . . . (see page 292) or else
      water from boiling the gluten

Combine all the ingredients listed under gluten balls with 3 cups water and bring to a boil. Cover, turn heat to low, and simmer for 15 minutes. Remove the balls with a slotted spoon and cool slightly. Reserve ¼ cup cooking water, if using it. Cut the balls into ⅓-inch-wide strips.

Add the ¼ cup stock or gluten cooking water gradually to the cornstarch and make a paste in a small cup. Add all the other ingredients for the sauce and mix.

Cut the broccoli into very slim flowerets that are about 2 inches long. Peel the carrot and cut at a slight diagonal into ⅛-inch-thick slices. Wipe the mushrooms with a damp cloth and cut them into ⅛-inch-thick slices, including the stem.

Heat the oil in a wok over a medium flame. When hot, put in the salt and garlic. Stir and fry until the garlic browns lightly. Now put in all the vegetables and the strips of wheat gluten. Stir-fry for about 2 minutes. Pour in the ¼ cup stock, cover immediately and cook for 30 seconds. Remove the cover and turn the flame to low. Give the cornstarch mixture a quick stir and pour it over the vegetables. Turn the heat to medium-low and cook, stirring, until the sauce thickens and reduces slightly. Serve at once.

For information about ingredients and basic techniques that may be unfamiliar, see General Information, pages 418–36.

FRIED WHEAT GLUTEN AND POTATO STEW

INDIAN STYLE

(serves 4)

A ¾-inch cube of fresh ginger, peeled
3 to 4 cloves garlic, peeled
4 fried wheat-gluten balls (see page 183)
3 medium-sized boiling potatoes
2 tablespoons vegetable oil
1 teaspoon whole cumin seeds
¼ teaspoon ground turmeric
⅛ teaspoon cayenne pepper
½ cup Tomato Sauce, homemade (see page 361)
  or canned
¾ teaspoon salt

Put the ginger and garlic into the container of an electric blender or food processor. Add ¼ cup water and blend.

Put the fried wheat-gluten balls in a bowl. Pour about 4 to 5 cups boiling water over them. Squeeze them a few times with a pair of spoons to get rid of the extra oil. Now take them out of the hot water and cut into halves.

Peel the potatoes and cut roughly into ¾- to 1-inch cubes.

Heat the oil in a 2½- to 3-quart pot over a medium flame. When hot, put in the cumin seeds. Stir once. Put in the turmeric and cayenne. Give another stir and pour in the ginger-garlic mixture, making sure you get all of it out of the blender container. Stir for a few seconds until the paste thickens. Put in the potato pieces and stir a few times. Now put in 1¾ cups water, the tomato sauce, salt, and wheat gluten. Stir to mix and bring to a boil. Cover, lower heat, and simmer for half an hour or until potatoes are tender. Check the salt.

SHREDDED WHEAT GLUTEN AND CABBAGE WITH FENNEL SEEDS

INDIAN STYLE

(serves 6)

About ¾ pound cabbage (½ a small-sized head)
4 fried wheat-gluten balls (see page 183)
3 tablespoons vegetable oil
1 teaspoon whole fennel seeds
1 teaspoon whole cumin seeds
1 teaspoon whole black mustard seeds
¼ teaspoon ground turmeric
⅛ teaspoon cayenne pepper
¾ teaspoon salt

Core the cabbage and cut it into very thin, long shreds.

Put the wheat-gluten balls in a bowl. Pour 4 to 5 cups boiling water over them. Squeeze them a few times with a pair of spoons to rid them of extra oil. Take them out of the water and cut them into ⅛-inch-thick strips.

Heat the oil in a wok over a medium flame. When hot, put in the fennel, cumin, and mustard seeds. As soon as the mustard seeds begin to pop, put in the cabbage and the wheat gluten. Stir for 10 seconds. Sprinkle the turmeric, cayenne, and salt over the top. Stir to mix. Add ¼ cup water, turn heat to low and partially cover. Simmer gently for 15 to 20 minutes or until cabbage and gluten are tender. Stir several times during this cooking period.

Ahtong's
BUDDHA'S DELIGHT
(A Mixed Chinese Stew)
HONG KONG

It is customary for many people in Hong Kong, especially those of Buddhist ancestry, to eat vegetarian food on the first day of the Chinese New Year. Large white radishes are hung in doorways for good luck—banging into them is considered auspicious—peach blossom branches and potted mandarin orange plants, all loaded with fruit, are decoratively scattered about the house. Fried melon seeds are nibbled on and, when it comes to sitting down and eating, many homes serve Buddha's Delight and rice.

In fact, just before New Year's Day, the grocery stores are filled with clear plastic packages containing all the dry ingredients needed to make this dish. The ingredients are many: dried black mushrooms; a dried seaweed that resembles crinkly hair; mung-bean cellophane noodles; dried bean-curd skin; tree ear fungus, both black and silver; ginkgo nuts; and red Chinese jujubes. To these dry ingredients are added fresh vegetables. The vegetables can vary. One may put in carrots and snow peas. Or one may add baby corn, straw mushrooms, and Chinese cabbage.·

There is a certain amount of preparation that has to be done in advance—a lot of soaking, the first ingredient requiring 6 to 8 hours. But the dish cooks quickly and easily.

(serves 6)

10 dried jujubes (red Chinese dates)
10 ginkgo nuts, shelled (or canned ginkgo nuts, shelled and peeled)
6 Chinese dried black mushrooms

Salt
5 tablespoons plus 1 teaspoon vegetable oil
2 ounces mung-bean "cellophane" noodles or threads
¼ cup dried hair seaweed, firmly packed
½ cup *shaohsing* wine or dry sherry
2 tablespoons tree ear fungus
2 tablespoons silver ear fungus (or white fungus)
4 rectangles dried bean-curd skin (about 5 × 1½ inches each)
5 1½-inch cubes fried bean curd, each cut diagonally into two pieces
3 fried wheat-gluten balls, each cut into 4 pieces
2 quarter-sized slices of fresh ginger
2 scallions, one cut into 2-inch lengths, the other into very fine slices
¼ cup coarsely julienned carrot
10 snow peas, trimmed with strings removed
1½ cups Delicious Stock . . . (see page 292)
1 tablespoon Chinese thin soy sauce
2 teaspoons sesame oil
1 tablespoon minced fresh Chinese parsley

Soak the dried jujubes in ⅓ cup water for 6 to 8 hours. Drain them and remove the seeds, if you wish.

Soak the ginkgo nuts, if you are using fresh ones, in ⅓ cup water for 2 hours. Then drain and peel them.

Rinse the Chinese mushrooms and soak them in 1 cup hot water for half an hour. Then simmer them, covered, in the same water with ¼ teaspoon salt and 1 teaspoon of the vegetable oil for 15

For information about ingredients and basic techniques that may be unfamiliar, see General Information, pages 418–36.

minutes. Cut off the coarse stems and discard. Slice the caps in half. Reserve the mushroom liquid in case you need it.

Soak the mung-bean noodles in 6 cups cold water for half an hour. Drain and put them in a bowl.

Soak the hair seaweed in a mixture of ½ cup hot water and ½ cup *shaohsing* wine or dry sherry for half an hour. Then swish the seaweed in its soaking liquid, rinsing it and separating the strands. Drain and put it in a saucer, separating the strands again.

Soak the tree ear fungus in 1 cup water for half an hour and the silver ear fungus in a separate cup of water the same amount of time. Drain both and rinse under running water. Feel with your fingers and snip off any hard, coarse sections or knots. Put them together in a bowl.

Cut each bean-curd skin, crosswise, into three pieces and rinse in hot water.

Put the fried bean curd and the wheat gluten in a sieve and pour about 6 cups boiling water over them. Gently squeeze the water out of them and put them together in a bowl.

Arrange all your ingredients near the stove. Now heat the 5 tablespoons oil in a wok or a wide saucepan over a medium flame. When hot, put in the ginger and the 2-inch lengths of scallion. Stir and fry until they turn brown. Remove the ginger and scallion pieces with a slotted spoon and discard them. Put in the tree ear and silver ear fungus. Stir once. Add the fried bean curd, wheat gluten, carrot, snow peas, ginkgo nuts, jujubes, and mushrooms. Stir and fry for 1 minute. Add the cello-

phane noodles, hair seaweed (make sure that the strands are separated), bean-curd skin, stock, salt, and soy sauce. Bring to a boil. Cover, lower heat and simmer gently for 5 minutes. There should be some liquid left at the bottom of the wok. If there is not, add some of the mushroom liquid. Add the sesame oil and stir. Turn off the heat.

Sprinkle with sliced scallions and minced Chinese parsley just before serving. (This dish can be made ahead of time and reheated.)

Eggs

Eggs have more usable protein than almost any other food on earth and, as a double blessing for us, there are such wonderful ways of cooking them. Nothing seems more perfect for a cold winter day than a cup of *chawanmushi*, that amazing cross between a soup and a savory custard. As you ease your spoon into the smooth, barely jelled, trembling mass, you might come across a crisp piece of water chestnut, a slice of mushroom, or even a noodle.

Chawanmushi is a Japanese dish. Asians have their own approach to eggs which makes them taste quite different from their Western counterparts. I once watched a Chinese mother in Singapore prepare a soft-boiled egg for her four-year-old daughter. After the egg had boiled in the usual way, it was removed from its shell and put in a bowl. Then, instead of seasoning it with salt and pepper, the mother dribbled a few drops of soy sauce and a few drops of sesame oil over it, stirred it up, and handed it to her daughter. The daughter kindly allowed me a taste. Just those tiny amounts of seasoning made the egg taste entirely different—and very good. You might also try eating hard-boiled eggs with salt and pepper, Chinese-style and fried eggs with salt and pepper, Indian-style.

Among the brunch dishes that I have added to my repertoire is the Persian *kookoo*. It is an egg pie, not entirely unlike a *frittata*, that is cooked with generous handfuls of fresh herbs, or with cauliflower, or zucchini, or what you will. It is an ideal food to serve to guests in the country and to take out cold on picnics.

Instead of making the more common type of European omelette, you could, instead, have Omelette with Bean Curd. Cut into squares and served with a dipping sauce, it may be eaten with plain rice and a crisp green salad. Or you could have the Indian Omelette with a Spicy Tomato Stuffing. It will perk up your appetite and make you hunger for more. I love to have it with toast and hot cups of tea.

A very charming dish from Korea consists of cooked egg strips, tied into bundles with blanched scallions. The bundles look very pretty and may be served at a buffet or as a first course.

If you are looking for a filling main course for dinner, try the Hard-Boiled Eggs in a Spicy Almond Sauce. It is rich, hot, nutty, and quite excellent when served with an Indian or Persian pilaf.

CHAWANMUSHI
(Steamed Savory Custards)

JAPAN

I do not know why savory custards are not eaten in this country. They are so delicate and delicious that they should be added to every American's repertoire of fine foods. If you just cannot imagine what a savory custard might taste like, think of a Southern corn pudding. Of course, no corn and no milk are used in a *chawanmushi* but the comparison does begin to suggest the possibilities of savory custards. Instead of milk, the Japanese use a delicate stock and then they add bits of vegetables and herbs for color and flavor, such as spinach, scallions, mushrooms, and ginger.

These custards are generally cooked and served in individual, lidded *chawanmushi* cups which resemble handleless teacups, only they are a bit taller. The custards are steamed. This is done by first filling the cups with the egg mixture, covering them, and then immersing them in simmering water in such a way that the water comes about three-quarters of the way up the sides of the cups. The steaming utensil is covered and the custards allowed to steam for about 13 minutes. In order to get the correct texture—the custards should just set, be free of bubbles, and they should not separate—several things should be watched for. 1. Do not let the steaming water bubble vigorously. This causes bubbles in the custard. The heat should be adjusted so the water simmers very, very gently. 2. Begin counting your 13 minutes from the moment you put your custard cups into the water and cover the steaming utensil. Then, if the custard is not set in the required time, give it another minute or so. Overcooking will cause the custards to separate.

To check if the custards have set, insert the tip of a pointed knife into one of them. 3. It is best not to let the custard cups rest on the bottom of the steaming utensil. Improvise a rack—this could be a steaming tray or a flat plate—that sits on a bowl or a set of bowls. Now you can pour in just the correct amount of water so the *chawanmushi* cups will be partially submerged.

What should you use for a steaming utensil and what if you have no *chawanmushi* cups? Any wide pot with a lid will do for a steaming utensil. Whether you need one such pot or two will depend upon the width of your cups, which should not be too crowded inside or they'll be hard to remove. You may use small custard cups, ramekins, small bowls—anything with the approximate capacity of 8 ounces. If the containers have lids, well and good. If not, cover each with aluminum foil, crimping the edges to seal as thoroughly as possible.

Once the custards are cooked, the cups have to be lifted out of the very hot water. In Asia, there are all kinds of gadgets that are specially engineered for this purpose. I have in my kitchen a three-pronged (it looks three-legged) piece of Chinese wizardry that can lift plates or cups out of hot water or steam. Then I have an Indian gadget that looks like a set of pliers. The end that grips is

For information about ingredients and basic techniques that may be unfamiliar, see General Information, pages 418–36.

CHAWANMUSHI WITH BEAN CURD, FRESH MUSHROOMS, AND SPINACH

JAPAN

angled, rather like a beak on a parrot's head. So *it* gets the brunt of the steam or hot water and not your hands. If you cannot get such gadgets in your local Oriental stores, the best solution is to ladle out some of the hot water so it is nowhere near the upper portions of the cups. Then, wearing an oven mitten, lift out the cups one by one. This has to be done rather quickly, as the custards should not go on cooking.

Chawanmushi should be served as soon as it is made. If there are lids, serve the custard covered. If you are using aluminum foil as a cover, take it off in the kitchen. Even though the custard has to be cooked just before it is eaten, the ingredients may be prepared well in advance. The stock may be prepared ahead of time, cooled, and mixed in with the eggs. This mixture may be refrigerated. It should be stirred and strained before being poured into the custard cups. The vegetables that are required may be cut and sliced beforehand, too.

In Japan, *chawanmushi* is often served like a soup course. You may serve it that way or else have it as a light lunch, followed by a green salad and fruit.

I have given two recipes for *chawanmushi*, one with dried mushrooms and water chestnuts and the other with bean curd, fresh mushrooms, and spinach. You can be as creative as you like with this dish, and add leftover vegetables like carrots, peas, and beans to it at will. The Japanese often put cooked noodles into a *chawanmushi* base and call this dish *odamakimushi*. That recipe follows the two recipes for *chawanmushi*.

Read general notes on *chawanmushi*, opposite

(serves 4)

1 4-ounce cake medium or slightly hard bean curd
2 tablespoons Japanese soy sauce
1 tablespoon *mirin*
2 teaspoons sesame oil
1 teaspoon sugar
3 medium-sized mushrooms
2¾ cups Japanese Stock (see page 291), at room temperature
4 large eggs
⅛ teaspoon salt, or to taste
½ teaspoon very finely grated ginger
4 tender spinach leaves, cut crosswise into ¼-inch-wide strips
4 very, very thin lemon slices
1 tablespoon very finely sliced scallion

You need 8 ¾-inch cubes of bean curd for this dish (save the remaining curd for a soup or a dressing). In a small bowl, mix 4 teaspoons soy sauce, 2 teaspoons *mirin*, 1 teaspoon sesame oil, and ½ teaspoon sugar. Add the bean-curd cubes and turn them around gently. Let them sit in this marinade for half an hour, turning them every 5 minutes or so.

Remove stems from mushrooms (reserve for another use) and wipe off the mushroom caps with a damp cloth, then cut into ¹⁄₁₆-inch slices.

Put 2 teaspoons soy sauce, 1 teaspoon *mirin*, 1 teaspoon sesame oil, ½ teaspoon sugar, ¼ cup of the stock, and the sliced mushrooms into a small pot. Bring to a simmer. Cover and simmer for 30 seconds. Turn off heat and uncover. Let the mushrooms cool in this liquid.

Get your steaming utensil ready. See pages 192–193 for details.

Beat the eggs gently in a bowl. Try not to create froth. Add the salt and the ginger. Slowly add the remaining 2½ cups stock, mixing gently as you do so.

Put 2 bean-curd cubes at the bottom of each of four 8-ounce-capacity *chawanmushi* cups. Lift the mushrooms out with a slotted spoon and divide them up among the four cups. (Save the mushroom liquid.) Stir the egg-stock mixture and pour it through a strainer into the four cups, dividing it up equally. Float the shredded spinach on top of the liquid in each cup. Put a thin slice of lemon on top of the spinach. Spoon 2 teaspoons of the mushroom liquid over each piece of lemon and then top the lemon with some scallion slices. Now cover the *chawanmushi* cups and steam according to directions in preceding recipe. Serve immediately.

CHAWANMUSHI WITH SHIITAKE MUSHROOMS, WATER CHESTNUTS, AND SNOW PEAS

JAPAN

Read general notes on *chawanmushi*, pages 192–3.

(serves 4)

2⅔ cups freshly made Japanese Stock (see page 291)
2 teaspoons Japanese soy sauce
1 teaspoon *mirin*
4 mushrooms reserved from stock
4 large eggs
⅛ to ¼ teaspoon salt, or to taste
1 fresh or canned water chestnut,
     peeled and quartered
1 tablespoon very finely sliced scallion, including
     green
2 snow peas, cut in half at a slight diagonal

Let the stock cool completely. Add the extra soy sauce and *mirin* to it.

Remove the coarse mushroom stems and slice each mushroom cap into ⅛-inch-wide slices.

Get your steaming utensil ready. See pages 192–3 for details.

Beat the eggs lightly. Try not to create froth. Add the salt and the stock, mixing gently as you do so. Taste for salt. You may want to add a bit more.

Divide the sliced mushrooms and quartered water chestnut among four 8-ounce *chawanmushi* cups. Pour in about ¾ cup of the egg-stock mixture through a strainer into each of the four cups. (Just divide the liquid evenly.) Now sprinkle the scallion over the liquid and then float a snow-pea half prettily over the top. Cover each cup with its lid or with a piece of aluminum foil. If using the foil, crinkle the edges to seal the cup.

For information about ingredients and basic techniques that may be unfamiliar, see General Information, pages 418–36.

Put the covered cups into barely simmering water, making sure that the water comes about three-quarters of the way up the sides of the cups. Cover the steaming utensil. Steam for about 13 minutes or until custard is just set. Turn off heat and immediately remove custard cups from the hot water. Serve at once. Diners should remove the lids of their cups and then eat the custard with a Chinese (or Japanese—they are the same, really) soupspoon. *Chawanmushi* seems to retain its heat for a long time, so let the first few portions in your spoon cool off slightly before you put them in your mouth.

ODAMAKIMUSHI
(Savory Custard with Noodles)

JAPAN

Read general notes on *chawanmushi*, pages 192–3.

(serves 4)

1¾ cups cooked *udon* noodles, rinsed and drained
2 tablespoons Japanese soy sauce
1 tablespoon *mirin*
1 teaspoon sugar
1 teaspoon sesame oil
4 large eggs
2⅔ cups Delicious Stock . . . (see page 292; or other vegetable stock), at room temperature or cold
¼ teaspoon salt
4 squares of *nori*, 2½ × ½ inches
1 scallion, sliced very fine, including green
4 smallish mushrooms

Put the noodles in a bowl. Mix the soy sauce, *mirin*, sugar, and sesame oil together and pour over the noodles. Toss to mix and set aside for 15 minutes.

Beat the eggs well but not to a froth. Add the stock and the salt. Beat gently to mix. Strain.

Divide the noodles among four 12-ounce bowls. Stir the egg mixture and divide it evenly among the four bowls. Float a square of *nori* in the center of each bowl. Sprinkle the scallion slices over the *nori*. Cut each mushroom into 4 slices and float the slices just outside the *nori*. Cover each bowl with a lid or with a piece of aluminum foil. If using foil, crinkle the edges to seal the bowl.

Put the covered bowls in barely simmering water, making sure that the water comes three-quarters of the way up the sides of the bowls. Cover the steaming utensil. Steam for about 13 minutes or until custards are just set. Turn off the heat and immediately remove the custard bowls from the hot water. Serve right away.

SCRAMBLED EGGS WITH CABBAGE

JAPAN

I make all my scrambled eggs in nonstick skillets. You can, of course, use a heavy, well-seasoned skillet instead.

(serves 2)

3 medium-sized dried *shiitake* mushrooms
2 large eggs
¼ teaspoon plus ⅛ teaspoon salt
1 tablespoon *dashi* (see page 291)
½ teaspoon sugar
¾ teaspoon Japanese soy sauce
¾ teaspoon *mirin*
2 tablespoons vegetable oil
2 cups cabbage leaves cut into ½-inch squares

Soak the *shiitake* mushrooms in 1 cup hot water for half an hour; you may use mushrooms left from making *dashi*.

Beat the eggs lightly. Add the ¼ teaspoon salt, *dashi*, sugar, soy sauce, and *mirin*.

Drain the mushrooms (save the soaking liquid for stock). Cut off and discard their coarse stems and then quarter the mushroom caps.

Heat the oil in a 7- to 8-inch nonstick skillet over a medium flame. When hot, put in the mushrooms and sauté them for about 30 seconds. Add the cabbage and sauté it for about 2 minutes or until it is wilted but still slightly crunchy. Sprinkle with ⅛ teaspoon salt and stir.

Strain the eggs into the skillet and stir them around, "scrambling" them to the consistency you like. Try and keep them on the soft side. Remove from skillet as soon as eggs are done.

For information about ingredients and basic techniques that may be unfamiliar, see General Information, pages 418–36.

Yien-koo's

SCRAMBLED EGGS WITH CHINESE CHIVES

CHINA

(serves 2)

3 tablespoons peanut oil
⅛ teaspoon salt, or to taste
About 2 tablespoons Chinese chives, cut into
   1½-inch lengths
4 large eggs, beaten

Heat the oil in an 8- to 10-inch, well-seasoned or nonstick skillet over a medium-high flame. Add the salt to the skillet and stir it around. Put in the chives and stir-fry them for 3 to 4 seconds. Now put in the eggs. Stir them gently 3 to 4 times in the next 5 to 10 seconds. The eggs should be very softly scrambled. Empty eggs immediately onto warm plates and serve with plain rice, Chinese style, or with toast.

SCRAMBLED EGGS WITH SPICY TOMATOES

INDIA

I like to make this dish very hot (chili hot) but you could leave out the green chilies and still have a very tasty dish. Also, if you have no access to good tomatoes, use canned ones. Just drain them well before chopping them. You should end up with about 2 cups of drained, chopped tomatoes.

The spicy tomato sauce used to make these scrambled eggs is very interesting in its own right. You can serve it under or over fried eggs to have an Indian version of the Mexican *huevos rancheros*.

You could make a Persian-style *kookoo* with it (see page 202), or you could use it to stuff an omelette (see opposite column).

The thick sauce is nice to have around in the refrigerator or freezer. It serves as an excellent relish and turns into a superb sauce for pasta.

(serves 4)

THE SPICY TOMATO SAUCE

1 pound red-ripe tomatoes, peeled
3 tablespoons vegetable oil
1½ teaspoons whole black mustard seeds
1 cup very finely sliced scallions (about 4 whole scallions, including green)
2 large cloves garlic, peeled and minced (about 1 tablespoon)
½ teaspoon finely grated fresh ginger
3 tablespoons finely minced fresh Chinese parsley
1 fresh hot green chili (or to taste), minced
½ to ¾ teaspoon salt
⅟₁₆ teaspoon freshly ground black pepper

7 large eggs
Salt to taste

Chop the tomatoes very fine.

Heat the oil in an 8-inch, very well-seasoned or nonstick skillet over a medium-low flame. When hot, put in the mustard seeds. As soon as the mustard seeds begin to pop (this takes just a few seconds), put in the sliced scallions and garlic. Stir and fry for about 3 minutes or until the scallion whites are almost translucent but not browned at all. Now add the tomato pulp, the ginger, Chinese parsley, and the green chili. Stir and fry over medium heat for 6 to 8 minutes. The tomatoes should not remain watery. Add ½ teaspoon salt and the black pepper. Mix, and correct seasonings. Turn off heat.

Beat the eggs lightly with a fork or a whisk. Add less than ¼ teaspoon salt to the eggs and mix.

Bring the sauce in the skillet to a simmer. Turn heat to low. Add the eggs to the skillet. Stir gently but continuously to scramble the eggs. Remove from the fire when the degree of doneness has been achieved. Serve immediately.

OMELETTE WITH A SPICY TOMATO STUFFING

INDIA
(serves 2)

6 large eggs
About ⅛ teaspoon salt, or to taste
2 tablespoons unsalted butter
Spicy tomato sauce (see preceding recipe), heated

Put the eggs in a bowl. Add 2 tablespoons water and the salt. Beat thoroughly until eggs are light and bubbly.

Heat 1 tablespoon butter in a 7- to 8-inch, very well-seasoned or nonstick skillet over a medium flame. When the butter has melted and is foaming, pour in half the beaten eggs. Keep stirring the eggs with the flat bottom of a fork or with a narrow plastic spatula until the eggs begin to set. (Those who like their omelettes fairly firm should cover the skillet for a minute and turn the heat to low.) Spread half the tomato sauce over the half of the omelette that is nearest you. Now slide your spatula under the half of the omelette that is farthest from you and fold it over the tomato mixture. Slide the folded omelette onto a warm plate.

Make a second omelette the same way.

OMELETTE WITH BEAN CURD

JAPAN

This is a thick Japanese omelette that is cut into squares and served with a dipping sauce. It is delicious and very nourishing at the same time. Unlike French omelettes, it can be served several hours after it is made and at room temperature. It seems to be equally popular as an appetizer and as a main course.

Like most of my egg dishes, I make this omelette in a nonstick skillet. A heavy, well-seasoned skillet would also work well. For this dish you could use bean curd that has been sitting around in the refrigerator for a few days.

(Serves 4 as a main course,
up to 24 as an appetizer)

6   ounces hard bean curd (about 1½ cakes)
3   medium-sized dried *shiitake* mushrooms
½   teaspoon salt
½   teaspoon sugar
2   tablespoons shelled fresh or defrosted frozen peas
2   large eggs
1   teaspoon *mirin*
1   tablespoon Japanese soy sauce
½   teaspoon all-purpose white flour
A dash of 7-spice seasoning
1   tablespoon vegetable oil

Put a piece of paper towel on a slightly tilted board and let the bean curd sit on it for an hour. Soak the mushrooms in 1 cup hot water for half an hour. Put the bean curd on a plate and mash it up with a fork. Now put the bean curd in the center of a dish towel. Bring the ends of the towel together and squeeze out as much liquid as you can. Set the bean curd aside.

Bring 1 cup of water to a boil in a small pot. Add ¼ teaspoon of the salt, ¼ teaspoon of the sugar, and the peas. Boil gently for about 3 minutes or until peas are just cooked through. Drain through a strainer. Put the strainer under cold running water and cool off the peas. Set the peas aside.

Drain the mushrooms (save the liquid for stock). Cut off the coarse stems and slice the caps into ¹⁄₁₆-inch-wide strips. Set aside.

Beat the eggs lightly. Add ¼ teaspoon salt, ¼ teaspoon sugar, *mirin*, soy sauce, flour, and the 7-spice seasoning. Mix well. Now add the bean curd, peas, and mushrooms. Mix again.

Heat the oil in a 7- to 8-inch-wide, nonstick skillet over a lowish flame. When hot, pour the egg-bean curd mixture in the center of the skillet. Using a plastic spatula, spread the mixture so it forms a square cake, about 6½ × 6½ inches and flat on the top. Tidy up the edges by pushing inward with the spatula. Make neat corners, if possible. Cover, and let the omelette cook for about 10 minutes or until it is quite set. It will get lightly browned on the bottom.

Remove omelette and place, brown side down, on a flat plate large enough to hold it. Cut into roughly 1-inch squares. (Smaller squares—½ inch in length and width—may be cut if serving this omelette with drinks.) Serve omelette hot, warm, or at room temperature. Once it has cooled off, it should be covered to prevent it from drying out. With it, pass Japanese Dipping Sauce (see page 357).

For information about ingredients and basic techniques that may be unfamiliar, see General Information, pages 418–36.

INDONESIAN OMELETTE: Without too much trouble, this very Japanese dish can be transformed into an Indonesian one! Just put the omelette cubes on a bed of lightly sautéed and lightly salted mung-bean sprouts. Sprinkle some chopped-up Chinese parsley as well as some Crisply Fried Onions over the top and serve with Spicy Peanut Sambal.

EGG FU YUNG

AMERICAN CHINESE

When I first came to New York and was scouting around for cheap places to eat, I was taken to a Chinese restaurant on Eighth Avenue in the Times Square area and advised to order a specialty called "egg foo yong." It consisted of a thick, round omelette, filled with bean sprouts and scallions and doused with a tasty brownish sauce. I loved it. Now my sophisticated Chinese friends tell me that the dish I ate was not authentically Chinese. Well, all that I can say to them is that it is too late. I have acquired a taste for it and refuse to give it up. Here is my vegetarian version of it, which is best eaten with rice. I make rather a lot of sauce because I like to spoon it over the rice.

(serves 2–4)

FOR THE SAUCE
½ cup fresh or frozen peas
1¼ cups Delicious Stock . . . (see page 292)
2½ teaspoons cornstarch
¾ teaspoon Marmite
1 tablespoon *shaohsing* wine or dry sherry
¼ teaspoon salt

Freshly ground black pepper
1½ tablespoons vegetable oil
5 medium-sized mushrooms, sliced

FOR THE OMELETTE
4 large eggs
2 scallions, sliced fine, including green
¾ cup mung-bean sprouts, washed and drained
⅛ teaspoon salt
Freshly ground black pepper
4 tablespoons vegetable oil

Drop the peas in 2 cups rapidly boiling water for 2 to 5 minutes or until they are just cooked through. Drain and rinse immediately under running water to set their bright-green color. These peas will now be added to the sauce just before serving.

Slowly add ¼ cup stock to the cornstarch, mixing it well as you do so. Also add the Marmite, *shaohsing* wine, the ¼ teaspoon salt, and some black pepper. Mix until Marmite is dissolved. Add the remaining 1 cup stock and mix.

Over a medium flame, heat the 1½ tablespoons of oil in a small saucepan. When hot, put in the mushrooms. Stir and fry for 1 minute. Give the stock mixture a stir and pour it in. Bring to a simmer. Turn heat to low and simmer for 2 minutes. Keep the sauce warm.

Beat the eggs but not to a froth. Add the scallions, bean sprouts, ⅛ teaspoon salt, and some black pepper. Mix.

Heat the 4 tablespoons oil in a nonstick or well-seasoned 8-inch skillet over a medium flame. When hot, pour in the egg mixture. Now, working quickly with a spatula, collect the solids in the center. As the liquid flows to the outer edges and sets slightly, fold it over the center. Keep doing this on all sides until you have a 6-inch, cakelike omelette. Turn the heat down and cover. The omelette may turn slightly brown at the bottom. It should definitely set properly and not be runny in the middle. This will take about 2 minutes. Using one large or two smaller spatulas, turn the cake over and cook the second side on low heat for a couple of minutes.

Put the omelette cake into the center of a warm serving platter. Add the peas to the warm sauce and spoon about half the sauce over the omelette. The rest of the sauce may be served on the side.

DATÉMAKI
(Japanese Rolled Omelette)
JAPAN

Datémaki is a very delicate Japanese omelette that is made up of several rolled layers. It looks initially like a log and, in the stores in Japan that specialize in the product, it is sold in various sizes. The logs are then sliced into "wheels" and served as appetizers, first courses, or on top of rice for lunch. A dipping sauce is often served on the side.

This omelette is traditionally made in rectangular skillets. I have one that might be considered small—about 5 inches wide, 7½ inches long, and 1 inch in height. It is made of tin-lined copper. You can get inexpensive rectangular skillets in any Japanese food store. The kind that are easiest to use are lined with a nonstick surface.

(Serves 4–6 as an appetizer)

3 large eggs
¼ cup *dashi* (see page 291)
⅛ to ¼ teaspoon salt, or to taste

¼ teaspoon Japanese soy sauce
¼ teaspoon sugar
About 2 tablespoons vegetable oil

Beat the eggs lightly in a bowl. Add the *dashi*, salt, soy sauce, and sugar. Mix.
1. Brush a 5 × 7½-inch *datémaki* skillet with oil and let it heat on a lowish flame. 2. When hot, pour in about 3 tablespoons of batter. Tilt the skillet to spread it around evenly. It should cover the entire bottom of the skillet. Let the batter set. 3. Now roll it toward you in as tight a roll as you can manage. You may use chopsticks or a spatula to do this. Brush the skillet again with oil. 4. Push the roll away from you so it rests at the far end of the skillet. Brush the end near you with oil. 5. Pour in another 3 tablespoons of batter and spread it around, lifting the roll a little so the batter can flow under it. Let this second layer set. Now roll toward you again, this time incorporating the new layer. The first roll will now be inside the second one. Push the roll toward the far end of the skillet. Keep repeating this process until all the batter is used up. Remove the hot roll from the skillet and place it at one end of a bamboo *sudare* mat. Roll the mat tightly around the *datémaki* and set aside to cool. The omelette will pick up the ridges obligingly provided by the bamboo strips.

For information about ingredients and basic techniques that may be unfamiliar, see General Information, pages 418–36.

NIGIRI-ZUSHI
(Sushi Rice with Datémaki)
JAPAN

To make Nigiri-Zushi, make small ovals of Sushi Rice (see page 124), using about 1½ tablespoons of rice for each oval. Wet your hands to help you form the ovals more easily. Dab a little *wasabi* (see page 360) on top of each oval. Balance a slice of *datémaki* over the *wasabi* and serve with a little soy sauce and some pickled ginger, *amazu shoga* (available in Japanese stores).

To serve, remove the mat and slice *datémak* into ⅓-inch-thick rounds. Offer Japanese Dipping Sauce on the side.

Kookoos

These are thick Persian versions of the omelette which sometimes border on being soufflés. Several eggs are beaten and then combined with herbs and/or vegetables. The mixture is cooked slowly in a skillet on top of the stove (this is the more traditional method) until it acquires a slightly crusty bottom. Then it is turned over to cook on the second side. The pielike omelette is cut into wedges and served hot, warm, or even cold. It is considered excellent picnic fare and is usually accompanied by yogurt. *Kookoos* can also be made in the oven.

Like omelettes, *kookoos* may be cooked with all manner of vegetables and herbs. I have given recipes here for *kookoos* with smoked eggplant, with fresh herbs, with cauliflower, with zucchini, and with tomatoes and scallions. You can make your own combinations using asparagus, green peas (purée them), mushrooms, and green peppers.

Well-seasoned omelette pans or nonstick skillets are the ideal utensils for cooking *kookoos* on top of the stove. When I bake the soufflélike *kookoos* in the oven, I use a nonstick cake tin.

KOOKOO WITH CAULIFLOWER AND PARSLEY
IRAN

This *kookoo* is a great favorite with my family. We often have it for Sunday lunches, accompanied by a green salad, French bread, and lots of tea. Leftovers, if any, are covered and refrigerated. Then when a hungry child comes in later, saying, "What is there to eat in the house?" he can be led directly to a wedge of cauliflower *kookoo*.

I make the *kookoo* in a nonstick skillet that measures 7½ inches in diameter at the bottom and 10 inches across the top. So my *kookoo* ends up being a little over 1 inch high at its center and it takes 25 easy minutes of cooking time. If your skillet has a different set of measurements, you may have to adjust your cooking time and your heat. Remember that the *kookoo* should turn a brown color on the bottom, it should be somewhat crisp at the edges, and the top should end up with brown specks on it. And, of course, it should cook through. *Kookoos* are not runny in the center. Instead, they are slightly spongy.

You will need only half a medium-sized head of cauliflower to make this dish. A 2-pound head

---

For information about ingredients and basic techniques that may be unfamiliar, see General Information, pages 418–36.

may be considered a medium-sized head, I suppose. At any rate, use a 1-pound section of cauliflower.

(Serves 6)

1 pound cauliflower (see note above)
1 tablespoon plus ¾ teaspoon salt
2 tablespoons vegetable oil
3 cloves garlic, peeled and minced
⅓ cup finely sliced scallions, including green
Freshly ground black pepper
7 large eggs
¾ teaspoon baking soda
2 tablespoons finely minced parsley
1 tablespoon unsalted butter

Break the cauliflower up into flowerets, about 1½ inches at the top and 1½ to 2 inches long.

Bring 3 quarts of water to a boil in a 4½-quart pot. Add 1 tablespoon salt to it. When the water is at a rolling boil, drop in the flowerets of cauliflower. Boil rapidly for about 2 minutes. The cauliflower should be cooked through but still crunchy. Drain the cauliflower, run it quickly under cold water while still in the sieve or colander, let it drain thoroughly again, and then mince it.

Heat oil in an 8-inch skillet over medium heat. When hot, put in the minced garlic. Stir garlic around for about 20 seconds. Now put in the scallions. Stir and cook for another 30 seconds. Add the minced cauliflower, ½ teaspoon salt, and a generous amount of freshly ground black pepper. Stir and cook for 2 to 3 minutes. Turn off the heat and let the cauliflower cool slightly.

Beat the eggs well in a large bowl. Add ¼ teaspoon salt,

some black pepper, and the baking soda. Mix thoroughly. Add the cauliflower and the parsley. Mix again.

Heat the butter in a nonstick skillet that is about 7½ inches wide at the bottom (see note above) over a low flame. When hot, pour in the egg-cauliflower mixture. Cover, and let the *kookoo* cook for 20 minutes. It should now be brown on the bottom and slightly crisp at the edges. Turn the *kookoo* over. I just slide a plastic spatula under the *kookoo*, lift it up an inch, tilt the skillet, and turn the *kookoo* over, using the side of the skillet as an aid. If you are unsure about turning over such a large, thick "pie," you can put a plate over your skillet and then flip the skillet over the plate so that the *kookoo* lands on the plate with its bottom side up. You can then slide the *kookoo* back into the skillet.

Cook the *kookoo* on the second side, uncovered, also on low heat, for about 5 minutes, or until it develops brown spots.

Put the pielike *kookoo* on a plate, brown side down and serve hot, warm or cold, cut into wedges.

KOOKOO WITH ZUCCHINI, DILL, AND RAISINS

IRAN

I make this *kookoo* in a nonstick skillet that measures 7½ inches in diameter at the bottom and 10 inches across at the top, so my *kookoo* ends up being about 1 inch high in the center and takes about 20 minutes of cooking time. If your skillet has a different set of measurements, you may have to adjust your cooking time and your heat. Remember that your *kookoo* should turn a brownish color on the bottom, it should be somewhat crisp at the edges, and the top should end up with brown specks on it. And, of course, it should cook through. *Kookoos* are not runny in the center. Instead, they are slightly spongy.

(Serves 6)

2   tablespoons golden raisins
2   medium-sized zucchini (¾ pound in all), trimmed
      and grated
1   teaspoon salt
7   large eggs
½   teaspoon baking soda
⅓   cup minced fresh dill, firmly packed
⅓   cup finely sliced scallions, including green
1   tablespoon unsalted butter

Soak the raisins in 1 cup hot water for 1 hour. Put the grated zucchini and ¾ teaspoon salt into a bowl. Mix well and set aside for half an hour.

After half an hour, take small amounts of the grated zucchini between your two palms and squeeze out as much moisture as possible. Do all the zucchini this way and set aside.

Beat the eggs well in a large bowl. Add ¼ teaspoon salt, the baking soda, drained raisins, dill, and scallions. Mix. Now add the zucchini and mix it in, making sure that it is not bunched up anywhere but is well distributed.

Heat the butter in a 7½-inch-wide (measured at the bottom), nonstick skillet over a low flame. When hot, pour in the egg-zucchini mixture. Cover, and let the *kookoo* cook for 15 minutes. It should now be brown at the bottom and slightly crisp at the edges. Now turn the *kookoo* over. I just slide a plastic spatula under the *kookoo*, lift it up an inch, tilt the skillet, and turn the *kookoo* over, using the side of the skillet as an aid. If you are unsure about turning over such a large, thick pie, you can put a plate over your skillet and then flip the skillet over the plate so that the *kookoo* lands on the plate with its bottom side up. You can then slide the *kookoo* back into the skillet.

Cook the *kookoo* on the second side, uncovered, also on low heat, for about 5 minutes, or until it develops brown spots. Put the pielike *kookoo* on a plate, with its brown side down. Now cut it, just like a pie, into wedges. Serve hot, warm, or cool.

For information about ingredients and basic techniques that may be unfamiliar, see General Information, pages 418–36.

KOOKOO WITH POTATOES

IRAN

(Serves 6)

2 medium-sized boiling potatoes
Salt
Freshly ground black pepper
3 tablespoons vegetable oil
8 eggs
½ teaspoon baking soda
¼ cup minced fresh parsley
2 scallions, cut into fine slices halfway up their
    green sections

Peel the potatoes and slice them crosswise very,
very thin, just as you would potato chips. I use a
mandolin to do this slicing. Starting from the outside and going around in rings of overlapping
slices, line the bottom of a 7- to 8-inch nonstick
skillet with the cut potatoes. Not only should the
slices overlap as you build each ring, but the rings
should overlap slightly as well. Sprinkle about ⅛
teaspoon salt and some black pepper over the
potatoes. Dribble the oil over them. Set the skillet
over a low flame, cover, and cook for 10 minutes.

Meanwhile, beat the eggs well. Add the baking
soda, parsley, scallions, as well as ½ teaspoon salt
and some black pepper. Mix. Pour this egg mixture
over the potatoes. Cover tightly and continue to
cook over low heat for 20 minutes.

Slide the *kookoo* onto a round serving platter.
Cut into wedges and serve hot, at room temperature, or cold.

KOOKOO MADE WITH SPICY, INDIAN-STYLE TOMATOES

(Serves 6)

Spicy tomato sauce (see page 197)
7 large eggs
⅛ to ¼ teaspoon salt, or to taste
½ teaspoon baking soda
1 tablespoon unsalted butter
1 tablespoon lightly roasted sesame seeds

Let the tomato sauce cool and come to room temperature.

Beat the eggs well with a fork or a whisk in a
large bowl. Add the salt (I usually need a little less
than ¼ teaspoon), baking soda, and the tomato
sauce. Mix well.

Heat the butter in a nonstick, 7- to 8-inch skillet
over a low flame. Pour in the egg-tomato combination. Cover, and proceed to make the *kookoo* as
in the recipe for Kookoo with Zucchini, Dill, and
Raisins (see opposite page) *but with this difference*:
After the *kookoo* has cooked for 6 minutes, lift the
lid, quickly sprinkle the sesame seeds over the top,
and cover again. Follow all the other steps in the
recipe, including the turning over of the *kookoo*,
in exactly the same way.

Like all *kookoos*, this may be served hot, warm,
or cold. Put the pielike *kookoo* on a plate with its
brown side down and cut it, just like a pie, into
wedges.

KOOKOO WITH ROASTED EGGPLANT

IRAN

Eggplants roasted over flames have their own very special smoky taste. In my New York apartment, I do this roasting over a gas burner fitted with an aluminum-foil liner. You could also do the roasting under a broiler. As the eggplant can burst, it is a good idea to prick it all over with a fork first.

(Serves 4–6)

1   medium-sized eggplant (about ¾ pound)
2 to 3 teaspoons lemon juice
½ teaspoon salt
2   tablespoons very finely minced parsley
2   tablespoons very finely sliced scallions
2   teaspoons melted unsalted butter or vegetable oil
6   large eggs at room temperature
Freshly ground black pepper

Prick the eggplant in 5 to 6 places with a fork. Now lay the eggplant directly over or under a flame. If you are roasting on top of the stove, keep the heat on low. If you are roasting under the broiler, keep the eggplant a few inches away from the heat. As one side gets charred, turn the eggplant over slightly, using a pair of tongs to do so. Do the entire eggplant this way. It should get very limp by the time it finishes roasting, which may take about 25 minutes.

Peel the eggplant under cold, running water and leave to drain in a colander for 5 minutes. Mince the eggplant and put it in a large bowl. Add the lemon juice and about ¼ teaspoon salt. Adjust the salt and lemon juice according to your taste. Now add the parsley and scallions. Mix and set aside.

Preheat oven to 350° F. Brush a nonstick round cake tin, 9 × 1½ inches, with the butter or oil.

Separate the eggs. Beat the yolks well. Add ¼ teaspoon salt and pepper to them. Mix. Fold the beaten egg yolks into the eggplant.

Beat the egg whites until they stand in stiff peaks (just as you would for a soufflé). Empty the egg whites on top of the eggplant-egg yolk mixture. Using a rubber spatula, fold the egg whites gently into the eggplant-egg yolk mixture, taking care not to deflate them. When well mixed, pour the contents of the large bowl into the cake tin. Put the cake tin in the oven and bake for 45 minutes.

This particular *kookoo* does rise like a soufflé and is a delicate treat if eaten the second it comes out of the oven. However, it is still very good a few (or several) hours later, eaten warm or cold. Plain yogurt or yogurt relishes are always served with *kookoos*.

EGG STRANDS

ALL OF EAST AND SOUTHEAST ASIA

These strands, used mainly for garnishing and salads, may be seasoned before being cooked with sugar and salt, or they may be left unseasoned, depending upon how they are to be used. I use a nonstick skillet to make the initial pancakes but you could also try a very well-seasoned cast-iron skillet.

(makes about 1½ cups)

3   large eggs
1½ teaspoons sugar
About ⅛ teaspoon salt
About 2 teaspoons vegetable oil

For information about ingredients and basic techniques that may be unfamiliar, see General Information, pages 418–36.

Combine the eggs, sugar, salt, and 3 teaspoons water and beat well but not to a froth.

Brush a 7- to 8-inch nonstick skillet lightly with about ½ teaspoon oil and heat on a medium flame. When hot, but not smoking, 1. pour in a quarter of the egg mixture, just enough to barely cover the bottom of the skillet. You will have to tilt the skillet around quickly in order to let the egg mixture flow evenly to the edges. Let the mixture set, which it will do quite quickly. 2. Now turn the pancake over carefully. I loosen the edges first with a flexible spatula, then ease the spatula to the middle of the pancake before flipping it over. Cook for a few seconds on the other side, just until it is firm. Remove the pancake and put it on a plate. Cover loosely with waxed paper or aluminum foil and leave to cool. Make 4 pancakes this way, putting each on its own plate for faster cooling.

3. Roll up each pancake and 4. cut it crosswise at ⅛-inch intervals. Put the egg strands in a closed container. They may now be used to garnish rice and noodle dishes, soups, vegetables, and salads.

EGG BUNDLES

KOREA

Here rectangular egg "pancakes" are cut into neat strips and the strips tied into bundles with blanched scallions. This dish, served with a dipping sauce, is as pretty as it is tasty and makes an excellent first course for almost any kind of dinner. Rectangular skillets, which are widely used in Korea and Japan to make a vast variety of dishes, are now available here in the larger Japanese and Korean stores. Even though I brought back a tin-lined, heavy copper skillet from Japan, I actually prefer to use a much cheaper nonstick skillet that I found in a Japanese store in New York. It measures 5 × 6 inches and is just perfect for such egg dishes. If you do not have access to a small rectangular skillet, use a 6-inch crepe pan or a 6-inch nonstick skillet. Increase the amount of eggs to 5 and be prepared for some waste. After the two egg "pancakes" are made, trim the edges so you have a neat square.

(serves 4–6)

4 large eggs
2 teaspoons vegetable oil
2 teaspoons salt
12 scallions, trimmed and washed

Beat the eggs but not to a froth. Put 1 teaspoon of oil into the skillet. Spread it around and heat it over a medium-low flame. When hot, pour in half the beaten eggs. Turn heat to low and cover loosely (with aluminum foil, if necessary). Cook for 5 to 6 minutes or until the bottom of the "pancake" is no longer soft. Ease a spatula under the "pancake" and turn it over. Cook the other side for 2 to 3 minutes or until it, too, is firm. Remove the "pancake." Add another teaspoon of oil to the skillet and make the second "pancake" the same way. Allow both "pancakes" to cool. Then cut them into strips that are about 2½ inches long and ¼-inch wide.

Bring 10 cups of water to a rolling boil in a 4-quart pot. Add the salt. Put the scallions, bulbs first, into the water. Like spaghetti, the upper ends of the scallions will have to be eased into the water as they soften. Boil rapidly for 2 minutes. You may have to hold the scallions down with a spoon so they stay submerged. Drain the scallions in a colander and rinse immediately under cold running water. Pat the scallions dry. Split each scallion lengthwise into two or more strands by first cutting the bulb with a knife and then tearing upward.

Now put four egg strips together to form a neat bundle. Place the bulb end of a scallion strip on the center of the bundle and then wrap round and round over it. Tuck the end of the strand underneath the binding. It will hold. Make as many bundles as you can this way.

Arrange bundles prettily on a round or rectangular platter. If not to be eaten immediately, cover dish with plastic wrap and refrigerate for a few hours. Korean Dipping Sauce Number 2 (see page 358) should be served on the side.

For information about ingredients and basic techniques that may be unfamiliar, see General Information, pages 418–36.

Jhab's
PARSI-STYLE EGGS WITH OKRA
(Bhinda par Inda)

INDIA

The Parsis of western India are ancient immigrants from Persia and, like modern Iranis, love eggs in all forms. They often break eggs over cooked okra and then bake them until they are done. The eggs are sometimes beaten before being put over the okra, and at other times they are left whole with their yolks intact. This egg dish can also be cooked over the stove and that is how I have chosen to do it.

Make the okra according to the recipe for Whole Okra (see page 44) *but with this difference*: After trimming the okra, cut it into ⅓-inch rounds. Now proceed with the recipe. Keep the okra warm in an 8-inch skillet.

(serves 6)

6 large eggs
⅛ teaspoon salt
¹⁄₁₆ teaspoon freshly ground black pepper
Okra cooked as described above

Separate the eggs. Put the whites into a large bowl and beat with a whisk until soft peaks form. Put the yolks into another large bowl and beat until smooth. Add the salt and pepper to the yolks and beat once more. Empty the egg whites over the yolks. Fold the egg whites gently into the yolks with a rubber spatula.

Pour the eggs over the okra. Cover and cook on low heat until the eggs have set to the desired consistency. Serve the portions straight from the skillet.

SOY-SAUCE EGGS

THAILAND/CHINA

These eggs may be eaten for breakfast with rice or congee or as snacks. They may also be taken on picnics.

(makes 4 eggs)

4 large hard-boiled eggs, peeled
2 tablespoons vegetable oil
3 to 4 cloves garlic, peeled and mashed to a pulp
¼ cup Chinese dark soy sauce
2 tablespoons palm sugar or dark brown sugar

Using a very sharp, pointed knife, score the eggs lengthwise in such a way that the scored lines are at ¼-inch intervals at the widest part of the egg. Do not let the lines meet anywhere. Instead, stop a quarter of an inch before you reach the top or bottom of the egg.

Put the oil in a small, 1½-quart pot and heat over a medium flame. Put in the garlic. Stir and fry until it browns lightly. Now add the soy sauce and sugar. Bring to a simmer and mix. Turn heat to low. Add the eggs and continue to simmer and cook over low heat. As you do this, turn the eggs around again and again and spoon some sauce over them as well. Make sure that they pick up the soy-sauce color evenly. Keep doing this until the soy sauce is reduced to a thick syrup. Remove the eggs from the syrup. The eggs should either be eaten as soon as they are made or else put in a tightly covered container so they do not harden.

HARD-BOILED EGGS WITH STRAW MUSHROOMS

THAILAND/INDONESIA

(serves 4 with other dishes)

1   whole hot dried red pepper, or more to taste
1   teaspoon sliced, dried lemon grass
4   tablespoons vegetable oil
½ cup minced, peeled shallots
2   cloves garlic, peeled and minced
A ¾-inch cube of peeled fresh ginger, minced
1   cup spicy tomato sauce, homemade (see page 197) or canned
¾ cup drained, canned straw mushrooms
1   tablespoon lime or lemon juice
1   cup coconut milk, fresh or canned
1¼ teaspoons salt, or to taste
2   teaspoons sugar
4   large hard-boiled eggs, peeled

Put the red pepper and lemon grass into the container of a clean coffee grinder and grind until fairly fine.

Over a medium flame, heat the oil in a 7- to 8-inch sauté pan or skillet. Put in the shallots, garlic, and ginger, as well as the red pepper-lemon grass mixture. Stir and fry for 4 to 5 minutes or until shallots are very lightly browned. Now put in the tomato sauce, straw mushrooms, lime juice, coconut milk, salt, and sugar. Stir and bring to a simmer. Turn heat to low and simmer gently for 7 to 8 minutes.

Meanwhile, using a sharp, pointed knife, score the eggs lengthwise in such a way that the scored lines are at ¼-inch intervals at the widest part of the egg. Do not let the lines meet anywhere. Instead, stop a quarter of an inch before you reach the top or bottom of the egg.

Put the eggs into the sauté pan and spoon some of the sauce over them. Simmer gently for 5 minutes, spooning the sauce over the eggs again and again.

EGGS, POTATOES, AND CAULIFLOWER

INDIA

This dish can easily be made ahead of time and reheated. I love it with Uppama and Yogurt with Chickpeas and Tomatoes (see pages 158 and 222).

(serves 4–6)

1   pound cauliflower (½ small head)
1   cup freshly grated coconut
2½ teaspoons salt

2   smallish tomatoes (¼ pound), peeled
A 1-inch cube of fresh ginger, peeled and cut into 3 or 4 pieces
6 to 7 cloves garlic, peeled
4   tablespoons vegetable oil
½ teaspoon whole fenugreek seeds
A 1-inch stick of cinnamon
1   medium-sized onion, peeled and finely chopped

For information about ingredients and basic techniques that may be unfamiliar, see General Information, pages 418–36.

1 to 2 fresh hot green chilies, minced
½ teaspoon ground turmeric
5 to 6 fresh curry leaves, if available, or 10 dried ones
2 medium-sized boiling potatoes, boiled, cooled, peeled, and cut into ¾-inch dice
4 hard-boiled eggs, peeled and cut in half crosswise
2 tablespoons lemon juice
½ teaspoon *garam masala*

Break the cauliflower into flowerets 1½ inches long and ¾ inch at the top.

Put the coconut into the container of a food processor or blender and turn the machine on. Slowly add 1 cup hot water. Let the machine run for 1 minute. Strain this mixture through a double thickness of cheesecloth, squeezing out as much liquid as you can. This is the first coconut milk. Set it aside.

Put the coconut that remains in the cheesecloth back into the processor or blender and repeat the process with another cup of hot water. After this coconut milk has been strained, set it aside separately from the first. This is the second coconut milk.

Bring about 4 quarts of water to a rolling boil in a large pot. Add 1 teaspoon salt to the water. Drop in the cauliflower. Let the water return to a boil and then boil rapidly for 30 seconds. Drain the cauliflower and rinse it immediately under cold running water.

Dice the tomatoes into ¼-inch pieces.

Put the ginger, garlic, and ¼ cup water into the container of a blender or food processor and blend until you have a paste.

Heat the oil in a 9- to 10-inch sauté pan or skillet over a medium flame. When hot, first put in the fenugreek seeds and, a couple of seconds later, the cinnamon stick. Now put in the onion. Stir and fry on medium heat for about 2 minutes. Add the ginger-garlic paste and the minced chili. Stir and fry for another minute. Add the tomatoes, turmeric, and curry leaves. Keep stirring and frying for 2 minutes. Now add half of the second coconut milk, cover, turn heat to low and simmer for 10 minutes.

Uncover, add the potatoes, cauliflower, 1½ teaspoons salt, and the remaining half of the second coconut milk. Stir gently to mix and bring to a simmer. Cover, and simmer on low heat for 5 minutes, stirring once or twice during this period. Uncover again and put in the halved eggs, cut side up, the first coconut milk, and the lemon juice. Mix very gently, spooning the sauce over the eggs. Cover and simmer another 5 minutes. Sprinkle in the *garam masala.* Mix gently.

Jyothi's
EGGS PULUSU
INDIA

Here is a simple, exceedingly pleasant dish from South India that may be eaten with rice, or, as one of my daughters seems to prefer, on slices of toasted bread.

(serves 4 with other dishes)

1   teaspoon ground cumin seeds
1   teaspoon ground coriander seeds
½   teaspoon ground turmeric
¼   teaspoon cayenne pepper
3   tablespoons vegetable oil
1   medium-sized onion, peeled and minced
2   tablespoons tamarind paste
1   teaspoon salt
4   large hard-boiled eggs, peeled and cut in half crosswise

Mix together the cumin, coriander, turmeric and cayenne in a small cup.

Over a medium-low flame, heat the oil in a sauté pan or skillet that is about 7 to 8 inches wide. Put in the onion. Sauté, stirring, for about 5 minutes. Put in the spice mixture and sauté for another minute. Now put in the tamarind paste, 1 cup water, and the salt. Cover and simmer on low heat for 2 to 3 minutes. Put in the eggs, cut side up, and spoon some of the sauce over them. Cook the eggs gently for 3 to 4 minutes, spooning the sauce over them again and again.

HARD-BOILED EGGS IN A SPICY ALMOND SAUCE
INDIA

You may eat this dish with rice or with any bread. I often have it for lunch or dinner with thick slices of French bread and a green salad.

(serves 4)

¼   cup blanched, slivered almonds
2   teaspoons whole cumin seeds
2   tablespoons white poppy seeds
1   teaspoon ground coriander seeds
1   whole dried hot red pepper
5   tablespoons vegetable oil
3   whole cardamom pods
1   medium-sized onion, peeled and finely minced
4   cloves garlic, peeled and finely minced
A ¾-inch cube of fresh ginger, peeled and finely minced
¼   cup plain yogurt
¼   cup spicy tomato sauce, homemade (see page 197) or canned
1   teaspoon salt, or to taste
½   cup heavy cream
1   tablespoon lemon juice
½   teaspoon *garam masala*
4   hard-boiled eggs, peeled and cut in half crosswise

Put the almonds in a small, heavy skillet (cast iron would be best) and stir them around over medium-low heat until they are lightly browned. Then put them into the container of a clean coffee grinder and pulverize them. Remove from coffee grinder.

Put 1 teaspoon of the cumin seeds, the poppy seeds, coriander seeds, and red pepper into the same skillet. Stir and dry-roast over medium-low

---

For information about ingredients and basic techniques that may be unfamiliar, see General Information, pages 418–36.

heat until the poppy seeds are a few shades darker (they turn grayish) and a pleasant "roasted" aroma arises from the skillet. This takes just a few minutes. Put these spices in the coffee grinder and pulverize. Leave in coffee grinder.

Heat the oil in a 7- to 8-inch sauté pan or skillet over a medium flame. When hot, put in the remaining 1 teaspoon cumin seeds and the whole cardamom pods. Stir and fry for a few seconds until the cardamoms turn a shade darker. Put in the minced onion, garlic, and ginger. Stir and fry for about 5 minutes or until the onion mixture is lightly browned. Now put in 1 tablespoon of the yogurt. Stir and cook for about 30 seconds or until the yogurt is incorporated into the onion mixture. Add the remaining yogurt 1 tablespoon at a time in exactly the same way. Now put in the tomato sauce, also 1 tablespoon at a time, incorporating it into the sauce each time just as you did the yogurt. Put in the ground spices sitting in the coffee grinder and stir for 10 seconds. Put in the ground almonds and stir for another 10 seconds. Add 1 cup water and the salt. Bring to a simmer. Cover, turn heat to very low and simmer gently for 5 minutes.

Add the cream, lemon juice, and *garam masala*. Stir to mix. Simmer, uncovered, on very low heat for 4 to 5 minutes. Put the eggs into the sauce, cut side up, laying them out in a single layer. Spoon some sauce over them. Simmer the eggs very gently for 7 to 8 minutes, spooning the sauce over them frequently as you do so. Spoon off any oil that surfaces to the top.

Milk Products

Just as products of the soy bean, such as soy milk and bean curd, help sustain vegetarians in East Asia, products made out of milk give nutritional balance to most vegetarian meals in South Asia. And these products are as varied as those derived from the soy bean.

It would be quite conceivable for an Indian to eat, say, a soft yogurt cheese flavored with fresh Chinese parsley for breakfast, have a cumin-flavored glass of buttermilk as a mid-morning snack, have *paneer* (milk-cheese cubes) and peas for lunch, and have a steamed yogurt custard with dinner. Oh yes, I forgot tea-time. For tea, the entire family might go out to the bazaar and eat *dahi-baras* out of disposable leaf-plates. *Dahi-baras* are fried, split-pea patties that are dunked in beaten yogurt, showered with ground spices, and then served with a generous swirl of a brown, hot, sweet, and sour tamarind-mint chutney.

Yogurt itself is eaten in so many different ways. When sweetened and flavored with saffron, it becomes the West Indian *shrikhand*; when beaten together with grated cucumber and mint, it becomes a North Indian *raita*; when added to sautéed zucchini, it becomes a South Indian accompaniment for rice; and when mixed with chickpea flour, it becomes the all-Indian *karhi*. *Karhis* are a very interesting food. They may be thick or thin but are always souplike. They may well have originated with the desire to have a heated yogurt dish. Yogurt, of course, curdles when it is heated, disintegrating into the most inedible particles. The way to avoid this is to blend it with some flour before it is cooked. In India, this flour is invariably chickpea flour, as it has so much flavor of its own. After the basic *karhi* is made, it is enriched with spices, vegetables, and sometimes even dumplings. Today, nothing evokes my childhood more than the sight of two big bowls, one containing steaming hot *karhi*, and the other, steaming hot *basmati* rice.

There are many dishes made with heated yogurt in the Middle East as well. The grandest of them all, I think, is Stuffed Zucchini in a Hot Yogurt Sauce. A whole zucchini is stuffed with an absolutely delicious mixture of bulgar wheat, red lentils, tomatoes, and parsley. It is steamed lightly, cut into thick rounds, and then served with a hot yogurt sauce that is stabilized, not with chickpea flour, but with a small amount of cornstarch.

YOGURT

For those of us who have grown up with it, yogurt is a protein-rich, easy-to-digest, tasty, versatile food that may be eaten plain or used in the making of soups, cold drinks, breads, sauces, relishes, and all manner of main dishes. But while all of us in West, Central, and South Asia—the regions where yogurt has always been abundantly eaten—believe that yogurt, especially when combined with milled rice, has a very settling effect on queasy stomachs, we have not endowed it with any greater powers. Nor do we fuss and fret when we make it—an activity that is carried on in our homes on a daily basis. We take it for granted that on some days the yogurt will turn out excellently and that on other days it will not be quite as good. On hot days it will set quickly and sour easily, while on cold days we may almost have to pray to get it to set and its taste might remain colorlessly bland. At least once a month my brother in India turns to his wife at the dining table, just as I remember my father and grandfather doing, and makes a bit of a face. "So," he says, "your yogurt didn't turn out too well?" She, just as my mother and grandmother before her, grunts as if to say, how little you understand, and goes on eating. Of course there are no thermometers for yogurt in Asia but then neither are there great pangs of anxiety. In my family, yogurt has always been made as the last thing at night. After that everyone goes to sleep and just *expects* to have yogurt for lunch the following day.

Here are some things to keep in mind when making yogurt:

Use a good starter. This starter consists of a few tablespoons of yogurt, commercial or homemade. The quality of your own yogurt will depend on the taste, freshness, and sourness of your starter. Pick a starter from a yogurt you like. In Asia, good starters are often "borrowed" from neighbors.

You may make your yogurt from whole milk, skimmed milk, or reconstituted dried milk.

Yogurt sets best at a temperature of 85° to 100° F. If you do not have an electric yogurtmaker, see how you can approximate this temperature. You could use a stove oven with the pilot light turned on, you could wrap your yogurt bowl loosely in an electric blanket, or you could find a warm spot in your attic or basement.

MAKING YOUR OWN YOGURT

(makes 1 quart)

1 quart milk
2 tablespoons plain yogurt

Put the milk in a heavy pot and bring to a boil. As soon as the milk begins to rise, turn the heat to very low and simmer for a minute. Turn the heat off and let the milk cool to anywhere between 100° to 110° F. It should feel slightly warm to the touch. A skin will probably form on top of the milk. You may either remove it or just stir it in.

While the milk cools, put the yogurt into a nonmetallic bowl. Beat it with a whisk until it is smooth and creamy. When the milk has reached the required temperature, add a tablespoon of it at a time to the yogurt and whisk it in. After you have added ¼ cup, the rest may be poured in a bit faster. Keep beating gently as you pour. Now cover the bowl with a plastic wrap and then wrap a large, heavy towel all around it in such a way that you do not tilt the bowl in one direction or another. Place the wrapped bowl in an unused oven or other undrafty place for about 8 hours or until set. If you have a pilot light going in the oven, the yogurt is apt to set more quickly—about 6 to 7 hours. Once set, the yogurt should be refrigerated.

The yogurt should be good for at least 4 days. A second batch may be prepared by using 2 tablespoons of this first batch.

NOTE: You may prepare half this amount of yogurt by halving the ingredients.

YOGURT WITH DILL

IRAN

(serves 2 to 4)

1 cup plain yogurt
⅓ to ½ teaspoon salt
2 tablespoons finely minced fresh dill

Put the yogurt and salt in a bowl. Beat with a fork or whisk until smooth and creamy. Add the dill and mix. Serve cold.

Alun's
YOGURT WITH GARLIC

TURKEY

This yogurt dish may be served as a relish or it may be used as a sauce over cooked vegetables. Of course, it also tastes quite wonderful if eaten plain, with a spoon. Some minced fresh mint may be added to it, if you like.

(serves 1–4)

1 cup plain yogurt
¼ teaspoon salt, or to taste
1 clove garlic, mashed to a pulp in a mortar
1⁄16 teaspoon freshly ground black pepper
2 teaspoons fruity olive oil

Put the yogurt in a bowl. Beat gently with a fork or whisk until smooth and creamy. Now add all the other ingredients. Beat to mix. Cover and chill until needed.

For information about ingredients and basic techniques that may be unfamiliar, see General Information, pages 418–36.

YOGURT WITH CUCUMBER, RAISINS, AND ALMONDS

IRAN

When almonds are left to soak for a length of time, they become rather like green almonds—white, tender, crunchy, and quite unlike their more "nutty" selves. They can be eaten just as they are (I love them that way) or they can be combined with other foods. They taste very nice in this yogurt dish, where they are combined with raisins and cucumbers. Serve as a snack or as part of a Persian or Indian meal.

(serves 4–6)

2　cups plain yogurt
1　teaspoon salt
⅛ to ¼ teaspoon freshly ground black pepper
1　cucumber
¼ cup golden raisins, soaked in 1 cup hot water for 1 hour and then drained
2　tablespoons halved, blanched almonds, soaked in 1 cup hot water 6 hours (or overnight) and then drained

Put the yogurt in a bowl and add the salt and pepper. Beat the yogurt lightly with a fork or whisk until smooth and creamy.

Peel the cucumber and cut it in half lengthwise. Remove the seeds if they are large. Now cut the cucumber into ¼-inch dice. Put the diced cucumber as well as the raisins and almonds into the yogurt. Mix well. Serve chilled.

YOGURT WITH FRESH MINT, RAISINS, AND WALNUTS

IRAN

Have this yogurt as a relish with any Persian or Indian meal. Or serve it in small bowls as a first course.

(serves 4–6)

2　cups plain yogurt
¾ teaspoon salt
⅛ to ¼ teaspoon freshly ground black pepper
¼ cup finely minced fresh mint leaves
¼ cup golden raisins, soaked in 1 cup hot water 1 hour and drained
2　tablespoons chopped walnuts

Put the yogurt in a bowl. Add the salt and pepper. Beat the yogurt with a fork or whisk until smooth and creamy. Add all the other ingredients and mix.

YOGURT WITH CUCUMBER AND CRUSHED MUSTARD SEEDS

INDIA

This relish goes well with almost all Indian meals.

(serves 4)

1　cup plain yogurt
½ teaspoon salt
¹⁄₁₆ teaspoon freshly ground black pepper

For information about ingredients and basic techniques that may be unfamiliar, see General Information, pages 418–36.

⅛ teaspoon cayenne pepper, or to taste
2 tablespoons finely minced fresh Chinese parsley
1 teaspoon lightly ground black mustard seeds
1 cucumber, peeled and coarsely grated

Put the yogurt in a bowl. Beat gently with a thin whisk until creamy. Add all the other ingredients. Mix well and chill.

YOGURT WITH CUCUMBER AND MINT

INDIA

(serves 6)

2 cups plain yogurt
1 cucumber, peeled and cut into ¾-inch dice
2 tablespoons finely minced fresh mint
¾ teaspoon salt
¾ teaspoon ground roasted cumin seeds
¼ teaspoon cayenne pepper (optional)
Freshly ground black pepper
Garnish: 1 small sprig mint

Put the yogurt in a bowl. Beat lightly with a fork or whisk until smooth and creamy. Add the cucumber, mint, salt, ½ teaspoon of the cumin, ⅛ teaspoon cayenne, and a little black pepper. Mix. Empty into a serving bowl. Sprinkle the remaining ¼ teaspoon cumin, ⅛ teaspoon cayenne, and some black pepper over the top. Plant the mint sprig in the center.

YOGURT WITH ROASTED EGGPLANT

MIDDLE EAST

(serves 6)

2 scallions
1 medium-sized eggplant (about ¾ pound)
2 cups plain yogurt
1 clove garlic, peeled and mashed to a pulp
3 tablespoons minced fresh mint
¾ to 1 teaspoon salt
2 tablespoons olive oil
Freshly ground black pepper

Cut the scallions into paper-thin rounds three-quarters of the way up their green sections. Put in a bowl. Pour 4 cups of ice water over them. Cover and refrigerate for an hour.

Prick the eggplant in five to six places with a fork. Now lay it directly over or under a flame. If you are roasting it on top of the stove, keep the heat on low. If you are roasting it under the broiler, keep the eggplant a few inches away from the heat. As one side gets charred, turn the eggplant over slightly, using a pair of tongs to do so. Roast the entire eggplant this way. It should turn very limp by the time it is done.

Peel the eggplant under cold running water and leave it to drain in a colander for 5 minutes. Then mince the flesh.

Put the yogurt in a bowl and beat lightly with a fork or a whisk until smooth and creamy. Add the eggplant, garlic, mint, salt, olive oil, and black pepper. Drain the scallions and pat dry. Add them to the yogurt and mix.

Serve at room temperature or chilled.

CELERY ROOT WITH YOGURT

I was trying to work out a low-calorie version of *celery rémoulade* using yogurt instead of mayonnaise and I came up with this deliciously refreshing recipe. Serve it chilled as a first course or as a salad.

(serves 4)

1 celery root, about ½ pound in weight (without leaves)
1 teaspoon salt
1 teaspoon lemon juice
8 tablespoons plain yogurt (low-fat, if preferred)
1 tablespoon finely minced parsley
Freshly ground black pepper

Peel the celery root. Cut it in half, lengthwise. Cut each half into very fine slices and cut the slices into fine, matchstick, julienne strips. Put the strips into a stainless-steel or nonmetallic bowl. Add ¾ teaspoon salt and the lemon juice. Toss well and leave for half an hour.

Drain the celery-root strips. Add the yogurt, parsley, ¼ teaspoon salt, and some freshly ground pepper to them. Mix well, cover, and refrigerate for a couple of hours or overnight, if you so desire.

YOGURT WITH SPINACH AND PARSLEY

MIDDLE EAST

(Serves 6)

5 tablespoons olive oil
1 medium-sized onion, peeled and finely chopped
2 cloves garlic, peeled and mashed to a pulp
¼ cup finely minced fresh parsley
2 teaspoons salt
1 teaspoon sugar
10 to 16 ounces fresh spinach, trimmed and washed or frozen spinach, cooked, drained, squeezed, then minced
2 cups plain yogurt
Freshly ground black pepper

Heat the oil in a 7- to 8-inch skillet over a medium flame. Put in the onion. Stir and fry, turning the heat down when necessary, until the onion is soft. If the onion picks up a few specks of brown color, it will not hurt. Put in the garlic. Stir and sauté for 15 seconds. Put in the parsley and sauté for another 15 seconds. Turn off the heat and allow this mixture to cool in the skillet.

Bring 4 quarts of water to a rolling boil in a large pot. Add 1 teaspoon salt, 1 teaspoon sugar, and the spinach. Boil rapidly for 2 to 3 minutes. Drain and rinse under cold running water. Squeeze out as much liquid as you can from the spinach and then mince it.

Put the yogurt into a bowl and beat it lightly with a fork or a whisk until it is smooth and creamy. Add all the ingredients in the skillet, the spinach, the remaining 1 teaspoon salt, and some freshly ground pepper. Mix.

Serve dish chilled or at room temperature.

For information about ingredients and basic techniques that may be unfamiliar, see General Information, pages 418–36.

YOGURT WITH BANANA IN THE GUJARATI STYLE

INDIA

(serves 4)

1 cup plain yogurt (preferably whole-milk)
⅓ to ½ teaspoon salt
1/16 teaspoon freshly ground black pepper
½ to 1 fresh hot green chili, or to taste, very finely
    minced (optional)
1 teaspoon sugar
1 firm but ripe medium-sized banana, sliced into
    ¼-inch-thick rounds

Put the yogurt in a bowl. Beat gently with a whisk until creamy. Add the other ingredients and mix.

Refrigerate until you are ready to eat.

As a slight variation, you might like to add 1 teaspoon lightly ground black mustard seeds to the yogurt as well. This makes the dish a bit more pungent.

Another possible variation is to substitute for banana 1 cup ripe mango that has been peeled and diced into ½-inch cubes. If you like, you may add a teaspoon of lightly ground black mustard seeds to this relish as well.

CAULIFLOWER AND PEAS WITH YOGURT

INDIA

This is a lovely, saladlike dish that can almost be eaten by itself as a very light lunch. It can be made several hours ahead of time and refrigerated.

(serves 4–6)

1 pound cauliflower (half a head)
2¾ teaspoons salt
¼ cup shelled fresh (or defrosted frozen) peas
2 cups plain yogurt
½ teaspoon ground roasted cumin seeds
1/16 teaspoon freshly ground black pepper, or more
    to taste
1/16 to ⅛ teaspoon cayenne pepper (optional)

Break the cauliflower into flowerets that are about 1½ inches long and 1-inch wide at the top.

Bring 3 cups of water to a boil in a large pot. Add 2 teaspoons salt. When the water is at a rolling boil, drop in the cauliflower and peas. Boil vigorously for about 2 minutes or until cauliflower is just cooked but still slightly crunchy. Drain vegetables in a sieve and run under cold water to cool off. Leave in the sieve to drain some more.

Put the yogurt in a bowl. Beat it lightly with a fork or whisk until smooth and creamy. Add the remaining ¾ teaspoon salt, cumin, black pepper, and cayenne. Mix. Fold in the cauliflower and peas. Cover, and refrigerate until ready to eat.

YOGURT WITH POTATOES AND CHICKPEAS IN THE DELHI STYLE

INDIA

In Delhi, this combination is generally eaten as a snack but you could serve it as a spicy salad.

(Serves 4–6)

1   medium-sized boiling potato (about ¼ pound)
1   cup homemade (see page 83) or canned, drained chickpeas
2   cups plain yogurt
1 to 1½ teaspoons salt
¼   teaspoon freshly ground black pepper
1   teaspoon ground roasted cumin seeds
⅛ to ¼ teaspoon cayenne pepper
½   fresh hot green chili, finely minced
1   tablespoon finely minced fresh Chinese parsley

Boil the potato until tender, then peel and cut into ½-inch dice.

Put the chickpeas in a sieve and wash them well if they are canned.

Put the yogurt in a bowl. Beat with a fork or whisk until creamy. Now put in the chickpeas as well as all the other ingredients. Mix. Check seasonings. You can make this dish as hot as you like. Refrigerate until ready to eat.

If you like, ¼ cup of Tamarind-Mint Chutney for Snack Foods (see page 364), may be swirled over the chickpeas before they are served.

YOGURT WITH CHICKPEAS AND TOMATOES

INDIA

While canned chickpeas are very convenient to use, saving all the time and labor of soaking and boiling, I cannot say that I like their taste too much for dishes that require no cooking and that are not heavily spiced. However, there is a way to get rid of their tinny taste. I drain the chickpeas and wash them thoroughly in cold water. Then I simmer them in water that has been flavored with spices for a bare 5 minutes, letting them cool in the liquid. If you are in a rush, this extra step may be eliminated.

(serves 4–6)

1   cup drained, canned chickpeas (about half a 20-ounce can)
A 1-inch-long stick of cinnamon
8   whole cloves
1   teaspoon whole black peppercorns
1   bay leaf
1   teaspoon whole cumin seeds
1   teaspoon whole fennel seeds
1   teaspoon salt
1½ cups plain yogurt
2   smallish tomatoes (about ¼ pound), peeled, and cut into ¼-inch dice
½   teaspoon ground roasted cumin seeds
⅛   teaspoon freshly ground black pepper
⅛ to ¼ teaspoon cayenne pepper (optional)
1   tablespoon minced fresh Chinese parsley (optional)

Put the chickpeas in a strainer under running water and wash them well. Leave to drain in the strainer.

For information about ingredients and basic techniques that may be unfamiliar, see General Information, pages 418–36.

Tie the cinnamon, cloves, peppercorns, bay leaf, cumin, and fennel seeds in a cheesecloth bundle. Bring 3 cups of water to a boil. Put in the cheesecloth bundle as well as ½ teaspoon of the salt. Cover, lower heat, and simmer 15 minutes.

Put the chickpeas into the simmering liquid and bring to a boil. Cover, lower heat, and simmer for 5 minutes. Uncover and let the chickpeas cool in the liquid. Drain.

In a bowl, combine the yogurt, chickpeas, tomatoes, the remaining ½ teaspoon salt, the cumin, black pepper, cayenne, and Chinese parsley. Mix. Cover and refrigerate until ready to eat.

YOGURT WITH FRIED OKRA

INDIA

For this very tasty dish, the yogurt may be prepared, covered, and refrigerated ahead of time. The okra, onions, and green chili may be sliced ahead of time also. But you do need to fry the vegetables as you do in the recipe for okra with onion and green chili just before you eat or else they get too soggy. The frying takes only about 10 minutes.

(serves 4)

1½ cups plain yogurt
½ teaspoon salt
¹⁄₁₆ teaspoon freshly ground black pepper

Okra cooked according to recipe for Okra Fried with Onion and Green Chili (see page 46)

Put the yogurt in a bowl. Add the salt and black pepper. Beat gently with a fork or whisk until smooth and creamy. Fold in the okra mixture and serve at once.

YOGURT WITH WHITE RADISH

INDIA

White radishes are available in most Oriental markets. Sometimes incorrectly labeled "horseradish," they can be sweet or sharp like their cousins, the red radishes. The taste of this dish will vary according to the pungency of the vegetable. The two radishes used in this recipe were about 1½ inches in diameter and weighed about 1½ pounds. White radishes of any size will do. This is a South Indian dish.

(serves 6)

2 tablespoons vegetable oil
1½ teaspoons black mustard seeds
1½ pounds white radish, trimmed, peeled, and cut into ½-inch dice
1 fresh hot green chili, sliced
1½ teaspoons salt
3 tablespoons chopped Chinese parsley
2 cups plain yogurt
¹⁄₁₆ teaspoon freshly ground black pepper

Heat the oil in a saucepan on a medium-high flame. When very hot, put in the mustard seeds. As soon as the seeds begin to pop (this will happen almost immediately), put in the diced radish, green chili, ½ teaspoon salt, and 2 tablespoons water. Stir and bring to a bubble. Cover. Turn heat to very low and steam gently for about 10 minutes or until radish is tender but still somewhat crisp. Add the Chinese parsley, stir, and leave uncovered. Let cool slightly.

Put yogurt in a serving bowl. Add 1 teaspoon salt and the black pepper. Beat with a fork or a whisk until smooth and creamy. Now empty the contents of the saucepan into the bowl. Mix well.

This yogurt dish goes well with most Indian food. It can be served at room temperature or cold.

YOGURT WITH ZUCCHINI

INDIA

This is an absolutely wonderful dish that may be served warm or cold. I find that I can eat it by the spoonful, all by itself. I often do!

(serves 4–6)

2   medium-sized zucchini (about 12
     to 14 ounces)
¾ teaspoon salt
1   medium-sized onion
1½ cups plain yogurt

3   tablespoons vegetable oil
1   teaspoon whole black mustard seeds
⅟16 teaspoon freshly ground black pepper
⅟16 teaspoon cayenne pepper (use as much
     as you like)

Trim the zucchini and grate it coarsely. Put it into a bowl and sprinkle with ½ teaspoon salt. Toss to mix and set aside for half an hour. Drain the zucchini and press out as much liquid as you can. Separate the zucchini shreds so you do not have lumps.

Peel the onion, cut it in half lengthwise, and then cut into fine, half-moon-shaped slices.

Put the yogurt in a bowl. Beat it lightly with a fork or whisk until it is smooth and creamy.

Heat the oil in an 8-inch skillet over a medium flame. When hot, put in the mustard seeds. As soon as the mustard seeds begin to pop (this just takes a few seconds), put in the onion. Stir and fry it for about 2 minutes or until the slices are translucent. Add the zucchini. Stir and fry for another 3 minutes. Turn off the heat and let the zucchini cool slightly. When cooled, fold it into the yogurt. Add the remaining ¼ teaspoon salt, pepper, and cayenne. If you wish to eat the dish cold, cover and refrigerate it. If you wish to eat it warm, put the yogurt-zucchini combination in a double boiler over a low flame. Then heat, stirring in one direction, until warm. *Do not let it boil.*

For information about ingredients and basic techniques that may be unfamiliar, see General Information, pages 418–36.

DAHI-BARAS
(Dal Patties in Yogurt)
INDIA

In this dish, yogurt, nicely seasoned with salt, pepper, and cumin, is poured over flat patties that look rather like potato cakes. These patties are made out of *urad dal*, a split pea that has been soaked overnight and then ground. In India, this grinding is done on a heavy grinding stone, after which the paste has to be beaten in order to make it somewhat airier. In American kitchens, these two steps can be combined in a food processor or blender.

(makes 12 patties)

FOR THE PATTIES

1 cup *urad dal*, picked over, washed, and drained
¾ teaspoon salt
⅛ teaspoon baking soda
⅛ teaspoon cayenne pepper
½ fresh hot green chili, coarsely chopped
Vegetable oil for deep frying

FOR THE YOGURT

3 cups plain yogurt
1 teaspoon salt
1 teaspoon ground roasted cumin seeds
¼ teaspoon cayenne pepper
Freshly ground black pepper

FOR THE GARNISHING

¼ cup Tamarind-Mint Chutney
   for Snack Foods (see page 364), optional
⅛ teaspoon cayenne pepper
⅛ teaspoon salt
⅛ teaspoon ground roasted cumin seeds

Freshly ground black pepper
1 tablespoon minced fresh Chinese parsley
   (optional)

Soak the *dal* in 5 cups of water for 13 to 14 hours. Drain. Put in a food processor or blender, add ¼ cup water, the ¾ teaspoon salt, baking soda, ⅛ teaspoon cayenne, and the green chili. Blend, pushing down with a rubber spatula, if necessary, until you have a smooth paste. Now let the machine run for another 5 minutes so the mixture gets lighter and airier. Spread out a wet, smooth dishcloth (one without ridges) or a wet 16-inch square torn out from an old, clean sheet, somewhere near the stove. Put a bowl of water near the stove as well. Now, working with wet hands, form twelve equal-sized balls and put them down at some distance from each other on the wet cloth. Using wet fingers, press down on the balls to form patties that are about 2½ inches in diameter and a little less than ¼ inch thick.

Set a large bowl of hot water on or near the stove.

Put 2 inches of oil in a wok or skillet and heat over a medium-low flame. When it is hot, carefully ease one of the patties off the cloth and slip it into the oil. It helps if you lift the cloth under the patty slightly as you do this.

Working quickly, put as many patties into the oil as the wok can hold in a single layer. Fry them for 5 to 6 minutes, turning them halfway through, until they are a reddish-golden color. Remove the patties with a slotted spoon and put them in the hot water. Make all the patties this way. Let them sit in the hot water for 15 to 20 minutes. Then lift out one patty at a time, put it on the palm of one hand and squeeze down gently with the other to expel some of the water. Do the same to all the patties. Lay the patties out in a single layer on a large serving platter. (You may cover the patties with plastic wrap and refrigerate for several hours.)

Put the yogurt in a bowl and beat lightly with a fork or whisk until smooth and creamy. Add all the other ingredients listed under "For the yogurt." Mix. Pour this yogurt over the patties, making sure that some goes under them as well.

If you are using the Tamarind-Mint Chutney, swirl it over the patties in such a way that both the white color of the yogurt and the brown of the chutney are clearly visible. Sprinkle all the other garnishing ingredients evenly over the top.

This dish is served either at room temperature or cold.

YOGURT WITH GREEN BEANS AND NAVY BEANS
MIDDLE EAST

This yogurt dish is served hot, not warm or cold. Heating yogurt can sometimes be problematic, as it curdles easily. But there is an easy solution to this problem, one that is used widely in West and South Asia. Adding a small amount of flour, almost any flour, holds yogurt together, even when it boils.

I have used dried navy beans for this dish. You could, if you like, use the cooked, canned variety. Just drain them and rinse them off.

(serves 4)

¼ cup dried navy beans, picked over, washed, and drained
2¾ teaspoons salt
1 tablespoon olive oil
6 ounces fresh green beans, cut into ¾-inch-long segments
1¼ teaspoons cornstarch
1½ cups plain yogurt
1 to 2 cloves garlic, peeled and mashed to a pulp
Freshly ground black pepper

Put the navy beans and 3 cups water in a small pot and bring to a boil. Cover, lower heat and simmer for 2 minutes. Turn off the flame and let the pot sit, covered, for 1 hour. Bring the beans to a boil again. Turn heat to low and simmer, covered, for 45 minutes or until beans are tender but still retain their shape. Drain. (You could save the liquid for soup.) Put the beans in a bowl. Add ¼ teaspoon salt and the olive oil. Mix.

Bring 2 quarts of water to a rapid boil. Add 2

teaspoons salt and the green beans. Boil rapidly for 3 to 4 minutes or until beans are just tender. Drain and rinse under cold running water. Set aside in a colander.

Put the cornstarch in a bowl. Add 1 tablespoon water and mix. Add the yogurt. Beat lightly with a fork or whisk until smooth and creamy.

Put the yogurt mixture in a 1½-quart pot and set it over a medium-low flame. Heat slowly, stirring in one direction as you do so. When the yogurt starts to bubble, turn heat to low and cook, still stirring in the same direction, for another 5 minutes. Add the garlic, ½ teaspoon salt, some black pepper, the green beans, and the navy beans. Stir gently to mix. Cook over a low flame until the beans are heated through.

SPICED, HEATED YOGURT

INDIA

This very tasty dish is traditionally served warm but it may be served cold. It is normally offered in individual bowls and is eaten with Indian rice dishes and Indian breads. I sometimes serve it in quite another way. I use it as a sauce for cooked vegetables. You could blanch vegetables like cauliflower, green beans, peas, carrots, shredded cabbage, and zucchini in salted water, drain and then fold them into this yogurt. You could also pour the yogurt over boiled, diced potatoes and over slices of fried eggplant.

(serves 3–4)

1½ cups plain yogurt
½ teaspoon very finely grated ginger
2 cloves garlic, peeled and mashed to a pulp
½ to 1 fresh hot green chili, minced
¼ teaspoon ground turmeric
1 teaspoon ground coriander
⅛ teaspoon cayenne pepper (optional)
3 tablespoons vegetable oil
¼ teaspoon whole cumin seeds
1 medium-sized onion, peeled and very finely chopped
½ teaspoon salt
1/16 teaspoon freshly ground black pepper

Put the yogurt in a bowl. Beat it lightly with a fork or whisk until smooth and creamy.

Put the ginger, garlic, chili, turmeric, coriander, and cayenne pepper, if you want to use it, in a small bowl with 1 tablespoon water and mix well.

Heat the oil in a 7- to 8-inch skillet over a medium flame. When hot, put in the cumin seeds. A few seconds later, put in the onion. Stir and fry for about 3 minutes. Do not let the onion brown. Now put in all the spices that are in the small cup. Stir and fry for 1 minute. Turn off the heat and let the spice mixture cool. Empty the spices and the frying oil into the bowl with the yogurt. Add the salt and pepper. Mix well. The yogurt may now be heated in a double boiler or it may be put in the skillet used for cooking the spices and then heated over a low flame. Stir gently *all the time* and *do not let the yogurt come to a boil.* Just heat until the yogurt is warm.

STUFFED ZUCCHINI IN A HOT YOGURT SAUCE
MIDDLE EAST

This is an exceedingly elegant main dish. Bright-green zucchini halves stuffed with a really delicious mixture of bulgar wheat, red lentils (called *masoor dal* in Indian stores and Egyptian lentils in some Middle Eastern stores), tomatoes, and parsley are served with a garlicky yogurt sauce.

I use medium-sized zucchini for this, each about ½ pound in weight, about 7½ inches long, and about 1½ to 2 inches in diameter at the center. If your zucchini are of a different size, you may have to adjust the amount of stuffing and the steaming time. It is useful to know that the zucchini may easily be stuffed ahead of time and refrigerated. All the ingredients for the sauce can also be mixed ahead of time. The final cooking, both of the zucchini and the sauce, may be done simultaneously, about 15 minutes before you sit down to eat.

(serves 4)

4   medium-sized zucchini (about 2 pounds; see note
     above)
Salt

FOR THE STUFFING
¼ cup *masoor dal*
½ cup fine-grained bulgar wheat
3   tablespoons olive oil
1   medium-sized onion, peeled and finely chopped
½ good-sized tomato, peeled and minced (about
     ½ cup)
1   clove garlic, peeled and mashed to a pulp
1   teaspoon salt
4   teaspoons lemon juice

¼ cup minced fresh parsley
Freshly ground black pepper

FOR THE YOGURT SAUCE
2   teaspoons cornstarch
2½ cups plain yogurt
1¼ teaspoons salt, or to taste
1   clove garlic, peeled and mashed to a pulp
Freshly ground black pepper

Wash the zucchini well but do not trim the ends. Cut each zucchini in half, crosswise. Now, using a grapefruit spoon or something similar, work your way into each zucchini half from the cut section and take out all the seeded portion. You should be left with eight hollow shells. Sprinkle about ¹⁄₁₆ teaspoon salt into each shell, spreading it about inside. Stand the shells, cut side up, in a bowl. Rub the outsides of the shells with another ¼ teaspoon salt. Set aside for 1 to 1½ hours.

Meanwhile, pick over the lentils, wash them, and then drain them. Put them in a small pot. Add 2 cups water and bring to a simmer. Lower heat and simmer gently for 2 minutes. Turn off the heat and let the lentils sit, covered, for 45 minutes.

Put the bulgar wheat in a bowl. Cover with 3 cups water and set aside for 1 hour.

When the lentils have finished sitting for 45 minutes, bring them to a simmer again. Turn heat to low and simmer for 10 to 12 minutes or until lentils are tender. Drain and put in a bowl. (The liquid may be saved for soup.)

Drain the bulgar wheat and squeeze out as much

For information about ingredients and basic techniques that may be unfamiliar, see General Information, pages 418–36.

liquid as you can easily. Put the wheat into the same bowl as the lentils.

Heat the olive oil in a 7- to 8-inch skillet over a medium flame. Put in the onion and sauté for about 2 minutes. Add the tomato and sauté for another 2 minutes. Put all the contents of the skillet into the bowl with the lentils and the wheat. Add all the other ingredients for the stuffing as well and mix.

Arrange an apparatus for steaming. I use a large pot to hold a few inches of water and set a colander on top of it. The water should not touch the bottom of the colander. Bring the water in the pot to a boil.

As you wait for this, turn the zucchini halves upside down to rid them of any accumulated liquid and then stuff them with the wheat-lentil mix-ture. Once the water is boiling rapidly, stand the zucchini halves in the colander, cut side up. Put a cover over the colander and steam for 10 to 15 minutes or until zucchini shells are just tender.

While the zucchini steams, make the sauce. Put the cornstarch in a bowl. Add 1 tablespoon water and mix. Add the yogurt. Beat with a fork or whisk until smooth and creamy.

Put the yogurt into a heavy saucepan and set over medium-low heat. Bring to a simmer, stirring constantly in one direction as you do so. When the yogurt begins to bubble, turn heat to low and cook 5 minutes, stirring gently in the same direction. Add all the other ingredients for the yogurt sauce and mix.

Put the zucchini on a serving platter or in individual plates. Spoon some sauce over them.

Karhis

Karhis are souplike dishes from India made out of yogurt or buttermilk and chickpea flour. The chickpea flour holds the yogurt or buttermilk together and prevents it from curdling as it heats, giving a very special flavor—and nutritional value—to the dish. I adored karhis as a child and continue to love them today. Give me a bowl of rice topped with some karhi and I begin to purr.

There are different types of karhis in India. In western states like Gujarat, karhis cook in 10 minutes, are very thin, and generally combine both sweet and tart flavors. Northern karhis cook slowly and long, are much thicker—they use more chickpea flour—and do not have even a hint of sweetness. All karhis may be made plain, or with the addition of vegetables and dumplings.

AALAN KA SAAG
(Karhi with Spinach)
INDIA

I have only had this exceedingly tasty and nutritious dish in my family. It is like a thick soup and is either eaten with Indian breads or with plain rice. It calls for sour yogurt which you can provide either by leaving freshly made yogurt unrefrigerated for 24 hours or by using old, and therefore already soured, yogurt. If you cannot get fresh spinach, frozen leaf spinach, cooked according to instructions and then drained, may be substituted.

(serves 8)

¾   cup chickpea flour
½   teaspoon turmeric
1   cup sour yogurt
2   tablespoons *mung dal*, picked over, washed, and drained (optional)
1½ pounds fresh spinach, washed, drained, and chopped
2½ teaspoons salt, or to taste
2   tablespoons lemon juice
⅛   teaspoon cayenne pepper
Freshly ground black pepper
2   tablespoons vegetable oil
A generous pinch of ground asafetida
1   teaspoon whole cumin seeds
2   whole dried hot red peppers

Sift the chickpea flour and turmeric into a bowl. Add ½ cup water, a little bit at a time, and keep stirring until you have a smooth paste.

Put the yogurt into a second bowl and beat it lightly with a whisk until it is smooth and creamy. Add 5 cups of water to the yogurt, beating lightly.

Add the yogurt mixture slowly to the chickpea-flour mixture, beating gently as you mix the two. Now empty this combination into a heavy 4-quart pot and bring to a simmer over a medium heat. Add the *mung dal*, spinach, salt, lemon juice, and cayenne. Bring to a simmer again. Cover, turn heat to low and simmer very gently for 1½ hours. Stir every 10 minutes or so. If the *aalan ka saag* gets too thick, thin it out with a little hot water. It should have the consistency of a pea soup. Check the salt and add some freshly ground black pepper. Turn off the heat but leave the pot covered.

Heat the oil in a small skillet or a very small pot over a medium flame. When very hot, add the asafetida, then, a second later, the cumin seeds, and 2 seconds later, the red peppers. As soon as the peppers turn dark on one side, turn them over. As soon as the second side darkens, pour the oil and all the spices in it over the *aalan ka saag*. Cover the *aalan ka saag* again immediately and let it stay covered until the sizzling noises stop. You may now stir the contents of the pot.

For information about ingredients and basic techniques that may be unfamiliar, see General Information, pages 418–36.

PLAIN GUJARATI KARHI
INDIA

If you want a very simple lunch or dinner, put some plain rice in a bowl, pour the *karhi* on top, and eat with a spoon. You might serve the Gujarati Carrot Salad (see page 319) on the side.

(serves 4)

2   tablespoons chickpea flour, sifted
2   cups sour yogurt (see introduction to preceding recipe)
1   teaspoon whole cumin seeds
½   teaspoon whole fenugreek seeds
½ to ¾ teaspoon salt
1½ teaspoons sugar
½ to 1 fresh hot green chili, chopped (optional)
1   tablespoon vegetable oil
A generous pinch of ground asafetida
A ¾-inch stick of cinnamon
5   whole cloves
1   dried hot red pepper
6   dried or preferably fresh curry leaves
½   teaspoon finely grated fresh ginger
2   tablespoons minced Chinese parsley

Put the chickpea flour in a 4-cup bowl. Slowly add 2 tablespoons of water so you have a smooth paste. Put the yogurt in another 4-cup bowl. Beat it with a narrow whisk or fork until it becomes smooth and pastelike. Slowly add a cup of water to the yogurt, beating as you do so. Now pour the yogurt mixture into the chickpea mixture little by little, beating all the time.

Pour the contents of the full bowl into a heavy 2-quart pot. Add ½ teaspoon of the whole cumin seeds and ¼ teaspoon of the whole fenugreek seeds. Bring to a boil. Cover, but leave the lid very slightly ajar. Turn heat to low and simmer very gently for 7 to 8 minutes. Add the salt, sugar, and chopped green chili. Cover and cook another 2 minutes. Turn off heat and leave *karhi* covered.

Heat the oil in a very small skillet or small pot over a medium flame. When hot, put in the following spices very quickly and in this order: first the asafetida; then, all together, the cinnamon, cloves, ½ teaspoon whole cumin seeds, and ¼ teaspoon whole fenugreek seeds; then the red pepper and curry leaves. Shake the spices once and immediately empty oil and spices from skillet into the pot with the *karhi*. Cover *karhi* again as soon as this is done. Let the *karhi* rest for 5 minutes. Now put in the grated ginger and Chinese parsley and serve hot.

GUJARATI KARHI WITH OKRA
INDIA

(serves 4)

Follow the preceding recipe through the first paragraph. Pour the contents of the full bowl into a heavy 2-quart pot. Add the ½ teaspoon whole cumin seeds, ¼ teaspoon whole fenugreek seeds, *and* 1¼ cups (buy ¼ pound) okra, trimmed at the ends and sliced into ⅛-inch rounds. Now follow the rest of the recipe. You might add all the ¾ teaspoon salt.

SPICED BUTTERMILK TO EAT WITH INDIAN RICE DISHES

INDIA

In South India, meals often end with plain rice, buttermilk, and pickles. The buttermilk can be unseasoned, or it can be spiced, as in this recipe. It is generally served in small individual bowls and is then poured over the rice on one's plate—or banana leaf! South Indians manage to pick up this wet, souplike combination very deftly with their fingers. For those who are not South Indian, the feat is somewhat more elusive. When serving American guests, I find it more convenient to put small mounds of rice in the center of individual plates and then pass the buttermilk around in a gravy boat. And I supply soupspoons. It may also be served as part of an Indian meal, with *dals* and vegetables.

(serves 2)

1   cup buttermilk
2   teaspoons vegetable oil
¼   teaspoon whole black mustard seeds
¼   teaspoon whole cumin seeds
⅛   teaspoon finely grated ginger
⅓   fresh hot green chili, finely sliced (optional)
⅛   teaspoon salt
Freshly ground black pepper

Put the buttermilk into a serving gravy bowl.

Heat the oil in a small heavy skillet or other small pot over a medium flame. When hot, put in the mustard seeds and cumin seeds. As soon as the mustard seeds begin to pop (this just takes a few seconds), turn off the heat and allow the oil to cool a little. Now pour it over the buttermilk. Add the ginger, green chilies, salt, and pepper. Mix well.

SPICED BUTTERMILK WITH TOMATO

INDIA

This soupy South Indian dish, like the one just before it, is meant to be eaten with rice. Here chopped-up tomatoes and garlic are added to the buttermilk to give it a slightly different flavor.

(serves 2)

1   tablespoon vegetable oil
4   cloves garlic, peeled
⅓ to ½ fresh hot green chili, cut into fine slices (optional)
¼   teaspoon whole cumin seeds
⅛   teaspoon ground turmeric
1   medium-sized, red-ripe tomato, peeled and seeded, and finely chopped
¼   teaspoon salt, or to taste
1   cup buttermilk
Freshly ground black pepper

Heat the oil in a small pot over a medium flame. When hot, put in the garlic and green chili. Stir and fry until the garlic turns a light-brown color. Add the whole cumin seeds and stir for 2 seconds. Put in the turmeric and the tomato. Stir once. Now add ¾ cup water and the salt. Bring to a simmer. Cover, turn heat to low, and simmer for 10 to 15 minutes or until tomatoes are quite tender. Uncover and allow to cool off slightly. Add the buttermilk and black pepper. Stir to mix. Taste for seasonings. Serve at room temperature.

For information about ingredients and basic techniques that may be unfamiliar, see General Information, pages 418–36.

SPICED BUTTERMILK WITH COCONUT AND SHALLOTS

INDIA

Here is another South Indian buttermilk dish that is meant to be eaten with rice. For details, see opposite page. The buttermilk for this should be quite sour. You could, if you like, add a little lemon juice to achieve this. Or else you could try leaving the buttermilk unrefrigerated for 12 to 24 hours before seasoning it.

(serves 2)

2   tablespoons vegetable oil
¼   teaspoon *urad dal*
½   teaspoon whole black mustard seeds
8   dried or fresh curry leaves (optional)
1   dried hot red pepper
2 to 3 good-sized shallots, peeled and cut into slivers
1   quarter-sized slice of fresh ginger, peeled and cut into thin slivers
5   fenugreek seeds
½   cup grated fresh coconut
¼   teaspoon cayenne, or to taste
⅛   teaspoon ground turmeric
¼   teaspoon ground cumin seeds
¼   teaspoon salt
Freshly ground black pepper

Put the oil in a saucepan that is about 6 inches in diameter and heat it over a medium flame. When hot, put in the *urad dal* and the mustard seeds. As soon as the mustard seeds begin to pop, add the curry leaves and the red pepper. Stir for a few seconds until the red pepper swells and turns dark. Put in the shallots and the ginger. Stir and fry until the shallots are very lightly browned. Now put in the fenugreek seeds, coconut, cayenne, turmeric, and cumin. Stir and fry for 1 minute. Empty into a small serving bowl. Pour the buttermilk over the coconut mixture. Add the salt and the pepper. Mix and taste for seasonings.

Soft Yogurt Cheeses

While cheeses like *paneer* (see page 237) may be made by curdling milk, tying the curds in cheesecloth, and letting the whey drip overnight, another kind of soft cheese very popular in the Middle East and India is made with yogurt. Yogurt is tied up in cheesecloth and left to drip from 3 to 8 hours—the 3 hours making for a very soft, creamy cheese and the 8 a slightly firmer but still creamy variety.

Some people prefer to salt the yogurt before they hang it up. I generally leave my salting and spicing to last-minute moods, preferring to do it when the yogurt has turned to cheese. This spicing can take any form that one fancies. In Iran, where tarragon, parsley, Chinese parsley, dill, mint, and chives are loved so much that they are munched by themselves, fresh herbs are often chopped and mixed in with the cheese. In Kuwait, on a burning summer morning, our family once had a wonderful—and simple—breakfast consisting of pitalike breads, olives, and cool yogurt cheese over which some olive oil had been floated. In parts of the Middle East little balls of yogurt cheese are first rolled in paprika, then some olive oil is dribbled over them and the dish eaten at breakfast. In Gujarat, India, I was once served a yogurt cheese that had chopped scallions and Chinese parsley in it; Gujarat has also developed a strained, saffron-enriched, and slightly sweetened yogurt cheese which is served in small individual bowls as part of the main meal, especially at banquets and weddings.

Yogurt cheeses are lighter and less caloric than cream cheeses. They are ideal to serve at breakfast and to put out at parties as dips and spreads.

HOW TO MAKE SOFT YOGURT CHEESE

Whole-milk yogurt makes a creamier cheese. You may, if you prefer, substitute skimmed-milk yogurt. I have not put any salt in this recipe. If you wish to add salt—and you should if you are going to eat it plain—sprinkle ¼ teaspoon over the yogurt before you hang it up.

(makes 1 cup)

1 pound (16 ounces) whole-milk yogurt

Balance a strainer over a bowl. Line the strainer with a tripled thickness of cheesecloth, about 14 inches square. Put the yogurt in the middle of the cheesecloth. Bring the four corners of the cheesecloth together. Now tie the yogurt so as to make a loose bundle. You can do this tying by using one of the four corners of the cheesecloth or by using a

piece of twine. Alternatively, you could sew a cheesecloth bag, put the yogurt inside the bag, and then tie the bag. Suspend the bundle or bag of yogurt where it can drip. I tie mine to the faucet of the kitchen sink. Let it drip for 3 to 8 hours, as your recipe requires. Remove cheese from cheesecloth. Refrigerate until needed in a closed plastic container. If adding herbs or spices, do this before you refrigerate it.

SOFT YOGURT CHEESE WITH DILL
IRAN

Again, this cheese is wonderful for breakfast, along with crisp flat breads, apples, pears, grapes, pomegranates, and figs.

It is good, too, for lunch, again with a Scandinavian crisp whole-wheat bread and a slice of melon. And, it is quite excellent as a spread for crisp breads at parties.

(makes 1 cup)

1 pound (16 ounces) whole-milk yogurt
¼ teaspoon salt
1 cup finely chopped dill

Follow directions for making soft yogurt cheese on opposite page, using 1 pound of whole-milk yogurt. Let the yogurt drip for 8 hours.

Combine yogurt cheese with all the other ingredients in a stainless-steel or nonmetallic bowl. Mix well. Cover and refrigerate for at least 1 hour. If some liquid accumulates, just discard it before you serve.

For information about ingredients and basic techniques that may be unfamiliar, see General Information, pages 418–36.

SOFT YOGURT CHEESE WITH CHINESE PARSLEY AND SCALLIONS GUJARATI STYLE
INDIA

This Gujarati dish is generally served at breakfast and eaten with *khakra*, a fine, crisp bread, any sprouted mung-bean dish, and a fresh green chutney, like Fresh Chinese Parsley and Mint Chutney (see page 364). Because *khakra* is a fairly complicated bread to master I have not included a recipe, but you could substitute Scandinavian whole-wheat flat breads as they are similar to *khakras*. I often put this cheese out in a 1-cup-sized ceramic bowl, filling it all the way to the top and then either smoothing the top or making a design in it with the flat side of a knife as one would with frosting. This cheese may be served as a spread with crackers and crisp breads.

Make sure that the Chinese parsley is thoroughly dry before you mince it.

(makes about 1 cup)

1   pound (16 ounces) whole-milk yogurt
2   tablespoons finely minced fresh Chinese parsley
1   teaspoon finely minced white part of scallion
¼   teaspoon salt
½   teaspoon sugar

Follow directions for making soft yogurt cheese on opposite page, using 1 pound of whole-milk yogurt. Let the yogurt drip for 4 to 5 hours.

Combine the yogurt cheese with all the other ingredients in a stainless-steel or nonmetallic bowl. Mix well. Cover and refrigerate for at least 1 hour. If some liquid accumulates, just discard it before you serve.

SOFT YOGURT CHEESE WITH CRUSHED BLACK PEPPER
INDIA

You could substitute crushed green peppercorns in this recipe, if you like.

(makes 1 cup)

1   pound (16 ounces) whole-milk yogurt
¼   teaspoon salt
¼ to ½ teaspoon crushed, or very coarsely ground black peppercorns

Follow directions for making soft yogurt cheese on opposite page, using 1 pound of whole-milk yogurt. Let yogurt drip for 4 to 5 hours.

Combine yogurt cheese with all other ingredients in a stainless-steel or nonmetallic bowl. Mix well. Cover and refrigerate for at least 1 hour. If some liquid accumulates, just discard it before you serve.

SOFT YOGURT CHEESE WITH CHIVES AND PARSLEY

IRAN

Be sure that the chives and parsley are thoroughly dry before mincing them.

(makes 1 cup)

1   pound (16 ounces) whole-milk yogurt
¼   teaspoon salt
1   tablespoon very finely sliced chives
1   tablespoon finely minced parsley

Follow directions for making soft yogurt cheese on page 234, using 1 pound of whole-milk yogurt. Let the cheese drip for 8 hours.

Combine yogurt cheese with all the other ingredients in a stainless steel or nonmetallic bowl. Mix well. Cover and refrigerate for at least 1 hour. If some liquid accumulates, just discard it before you serve.

SOFT YOGURT CHEESE WITH PAPRIKA AND OLIVE OIL

MIDDLE EAST

(makes 1 cup)

1   pound (16 ounces) whole-milk yogurt
¼   teaspoon salt
¼ to ⅓ teaspoon sweet paprika
1   tablespoon fruity olive oil

Follow directions for making soft yogurt cheese on page 234, using 1 pound of whole-milk yogurt. Let the cheese drip for 8 hours.

Put the cheese and salt in a stainless-steel or nonmetallic bowl. Mix well. Cover and refrigerate until ready to serve.

Spread the cheese out in a shallow, saucerlike bowl and sprinkle the paprika over it. Dribble the oil over the cheese and serve with whole-wheat pita bread and olives (Middle Eastern olives, black or dark green, in oil).

SOFT YOGURT CHEESE WITH FRESH TARRAGON

IRAN

(makes 1 cup)

1   pound (16 ounces) whole-milk yogurt
¼   teaspoon salt
⅛   teaspoon freshly ground black pepper
1   tablespoon finely minced fresh tarragon

Follow directions for making soft yogurt cheese on page 234, using 1 pound of whole-milk yogurt. Let the yogurt drip for 8 hours.

Combine yogurt cheese with all the other ingredients in a stainless-steel or nonmetallic bowl. Mix well. Cover and refrigerate for at least 1 hour. If some liquid accumulates, just discard it before you serve.

For information about ingredients and basic techniques that may be unfamiliar, see General Information, pages 418–36.

SHRIKHAND
(Sweet Soft Yogurt Cheese with Saffron)
INDIA

This Gujarati cheese, made by hanging yogurt up for just 3 hours, has the consistency of a very, very thick cream. The use of saffron and pistachios makes it somewhat expensive, hence it is generally reserved for weddings and banquets.

You may serve this cheese with a meal or after it. If you serve it as dessert, you may wish to make it even sweeter.

This recipe may be doubled easily by doubling all the ingredients. The time for hanging up the yogurt will, of course, remain the same.

(makes about 1 cup and serves 2)

16 ounces (2 cups) plain yogurt, preferably made from whole milk
¼ teaspoon leaf saffron
2 teaspoons warm milk
¼ cup superfine sugar
⅛ teaspoon cardamom seeds
1 teaspoon shelled, unsalted pistachios, cut into slivers

Follow the directions for making soft yogurt cheese on page 234. Hang the yogurt up for just 3 hours.

Meanwhile, soak the saffron in the milk for about 1 hour.

Combine the yogurt cheese, saffron milk, and sugar in a bowl. Mix well with a fork or whisk until creamy. Push this mixture through a very fine sieve to make sure that there are no lumps left. Crush the cardamom seeds to a powder in a mortar and add them to the yogurt. Spoon this mixture neatly into two small bowls. Sprinkle the pistachios over the top. Cover tautly with plastic wrap and chill until ready to eat.

Paneer (Milk Cheese)

In order to get a balanced intake of protein, most Indians tend to eat quite a few milk products at each meal, ranging from plain glasses of cold buttermilk to complicated milk-based sweets. Because of the generally high temperatures in the nation, cheeses, as understood in the West, have never been made in India. But the life of milk has to be stretched in every possible way that the climate allows, and various fresh cheeses—all with the short life of 24 to 48 hours—have been concocted since earliest times with great success.

Paneer is one such cheese and it is made with curdled milk. Actually, *paneer* simply means cheese in most North Indian languages but because *this* particular cheese is popular and well known, it seems to have appropriated the name for itself. Whenever a North Indian says that he has cooked a dish of *paneer*, it is probably this *paneer* that he is referring to. As fresh *paneer* is readily available in Indian bazaars and grocery stores (just as bean curd is in China and Japan), it is seldom made at home. However, making it is not too complicated, though it does require an overnight wait.

PANEER
(Fresh Cheese)
INDIA

(This amount, when mixed with
vegetables, will serve 6)

5 cups whole milk
2½ tablespoons lemon juice

Bring the milk to a boil. As soon as it begins to bubble, put in the lemon juice, stir once, and take the pot off the heat. Leave it for 15 minutes. The milk will curdle and the curds will separate from the whey.

Strain the curds through 3 layers of cheesecloth. Squeeze out as much whey as you can easily. (Do not discard this whey. Refrigerate it and use it in cooking instead of water.) Tie up the curds in the cheesecloth, using twine to make a small, round bundle. Use sufficient twine, as you now need to hang up this bundle somewhere to drip overnight. (I just hang it on the faucet in the sink.)

Next morning, remove the hanging bundle and untie it. Gently flatten it out to make a 4-inch patty, keeping the cheese loosely wrapped in the cheesecloth. Put the cheesecloth-wrapped cheese patty on a sturdy plate

and place a very heavy object (5 to 6 pounds) on top of it. I use one of my very heavy, porcelain-covered cast-iron pots filled with water. If the pot seems in danger of tipping over to one side, I balance it by standing appropriately sized jars under its two handles. Leave the weight on the cheese for 4 to 5 hours. After the cheese has been pressed, it should be ½- to ¾-inch thick.

Remove the cheese from the cheesecloth and, with a sharp knife, cut it into cubes, diamond shapes, or rectangles. If your cheese has pressed down to ½ inch, diamonds or rectangles no longer than an inch are best. If the cheese is about ¾-inch thick, it can be cubed.

NOTE: Some people like to add a little freshly ground pepper and some finely minced Chinese parsley—1 tablespoon—to the curds just after the whey has been strained, before it is tied and hung up.

Paneer, once made, is quite crumbly and breakable. Because of this, it is generally fried and lightly browned before it is cooked. It is a good idea to do this frying in a well-seasoned cast-iron or teflon-lined skillet, as the cheese tends to stick a bit. There are some dishes in which the cheese is not fried at all.

For information about ingredients and basic techniques that may be unfamiliar, see General Information, pages 418–36.

Rather like bean curd, fresh *paneer* has very little taste of its own. It does have texture—and lots of protein. The taste comes from the flavors of the foods with which it is cooked. In a very traditional dish from the Punjab, *paneer* is combined with peas and tomatoes. It is frequently cooked with puréed spinach. It can also be crumbled and added to various grated vegetables (like squash and zucchini) to form "meatballs." It can be crumbled, layered with partially cooked rice, and baked.

MATAR PANEER
(Peas with Paneer)
INDIA

This Punjabi dish, with some variation in the spices, is eaten over all of North India. Indian restaurants, whether in India or outside it, almost always serve it on their *thali*, or vegetarian platter. (As an interesting variation, you could substitute a diced 6-ounce cake of regular bean curd for the *paneer*.)

(serves 6)

1 medium-sized onion, peeled and chopped
About a 1-inch cube fresh ginger, peeled and
    chopped
6 tablespoons vegetable oil
Paneer, see opposite page (plus 2 cups of the whey)
1 whole dried hot red pepper
1 tablespoon ground coriander seeds

¼ teaspoon ground turmeric
3 medium-sized tomatoes, peeled and minced
1 teaspoon salt
⅛ teaspoon freshly ground black pepper
3 cups shelled fresh or 2 packages defrosted frozen
    peas

Put the chopped onion and ginger into the container of an electric blender or food processor along with ⅓ cup water and blend until you have a smooth paste. Leave paste in the blender container.

Heat the oil in a heavy, 10-inch-wide pot (preferably teflon-lined) over a medium flame. When hot, put in the pieces of *paneer* in a single layer and fry them until they are a golden brown on all sides. This happens pretty fast. With a slotted spoon remove fried *paneer* to a plate. Put the dried red pepper into the same oil. Within 2 seconds, turn the pepper over so that it browns on both sides. Now put in the contents of the blender (keep your face averted as the paste might splatter). Fry, stirring constantly, for about 10–12 minutes, or until paste turns a light-brown color.

Add the coriander and turmeric and fry, stirring, for another minute. Put in the minced tomatoes. Stir and fry for another 3 to 4 minutes or until tomatoes turn a dark, reddish-brown shade. Now pour in 2 cups of the whey. Add the salt and the black pepper. Mix well and bring to a boil. Cover, lower heat, and simmer gently for 10 minutes. Lift cover and put in the *paneer* pieces and the peas. Cover and simmer for 10 minutes or until peas are cooked.

SAAG PANEER
(Spinach with Paneer)
INDIA

Saag paneer, a combination of greens and *paneer*, is eaten all over North India with slight variations in the spices. The greens change with the seasons and local preferences: fenugreek greens, collard greens, beet greens, escarole, mustard greens—all can be used. In India, the spinach, which turns into a sauce for the *paneer*, is sometimes creamed. At other times it is left in its chopped state, thus allowing it to stand in equal partnership with the *paneer*. I like the latter method because this way the spinach retains its texture.

I use a 12-inch-wide, 4-inch-high, nonstick sauté pan to make this dish. If you do not have such a pan, fry the *paneer* separately, in a teflon or a well-seasoned cast-iron skillet. Then transfer the oil to a pot large enough to hold the raw spinach, and continue the cooking.

For this recipe, I have used fresh spinach because I prefer its taste. You could use two packages of frozen, chopped spinach if you like. Cook spinach according to package directions, drain well, and proceed with the recipe. Do not salt the spinach twice and remember to cook it very briefly with the ginger-garlic mixture.

For a quick lunch, heat up leftover *Saag Paneer* and stuff it into whole-wheat pita bread halves with thin slices of raw onion and tomato.

(serves 4–6)

A 1-inch cube of fresh ginger, peeled and coarsely chopped
3 to 6 cloves garlic, peeled
½ to 1 fresh hot green chili, sliced roughly

Paneer (see page 238)
Salt
¼ teaspoon *garam masala*
⅛ teaspoon cayenne pepper (optional)
6 tablespoons vegetable oil
1½ pounds spinach, washed, trimmed, and very finely chopped
3 tablespoons heavy cream

Put the ginger, garlic, and green chili into the container of an electric blender or food processor along with ¼ cup water. Blend until you have a smooth paste. You may need to push down with a rubber spatula once.

Heat the oil in a large, wide, preferably nonstick sauté pan over a medium flame. Put in all the pieces of *paneer* and fry them, turning them over gently with a slotted spatula, until they are golden brown on all sides. (This happens fairly quickly.) Remove *paneer* with a slotted spoon and place on a plate in a single layer. Sprinkle *paneer* quickly with the ⅛ teaspoon salt, the *garam masala*, and the cayenne pepper. Set aside.

Put the paste from the blender into the hot oil in your pan (keep face averted) and fry it, stirring constantly, for about 30 seconds. Now put in the spinach and ½ teaspoon salt. Stir the spinach around for 1 minute. Cover the pan, lower the heat, and let the spinach cook gently with the ginger-garlic paste for 15 minutes. There should be enough water clinging to the spinach leaves to cook them. If all the water evaporates, add 1 to 2 tablespoons and continue cooking.

For information about ingredients and basic techniques that may be unfamiliar, see General Information, pages 418–36.

Now put in the *paneer* and cream, stir gently, and bring to a simmer. Cover, and continue cooking on low heat for another 10 minutes. Stir once or twice during this period.

BHAPA DOI
(Steamed Yogurt, Bengali Style)
INDIA

Bhapa doi may be described as a sweet Bengali custard made with boiled-down (and thus thickened) milk and yogurt. Traditionally it is served with meals, though it could easily be served as a dessert or a snack. The Bengalis often use raw palm sugar as the sweetening agent, a sugar that is available in Indian, Chinese, and Thai grocery stores. Jaggery (available only in Indian stores) or brown sugar may be substituted. I tend to go very light on the sugar. If you feel that the custard is not sweet enough for your taste (the time to taste it is just before the steaming), add more sugar.

Bengalis often add saffron to this custard. You may, if you like, throw in ¼ teaspoon leaf saffron into the milk while it is cooking down.

(To my amazement, I found that a kind of yogurt known as *ryazhenka*, which is found in Soviet cities like Moscow and Leningrad today, closely resembles the Bengalis' *bhapa doi*. Yogurt was, supposedly, introduced to the Russians by the Mongols. As the Mongols began raiding India as early as the thirteenth century and finally managed to conquer it in the sixteenth century, the connection between the two yogurt dishes may be more than coincidental.)

(serves 4–6)

5 cups milk
2 tablespoons sugar
⅔ cup plain yogurt (preferably whole-milk)
1 tablespoon pistachios, slivered

Put the milk in a heavy pot. Bring to a boil, being careful not to let it bubble over. Turn heat to low and simmer, stirring, until reduced to 2½ cups. Stir in the sugar and allow to cool. Strain.

Beat yogurt lightly until it is smooth and creamy. (Avoid making bubbles.) Pour in the cooled milk, a little at a time, mixing it in as you do so. Pour the yogurt-milk mixture into a serving dish capable of being steamed (I often use a soufflé or custard dish). Cover tightly with aluminum foil or a lid.

In a larger pan that can hold the serving dish, place a trivet to hold the custard an inch above the bottom. Now pour in an inch of water and bring it to a boil. Place the covered serving dish with the yogurt-milk mixture on the trivet. Cover the steaming pan. Lower heat and simmer very, very gently until yogurt sets, about 15 minutes.

Lift custard container out carefully, without tilting. Uncover and allow to cool.

Garnish with slivered pistachios, cover and refrigerate.

Noodles, Pancakes, and Breads

Asian noodles, made from both grain flours and bean flours, can be thick and starchy as well as threadlike, transparent, and slippery. And, rather like Italian pasta, they may be tossed with cold sauces, hot sauces, and sautéed vegetables.

If you are looking for pleasant first courses to serve during the hot summer months, I cannot imagine anything nicer than Cold Noodles with a Peanut Sauce or Cold Noodles with Sesame Sauce, both of Chinese origin. Or you might serve your noodles the Japanese way, on a bed of ice, with cooling dipping sauces and crisp relishes on the side.

For heartier winter fare, you might try Noodles with Spinach and Mung-Bean Sprouts. I had this extraordinary dish on Cheju Island in South Korea. A mound of freshly cooked noodles was piled in a bowl, standing like a rising island in a sea of steaming broth. The noodles were topped with blanched, seasoned spinach and the spinach topped with blanched, seasoned bean sprouts. The entire hillock had been sprinkled with roasted sesame seeds and crushed red pepper. All we had to do was mix the noodles at the table and eat it with healthy bites of fiery *kimchee* pickles.

Among the more soothing noodle dishes, and one which my children invariably ask for when they return home for vacations, is Crisp-Soft Noodles with a Broccoli, Mushroom, and Zucchini Topping. It looks quite grand. Cooked noodles are fried into a cake, which turns brownish and crisp on the outside but stays quite soft inside. The cake is then smothered with sauced, stir-fried vegetables.

Even though Oriental noodles are used for most of the dishes here, you may use any other pasta of your choice. Spaghetti, spaghettini, and linguini make perfectly fine substitutes.

Pancakes in Asia are made from a variety of beans and grains, the method of cooking depending upon the type of batter. Hoppers from Sri Lanka, for example, are made with a leavened white flour and rice-flour batter. They are cooked, covered, in a wok, and end up with lots of muffinlike holes. I like to eat them with butter and jam, though the more traditional way would be to dip them into mouth-burning *sambals*.

The Filipino Lumpia is no more than a very thin skin made with cornstarch, eggs, and water. It, too, is cooked traditionally in a wok, though I find it more convenient to use a nonstick skillet. The skins are used to enclose a stuffing that can vary from lettuce and fresh heart of palm (when one says *fresh* heart of palm in the Philippines, it usually means that the palm has been felled that morning) to lettuce and sautéed vegetables. The pancakes are wrapped or "packaged" most amusingly to resemble vases, with the greens all popping out enthusiastically from one side.

It is not always easy to separate breads and

pancakes in Asia as they are often eaten in the same way. This is certainly true of many pancakes from India.

Indian pancakes, made out of bean flour, soaked bean, or soaked rice and bean batters, are among India's favorite breakfast and snack foods. Generally speaking, Indian pancakes are made without eggs, white flour, or leavening agents, though in some cases the batter is allowed to stand long enough to ferment naturally. Sometimes the batter is seasoned just with salt. At other times, especially when the pancake is not going to be stuffed, minced ginger, Chinese parsley, and green chilies are mixed in.

Cooking these Indian-style pancakes—and here I include the Korean Bindaetuk, made from mung beans, because it is very similar—is quite an art but one which is not at all difficult to master. In India, the pancakes are always cooked on seasoned, cast-iron griddles. As the batters have a tendency to stick to the griddles, Indian cooks use various methods to make their griddles as "nonstick" as possible. One South Indian housewife I know always grates her coconut onto her griddle, using it as a platter. The natural oil released by the coconut keeps her griddle permanently seasoned. She does not, of course, ever wash it. Another South Indian chef rubs heated griddles with cut onion halves. This simple procedure, he says, makes his griddles "nonstick." My own feeling on the matter is that since one can now buy real nonstick griddles and skillets, why work so hard on cast-iron ones?

The general method for making Indian pancakes is the same: A batter is made, most frequently with beans, or rice and beans that have been soaked and ground. In India, this grinding is done on heavy grinding stones. Here in America it can be done with the greatest of ease in blenders and food processors. This much of the pancake-making process is simplicity itself. The moment of truth comes in spreading out the batter.

Unlike white-flour and egg batters, bean batters do not flow. You cannot tilt your skillet around expertly and have the batter flow to the edges as it would for a crepe. Instead, the batter will sit obstinately like a lump in the center of your skillet. It has to be coaxed to move. This is best done with a round soupspoon.

The first step should be to grease the nonstick skillet very lightly and heat it. Then, drop a blob of batter in the center. Next, put the rounded bottom of the soupspoon *very lightly* on the center of this blob of batter and, using a slow, gentle, but continuous spiral motion, spread the batter outward with the back of the spoon. You can make the pancakes as thin as you like. You may not be able to manage a "continuous spiral" motion the first time around. Do not worry about that. As long as you get the batter to spread, basically using circular motions, that is good enough. Because nonstick skillets have no grip, if you push too hard with the spoon, the entire batter may begin to move. If you have that problem, use a lighter touch and try *not* greasing the skillet before you put in the pancake.

Many of the batters for Indian pancakes can be made ahead of time and refrigerated. So if you want to eat the pancakes for breakfast, you can easily make the batter the night before. Sometimes the pancakes themselves can be made ahead of time and wrapped in aluminum foil. They can then be reheated by being placed in a medium-hot oven for about 15 minutes, still covered in foil.

BREADS

Oven breads, griddle breads, skillet breads, steamed breads, and deep-fried breads, Asia has them all.

When ovens are used, they tend to be made out of clay, stones, or bricks. Sometimes they are even built inside pits. Yeast dough is rolled or patted into round or leaf shapes and then slapped onto the walls or floor of the oven to make breads such as pitas and *naans*. Similar oven breads can be found all over the Caucasus-Caspian Sea region and down through Iran, Afghanistan, and Pakistan into northern India.

Griddle and skillet breads include the *rotis* and *parathas* of India and the Chinese *yow bing*. No yeast is added to the flour. *Rotis* are made with just whole-wheat flour and water and are similar to tortillas except that they puff up like balloons and are much more delicate. Some people serve their *rotis* plain, others smear them with *ghee* as soon as they are made. *Parathas* and *yow bing* are somewhat grander skillet breads. During the process of rolling them out and folding them, several layers of oil are incorporated inside. As they cook, they turn all flaky. *Yow bing* is stuffed with lots of scallions to make it entirely irresistible.

I think Asians do much more steaming than we do here and a great many cakes, buns, breads, and muffins are cooked by this method. *Putu*, for example, is a Filipino muffin made with rice flour and baking powder. Originally, it was steamed in banana-leaf cups but now even the Filipinos have begun to use muffin tins. Chinese buns are made out of white flour and yeast. They puff up into spongy balls as they steam. India has all manner of steamed, savory cakes. *Idlis*, which emerge from the steamer looking like small, harmless flying saucers, are made here from a well-spiced mixture of yogurt and cream of wheat. Served with coffee or buttermilk, they are as common a breakfast food in South India as croissants and coffee are in France.

And then there are the deep-fried breads, such as the Indian *pooris* which puff up into balls in seconds and are quite marvelous when torn and eaten with vegetables.

I have noticed that when making flat Indian breads, it is best to use *ata* or "chappati flour," which is available in Indian grocery stores. It is usually made from hard wheat which is low in gluten. Failing that, you could mix whole-wheat or white flour with cake flour in equal proportions to get a less elastic dough.

COLD NOODLES WITH SESAME SAUCE

CHINA

This is a lovely dish to have in the summer. It is best to use fresh (or frozen) Chinese egg noodles, the kind used to make *lo mein*, but if you have no access to them, dry spaghettini or thin Japanese buckwheat noodles—*ki soba*—may be substituted; be sure to cook them *al dente*. The noodles are served topped with the ground sesame-seed dressing which, in turn, is topped with very finely sliced cucumbers and roasted sesame seeds.

You may, if you like, serve these noodles as a hot dish, in which case do not rinse the noodles after draining them; toss them, while still very hot, first with the 1 tablespoon sesame oil and then with the sesame sauce.

(serves 4 if eaten with other dishes)

1   medium-sized cucumber
½ pound fresh thin Chinese egg noodles (or see above suggestions)
1   tablespoon plus 1 teaspoon sesame oil
4   tablespoons roasted sesame seeds (3 of them ground)
1   tablespoon Chinese thin soy sauce
1   tablespoon Chinese dark soy sauce
2   teaspoons Chinese black vinegar
1½ teaspoons sugar
⅛ teaspoon cayenne pepper
½ teaspoon salt
⅛ teaspoon freshly ground white pepper
1   tablespoon vegetable oil
1   tablespoon Vegetable Stock (see page 292), mushroom soaking liquid, or water

Peel the cucumber, cut it in half lengthwise, and remove all the seeds. Cut into fine julienne strips. Put in a plastic bag and refrigerate.

Bring 10 cups of water to boil in a large pot. Separate the strands of noodles and, when the water is at a rolling boil, drop them in. Let the water come to a boil again. Pour in 1 cup of cold water from the faucet. The boiling will subside. Let the water come to a second boil. Pour in a second cup of cold water. Let the water come to a third boil. Drain the noodles in a colander, then run cold water over the noodles and rinse them off. Let them drain for 5 minutes. Put the noodles in a serving bowl. Add the 1 tablespoon sesame oil to them and toss. You can, if you like, cover and refrigerate the noodles at this stage for a couple of hours.

Combine the 1 teaspoon sesame oil, the *ground* sesame seeds, thin soy sauce, dark soy sauce, vinegar, sugar, cayenne, salt, white pepper, vegetable oil, and stock in a small bowl. Mix well and beat with a fork until you have a smooth paste (you may do this in a food processor or blender).

When ready to serve, pour the sauce over the noodles. Put the julienned cucumber in a little heap on top of the mound of noodles, and top the cucumbers with the remaining roasted whole sesame seeds. Take the noodle bowl to the table this way. The noodles should be tossed—with chopsticks preferably—at the table.

For information about ingredients and basic techniques that may be unfamiliar, see General Information, pages 418–36.

COLD NOODLES WITH A PEANUT SAUCE

CHINA

Cold noodle dishes are lovely to serve in the summer months. As in the preceding recipe, you need fresh thin Chinese egg noodles, the kind that are used in *lo mein*. If you have no access to them, use spaghettini or thin Japanese buckwheat noodles— *ki soba*—cooked *al dente*. The noodles are tossed with a ground peanut dressing and served topped with sliced scallion shreds and some crushed peanuts.

This dish may also be served hot. Do not rinse the noodles after draining them and toss, while still very hot, first with the 1 tablespoon sesame oil and then with the peanut sauce.

(serves 4 if eaten with other dishes)

½ pound fresh thin Chinese egg noodles
   (or see above)
2 tablespoons sesame oil
¼ cup plus 1 tablespoon shelled, salted roasted
   peanuts
1 clove garlic, peeled
1 tablespoon peanut oil
1 tablespoon Chinese thin soy sauce
2 teaspoons Chinese black vinegar
1 teaspoon sugar
⅛ teaspoon cayenne pepper
A 2½-inch piece scallion bottom, cut lengthwise
   into very, very fine strips

Bring 10 cups of water to a boil in a large pot. Separate the strands of noodles and, when the water is at a rolling boil, drop them in. Let the water come to a boil again. Pour in 1 cup of cold water from the faucet. The boiling will subside. Let the water come to a second boil. Pour in a second cup of cold water. Let the water come to a third boil. Drain the noodles in a colander, run cold water over them and rinse. Let them drain for 5 minutes. Put the noodles in a serving bowl. Add 1 tablespoon of the sesame oil to them and toss. You can, if you like, cover, and refrigerate the noodles at this stage for a couple of hours.

Combine the ¼ cup peanuts, 1 tablespoon sesame oil, garlic, peanut oil, soy sauce, vinegar, sugar, cayenne, and ¼ cup water in a food processor or blender. Blend until you have a smooth sauce.

Crush the remaining 1 tablespoon peanuts to a coarse crumb texture in a spice grinder, mortar, or food processor.

When you are ready to eat, pour the sauce over the noodles and toss. Garnish by putting the strips of scallions in a heap on top of the mound of noodles and top with the peanut crumbs.
Serve this way and toss the noodles
at the table, preferably
with chopsticks.

HOT OR COLD NOODLES WITH A SOY-SAUCE DRESSING

CHINA

(serves 4)

½ pound fresh thin Chinese egg noodles (for substitute, see page 246)
2 tablespoons sesame oil
3 tablespoons Chinese thin soy sauce
1 tablespoon distilled white vinegar
1 clove garlic, peeled and mashed to a pulp
½ teaspoon sugar
1 cup fresh, crisp mung-bean sprouts, firmly packed
4 crisp inner romaine leaves, cut crosswise into ¼-inch-wide shreds

Bring 10 cups of water to a boil in a large pot. Separate the strands of noodles and, when the water is at a rolling boil, drop them in. Let the water come to a boil again. Pour in 1 cup of cold water from the faucet. The boiling will subside. Let the water come to a second boil. Pour in a second cup of cold water. Let the water come to a third boil. Drain the noodles in a colander. Run cold water over the noodles and rinse them off. Put the noodles in a serving bowl. Add 1 tablespoon of the sesame oil and toss. You can, if you like, cover and refrigerate the noodles at this stage for a couple of hours.

Combine the remaining 1 tablespoon sesame oil, the soy sauce, vinegar, garlic, and sugar in a small bowl. Set aside.

Wash the mung-bean sprouts thoroughly, drain, and pat them dry.

Just before you get ready to eat, distribute the lettuce and bean sprouts over the noodles. Stir the dressing, pour it over the noodles and vegetables, and toss.

For information about ingredients and basic techniques that may be unfamiliar, see General Information, pages 418–36.

COLD, SUMMER NOODLES

JAPAN

This is very much a summer dish. I know of a restaurant in Kyoto, set right on the river, where thin *somen* noodles, awash in ice water, float by the customers in a man-made stream that runs along the dining tables. Diners are provided with sauces, seasonings, cold barley tea— and chopsticks with which to fish out the moving noodles.

If you cannot find the very thin *somen* noodles, use spaghettini. Just cook it *al dente*, drain and rinse it out well in cold running water. The 1-pound *somen* packets I get in my area are divided into five portions with ribbons. I cook three portions— about 9 ounces—for four people.

Japanese cucumbers are singularly free of large seeds. The closest thing in America is the pickling cucumber. I used two of those in this recipe. You may use the large, regular cucumbers. Just scrape out the seeds first.

(serves 4)

9 ounces *somen*

FOR THE DIPPING SAUCE
2 scallions
1 cup Delicious Stock . . . (see page 292) or *dashi* (see page 291)

6 tablespoons *mirin*
6 tablespoons Japanese soy sauce
⅛ teaspoon 7-spice seasoning
1 teaspoon very finely grated fresh ginger

FOR THE CUCUMBER RELISH
1½ cups peeled cucumber, cut into julienne strips
1 tablespoon Japanese rice vinegar
1 tablespoon sugar
4 teaspoons Japanese soy sauce
1 teaspoon roasted and lightly crushed sesame
  seeds
About 16 ice cubes

Bring 3 cups of water to a rolling boil. Put in a third of the noodles. Stir quickly to separate them. Put in another third of the noodles. Stir briskly again. Put in the remaining noodles and stir briskly. When the noodle water comes to a second boil, pour in 1 cup of cold faucet water. When the noodle water comes to a third boil, empty the contents of the pot into a colander set in the sink. Rinse the noodles well in running water. Put the noodles in a bowl, cover with water, and refrigerate for at least 1 hour.

Cut the scallions into fine rings. Put in a bowl of water and refrigerate for at least 1 hour.

Combine the stock, *mirin*, soy sauce, and 7-spice seasoning in a bowl. Put the grated ginger in a small sieve and lower it partially into the stock mixture. Stir the ginger around to release its juice. Lift up the sieve. Press the ginger with the back of a spoon to release more of the juice. Refrigerate the stock.

Put the cucumber in a small plastic container, cover tightly, and refrigerate. Combine all the seasonings except sesame seeds for the cucumber relish in a small bowl. Mix well until the sugar is dissolved. Refrigerate separately.

To assemble the dish, crack each ice cube into two to three pieces. Put some ice at the bottom of four chilled bowls. Drain the noodles and divide them up among the bowls. Tuck some ice all around them and even lay some over. Pour the dipping sauce into four smaller bowls. Remove the scallions from their water and scatter them over the dipping sauce. Pour the seasoning sauce for the cucumber relish over the julienned cucumbers and toss. Divide this relish among four small bowls. Sprinkle the sesame seeds over the cucumbers. To eat, pick up some noodles with chopsticks (or a fork), dunk in the dipping sauce, and then suck them in. Refresh yourself now and then with some of the cucumber.

NOODLES WITH A HOT-AND-SOUR BEAN SAUCE

CHINA

(serves 4–6)

8   Chinese dried black mushrooms
2   teaspoons cornstarch
½ cup bean paste
1   tablespoon Chinese thin soy sauce
3   tablespoons white distilled vinegar
3½ tablespoons sugar
2   tablespoons chili paste with soy beans and garlic
1   tablespoon sesame oil
2   tablespoons vegetable oil
3   cloves garlic, peeled and minced
3   quarter-sized slices of fresh ginger, minced
3   scallions, cut into fine rings, including green
1   tablespoon roasted and very lightly crushed sesame seeds
¾ pound fresh Chinese *lo-mein* egg noodles (or spaghettini cooked *al dente*)

Soak the mushrooms in 1½ cups hot water for half an hour. Lift out of the soaking liquid. Remove the hard stems and cut the caps into ⅛-inch-wide strips.

Put the cornstarch into a bowl. Slowly mix in 1¼ cup water. Add the bean paste, soy sauce, vinegar, sugar, chili paste, and sesame oil. Stir to mix.

Heat the vegetable oil in a wok or pot over a medium flame. When hot, put in the garlic and ginger. Stir briskly and fry for 5 seconds. Add the mushrooms and scallions. Stir and fry for another minute. Turn heat to low. Give the cornstarch mixture a quick stir and pour it into the wok. Turn heat up to medium-low and cook for a minute or two or until the sauce thickens. Add the sesame seeds and mix. (This sauce may be made ahead of time and reheated.)

Bring 3 quarts of water to a rolling boil. Separate the strands of noodles gently and drop into the water. When the water comes to a second boil, pour in 1 cup of cold faucet water. When the water comes to a boil for a third time, pour in another cup of cold faucet water. When the water comes to a boil for the fourth time, empty the contents of the pot into a colander set in the sink. Put the noodles in a bowl. Spoon as much of the sauce as you think you need over the noodles. Toss and serve.

THICK NOODLES IN A WINTER STEW

JAPAN

This is a one-pot, Hokkaido-style dish that may be cooked at the table in a hot pot or in a not-very-large electric skillet. It may also be cooked in a pretty, casserole-type pot in the kitchen and then brought to the table in the same pot.

Udon, the thick, dried noodles that are used in

For information about ingredients and basic techniques that may be unfamiliar, see General Information, pages 418–36.

this stew, may be made out of white or whole-wheat flour and you can find them in Japanese, Korean, and health-food stores. If you cannot find *udon*, use spaghetti. Time it so that it is ready just when the vegetables have finished cooking, then drain and add directly to the stew.

If you cannot find fresh water chestnuts in your area, just leave them out.

(serves 4)

8   dried *shiitake* mushrooms
⅓ pound *udon*
2   scallions
1   carrot
4   Chinese cabbage leaves or 5 of the softer leaves from a regular cabbage
4   fresh water chestnuts
About 4 to 6 ounces medium bean curd
4   cups Delicious Stock . . . (see page 292)
¼ teaspoon salt
1   teaspoon Japanese soy sauce
1   teaspoon *mirin*
8   pieces peeled white radish, about ½-inch thick and 1 inch across

FOR THE DIPPING SAUCE
½ cup Japanese soy sauce
½ cup lemon juice

Soak the mushrooms in a cup of hot water for half an hour. Lift them out of the hot water and cut off the hard stems. Cut each cap in half.

Cook *udon* according to package instructions. Drain immediately and rinse under cold running water. Put in a bowl and cover with cold water.

Cut the scallions into 2-inch lengths.

Peel the carrot and cut into ½-inch-thick rounds.

Lay the cabbage leaves one on top of the other and cut, crosswise, at 1-inch intervals.

Peel the water chestnuts and cut into halves.

Cut the bean curd into ½- to ¾-inch cubes.

Combine the stock, salt, 1 teaspoon soy sauce, and *mirin* in a bowl.

Mix the ingredients for the dipping sauce and divide among four small, shallow bowls (or as many bowls as there are people). Set these bowls up at the table. Also arrange chopsticks, soupspoons, and eating bowls at each setting. Drain the noodles. You may now proceed to cook at the table or in the kitchen.

Heat the stock. When it is simmering, put in the scallions and radish pieces. Simmer for a minute. Put in the carrot. Simmer another minute. Put in the water chestnuts. Simmer a minute. Put in the cabbage and mushrooms. Cook for 6 minutes more or until all vegetables are just tender. Put in the noodles and the bean curd and cook until they are just heated through. (If you are "cooking" at the table, the noodles and the bean curd would be dipped by each diner, one mouthful amount at a time, in the barely simmering broth and heated through.) Either pick choice ingredients out of the common pot, dip in the sauce and eat, or else serve yourselves in the bowls.

NOODLES WITH TEMPURA VEGETABLES
JAPAN

The Japanese seem to love everything about tempura, or batter-fried foods. Even the tiny pieces of batter that float free of the vegetables are scooped up to be used later in soups as dumplings. Leftover vegetables have another use. They are mounted over hot noodles (or rice), the combination moistened with some broth, and then quickly slurped up for thousands of quick lunches and quick dinners throughout the country.

(serves 4)

4   cups Delicious Stock . . . (see page 292)
2   teaspoons Japanese soy sauce
2   teaspoons *mirin*
½ pound *soba* noodles
16 to 20 pieces Tempura (see page 75)

2   scallions, cut into fine rounds
About ¼ teaspoon 7-spice seasoning
Additional soy sauce

Combine the stock, 2 teaspoons soy sauce, and *mirin* and bring to a simmer. Leave on a very low flame.

Cook the noodles according to the instructions on the packet. Drain them and divide among four bowls. Put 4 to 5 pieces of tempura over each mound of noodles. Pour the hot broth over the tempura and noodles. Scatter the scallions over the top and sprinkle some 7-spice seasoning into each bowl. Cover the bowls immediately and leave for 3 to 4 minutes.

Serve extra soy sauce on the side.

CRISP-SOFT NOODLES
WITH A BROCCOLI, MUSHROOM, AND ZUCCHINI TOPPING
CHINA

Here is another dish that our family eats with great relish. I learned how to make it from a Jamaican-Chinese immigrant who owned a tiny restaurant near an Off-Broadway theater where I worked many years ago. I had hardly any money then and this dish was cheap. The Jamaican lady put in any scraps of vegetables that she happened to have lying around—I remember that there were always more onions than I cared for—and, because she

had grown quite fond of me during the course of a long run, a good bit of cayenne pepper to please my Indian palate. This dish is somewhat more elegant—there is no cayenne in it, though you could add that, if you like, and it has positively *no* onions.

My Jamaican friend used a wok to fry her noodles. I find it much easier to use a nonstick skillet.

You do need a large, preferably round platter to

For information about ingredients and basic techniques that may be unfamiliar, see General Information, pages 418–36.

serve the noodles, at least as large as the bottom circumference of your skillet and with some depth so it can hold the vegetables and sauce.

(serves 4)

½ pound fresh Chinese *lo mein* egg noodles
1   medium-sized zucchini
1   teaspoon salt
About half a bunch of broccoli (about 2 cups, when cut)
8   medium-sized mushrooms
2   teaspoons cornstarch
¾   cup Delicious Stock . . . (see page 292)
2   tablespoons bean sauce
2   teaspoons sugar
1   tablespoon sesame oil
7   tablespoons vegetable oil
2   cloves garlic, peeled and minced
1   quarter-sized slice of fresh ginger, minced
1   tablespoon *shaohsing* wine or dry sherry

Bring 13 cups of water to a rolling boil. Gently separate the noodle strands and drop them into the water. When the water comes to a second boil, pour in 1 cup of cold faucet water. When the water comes to a third boil, pour in another cup of cold faucet water. When the water comes to a fourth boil, empty the contents of the pot into a colander set in the sink. Rinse the noodles under running water, washing off a lot of the starch. Leave to drain for at least half an hour.

Trim the zucchini ends and then cut it in half, lengthwise. Cut the halves crosswise at ¼-inch intervals. Put the zucchini in a bowl. Sprinkle ¼ teaspoon salt over it and mix. Set aside for half an hour. Drain and pat dry.

Cut the broccoli into slim flowerets, not more than 2 inches long. You can use some of the stems, too. Just peel and cut them into ¼-inch-thick strips. In all, you should have about 2 cups.

Wipe off the mushrooms and then cut them, stem and all, into ¼-inch-thick slices.

Put the cornstarch in a small bowl. Slowly add the stock, mixing as you do so. Add the bean sauce, sugar, and sesame oil. Mix well.

Heat 3 tablespoons of the vegetable oil in a 7- to 8-inch, nonstick skillet over a medium flame. When the oil is hot, put in the noodles, spreading them out evenly over the entire bottom of the skillet. Fry without stirring for about 4 minutes or until the bottom of the noodle patty is a reddish-golden color and is crisp. Now slip one spatula under the noodles and hold the top of the patty with another spatula. Turn the patty over. Dribble another tablespoon of vegetable oil along the edges of the skillet, allowing it to slither downward. Cook the second side until it, too, has turned a reddish-golden color. Carefully lift up the patty and put it on a warm platter.

Heat 3 tablespoons of vegetable oil in a wok or skillet over a medium flame. When hot, put in the garlic and ginger. Stir a couple of times. Put in the mushrooms, broccoli, and ¾ teaspoon salt. Stir and fry, turning the vegetables around briskly. Put in the zucchini. Stir and fry for another 30 seconds. Now add the wine, cover immediately and turn heat to low. Cook for 1 minute. Uncover, give the cornstarch mixture a quick stir and pour it over the vegetables. Turn heat up a bit and cook, stirring gently, until the sauce thickens. Spoon the vegetables and sauce over the noodles and serve immediately.

NOODLES WITH SPINACH AND MUNG-BEAN SPROUTS

KOREA

This dish should be served surrounded by several small bowls of seasonings and relishes. Of these, perhaps the most essential are finely crushed dried hot red peppers, soy sauce, and Cabbage Kimchee. The ideal eating implements would be chopsticks and a soupspoon for each person. Of course, you can use whatever you feel comfortable with.

I have used the fresh *lo mein* egg noodles for this dish but you could use spaghetti or linguini, cooked according to instructions, then rinsed under cold, running water.

(serves 4)

5   Chinese dried black mushrooms
½ pound fresh Chinese *lo mein* egg noodles
1   pound fresh spinach
2   teaspoons salt
1   tablespoon sugar
1   cup fresh mung-bean sprouts, washed and drained
3   tablespoons Japanese soy sauce
1   tablespoon sesame oil
2   cups Delicious Stock . . . (see page 292)
1   tablespoon fresh Chinese chives or scallion tops, cut into ½-inch lengths
1   tablespoon roasted and lightly crushed sesame seeds
⅛ teaspoon finely crushed dried hot red pepper or cayenne pepper

TO SERVE ON THE SIDE

A very small bowl with finely crushed dried hot red pepper or cayenne pepper
A very small bowl with Japanese soy sauce in it

A bowl of Cabbage Kimchee, homemade (see page 379) or store-bought

Soak the mushrooms in 1 cup hot water for half an hour. Lift them out of the water and cut off the hard stems. Cut the caps into ⅛-inch-wide strips. Bring 3 quarts of water to a rolling boil. Gently separate the noodle strands and drop them into the water. When the water comes to a second boil, pour in 1 cup of cold faucet water. When the water comes to a third boil, pour in another cup of cold faucet water. When the water comes to a fourth boil, empty the contents of the pot into a colander set in the sink. Wash the noodles in cold running water and leave to drain.

Wash the spinach and separate the leaves. Do not discard the pinkish roots, if there are any. Just peel and then quarter them lengthwise.

Bring 3 cups of water with the salt and 1 teaspoon of the sugar to a rolling boil. Put the bean sprouts into a small sieve and lower the sieve into the water. After the water comes to a boil again, cook the sprouts for about 20 seconds. Drain and rinse under running water. Set the sieve on a bowl and leave to drain.

Drop the spinach into the same water and boil for about 2 minutes or until it has wilted completely. Drain in a large sieve or colander and rinse under running water. Leave to drain.

Mix together 2 tablespoons soy sauce, 2 teaspoons sugar, and the 1 tablespoon sesame oil in a small cup.

Just before you sit down to eat, add 1 tablespoon soy sauce to the stock and heat it. Drop the noodles into the stock. As soon as the noodles have heated through, remove them with a slotted spoon or a pair of tongs and pile them in the center of a

---

For information about ingredients and basic techniques that may be unfamiliar, see General Information, pages 418–36.

serving bowl. Keep warm. Put the spinach and mushrooms into the stock. When they have heated through, lift them out with a slotted spoon and put them in a work bowl. Put the sprouts into the same stock. When they have heated through, lift them out also with a slotted spoon and put them in another work bowl. Quickly season the spinach and mushrooms with 2 tablespoons of the soy mixture and the sprouts with the remaining soy mixture. Heap the spinach over the noodles and the sprouts over the spinach. Pour the remaining stock around the mound of noodles and vegetables. Scatter the chives on top of the mound. Sprinkle the sesame seeds and the ⅛ teaspoon cayenne pepper over the entire dish. Serve at once, with the suggested seasonings and *kimchee.*

VEGETARIAN MEE KROB
(Crisp Noodles with Pressed Bean Curd and Eggs)
THAILAND

A very fine rice vermicelli, called *mee* in Thailand, is used to make this dish. The vermicelli is first fried until it is crisp and then tossed with a hot, sweet, salty, and sour combination of pork, shrimp, pressed bean curd, and eggs. (I have eliminated the pork and shrimp.) This combination has to be cooked until it is quite dry, else the vermicelli turns soggy.

Mee may be bought from Thai grocery stores. Get the thinnest variety available. Fine Chinese rice sticks may be used as a substitute.

(serves 4–6)

6 ounces *mee* (see above)
Vegetable oil for deep frying, about 2 cups
½ cup very finely chopped, peeled shallots
1 tablespoon peeled and minced garlic
1 to 2 fresh hot green chilies, minced
1 cake pressed bean curd, cut into julienne strips
5 large eggs
1½ teaspoons salt
2 tablespoons Japanese soy sauce
¼ cup distilled white vinegar
2 tablespoons sugar
2 tablespoons tomato ketchup
¼ to ½ teaspoon cayenne pepper
Freshly ground black pepper
Peel from ½ lemon, cut into very thin, 1-inch-long strips
¼ cup fresh Chinese (or other) chives, cut into ½-inch lengths
¼ cup fresh Chinese parsley leaves
1 cup fresh mung-bean sprouts, washed, drained, and patted dry
Garnish: additional parsley sprigs

Soak the *mee* in hot, not boiling, water for a minute or until they soften. Drain immediately.

Line two large platters with paper towels and keep nearby.

Heat the oil over a high flame. When very hot, throw in a small handful of *mee.* Fry for about 30 to 40 seconds, then turn over what will look like a thin pancake of vermicelli. Fry for 30 to 40 seconds on the second side. The *mee* should turn a lovely reddish-golden color and be quite crisp. Remove it with a slotted spoon and leave to drain on the paper towels. Fry all the *mee* this way.

Take the wok off the flame and remove all but ¼ cup of the oil. Heat this over a medium flame. Put in the shallots, garlic, and green chili. Stir and fry until the shallots are lightly browned. Put in the bean curd and stir for a minute. Now break all the eggs into the wok. Stir for a minute, breaking up the yolks. Add the salt, soy sauce, vinegar, sugar, ketchup, cayenne, and lots of black pepper. Stir and fry until the eggs have solidified completely. Turn the heat to medium-low. Continue stirring and frying another 15 to 20 minutes or until the mixture is completely dry, lowering heat if necessary.

Just before you are ready to eat, toss the *mee* with the egg mixture, the lemon peel, chives, and Chinese parsley leaves. Arrange on a platter. Scatter the bean sprouts over the top and garnish with the additional parsley sprigs.

NOODLES WITH QUAIL EGGS, MUSHROOMS, SPINACH, AND YUBA

JAPAN

This dish tastes best with freshly boiled quail eggs. If you cannot find them, use 2 small chicken eggs, hard-boiled, peeled, and cut into halves.

Yuba is the Japanese name for the skin that forms on top of cooling soy-bean milk. When fresh, this skin is creamy and quite heavenly. It can only be purchased in its dried form here and therefore needs to be reconstituted by a soaking in water. The trouble is that there are so many forms of dried soy-milk skin in Oriental markets, each requiring a different soaking time, and each with a different shape and thickness. Japanese stores sell

very fine, flaky *yuba* rolls, all tied with a *konbu* "thread." These would be ideal for this dish. They require about 15 minutes of soaking. Chinese stores sell packets of what is called "Dried Bean Curd, Slice Type." These slices need to be soaked for 45 minutes and then cut into 1-inch squares.

(serves 4)

8 small *yuba* rolls or 8 1-inch squares of bean-curd skin
4 dried *shiitake* mushrooms
½ pound *udon* or *soba* (Japanese noodles)
4 quail eggs
¼ pound fresh spinach leaves
4 cups Delicious Stock . . . (see page 292)
¼ teaspoon salt
1 tablespoon plus extra Japanese soy sauce
1 tablespoon *mirin*
2 teaspoons very finely grated fresh ginger

Soak the *yuba* in 2 cups water until it is creamy in color and soft (see note above).

Soak the mushrooms in ¾ cup hot water for half an hour. Lift out of the water. Cut off the hard stems and cut each cap into ⅛-inch-thick strips.

Cook the noodles according to package instructions. Drain and rinse under cold running water.

Cook the quail eggs 5 minutes in barely simmering water. Cool in cold water and peel.

Bring 3 cups of water to a rolling boil. Throw in the spinach leaves and cook rapidly for 2 minutes. Drain and rinse under cold water. Leave to drain.

Bring the stock to a boil. Add the salt, 1 tablespoon soy sauce, and *mirin*. Put in the noodles and heat through. Remove the noodles with tongs and divide among four bowls. Put in the spinach and mushrooms. When they have heated through, lift them out with a slotted spoon and lay them on top

---

For information about ingredients and basic techniques that may be unfamiliar, see General Information, pages 418–36.

of the noodles. Drop in the *yuba* and eggs. Simmer for 30 seconds. Lift out of the liquid and place somewhere near the vegetables. Pour some of the broth into each bowl. Divide the ginger into four neat heaps and place each in a tiny saucer. Offer extra soy sauce that may be mixed with the ginger and used for added seasoning.

VEGETABLE LO MEIN

CHINA
                                        (serves 4–6)

½ pound fresh Chinese *lo mein* egg noodles
5   medium-sized Chinese dried black mushrooms
6   stalks (about 10 to 12 ounces) *choy sum*
About 6 ounces cabbage (¼ small-sized head)
1   fresh hot green chili
2   scallions
2   cloves garlic, peeled
1   cup mung-bean sprouts
¼   cup Chinese dark soy sauce
1   tablespoon sesame oil
2¾ teaspoons sugar
⅛   teaspoon cayenne pepper
Freshly ground black pepper
6   tablespoons vegetable oil
Salt
½   cup Delicious Stock . . . (see page 292)
¼   cup fresh Chinese (or other) chives, cut into
    1½-inch lengths

Bring 13 cups of water to a rolling boil. Gently separate the noodle strands and drop them into the water. When the water comes to a second boil, pour in 1 cup of cold faucet water. When the water comes to a third boil, pour in another cup of cold faucet water. When the water comes to a fourth boil, empty the contents of the pot into a colander set in the sink. Rinse the noodles thoroughly in cold running water, washing away any extra starch. Leave the noodles in the colander to drain for half an hour.

Soak the mushrooms in 1 cup hot water for half an hour. Lift them out of the water and cut off their hard stems. Cut the mushroom caps into ⅛-inch-wide strips.

Cut the leaves of the *choy sum* crosswise into ⅛-inch-wide strips. Cut the stems lengthwise into thin, 2- to 3-inch-long strips, peeling them wherever the skin seems too coarse.

Core the cabbage and cut it into long, ⅛-inch-wide strips.

Cut the green chili into ⅛-inch-thick strips. Seed it if you do not want the dish to be somewhat hot.

Cut the scallions into 2½-inch-long sections and then cut these sections lengthwise into very thin strips.

Cut the garlic into very thin strips.

Wash the bean sprouts well and leave to drain.

In a cup, mix together the soy sauce, sesame oil, 2 teaspoons sugar, cayenne pepper, and black pepper.

Heat 3 tablespoons of vegetable oil in a large wok over a medium flame. Put in the garlic and give it a few stirs. Put in the green chili and give another few stirs. Put in the mushrooms. Stir for 5 seconds. Now add the *choy sum*, cabbage, scallions, ¾ teaspoon salt, and ¾ teaspoon sugar. Stir-fry for about 3 minutes or until the vegetables wilt. Remove the vegetables and put them in a bowl.

Add another 3 tablespoons of vegetable oil to the wok. When it is hot, put in the drained noodles. Let the noodles just sit for a few seconds.

Then stir-fry them for another few seconds. Put in the stock and turn the heat up slightly. Stir gently and cook until all the liquid seems absorbed. Put in the soy-sauce mixture and stir to mix. Put back the cooked vegetables. Stir gently to mix. Put in the bean sprouts and chives. Stir-fry another 2 minutes.

CHAPCHAE
(Cellophane Noodles with Vegetables)
KOREA

(serves 4)

2 ounces "cellophane" mung-bean noodles
6 Chinese dried black mushrooms
⅓ pound tender spinach leaves
1 carrot
1 small zucchini
3 medium-sized mushrooms
2 Chinese cabbage leaves
4 scallions
4 tablespoons vegetable oil
1 tablespoon sesame oil
3 cloves garlic, peeled and minced
1 tablespoon Japanese soy sauce
1 teaspoon sugar
½ teaspoon salt

Soak the noodles in 6 cups of water for half an hour. Drain.

Soak the Chinese mushrooms in 1 cup hot water for 20 minutes. When they have softened, cut off the hard stems and slice the caps fine.

Drop the spinach into 10 cups of boiling water. Boil rapidly for 2 minutes. Drain. Run under cold water. Squeeze out as much moisture as possible.

Peel the carrot, cut into 3 sections and then into fine julienne strips.

Trim the zucchini ends and cut into fine julienne strips.

Wipe off the fresh mushrooms and break off their stems. Cut the caps into very fine slices. Cut the nonwoody part of the stems into matchstick pieces.

Cut away and discard the curly, tender part of the cabbage leaves. Save only the V-shaped core of the leaves. Cut this into julienne strips.

Cut the scallions into 2½-inch sections. Quarter the section with the bulb lengthwise.

Combine the Chinese mushrooms, spinach, carrot, zucchini, mushrooms, cabbage, and scallions in a bowl. Mix well, separating all the spinach leaves.

Heat the vegetable oil and the sesame oil in a wok or a 10-inch sauté pan over a medium-high flame. When hot, put in the garlic. Stir and fry for 10 seconds. Add all the vegetables in the bowl. Stir and fry for 3 to 4 minutes or until the vegetables are tender-crisp. Turn the heat to low. Add the drained noodles, soy sauce, sugar, and salt. Stir well, distributing the noodles evenly, and cook 2 to 3 minutes. Taste for seasonings.

For information about ingredients and basic techniques that may be unfamiliar, see General Information, pages 418–36.

BIBINGKA
(Sweet Rice Pancake)
PHILIPPINES

Everywhere the colonial Portuguese went, they taught the locals to make sweetmeats out of eggs. On India's west coast they taught the Goans to make a cake of stacked pancakes that used forty eggs; Thais were taught how to make glazed egg yolks and sweet egg-yolk vermicelli; and in the Philippines, *bibingka* soon became dominant among snack-time favorites. In its simplest form the *bibingka* is made from fermented ground rice, eggs, sugar, and either coconut milk or water. These days the natural fermentation process is replaced by the faster-working baking powder. More elaborate *bibingkas* are studded with pieces of carabao cheese and salted, boiled duck eggs. When the *bibingka* is served, it is smeared with butter and then dusted with confectioners' sugar as well as freshly grated coconut.

Traditionally, *bibingkas* are cooked in banana-leaf-lined clay baking trays placed over live charcoal. These individual baking trays are covered with a second tray that holds more live charcoal. I have made my *bibingka* quite a bit larger and cooked it in an oven. Instead of ground rice, I have used rice powder.

In the Philippines, these pancakes are often served with hot Salabat (ginger tea).

(serves 6)

2 large eggs
⅓ cup sugar
1 cup rice powder (rice flour)
2 teaspoons baking powder

About 2 tablespoons unsalted butter
1 tablespoon or more confectioners' sugar
¼ cup or more freshly grated coconut

Preheat oven to 400° F.

Beat the eggs and sugar together until light and creamy. In a blender or food processor, combine the rice powder, baking powder, and ½ cup water. Let the machine run for 3 to 4 minutes or until the batter is smooth and satiny. If some rice flour clings to the sides of the container, release it with a rubber spatula. Pour the rice-flour mixture into the egg mixture and fold it in. It should be thoroughly blended.

Grease an 8-inch cake tin generously with butter and pour the batter into it. Bake about 15 to 20 minutes or until batter has just set and a toothpick inserted inside the pancake comes out clean. Remove the pancake from the baking tin and put it on a plate. Smear with butter—as much butter as pleases you—and then dust first with the confectioners' sugar and then the coconut. Serve hot.

Mrs. Roxas'
LUMPIA
(Vegetables Wrapped in Pancakes)
PHILIPPINES

You could stuff these pancakes yourself for your family and friends or, better still, you could teach them to do it themselves. It is great fun and keeps everyone gainfully employed. Each pancake contains a crisp leaf of lettuce, which sticks out merrily like a plume at the top, as well as some stir-fried vegetables which stay discreetly inside. Lumpia is considered "finger-food" and is generally not eaten with cutlery.

Lumpia pancakes may be made several hours in advance and kept covered between sheets of waxed paper.

(makes 8 stuffed pancakes)

FOR THE PANCAKES
½ cup cornstarch
2 large eggs, separated
About 2 teaspoons vegetable oil

FOR THE STUFFING
4 tablespoons vegetable oil
2 teaspoons peeled and minced garlic
½ cup onion, peeled and sliced into fine half rings
4 cups finely shredded cabbage
⅓ cup carrot, peeled and cut into ¼-inch dice
¼ cup celery, cut into ¼-inch dice
¾ cup fresh green beans, cut crosswise at ⅛-inch intervals
¾ teaspoon salt, or to taste
Freshly ground black pepper
8 crisp romaine leaves

FOR THE SAUCE
1 tablespoon cornstarch
½ cup Delicious Stock . . .
    (see page 292) or any vegetable stock
½ cup dark brown sugar
1½ tablespoons Japanese soy sauce
1 tablespoon lightly crushed, fried, or roasted peanuts (optional)
A few drops of Tabasco sauce (optional)

Make the pancakes first. Mix the cornstarch slowly with 1 cup water. In a separate bowl, beat the whites of the eggs until frothy. Fold in the yolks, beating lightly to mix. Give the cornstarch mixture a stir and pour it into the bowl with the eggs. Strain the batter.

Heat an 8-inch, nonstick skillet over a low flame. When hot, pour in ¼ teaspoon oil and spread it with a piece of paper towel or brush. Stir the batter and pour ¼ cup into the skillet. Quickly tilt the skillet in a circular motion so the batter covers the entire bottom surface. Cook on low heat for about 1½ minutes or until the batter has set. Peel off the thin pancake (I find it easier to use my fingers) and put the pancake on a large plate. Cover with a sheet of waxed paper. Make all the pancakes this way, stirring the batter each time. Stack the pancakes on top of each other, with a layer of waxed paper in between. Cover the pancakes with an inverted plate.

Make the stuffing next. Heat the oil in a wok or

For information about ingredients and basic techniques that may be unfamiliar, see General Information, pages 418–36.

skillet over
a medium flame.
Put in the garlic.
Stir for a few seconds
or until the garlic browns
lightly. Put in the onion and stir-fry
for 30 seconds. Put in the cabbage and stir-fry for
about 1 minute or until the cabbage wilts. Put in
the carrot, celery, green beans, and salt. Turn heat
to low. Stir and cook another 6 to 8 minutes or
until all vegetables are cooked but still crisp. Add
some freshly ground black pepper and mix. Leave
until the mixture reaches room temperature.

Wash the lettuce leaves and pat them with a dish
towel until they are completely dry. If not used
immediately, refrigerate in a plastic bag.

Make the sauce. Mix together the cornstarch
and ½ cup water until smooth. Add the stock,
sugar, and soy sauce. Heat in a small pot over a
lowish flame, stirring as you do so. When the
sauce thickens, turn off the flame. Add the peanuts

and Tabasco, if you want to. The sauce may be
served lukewarm or at room temperature.

Assemble the *lumpia* as illustrated. 1. Lay a
pancake in front of you. Put a lettuce leaf down in
the center, its pointed end away from you and
protruding a few inches outside the pancake. Divide
the vegetable stuffing into eight parts. Lay one part
along the length of the lettuce leaf that is inside the
pancake. 2. Fold the left side of the pancake tightly
over the vegetable stuffing. 3. Fold the bottom of
the pancake—that is, the end nearest you—over
the stuffing. Now fold the right side of the pancake
over the stuffing to form a roll. 4. Dribble some
sauce inside the roll from its open end and start
eating.

Neela's

CHAURA NA POORA
(Black-Eyed Pea Pancakes)
INDIA

This scrumptious savory pancake, given here with its Gujarati name, is eaten in western and southern India. It is spicy, light, but quite satisfying, and exceedingly nourishing. It can be eaten at any time of the day, but is ideal for breakfasts and snacks. To make it, black-eyed peas have to be soaked overnight in water. Next morning, their skins are rubbed off and the beans are ground in a food processor or blender into a batter. Ginger, garlic, green chilies, Chinese parsley, salt, and turmeric are added to the batter and then the pancakes are cooked on a nonstick griddle or skillet. Please read the section on Indian Pancakes, page 244, especially the part that deals with cooking the pancakes, before you make *chaura na poora*. Also, remember that the batter can be made up to 24 hours in advance and then covered and refrigerated. Stir it well before you begin cooking.

(makes 12–14 pancakes)

1½ cups dried black-eyed peas, picked over, rinsed, and drained
A ¾-inch cube of fresh ginger, peeled, and cut into 4 pieces
5 cloves garlic, peeled
1 to 2 fresh hot green chilies, cut into quarters
1 teaspoon salt
¼ teaspoon ground turmeric
1 tablespoon minced Chinese parsley
About ¾ cup vegetable oil

Soak the peas for 12 to 16 hours in a bowl filled with 4 cups of water. Then peel the peas by dip-ping your hands into the bowl of peas and water and rubbing them between your two palms. Drain and spread the peas out on a large platter and pick off the skins that have been loosened. (Do not worry if not all the skins have come loose.)

Start your food processor with the metal blade in place. Through the funnel, drop in the ginger pieces first, followed by the garlic cloves and the green chili (or chilies). When they are minced, stop the machine and put in all the drained black-eyed peas. Start the machine again and let it run until the peas turn pastelike. Now stop the machine and add 1⅓ cups water, the salt, turmeric, and Chinese parsley. Run the machine for another minute to make a thickish batter. Empty batter into a bowl. (This batter can also be made in an electric blender.)

See that you have everything you need for *poora*-making. Not far from your nonstick skillet should be your oil (take it out in a cup) and a teaspoon, a rounded soupspoon for spreading out the batter, your bowl of batter, a ⅓-cup measuring cup, and a plastic spatula. Also have a plate beside you on which you can put the *pooras* as they are cooked.

Pour 1 teaspoon of oil into an 8-inch nonstick skillet. Spread the oil around by tilting the skillet. Now put the skillet to heat over a medium-low flame. When the oil is hot, stir the batter well, scoop up ⅓ cup, and flop this down in the center of your heated skillet. Let it just sit there for 3 to 4 seconds. Now place the rounded bottom of your soupspoon very lightly on the center of your blob of batter. Using a slow, gentle, and continuous spiral motion, spread the batter outward with the back of the soupspoon. You should now have a pancake about 6 to 7 inches in diameter. Dribble ½ teaspoon of oil over the pancake and another ½

For information about ingredients and basic techniques that may be unfamiliar, see General Information, pages 418–36.

teaspoon just outside its edges. Using your plastic spatula, spread the oil on top of the pancake and also smooth out any lumps or ridges. Let the pancake cook for about 2 minutes on the first side or until it turns a nice reddish color. Flip the pancake over with the plastic spatula and cook the other side for about 2 minutes or until it develops small red spots. Remove the pancake and put it on a plate. Make all the pancakes this way, *making sure you stir the batter before you make each pancake.* (If you do not do this, you will be left with a very watery batter toward the end.) Stack the pancakes one on top of the other. If not eating immediately, wrap the whole stack of pancakes in aluminum foil. This way, they can be eaten a couple of hours later at room temperature or reheated, still wrapped in foil, in a 450° F oven for 15 minutes.

These pancakes are always served with their first side up (the first side that was cooked, that is) and eaten with relishes, pickles, chutney, or cooked vegetables.

Mrs. Patel's
MUNG DAL NA POORA
(Savory Mung-Dal Pancakes with Onions)
INDIA

Like the *poora* made out of black-eyed peas, this pancake, too, is light, spicy, and very nourishing— ideal food for breakfasts and snacks. Because *mung dal* is hulled and split, it needs only 4 to 5 hours of soaking. Minced onions are added to the batter to give it an edge (you may use very finely sliced scallions instead of onions). This *poora* is slightly thicker than the black-eyed-pea *poora* mainly because it has onions in it. Without the onions, you could spread it out much thinner. Though the use of baking soda is not traditional to Indian pancakes, Mrs. Patel, a very talented cook (and doctor) from Bombay, does add a little bit to her batter to give extra lightness to her pancakes. Please read the section on Indian pancakes (page 244), especially the part that deals with cooking the pancakes, before you make these *pooras*. If you wish to eat them for breakfast, remember that the batter can be made a day ahead and refrigerated. Add the onions and baking soda just before you get ready to do the cooking and stir the batter well before you make each pancake. Served with yogurt relishes and sweet chutney, these pancakes take the place of bread.

(makes about 9 pancakes)

1 cup *mung dal*, picked over, washed, and drained
A ¾-inch cube of fresh ginger, peeled, and cut into 3 to 4 pieces
3 cloves of garlic, peeled
1 to 2 fresh hot green chilies, cut into 3 pieces each
1 teaspoon salt
¼ teaspoon baking soda
¼ teaspoon turmeric
2 tablespoons finely minced Chinese parsley
1 smallish onion, peeled, and finely minced
About ½ cup vegetable oil

Put the *dal* in a bowl. Add 4 cups of water and soak for 5 hours. Drain.

Start your food processor with the metal blade

in place. (You could also use an electric blender to make this batter.) Through the funnel, drop in the ginger pieces first, then the garlic, and finally the green chili (or chilies). When they are minced, stop the machine and put in the drained *mung dal*. Start the machine and let it run until the *dal* turns pastelike. Now stop the machine and add ½ cup water, the salt, baking soda, and turmeric. Run the machine for another 2 minutes to make a thick batter. Empty the batter into a bowl and mix in the parsley and onion thoroughly.

See that you have everything you need for *poora*-making. Not far from your nonstick skillet should be your oil and a teaspoon, a rounded soupspoon for spreading out the batter, your bowl of batter, a ⅓-cup measuring cup, and a plastic spatula. Also a plate for the cooked *pooras*.

Pour 1 teaspoon of oil into an 8-inch, nonstick skillet. Spread the oil around by tilting the skillet. Now put the skillet to heat over a medium-low flame. When the oil is hot, stir the batter well and remove ⅓ cup of it from the bowl. Plop this ⅓ cup of batter down in the center of your heated skillet. Let it just sit there for 3 to 4 seconds. Now place the rounded bottom of your soupspoon very lightly on the center of your blob of batter. Using a slow, gentle, and continuous spiral motion, spread the batter outward with the back of the soupspoon. Make a pancake that is about 5½ inches in diameter. Dribble ½ teaspoon oil over the pancake and another ½ teaspoon just outside its edges. Using the plastic spatula, spread out the oil on top of the pancake and also smooth out any lumps or ridges. Cover the skillet and let the pancake cook for about 2 minutes or until its underside turns a nice reddish color. Uncover and turn the pancake over. Let the second side cook, uncovered, for

For information about ingredients and basic techniques that may be unfamiliar, see General Information, pages 418–36.

about 1½ minutes or until it develops small red spots. Remove the pancake and put it on a plate. Make all the pancakes this way, *making sure you stir the batter before you make each pancake.* Stack the pancakes one on top of the other. If not eating immediately, wrap the whole stack of pancakes in aluminum foil. This way, they can be eaten a couple of hours later at room temperature, or reheated, still wrapped in foil, in a 450° F oven for 15 minutes.

These *pooras* are served either with yogurt relishes or with sweet chutneys (like Apricot Chutney with Raisins and Currants, page 366).

CHICKPEA-FLOUR PANCAKES

INDIA

This is the Indian pancake that most resembles the *socca* of Nice. I happen to think that the Indian version, which gets crispy on the bottom while retaining a silkiness on the top, is much more delicate. The ideal utensil for cooking this is a nonstick skillet. I use one that is 7½ inches in diameter at the bottom. If yours is larger or smaller, you will have to adjust the amount of batter you pour in. Unlike other Indian pancakes, the batter here is thin and can be spread around by tilting the skillet in different directions, just as you would for a crepe. In fact, this pancake ends up by being about as thin as a crepe, though for some reason it starts off looking a bit thicker when first poured into the skillet. The chickpea-flour batter tends to "set" quickly, just as egg batters do, so you have to move your wrist with a certain degree of urgency.

(makes 4 large pancakes)

1 cup chickpea flour, firmly packed
½ teaspoon salt
½ teaspoon ground turmeric
⅛ to ¼ teaspoon cayenne pepper
About ¼ cup vegetable oil

Sift the chickpea flour into a bowl. Slowly add 1 cup water, 2 tablespoons at a time. After each addition stir well with a wooden spoon, breaking up all lumps. Now add another ½ cup water, the salt, turmeric, and cayenne. Stir to mix.

Put a small cup with the oil, as well as a pastry brush, a teaspoon, and a ½-cup measuring cup somewhere near your skillet. Have plates ready so you can serve the pancakes as soon as they are made. Each pancake takes about 7 to 8 minutes to cook. If you have two similar skillets, you can have them both going at the same time.

Brush a 7- to 8-inch, nonstick skillet with about 1 teaspoon of oil. Let the oil heat on a lowish flame. When it is hot, stir the batter well and remove ½ cup from the bowl. Pour this into the skillet. Now tilt the skillet around to spread the batter to the very edges. Keep doing this until all the batter in the skillet is evenly distributed and is set. Dribble 1 teaspoon of oil around the edges of the pancake and another teaspoon over the pancake. Cover the skillet and let the pancake cook for 7 to 8 minutes. It should be slightly crisp at the edges and on the bottom. Carefully ease a plastic spatula around the edges of the pancake. Now ease the spatula under the pancake. Lift it up and put it on a plate. It is best if eaten at once. Otherwise, cover the plate with another inverted plate. Do all pancakes this way.

Serve with any chutney, sambal, or dipping sauce of your choice.

SOUTH INDIAN DOSAS
(Rice and Urad-Dal Pancakes)
INDIA

Dosas, plain or stuffed, may be served at breakfast, brunch, lunch, or as a snack. In South India, they are often accompanied by glasses of buttermilk or cups of steaming hot, sweet, milky coffee. *Dosas* may also be served as any Indian bread might be, with an assortment of vegetables and relishes.

Please read the section on Indian pancakes (page 244), especially the part that deals with cooking the pancakes, before making these *dosas*. Since the *dal* and rice must be soaked 8 hours and paste must ferment almost a day, plan ahead.

(makes 8 pancakes)

½ cup *urad dal*
1 cup long-grain rice
¾ teaspoon salt
¾ teaspoon ground cumin seeds
About ½ cup vegetable oil

Pick over the *urad dal*, wash well, drain, and then soak in 2 cups water for 8 hours.

Wash the rice well, drain, and then soak in 3 cups water for 8 hours.

Drain the *dal*. Put it into the container of a food processor (with the metal blade in place) or a blender. Run the machine for 2 minutes, pushing down the *dal* with a rubber spatula every now and then. Now add 2 tablespoons of water and let the machine run another minute. Add another 2 tablespoons of water and let the machine run another minute. Keep doing this until you have added ¾ cup water. The *dal* should be very well ground, light, and fluffy. Put this paste into a bowl.

Drain the rice. Put it into the container of the food processor or blender. Run the machine for 2 minutes, pushing down the rice with a rubber spatula every now and then. Now add 2 tablespoons of water and run the machine for 1 minute. Add another 2 tablespoons of water and run the machine for another minute. Keep doing this until you have added ¾ cup water and the rice is reduced to *very* fine, semolinalike grains. Pour this rice paste over the *dal* paste. Mix. Cover, and leave to ferment in a warm place for 16 to 20 hours.

See that you have everything ready for *dosa*-making. Not far from your 8-inch, nonstick skillet should be your oil (take it out in a cup), a teaspoon, a rounded soupspoon, your bowl of batter, a ½-cup measuring cup, and a plastic spatula. Also have a plate beside you on which you can put the *dosas* as they cook. If you like, this plate may be kept in a warming oven.

The batter should by now have a frothy, fermented look. Add the salt and cumin to it and stir. Heat 1½ teaspoons of oil in the nonstick skillet over a medium-low flame. Remove ½ cup of the batter and pour it into the middle of the skillet. Let it sit there for 3 to 4 seconds. Place the rounded bottom of the soupspoon very lightly in the center of the batter. Using a slow, gentle, and continuous spiral motion, spread the batter outward with the back of the soupspoon until you have a pancake that is about 7 inches in diameter. Dribble ½ teaspoon oil over the pancake and another ½ just around its edges. Using a plastic spatula, spread out the oil on top of the pancake and also smooth out any lumps or ridges. Cover the skillet. Cook for about 1½ to 2 minutes on the first side or until the *dosa* turns a nice, reddish-brown color. Lower your heat, if necessary. Turn the *dosa* over and

---

For information about ingredients and basic techniques that may be unfamiliar, see General Information, pages 418–36.

cook, uncovered, for another minute, or until the second side develops reddish spots. Put the cooked *dosa* on a warm plate. Stir the batter and make another *dosa*, just as you made the first. Make all *dosas* this way. Serve with the first side cooked up, accompanied by South Indian Coconut Chutney.

TO MAKE STUFFED DOSAS OR MASALA DOSAS (AS THEY ARE CALLED IN INDIA):

Make a recipe of Potatoes and Onions (see page 48) first. This dish may even be made a day ahead of time and then reheated. Now make the *dosas*. Lay out each *dosa* on an individual plate, with its "good" side—the side that was cooked first—down. Spread 3 to 4 tablespoons of the heated potato stuffing over half the *dosa*. Fold the *dosa* over to form a capital "D." Once the *dosa* is stuffed, it should be served immediately.

RICE-FLOUR DOSAS WITH MUSTARD SEEDS AND BLACK PEPPER

INDIA

The batter for these pancakes may be made almost entirely in a food processor or blender. It may also be made several hours in advance. Please read general notes on Indian pancakes (page 244).

(makes 8 pancake-breads)

1 cup all-purpose white flour
1 cup rice flour (also called rice powder)
⅛ to ¼ teaspoon cayenne pepper
½ cup peeled and chopped onion
¼ cup freshly grated coconut
1¼ teaspoons salt
1 cup plain yogurt (the sourer the better)
About 7 tablespoons vegetable oil
1 teaspoon whole black mustard seeds
¾ to 1 teaspoon coarsely crushed or very coarsely ground black peppercorns

Put the white flour, rice flour, cayenne, onion, coconut, salt, yogurt, and ¾ cup water into the container of a food processor or blender. Blend until smooth and pour into a bowl.

Heat 1 tablespoon oil in a small skillet or pot over a medium flame. When hot, put in the mustard seeds. As soon as the mustard seeds begin to pop (almost immediately), pour the seeds and oil over the batter. Add the black pepper and mix thoroughly.

See that you have everything you need for making the pancakes: a 7- to 8-inch, nonstick skillet, a cup containing oil, a teaspoon, a rounded soupspoon for spreading out the batter, and a ⅓-cup measuring cup. You also need a plate to hold the pancakes and a second plate that you can invert over the first to keep the pancakes warm and moist.

Set the skillet over medium-low heat. Dribble ½ teaspoon oil into it. When the skillet is hot, pick up ⅓ cup of batter and plop it right in the center of the skillet. Immediately put the rounded bottom of a soupspoon very lightly on the blob of batter and, using a gentle but continuous spiral motion, spread the batter outward. You should end up with a pancake 6 to 7 inches in diameter (the thinner, the better). Dribble ½ teaspoon of oil over the pancake and another teaspoon just outside its edges. Cover and cook for 3½ to 5 minutes or until the pancake has turned a reddish-gold color on the bottom and is slightly crisp along the edges. It may not color uniformly. Remove the cover and turn the pancake over. Cook the second side uncovered until it, too, has developed reddish-gold spots, about 4 minutes. Remove with a spatula and keep on the nearby plate. Cover with the second inverted plate. Make all the pancakes this way, stacking them all on the same plate.

If you wish to reheat these pancakes, cover them well in aluminum foil, and place in a 400° F oven for about 15 minutes.

Serve with South Indian Coconut Chutney or any vegetables of your choice.

SEMOLINA DOSAS WITH CUMIN SEEDS
INDIA

The batter for these pancakes may be made several hours in advance.

(makes 8 pancake-breads)

1¾ cups fine-grained semolina
1   tablespoon all-purpose white flour
½ to 1 fresh hot green chili
1   cup plain yogurt
1   teaspoon salt
About 7 tablespoons vegetable oil
1   teaspoon whole cumin seeds

Put the semolina, white flour, chili, yogurt, salt, and 1 cup water into the container of a food processor or blender. Blend until smooth. Empty the batter into a bowl.

Heat 1 tablespoon oil in a small skillet or pot over a medium flame. When hot, put in the cumin seeds. Stir for a few seconds. Now pour the seeds and oil over the batter. Stir to mix. Cover and set aside for half an hour.

Now make the pancakes following the directions detailed in the preceding recipe, Rice-Flour Dosas with Mustard Seeds and Black Pepper.

Serve with South Indian Coconut Chutney and/or any vebetables of your choice.

BINDAETUK
(Mung-Bean Pancakes)
KOREA

It is surprising how similar these pancakes are to the mung-bean pancakes made miles away in India. When I first saw them in Seoul and asked what they were, I was told that they were "Korean pizzas." They are a popular street snack but they are also made in homes on festive occasions like birthdays, weddings, and New Year's Day. The street version is usually a fairly thick, 7-inch round. In homes and in restaurants, the pancakes can be much smaller. The batter not only contains soaked and ground mung beans but a little glutinous rice, mung-bean sprouts, onions, and green peppers. *Bindaetuk* are eaten with a soy-based dipping sauce.

The method for making these pancakes is very similar to that for making Mung Dal Na Poora

---

For information about ingredients and basic techniques that may be unfamiliar, see General Information, pages 418–36.

(see page 263)—read the general notes on Indian pancakes (page 244) before making *bindaetuk*. I have used whole mung beans for this recipe because that is what the Koreans use. You could, if you like, use mung *dal* instead, which would allow you to lessen the soaking time to 5 hours and do away with the problem of rubbing away the green skin.

(makes about 8 pancakes)

2   tablespoons glutinous rice
1   cup whole mung beans
1   cup mung-bean sprouts
2   scallions, cut into thin rounds, including green
⅓   cup green pepper, cut into ¼-inch dice
⅓   cup finely chopped onion
¼   teaspoon baking soda
2   teaspoons sesame oil
1   tablespoon roasted and lightly crushed sesame seeds
2   teaspoons Japanese soy sauce
1   teaspoon salt
About ¾ cup vegetable oil

Wash the rice and drain.

Pick over the mung beans and wash them. Drain. Put the rice and beans in a bowl. Add 5 cups water and set aside for 10 hours. Now dip your two hands into the soaking water and rub the beans between your palms to loosen the skins. Pour off the water. A lot of the skins will float away with the water. Add more water to the bowl. Rub the beans again. Pour this water off, too. Keep doing this until nearly all the skins have been removed. Drain the rice and bean mixture thoroughly and put it into the container of a food processor. Turn the machine on and blend until you have a thick paste, stopping the machine and pushing down the batter with a rubber spatula, if necessary. Slowly add ¾ cup water to the running machine and blend again.

Empty the batter into a bowl.

Bring 8 cups of water to a boil and drop in the mung sprouts. Boil rapidly for 2 minutes and drain. Squeeze out as much moisture as possible. Separate the sprouts and add them to the batter. Also add the scallions, green pepper, onion, baking soda, sesame oil, sesame seeds, soy sauce, and salt. Mix well.

Brush a 7-inch, nonstick skillet with about 1 teaspoon oil and heat over a medium-low flame. When the oil is hot, pour ⅓ cup of the batter into the center of the skillet. Place the rounded bottom of a soupspoon very lightly on the center of the blob of batter. Using a gentle but continuous spiral motion, spread the batter outward with the back of the spoon until you have a 5-inch pancake. Dribble 1 teaspoon of oil on top of the pancake and another teaspoon around it. Cover the skillet. Adjust the heat so the bottom of the pancake turns a nice reddish-brown color in 2½ to 3 minutes. Turn the pancake over, dribble another teaspoon of oil around the outside of the pancake and cook, uncovered, for another 2½ to 3 minutes. Do all the pancakes this way, adding oil to the skillet each time.

Serve *bindaetuk* hot, with Korean Dipping Sauce Number 3 (see page 358).

HOPPERS
(Yeast Pancakes)
SRI LANKA

If a French crepe were to marry an American "English" muffin, the couple would probably become the proud parents of a Sri Lankan hopper. The hopper has the softness, delicacy, and pliability of the crepe teamed with the airy, hole-filled, puffy, and browned-on-the-outside quality of the muffin. What is more, it is quite easy to make, especially if your freezer already has grated fresh coconut sitting expectantly in a plastic container.

The hopper is not baked. Nor is it made in a crepe pan. Instead, it is cooked, covered, in a wok which allows it to be thicker, whiter, and softer in the center and crisp around its delicate browned edges. The batter is a simple one containing white flour, rice flour, and yeast. (The traditional leavening agent used to be palm toddy. Many people use yeast as a substitute now.) The batter, once made, needs to ferment overnight. In the morning it is thinned out with coconut milk.

The word "hopper" is, of course, European, and a distortion of the Tamil word *appam* (which comes from the Tamil word *apu*, "to clap with the hands" and thus form flat breads). Sixteenth-century Europeans who traveled through South India, where this dish probably originated, were quite taken with the bread and began to pronounce its name fairly accurately. By the early eighteenth century they were calling it "oppers" and in the nineteenth century, when it was quite the preferred "morning's repast" of British residents in Sri Lanka, the name had become "hoppers."

Traditionally, Sri Lankan hoppers are eaten for breakfast or as snacks, accompanied by a fiery hot *sambal* or sauce that has ground, dried Maldive fish in it. I have worked out an equally fiery vegetarian *sambal* for those who wish to eat their hoppers that way (see Spicy Peanut Sambal, page 363). Hoppers can also be eaten with syrups or honey. I find that I have a weakness for eating hot hoppers smeared with butter and raspberry jam! You could also eat hoppers as a bread with an Indian meal. They are good any way you eat them.

To make hoppers more quickly, you can have two small round-bottomed woks going at the same time.

(makes 8 hoppers)

1   teaspoon active dry yeast
1   tablespoon sugar
1   teaspoon salt
1½ cups unbleached, all-purpose white flour, sifted
½ cup rice flour (also called rice powder), sifted
1   cup coconut milk, at room temperature
About 3 tablespoons vegetable oil

Put the yeast in a large bowl. Slowly add 1 cup lukewarm water, stirring all the time. Add the sugar and salt and mix.

Slowly add the white flour and the rice flour, mixing with a wooden spoon as you do so. You should end up with a very thick, pasty, doughlike batter. Cover the bowl with a lightly dampened dish towel (do not let the towel touch the batter) and leave it in a dark, warm spot for 10 hours. (I leave mine on an oven shelf.)

The batter should now have risen and become filled with air bubbles. Slowly add the coconut

---

For information about ingredients and basic techniques that may be unfamiliar, see General Information, pages 418–36.

milk, mixing thoroughly as you do so. The batter will deflate; let it sit for 10 minutes as you get yourself organized for making hoppers.

Set up your wok or *karhai*, with its lid handy. Have near you: the oil in a cup, with a pastry brush alongside; two 6- to 7-inch plates to hold the hoppers as they get done; the batter; a ⅓-cup measuring cup; and a spatula, curved if possible.

Turn the flame under your wok on low and brush the center of the wok—a diameter of about 7 inches—with approximately 1 teaspoon oil. Let the wok heat. Now pour in ⅓ cup of the batter. Quickly pick the wok up by its two handles (if it has one handle, wear an oven mitt and put your second hand where the second handle would be). Swish the batter around by moving your arms in a circular motion so the batter covers ¾ inch more than its original radius (see drawing). Cover the wok and let the hopper cook on low heat for about 11 to 12 minutes or until the center resembles a thin muffin, the outer edges turn light brown and crisp, and the bottom is a nice reddish-golden color. Remember that the time taken for the hopper to cook might vary with the size and shape of your wok or *karhai*.

Lift the hopper up with the spatula and put it on a plate. Cover the plate with another plate, the second inverted over the first.

Make all the hoppers this way.

Hoppers are best eaten soon after they are made. If you wish to reheat them, divide the eight hoppers into two stacks, wrap each stack in aluminum foil, and heat in an oven preheated to 400° F for 10 minutes.

EGG HOPPERS
(Yeast Pancakes with Eggs)
SRI LANKA

(makes 8 egg hoppers)

Egg hoppers are hoppers with whole eggs embedded in them. To make them, you need all the ingredients for hoppers (see preceding recipe) plus 8 large eggs. These pancakes may be served as a light lunch, accompanied by a green salad.

Make the batter for hoppers exactly as in the preceding recipe, letting it ferment for 10 hours and mixing it afterward with coconut milk.

As you get ready to cook the hoppers, have the 8 eggs nearby as well and a cup to break them into.

Break open an egg and put it carefully into the cup reserved for the purpose without breaking the yolk.

Pour the batter into the oiled wok as in the preceding recipe, swishing it around in a circular motion. Cover, and let the batter set for 20 to 30 seconds. Remove cover. Make a space in the center of the batter with a spoon—do not go all the way to the bottom—and carefully slide the egg into this space. The yolk should nestle in the hole you created while the white should spread around part of the hopper. Now cover and cook the hopper as in the preceding recipe. Keep each egg hopper, covered, on a separate plate. It is really best to eat these as soon as they are made, though you can keep them covered in a warming oven.

Make all egg hoppers as you made the first one.

STEAMED BUNS
CHINA

These white, spongy buns may be eaten with almost any sauced food. I love them with Hard-Boiled Eggs in a Spicy Almond Sauce or Stewed Beets with Tomatoes and Potato Stew. As with my other leavened breads, I have used Pillsbury's new Bread Flour which is high in both protein and gluten.

(makes 12 buns)

1 teaspoon active dry yeast
1 teaspoon plus 3 tablespoons sugar
3½ cups Pillsbury's Bread Flour or all-purpose
   white flour

Combine the yeast, 1 teaspoon sugar, and ¼ cup lukewarm water in a cup. Set aside for 5 to 6 minutes.

Put the flour into a warm bowl. Add the 3 tablespoons sugar and mix gently. Make a depression in the center of the flour and pour in the yeast mixture and 1 cup lukewarm water. Gather the dough together to form a ball, adding more warm water as you need it. You will probably need to add another ¼ cup water. Knead the dough for 10 to 12 minutes or until smooth. Form a ball and put it in a large bowl. Cover the bowl with a damp cloth and set it aside in a warm place for about 2 hours or until the dough has doubled in bulk.

Punch down the dough and knead again for 2 to 3 minutes. Working on a lightly floured surface, make a 12-inch roll out of the dough. Cut the roll into twelve equal parts. Form a ball out of each part. Dust a baking sheet lightly with flour and lay

---

For information about ingredients and basic techniques that may be unfamiliar, see General Information, pages 418–36.

the balls on it, at least 2 inches apart. Cover with a dry dishcloth and let them rise for 45 minutes.

Set up your steaming equipment. I use a wok filled with water over which I set up several tiers of bamboo steamers. The water in the wok should never touch the buns. Line the bamboo steamers with wet cheesecloth. Place as many buns in a tier as you can, making sure that they are at least 2 inches apart. Cover and steam over high heat for 15 minutes. If the water in the wok starts to boil away, be sure to replenish it with more boiling water. After the 15 minutes of steaming, turn off the heat. Let the buns sit, covered and undisturbed, for another 10 minutes. If not eating immediately, allow the buns to cool. You may now pack them in plastic bags and either refrigerate them or freeze them. To reheat, steam again until heated through.

ROTI
(Flat Whole-Wheat Bread)
INDIA

(makes 12 rotis)

2 cups *chappati* flour
    or 1 cup whole-wheat flour mixed with 1 cup
    cake flour (*not* the self-rising kind)
Additional flour for dusting

Put the flour in a bowl. Slowly add enough water so that you will be able to gather the flour together and make a soft dough. You may need about 2½ tablespoons less than a cup of water. Knead the dough for 7 to 8 minutes or until it is smooth. Make a ball and put it inside a bowl. Cover the bowl with a damp dishcloth and set it aside for half an hour.

If the dough looks very runny, flour your hands and knead for another few minutes. Form twelve equal balls and dust each with a little flour. Keep them covered.

Set a cast-iron griddle or skillet to heat over a medium-low flame. Allow at least 5 minutes for that. Keep about a cup of dusting flour near you. Remove a ball of dough and flatten it between the palms of your hands. Dust it on both sides with flour. Roll it out, as thinly and evenly as you can, aiming for a 5½-inch round. When the griddle is hot, slap the *roti* onto its heated surface. Cook for about a minute or until soft bubbles begin to form. Turn the *roti* over. (Most Indians use their hands to do this.) Cook for half a minute on the second side. If you have a gas fire, light a second burner on a medium flame and put the *roti* directly on it. Using tongs with rounded ends, rotate the *roti* so that all areas are exposed to the shooting flames.

Take 5 seconds to do this. Turn the *roti* over and repeat for about 3 seconds. The *roti* should puff up. Put the *roti* on a plate and cover with a clean dish towel. Make all *roti* this way. If you have an electric stove, place the griddle and *roti* under a broiler for a few seconds, until the *roti* puffs up. Serve hot.

PARATHA
(Whole-Wheat Griddle Bread)
INDIA

(makes 6 big parathas)

1   cup whole-wheat flour plus 1 cup cake flour
    or 2 cups *chappati* flour
Additional flour for dusting
½ teaspoon salt
About 9 tablespoons vegetable oil

Put the flour and salt into a bowl. Dribble 2 tablespoons of oil over the flour and rub it in with your fingertips. Slowly add about ¾ cup plus 1 tablespoon water, gathering the dough together into a ball as you do so. You should end up with a soft dough. Knead the dough for 10 minutes and then make a ball. Put the ball in a bowl and cover the bowl with a damp dishcloth. Set the dough aside for half an hour.

Knead the dough again and divide it into six parts. Keep five parts covered with a damp cloth as you work with the sixth. Make a round patty out of it and then roll it out on a floured surface until you have a 6-inch round. Dust with extra flour whenever necessary. Spread about 1½ teaspoons oil on the top of this round. Gather the edges of the round together, forming pleats as you go. Soon you will have a closed pouch. Give the top of the pleats a small twist to close the pouch. Dust the pouch lightly with flour and put it, pleated side down, on a floured surface. Roll it out until it is about 7 inches in diameter. Heat a cast-iron griddle or skillet over a medium-low flame. When hot, spread a teaspoon of oil on it and slap the *paratha* onto its heated surface. Cook for about 2 minutes. The top of the paratha should now have turned fairly pale. Spread a teaspoon of oil over it with the back of a spoon. Cook another minute or so, turning the heat down a bit if necessary. The first side should have developed some pale, reddish-brown spots. Turn the *paratha* over and cook the second side for about 3 to 3½ minutes or until it, too, develops pale, reddish-brown spots. Take the *paratha* off the fire and wrap in aluminum foil. Make all the *parathas* this way, stacking them in the same aluminum-foil bundle. (*Parathas* may be reheated in the foil; place in a 350° F oven for about 15 minutes.)

For information about ingredients and basic techniques that may be unfamiliar, see General Information, pages 418–36.

STUFFED PARATHAS
(Stuffed Whole-Wheat Griddle Breads)

INDIA

(makes 8 parathas)

2 cups *chappati* flour
  or 1 cup whole-wheat flour plus 1 cup plain
  cake flour
Additional flour for dusting
½ teaspoon salt plus some more for sprinkling
2 tablespoons unsalted butter, cut into 6 pats
6 tablespoons peeled, finely grated,
  and well-squeezed white radish
¼ teaspoon *garam masala*
½ teaspoon ground cumin seeds
½ to 1 finely minced fresh hot green chili
¼ teaspoon ground dried ginger
1 tablespoon minced fresh Chinese parsley
¼ teaspoon *ajwain* seeds
6 tablespoons *ghee* or vegetable oil

Put the flour, ½ teaspoon salt, and butter into the container of a food processor with the metal blade in place. Turn on the machine for 30 seconds. Now pour in ½ cup plus 3 tablespoons water for the *chappati* flour and about 2 tablespoons more for the whole-wheat mixture. Let the machine run until you have a ball of dough. Take the ball out and knead it for 10 minutes. You should have a soft but workable dough. If you do not have a processor, put the flour, salt, and slightly softened butter into a bowl. Rub with your fingers until you have the consistency of fine bread crumbs. Add the same amount of water as above and gather into a ball. Knead for 10 minutes. Form a ball with the dough and put inside a bowl. Cover the bowl with a damp cloth and set aside for ½ to 1 hour.

Combine the white radish, *garam masala*, cumin

seeds, green chili, ginger, and Chinese parsley. Crush the *ajwain* seeds lightly in a mortar and add them to this mixture as well. This is the stuffing.

Heat a cast-iron griddle or a cast-iron skillet (about 8 inches in diameter) over medium-low heat for about 10 minutes.

As the griddle heats, divide the dough into eight balls. Keep seven of them covered with plastic wrap. Roll the eighth ball out on a floured board until it is 3½ inches in diameter. Place a heaping teaspoon of stuffing in its center. Sprinkle the stuffing with a little salt. 1. Now gather the edges of the dough round and bring toward the center, 2. twisting them slightly to form a closed ball. Flatten the ball. Sprinkle it lightly with flour and roll out on a floured board until you have a 6-inch round.

Place the *paratha* on the heated griddle. Let it cook slowly until its underside develops light-brown spots. Turn and cook the same way on the other side. Now dribble 1 teaspoon of *ghee* along the edges of the *paratha* so it goes under it, and 1 teaspoon on top. Turn the *paratha* over again and cook for about a minute. Turn a fourth time and cook, slowly, another minute. In all, the *paratha* should cook about 5 minutes and not remain raw inside. It should also not burn, so adjust your heat accordingly. Wrap the *paratha* first in a paper towel and then in a large piece of aluminum foil. Do all *parathas* this way, stacking them one on top of the other in the same piece of foil.

Shalimar's
WONDERFUL FLAKY PARATHAS
(Flat Griddle Breads)
INDIA

Shalimar, one of the older Indian restaurants in New York City, makes some of the best *parathas* this side of the Atlantic. These are not the simple, everyday *parathas* that I have described and given a recipe for in my first cookbook, *An Invitation to Indian Cooking*, nor does their distinction come from being stuffed or cooked in a *tandoor* (clay oven). They are "plain" *parathas*, but so crisp and flaky that they are an absolute joy to eat.

The best utensil for cooking these *parathas* is a cast-iron griddle or cast-iron skillet. The *parathas* are fairly large—about 9 inches in diameter—so you should use a griddle or skillet that can accommodate them easily.

For information about ingredients and basic techniques that may be unfamiliar, see General Information, pages 418–36.

(makes 6 large parathas)

3 cups all-purpose, unbleached white flour, plus some extra flour for dusting
½ cup finely ground whole-wheat flour
½ teaspoon salt
About 1½ cups melted *ghee* or melted margarine

Sift the white flour, whole-wheat flour, and salt into a bowl. Add 5 tablespoons of melted *ghee* and rub it into the flour until the mixture resembles coarse bread crumbs. Very slowly add 1 cup plus 1 tablespoon water or just enough to make a very soft, pliable dough. Work the water into the flour. Gather the dough into a ball. Knead the ball for 10 minutes or until the dough is smooth and elastic. Roll the dough into a ball. Rub the ball with a little melted *ghee* and put it in a plastic bag. Set aside for half an hour.

Knead the dough again and divide it into six equal parts. Keep all the parts that you are not working with covered with plastic wrap. Take one part and roll it into a ball. Flatten the ball. Sprinkle some flour over the area where you will make the *paratha*. Using a rolling pin, roll out the ball until it is a round, about 9 inches in diameter. If it seems to stick, sprinkle a little flour both on the rolling surface and on the *paratha*. Brush the round with melted *ghee*. Now, starting at the edge farthest away from you and using both hands, begin rolling up the *paratha* tightly toward you. Once you have completed the process, you should have a 9-inch-long "rope" in front of you. Brush the top of this "rope" with more melted *ghee*. 1. Coil the rope so as to form a tight cone. Flatten the cone into a patty. Press down on the patty a bit to make sure that it will not open up. Now put the patty on a plate and cover it with plastic wrap. Take the other five remaining parts of dough and work them, one at a time, into similar patties. Put all the patties onto the same plate in a single layer. Make sure they are well covered and then refrigerate them for 1 to 2 hours. (You may even refrigerate them overnight.)

Heat a large cast-iron griddle or skillet over a medium-low flame for 10 minutes. Turn the heat down a bit to low (not *very* low). Flour your rolling surface. 2. Take one patty and roll it out with a rolling pin until it is about 9 inches in diameter, dusting with flour whenever necessary. Brush the griddle lightly with melted *ghee*. Put the *paratha* on the hot griddle and let it cook for about 3 minutes. The top of the *paratha* should now have turned whitish. Brush the top of the *paratha* with melted *ghee* and let the bread cook, on the same side, for another 3 minutes. The first side, which should now have cooked 6 minutes, should have nice brown specks on it. If it is too dark, your heat is too high. Adjust it. Turn the *paratha* over and cook the second side for 5 to 6 minutes. It, too, should get nice medium-brown specks on it. The

paratha should be crisp and flaky outside, soft and pliable (but not uncooked) inside.

Take the *paratha* off the griddle, cut it into four quarters, and eat it immediately. If such hasty consumption is impractical, wrap the *paratha* in aluminum foil and put it in a warming oven. Do all *parathas* this way. As they are cooked, stack the *parathas* on top of each other and keep them covered.

Juji's
NAAN
(Leavened Flat Breads)
SOVIET CENTRAL ASIA, AFGHANISTAN,
PAKISTAN, AND INDIA

Some version of the *naan* is made all the way from the southern part of the Soviet Union to North India, often in clay, brick, and stone ovens. The version here, simplified for home kitchens, is cooked on top of the stove and under the broiler.

(makes 9 breads)

3¾ cups unbleached, all-purpose white flour
1 teaspoon baking powder
¼ teaspoon salt
About 1¾ cups plain yogurt
Soft unsalted butter (optional)

Sift the flour, baking powder, and salt into a bowl. Slowly add as much yogurt as you need to gather the flour together and make a soft, resilient dough. Knead for about 10 minutes and form a ball. Put the ball in a bowl and cover the bowl with a damp dishcloth. Set aside in a warm place for 1½-2 hours. Knead the dough again and divide into nine equal parts. Keep them covered.

Heat a cast-iron skillet or griddle over a lowish flame.

Preheat the broiler.

Take one of the parts of dough and make a ball out of it. Flatten it and then roll it out on a lightly floured surface until you have a round that is about ⅛-inch thick. When the skillet is very hot, pick up the *naan* and slap it onto the heated surface. Let it cook slowly for about 4 to 5 minutes. It will either puff up completely or partially. Now put the whole skillet under the broiler for 1 to 1½ minutes or until the puffing-up process completes

itself and there are a few reddish spots on the *naan*. Remove the *naan* with a spatula and brush with butter if you like. Make all the *naans* this way, keeping them stacked and covered with a clean dishcloth. Serve hot.

If you wish to have the *naans* later, wrap them in a plastic bag when they have cooled. Before you eat, wrap as many as you need in aluminum foil and heat in a 400° F oven for 15 minutes.

PITA BREAD
(Pocket Breads)
MIDDLE EAST

These round, all-purpose breads are now available throughout this country. If you wish to make them at home—and it is certainly cheaper to do so—here is a recipe. I have used Pillsbury's new Bread Flour which is high in both protein and gluten. If you cannot find it, use an all-purpose white flour or 3¼ cups white flour and ¼ cup gluten flour.

If you have a gas oven, the baking is best done on the floor of the oven. If you have an electric oven, do the cooking in the middle of the oven.

(makes 12 breads)

3½ cups Pillsbury's Bread Flour, plus some extra
    for dusting
1 teaspoon salt

For information about ingredients and basic techniques that may be unfamiliar, see General Information, pages 418–36.

1 packet active dry yeast
1 teaspoon sugar
1 tablespoon olive oil

Sift the flour and salt into a large, warmed bowl. Leave in a warm place.

Combine the yeast, sugar, and ¼ cup lukewarm water in a small cup. Mix and set aside for 5 to 6 minutes.

Make a depression in the center of the flour. Pour in the yeast mixture, 1 cup lukewarm water, and the olive oil. Gently gather the dough to form a ball, adding more lukewarm water as you need it. You will probably need another 3 tablespoons. Once you have a ball, knead it for 10 minutes or until it is smooth. Put the ball in a large bowl and cover the bowl with a damp cloth. Set aside for 1½ to 2 hours in a warm, draftfree place until it has doubled in bulk.

Punch the dough down again and knead until smooth. Working on a surface dusted lightly with flour, make a long (12 inches or so) roll and then cut it into twelve equal parts. Roll each into ¼-inch-thick rounds and lay these rounds on baking sheets that have been lightly dusted with flour. (I use two large baking sheets.) Cover first with a dry dishcloth, lightly dusted with flour, and then with a damp cloth. You may also cover with a thick plastic sheet that has been dusted with flour. Set aside in a warm, draft-free place for 45 minutes.

Sometime during this second rising, preheat your oven to its highest temperature. If you have a gas oven with a broiler underneath, turn it to "broil."

Put a large cast-iron skillet or griddle on the floor of your oven if it is gas and in the middle of your oven if it is electric. Allow it to heat. Put one or two pita breads in the hot skillet (this will depend upon the size of your skillet—my 14-inch skillet holds two) and immediately return it to its place in the oven. Cook for 2½ to 3 minutes. The breads will puff up. You may take the breads off the skillet the way they are, or else put them under a broiler for a minute if you want the tops to brown lightly. As the breads get done, wrap them in a damp dish towel to cool them off (this gives them their leathery look) and then put them in plastic bags. You may freeze the pita bread, if you like.

To reheat *pitas*, put them under a broiler for a couple of minutes.

Glenda Barretto's
PUTU
(Ground Rice Muffins)
PHILIPPINES

Traditionally, these muffins are made out of rice that has been soaked overnight and then ground to a thick, satiny paste. Since I have been unable to find a machine here that can grind out such a paste, I have resorted to using rice powder (also called rice flour). It is best to use a rice powder of Chinese or Filipino origin.

In the Philippines, these muffins are steamed in

banana-leaf cups. Other than the subtle flavor the leaves provide, muffin tins work just as well. If your steaming apparatus is similar to mine—here I use a bamboo steamer set over a wok that is half filled with water—it might be easier to steam in two batches, using six-muffin tins. A single twelve-muffin tin would just be too large.

In the Philippines, *putu* is eaten with morning chocolate and with thick stews.

(makes 12 small muffins)

1¾ cups rice powder
¼ teaspoon salt
1½ teaspoons baking powder
½ cup sugar

Put the rice powder into the container of a food processor or blender. Add 1 cup water and blend until well mixed. Stop the machine and release any flour sticking to the sides of the container with a spatula, if necessary. Let the machine run for 3 to 4 minutes or until the mixture appears smooth and satiny. Add the salt, baking powder, and sugar. Blend to mix. Pour this batter into two six-muffin tins filling each mold only half full. Steam one tin at a time, covered, over rapidly boiling water, for about 15 minutes or until a toothpick inserted inside a muffin comes out clean. As soon as you remove a muffin tin, put it in a shallow pan of cold water. This loosens the muffins from the molds.

CREAM OF WHEAT IDLIS
(Savory Cakes)
INDIA

Idlis are a breakfast and snack food all over South India. They are round, slightly tart cakes, about 2½ to 3 inches in diameter and about ¾ inch thick in the center. Rather like Madeleines, they taper off toward the edges. The most common *idlis* are made out of a fermented batter of ground rice and *dal*. But there are other much simpler, quick-cooking variations. This is one of them. It is made from the supermarket variety of regular cream of wheat and may be served in its traditional way with *sambar*, chutneys, and relishes or it may be served as the grain in any combination of foods that you like. Since it contains both wheat and yogurt, a meal needs only the addition of a bean dish and a vegetable to be nutritionally balanced.

Idlis need to be steamed over rapidly boiling water. The special steaming molds used in South India are now available in most Indian grocery stores. They consist of a central trunk on which several discs may be fitted at spaced intervals. Each disc is filled with tiny steam holes. It also has round depressions in it which act as molds for the *idlis*. The entire "tree" is placed over boiling water, covered, and steamed.

If you cannot find the *idli* molds, it is not hard to improvise. Use a steaming trivet, about 6 inches in diameter, and put it inside a colander. It will probably come to rest somewhere above the bottom of a rounded colander. Line the trivet and the sides of the colander with a double layer of wet cheesecloth. Pour a ½-inch thickness of batter into the cheesecloth, cover the colander, and then fold the overhanging edges of cheesecloth over the lid

For information about ingredients and basic techniques that may be unfamiliar, see General Information, pages 418–36.

so they do not burn. The colander should be set over a pot of boiling water in such a way that the water stays below the level of the *idlis*. Instead of ending up with lots of small *idlis*, you will have large cakes which you can cut up into diamonds, squares, or wedges.

Whatever method of steaming you use, have plenty of extra boiling water at hand to replenish the water in your steamer.

(makes 12 small cakes)

2 tablespoons vegetable oil plus a little more for greasing the molds
1 teaspoon whole black mustard seeds

1 cup regular cream of wheat
3 tablespoons freshly grated coconut
¾ teaspoon salt
1 to 2 fresh hot green chilies, minced
1½ cups plain yogurt (the sourer the better)

Heat the 2 tablespoons oil in a skillet over a medium flame. When the oil is hot, put in the mustard seeds. As soon as the mustard seeds begin to pop, turn the heat to medium-low and put in the cream of wheat. Sauté for 2 to 3 minutes. The cream of wheat should not brown. Remove the skillet from the fire. Add the coconut, salt, and green chilies. Mix and allow to cool somewhat. Add the yogurt and mix. You should have a thick batter.

Prepare your steaming apparatus and get the water to a rolling boil. (See note at the top of the recipe.) Oil the *idli* molds and fill each with the batter. Cover and steam for 20 minutes. Ease each *idli* out with the help of a knife and serve hot with its smoother underside up.

Sudha Doshi's

MUNG DAL DHOKLA
(Savory Cakes Made with Mung Dal)
INDIA

Dhoklas are served at room temperature and may be eaten at a meal or as a snack with a drink of tea, coffee, lemonade, *lassi*, or *thandai*.

(makes 25–30 cubes)

1   cup *mung dal*, picked over, washed, and drained
1   ¾-inch cube of fresh ginger, peeled and coarsely chopped
2   fresh hot green chilies, coarsely chopped
2   tablespoons plain yogurt
1   tablespoon lemon juice
1   teaspoon salt
¼   teaspoon ground turmeric
1   tablespoon plus ¼ cup vegetable oil
1   tablespoon Eno sparkling antacid
¹⁄₁₆ teaspoon ground asafetida
1   tablespoon whole black mustard seeds
2   tablespoons sesame seeds
¼   cup finely chopped Chinese parsley
¼   cup grated fresh coconut

Pick over the *dal*, then wash, and drain. Soak in 3 cups of water for 3 hours. Drain.

In the container of an electric blender or food processor, combine the ginger, green chilies, yogurt, lemon juice, and 1 cup water. Blend thoroughly. Now add the drained *dal*, and salt, and turmeric. Blend again until you have a fairly smooth batter. Let the batter rest, unrefrigerated, for 2 to 3 hours.

Arrange a utensil for steaming. (I use a bamboo steamer with a domed lid which I place inside a wok. If you decide to put a trivet inside a large pot, make sure that the pot is wide enough to hold an 8-inch cake tin easily. Also, line the lid of your pot with a dish towel so droplets of water will not fall onto the steaming *dhokla*.) Rub the inside of an 8-inch round cake pan with 1½ teaspoons of the oil. Pour enough water into the steaming utensil so it stays just below the cake tin. (If using a wok, pour in enough water so it stays just below the bottom of the bamboo steamer. If using a trivet inside a pot, the water should stay ¼ inch below the top of the trivet.) Bring the water to a boil. Keep an extra kettle of boiling water handy in case you begin to run low on the steaming water.

Stir the batter and pour half of it (about 1½ cups) into a clean bowl. Stir it again. Now sprinkle 1½ teaspoons of the Eno antacid over the batter and immediately begin to stir *gently* and in *one direction*. Keep stirring slowly, even as the batter froths and foams, until it is well mixed. Pour this batter into the cake tin and place the cake tin in the steamer. Cover and steam for 10 minutes or until a toothpick inserted into the *dhokla* comes out clean. Remove the cake tin from the steamer and let it sit for 10 minutes. Meanwhile prepare a second batch for steaming just as you did the first, using a fresh cake tin. Put it to steam, removing it after 10 minutes also.

Cut the first *dhokla* into 1½-inch squares. When the second *dhokla* has rested for 10 minutes, cut it into similar squares. If not eating immediately, let the squares cool completely in the tins and then cover with aluminum foil or plastic wrap. They can stay this way, unrefrigerated, for 4 to 5 hours.

Just before serving, take squares carefully out of the cake tins and arrange neatly in a single layer on one or two serving platters. (I arrange them in the same circular shape as the cake tin.) Heat the ¼ cup oil in a small skillet or small pot over a medium

---

For information about ingredients and basic techniques that may be unfamiliar, see General Information, pages 418–36.

flame. When hot, put in the asafetida, mustard and sesame seeds, immediately covering the skillet with a mesh splatter shield. Keep shaking the skillet. When the sesame seeds have browned lightly (this happens very quickly), turn off heat and remove splatter shield. Quickly spoon the oil and seeds evenly over the *dhoklas*. Garnish the *dhoklas* with sprinklings of Chinese parsley and fresh coconut.

Hsu Hung Ying's
YOW BING
(Fried Bread with Scallions)
TAIWAN

This bread may be eaten with Chinese Dipping Sauce (see page 357).

(makes 4 very large breads)

About 2 to 3 cups all-purpose unbleached white flour
4   teaspoons vegetable oil
1¼ teaspoons salt
¾ cup very finely sliced scallions
Vegetable oil for shallow frying

Put 1½ cups flour in a bowl. Pour ¾ cup very hot (but not boiling) water over it. Stir quickly with a pair of chopsticks or with a wooden spoon. Begin to add flour, a little at a time, and try to gather the flour into a ball. You will need at least ½ cup of flour or more. The dough should remain soft. Take the dough out of the bowl and knead for 10 minutes, adding more flour if it is too sticky. Form a ball and put it in a bowl. Cover the bowl with a damp dishcloth and set aside for an hour.

Flour your work surface and knead the dough again. Roll the dough out into an oval shape that is about ¼- to ⅛-inch thick. As you do this, keep lifting up the dough and dusting its underside as well as the top with flour. Spread 4 teaspoons of oil over the surface of the dough. Then sprinkle the salt over it evenly. Scatter the scallions evenly over the salt. Using both hands, roll the dough tightly away from you. You should now have a long stuffed roll. (If the dough sticks at all to the work surface, use a knife to release it.) Now cut the roll into four equal sections. Dust each lightly with flour. Pick up one section at a time with two hands and give it a few twists along its length. Now bring the ends of the section together to form a patty. Flatten the patty somewhat and dust it lightly with flour. Make four patties this way, dusting each with flour and setting them down on a floured surface at some distance from each other so they do not stick together.

On a floured surface, roll out one patty until you have an ⅛-inch-thick round. You may need to dust it with flour several times during this rolling.

Cover a 10- to 12-inch heavy skillet with a thick coating of oil and heat over a medium-low flame. When it is hot, put in the bread. Cook it for about 2 minutes, pressing down now and then so all parts touch the bottom of the skillet. Turn the bread over and cook the second side the same way for 2 minutes. Now turn back to the first side. Keep doing this until both sides develop reddish-gold spots and the bread is cooked through. Remove with a slotted spatula and place on a plate lined with a paper towel. Make all the breads this way, stacking one on top of the other, between layers of paper towel. Replenish the oil, whenever necessary. Serve hot, each bread cut in quarters.

POORIS
(Deep-Fried Breads)

INDIA

Pooris may be made out of all kinds of flours. Here is a flour combination that makes wonderfully soft, pliable *pooris*. Make sure that your cake flour is *not* the self-rising kind.

(makes 8 large pooris)

⅓ cup whole-wheat flour
⅓ cup white cake flour plus some extra for dusting
⅓ cup fine-grained semolina
¼ teaspoon salt
1 tablespoon vegetable oil
Vegetable oil for deep frying

Put the whole-wheat flour, the ⅓ cup cake flour, and semolina into a bowl. Add the salt. Dribble 1 tablespoon oil over the flours and rub it in with your fingertips. Add water, a little bit at a time, and gather the dough together to make a ball. As you need a fairly soft dough, the amount of water may well be around ½ cup plus 1 tablespoon. Knead the dough for 10 minutes or until it is smooth. Put the dough in a bowl and cover with a damp dishcloth. Set aside for half an hour.

Put the oil for deep frying in a wok and set it to heat on a flame that is slightly lower than medium. Knead the dough again and divide it into twelve equal parts. Keep the parts you are not working with covered with the damp dishcloth. Make a round ball out of one of the parts and then flatten it with your palm to form a patty. Sprinkle a little flour on it. Flour your work surface and roll out the patty into a 5½-inch round.

When the oil in the wok is very hot (it should not be smoking, though), pick up the rolled-out *poori* and take it as close as possible to the oil. Lay it over the oil, making sure that it does not double over. (If the *poori* sinks quietly to the bottom of the wok, the oil is not hot enough.) The *poori* will start sizzling. Using quick but very gentle taps with the back of a slotted spoon, keep pushing the *poori* slightly under the oil. Within seconds, it should balloon. Turn it over and cook the second side for a few seconds. Remove with a slotted spoon and place in a bowl lined with paper towels. Cover the bowl with a plate or lid. Make all the *pooris* this way. (Keep an eye on the oil as you are rolling out the *pooris*. If it starts to overheat, remove it from the flame for a while.)

Ideally, *pooris* should be eaten as soon as they are made. If you keep them tightly covered, you may eat them somewhat later at room temperature. They will have deflated but will still taste good.

For information about ingredients and basic techniques that may be unfamiliar, see General Information, pages 418–36.

BANANA POORIS
INDIA

These *pooris* are flavored with freshly mashed bananas and may be eaten with a regular Indian meal or may be sprinkled with confectioners' sugar and eaten at tea-time. They are excellent either way. Care must be taken to roll these *pooris* out as thinly as possible or the inside will not cook properly. As with the potato *pooris* which follow, you should start off with a fairly stiff dough. The dough will soften as it "rests." Make sure your cake flour is not the self-rising kind.

(makes 8 pooris)

About 1 ripe banana or less
½ cup cake flour
¾ cup all-purpose, unbleached white flour
Vegetable oil for deep frying
4   teaspoons confectioners' sugar (optional)
About 1½ tablespoons vegetable oil

Mash the banana thoroughly. You may do this in a food processor or blender. You will need 4 tablespoons of banana paste.

Sift the two flours into a bowl. Add 1 tablespoon oil. Rub the oil into the flour until the mixture resembles coarse bread crumbs. Add the 4 tablespoons banana paste and rub that into the flour as well, making sure to distribute it as thoroughly as possible. Now add about 1 tablespoon of water and gather the dough into a ball. Knead for about 10 minutes. You should have a fairly stiff dough. Make a ball out of the dough and rub the ball with a little oil. Put the ball in a plastic bag and set it aside for 1 hour.

The dough ball should be softer now. Knead it again for a couple of minutes. Divide the dough into eight equal parts. Keep all the parts covered with plastic wrap.

Heat the oil for deep frying in a wok or *karhai* over a medium flame. You should have a good 2½ inches in the center of the wok. Wait for the oil to get very hot.

As the oil heats, lightly flour your work surface. Take out one part of the dough and make a ball out of it in your palms. Flatten the ball and flour it lightly. Now roll it out evenly with a rolling pin, sprinkling the surface and the *poori* with flour whenever you need to, until you have a round that is about 4½ to 5 inches in diameter.

Fry the *poori* in the hot oil as in the directions given on page 284. Put the cooked *poori* on a platter lined with paper towels. Do all the *pooris* this way. If the *pooris* are to be eaten sweet, they should be eaten as soon as they are made, each sprinkled with about ½ teaspoon of confectioners' sugar. If the *pooris* are to be eaten up to half an hour later with a meal, they may be put into a bowl or deep plate lined with paper towels and then covered with an inverted plate.

POTATO POORIS

INDIA

The dough for these *pooris* has both white flour and mashed potatoes in it, making for a very interesting taste. I have seasoned my dough with just salt, cumin, and *garam masala*, though you could add cayenne and very finely minced Chinese parsley as well. I love the smell of these *pooris*: If one could bottle the smell of a traditional Delhi or Uttar Pradesh kitchen at a time when a banquet was being prepared, one would probably come up with the delicate aroma of these fried potato breads.

Make sure that your cake flour is not the self-rising kind.

(makes 8 pooris)

1   medium-sized boiling potato, freshly boiled in its jacket
½ cup cake flour
¾ cup all-purpose, unbleached white flour
½ teaspoon salt
½ teaspoon ground cumin seeds
½ teaspoon *garam masala*
About 1½ tablespoons vegetable oil
Vegetable oil for deep frying

Peel the potato while it is still hot and mash it well. (I put the hot potato through a ricer.) You should have a heaping half-cup, loosely packed. Let it cool off a bit.

Sift the two flours, salt, cumin, and *garam masala* into a bowl. Add the potato and rub it into the flours, distributing it as thoroughly as you can. Add 4 teaspoons oil and rub that in as well. Collect the dough and try to form a ball. You may need to add a tablespoon of water. The ball will be hard but this is as it should be. Knead the dough for 10 minutes. Form a ball again. Rub the ball lightly with a little oil and put it in a plastic bag. Set it aside for 15 minutes.

Knead the dough again for a couple of minutes. Divide the dough into eight equal parts. Keep them covered with a plastic wrap.

Heat oil for deep frying in a wok or *karhai* over a medium flame. You should have a good 2½ inches in the center of the wok. Wait for the oil to get very hot.

As the oil heats, lightly flour your work surface. Take one part of the dough and make a ball out of it in your hands. Flatten the ball and flour it lightly. Now roll it out evenly with a rolling pin, sprinkling the surface and the *poori* with flour whenever you need to, until you have a round that is about 5½-6 inches in diameter.

Fry the *poori* in the hot oil as in the directions given on page 284. Put the cooked *poori* on a platter lined with paper towels and continue with the rest. If the *pooris* are not going to be eaten within 10 to 15 minutes, they should be kept covered. Put them on a deep plate or a bowl lined with paper towels and cover with an inverted plate. You can keep the *pooris* this way for half an hour in a warm spot.

For information about ingredients and basic techniques that may be unfamiliar, see General Information, pages 418–36.

BHATURAS
(Deep-Fried Leavened Breads)
INDIA

(makes 24 breads)

1   pound (about 3½ cups) unbleached, white flour
½ teaspoon salt
1   teaspoon baking soda
2   teaspoons sugar
½ cup plain, slightly warmed yogurt
2   large eggs, at room temperature
2   teaspoons vegetable oil
Vegetable oil for deep frying
Additional flour for kneading and rolling

Sift the flour, salt, and baking soda into a warm bowl. Add sugar, yogurt, and eggs. Mix well. Now add lukewarm water, a little at a time, until the dough holds together in a ball. (You will need a little less than half a cup.) Knead well for 10 to 15 minutes or until the dough is smooth and elastic but soft. Form the dough into a ball. Rub the ball with about 2 teaspoons of oil and place in a clean bowl. Cover the bowl with plastic wrap or a wet towel and leave in a warm, draft-free area to rise for 5 hours (or overnight in a 68° to 75° F kitchen).

Knead dough again. Divide it into twenty-four equal balls and keep them covered. Line a platter with paper towels and keep near stove. Heat about 2 inches of oil in a deep skillet over a medium flame. (A wok could be used instead.) Let it get smoking hot. Meanwhile roll out each ball until it is about 5½ inches in diameter, dusting with flour if it sticks. As soon as it is rolled out, drop into the hot fat. It will first sink to the bottom and then, in a few seconds, rise and sizzle. Press down on it gently, again and again, with the back of a slotted spoon, using quick, light strokes. The bread should puff up and turn golden on its underside. Turn it over and let the other side turn light brown. The entire process should take less than 1 minute. Put the *bhatura* on the lined platter and cover with a lined plate or inverted bowl. Do all *bhaturas* this way and keep covered.

Soups

Perhaps the hardest thing for vegetarians to arrive at is a good, sound stock. I remember once when I was shepherding an out-of-town vegetarian friend through New York's eateries, he was willing to go to most places—but not Chinese restaurants. "It's the stock," he said. "Even when you order stir-fried greens, you just know that they will put a little meat stock in it." Which is probably true. A good stock enriches the simplest of dishes very quickly. For light, brothy soups, it is absolutely essential. You can, of course, use the water left over from boiling beans and vegetables. But some soups demand that the broth have more taste and character.

The classical Japanese vegetarian stock—*dashi*—uses *kombu* (dried kelp) and dried *shiitake* mushrooms, plus seasonings such as soy sauce and *mirin* (sweet *sake*). It is light and delicate, with its quality depending upon the grade of *kombu*. The Chinese use the water left over from boiling soy beans or just plain water seasoned with soy sauce and monosodium glutamate. Even though msg is used from Korea down to Bali, I never cook with it. It is unnecessary. I have devised quite a wonderful stock of my own that uses soy-bean sprouts and dried mushrooms—Chinese or Japanese—as a base. I add some scallions, a carrot, lettuce leaves, soy sauce, sesame oil, and a little sugar for extra flavor. That sugar is important as it balances the soy sauce and brings out the flavor of the stock. I've called this stock Delicious Stock Made with Soy-Bean Sprouts and you will find it on page 292. There are a few other stocks, too, for you to exper-iment with. See what you like and add extra seasonings as you see fit.

A good stock is essential for soups such as Clear Soup with Soft Bean Curd and Celery Cabbage, Hot-and-Sour Soup, and Thai Noodle Soup. My favorite cold soup, Naeng Myon, would taste quite insipid without it. I am just waiting for the day when *naeng myon* is served in every vegetarian restaurant. It consists of a mound of thin noodles in cold broth. The noodles are covered with sliced hard-boiled eggs, sliced cucumber, sliced white rad-ish pickle, and slices of crisp Korean pear-apple (hard pears may be substituted). This is topped with sliced hot chilies, scallions, and roasted ses-ame seeds. The soup is served with an array of additional sauces. It is spectacular in every way.

Needless to say, not all soups require stock. The very pleasant cold yogurt soups from Iran and the Caucasus region require only soothing vegetables such as cucumber or else varying combinations of nuts, dried fruit, fresh herbs, grains, and beans. Some vegetable soups, such as those made with tomatoes and potatoes, require no assistance either. And then there is the whole world of thick and thin bean and split-pea soups that tend to create their own broth.

Asia has several types of bean and split-pea soups. Those in Japan are made out of fermented bean and grain pastes known as *miso*. *Miso* comes in various hues according to the bean and grain used, ranging from dark brown, red, ochre, and yellow to white. The degree of saltiness and sweet-ness varies in each one of them. *Miso* is now available in America not just in Japanese stores, but in most health-food stores as well. I have identified the pastes by color as that is how they are sometimes sold. The two *miso* soups here, one with bean curd and the other with carrot and mushrooms, should give you a good idea of how these soups are put together. You can improvise your own *miso* soups after that, putting anything into them that you fancy.

When split peas are cooked—and in many Indian homes they are cooked for every single meal—a thin liquid rises to the top while the heavier split peas sink to the bottom. In South India, this thin liquid is removed to make *rasam*, a tart, tamarind-flavored, soupy dish that is either drunk at the start of a meal or else eaten with rice. The thicker split peas—or *dal*—are used to make *sambar*. This way the same *dals* end up doing double duty most efficiently.

The Middle East has many thick, hearty bean soups, such as Chickpea Soup and Navy Bean and Celery Root Soup, that are almost a meal in themselves. All that you need to serve with them is some pita bread, a yogurt cheese, and a crisp salad.

DASHI
(Kombu and Shiitake Mushroom Stock)
JAPAN

This is the basic, classical Japanese stock used for cooking vegetables and for making vegetarian soups. It requires *kombu*, a long, leaflike kelp, filled with vitamins, calcium, and flavor. *Dashi* may be refrigerated and will keep for 3 to 4 days.

(makes 3 cups)

1   piece of *kombu*, about 4 × 7 inches
5   medium-sized dried *shiitake* (or Chinese black) mushrooms
1   teaspoon Japanese soy sauce
½   teaspoon *mirin*

Wipe the *kombu* lightly with a damp cloth and put it into a 2- to 3-quart pot. Add 3 cups water and bring to a boil. When the water begins to boil rapidly, remove the *kombu* with a pair of tongs (save it for Kombu Relish or for making a second stock) and turn off the heat. Rinse the mushrooms quickly and throw them into the hot liquid. Let them soak for 30 minutes. Remove the mushrooms (they can be used in soups and other dishes). Add the soy sauce and *mirin*. Strain the stock through three layers of cheesecloth if the mushrooms have left any grit at the bottom of your pot.

JAPANESE STOCK
JAPAN

This is a richer and somewhat less austere stock than the preceding Dashi. It may also be used for cooking vegetables and for making Japanese soups.

(makes 2⅔ cups)

8   medium-sized dried *shiitake* (or Chinese black) mushrooms
6   scallions, each cut into 3 sections
2   carrots, trimmed, peeled, and each cut into 3 sections
½   teaspoon salt
1   4-inch square of *kombu*
2   teaspoons Japanese soy sauce
¼   teaspoon sugar
1   teaspoon *mirin*
½   teaspoon sesame oil

Rinse off the mushrooms quickly. In a small pot, combine the mushrooms, scallions, carrots, 3 cups water, and ¼ teaspoon of the salt. Cover and simmer gently on a low flame for 30 minutes. Wipe the *kombu* lightly with a damp cloth and put into the pot. Simmer for 1 minute. Turn off the heat and strain the stock immediately through three layers of cheesecloth. (The *kombu* may be saved to make Kombu Relish.) Add the remaining ¼ teaspoon salt, soy sauce, sugar, *mirin*, and sesame oil to the stock. Stir to mix.

For information about ingredients and basic techniques that may be unfamiliar, see General Information, pages 418–36.

DELICIOUS STOCK MADE WITH SOY-BEAN SPROUTS

This tasty stock may be used for any Asian soup.

(makes 5 cups)

2   cups soy-bean sprouts
16 medium-sized dried *shiitake* (or Chinese black) mushrooms
1   carrot, peeled
6   outer lettuce leaves
5   scallions
1   teaspoon salt
2   teaspoons Japanese soy sauce
1   teaspoon sesame oil
½   teaspoon sugar

Wash the sprouts well and drain them. Rinse off the mushrooms quickly. In a large pot, combine the sprouts, mushrooms, carrot, lettuce, scallions, salt, and 8 cups water. Bring to a boil. Cover, turn heat to low and simmer for 1 hour. Strain the stock through three layers of cheesecloth. Add the soy sauce, sesame oil, and sugar. Mix. Bring the stock to a boil again and reduce it until you have 5 cups.

This stock may be refrigerated for 2 to 3 days or else frozen.

VEGETABLE STOCK
(For Chinese Dishes and Soups)

Vegetable stocks do not taste like meat stocks. They have their own delicate taste which can vary with the vegetables that you happen to have around in your refrigerator. You could add shelled pea pods, celery, parsnips, zucchini and yellow squash tips, fresh mushroom stems, asparagus bottoms, watercress stems, green peppers, and parsley.

(makes 4 cups)

16 medium-sized dried *shiitake* (or Chinese black) mushrooms
4   carrots, washed and scrubbed
8   whole scallions
6   outer lettuce leaves
1   teaspoon salt
1   teaspoon Chinese thin soy sauce
2   teaspoons sesame oil
¼   teaspoon sugar

Rinse the mushrooms quickly in cold water. Wash and scrub the carrots, leaving 4 inches of their tops on, if possible.

Combine the mushrooms, carrots, scallions, lettuce, salt, and 5 cups water in a 4-quart pot and bring to a boil. Cover, lower heat and simmer for half an hour. Strain the stock through three layers of cheesecloth. (Discard all the vegetables except the mushrooms. Save the mushrooms for other dishes— you can slice and put them in scrambled eggs, you can put them in soups, you can put them in fried rice, and you can stir-fry them with various greens.) Boil down the stock to 4 cups. Add the soy sauce, sesame oil, and sugar. Mix and check seasonings.

For information about ingredients and basic techniques that may be unfamiliar, see General Information, pages 418–36.

Alun's
CACIK
(Cold Yogurt Soup in a Turkish Style)
TURKEY

This is an excellent soup to have on hot summer days.

(serves 4–6)

1 medium-sized cucumber
¾ teaspoon salt, or to taste
2 cups plain yogurt
½ cup milk
1 clove garlic, peeled and mashed to a pulp in a mortar
1 tablespoon fruity olive oil

Peel the cucumber. Cut it in half lengthwise and scrape out all the seeds with a grapefruit spoon. Now cut the cucumber into ¼-inch dice. Sprinkle with ¼ teaspoon salt and set aside for half an hour. Squeeze out as much moisture as you can.

Put the yogurt in a bowl. Beat with a fork or whisk until it is smooth and creamy. Slowly add the milk, beating gently as you do so.

Add the cucumbers to the yogurt, along with the remaining ½ teaspoon salt, garlic, and olive oil. Mix well and chill until ready to serve.

PERSIAN-STYLE COLD YOGURT SOUP
IRAN

(serves 4–6)

2 tablespoons golden raisins
1 cucumber
2 cups plain yogurt
¾ teaspoon salt
⅛ teaspoon freshly ground black pepper
1 cup heavy cream
2 tablespoons very finely sliced tender green of scallions
3 tablespoons coarsely chopped walnuts
1 tablespoon minced fresh dill

Soak the raisins in 1 cup hot water for 1 hour, then drain.

Peel the cucumber. Remove seeds if they are very large, then grate the cucumber.

Put yogurt, salt, and pepper into a bowl. Beat yogurt with a fork or whisk until it is creamy. Slowly add 1 cup ice water and then the cream, beating as you do so. Now add all the other ingredients. Mix well.

If the soup is not to be drunk immediately, it should be refrigerated. It is best served on hot days.

NAENG MYON
(Cold Noodle Soup)
KOREA

This is easily one of the greatest cold soups on this earth. I often had it for lunch in Korea. As it is almost a meal in itself, not much else needs to be served with it except, of course, some *kimchee*. And even though it has many parts to it, these various components as well as the sauces may be made in advance and refrigerated.

In the dining room of Seoul's King Sejong Hotel, a separate buffet table is set aside, loaded with all the prepared components of the more common, nonvegetarian version of this soup. Diners come with empty soup bowls and put the soup together themselves. Cold, cooked noodles are first piled in the center of the bowl. Cold broth is then ladled over the noodles. Various fruits and vegetables, all sliced thin, are laid over the noodles like the rays of the sun. The central "sun" consists of slices of hard-boiled egg. The soup is then seasoned to taste with various sauces which include prepared English-type mustard, a soy-vinegar sauce, and the cool liquid from Dong Chimi, the white radish water *kimchee*.

Additional seasonings, such as sliced chilies, sliced scallions, sliced Chinese chives, and roasted sesame seeds are sprinkled over the top.

I developed such a passion for this soup that I found myself hunting for it in every Korean city. In Pusan, I discovered a very interesting variation. The vegetables and fruit had been cut into very fine julienne strips. The hard-boiled eggs had been replaced by very fine Egg Strands (see page 206). All of these had been piled on top of the noodles in a big mound.

(serves 4)

½ pound thin Japanese or Korean buckwheat noodles*

5 cups Delicious Stock . . . (see page 292), refrigerated at least 3 hours

1 teaspoon sesame oil

1 large or 2 small cucumbers

2 cold hard-boiled eggs

8 rectangles Dong Chimi (pickled white radish, see page 382)

½ pear-apple, if available, or a whole, very hard and crunchy pear

*NOTE: If you can't get the buckwheat noodles, substitute thin linguini, spaghettini, or fresh Chinese noodles.

For information about ingredients and basic techniques that may be unfamiliar, see General Information, pages 418–36.

SAUCES FOR NAENG MYON

Mustard Sauce: Put 4 teaspoons of dry English mustard in a small cup, add 4 teaspoons water and mix.

Korean Dipping Sauce Number 3 (see page 358)

1   cup cold liquid from the Korean water pickle, Dong Chimi (see page 382): Stir before pouring the liquid out.

ADDITIONAL OPTIONAL SEASONINGS

1 to 2 fresh hot green chilies, sliced into very, very fine rounds

A ¾-inch cube of peeled fresh ginger, cut into very fine shreds

1½ tablespoons roasted and lightly crushed sesame seeds

2   tablespoons very finely sliced scallions or Chinese chives

Cook the noodles according to the instructions on the package. (Directions for cooking Chinese noodles are given on page 246.) Drain the noodles in a colander and rinse thoroughly under cold running water. Put the noodles in a bowl. Toss with ½ cup of the stock and the sesame oil. Cover and set aside.

Unless the cucumber is waxed, do not peel it. Scrub under running water and, if the cucumber is long, cut into 2- to 2½-inch chunks. Trim away the ends. Now cut lengthwise into ⅛-inch-thick slices. Cut these slices, lengthwise, in half. Ideally, you should end up with rectangles that are 2 inches long, ¾ inch wide, and ⅛ inch thick. The ends that are almost all skin may be discarded.

Peel the eggs and cut them crosswise into ¼-inch-thick slices.

Cut the rectangles of pickled white radish lengthwise into slices that are about 1½ inches long, ½ inch wide, and ⅛ inch thick.

Peel the pear-apple or pear and core it. Cut it into ⅛-inch-thick slices. The pear should be cut at the last minute so it does not discolor.

To serve, divide the noodles among four bowls. Pour one-quarter of the stock over each pile of noodles. Put a few neatly overlapping egg slices right on top of the noodles in the center. Arrange a few slices each of the vegetables and fruit all around like slightly overlapping rays of the sun. Put the mustard sauce in a very small bowl and the dipping sauce and pickle water in slightly larger bowls. Put the optional seasonings in shallow bowls or saucers. The sauces and seasonings should be passed around to each diner. Diners should put in whatever they want and as much as they like. Offer chopsticks and soupspoons as eating implements. Serve Cabbage Kimchee (see page 379) on the side.

COLD YOGURT SOUP WITH BARLEY

CAUCASUS

(serves 4)

¼ cup hulled barley, washed and drained
3 tablespoons unsalted butter or vegetable oil
3 tablespoons finely chopped fresh mint
1 small onion, peeled and finely chopped
2 cups yogurt
1 cup milk
¾ teaspoon salt
Freshly ground black pepper

Put the barley and 2 cups water in a small pot and bring to a boil. Cover, turn heat to low and simmer for 50 to 60 minutes or until barley is tender. Pour the contents of the pot into a sieve to drain. Hold the sieve under running water and rinse the barley. Set the sieve over a bowl and leave to drain.

Heat the butter or oil in a skillet over a low flame. Put in the mint and onion. Stir and sauté gently for 5 to 6 minutes or until onion is quite tender but not at all brown. Turn the heat off under the skillet and let the mixture cool slightly.

Put the yogurt in a bowl. Beat lightly with a fork or whisk until smooth and creamy. Add the milk. Beat again to mix. Now add the barley, salt, black pepper, and the mixture in the skillet. Stir to mix. Refrigerate until ready to eat.

Gary Jenanyan's
TAN ABOUR
(Cold Yogurt Soup with Chickpeas and Wheat)

TURKEY/ARMENIA

Gary lives in California and it was his maternal grandfather, still hale and hearty in his nineties, who brought this simple recipe out with him when he fled Turkey during the massacre of the Armenians by the Turks. It is a dish that is eaten in their house almost every day.

I often double this recipe and leave whatever is uneaten in the refrigerator. It keeps beautifully for days and may be served as a soup course or for breakfast or lunch.

(serves 4)

¼ cup whole-wheat berries, picked over, washed, and drained
½ cup dried chickpeas, picked over, washed, and drained
Salt
2 cups plain yogurt
2 tablespoons minced fresh mint

Soak the wheat in 1½ cups water for 12 hours.

Soak the chickpeas in 3 cups water for 12 hours.

Drain and rinse the wheat. Put it in a small pot along with 3 cups water and bring to a boil. Cover partially, turn heat to low and simmer for 45 minutes. Add ½ teaspoon salt and simmer another 30 minutes. Drain and rinse.

While the wheat is cooking, drain and rinse the chickpeas and put them in another pot with 4 cups water. Bring to a boil. Cover partially, turn heat to low and simmer for 45 minutes. Add 1 teaspoon salt and simmer for 30 minutes or until chickpeas are tender. Drain and put in a bowl. Cover with

---

For information about ingredients and basic techniques that may be unfamiliar, see General Information, pages 418–36.

cold water. Rub the chickpeas gently with your hands to loosen the skins. Pour off the water and the loosened skins. Cover the chickpeas again with water. Rub to remove more skins. Keep doing this until most of the skins have been taken off. Drain. (The removal of the skins is not essential to this soup. I just think that it improves both the taste and appearance somewhat.)

Put the yogurt in a bowl. Beat lightly with a fork or whisk until smooth and creamy. Add the mint, wheat, and chickpeas. Stir to mix. While it is not common to add salt at this stage, you may do so if you wish.

CLEAR SOUP WITH ENOK MUSHROOMS, BEAN-CURD SKINS, AND SPINACH

JAPAN

Now that the tiny fresh Japanese mushrooms— *enoki-dake* or enok mushrooms—are beginning to find their way into specialty grocery stores in America, do experiment with using them in soups, salads, and sautéed dishes. Apart from their fine, delicate flavor and very smooth texture, they are rich in vitamins.

Before you use these mushrooms, trim off about 1 inch of the lower stems and then rinse them off.

(serves 4)

1 sheet dried bean-curd skin, about 5 × 1½ × ⅟₃₂ inches.
4 cups Japanese Stock (see page 291)
½ cup trimmed and rinsed enok mushrooms
12 spinach leaves, well washed
1 teaspoon lemon juice
8 slivers of lemon peel, each about 1-inch long

Rinse the bean-curd skin in hot water, then soak in hot water for 10 minutes. Drain and cut it crosswise into ⅟₁₆-inch-wide strips.

Bring the Japanese Stock to a boil in a 2-quart pot. Add the bean-curd-skin strips, enok mushrooms, and spinach leaves. Simmer the soup on medium heat until the spinach leaves have wilted, about 1 minute. Add the lemon juice, stir, and taste for seasonings. I usually do not need any more salt than is in the broth but you might want a bit more.

Divide the soup among four soup bowls. Garnish each bowl with 2 slivers of lemon peel and serve immediately. The Japanese like to drink their soup directly from the soup bowls. Solids are picked up with chopsticks.

CLEAR SOUP WITH SOFT BEAN CURD AND CELERY CABBAGE
CHINA

This is a light, very pleasant soup.

(serves 6)

4   cups Vegetable Stock (see page 292)
¼   teaspoon salt
2   well-packed cups Chinese cabbage or celery cabbage, cut into 1¼-inch-wide strips
1   pound soft or medium bean curd, cut into approximately 1-inch cubes

Heat the stock in a wide pot or a casserole-type dish that can be taken to the table, over a medium-high flame. When it is simmering, put in the salt and the cabbage. Cover, lower flame, and simmer gently for about 3 minutes or until the cabbage is just tender. Uncover, and put in the bean-curd cubes. Cook, uncovered, for another minute to allow the bean curd to heat through. Serve immediately in a large, warmed soup tureen or in the casserole dish in which it was cooked.

SWEET CORN AND EGG SOUP
CHINA

(serves 4)

4   cups Vegetable Stock (see page 292)
2   teaspoons cornstarch
2   teaspoons sesame oil
2   small or 1½ large eggs
1   cup canned sweet, cream-style corn
⅓ to ½ teaspoon salt
⅛ teaspoon freshly ground white pepper
¾ teaspoon Chinese thin soy sauce
2   teaspoons very finely sliced scallions

Remove ¼ cup of cool stock and slowly mix it with the cornstarch to make a smooth paste. Add 1 teaspoon sesame oil and set this mixture aside. Beat the eggs lightly (they should not froth) and add the remaining 1 teaspoon sesame oil to it. Mix well and set aside.

Heat the remaining 3¾ cups stock in a 2- to 3-quart pot over a medium-high flame. When hot, add the corn, salt, pepper, and soy sauce. Bring to a simmer and turn heat to low. Stir the cornstarch mixture and pour it into the hot stock. Stir and cook on low heat until the mixture thickens slightly. Turn off the heat. Immediately pour in the egg mixture in a slow, steady stream, covering the entire surface of the soup with it. Stir gently.

Pour the soup into individual bowls and sprinkle each bowl with some of the sliced scallions.

For information about ingredients and basic techniques that may be unfamiliar, see General Information, pages 418–36.

CLEAR SOUP WITH CUCUMBER, COOKED WITH THAI SEASONINGS

WHITE RADISH SOUP

KOREA

This was one of my favorite breakfast soups in Korea. It is very soothing and warming, especially on cold, blustery days.

(serves 4–6)

6 cups Delicious Stock . . . (see page 292)
16 Chinese mushrooms (from the above stock)*
1 pound white radish, peeled and cut into ¾-inch dice
3 cups mung-bean sprouts, washed and drained
½ to 1 teaspoon Japanese soy sauce
½ teaspoon sugar

*NOTE: If you haven't saved the mushrooms from the stock, soak 16 Chinese dried black mushrooms in 1½ cups hot water for ½ hour.

Put the stock to boil in a 3½-quart pot. Meanwhile, cut off the hard mushroom stems and then cut the caps into fine slices.

Put the mushrooms and diced radish into the boiling stock. Cover, turn down heat, and simmer gently for about 10 minutes or until the radish pieces are tender. Add the sprouts and bring to a boil again. Cover, turn heat down and simmer 3 to 4 minutes. Taste the soup. Add the soy sauce according to the saltiness you think you need. Add the sugar and mix gently.

This is quite a wonderful soup, especially for those who like Thai seasonings like lemon grass and kaffir lime leaves. You will not find this soup in Thailand. It is my own vegetarian adaptation of a popular shrimp soup. The main "solid" in this clear soup consists of julienned cucumbers, which I barely cook, so they stay very crisp. I prefer to use Kirby or pickling cucumbers which I can get almost all year round in New York City. They have small, tender seeds which are ideal if one wishes to cut the entire cucumber into julienne strips. If you cannot find pickling cucumbers, or English cucumbers which also have small seeds, use the regular cucumber. Peel it, cut it in half lengthwise, and then scoop out all the seeds. Cut the cucumber shell into julienne strips.

(serves 4)

4 cups Vegetable Stock (see page 292) or Delicious Stock . . . (see page 292)
12 to 16 whole stalks of fresh Chinese parsley
8 dried kaffir lime leaves
1 tablespoon dried, sliced lemon grass
About ½ teaspoon salt
4 teaspoons lime or lemon juice
1 cup julienned cucumber (see note above)
Freshly ground black pepper to taste
1 tablespoon chopped Chinese parsley
1 tablespoon finely sliced scallions
About 1 teaspoon very, very finely minced fresh hot green chilies (optional)

Combine the stock, Chinese parsley stalks, kaffir lime leaves, and lemon grass in a 2- to 3-quart pot and bring to a boil. Cover, lower heat, and simmer gently for 20 minutes. Strain. Add the salt, lime or lemon juice, and cucumber. Stir and bring to a boil again. Turn heat to low and simmer, uncovered, for 15 seconds. Turn the heat off. Add the black pepper.

Pour soup into individual bowls and garnish with the chopped Chinese parsley, scallions, and green chilies.

CHINESE-STYLE NOODLE SOUP

HONG KONG

The noodle "soups" of Eastern Asia are much more substantial than their American counterparts. Each soup bowl does, of course, have some clear broth in it but it is also quite filled with a generous quantity of noodles and vegetables—enough to make a very satisfying lunch or snack. In Hong Kong's noodle restaurants—sometimes they are just little sheds—the kitchens have huge cauldrons of simmering stock. As orders come in, fresh noodles are put into a sieve and the sieve is lowered into the simmering stock. Chopsticks are used to separate the strands. As soon as the noodles are cooked, and this takes almost no time at all, they are put into individual bowls which sit ready with some sliced scallions and droplets of soy sauce in them. Then vegetables—it could be *bok choy*, *choy sum*, celery cabbage, spinach, or bean sprouts—are put into the sieve and lowered into the broth. These

are emptied on top of the noodles. A little broth is ladled in, some chopped Chinese parsley is sprinkled on the top, and the bowls are ready to be carried to the table. Diners are offered a variety of sauces to season their soups further—hot chili sauces (the red and green commercial kind), hot oil, soy sauce, and vinegar are always on the table.

(serves 4–6)

¼ pound thin, fresh Chinese *lo-mein* egg noodles,* or 2 cups freshly cooked spaghettini
4 cups Vegetable Stock (see page 292) or Delicious Stock . . . (see page 292)
1 medium-sized carrot, peeled, and cut at a slight diagonal into 1/16-inch-thick slices
2 cups celery cabbage, cut crosswise into 1-inch-wide strips
20 tender leaves of either *choy sum* or spinach
2 scallions cut into very fine rounds, including ¾ of one green
About ¼ teaspoon salt
2 tablespoons chopped fresh Chinese parsley

*NOTE: Use 2 cups freshly cooked spaghettini if you can't find the thin, fresh Chinese egg noodles.

Bring 8 cups of water to a boil in a large pot. Separate the noodles and when the water is at a rolling boil, drop them in. Let the water come to a boil again. Put in 1 cup of cold faucet water. The boiling will subside. Bring the water to a third boil. Pour in a second cup of cold water. Let the water come to a fourth boil. Turn off the heat and drain the noodles in a colander. Run cold water over the noodles and rinse them off. Leave to drain. (If you are using freshly cooked spaghettini, drain and rinse it off as well.)

For information about ingredients and basic techniques that may be unfamiliar, see General Information, pages 418–36.

Heat the Vegetable Stock in a 3-quart pot. Add the carrot, cabbage, *choy sum*, and scallions. Simmer, uncovered, on medium heat for a minute or until vegetables are just done. Add the noodles and bring to a simmer again. Let the noodles heat through. Add the salt, stir, then taste and correct seasoning, if necessary.

Divide the soup evenly among all the soup bowls. Sprinkle the Chinese parsley over the top. These soups are generally eaten with both chopsticks and soupspoons. Extra sauces (see note above) should be offered at the table.

THAI NOODLE SOUP
THAILAND

In Thailand, this soup is made with chicken stock and seasoned with fish sauce. I have taken the liberty of changing the dish somewhat. Instead of the chicken stock, I use a vegetable stock; for the fish sauce, I have substituted soy sauce. You may use mushroom soy, if you prefer.

Noodles are Thailand's favorite lunch and snack food. Any visitor to Bangkok will find the city dotted with noodle shops, all set up with Formica-topped tables, as well as with basket-toting noodle vendors who squat on sidewalks, hoping to catch the hungry and the greedy as they rush by.

Thai noodle shops generally offer several kinds of noodles. I have a preference for the fresh Chinese *lo-mein* noodles but you could use Japanese whole wheat or buckwheat *soba* or *udon* or *somen* or you could use spaghettini or linguini. In a seasoning combination typical of many Thai foods, this soup has hot, sweet, sour, and salty flavorings. Apart from being exceedingly tasty, it is also quite nourishing, as it is always topped with fresh bean sprouts, green beans, Chinese parsley, and crushed peanuts.

(serves 6)

½ pound fresh Chinese *lo-mein* egg noodles (for substitutes, see above)
2 tablespoons finely sliced fresh hot green chilies
4 tablespoons Japanese rice vinegar
½ cup Chinese or Japanese soy sauce
¾ cup roasted or fried unsalted peanuts (see page 322)
2 cups washed and drained mung-bean sprouts
Granulated sugar to pass around
9 cups Vegetable Stock (see page 292) or Delicious Stock . . . (see page 292)
4 to 5 ounces fresh green beans cut into ¾-inch pieces

Bring 4 quarts of water to a boil in a large pot. Separate the noodles and when the water is at a rolling boil, drop them in. Let the water come to a boil again. Put in 1 cup of cold faucet water. The boiling will subside. Bring the water to a third boil. Pour in a second cup of cold water. Let the water come to a fourth boil. Turn off the heat and drain the noodles in a colander. Run cold water over the noodles and rinse them off. Leave to drain. (If you are using dried noodles, cook them according to package instructions, then drain and rinse them off.)

Set up the seasonings and extras that go on top of the noodles. You will need four bowls for this. Combine the green chilies and the vinegar and put the mixture in one small bowl; the soy sauce should be poured into another small bowl; crush the peanuts or grind them coarsely in a clean coffee grinder and put them in the third bowl; put the bean sprouts in a larger bowl. Arrange these four bowls as well as the sugar bowl neatly in the center of the dining table.

Bring the stock to a boil. Throw in the green beans and let them boil for a minute. Now add the noodles and let them heat through.

Divide the soup among individual bowls. Diners should put bean sprouts over their soup and then season it, to taste, with the chili-vinegar mixture, soy sauce, peanuts, and sugar. (I rarely use more than a half teaspoon of sugar.)

HOT-AND-SOUR SOUP

CHINA

(serves 4)

1   tablespoon tree ear fungus
6   Chinese dried black mushrooms
24 dried day-lily buds
4   cups Vegetable Stock (see page 292)
2   teaspoons cornstarch
2   teaspoons sesame oil
1   large egg
¼ cup finely julienned bamboo-shoot strips
4   ounces medium bean curd, cut into julienne
     strips
⅓ to ½ teaspoon salt
2   tablespoons distilled white vinegar
¼ to ½ teaspoon freshly ground white pepper
2   teaspoons Chinese thin soy sauce
2   teaspoons very finely sliced scallions

Soak the tree ear fungus and Chinese mushrooms in 1 cup water each for half an hour, and the day-lily buds in 1½ cups water for half an hour.

Drain the tree ear fungus and rinse it. Feel for any hard knots with your fingers. Cut off and discard them. Now cut the fungus into long strips, about ¼-inch wide.

Remove the mushrooms from their soaking liquid. (Save the liquid for stock or for cooking vegetables.) Cut off and discard the coarse stems and then cut the caps into ¼-inch-wide strips.

Remove the day-lily buds from their soaking liquid. Cut off and discard the hard knots that can sometimes be found at one end.

Remove ¼ cup of the stock and set the remainder to heat in a 3-quart pot over a medium-high flame.

Put the cornstarch into a small bowl. Slowly add the ¼ cup cold stock and 1 teaspoon sesame oil. Set aside.

Beat the egg very lightly. (Do not let it froth.) Mix in 1 teaspoon sesame oil and set aside.

The stock should now be boiling. Add the tree ear fungus, mushrooms, day-lily buds, bamboo-shoot strips, bean-curd strips, and salt to it. Bring to a simmer. Turn heat to low and simmer, uncovered, for 5 minutes. Now add the vinegar, white pepper, and soy sauce. Bring to a simmer. Stir the cornstarch and stock mixture and add it to the pot. Stir and cook until the soup thickens slightly. Turn off the heat. Immediately pour in the beaten egg mixture in a steady stream, covering the surface of the soup with it. Stir gently.

Pour soup into individual bowls. Sprinkle with the sliced scallions and serve hot.

For information about ingredients and basic techniques that may be unfamiliar, see General Information, pages 418–36.

QUAIL-EGG SOUP

CHINA

Apart from being a very tasty soup, this is also a very pretty soup—the kind that elicits exclamatory gasps when it first appears on the table. In order to get full dramatic mileage out of your efforts, bring the soup to the table in a single Chinese serving bowl. If you do not have a Chinese serving bowl, use a light-colored or white ceramic or porcelain bowl of roughly a 6- to 7-cup capacity. (There are actually only 4 cups of broth.) Let me describe to you what the soup looks like when it first appears on the table. The bowl is lined with the bright-green stalks and leaves of the Chinese vegetable, *choy sum*, to form a kind of nest. The quail eggs, steamed in small dishes so they form tiny flying-saucer-shaped discs, are placed on top of the green nest. Steaming hot broth seems to hold this nest and its contents in suspension. It is quite a sight.

Choy sum is the best green for this soup. However, if you live in an area quite devoid of Chinese grocery stores, substitute 1½ pounds of fresh spinach. If you do have access to *choy sum*, buy about 1½ pounds. You actually need ¾ to 1 pound of trimmed *choy sum*. As it is hard to calculate exactly how much will need to be trimmed away, it is best to buy a little extra. If some *choy sum* is left, you can always steam it the following day. It is such a tasty vegetable.

Fresh quail eggs are available in Chinese markets (look for a store that sells poultry and fish) and in specialty grocery stores. If you just cannot get quail eggs, use the smallest hen's eggs that you can find, one per person, and steam them in the

saucers of demitasse coffee cups. For steaming the quail eggs, you need the tiny, shallow, bowl-like dishes that Chinese restaurants use for serving soy sauce, duck sauce, and mustard. I have a collection of such dishes and the ones that I prefer measure about 2⅔ inches in diameter (inside) and about ¾ inch in depth (inside). You need to steam 12 eggs but they may be done in several batches, reusing the dishes.

(serves 4–6)

About 3 teaspoons sesame oil
12 fresh quail eggs
12 single, unblemished leaves of fresh Chinese parsley
Choy sum (see note above for quantity)
2 teaspoons salt
3 tablespoons vegetable oil
2 cloves garlic, peeled and minced
2 scallions, trimmed and cut into fine rings, including three-quarters of the green
1 tablespoon Chinese thin soy sauce
4 cups Vegetable Stock (see page 292) or Delicious Stock . . . (see page 292), steaming hot

Get your steaming equipment ready. If you are using a Chinese bamboo steamer set inside a wok, make sure that you put just enough water inside the wok so it stays below the slats on the "floor" of the steamer. Do not put the steamer over the water yet. Bring the water to a boil first. (If you do not have a bamboo steamer, set a trivet inside a large pot. Set a plate over the trivet. Pour just enough water into the pot so it stays below the plate. Bring the water to a boil. The egg dishes can then be put on the plate and the pot covered for steaming.)

Use 1½ teaspoons sesame oil to grease the small soy-sauce dishes generously (see note above). Crack open a quail egg near its middle and empty the whole egg into the soy-sauce dish. Do not let the yolk break. Do all eggs this way. Place a single unblemished Chinese parsley leaf on the center of each egg yolk. Put the dishes in the steamer in a single layer (you may need to do more than one batch) set over the boiling water, cover, and steam for 2½ to 4 minutes or until it the whites of the eggs are set and the yolks are semihard. Remove from the hot water, uncover, and set aside.

Trim the *choy sum* by cutting off and discarding the tough lower sections. Pull off the larger leaves on the lusher stalks to thin them out. Arrange these leaves as well as the remaining *choy sum* so that all the stalks and stems face one direction and the leaves the opposite direction. You will have to keep this "bundle" shape throughout the cooking.

Bring 8 cups of water with 2 teaspoons salt to a rolling boil. Heat 3 tablespoons of vegetable oil in a wok over high heat. When hot, put in the garlic. Stir the garlic around until it has browned. Pour in the boiling water (keep your face averted). Put in the *choy sum*, still preserving its "bundle" form. Make sure that the stem ends are completely submerged. Cover and boil vigorously for 2 minutes or until the *choy sum* is just tender. Drain the *choy sum* by pouring the water out of the wok. Lift the whole *choy-sum* bundle up with a pair of tongs and place it on a chopping board. Cut the *choy sum* into 3- to 4-inch lengths. Work quickly now.

Put the scallions, soy sauce, and 1½ teaspoons sesame oil in the center of a warmed soup bowl. Arrange the *choy sum* pieces around the seasonings in such a way so that they seem to radiate from the scallions and go up the sides of the bowl. Slide the quail eggs out of their dishes and place them, Chinese parsley leaf up, over the green nest. Pour the steaming broth over the eggs and serve at once.

Take the serving bowl to the table and then ladle out portions into individual soup bowls.

BEET AND TOMATO SOUP
INDIA

This simple dish was probably concocted by English families in India who were quite taken with Indian spices but yearned to have elegant European soups on their tables. In the nineteenth century, the soup was probably thickened with flour. I prefer it unthickened. The use of cream is entirely up to you. Without it, the soup is light and brothlike; you could serve thin slices of oven-crisped bread with it. Actually, I often drink it like broth when I am working late into the night. When thickened with cream, the soup becomes slightly richer and needs no accompaniment.

For information about ingredients and basic techniques that may be unfamiliar, see General Information, pages 418–36.

It is very easy to double or triple the recipe by doubling or tripling the ingredients. The cooking time remains exactly the same.

(makes about 2½ cups and serves 2–3)

½ pound fresh beets (about 3 medium-sized beets)
1 teaspoon *ghee*
½ teaspoon whole cumin seeds
1 teaspoon whole black peppercorns
4 whole cloves
A ¾-inch piece of stick cinnamon
3 medium-sized tomatoes, peeled and then chopped (or equivalent amount of canned tomatoes)
½ or more teaspoon salt
¼ cup cream (optional)

Peel the beets and cut them into large dice. Put them into the container of a food processor or blender along with 1½ cups water. Blend for 1 minute. Strain the juice through a fine sieve, getting out as much of the liquid as possible.

Heat the *ghee* in a 1½- to 2-quart pot over a medium flame. As soon as it is hot, put in the cumin seeds, black peppercorns, cloves, and cinnamon. Stir for a second and then put in the chopped tomatoes. Stir for another 3 to 4 seconds and add the beet juice, salt, as well as another ½ cup of water. Bring to a boil, cover, turn heat to low and simmer 10 minutes. Strain. Add cream if you desire and reheat.

MY CREAM OF TOMATO SOUP
INDIA

Cream of tomato soup has been adopted by India with a passion. The same small coffeehouses that offer the most traditional *dosas* and vegetable *pakoris* also have, to the surprise of many Americans, tomato soup on their menus. When cooking tomato soup in their homes, most Indians cannot resist putting in a few spices or herbs. My sister-in-law, for example, puts in fresh curry leaves from the tree that grows just outside her kitchen door. The soup immediately becomes very aromatic. In New York, I put in dried curry leaves, more for the aroma I remember than for the limited flavor provided by the dried leaves, as well as ginger, ground roasted cumin, and a few other things besides. Here is my tomato soup, which can be had hot or cold.

(serves 4–6)

1½ pounds red-ripe tomatoes, chopped
1 tablespoon dried, sliced lemon grass
1 tablespoon dried or fresh curry leaves
1 quarter-sized slice fresh ginger
1¼ teaspoons salt
4 tablespoons unsalted butter
2 tablespoons all-purpose unbleached white flour
½ cup heavy cream
2½ cups milk
½ teaspoon ground roasted cumin seeds
1/16 to ⅛ teaspoon freshly ground black pepper
⅛ teaspoon cayenne pepper
2 teaspoons lime or lemon juice
1 tablespoon minced fresh Chinese parsley

Combine the tomatoes, lemon grass, curry leaves, ginger, ½ teaspoon salt, and ½ cup water in a 2½-quart pot and bring to a boil. Cover, lower heat, and simmer gently for 15 minutes. Uncover, turn heat to medium, and simmer a little more aggressively for another 15 minutes. Put the tomatoes through a sieve. You should have about 2 cups of thick tomato juice. Bring this juice to a simmer and keep on a very low flame.

Melt the butter in a heavy saucepan. Add the flour. Stir and cook the flour on low heat for 2 to 3 minutes. Do not let it brown. Now pour in the hot tomato juice, stirring all the time. Add the cream and the remaining ¾ teaspoon salt. Stir to mix and bring to a simmer. Add all the other ingredients except the Chinese parsley. Stir to mix. Heat over a medium flame. As soon as the soup is about to come to a boil, turn off the heat. Ladle the soup into warmed soup bowls and serve garnished with a little minced Chinese parsley. If you wish to serve the soup cold, stir it occasionally as it cools so it does not form a thick film. Then cover and refrigerate.

CALDO VERDE
(Green Soup)
INDIA

This hearty soup is served in the former Portuguese colony of Goa on the west coast of India. It is not unlike a basic leek and potato soup, only it is flavored with *couve*—kale, garlic, and olive oil.

(serves 6)

4 medium-sized potatoes, peeled and chopped into ¾-inch dice
1 medium-sized onion, peeled and coarsely chopped
2 cups coarsely chopped kale leaves, firmly packed
12 cloves garlic, peeled
1¼ teaspoons salt
1 tablespoon fruity olive oil
Freshly ground black pepper

In a large pot, combine the potatoes, onion, kale, garlic, and salt. Add 6 cups water and bring to a boil. Cover, lower heat, and simmer very gently for 1 hour and 15 minutes or until kale is quite tender.

In as many batches as necessary, pour the soup into the container of an electric blender or food processor and blend until you have a smooth texture. Pour soup back into soup pot and taste for seasonings. Add more water if the soup seems too thick. Just before serving, add the olive oil and black pepper.

For information about ingredients and basic techniques that may be unfamiliar, see General Information, pages 418–36.

MISO SOUP WITH BEAN CURD

JAPAN

(serves 4–5)

1 strip *kombu*, about 11 × 3 inches
4 tablespoons dark yellow *miso*
1 cake fresh bean curd, cut into ½-inch cubes
2 scallions, trimmed and sliced into very fine
  rounds, including half their green

Bring 4 cups water to a boil in a 2½-quart pot. Wipe the *kombu* with a damp cloth, then drop into the water, making sure that it is well submerged. Turn off the heat. Leave *kombu* in the water 2 to 3 minutes. Remove the *kombu*. (Do not discard it. It can be reused to flavor a second broth or to make Kombu Relish.)

Partially submerge a small sieve in the *kombu* broth. Put the *miso* into the sieve and push it through with a wooden spoon. If any little pieces are left in the sieve, they may be discarded. Add the bean curd and bring to a boil. As soon as the first bubbles form, turn off the heat. Stir in the scallions and serve immediately in covered Japanese laquer bowls or in ceramic bowls.

MISO SOUP WITH CARROTS AND MUSHROOMS

JAPAN

(serves 4)

1   strip *kombu*, about 7 × 4 inches
1   carrot, peeled, and cut into very fine julienne matchsticks
½   medium-sized onion, peeled, and sliced into very fine half rings
4   medium-sized mushrooms, wiped, and cut into very thin slices
A piece of lemon peel, 1 inch long and ⅓ inch wide, cut lengthwise into very fine, long slivers
4   tablespoons red (its actual color is a rich brown) *miso*
⅛   teaspoon 7-spice seasoning

Bring 4 cups of water to a boil in a 2½-quart pot. Wipe the *kombu* lightly with a damp cloth, then drop into the water, making sure that it is well submerged. Turn off the heat. Leave *kombu* in the water 2 to 3 minutes. Remove the *kombu*. (This *kombu* may be reused to make Kombu Relish.)

Add the carrot, onion, mushrooms, and lemon peel to the *kombu* broth. Bring to a boil again, cover, and simmer on low heat for 5 minutes. Turn off the heat. Put *miso* in a small sieve. Partially submerge the sieve in the soup and press out the *miso* with a wooden spoon. Bring to a boil again. Just as the first bubbles form, turn off the heat. Stir the soup and ladle it into soup bowls (lidded Japanese bowls are best). Sprinkle each bowlful with some of the 7-spice seasoning and serve immediately.

Jyothi Baswan's

RASAM
(A Tomato, Tamarind, and Dal Broth)

INDIA

Rasam is a thin South Indian broth that is served in clear glasses, cups, or small bowls and then either sipped as an appetizer or else eaten with rice. I love to serve it in cups as a soup and find that it makes a light, spicy, and very refreshing first course.

When *dals* (split peas) are boiled in water, the heavy grains sink to the bottom and a thin broth separates itself and rises to the top. South Indians, who cook *dals* for almost every meal, manage very cleverly to make two dishes out of the contents of the same pot. The thin broth is removed to make *rasam* while the thicker *dal* is used to make dishes like *sambar*.

There are many types of *rasam*. The most common kind combines tomatoes, tamarind, and thin *dal* water to produce a broth that has herbs, seeds, and bits of tomato floating around in it. I find it much more convenient to strain the broth before serving it.

Another thing: *rasam* has a kind of sediment—a quite tasty sediment, I might add—that sinks to the bottom of the pot. South Indian housewives feel obliged by custom to serve honored guests the lighter top broth and to eat the leftover sediment themselves. I prefer to divide the broth and sediment more equally. So I just give the broth a good stir before ladling it out into cups. As diners sip the broth, the thicker particles begin collecting at the bottom of their cups. A spoon may be used to finish them off.

For information about ingredients and basic techniques that may be unfamiliar, see General Information, pages 418–36.

(serves 4–6)

½ cup *toovar dal* (also called *arhar dal*), picked over, washed, and drained

2 quarter-sized slices of fresh ginger

½ teaspoon ground turmeric

1 pound red-ripe tomatoes (about 2 large ones), chopped

4 teaspoons tamarind paste, or to taste

2½ teaspoons salt, or to taste

7 cloves garlic, peeled and lightly crushed

1 whole, dried hot red pepper, or more to taste

1½ tablespoons dried curry leaves

10 to 15 fresh Chinese parsley stalks

A generous pinch of ground asafetida

¾ teaspoon ground cumin seeds

¾ teaspoon ground coriander seeds

2 teaspoons vegetable oil

¾ teaspoon whole black mustard seeds

¾ teaspoon whole cumin seeds

½ teaspoon *urad dal*

2 teaspoons finely chopped fresh Chinese parsley leaves

Put the *toovar dal*, 4 cups water, ginger, and ¼ teaspoon turmeric in a small pot and bring to a boil. Cover, leaving the lid slightly ajar, turn heat to low and simmer for 1½ hours. Stir 3 to 4 times in the last half hour, mashing the *dal* slightly as you do so. Turn the heat off and let the *dal* sit, covered, for 10 minutes.

Meanwhile, combine the tomatoes, tamarind paste, ¼ teaspoon turmeric, salt, 5 of the garlic cloves, red pepper, 1 tablespoon of the curry leaves, Chinese parsley stalks, asafetida, ground cumin, ground coriander, and 4 cups water in a pot. Bring to a boil. Cover, turn heat to low and simmer for 1½ hours.

In the *dal* pot, a thin broth will have risen to the top. Take out a cup of this and add it to the pot with the tomatoes. Now take out ¼ cup of the thick *dal*, mash it slightly and add it to the tomato pot as well. Strain this mixture through a sieve, extracting as much liquid as you can. (Any remaining thick *dal* may be refrigerated and added to other soups.)

Put the strained liquid in a pot and bring to a boil. Cover, and turn off the heat.

Put the oil in a small skillet and heat over a medium flame. When hot, put in the remaining 2 garlic cloves, the mustard seeds, whole cumin seeds, *urad dal*, and the remaining ½ tablespoon curry leaves. As soon as the mustard seeds begin to pop and the garlic darkens—this just takes a few seconds—pour the contents of the skillet into the hot soup and cover it again immediately. Let the pot sit, covered, for 5 minutes or longer. Now strain the soup and ladle it into cups. Sprinkle the chopped parsley over the top. If the soup has cooled off, you may reheat it before serving.

MASOOR DAL SOUP

INDIA

(serves 4)

10 whole cloves
2 bay leaves
1 teaspoon whole black peppercorns
1 cup *masoor dal* * picked over, washed, and
   drained
½ teaspoon ground turmeric
1¼ to 1½ teaspoons salt
1 tablespoon lime juice
⅛ teaspoon cayenne pepper (use as desired)

*NOTE: These are called red lentils or Egyptian lentils in health-food stores.

Tie the cloves, bay leaves, and peppercorns in a piece of cheesecloth.

Put the *dal* and 5 cups water into a heavy 2½- to 3-quart pot and bring to a boil. Remove the scum that rises to the top and discard it. Add the spice bundle and the turmeric to the pot. Turn heat to low, cover so the lid is very slightly ajar, and simmer very gently for 1½ hours. Remove the spice bundle and discard it. Put the soup in a blender or food processor (you may have to do this in two batches) and blend until it is smooth. Add the salt, lime juice, and cayenne. Stir to mix.

This soup may easily be made ahead of time and reheated. I like to serve mine with homemade croutons on the side.

TO MAKE CROUTONS: Cut 2 slices of bread into ½-inch cubes. Heat enough oil in a skillet so you have about ½ inch at the bottom. Do this over medium heat. Put in as many croutons as the skillet will hold in a single layer. Stir and fry them until they turn a golden-brown color. Remove with a slotted spoon and drain on paper towels. (Make all croutons this way.)

RED BEAN SOUP

INDIAN STYLE

Here I have converted a Punjabi method of cooking beans into a puréed soup.

(serves 4)

1 cup small red *azuki* beans, picked over, washed,
   and drained
1 medium-sized onion, peeled and chopped
2 cloves garlic, peeled
2 quarter-sized slices of fresh ginger
1 whole dried hot red pepper
1¼ teaspoons salt, or to taste
Freshly ground black pepper
¼ cup plain yogurt
¾ cup heavy cream
2 tablespoons *ghee* or vegetable oil
½ teaspoon whole cumin seeds

Put the beans and 4 cups water in a pot and bring to a boil. Cover, turn heat to low, and simmer for 2 minutes. Turn off the heat and let the pot sit, covered, for 1 hour. Bring to a boil again. Cover, turn heat to low and simmer for 30 minutes. Add

For information about ingredients and basic techniques that may be unfamiliar, see General Information, pages 418–36.

the onion, garlic, ginger, and red pepper and simmer, covered, for another 30 minutes. Remove the slices of ginger and the red pepper. Add the salt and black pepper and mix.

Put the beans into the container of a food processor or blender and blend until you have a smooth soup. If you like, you may push the soup through a sieve to remove the bean skins but this is not essential.

Put the yogurt into a bowl and beat with a fork or whisk until smooth and creamy. Slowly add a ladleful of soup, mixing it in as you do so. Add another ladle of soup and mix that in as well. Pour in all the soup, mix, then return soup to a clean pot. Add the cream, mix, and heat over a low flame.

Put the *ghee* in a small skillet or small pot and heat over a medium flame. When hot, put in the cumin seeds. Let the seeds sizzle for a few seconds. Now pour the contents of the skillet into the soup. Stir to mix.

Serve the soup nice and hot.

CREAM OF LENTIL SOUP
INDIAN STYLE

Here is a simple, soothing soup that I often serve to my family. With it, I offer thin slices of French bread which I crisp up in a slow oven and—would you believe it—radishes! They are a wonderful accompaniment and, with their inner leaves left on, they add a nice splash of color as well. I put the soup in individual bowls, set the bowls on small plates, and then arrange a slice of bread and a radish on each plate.

(serves 4)

1 cup lentils, picked over, washed, and drained
1 medium-sized onion, peeled and chopped
1 teaspoon salt, or to taste
Freshly ground black pepper
1 cup heavy cream
¼ teaspoon ground, roasted cumin seeds
2 teaspoons lemon juice, or to taste

Put the lentils, onion, and 3 cups water in a pot and bring to a boil. Cover, turn heat to low and simmer gently for 1 hour. Purée the lentil mixture in a food processor or blender. Add ¾ cup water and blend again to mix. Push this mixture through a sieve into a clean pot. Make sure you push all the pulp through and leave only a small quantity of skins behind. Add the salt, pepper, cream, cumin, and lemon juice. Mix and bring to a simmer. Taste for seasonings.

NAVY BEAN AND CELERY ROOT SOUP
MIDDLE EAST

This is a hearty soup, ideal for cold winter days, that may be served as a meal in itself. Some crusty French or pita bread, a yogurt cheese, and some olives would be all that would be required as accompaniments. You may sour this soup with either vinegar or lemon juice. Each gives its own taste and both are traditional.

(serves 4)

1   cup navy beans, picked over, washed, and drained
1   celery root (about ½ pound), peeled, and cut into ¼-inch dice
4   medium-sized tomatoes, peeled, and minced
1   medium-sized onion, peeled, and cut into ¼-inch dice
3   cloves garlic, peeled, and minced
½ cup finely chopped fresh parsley
¼ teaspoon dried rosemary
¼ teaspoon dried thyme
2   teaspoons salt, or to taste
Freshly ground black pepper
4   teaspoons white, distilled vinegar or lemon juice, or to taste
2   tablespoons olive oil

Put the beans and 4 cups water in a pot and bring to a boil. Cover, turn heat to low and simmer for 2 minutes. Turn off the heat and let the pot sit, covered, for 1 hour. Bring the contents of the pot to a boil again. Cover, turn heat to low and simmer for 45 minutes. Add the celery root, tomatoes, onion, garlic, and parsley. Crush the rosemary and

thyme together and add along with 1 cup water. Bring to a boil. Cover, turn heat to low and simmer for 20 minutes. Uncover, and add the salt, some black pepper, the vinegar or lemon juice, as well as the oil. Cook, uncovered, on low heat, for another 15 minutes, stirring the soup every now and then and also mashing some of it against the sides of the pot with the back of a large spoon. If the soup seems too thick, you may thin it out with some water.

CHICKPEA SOUP
MIDDLE EAST

This thick, stewlike soup is eaten in many countries of the Middle East, often forming the centerpiece of simple peasant meals. Salads, olives, bread, and yogurt dishes are served on the side. Although soaked chickpeas are generally tender enough to eat after an hour of cooking, it is important here that they cook longer. This way the chickpeas themselves get somewhat softer, the liquid thickens considerably, and the soup develops a cohesion that it would otherwise lack.

It might be a good idea to taste the soup before putting in the lemon juice. Chickpea broth has a natural sweetness that you may prefer to leave untouched.

For information about ingredients and basic techniques that may be unfamiliar, see General Information, pages 418–36.

CHICKPEA, CABBAGE, AND DILL SOUP
MIDDLE EAST

(serves 6)

(serves 4–6)

2 cups dried chickpeas, picked over, washed, and drained
2 medium-sized onions, peeled, and chopped
2 medium-sized boiling potatoes, peeled, and cut into ½-inch dice
1 tablespoon salt, or to taste
½ teaspoon ground turmeric
1 teaspoon ground cumin seeds
1 teaspoon ground coriander seeds
⅛ teaspoon cayenne pepper, or to taste
Freshly ground black pepper
2 tablespoons lemon juice

Soak the chickpeas in 8 cups of water for 12 hours. Drain and rinse thoroughly. Put the chickpeas, onions, and 8 cups water into a large pot and bring to a boil. Cover partially, turn heat to low, and simmer gently for 1 hour. Add the potatoes, salt, turmeric, cumin, coriander, cayenne, and another ¾ cup water. Bring to a boil. Cover and simmer on very low heat for another 1½ hours. Stir a few times during this period. Check seasonings. Add the black pepper and lemon juice. Stir to mix.

1 cup dried chickpeas, picked over, washed, and drained
1 medium-sized onion, peeled and chopped
1 medium-sized boiling potato, peeled and cut into ½-inch dice
1 good-sized tomato, peeled and cut into ½-inch dice
2 cups cabbage, cut into ½-inch squares
¾ cup chopped fresh dill, firmly packed
2 teaspoons tomato paste
2 teaspoons salt, or to taste
Freshly ground black pepper

Soak the chickpeas in 4 cups water for 12 hours. Drain and rinse thoroughly. Put the chickpeas, onion, and 4 cups water into a 3½-quart pot and bring to a boil. Cover partially, turn heat to low, and simmer gently for 1 hour. Add the potato, tomato, cabbage, dill, tomato paste, salt, and ½ cup water. Bring to a boil. Cover, turn heat to very low and simmer for 1½ hours. Add the black pepper and mix.

Little Salads, Appetizers, Snacks, and Drinks

Spicy nibbling food that could be taken along on car trips, split-pea wafers that may be served with drinks, the cold eggplant dip that is fun to eat with pita bread, the cold yogurt or strawberry drink that is so refreshing in summer—well, they are all here. This is the catch-all chapter for the good things that do not quite fit anywhere else in this book.

I would not dream of traveling, even from New York to Poughkeepsie, without some *cheewra* (or, for that matter, writing without it—I'm eating some now). Before America discovered granola, India had *cheewra*, one of the most satisfying hot, sweet, salty, and sour mixtures of seeds, nuts, dried fruit, beans, and grains that you can ever hope to encounter. It is not eaten with milk as a breakfast food but devoured, plain and unadulterated, as a snack between meals. I grew up with it in India and my children seem to be thriving on it in America.

Then there are the Middle Eastern *dolma*, vine-leaf rolls stuffed with a mixture of rice, pine nuts, and herbs. The rolls are cooked slowly in a garlicky oil and lemon dressing. By the time they are done, it is really hard to keep one's hands off them. They make a very pleasant first course and are also perfect picnic food. An equally pleasant first course from Armenia is Artichoke Hearts and Potatoes Cooked in Oil and Lemon. Rather like *dolma*, this may be made ahead of time and refrigerated.

My mother's Fresh Peach Salad, on the other hand, cannot be prepared ahead of time as it wilts in the most pathetic manner. If you want to eat this salad in the true bazaar style, serve it on large leaves and eat it with toothpicks.

I have included a recipe for the classical, flaky *samosas*, deep-fried pastry cones filled with spicy potatoes and peas. They should be fried slowly so that they turn nice and crisp—and then they should be eaten with dollops of the sweet-and-sour Tamarind-Mint Chutney. Among the drinks, you will find quite a few made with yogurt and buttermilk. My mother always kept big pitchers of these in the refrigerator during the summer months, all nicely seasoned with salt, pepper, and roasted cumin. We would come home from school, peel off our shoes and socks, and run to the refrigerator. One healthy swig and the whole hot, bothersome school day would be left far behind us.

CARROT AND WHITE RADISH SALAD
KOREA

(serves 4–6)

1 medium-sized carrot
½ pound white radish
1 teaspoon salt
1 tablespoon sesame oil
1 tablespoon rice vinegar
¼ teaspoon Japanese soy sauce
¼ teaspoon sugar
Dash of cayenne pepper

Peel the carrot and cut it into thin, diagonal slices. Cut these slices into slim julienne strips.

Peel the radish and cut it into julienne strips that are about the same size as the carrot strips.

Put the carrot and radish in a bowl. Add the salt, mix well, and set aside for an hour. Drain thoroughly, pressing out as much liquid as possible. Put the vegetables in a serving bowl. Add the sesame oil, vinegar, soy sauce, sugar, and cayenne. Mix.

SAWSAWANG KAMATIS
(Filipino Tomato Salad)
PHILIPPINES

In this simple salad, the souring agent is green mango, the kind that is dark green on the outside, quite hard, and has not given a single thought to ripening. If you cannot find such a fruit, use lime juice as a substitute.

(serves 4–6)

¾ pound red-ripe tomatoes
1 teaspoon coarsely grated fresh ginger
2 tablespoons peeled, chopped green mango
    or 1 tablespoon lime juice
1 scallion, finely sliced
¼ to ⅓ teaspoon salt
Freshly ground black pepper

Cut the tomatoes into ⅛-inch-thick rounds and arrange them in a single layer in a platter. Sprinkle the ginger, green mango, and scallion evenly over the tomatoes. Now sprinkle the salt and pepper over the top.

JAPANESE CUCUMBER SALAD
JAPAN

(serves 6)

6 pickling cucumbers* (about 1½ pounds)

1 teaspoon salt
1 tablespoon soy sauce
1½ tablespoons rice vinegar
1 tablespoon lightly crushed, roasted sesame seeds

*NOTE: Regular cucumbers may be substituted if they do not have overdeveloped seeds; also, peel them if they have been waxed.

Wash cucumbers well, scrubbing them if necessary. Slice, unpeeled, into very, very fine rounds either by hand or with the slicing blade of a food processor. Put cucumber slices in a bowl, sprinkle with salt, mix well, and set aside for an hour.

For information about ingredients and basic techniques that may be unfamiliar, see General Information, pages 418–36.

Squeeze cucumber slices and discard all accumulated liquid. Now add the soy sauce, vinegar, and sesame seeds. Mix well and check seasonings.

This dish may be refrigerated for a few hours prior to eating or it may be served at room temperature.

WATERCRESS SALAD WITH SESAME SEEDS
JAPAN

(serves 4)

2 bunches fresh watercress
1½ tablespoons rice vinegar
2 tablespoons soy sauce
½ teaspoon sugar
1 tablespoon crushed, roasted sesame seeds

Trim away about 1½ inches of the coarser watercress stems. Wash watercress.

Bring 4 cups of water to a boil. Add the watercress. Boil on medium heat for about 5 minutes or until watercress is just tender. Drain in a colander and run cold water over the watercress to fix the bright-green color. Drain, squeezing out as much water as possible.

Separate watercress sprigs so they are not in a tight wad and place in a bowl. Mix the vinegar, soy sauce, sugar, and sesame seeds in a small cup. Pour this dressing over the watercress and mix well.

Make four mounds of the watercress salad and place a mound each in the center of four small Oriental bowls or small plates. Serve cold or at room temperature.

CELERY, CARROT, AND CUCUMBER SALAD
HONG KONG

You could add peeled and julienned broccoli stems or kohlrabi to this salad as well.

(serves 4)

2½ celery sticks
1 carrot
1 cucumber
1 tablespoon Chinese light soy sauce
2 teaspoons distilled white vinegar
1 teaspoon sesame oil
½ clove garlic, peeled and mashed to a pulp

Cut the celery into thin, 2½-inch-long matchsticks.

Peel the carrot and cut into ⅟₁₆-inch-thick diagonal slices. Cut the slices into thin matchsticks.

Peel the cucumber and cut in half, lengthwise. Scoop out the seeds and discard them. Cut the cucumber shells into matchsticks.

If you are not eating immediately, put the vegetables into a plastic bag and refrigerate.

Meanwhile, mix the soy sauce, vinegar, sesame oil, and garlic.

Just before eating, put the salad into a bowl, pour the dressing over it, and mix.

KOREAN-STYLE CUCUMBER SALAD

KOREA

I use pickling cucumbers for this salad. As a substitute you may use European cucumbers or regular cucumbers with their seeds removed.

(serves 6)

3   pounds pickling cucumbers, peeled
1   medium-sized onion, peeled
1   tablespoon plus 1 teaspoon kosher salt
3½ tablespoons lemon juice
About ¼ to ½ teaspoon cayenne pepper
2   tablespoons crushed, roasted sesame seeds
1½ tablespoons sesame oil

Cut the cucumbers and onion into very fine slices (a food processor may be used for this). Sprinkle with salt, mix well, and set aside in a bowl for an hour.

Drain all the accumulated liquid and discard. Add the lemon juice, cayenne pepper (Koreans like this dish very hot), sesame seeds, and sesame oil. Mix well, cover, and refrigerate. Serve cold or at room temperature.

CUCUMBER AND DRIED SHIITAKE MUSHROOM SALAD

JAPAN

(serves 2)

1   small cucumber (about 6½ ounces)*
1   teaspoon salt
5   medium-sized dried *shiitake* mushrooms
2   teaspoons sesame seeds, roasted and crushed coarsely
2   teaspoons Japanese rice vinegar
1   teaspoon *mirin*
½   teaspoon sugar
2 to 3 drops Japanese soy sauce

*NOTE: If small Kirby pickling cucumber isn't available, use part of an English cucumber.

Peel the cucumber and cut it in half, lengthwise. Then cut it into very thin, half-moon-shaped slices. Sprinkle with salt and mix well. Set aside for an hour. Rinse under cold water to wash off salt. Squeeze out as much liquid as possible.

Soak the mushrooms in ½ cup boiling water for half an hour. Remove coarse stems and cut mushroom caps into ⅛-inch-wide slices.

Combine cucumber, mushrooms, sesame seeds, vinegar, *mirin*, sugar, and soy sauce. Mix well.

For information about ingredients and basic techniques that may be unfamiliar, see General Information, pages 418–36.

GUJARATI CARROT SALAD

INDIA

(serves 4)

3   carrots (about ¾ pound), trimmed, peeled, and
    grated
¼   teaspoon salt
2   tablespoons vegetable oil
1½ teaspoons whole black mustard seeds

In a bowl, toss the grated carrots with the salt.
Heat the oil in a small skillet or small pot over a
medium flame. When hot, put in the mustard seeds.
As soon as the mustard seeds begin to pop (this
will take just a few seconds), pour the contents of
the skillet—oil and mustard seeds—over the carrots. Stir to mix.

GUJARATI CUCUMBER AND PEANUT SALAD

INDIA

For this recipe, either raw or boiled peanuts may
be used. (For more on cooking with peanuts, see
page 106.) I happen to like the chestnutlike flavor
of boiled peanuts.

(serves 4)

1   cup raw, shelled, skinless peanuts
¾   pound cucumbers (small pickling preferred),
    peeled and cut into ⅓-inch dice
2   tablespoons roasted sesame seeds
⅓   cup freshly grated coconut

½ to 1 fresh hot green chili, minced (or use ⅛
    teaspoon cayenne pepper)
2   tablespoons finely chopped Chinese parsley
2   tablespoons vegetable oil
1½ teaspoons whole black mustard seeds
½   teaspoon salt
1   tablespoon lemon juice

If you are using the peanuts raw, crush them lightly. This may be done in a mortar, a food processor,
or you can place the peanuts between two sheets of
waxed paper and hit them lightly with a rolling
pin. Each whole peanut should break up into 8 to
10 pieces. If you wish to boil the peanuts, soak
them in 2 cups of water for 3 to 4 hours and then
boil them, covered, in the same water for about 15
minutes. Drain and let cool. Do not crush the
boiled peanuts.

In a serving dish, combine the peanuts (raw or
boiled), the diced cucumbers, sesame seeds, coconut, green chili, and Chinese parsley. Mix.

Heat the oil in a small skillet or a small pot over
a medium flame. When hot, put in the mustard
seeds. As soon as the seeds begin to pop (this just
takes a few seconds), pour the contents of the
skillet—oil and seeds—over
the salad. Stir again.
Just before serving,
add the salt and lemon
juice. Mix well.

FRESH PEACH SALAD

INDIA

This is a wonderful salad to make when the fresh fruit is in season. As peaches discolor and turn very limp and watery if left in spices for too long, the salad should be made just before you sit down to eat. In India, such savory fruit salads are served with meals or as snacks and may be made with a variety of fruit. Peeled and sliced bananas, peeled and sliced guavas, even peeled orange segments may be used—singly or in any preferred combination. Of course the salt, sugar, and lemon juice have to be balanced with the natural qualities of the fruit that is being used.

My mother often made savory fruit salads to go with our lunches. Lunch could consist of a simple rice dish—perhaps Rice with Sautéed Onions and Mushrooms; a *dal*—perhaps Chana Dal with Cucumber; a vegetable—perhaps Cauliflower and Potatoes cooked with Fenugreek and Fennel Seeds; a glass of ice-cold buttermilk, and a fruit salad to perk up the meal. We did not always leave it to our mother to make the salad. In the late afternoon, with tea-time still far away and hunger pangs distracting us from our homework, we took to concocting these salads ourselves. Perhaps as a result of this, I often offer such salads to my children when they come in from school.

I might add that I have frequently served this salad as a first course at a Western-style meal.

(serves 6)

2½ pounds fresh peaches, peeled and sliced
3   tablespoons sugar
¾ teaspoon salt

Freshly ground black pepper, to taste
1½ teaspoons ground, roasted cumin seeds
1½ tablespoons lemon juice
⅛ to ¼ teaspoon cayenne pepper

Combine all ingredients in a glass, ceramic, or stainless-steel serving dish. Serve at room temperature.

FRIED, MUNCHABLE MUNG DAL

INDIA

As a child, this was one of my favorite snack foods. I would buy it in a little paper cone from the bazaar, empty it into my pockets, and then munch it quietly as I accompanied my mother on her shopping sprees. While my mother searched for the perfect gold brocade Benarasi border to match her latest chiffon sari from France, I kept myself busy with the mung *dal*. When I grew up and had my own children in America, I took them to India as little tots. Imagine my sense of *déjà vu* as I watched them fall upon the crunchy fried mung *dal* with the same mindless pleasure that I had exhibited decades earlier. I found myself complaining, just as my mother had done, of finding mung *dal* in little coat pockets, all mixed up with unidentifiable fluff.

This is not a spicy snack. It is generally seasoned with just salt and, if one likes, some black pepper. Cayenne may be sprinkled over it, if one so wishes. And there is no particular time of the day when it meant to be eaten. Like peanuts, fried mung *dal* is eaten whenever one feels like eating it, as a snack or with drinks.

For information about ingredients and basic techniques that may be unfamiliar, see General Information, pages 418–36.

NOTE: Although this *dal* is deep-fried and appears oily when first removed from the fire, it does not remain oily if handled properly.

(makes 1½ cups)

1 cup mung *dal*
Vegetable oil for deep frying
½ teaspoon salt
Freshly ground black pepper to taste

Pick over the *dal* and wash it in several changes of water. Drain. Soak the *dal* in 5 cups of water for 5 to 8 hours. Drain thoroughly. Dry off *dal* by rubbing gently in a towel.

Heat oil for deep frying in a wok over a medium flame. You should have a good 2½ inches of oil in the center of the wok. Line two plates with paper towels and keep them beside you. Have a fine, medium-sized sieve handy that you can lower into the oil.

When the oil has heated, lower the sieve into it. Put two modest handfuls of *dal* into the oil in the sieve. The *dal* will begin to sizzle and the oil will bubble. When the sizzling and bubbling subside (about 1½ minutes), the *dal* should be a golden color (not brown), crunchy, and done. Lift up the sieve, shake it gently to drain off the oil, and then empty the *dal* onto one of the two plates. Keep doing this until all the *dal* is cooked, dividing it up between the two plates.

Change the paper towels on the plates again and again until they no longer appear oily. You may also rub the top of the *dal* with paper towels. (But do this fairly quickly, as you should salt the *dal* while it is still hot.) Consolidate the *dal* on one plate, lined with a fresh paper towel. Sprinkle with salt and pepper. Mix and allow to cool completely.

Put the *dal* in a jar and cover with a tight lid. If kept in a tightly lidded jar, the *dal* will stay fresh for several weeks.

FRIED, MUNCHABLE SOY BEANS
CHINA

You may salt these beans or not, just as you like. I actually prefer them unsalted.

(makes 1¾ cups)

1 cup yellow soy beans, picked over, washed, and drained
Vegetable oil for deep frying
Salt (optional)

Soak the beans in 4 cups water for 5 to 6 hours. Drain, removing any skins that may have come loose. Pat the beans dry. There should be no external moisture clinging to them. If it is a dry, sunny day, spread out the beans on a tray and leave them in the sun for a couple of hours. If you have no access to the sun, spread the beans out on a tray and leave them in a dry, airy place for a couple of hours.

Put the oil in a wok and heat over a flame that is slightly lower than medium. When the oil is hot, put in all the soy beans. Stir and fry for 6 to 7 minutes or until the beans turn a shade darker and turn crisp on the outside. Remove with a mesh strainer or a small-holed slotted spoon and spread out on paper towels to drain. Change the paper towels a few times. Rub the beans gently with paper towels as well to remove as much oil as possible.

If you like, sprinkle a little salt over the top and mix.

PEANUTS, FRIED AND ROASTED

Fried and roasted peanuts are used in many parts of South, Southeast, and East Asia in main dishes as well as in sauces, and as toppings for both sweet and savory dishes. While it is perfectly all right to use shelled but unskinned raw peanuts for snack foods, it is best to use the shelled, skinned raw peanuts for all other recipes. Such peanuts are available in varying sizes at health-food, Oriental, and Indian grocery stores.

(2 cups)

Vegetable oil, as and if needed
2 cups shelled, skinned raw peanuts
¾ to 1 teaspoon salt, if desired

DEEP FRYING: This is by far the best method for frying peanuts as there is no chance of burning or browning them unevenly. I like to use my deeper Indian wok for this but you could use a Chinese wok as well. Heat enough oil over a medium flame so you have about 2½ to 3 inches of it in the middle of the wok. Now put a cup of peanuts into a sieve that is about 8 inches in diameter at the top and has a handle. When the oil has heated, lower the sieve into the oil. As soon as the peanuts have turned a golden color, lift the sieve out of the oil.

Let it drain over the oil for a few seconds. Now put the peanuts on paper towels (my mother used brown-paper bags for this) and sprinkle them with half the salt. Do a second batch the same way.

SHALLOW FRYING: Even though less oil is used in this method, the advantage is somewhat nullified by the uneven color of the end product. This unevenness may well have to do with not being able to remove all the peanuts from the oil at the same time. However, there is a way around it. Heat enough oil in a skillet over a medium flame so you have ¼ inch at the bottom of the skillet. While it heats, place a sieve over a bowl. Put as many peanuts into the hot oil as the skillet will hold in a single layer. Stir and fry until the peanuts turn a golden color. Now empty the contents of the skillet into the sieve. Let the peanuts drain briefly and then empty them onto paper towels and sprinkle some salt on them if you want to. Put the oil in the bowl back into the skillet and do a second batch and, if necessary, a third batch the same way.

ROASTING: Raw, shelled, or unshelled peanuts are generally not roasted in ovens in Asia. The most common method is to put them into a heavy wok and then to stir and cook them over a lowish flame until they give off a roasted aroma. A cast-iron skillet may be used instead of a wok. Put all the peanuts into the wok or skillet. Stir constantly and cook over a lowish flame until the peanuts look and smell roasted. Put into a bowl and sprinkle with salt, if desired.

When the fried and roasted peanuts have cooled, they may be stored in airtight bottles or tins for several weeks.

For information about ingredients and basic techniques that may be unfamiliar, see General Information, pages 418–36.

PAPADUM
(Dal Wafers)
INDIA

(serves 6)

Called *papadum* in South India and *papar* in the North, these thin wafers (generally made out of *dal* but occasionally out of potatoes and sago as well) are served at most vegetarian meals. Southerners often crush them toward the end of their meals and then mix them with rice, yogurt, and pickles for a simple finale. North Indians prefer to nibble them along with their meal, dipping them now and then into the yogurt for a variation. Both Northerners and Southerners have developed the habit of serving *papadum* as a convenient cocktail snack.

Although members of my grandmother's generation did, now and then, make their own *papadum*—I remember thousands of yellow discs drying on cots set out in a sunny courtyard—very few people make them at home anymore. Almost all grocery stores carry them, nicely rolled out and dried. All that then remains to be done is to cook them.

The quickest—and most traditional—way of cooking *papadum* is to deep fry them. This takes just a few seconds and allows the *papadum* to expand to their maximum size and turn quite light and airy. *Papadum* may also be toasted, either in a toaster-oven or over a direct flame. They are less caloric this way but they do not expand quite as much.

Papadum may be bought plain, flavored with garlic, dotted with black pepper or dotted with red pepper.

6 *papadum*
Vegetable oil for deep frying (optional)

FRYING METHOD: Break each *papadum* into two pieces.

Set the oil to heat in a wok or skillet over a medium flame. When hot, drop in a *papadum* half. Within seconds, it will expand. (If it browns at all, the oil is too hot. It should remain a pale yellow color.) Turn the *papadum* over and cook the second side for a few seconds. Remove with a slotted spoon and drain on paper towels. Do all the *papadum* this way.

THE TOASTING METHOD: Break each papadum into two pieces. Lay two halves inside the toaster-oven set at "medium" toast. Now watch through the glass window. The *papadum* will begin to bubble, expand slightly, and turn lighter in color. As soon as all of it is this lighter color, remove it from the oven. Do not let it brown. Do all the *papadum* pieces this way.

If you wish to toast directly over the flame, do not break the *papadum* in half. Turn the flame on to low. Hold a *papadum* with a pair of tongs about half an inch above the flame. As one part of the *papadum* bubbles and turns lighter in color, put another part of the *papadum* above the flame. Keep doing this until the entire *papadum* is toasted.

GREEN PLANTAIN WAFERS

INDIA

Plantain wafers, in some form or other, are eaten in most tropical countries. The unusual quality of the Indian wafer comes from the use of turmeric. Like potato chips, they may be eaten at almost any time of the day or night. They are excellent to take on long car rides and on picnics.

(serves 4
as a snack)

2   green plaintains
¼ teaspoon ground turmeric
1¼ teaspoons salt
Vegetable oil for deep frying*

*NOTE: South Indians would use coconut oil for this recipe.

Peel the plantains with a knife, removing all the green skin. Using a food processor with the slicing blade, a mandolin, or a potato-slicing gadget, slice the plantains into very, very thin rounds (rather like potato chips) and soak in ice water for 30 minutes. Drain and pat dry.

In a small bowl or cup, combine the turmeric and salt with 2 tablespoons of warm water.

Heat the oil in a wok or deep-frying utensil over a medium flame. You should have about 1½ inches of oil. When the oil is hot, put in as many plantain wafers as will fit in a slightly overlapping single layer. Dip your fingertips into the turmeric-salt solution and sprinkle whatever liquid you pick up over the wafers. This has to be done in a fast motion, as soon as the wafers are put into the oil. Fry wafers 1½ to 2 minutes, turning them over midway during this cooking time. Wafers should be crisp but retain their yellow color. Remove with a slotted spoon and drain on a platter lined with paper towels. Do all the wafers this way. Cool the wafers and then store them in airtight jars. They should stay fresh for 3 to 4 days.

ROASTED LAVER

KOREA

For this recipe you need sheets of the dark-green, paperlike dried laver that the Japanese call *nori* and the Koreans call *kim*. The sheets come in different sizes and in different qualities. For each sheet that is roughly 6 × 7 inches, brush both sides lightly with sesame oil—a teaspoon should be enough for both sides—and then sprinkle very lightly with salt. Now hold the *nori* with a pair of tongs and wave over a lowish fire, keeping it about 3 inches away from the flame. Roast for about 5 seconds on each side. Offer each person one sheet of *nori*, cut into halves or quarters.

For information about ingredients and basic techniques that may be unfamiliar, see General Information, pages 418–36.

ROASTED MONUKKA RAISINS

INDIA

It was so strange to find something called monukka raisins in my local health-food store. As a child, one of my favorite treats was to ask the cook to prepare what *we*, in India, called monukka. This was a large, dark raisin that the cook would thread on a slim wooden skewer—he would actually thread a whole garland of them—and then wave them over the charcoal fire in our stove. The outside edges of the raisins would get slightly blackened. He would hand me the skewer and I would wander off into the vegetable garden, stingily pulling off one raisin at a time and gobbling it up. By the time I had inspected the tomatoes and the beans and the peas, all the raisins would be gone and it would be time to return to the kitchen for another freshly roasted, hot batch of skewered monukka.

If you want to roast some monukka, thread about 3 inches of them, all tightly packed, onto a long metal skewer. Now wave this skewer over a low flame, holding it about 1½ inches away from the source of heat. Every 1 second, turn the skewer a bit. It takes no time at all to roast a batch. The raisins burn quickly, so watch what you are doing. Roast more as you need them. If you have a campfire, roast monukka instead of marshmallows!

KHARI POORI
(Savory Cookies with Peppercorns)

INDIA

These savory, deep-fried "cookies" are made with a combination of whole-wheat and white flour. In Gujarat, *khari pooris* or "salty *pooris*" are often studded with crushed black peppercorns.

These *pooris* are generally eaten as a snack, accompanied by *lassi*, buttermilk, or tea. They can be eaten plain, or they may be smeared with hot pickles or sweet chutneys (like the Apricot Chutney). *Khari pooris* have been a standard "journey food" in India for centuries. Packed into tins and bags, the *pooris* are still carried on long bullock-cart, car, rail, and airplane trips. You could take them on picnics or hiking trips. You could also serve them with drinks.

(makes about 50)

1 cup finely ground whole-wheat flour
1 cup unbleached white flour
1 teaspoon salt
1 tablespoon coarsely crushed black pepper
3½ tablespoons vegetable oil or softened unsalted butter *plus* oil for deep-frying

Sift the whole-wheat flour, white flour, and salt into a bowl. Add the black pepper as well as the 3½ tablespoons oil or butter. Rub the oil or butter into the flour with your fingers until the flour resembles coarse oatmeal. Now slowly add very hot water—about ½ cup plus 3 tablespoons—and begin to gather the flour together. Squeeze the dough into a ball. It should just about hold. Do *not* knead.

Break the dough into about 50 balls. Keep them

covered with a plastic wrap or lightly dampened towel.

Heat about 1½ to 2 inches of oil in any utensil for deep frying (an Indian *karhai* or Chinese wok is an ideal utensil for this) over a medium flame. While the oil is heating, begin to roll out the *pooris*. Take each dough ball, flatten it, and roll it into a very rough round, about 2 inches in diameter. (Don't worry about the cracked edges.) Roll and fry as many *pooris* as your frying utensil will hold in a single layer. Fry 2 to 3 minutes on each side or until *pooris* are lightly browned on both sides and crisp. Adjust heat, if necessary. Remove *pooris* with a slotted spoon and drain on paper towels. Make all *pooris* this way. Allow them to cool and then store them in an airtight container. *Khari pooris* do not need refrigeration and will stay fresh for several weeks.

MUTTHRIES
(Savory Cookies with Ajwain Seeds)
INDIA

While the preceding recipe for savory cookies (*khari poori*) is from the western state of Gujarat, this recipe is from my hometown, Delhi. The traditional method for making both styles of cookies is very similar, except that the Delhi version uses white flour as its base and the delicate *ajwain* seeds as a flavoring. You could, if you want the more traditional *mutthrie*, follow the preceding recipe and just substitute 2 teaspoons of *ajwain* seeds for the crushed black pepper. Or you could follow this new recipe that I have worked out in which, instead of deep frying the cookies, I bake them. The result is quite excellent. I love to eat these *mutthries* at tea-time with lots of Sweet Tomato Chutney smeared on them. You could also have them with butter and jam.

(makes about 28)

1¾ cups all-purpose unbleached white flour (plus a little more for dusting)
¾ teaspoon salt
1 teaspoon *ajwain* seeds
1 ice-cold stick (¼ pound) unsalted butter, cut into 8 pats
¼ cup ice water

Sift the flour and the salt and put into the container of a food processor with its metal blade fitted into place. Add the *ajwain* seeds and the butter. Turn the machine on and off quickly a few times until the flour resembles coarse bread crumbs. Turn the machine on and slowly pour in the cold water. Let the machine run for a few seconds more but stop it *before* the dough forms a ball. Empty the contents of the food processor onto a sheet of waxed paper. Form a very loose ball out of the dough.

(If you do not have a processor, put the sifted flour and salt into a chilled bowl. Add the *ajwain* seeds and the butter. Rub the butter in with your fingertips until the mixture resembles coarse bread

For information about ingredients and basic techniques that may be unfamiliar, see General Information, pages 418–36.

crumbs. Slowly pour in the cold water as you begin to gather the dough into a loose ball.)

With the heel of your hand, press down on the dough and stretch it along the waxed paper in a few quick strokes to blend the flour and butter. Do not overdo this. Gather the dough into a loose ball again, cover with the waxed paper, and refrigerate for an hour.

Spread out a clean sheet of waxed paper on a slightly dampened counter or board. (This prevents the waxed paper from sliding.) Dust lightly with flour. Put the ball of dough on the paper. Dust the top of the ball with a little flour. Put another sheet of waxed paper on top of the ball. Now begin to roll out the dough. Every now and then lift up the top waxed paper and dust with a little flour, then flip the dough over so the bottom waxed paper is on top. Remove it and dust this side of the dough, too. Put the waxed paper back and continue rolling out. Keep doing this until you have a round of dough that is about ¼-inch thick. Use a round cookie cutter (it could be scalloped at the edges) that is 2½ inches in diameter, and cut out as many cookies as you can. Put the cookies on a cold baking sheet, prod each of them several times with a fork, and refrigerate.

Gather the remaining dough and quickly form a loose ball. Wrap in a sheet of waxed paper and refrigerate for about half an hour or until cold enough to roll out again easily.

Repeat the process of rolling out the dough and making more cookies. Use up all the dough. Keep all the cookies refrigerated on the cookie sheet.

Preheat oven to 425° F.

Put the cookie sheet into the oven and bake cookies for about 20 minutes or until done. Let cookies cool. Store in an airtight container.

SAMOSAS
(Stuffed Savory Deep-Fried Pastry Cones)
INDIA

Like most Indian snack foods, *samosas* may be eaten at any time of the day or night, preferably with healthy swigs of tea, coffee, or fruit juice. On the streets in India, itinerant vendors serve them on leaves, with a little Tamarind-Mint Chutney (see page 364) on the side. "Take-out" *samosas* are invariably wrapped in two leaf bowls, one inverted over the other, while the chutney is handed over in a terra-cotta pot. At formal lunches and dinners, *samosas* are placed on the center of the *thali*—the individual food platter—along with rice and the bread, while all other foods—*dals*, numerous vegetables, relishes—surround it in small bowls.

Even though many homes like ours made fine *samosas*, experts like my mother and grandmother were of the secret belief (secret because the men in our family were firm, and often loquacious believers in clinical cleanliness) that the *best samosas* came from the open-to-the-elements, hygienically questionable stalls of the local bazaar. The best thing that I can say about my *samosas* is that they do happen to have a bazaar taste!

I have a *samosa* recipe in my first cookbook, *An Invitation to Indian Cooking*. That recipe makes a simplified *samosa* with a soft, whole-wheat wrapping—a kind of *samosa* that I made quite often for my children when they were little and dinner seemed more amusing to them if it came in a triangular wrapping. The recipe here is for the classical *samosa* with a crisp, flaky white-flour crust. For best results, the *samosas* should be fried quite slowly.

(makes 24 medium-sized samosas)

FOR THE PASTRY

1½ cups unbleached all-purpose white flour
¼ teaspoon salt
4 tablespoons soft, unsalted butter

FOR THE STUFFING

4 medium-sized potatoes, boiled unpeeled and cooled
4 tablespoons vegetable oil
1 medium-sized onion, peeled and minced
1 cup shelled fresh or defrosted frozen peas
1 tablespoon peeled and grated fresh ginger
1 fresh hot green chili, minced
3 tablespoons finely minced Chinese parsley
1½ teaspoons salt
1 teaspoon ground coriander
1 teaspoon *garam masala*
1 teaspoon ground roasted cumin seeds
¼ teaspoon cayenne pepper
2 tablespoons lemon juice or 1 tablespoon lemon juice and 1 tablespoon *amchoor*
1 teaspoon *anardana* (dried pomegranate seeds)

Oil for deep frying
Extra flour for dusting

Sift the flour and salt into a bowl. Add the softened butter and rub it in with your hands so that the flour resembles fine bread crumbs. Add warm water, a tablespoon at a time, and begin to gather the flour into a ball. You will need about 5 tablespoons of water. Form a ball and begin to knead it. Knead well for about 10 to 15 minutes or until dough is very soft and pliable. (If you have a food processor, put the steel blade in place and empty the sifted flour and salt into the container. Add the softened butter and turn on the machine. When you have a bread-crumb consistency, begin to add about 5 tablespoons of water slowly through the funnel. Stop when the dough forms a ball. Take out the ball and knead it for 5 to 10 minutes or until it is very soft and pliable.) Wrap the dough in plastic wrap and let it sit for an hour in the refrigerator. The dough can be made a day in advance and refrigerated.

Make the stuffing. Peel the potatoes and dice them into roughly ¼-inch pieces. Heat the 4 tablespoons oil in a 10- to 12-inch skillet over a medium flame. Put in the onion, stirring and frying until it turns a light-brown color. Add the peas, the ginger, green chili, Chinese parsley, and 3 tablespoons of water. Cover, lower heat and simmer very gently until peas are cooked. Stir every now and then and add additional water, a tablespoon at a time, if the skillet seems to dry out. Now put in the diced potatoes, salt, coriander, *garam masala*, roasted ground cumin, cayenne pepper, lemon juice (or lemon juice and *amchoor*), and *anardana*. Keep heat on low and mix the spices with the potatoes. Continue cooking gently, stirring frequently, for 3 to 4 minutes. Check salt and lemon juice. Turn off heat and leave potato mixture to cool.

Take the dough out of the refrigerator and knead again. Divide dough into twelve equal balls. Keep balls covered with plastic wrap.

Place a small bowl of water on your work surface. Lightly flour a pastry board. 1. Flatten one of the dough balls on it and then roll it out into a round about 6 inches in diameter. 2. Now cut the round in half with a sharp knife. 3. Pick up one half and form a cone, making a ¼-inch overlapping "seam" 4. and using a little water from the nearby bowl to seal the "seam" (see illustration). 5. Fill the cone with a heaping tablespoon of the stuffing.

For information about ingredients and basic techniques that may be unfamiliar, see General Information, pages 418–36.

Close the top of the cone by sticking the open edges of the triangle together, again with the help of a little water. This seam should also be ¼ inch wide. 6. Press the top seam again and, if possible, "flute" it with your fingers. Put the *samosa* on a platter in a cool spot. Make all 24 samosas this way.

Heat oil for deep frying (about 2½ inches deep) in a wok or other wide utensil over a medium-low flame. When the oil is hot, drop in the *samosas*, as many as will lie in a single layer. Fry them slowly until they are a golden brown, turning them over when one side seems done. When the second side of the *samosas* has turned a golden color, remove them from the oil with a slotted spoon and place them on a paper-towel-lined platter. Do all *samosas* this way.

Samosas may be served at room temperature or they may be served warm. *Samosas* may be made ahead of time (up to a day), refrigerated neatly layered in flat plastic containers, and then reheated in a 350° F oven. If you wish to freeze *samosas*, fry them partially, drain them, and freeze them in a single layer in flat plastic containers. When you wish to eat them, defrost and fry them a second time. Generally, *samosas* are served with a tart, spicy chutney, like Tamarind-Mint Chutney.

CHEEWRA
(A Melange of Nuts, Grains, Dried Fruit, and Spices)
INDIA

For those people who cannot stop at one peanut, this irresistible snack or "munch" food from Western India might well prove to be their undoing. I have to confess to you here and now that this cookbook might never have been finished without the necessary "breaks" for hot cups of Darjeeling tea and small bowls full of *cheewra*. A glorious, spicy, complex ancestor of granola, *cheewra* combines cashews, peanuts, split peas, puffed rice, sesame seeds, and raisins with spices like cloves and cinnamon. The roasted split peas (*chana dal*) and small variety of puffing rice (*poha*) used are available only in Indian shops, but you can substitute roasted chickpeas, available in nut shops and Middle Eastern stores, and commercial Rice Krispies (in this case the puffed rice wouldn't have to be fried). It is full of protein, extremely nourishing, and, with its delicate blending of sweet, sour, salty, and hot flavorings, so very satisfying. *Cheewra* can be eaten between meals, it can replace cookies and cake at tea-time, and it can also be served with drinks before dinner. It keeps very well for a couple of months if stored in airtight jars or plastic bags. Because many of the ingredients in this recipe need to be fried briefly, you might conclude that this snack would turn out to be greasy. It does not. *Cheewra* ends up with a very dry appearance, not unlike that of granola.

(enough to fill a 1½-quart jar)

3 whole cloves
A ¾-inch-long stick of cinnamon, broken into small pieces

For information about ingredients and basic techniques that may be unfamiliar, see General Information, pages 418–36.

½ teaspoon whole black peppercorns
Vegetable oil for deep frying
⅔ cup raw cashews, split in half lengthwise
⅔ cup raw peanuts, preferably without the brown
   inner skin
½ cup roasted *chana dal* or roasted chickpeas (see
   opposite page)
3 tablespoons golden raisins
2 cups *poha* or 3 cups Rice Krispies (see opposite
   page)
1½ tablespoons vegetable oil
A generous pinch of ground asafetida (optional)
½ tablespoon whole black mustard seeds
2½ tablespoons sliced fresh hot green chilies or 1
   to 1½ teaspoons cayenne pepper (optional)
3 tablespoons sesame seeds
¼ teaspoon ground turmeric
1¼ teaspoons salt
2½ teaspoons sugar
1½ teaspoons ground *amchoor*

Place cloves, cinnamon, and black peppercorns in a mortar and pound with a pestle until they are powdery. Set aside.

Line two large platters with paper towels.

Put 2½ inches of oil in a wok or other wide utensil for deep frying and heat over a medium flame. You will need a sieve or other fine mesh gadget that you can lower into the oil to fry the different batches of nuts, grain, and dried fruit. Once the oil is hot (a nut dropped into it should begin to sizzle immediately), put the cashews in the sieve and lower the sieve into the oil. When the cashews are a golden brown, lift up the sieve and empty the cashews on one of the platters lined with paper towels.

Now put the peanuts in the sieve and lower into the oil. Fry until the peanuts turn a golden brown. Spread out the peanuts near the cashews.

Put the *chana dal* (or roasted chickpeas) in the sieve and lower sieve into the hot oil. Fry until *dal* turns a shade darker. Spread *dal* out near the peanuts.

Put the raisins in the sieve. Lower sieve into the oil and fry until raisins puff up. Spread the raisins out near the *dal*.

To fry the *poha*, put the empty sieve into the hot oil. Sprinkle a small fistful of *poha* into the sieve. It will begin to froth immediately. As soon as the froth dies down, the *poha* is cooked (it takes just a few seconds). Empty the *poha* onto the second platter. Do all the *poha* this way in small batches. Turn the heat off under your deep-frying utensil. Remove the oily paper towels on the two platters and replace them with fresh paper towels.

Heat 1½ tablespoons fresh oil in a very small pot (like a butter-warmer) or in a small skillet over a medium flame. When hot, put in the asafetida and the mustard seeds. As soon as the mustard seeds begin to pop (this just takes a few seconds), put in the sliced green chilies and fry them, stirring, until all the moisture in them disappears and they turn crisp. (If you are using the cayenne pepper, hold on to it.) Add the sesame seeds and fry, stirring, until they turn a shade darker. Now add the turmeric (and cayenne, if you are using it) and stir for another second. Remove from heat.

In a large bowl, combine all the ingredients from the two platters: (the Rice Krispies, if you are using them), the freshly fried spices from the small pot with their oil, the pounded spices from the mortar, as well as the salt, sugar, and *amchoor*. Toss gently until well mixed. Allow to cool. Toss again and store in airtight jar.

POTATO SEV
(Snack Noodle)
INDIA

Sev is a kind of squiggly, crisp, vermicellilike snack food made out of chickpea flour. Indians, both in the north and the south, approach it with the same mindless devotion that Americans shower on potato chips—munching it in movie theaters, on trains, while listening to the radio, at college beer parties, at tea-parties, and even at formal cocktail parties.

Just as there are noodle machines for those who want to make fresh noodles in their own kitchens, there are *sev* machines for those who frown on the bazaar variety and wish to produce their own. These gadgets are fairly cheap and may be bought in America from Indian grocery stores. The most handsome *sev*-maker available at the moment is made out of brass and comes equipped with changeable discs. You attach the disc with the small holes, fill the container with the prepared dough, turn a handle around, and tiny wormlike *sev* come squiggling out, only to fall into hot oil to be deep fried instantly. If you do not have a *sev*-maker, a potato-ricer may be substituted.

(will serve 20 to accompany drinks)

2½ pounds boiling potatoes (about 8 to 9 medium-sized)
2½ well-packed cups chickpea flour, sifted
1 tablespoon and 1 teaspoon salt
About 1½ teaspoons cayenne pepper
2 tablespoons lemon juice
1 tablespoon sugar
Vegetable oil for deep frying

Boil potatoes. Peel them while they are still hot (hold them, one at a time, with a fork, and peel) and then put them through a potato-ricer or mash them well.

Since you need half as much chickpea flour as mashed potatoes, measure your mashed potatoes in cups. You should have 5 cups. If you have a little more or less, adjust the amount of your flour.

Put the riced potatoes in a large bowl. Add the chickpea flour, salt, cayenne pepper (1½ teaspoons will make the *sev* mildly hot; use more or less as desired), lemon juice, and sugar. Mix well and knead with the heel of your palm to make a dough. If the dough is sticky, add more chickpea flour.

Heat the oil in a wok or other deep-frying utensil over a medium flame. You will need about 2 inches of oil. Put a tangerine-sized ball of dough into a *sev* machine fitted with the disc that has the smallest holes. (If you do not have a *sev* machine, put the same amount of dough into a potato-ricer.) When the oil is hot, hold your *sev*-making gadget over it and push the dough through (by turning a

For information about ingredients and basic techniques that may be unfamiliar, see General Information, pages 418–37.

handle or by pressing, depending upon the machine). Squiggly *sev* will begin to drop into the hot oil. Move your machine around a bit so the entire surface of the oil is covered, up to a quarter inch in depth, with the *sev*. Let the *sev* fry for 1 to 1½ minutes or until they are a golden brown on the underside. Using a slotted spoon, turn the entire batch over and fry another 1 to 2 minutes. The *sev* should be a golden, honey color and crisp (they turn even crisper as they cool). Remove the *sev* with a slotted spoon and place on a platter lined with paper towels. Use a fork to separate the *sev* if they have bunched up. Now fry another batch. Continue this way in batches until the dough is used up.

When all the *sev* batches have cooled, store them in airtight cookie jars or large Mason jars. The *sev* will keep for several weeks.

COLD CHINESE-STYLE EGGPLANT

HONG KONG

In the Hong Kong restaurant where I was served this dish as an appetizer, the eggplant had been steamed in one of the many enormous aluminum steamers that seem to have become standard kitchen equipment in this part of the world, replacing the more charming bamboo steamers of the past. You may use any steaming contraption that is convenient. I just balance a colander on top of a pot of boiling water and then put a lid on top of the colander.

(serves 4)

1   large or 2 smaller eggplants (about 1 pound, 6 ounces)
4   teaspoons Chinese thin soy sauce
1   tablespoon distilled white vinegar
2   teaspoons sesame oil
1   clove garlic, peeled and mashed to a pulp
¼   teaspoon Hot Oil (see page 361), optional
⅛   teaspoon salt, or to taste
1   tablespoon very finely sliced scallions
1   tablespoon finely chopped fresh Chinese parsley (optional)

Set up your steaming equipment. Remember that the water in the lower container should not touch the bottom of the perforated steamer. There should be a lid to hold in the steam.

Peel the eggplant and cut it into large, 1-inch chunks.

Bring the steaming water to a boil. Put the eggplant in the perforated steamer, cover, and steam for 20 minutes or until eggplant is tender.

Put the eggplant in a bowl and mash lightly with a fork. You do *not* want a purée. Mix the soy sauce, vinegar, sesame oil, garlic, hot oil, and salt in a small bowl and pour over the eggplant. Mix. Cover and chill until ready to serve. Garnish with scallions and parsley before serving.

COLD EGGPLANT, DRESSED WITH YOGURT

MIDDLE EAST

Here is a very easy-to-make appetizer that is quite refreshing in its simple flavors. Serve it nicely chilled, with pita bread or crackers.

(serves 6)

1 large or 2 smaller eggplants (about 1½ pounds)
1 cup plain yogurt
¾ teaspoon salt, or to taste
Freshly ground black pepper
¼ teaspoon paprika
1 tablespoon olive oil

Follow the preceding recipe for directions on setting up steaming equipment, peeling, cutting, and steaming eggplant.

Remove the eggplant from the steamer. Put in a bowl and mash coarsely. Allow to cool. Beat the yogurt with a fork or whisk until smooth and creamy. Pour this over the eggplant. Add the salt and pepper. Mix and adjust seasonings. Sprinkle paprika over the top and then dribble some oil over the paprika.

BABA GHANOUSH
(Creamed Eggplant with Tahini)

MIDDLE EAST

This dish makes a good appetizer and may be used as a "dip."

(makes 2 cups)

1 medium-sized eggplant (about 1 pound)
1 to 2 cloves garlic, peeled
3 tablespoons *tahini*
3 to 4 tablespoons lemon juice
½ teaspoon salt, or to taste
1 tablespoon minced fresh parsley

Preheat the broiler.

Prick the eggplant with a fork (about 3 or 4 jabs to a side) and place on a foil-lined baking tray. Set under the broiler. When the skin gets charred on one side, give the eggplant a quarter turn. When this side gets charred, turn a little bit again. Continue until the entire skin is charred and the pulp is soft and mushy.

Peel away the charred skin. Quickly rinse off the peeled eggplant to remove little bits of charred skin and pat dry. In a blender or food processor combine the garlic, eggplant, *tahini*, lemon juice, and salt and blend until smooth. Or mash the garlic by hand; then mince the eggplant very fine on a chopping board and mash it with a fork; combine the garlic, eggplant, and *tahini* in a bowl and beat with a fork, adding the lemon juice and salt until well blended.

This dish may be prepared ahead of time and refrigerated for at least a day. Put the *baba ghanoush* in a bowl. Smooth over the top and garnish with the minced parsley. Serve at room temperature or cold with pieces of pita bread.

For information about ingredients and basic techniques that may be unfamiliar, see General Information, pages 418–36.

CHICKPEAS WITH TAHINI
MIDDLE EAST

This dish is usually served as a dip for pita bread and may be eaten at breakfast, along with goat's cheese, olives, and coffee, or it may be served as an appetizer with drinks.

(makes 2¼ cups and could serve 6–8 as a dip)

1 to 2 cloves garlic, peeled
2 cups cooked, drained chickpeas, home-made (see page 83) or canned
4 tablespoons lemon juice
½ teaspoon salt
3 tablespoons *tahini*
2 tablespoons cold water
¼ teaspoon paprika
2 tablespoons olive oil

(This dish is best made in a blender or food processor, though you could pound the garlic, salt, and chickpeas in a mortar and then add the lemon juice, *tahini*, and cold water.)

Start your food processor and then put in the garlic. As soon as the garlic is minced, put in the chickpeas, lemon juice, salt, *tahini*, and cold water. Blend until quite smooth. Add a little more cold water if you want it thinner.

Empty the contents of the food processor into a shallow, 6-inch-wide (approximately) bowl. Smooth over the top of the paste with a flattened knife. Sprinkle the paprika over the paste and then dribble the oil over it.

NAVY BEAN PURÉE WITH POMEGRANATE JUICE
MIDDLE EAST/CASPIAN SEA AREA

Purées made with dried beans and peas are generally seasoned with lemon juice and olive oil in this part of the world. What sometimes replaces the lemon juice is pomegranate juice, either bottled or fresh, which lends its own sweet-and-sour flavor to the purée.

This purée is eaten as a dip and served at breakfast or as a snack. Breads or crackers would be suitable accompaniments.

(makes 1 cup)

½ cup navy beans, picked over, washed, and drained
5½ teaspoons bottled pomegranate juice
5 tablespoons olive oil
¾ teaspoon salt
Freshly ground black pepper

Put the beans and 4 cups water in a pot and bring to a boil. Cover, turn heat to low and simmer for 2 minutes. Turn the heat off and let the pot sit, covered, for 1 hour. Bring the contents of the pot to a boil again. Cover, turn heat to low, and simmer for about 40 minutes or until the beans are tender. Drain. (The liquid may be served for a soup.)

Purée the beans, either by hand or in a food processor. Fold in the pomegranate juice and 4 tablespoons of the oil. Season with salt and pepper and mix. Put the purée in a serving bowl. Dribble the remaining 1 tablespoon oil over it.

ARTICHOKE HEARTS AND POTATOES COOKED IN OIL AND LEMON

ARMENIA

This delightful dish used to be served in New York's Sayat Nova restaurant as a first course. The restaurant, alas, is no more, but here is my version of their recipe.

(serves 4–6)

1 teaspoon whole fennel seeds
1 teaspoon whole black peppercorns
2 teaspoons whole coriander seeds
2 whole bay leaves
4 cloves garlic, peeled and lightly mashed
3 tablespoons lemon juice plus 1 whole lemon
½ cup olive oil
1½ teaspoons salt, or to taste
¼ teaspoon sugar
4 fresh medium or large artichokes
1 good-sized (about 8 ounces) boiling potato
1 smallish onion

Tie up the fennel, peppercorns, coriander seeds, bay leaves, and garlic in a cheesecloth bundle and drop into a 2½-quart pot. Add 2 cups water and bring to a boil. Cover, turn heat to low and simmer 20 minutes. Turn off the heat and remove the cheesecloth bundle, squeezing out as much liquid as possible. Add the lemon juice, olive oil, salt, and sugar. Mix and set aside.

Halve the lemon. Cut off the long artichoke stems, if there are any. 1. Starting near the stem end, press back the artichoke leaves, one by one, and then snap them off. Keep doing this until you have gone past the bowl part of the artichoke that harbors the heart and have reached the paler inner leaves. Using a sharp knife (a serrated one is particularly good), cut off the remaining leafy area and discard it. Immediately rub all cut sections with a lemon half. 2. Scoop away the "choke" in the center of the artichoke with a grapefruit spoon. Squeeze a little lemon juice into this area and rub it in. 3. Using a sharp paring knife, trim the outside of the artichoke bowl so there are no more dark green sections left and the bowl gets a smooth appearance. Rub these newly cut sections with lemon. Cut each artichoke heart into four, again rubbing cut sections with lemon. Cut and prepare the remaining artichokes the same way.

Peel the potato and cut into sections that seem roughly the same size as the pieces of artichoke heart.

Peel the onion and cut it into eight sections.

Put the artichoke hearts, potatoes, and onion

For information about ingredients and basic techniques that may be unfamiliar, see General Information, pages 418–36.

into the prepared liquid and
bring to a boil. Cover, lower heat and
simmer for about 12 minutes. Remove a
piece of potato and a piece of artichoke. Cut off
sections of each and taste for doneness and balance of salt and lemon. You may add more of
either seasoning at this time if you wish. Cover
and simmer another 3 to 7 minutes or until vegetables are tender. Uncover and cool the vegetables
in the liquid. You may refrigerate the contents of
the pot if you wish.

When serving, remove the cool (or cold) vegetables with a slotted spoon. Do not serve the liquid.

POTATO PATTIES STUFFED WITH SPICY PEAS

INDIA

These patties, often referred to as "potato cutlets" and "potato chops," may well be one of North India's favorite restaurant snacks. People on short breaks rush in for a quick coffee and patty just as Americans might for coffee and hamburger. The most common shape for these patties is the flattened teardrop. I prefer my patties smaller than normal and quite round.

You may serve these patties with Tamarind-Mint Chutney (see page 364) or Fresh Chinese Parsley and Mint Chutney (see page 364) or with plain old tomato ketchup.

(makes about 10 patties)

FOR THE POTATOES

4 medium-sized boiling potatoes (a little over 1 pound)
¾ teaspoon salt
Freshly ground black pepper
⅛ teaspoon cayenne pepper

FOR THE STUFFING

½ cup frozen peas
1 heaping tablespoon minced Chinese parsley
¼ teaspoon salt
⅛ teaspoon cayenne pepper
¼ teaspoon ground cumin seeds
¼ teaspoon ground coriander seeds
Freshly ground black pepper
1 teaspoon lemon juice

FOR THE CRUST

2 large eggs
1½ cups unflavored bread crumbs

½ teaspoon salt
Freshly ground black pepper
½ teaspoon ground turmeric
⅛ to ¼ teaspoon cayenne pepper
½ teaspoon ground cumin seeds

Vegetable oil for frying

Boil the potatoes in their jackets. Peel while still hot (you can hold up one at a time with a fork to do this) and mash with a fork. Add the seasonings for the potatoes, mix, and divide roughly into 10 patties.

Drop the peas into 2 cups of boiling water and boil rapidly for 2 minutes. Drain, rinse under cold water, and drain again. Mix the peas with all the ingredients for the stuffing. Mash lightly and divide into 10 parts.

Beat the eggs in a shallow, bowl-like dish. Put the crumbs in a separate dish. Put all the seasonings listed for the crust into the dish of crumbs and mix.

Put one part of the stuffing in the center of one of the patties. Now fold the potato mixture over it to form a rough ball. Flatten the ball gently and form a neat patty, about 2½ inches in diameter. Dip the patty first in the beaten egg and then in the crumbs. Pat down and set aside. Prepare all the patties this way.

In a skillet over a lowish flame, heat enough oil to cover the bottom by ⅛ inch. Put in as many patties as the skillet will hold in a single layer and fry until the bottoms turn a nice reddish color. Turn the patties over and cook the second side the same way. Remove with a slotted spatula. Fry all the patties this way, adding a little more oil for the second batch if you need to. Serve hot.

For information about ingredients and basic techniques that may be unfamiliar, see General Information, pages 418–36.

POTATO AND TEMPEH PATTIES
INDONESIA

This is a tasty and nourishing snack which may be served with Spicy Peanut Sambal (see page 363), Sambal Tomat (see page 362), or with ordinary tomato ketchup. You might even try thin slices of raw onion on top of it.

(makes 5 patties)

FOR THE POTATOES
10 to 12 ounces boiling potatoes
½ teaspoon salt
Freshly ground black pepper
¼ teaspoon ground cumin seeds
¼ teaspoon ground coriander seeds
⅛ teaspoon cayenne pepper
1 clove garlic, peeled and mashed to a pulp

FOR THE TEMPEH
2 ounces *tempeh*
⅛ teaspoon salt
Freshly ground black pepper
⅛ teaspoon ground cumin seeds
⅛ teaspoon ground coriander seeds
⅛ teaspoon cayenne pepper

FOR THE CRUST
1 large egg
¾ cup unseasoned bread crumbs

Vegetable oil for frying

Boil the potatoes in their jackets. Peel while still hot (you could hold one at a time with a fork) and then mash with the back of a fork. Add the seasoning for the potatoes and mix.

Mince the *tempeh* and mash with the back of a fork. Add the seasonings for the *tempeh* and mix.

Mix the mashed potato and mashed *tempeh*. Form 5 firm patties.

Beat the egg in a shallow, bowl-like dish and spread the bread crumbs in another similar dish. Dip the patties first in the egg and then in the crumbs. Pat the crumbs so they adhere.

In a skillet over a lowish flame, heat enough oil to cover the bottom by ⅛ inch. Put in the patties and fry until the bottom turns a nice, reddish color. Turn them over carefully and cook the second side in the same way. Remove with a slotted spatula and serve hot.

FILO PASTRIES
MIDDLE EAST

These small, buttery pastries make impressive appetizers. You could fill them with almost anything you fancy. My stuffing, containing feta cheese, herbs, and hard-boiled eggs, is a very traditional one.

Filo pastry, also called phyllo and fila, consists of large, paper-thin rectangles of dough. It is now so easily available in the freezers of specialty stores and Middle Eastern stores that there is no need to go through the cumbersome process of making it at home.

Filo pastry must be handled with care as it dries out very quickly. Every single sheet and part of a sheet not being used should be folded and covered. A Greek friend of mine uses heavy plastic sheets for this. You could also use kitchen parchment paper topped with a damp towel.

(makes 24 small pastries)

6   sheets filo pastry (less than ½ pound)
¼   pound feta cheese
2   large hard-boiled eggs, peeled
½   loosely packed cup of minced fresh parsley
2   tablespoons minced scallion, including some
     green
2   heaping tablespoons minced fresh dill
Freshly ground black pepper
⅛   teaspoon salt, or to taste
½   cup unsalted butter, melted

If the pastry is frozen, defrost it slowly according to package instructions.

Mash the feta cheese with the back of a fork. Mince the eggs. Mix together the cheese, eggs, parsley, scallion, dill, and a generous amount of black pepper. Taste for salt (the cheese is fairly salty) and add as much as you need. Mix and mash gently.

Generously butter a baking tray. Preheat the oven to 350° F. Remove one sheet of the pastry and cover up the rest. Cut this sheet lengthwise into four strips, each 3 inches wide. Fold up three of the strips and put them under the covers. Work fast now. Spread the remaining strip in front of you on a dry surface. Brush it generously with butter. Put 1 heaping teaspoon of the stuffing down on the place marked in the diagram. Fold a corner over the stuffing, forming a triangle. Continue to fold, forming triangles as you go, until the entire length of pastry has been used up. You will end up with a many-layered triangle. Place it, seam side down, on the tray. Brush the top with butter. Make all the pastries this way. Bake for 35 minutes or until pastry is golden brown.

For information about ingredients and basic techniques that may be unfamiliar, see General Information, pages 418–36.

DOLMA
(Stuffed Grape Leaves)
CAUCASUS/MIDDLE EAST

Almost every nation in the Middle East and Caucasus region makes a version of *dolma*. Along with rice, some people wrap bits of dried fruit inside the grape leaves, some add tomatoes, others dried peas and nuts, and the inclusion of herbs such as dill, mint, and parsley is not at all uncommon. Of all the *dolma* that I have eaten, the ones I like best are also the simplest. These are stuffed with rice, parsley, scallions, and pine nuts and then cooked in a garlicky oil and lemon dressing. I just cannot stop eating them.

Both fresh and prepared grape leaves may be used for the outer shells. If you use fresh leaves, pick tender ones that are about 4 inches across their widest section. Snip off their stems and then plunge them in boiling water for 2 to 3 minutes. You should start off with about 50 leaves. The prepared leaves come in cans and jars and are preserved in brine. The brine needs to be washed off before the leaves can be used.

Drain the grape leaves. Rinse them off, separating them as you do so. Put the leaves in a bowl and pour boiling water over them. Drain and rinse them off again.

Bring 10 cups of water to a rolling boil. Pour in the rice in a steady stream. Stir and bring to a boil again. Boil rapidly for 5 minutes. Drain immediately and rinse under cold water. Drain again.

In a bowl, mix together the rice, parsley, scallions, pine nuts, 1 teaspoon salt, and a generous amount of black pepper.

Line a wide, 3-quart-sized pot with some of the coarser or broken grape leaves.

Begin stuffing the leaves: Lay a leaf in front of you with the shiny side down and its stem end nearest you. Put a good heaping teaspoon (more for larger leaves) of the stuffing in a mound not too far from the stem. Fold the stem end of the leaf over the stuffing and hold it down. Next, fold the

(serves 8)

1-pound jar of prepared grape leaves
1   cup long-grain rice
1   well-packed cup of finely chopped fresh parsley
4   scallions, sliced fine, including green
¼ cup pine nuts, chopped
1½ teaspoons salt
Freshly ground black pepper
½ cup olive oil
¼ cup lemon juice
2   teaspoons sugar
3   cloves garlic, peeled and mashed to a pulp

SALABAT
(Ginger Tea)
MOST OF ASIA

Salabat is the Filipino name for it, but ginger tea is drunk from Syria to Korea. Syrians add cloves, cinnamon, and anise to it and serve it on festive occasions. My own grandmother served it to us in India when we had colds, saying that it would make us feel all better. It did. In the Philippines, *salabat* is often sweetened with honey or caramelized sugar and served just as tea might be, at breakfast and with all manner of sweet cakes and snacks. In Korea, whole dried fruit—such as persimmons—are sometimes dropped into the hot tea. As it cools, it picks up the subtle flavor of the fruit. This Korean tea is drunk cold, dotted with a few pine nuts—and, of course, you get to eat the fruit as well.

(serves 4)

2 1-inch cubes of fresh ginger
3 heaping tablespoons honey, or to taste

Peel the ginger and chop it coarsely. Put it into a pot along with 4 cups water and the honey. Bring to a boil. Cover, turn heat to low and simmer for 25 minutes. Uncover, turn up heat to medium-low, and cook another 15 minutes. You now should have 3 cups of liquid. Strain and serve.

two ends of the leaf to the left and right of the stuffing over it as well. Tightly roll the leaf away from you. Lay this roll neatly in the pot, seam side down. As you do each leaf, put it in the pot, forming tightly fitting rows. When the bottom of the pot is covered with one layer, do a second and, if necessary, a third layer.

Put the olive oil, lemon juice, sugar, ½ teaspoon salt, garlic, and some more black pepper in a bowl. Beat to mix. Add 1 cup water and mix again. Pour this mixture over the *dolma*. Lay a plate, turned upside down, over the *dolma* to prevent them from opening up. Bring to a boil. Cover the pot, turn heat to low and simmer for 1 hour. Every 10 minutes or so, lift up the plate and baste the upper leaves with the liquid. (A bulb baster is useful for this.) If all the liquid seems to evaporate, add some more water. At the end of the cooking time, just a little oil should be left at the bottom of the pot.

Let the dolma cool completely before serving them. They may be made 24 to 48 hours in advance, covered, and refrigerated.

For information about ingredients and basic techniques that may be unfamiliar, see General Information, pages 418–36.

FRESH GINGER-FLAVORED LIMEADE

INDIA

On summer days, limeade is often served in India flavored with fresh ginger. Here is a recipe to make one tall glassful. The recipe can easily be doubled or quadrupled. You can, if you like, substitute club soda for the ⅔ cup water.

(makes 1 tall glass)

5   tablespoons freshly squeezed lime juice
4   tablespoons sugar
¼ to ½ teaspoon finely grated fresh ginger
Ice cubes

Mix the lime juice and sugar in a small bowl. Put the grated ginger in a small strainer. Lower the bottom of the strainer into the sweetened lime juice. Stir the ginger around with a spoon. (The ginger will still be in the strainer.) Lift up the strainer and discard any remaining ginger pulp (there may not be much). Pour the ginger-flavored lime concentrate into a tall glass. Add ⅔ cup water and a few ice cubes. Stir.

INDIAN-STYLE HOT TEA WITH FRESH MINT

INDIA

(serves 4–6)

Cold tea with mint sprigs is very popular in America but hot tea with mint tastes equally good. To make it, put 2 tablespoons of black tea leaves into a tea pot that you have just heated by rinsing it with boiling water. Also put in 3 sprigs of fresh mint. Now pour in 5 cups of water that you have just brought to a rolling boil (put in 6 cups if you like your tea on the weaker side). Cover the tea pot and let the tea steep for 4 minutes. Stir the tea.

You may serve this tea with milk and sugar, with honey and lemon, or just plain.

HOT TEA WITH CARDAMOM AND CINNAMON

MIDDLE EAST/INDIA

(serves 4–6)

Put 2 tablespoons of black tea leaves into a tea pot that you have just heated by rinsing it with boiling water. Add 6 cardamom pods and a 2-inch piece of stick cinnamon. Now pour in 5 cups of water that you have just brought to a rolling boil (put in 6 cups if you like your tea on the weaker side). Cover the tea pot and let the tea steep for 4 minutes. Stir the tea.

You may serve this tea with milk and sugar (in India, it would be hot milk), honey and lemon, or just plain.

ANISE TEA

MIDDLE EAST

(serves 4)

Bring 4 cups of water to a boil. Throw in 4 teaspoons anise seeds, cover and steep for 10 minutes. Strain and bring to a boil again. Meanwhile, rinse out a tea pot with hot water to warm it. Put in 4 teaspoons black tea leaves. Now pour the boiling anise water over the tea leaves. Cover and steep for 3 to 4 minutes. If the tea is too strong for you, you may add more boiling water.

Serve plain or with honey and lemon or with milk and sugar.

OCHA
(Japanese Green Tea)

JAPAN

(serves 4–6)

I have used *bancha*, the cheapest type of Japanese leaf tea, to make this *ocha*.

Bring 4 cups of water to a rolling boil. Meanwhile, put ¼ cup green *bancha* tea leaves in a tea pot or divide them up among individual cups. Now pour the water over the leaves and let them steep for 2 minutes. If you have put your tea directly into tea cups, which the Japanese often do, the leaves will sink to the bottom by the time the steeping period is over.

You may, if you like, make your tea with roasted *bancha*. Just put the tea leaves in a heavy skillet over a lowish flame and stir them for a few minutes or until they smell roasted. Roasted *bancha* is excellent if it is strained, refrigerated, and served cold.

GINSENG TEA

KOREA

In Korea, this slow-growing root is prized for curing everything from insomnia to impotence. On the other hand, it is not supposed to be good for patients with high-blood pressure. Whether any of these claims have benefited from careful scientific scrutiny, I cannot tell. At any rate, ginseng tea is very popular in Korea and is becoming so here as well. I prefer the taste of the brew made from fresh roots, but as only instant tea, tea bags, and the dried root are available here, it is best to follow instructions on the package.

For information about ingredients and basic techniques that may be unfamiliar, see General Information, pages 418–36.

RICE TEA

EAST ASIA

(serves 4)

There are just so many versions of this tea that it would be impossible to enumerate them all. It probably all started with the East Asian love of rice and the resultant desire to see that no precious grain be wasted. When rice was cooked the traditional way in large heavy pots, some grains invariably stuck to the bottom of the pot and got slightly burnt. After all the nonburnt rice had been served, hot water was poured over the burnt section, brought to a boil, and served as rice tea. Some rice grains invariably accompanied the liquid. Needless to say, this tea was served at the end of a meal. It was considered to be a digestive.

It was not just poor peasants who drank such a tea. In Japan, for example, it was and is still served very formally at the end of the *kaiseki* meal that accompanies a tea ceremony. As electric rice-cookers replace the iron kettles of Japan, rice tea made with genuinely burnt rice is fast becoming a part of Japanese nostalgia. At one very formal Japanese vegetarian lunch I attended, the meal ended with a rice tea made, rather like barley tea, from roasted rice kernels.

In Hong Kong, I noticed something else. After a lunch was over, my Chinese companion poured the regular tea from his tea cup into his empty rice bowl. I asked if he was trying to cool off his tea. No, he answered, tea tasted much better when drunk from the rice bowl. It picked up the rice flavor, and a few odd remaining rice grains as well.

TO MAKE RICE TEA: Put 2 tablespoons rice in a small, cast-iron skillet and set over a medium-low flame. Stir the grains until they turn dark in spots and give out a nice roasted aroma. Put the rice kernels into a small pot. Add 4 cups boiling water. Simmer for 1 minute. Cover, and turn off the heat. Let the tea steep for 3 minutes. Strain and serve. (The Japanese do not strain the tea. They just leave a few grains sitting quietly at the bottom of each bowl.)

BORI CHA
(Barley Tea)

KOREA/JAPAN

(serves 4)

Korea is surrounded by mighty tea-drinking nations but its own people rarely touch the stuff, relying more on a drink made with roasted barley. In summer this brownish "tea" is served cold and in the winter it is served hot. It comes as automatically to tables as water does in America and tea in China and Japan. It is a most pleasant, smoky drink—quite free of caffeine.

Roasted barley is available in Korean and Japanese stores and is known as *bori cha* and *mugi cha* respectively.

TO MAKE BARLEY TEA: Put 2 tablespoons roasted barley and 4 cups water in a pot and bring to a boil. Turn heat down and simmer fairly aggressively for 5 minutes. Strain. Serve hot or chilled.

TAMARIND SHARBAT
(Tamarind Syrup)
MIDDLE EAST/SOUTH ASIA

Tamarind drinks, known variously as tamarind tea and tamarind water, are basically infusions made with the peeled pulp of the sweet-and-sour tamarind pods. They are meant to be particularly beneficial in hot weather and are supposed to bring down raging fevers as well. (Sleeping under the tamarind *tree*, however, is supposed to bring *on* fever.) As a child, I was given a cold infusion of tamarind and cumin seeds at least once every two weeks during the burning summer months. This would, I was told, cool my body and cleanse my system.

The recipe here is for the most common of all tamarind drinks found through much of Asia, the sweetened tamarind juice. I have seen it being sold in places as far from each other as the *souks* of Old Jerusalem and the bazaars of Old Delhi. It consists of a thick, concentrated syrup that is then diluted with cold water and ice.

(makes 1¼ cups and serves 5)

½ cup tamarind paste
1 cup sugar

Combine the tamarind paste, sugar, and ½ cup water in a small pot and bring to a simmer on a medium-low flame. Turn the heat to low and simmer, stirring frequently, until the sugar is completely melted. You should now have a syrup with the consistency of maple syrup. If it is thicker, add a bit more water and cook another minute. As the syrup cools, it will thicken. Remember that the syrup should end up being slightly thicker than maple syrup but still quite pourable. You will probably end up with about 1¼ cups syrup. This syrup may be bottled and kept for several days; it's not necessary to refrigerate.

To make a drink, combine ¼ cup Tamarind Sharbat, ½ cup water, and about 4 ice cubes. Stir to mix.

STRAWBERRY AND LEMON SHARBAT
(Strawberry and Lemon Syrup)
WEST AND SOUTH ASIA

Sharbats, concentrated syrups, may be made out of many fruits, vegetables, and aromatic seasonings. Raspberries, mangoes, sour cherries, oranges, limes, pomegranates, rhubarb, and mint may all be used. Once you understand the basic technique of making syrups, you can easily concoct your own recipes.

I have used frozen, sweetened strawberries here. If you can get cheap summer strawberries, substitute 1½ pounds of the fresh ones. Chop them up and increase the sugar and water by ½ cup each.

(makes 2¼ cups and serves 9)

2 10-ounce packages of frozen, sliced strawberries with sugar
2 cups sugar
½ cup lemon juice

For information about ingredients and basic techniques that may be unfamiliar, see General Information, pages 418–36.

Combine the strawberries, their liquid, sugar, lemon juice, and 1 cup water in an enameled or stainless-steel saucepan. Stir and bring to a simmer. Simmer on low heat, stirring gently, for 30 to 40 minutes. The liquid in the pan should resemble a thin syrup.

Line a sieve with two layers of cheesecloth and place the sieve over a bowl. Pour the contents of the pan into the sieve. The syrup will flow through into the bowl. Gently press the strawberry pulp with the back of a wooden spoon, pushing out as much liquid as possible. (The very thick strawberry pulp may be discarded or eaten as jam.) You should end up with about 2¼ cups of syrup.

Pour the syrup into a jar. Allow to cool and cover.

To make a drink, combine ¼ cup of the syrup, ½ cup water, and 4 ice cubes in a glass. Stir to mix.

QAHWAH
(Turkish Coffee)
MIDDLE EAST

What we call "Turkish" coffee is served all through the Middle East, by wandering Bedouins and more stationary city dwellers alike. Business is conducted over cups of this thick, sweet brew and no host lets a guest depart without at least a cup of it.

Turkish coffee is made from very finely ground—but not powdered—coffee beans. Sometimes a few cardamom seeds are ground with the coffee. As the coffee is thick and strong, it is generally drunk quite sweet. Heavy coffee grounds sink to the bottom of each cup and are not meant to be consumed. (Instead, the coffee cups are turned upside down and the grounds used for fortune-telling.) The froth at the top of each cup, on the other hand, *is* meant to be consumed.

In order to make this coffee properly and get an adequate amount of froth, it is best to buy a *tanaka*, the narrow-necked and long-handled pot available in most specialty stores and in Middle Eastern stores. The pots come in different sizes. There is even a 1-cup size. Turkish coffee is drunk from demitasse cups.

(serves 4)

2 to 4 teaspoons sugar, to taste
2 whole cardamom pods (optional)
4 heaping   teaspoons Turkish coffee

Put 4 demitasse cups worth of water into the *tanaka*. Add sugar and cardamom and bring to a boil. Add the coffee, stirring as you do so. The froth will begin rising to the top. As soon as it reaches the top, remove the pot from the fire. Let the froth subside. Put the *tanaka* back on the fire. As soon as the froth reaches the top, remove the pot again. Do this a third time. Now spoon the froth into 4 demitasse cups. Pour the coffee over the froth. (Discard the cardamom pods.) The froth will rise to the top of the cups.

BUTTERMILK

INDIA

Of all the dairy products, buttermilk is easily my favorite. By buttermilk I mean *real* buttermilk, the slightly tart, liquid residue which is left when cream is churned to make butter. Real buttermilk is much thinner than the cultured supermarket variety and was, until the turn of the century, used in America mainly to feed pigs. Known as *chha* or *chhaas* in northern India, it is a popular breakfast and lunchtime drink.

My problem with cultured, supermarket buttermilk is that while I know it to be nutritious, I find it hard to adjust to its thick texture. I have found a way around that. I just thin it down to the texture of real buttermilk with cold water!

(serves 2)

½ teaspoon whole cumin seeds, roasted and ground
1⅓ cups cold buttermilk
⅔ cup ice-cold water
½ teaspoon salt
Freshly ground pepper to taste
A pinch of cayenne pepper (optional)

Combine all ingredients in the container of an electric blender and blend for 3 seconds. You could, if you like, mix all the ingredients with a wire whip instead. Pour into two glasses and serve.

You may make this drink several hours ahead of time and store it, covered, in the refrigerator. Serve very cold and stir before serving.

SWEET LASSI
(Sweet Yogurt Drink)

INDIA

In this drink plain yogurt is thinned out with ice water and sweetened. Lassi may be drunk with meals or, as was generally done in my family, it can be served between lunch and dinner. In India, both the *lassi* and the preceding buttermilk drink are often served after vigorous games of tennis, badminton, or hockey.

(serves 2)

½ cup plain yogurt
1½ cups ice-cold water
1½ tablespoons sugar, or to taste
¼ teaspoon rose essence (optional)

Combine all ingredients in the container of an electric blender and blend for 3 seconds. Pour into two glasses and serve.

This drink may be made several hours ahead of time and stored, covered, in the refrigerator. It should be served very cold. Stir before serving.

For information about ingredients and basic techniques that may be unfamiliar, see General Information, pages 418–36.

SALTY LASSI
(Salty Yogurt Drink)
INDIA

This is very similar to the preceding Sweet Lassi, only it is salty.

(serves 2)

½ cup plain yogurt
1½ cups ice-cold water
¼ teaspoon salt, or to taste

Combine all ingredients in the container of an electric blender and blend for 3 seconds. Pour into 2 glasses and serve.

DOOGH
(Persian-Style Yogurt Drink, Flavored with Mint)
IRAN

Rather like salty Indian *lassi, doogh* is made out of thinned yogurt. It may be served plain or flavored with mint. I often freeze sprigs of fresh mint in ice cubes to serve with my *doogh*. To make these cubes, half fill your ice-cube trays with water. Let the ice form. Now lay a sprig of fresh mint (or a leaf) on top of each cube and pour a tablespoon of ice water over each sprig of mint and freeze again. Take the tray out once more and fill to the top with water. Let the cubes freeze.

Instead of thinning out the yogurt with water, you could use club soda instead.

(serves 2)

½ cup plain yogurt
1½ cups ice-cold water
¼ teaspoon salt, or to taste
4 ice cubes with mint in them (see above)
2 sprigs fresh mint

Put the yogurt in a bowl. Slowly add the ice water, beating with a fork or whisk as you do so. Season with salt to taste.

Pour *doogh* into 2 glasses. Put 2 ice cubes into each glass and garnish with a sprig of mint.

CALPIS

Japan, which has almost no tradition of consuming milk products, has come up with a new drink that is likely to prove very popular. It is called Calpis (one trade name I see around New York is "Calpico") and is based on nonfat dry milk that has been treated with lactic acid. The drink is milky white, with a slightly tart, slightly sweet, fruity flavor. It is most pleasant. What you buy in the bottle is a concentrate that can be diluted with cold water, hot water, or club soda. The directions for mixing the drink are on the bottle.

THANDAI
(A Milk and Almond Drink)
INDIA

This is a very refreshing, cool, summer drink made out of milk and almonds and sold from terra-cotta pots throughout the plains of North India. Normally, whole milk is used in the recipe but since very few people in India own refrigerators, the milk is always diluted with small chunks of block ice. I substitute cold skimmed milk for the whole milk and do without the ice. The end result tastes very much like the *thandai* in India. The second major ingredient is almonds. Almonds, besides providing extra nourishment, are very popular in India as they are supposed to sharpen the brain! The flavoring in this drink comes from the aromatic cardamom. If you wish to vary the flavor, you might substitute the cardamom seeds with fresh mint or fresh holy basil leaves. Holy basil (*Ocymun sanctum*), also of the mint family, is used frequently in Thai cooking. It is not easily available so you would probably have to grow it in your own garden or on your windowsill. In India, holy basil or *tulsi* is considered sacred to Vishnu, the Preserver. My grandmother grew plants of it just outside our family Prayer Room and used the leaves to make a "holy drink," not unlike *thandai*.

The recipe here would serve two people but it can easily be doubled or tripled. I tend to undersweeten most of my drinks, but *thandai* is generally drunk quite sweet. You can increase or decrease the suggested amount of sugar.

(serves 2)

Seeds from 1 cardamom pod (or 4 to 5 fresh mint leaves or fresh holy basil leaves)
2 cups very cold skimmed milk
12 blanched almonds, soaked in ⅔ cup water overnight or for at least 5 hours and then drained
1 tablespoon sugar

Crush the cardamom seeds finely in a small mortar or place seeds between two sheets of waxed paper and pound gently with the wide section of a hammer until you have a powder. (If you are using mint or holy basil leaves, throw them into the blender.)

Pour ½ cup of the milk into the container of an electric blender. Add cardamom powder, almonds, and sugar. Blend well. Stop the blender and pour

---

For information about ingredients and basic techniques that may be unfamiliar, see General Information, pages 418–36.

in the rest of the milk. Blend for just 1 second. Pour into two glasses and serve.

This drink can be made several hours ahead of time and stored, covered, in the refrigerator. It should be served *very* cold. Stand it in crushed ice, if necessary. Stir before serving. (If you have flavored your drink with fresh mint or holy basil, you might want to garnish your glasses with sprigs of the herbs.)

MILK WITH SAFFRON AND NUTS

INDIA

Many Indians begin their day with a hot glass of milk. Those who can afford it, add saffron and nuts to it as well. It is not an uncommon sight, even today, to see turbaned, liveried servants in the palaces of those who were once maharajas, moving about gracefully in the early morning hours, bearing silver trays that hold frothy glasses of saffron-colored milk. The froth is considered important in India and is made by pouring the milk from one glass to another several times. The distance between glasses sometimes reaches an impressive three feet! The same froth can, however, be created in a blender with much less fear of mishaps.

(makes 2 cups)

2 cups milk
3 cardamom pods, lightly crushed
A generous pinch of leaf saffron

2 teaspoons sugar, or
    to taste
1 teaspoon unsalted, peeled
    pistachios, cut into slivers

Combine the milk, cardamom pods, saffron, and sugar in a heavy pot and bring to a simmer. Turn heat to low and simmer the milk for 2 minutes.

Meanwhile, rinse out a blender container in very hot water. Strain the milk into it. Blend at high speed to make a froth. Pour into two glasses. Sprinkle the pistachios over the froth and serve immediately.

Condiments, Dips, Chutneys, and Relishes

"Nice flowers," my daughter said a few days ago as she glanced offhandedly at the dinner table on the way from the front door to her room. They weren't flowers at all but scallions that I had arranged, green side up, in a cut-glass, water-filled tumbler set in the center of our dining table. And the scallions were not decorative, but meant for eating. My mother used to arrange scallions that way. Somehow, I had forgotten about them until just the other day.

Table condiments in Asia can be very simple—scallions, onion slices, green chilies, roasted sesame seeds mixed with salt, salt mixed with Szechuan peppercorns, salt mixed with pepper and roasted cumin seeds, hot oil, red chilies pounded with garlic and salt and then soured with lemon juice, and crushed peanuts. Or they can get very elaborate—you might be served a rare pickle that was ten months in the making. Among the nicest part of Asian meals is just this—the number of condiments, pickles, sauces, dips, chutneys, relishes, and *sambals* that appear miraculously at the table, giving it variety and zest. Vegetarian food in particular gets such a boost from this approach. Each bite of the same food can be made to taste quite different, depending on what you eat it with or what you dip it in.

In Japan, for example, the simplest of bean-curd dishes, Udofu, is served with a heated sauce containing soy sauce, stock, and wine. But there are other condiments at the table as well, such as grated radish, grated ginger, shredded *nori* (laver), and sliced scallions. Each cube of bean curd can be eaten with a new combination of seasonings. Eating becomes quite an adventure.

Simple relishes and everyday chutneys in India may be made out of chopped-up tomatoes and puréed herbs such as Chinese parsley and mint. They are not only supposed to provide the much-needed contrasts of tastes but some very necessary vitamins as well.

Pickles in Asia enjoy an even higher status. Much time and effort goes into preparing them as whole families trim, peel, and cut vegetables. Koreans spend the late fall months making mountains of cabbage *kimchee*, generously flavored with garlic, ginger, scallions, and red pepper. They eat it in generous portions, too, at every single meal. Japanese pickles tend to be much more sedate, and served always in tiny portions. Many meals, all over Japan, end with the felicitous combination of plain rice, pickles, and tea. Indian pickles tend to be very hot and spicy. They sharpen appetites and give lethargic systems a fresh charge. In the Middle East, a great deal of pickling is done in vinegar. The addition of fresh herbs such as mint and dill gives the pickled vegetables an aromatic freshness.

All pickles and chutneys are palate-teasers and flavor-enhancers. They give color to the simplest of meals.

SALT AND PEPPER, INDIAN-STYLE

INDIA

On our dining table in India, we always had a spice mixture that we referred to as "Bauwa's salt." ("Bauwa" is what we called our mother.) It consisted of freshly ground coarse salt, freshly ground black pepper, and ground, roasted cumin seeds, all mixed together and put inside a cut-glass salt cellar. We used this mixture to season radishes, cucumber, tomato slices, guava wedges, tart apple slices, tangerine sections, and sometimes we even put it on buttered toast.

(makes 1⅔ tablespoons)

1   tablespoon kosher or coarse salt
1   teaspoon freshly ground black pepper
1   teaspoon freshly ground, roasted cumin seeds

Mix all the ingredients together.

It is best to keep this in a tightly closed jar and take it out as needed. Although this mixture is most aromatic and pungent when the spices have just been ground, you can store it for a few weeks.

SALT AND PEPPER, CHINESE-STYLE

CHINA

Here is a combination of salt and pepper with a slight difference. Instead of regular peppercorns, the highly fragrant Szechuan peppercorns are used. This salt makes an excellent dip for raw vegetables, for batter-fried vegetables, and even for some sour fruit such as green apples. You might also use it in place of salt when boiling vegetables. It gives them a special aroma.

(makes 3 tablespoons)

¼ cup coarse or kosher salt
1½ teaspoons Szechuan peppercorns

Put the salt and peppercorns in a small, heavy, cast-iron skillet and set it over a medium-low flame. Stir and cook for 4 to 5 minutes or until the salt turns slightly darker and the peppercorns not only darken but give off a wonderful aroma. Put the contents of the skillet into the container of a clean coffee grinder and grind.

For information about ingredients and basic techniques that may be unfamiliar, see General Information, pages 418–36.

GOMA SHIO
(Black Sesame Seeds and Salt)

JAPAN

This is a combination of roasted black sesame seeds and coarse salt that may be sprinkled over soups, vegetables, egg dishes, and rice dishes. Although sesame seeds do taste best when freshly roasted, you could store this mixture in a tightly lidded jar for a couple of weeks. I love it on lightly boiled vegetables like green beans and broccoli. It is also good on eggs, cucumber slices, tomatoes, white radish slices, light soups, and plain rice. It makes an excellent dip for raw vegetables.

(makes about 3 tablespoons)

2 tablespoons roasted black sesame seeds
1 tablespoon coarse salt or kosher salt

Mix together.

DRY NORTH INDIAN DIP

INDIA

Here is a wonderful dip for raw vegetables. Arrange them all around the bowl of spices and serve as a snack for children or with evening drinks. It may be frozen.

(makes 1 cup)

2 tablespoons whole coriander seeds
1 tablespoon whole cumin seeds
3 tablespoons sesame seeds
2 tablespoons kosher salt
¼ teaspoon cayenne pepper, or more to taste
¼ teaspoon freshly ground black pepper

Put the coriander seeds, cumin seeds, and sesame seeds into a small, heavy skillet over a medium-low flame. Stir and dry-roast the seeds gently until the seeds are a few shades darker and emit a deliciously nutty odor. Empty the spices onto a plate and let them cool slightly. Now put them into the container of a clean coffee grinder and grind as finely as possible.

Put the spice mixture into a serving bowl. Add the salt, cayenne, and black pepper. Mix.

Neela's
MAULKA PORI
(Dry South Indian Chutney)
INDIA

This is a South Indian fried spice combination that is used as a kind of relish with Indian pancakes, rice, and vegetable dishes. It is stored in jars (I know one South Indian vegetarian photographer who travels through Europe and America with a jar lovingly prepared by his wife) and can be sprinkled over foods as is or—and this is how it is commonly used—it can be mixed with oil or *ghee* before being served. Rather like Chinese hot oil, it can be used to season all kinds of foods, from soups to salads, or it can be placed on the edge of a dinner plate and eaten, in small amounts, like prepared English mustard. It should be eaten with discretion as it *very* hot. In this recipe you will notice the South Indian habit of using *dals* like spices.

(makes about ½ cup)

2   teaspoons vegetable oil
A generous pinch of ground asafetida
1   teaspoon whole cumin seeds
¼ cup *urad dal*
¼ cup *chana dal*
⅛ cup *toovar (arhar) dal*
2   teaspoons salt
10 whole dried hot red peppers
Extra vegetable oil or *ghee* to be used
     when serving

Heat the 2 teaspoons of oil in a small, heavy skillet over a medium flame. When hot, put in the asafetida and, a few seconds later, the cumin seeds. Stir and fry for 8 to 10 seconds. Now add the *urad dal*, *chana dal*, and *toovar dal*. Fry, stirring, until the *dals* turn reddish in color. Empty the contents of the skillet into a blender container. (If your blender will not grind *dals* well, you could empty contents of the skillet onto a paper towel. Let the spices drain for a minute and then put them into a coffee grinder reserved for spices. You can then proceed with the recipe.) Add the salt and red peppers. Pulverize the spices so they are coarsely powdered. Let the spices cool completely and then store in a tightly closed jar. This spice mixture should be good for 3 to 4 weeks.

To serve as a relish to be eaten with dinner, put as many teaspoons of the mixture into a small serving bowl as there are people eating. Add just as many teaspoons of vegetable oil or melted *ghee* and mix well. After that, people can serve themselves as much as they want.

For information about ingredients and basic techniques that may be unfamiliar, see General Information, pages 418–36.

TEMPURA DIPPING SAUCE

JAPAN

This is an excellent sauce for Japanese batter-fried foods. Pour it into individual bowls and serve with a dish like Tempura.

(makes 6 portions)

1   cup Japanese Stock (see page 291)
4   tablespoons Japanese soy sauce
4   tablespoons *mirin*
1   teaspoon sugar
4   tablespoons white radish,
     or 2 tablespoons peeled fresh ginger
     grated to a pulp

Combine all ingredients in a bowl.

CHINESE DIPPING SAUCE

CHINA

This sauce may be dribbled over congee or eggs or it could be used as a dipping sauce for batter-fried vegetables and breads. It could also be used as a dressing for cold noodles.

(serves about 4)

2   tablespoons Chinese thin soy sauce
1   teaspoon sesame oil
2½ teaspoons distilled white vinegar
1   teaspoon sugar
A few drops Hot Oil (see page 361)

Mix all the ingredients together.

JAPANESE DIPPING SAUCE

JAPAN

This recipe makes a very concentrated sauce. For dishes such as Japanese Omelette with Bean Curd (see page 198), you should thin it out with 2–4 tablespoons of *dashi*.

(serves 6)

4   tablespoons Japanese soy sauce
2   tablespoons *mirin*
1   tablespoon sesame oil
1½ teaspoons sugar
2–4 tablespoons *dashi* (see page 291), optional

Mix all ingredients together. If you are serving a Japanese-style meal, you might want to pour the sauce into small, individual bowls.

FILIPINO DIPPING SAUCE

PHILIPPINES

This sauce may be served with Ukoy or with any other batter-fried vegetables.

(serves 4)

4   tablespoons distilled white vinegar
½ teaspoon garlic, peeled and mashed
¼ teaspoon salt, or to taste

Mix all ingredients together and divide among four very small bowls.

KOREAN DIPPING SAUCE NUMBER I

KOREA

Serve this with *bindaetuk* or with batter-fried vegetables.

(serves 4)

4   tablespoons Japanese soy sauce
4   teaspoons rice vinegar
1   teaspoon sesame oil

Mix all ingredients.
To serve, divide sauce among four small saucers.

KOREAN DIPPING SAUCE NUMBER 2

KOREA

This sauce may be served with Sautéed Bean Curd, used as a dressing for noodles, and used as a dip for sliced vegetables.

(makes about 7 tablespoons)

4   tablespoons Japanese soy sauce
2½ tablespoons rice vinegar
1   teaspoon sugar
1   tablespoon very finely sliced scallions
1   clove garlic, peeled and mashed
1   teaspoon roasted and lightly crushed sesame seeds

Mix all ingredients together.

KOREAN DIPPING SAUCE NUMBER 3

KOREA

This sauce may be used to season the cold noodle soup, Naeng Myon; it may be used as a dip for vegetables or for cubes of hot or ice-cold bean curd; and it may be used to season Plain Japanese Rice for Korean-style rice dishes.

(makes about 7 tablespoons)

4   tablespoons Japanese soy sauce
2½ tablespoons rice vinegar
1   teaspoon sugar
1   tablespoon very finely sliced scallions
1   clove garlic, peeled and mashed

Mix all ingredients together.

For information about ingredients and basic techniques that may be unfamiliar, see General Information, pages 418–36.

SIMPLE KOREAN SAUCE

KOREA

This sauce may be used as a dip for vegetables, cooked and raw, or it may be used to season Korean rice dishes.

(serves 4–6)

3   tablespoons Japanese soy sauce
3   tablespoons sesame oil
¾   teaspoon sugar
1   teaspoon roasted and lightly crushed sesame seeds

Combine all ingredients. Mix again before serving, as the oil tends to rise to the top.

The sauce may be served in small individual saucers or in a somewhat larger single bowl.

SPICY KOREAN SAUCE

KOREA

This sauce may be used as a dipping sauce for Korean pancakes, raw vegetables, vegetable fritters, and bean curd. It may also be eaten with Korean rice dishes.

(makes about ½ cup)

6   tablespoons Japanese soy sauce
1   tablespoon sesame oil
½   teaspoon *kochu chang*; or more, as desired
½   teaspoon very finely minced garlic
1   tablespoon roasted and lightly crushed sesame seeds
1   teaspoon sugar
½   scallion, sliced into very fine rounds (bottom half only)

Combine all ingredients and mix well.

TAHINI DIPPING SAUCE

MIDDLE EAST

This simple sauce, with ground sesame paste, or *tahini*, as its base, is found all over the Middle East. It may be used as a dip for raw vegetables, pita bread, or, when thinned and mixed with chopped parsley, it can be used as a sauce for *falafel* (see variation below), the chickpea-flour "hamburgers" that are stuffed into pita-bread pockets along with shredded lettuce and sliced tomatoes.

(makes about ⅔ cup)

2 to 3 cloves garlic, peeled
¼ cup *tahini*
4 tablespoons lemon juice
¼ to ½ teaspoon salt
3 tablespoons cold water

Crush the cloves of garlic to a paste. Put this paste in a stainless-steel or nonmetallic bowl. Add the *tahini* and beat it in with a fork. Add the lemon juice, beating it in as you do so. Now add the salt and mix it in. Add the cold water, a little bit at a time, beating in as well. (You could do all this in a food processor or blender, too.) Check the balance of sour and salt. Adjust, if necessary.

VARIATION: FALAFEL SAUCE—Add 1 tablespoon very finely chopped parsley and 1 tablespoon more cold water.

WASABI
(Horseradish)
JAPAN

Wasabi is a pungent and nose-tingling Japanese horseradish paste that is best when made from the peeled and finely grated fresh vegetable. As this is not always available in the United States, the next best alternative is to use the dry, powdered variety which needs to be reconstituted (about ¾ teaspoon water to every teaspoon of the powder) or to use a processed packaged paste.

CRISPLY FRIED ONIONS

These onions are more than a garnish. They are sprinkled over many Asian dishes for extra flavor. You might try them over rice dishes, egg dishes, noodle dishes, and even in salads.

(makes about 1½ cups)

2 medium-sized onions, peeled
Vegetable oil for shallow frying

Cut the onions in half lengthwise, and then crosswise into very, very thin half rings. Press the half rings between layers of paper towel for half an hour.

Heat ½ inch of oil in an 8- to 9-inch skillet over a medium flame. When hot, put in the onions. Fry, stirring gently, until the onions are a reddish-brown color and no longer limp looking. Some onions will become dark brown and that is quite all right. Remove the onions with a slotted spoon and spread out on paper towels. Once the onions have drained and cooled, they should turn very crisp. You may now use them the same day or else store them in a tightly closed container for a few days.

For information about ingredients and basic techniques that may be unfamiliar, see General Information, pages 418–36.

HOT OIL

CHINA

This is the orange-colored oil that seems to sit permanently on tables in Chinese restaurants, along with soy sauce and vinegar. It is a hot seasoning that may be dribbled into soups and sauces, in the minutest quantities, of course.

For your oil to get a nice color, you need a cayenne pepper—or ground hot red chili pepper (same thing)—that is really bright red and not faded with time and exposure. I find that among the best places to buy this are Korean stores, with Indian and Chinese stores as a distant second choice. Koreans need that lovely bright-red color for their own *kimchees* and dressings and their stores seem to be constantly well supplied. Once the oil has been seasoned with the hot pepper, it needs to be strained properly. The best way seems to be to use a clean but discardable piece of cloth, such as a 10-inch square torn out from an old sheet or pillowcase.

(makes about ½ cup)

½ cup vegetable oil
1½ teaspoons ground hot red pepper (cayenne pepper or chili pepper)

Heat the oil in a small cast-iron skillet over a medium flame. As soon as the oil is hot—you will be able to tell as it will start swirling and moving—put in the red pepper. Stir once and turn off the heat. Let the oil cool off just slightly. Then strain it through a clean cloth and store it in a bottle with a well-fitting top.

If you wish to bring the oil to the table to offer as a seasoning, you could transfer it to a bottle with a narrow neck such as the old-fashioned bottles for table vinegar. Drops of Hot Oil may be put into congees, soups, and dipping sauces.

TOMATO SAUCE

This plain, simple sauce may be used for cooking all manner of bean, *paneer*, and vegetable dishes. Make it when good, red-ripe tomatoes are in season. You could easily double or quadruple this recipe. What you do not use immediately may be refrigerated or frozen.

(makes about 2 cups)

2 pounds red-ripe tomatoes or peeled canned tomatoes
½ teaspoon salt
½ teaspoon sugar

Chop up the tomatoes and put them into a heavy stainless-steel pot or a pot lined with a nonmetallic substance. Add the salt and the sugar and bring to a boil. Cook on medium heat, stirring frequently, until you reduce the contents of the pot by half. Push the tomatoes through a sieve in order to get rid of the skins. You could leave the tomato sauce this way, but if you want it any smoother, put it into an electric blender or food processor and blend for a minute.

CHILI SAMBAL
INDONESIA

In Indonesia, this *sambal* is made by pounding lots of fresh hot red peppers in a mortar and then adding tamarind paste and salt. It is quite fiery. I have calmed the fire somewhat in this recipe by adding some peanuts. It still remains very hot and should be approached with caution. This is a relish that should be spooned in a very small quantity onto one's plate. It can then be eaten with almost any food that needs pepping up. I love to put small amounts in soups and in dressings for green vegetables and beans.

(makes about 3 tablespoons)

¼ cup whole dried hot red peppers
2 tablespoons fried or roasted unsalted peanuts
2 tablespoons tamarind paste
⅓ teaspoon salt

Put the red pepper in a coffee grinder reserved for spices and grind to a powder. Add the peanuts and grind them as well. Empty into a small bowl. Add 2 teaspoons of water as well as all the other ingredients. Mix well.

SAMBAL TOMAT
(Hot Tomato Sambal)
INDONESIA

You need red-ripe tomatoes for this *sambal* but they can be fresh or canned. If fresh, peel them (see glossary); if canned, lift them out of their liquid. This is another hot relish that could be smeared on a cheese sandwich, eaten with Fried Preseasoned Tempeh, or served as a condiment at all South Asian, Southeast Asian, and even Mexican meals.

(makes about 2 tablespoons)

2 tablespoons vegetable oil
1 cup peeled tomatoes, chopped
½ teaspoon cayenne pepper
¼ teaspoon salt
2 teaspoons lime or lemon juice

Heat the oil in a heavy 6-inch saucepan over a medium flame. When hot, put in the tomatoes. Stir and cook for 10 to 12 minutes, turning the heat down as the oil separates and the tomatoes begin to fry. Stir continuously through this cooking period. The tomatoes should turn a nice darkish color. Lift the tomato mixture out of the oil and put it in a small bowl. Add all the other ingredients and mix.

For information about ingredients and basic techniques that may be unfamiliar, see General Information, pages 418–36.

SPICY PEANUT SAMBAL

INDONESIA

This hot, nutty sauce is generally served on the side with the saladlike dish, Pecel (see page 73), about 2 tablespoons per person—or else it may be used as a dip for potato chips, fried *tempeh* sticks, or for raw, cut vegetables. In Indonesia, I have always seen it made in a mortar but you could use a blender instead.

(makes about ½ cup)

3 to 4 fresh hot green chilies, sliced into thin rounds
4 cloves garlic, peeled
¼ cup fried or roasted unsalted peanuts
5 teaspoons Japanese soy sauce
4 teaspoons lime juice
4 teaspoons tamarind paste
4 teaspoons palm sugar

If you are using a mortar, pound the chilies and garlic first. When they are well mashed, add the peanuts. Pound them too. I like to leave the peanuts a little grainy, but you could pound them until they are quite smooth. Now add the soy sauce, lime juice, tamarind paste, and palm sugar. Pound gently to mix. Add about 2 tablespoons plus 2 teaspoons water to get a thickish sauce with about the consistency of prepared English mustard. If you are using a blender, put all ingredients, as well as 2 tablespoons plus 2 teaspoons water into the blender container. Blend until smooth. If the sauce seems too thick, add another teaspoon of water.

Usha's

HOT AND SPICY HYDERABADI TOMATO CHUTNEY

INDIA

This is a perky relish to have around in the refrigerator. A dollop of it could brighten up almost any meal. It *is* garlicky and it *is* hot. It is *not* sweet. Instead, it has the natural tartness of fresh tomatoes.

(makes ¾ cup)

1 pound red-ripe tomatoes, peeled, and finely chopped (about 1¾ cups)
1 teaspoon finely grated fresh ginger
1 teaspoon well-mashed garlic pulp
½ teaspoon ground turmeric
¼ teaspoon cayenne pepper
4 tablespoons vegetable oil
4 cloves garlic, peeled
1 teaspoon whole cumin seeds
½ teaspoon whole black mustard seeds
¼ teaspoon whole fenugreek seeds
2 whole dried hot red peppers
½ teaspoon salt, or to taste

Put the chopped tomatoes, ginger, garlic pulp (*not* the whole cloves), turmeric, and cayenne in a bowl and mix.

Heat the oil in a 7- to 8-inch skillet over a medium flame. When hot, put in the cloves of garlic. Stir and fry until they are brown. Add the cumin seeds, mustard seeds, and fenugreek seeds. Let the seeds sizzle for 2 seconds. Put in the red peppers. Stir them once; they should swell up and turn dark red. Now put in the tomato mixture (keep face averted). Stir and cook on medium heat for 10 to 12 minutes or until tomatoes are fairly dry. You should have about ¾ cup chutney, but this could vary with the water content of the tomatoes. Add the salt and mix it in.

Serve hot, cold, or at room temperature. Store in a jar in a refrigerator. The chutney should last at least a week.

FRESH CHINESE PARSLEY AND MINT CHUTNEY

INDIA

This chutney may be served with almost any Indian meal. It makes an excellent—and nutritious—dip for Vegetable Pakoris.

(serves 6)

¾ cup chopped fresh Chinese parsley,
  firmly packed
½ cup chopped fresh mint, firmly packed
1 fresh hot green chili (optional)
1 tablespoon lemon juice
¾ cup plain yogurt
¼ to ½ teaspoon salt

Put the Chinese parsley, mint, green chili, lemon juice, and 3 tablespoons water into the container of a blender or food processor. Blend until smooth, pushing down, if necessary, with a rubber spatula.

Beat the yogurt in a small bowl until it is creamy. Add the mixture from the blender and fold in. Add ¼ teaspoon of the salt, mix, and taste. Add more salt if you need it.

TAMARIND-MINT CHUTNEY FOR SNACK FOODS

INDIA

Throughout North India, there are certain chutneys that are associated just with snack foods, foods like *samosas* or potato patties, or lentil patties. These chutneys tend to be sour or sweet and sour and frequently they are poured over savory foods in order to provide a contrast of flavor. Here is a fairly typical sweet-and-sour chutney in which tamarind is combined with mint and Chinese parsley. It is quite wonderful when swirled over lightly beaten and seasoned yogurt.

(makes 1 cup)

1 heaping tablespoon chopped Chinese parsley
1 heaping tablespoon chopped mint
2 tablespoons chopped *gur* (jaggery) or
  dark brown sugar
A ¾-inch cube of fresh ginger, peeled and chopped
¼ teaspoon pounded or ground *kala namak* (black
  salt)
⅔ cup tamarind paste
⅛ teaspoon freshly ground black pepper
⅛ to ¼ teaspoon cayenne pepper
1 teaspoon ground, roasted cumin seeds

Put the Chinese parsley, mint, *gur*, ginger, *kala namak* and 4 tablespoons water into the container of an electric blender or food processor. Blend until you have a smooth paste. Mix contents of the blender with the tamarind paste (use a nonmetallic or stainless-steel bowl). Add all the remaining ingredients. Mix well and keep covered in the refrigerator until ready to use.

For information about ingredients and basic techniques that may be unfamiliar, see General Information, pages 418–36.

SOUTH INDIAN COCONUT CHUTNEY

INDIA

In South India, *chana dal*, small yellow split peas, are often used as a flavoring. They are fried in oil first and then either mixed with other roasted spices and ground or, as in this fresh coconut chutney, they are mixed with chutney ingredients and pulverized. The frying makes the *chana dal* very red and gives it an interesting nutty taste. This chutney may be eaten with Indian *dosas* and Mung Dal na Poora, with any batter-fried vegetables, or served as a dip for raw vegetables.

(makes about 1 cup)

1½ tablespoons *chana dal*
4   tablespoons vegetable oil
1   fresh hot green chili, sliced
½ cup chopped Chinese parsley
½ medium-sized coconut, split and grated
¼ to ½ teaspoon salt
4   tablespoons lime or lemon juice

Pick over the *dal*.

Heat the oil in a small skillet over a medium flame. Fry the *dal* in this oil until it is a rich reddish color. Remove *dal* with a slotted spoon (leave the oil behind—you do not need it) and put it into the container of an electric blender. Add the green chili, parsley, and ½ cup water. Blend until smooth. Now add the grated coconut, salt, and lime or lemon juice. Blend again, using a rubber spatula to push down the coconut, if necessary.

Pour the chutney into a stainless steel or nonmetallic bowl. It should have the consistency of thick batter. Add more water, if necessary. Check the salt and lemon juice. Cover and refrigerate.

Kamal's

SWEET TOMATO CHUTNEY

INDIA

This chutney may be served with almost all Indian meals. I love to eat it at tea-time, spread over freshly made *mutthries*. You could also eat it with toast!

(makes 2 cups)

2   pounds red-ripe tomatoes
¼ teaspoon whole fennel seeds
¼ teaspoon whole fenugreek seeds
2   cups distilled white vinegar
2   cups sugar
10 cloves garlic, peeled and very finely minced
½ teaspoon dried powdered ginger
2   bay leaves
¼ teaspoon ground mace
¼ teaspoon *garam masala*
¼ teaspoon cayenne pepper
About 1¼ teaspoons salt
¼ cup raisins

Wash the tomatoes and dry them thoroughly.

Grind the fennel and fenugreek seeds in a coffee grinder, spice grinder, or mortar.

Heat the vinegar in a 7½- to 8-inch-wide, heavy stainless-steel or porcelain-lined pot over a medium flame. When it begins to boil, put in as many of the tomatoes as the pot will hold in a single layer. Turn the tomatoes around for 15 to 20 seconds, then remove with a nonmetallic slotted spoon and place on a plate. Do all tomatoes this way. Turn the heat under the vinegar to a medium-low.

While the tomatoes cool, put the sugar into the vinegar and let it melt slowly. Peel the tomatoes and cut them into 1-inch cubes. Put the tomatoes and any accumulated liquid into the pot with the vinegar and the sugar. Add the ground fennel and fenugreek, the garlic, ginger, bay leaves, mace, *garam masala*, cayenne, and 1¼ teaspoons of the salt. Mix and bring to a boil. Now arrange the heat so that the chutney keeps boiling fairly rapidly—a medium-low temperature is usually about right—and let it cook this way for about 40 minutes. Stir every now and then during this period.

Add the raisins to the chutney and stir.

From now on the chutney needs to be watched more closely as it can stick on the bottom. Stir more frequently and continue to cook another 25 to 35 minutes or until chutney has thickened and is no longer watery. It should have a nice sheen to it. Remember that it will thicken some more as it cools. You should have about 2 cups. Taste for salt and add a bit more if you think you need it. Mix.

Allow the chutney to cool completely, put it in clean jars, and cover tightly. I keep my chutney in the refrigerator and it stays in perfect condition for months.

For information about ingredients and basic techniques that may be unfamiliar, see General Information, pages 418–36.

APRICOT CHUTNEY WITH RAISINS AND CURRANTS
INDIA

In North India, we often make a chutney out of the flesh of a sour, dried plum known as *aloo bokhara* (the plum of Bokhara). I have changed that recipe somewhat and used the more available dried apricots instead. I find that this sweet-and-sour, pectin-rich fruit makes for a superb chutney.

(makes about 4 cups)

1 pound dried apricots
10 large cloves garlic, peeled and coarsely chopped
A 1 × 3-inch piece of fresh ginger, peeled and
   coarsely chopped
1¼ cups red wine vinegar
2 cups sugar
¼ teaspoon salt
⅛ to ¾ teaspoon cayenne pepper
¾ cup golden raisins
½ cup currants

Put the apricots in a bowl. Pour 4 cups of hot water over them and let them soak for an hour.

Put the garlic and ginger into the container of an electric blender or a food processor along with ¼ cup of the vinegar. Blend until smooth.

Empty the apricots and their soaking liquid into a heavy stainless-steel or porcelain-lined pot. Add the garlic-ginger mixture, the remaining vinegar, sugar, salt, and cayenne. Bring to a boil. Simmer on a medium flame, stirring frequently, for 45 minutes. Do not let the chutney catch at the bottom of the pot. Lower heat if necessary. Add the raisins and currants and cook, stirring, another half hour or until chutney takes on a thick, glazed look. (Remember that the chutney will thicken slightly as it cools.) Let the chutney cool and store, refrigerated, in lidded glass or ceramic jars.

GOAN CABBAGE SALAD

INDIA

The Goan peasants on the west coast of India eat this salad with many of their simple meals. Though carrots are not normally added to the salad, I find that they provide a nice contrast of colors. This salad gets sharper in taste as the hours and days go on. It can be kept for several weeks. You could serve it with almost any bean dish in this book.

(serves 4–6)

4   cups finely shredded cabbage
1   carrot, trimmed, peeled, and cut into 1½-inch-long julienne strips
1 to 3 fresh hot green chilies, cut into fine, 1½-inch-long shreds
2½ cups distilled, white vinegar
1½ tablespoons salt

Put the shredded cabbage, carrot, and green chilies into a clean, wide-mouthed quart jar. Mix the vinegar with the salt and pour that into the jar. Mix with a clean spoon. Cover, and leave for an hour.

PICKLED GREEN CHILIES

INDIA

Here is my family's recipe for a fiery pickle that combines three of God's most potent creations—hot green chilies, cayenne, and mustard. It is astoundingly good but only recommended for the stout of heart. There is no getting away from it—it is hot. Just as the English use droplets of their "made" mustard on their foods, so do we in India add the minutest portions of this pickle to whatever else we may be eating. It works wonders with all kinds of foods, perking up anything from cheese sandwiches to tomato salads.

(makes about 1½ cups)

½ pound (about 2 well-packed cups) fresh hot green chilies
4   tablespoons whole black mustard seeds
4   teaspoons salt
1   teaspoon cayenne or other hot ground red pepper
A 1-inch cube of fresh ginger, peeled and minced
2   tablespoons mustard oil
3   tablespoons lemon juice

Wipe off each green chili with a damp cloth. Spread out on a tray and leave to dry in a sunny or airy place.

Grind the mustard seeds to a powder in a coffee grinder or other spice grinder.

Trim away the stems of the green chilies and then slice them crosswise into ⅛-inch-thick rounds. (You may want to wear fine rubber gloves while doing this. If not, refrain from touching any part of your face before washing your hands thoroughly with soap and water.)

Combine the green chilies, ground mustard, salt, cayenne, and ginger in a bowl. Mix well.

Heat the oil in a small skillet or a very small pot over a medium flame. As soon as the oil begins to smoke, turn off the flame and let the oil cool completely. Pour the oil over the seasoned green chilies and mix well. Put the chili mixture into a 2-cup jar or crock and cover with a nonmetallic lid. Put the jar in a warm sunny spot and let it get as many hours of sunlight as you can manage in the next twenty-four hours. Shake the jar a few times during this period.

On the following day, add the lemon juice. Put the lid back on and shake the jar thoroughly. For the next few days, put the jar out in a warm, sunny spot in the daytime and, if that spot is outdoors, bring the jar in at night. The pickle should take 3 to 4 days to mature in the summer and up to 7 days in the winter. The pickle is ready when it has turned slightly sour and the green chilies have lost their bright-green color. It may now be refrigerated.

My Grandmother's
SOUR LIME PICKLE
INDIA

This is a simple version of my grandmother's black lime pickle, the one I wrote about but did not give a recipe for in my last cookbook. It is salty and sour. The only "heat" it has comes from black pepper. I grew up on this pickle and can recall almost no picnic, banquet, or, for that matter, car journey, that wasn't associated with it. Apart from its excellent taste, my grandmother insisted that the pickle had a very "settling" effect on the stomach. As children, we often sucked on it the way American kids do on lollipops, while we watched an itinerant puppet show or giggled our way through a mock monkey wedding, another traveling show that still goes from house to house in India. My grandmother's pickle, which turned darker—and better—as the months rolled on, was quite unlike the yellowish or greenish sweet or hot lime pickles that we ate in other Indian homes. Ours was definitely considered superior.

(fills a 1-quart jar)

6   unblemished limes
1   teaspoon whole black peppercorns
4   large black cardamom pods
2   teaspoons whole cumin seeds
A 2-inch stick of cinnamon, broken up a bit
12 whole cloves
6   teaspoons salt
6   tablespoons lime juice

For information about ingredients and basic techniques that may be unfamiliar, see General Information, pages 418–36.

Wipe the 6 limes with a damp cloth and leave to dry off in the sun or in an airy place.

Put the black peppercorns, black cardamoms (skin and all), cumin seeds, cinnamon, and cloves into the container of a coffee grinder or other spice grinder. Grind as fine as possible. Empty the spices into a cup. Add the salt and mix.

Find a wide-mouthed jar or crock that will hold the 6 limes easily with enough room to shake them around. I use a jar with a 5-cup capacity.

Quarter the limes lengthwise in such a way that the four sections remain attached at the bottom. Remove seeds, if any.

Divide the spice mixture into six parts. "Stuff" one portion into each of the limes, rubbing the spices well into the cut section. Close up the limes and put them, cut side up, into the jar. Cover the jar with a nonmetallic lid and place it in a warm, sunny spot for as many hours of sunlight as you can manage to get in the next 24 hours.

On the following day, add the 6 tablespoons of lime juice to the pickle jar. Cover and shake well. For the next month, put the jar in a warm, sunny spot in the daytime and then, if that spot is outdoors, bring the pickle in at night. Shake the jar three or four times a day. The pickle is still not ready. You may discontinue putting it out in the sun, but continue to shake the jar for another month. You may now begin to remove wedges of the pickle for eating. Do not refrigerate the pickle and remember that it will keep improving with age.

To serve four people, remove two wedges and then cut each wedge into halves. Arrange these halves in a small, shallow bowl and set the bowl in the center of the table along with other chutneys and relishes.

CAULIFLOWER AND WHITE RADISH PICKLED IN WATER

INDIA

You may substitute turnip slices for the radish in this recipe. Peeled and sliced carrots, peeled and sliced kohlrabi, as well as scraped and sliced lotus roots, may also be added. Even though I have given cup measurements for the cut vegetables, it is best to weigh them.

(makes 3 cups)

½ pound cauliflower (½ smallish head)
½ pound white radish
1 tablespoon whole black mustard seeds
½ teaspoon ground turmeric
½ teaspoon cayenne or other ground hot
    red pepper
1½ teaspoons salt

Cut the cauliflower into slim flowerets that are about 1 to 1½ inches across at the head, ⅓ to ½ inch wide, and 1½ to 2 inches in length. You should have a little over 2 cups.

Peel the radish and cut it crosswise into ⅓-inch-thick rounds. Radish slices that are 1 inch in diameter or less may be left in rounds; radish slices that are 1½ inches in diameter should be cut into halves; radish slices that are bigger should be quartered. You should have about 1¾ cups.

Bring 3 quarts of water to a boil in a big pot. Throw in all the cut vegetables and bring to a boil again. Boil rapidly for 15 seconds and drain immediately, making sure that you save ½ cup of the boiling liquid. Spread the drained vegetables out on a platter and allow to cool off.

Grind the mustard seeds coarsely in a coffee grinder or other spice grinder.

Combine the vegetables, ground mustard seeds, turmeric, cayenne, and salt in a bowl. Mix well. Empty the contents of the bowl into a quart-sized jar or crock. Add the ½ cup warm reserved liquid. Cover with a nonmetallic lid and shake the jar well. For the next few days, put the jar in a warm, sunny spot in the daytime and if that spot is outdoors, bring the jar in at night. This pickle may take 4 days to mature in the summer and up to 8 days in the winter. Make sure to shake the jar at least three or four times a day. When the pickle is sour enough for your liking, it is ready. It may now be refrigerated.

Asha's
CARROT AND TURNIP PICKLE
INDIA

Traditionally, this sweet-and-sour pickle is sweetened with jaggery, a raw, lump sugar. Even though jaggery is available in most Indian grocery stores, it is generally rock-hard and not crumbly enough to use easily in this pickle. If you can manage to find soft, crumbly jaggery, do use it; if not, brown sugar makes an adequate substitute.

(makes about 3 cups)

½ pound carrots (about 2½ carrots)
½ pound young turnips (about 2 turnips)
5   tablespoons whole black mustard seeds
¾ to 1 teaspoon cayenne or other ground hot red
      pepper
2   teaspoons salt
1   cup mustard oil
About 3 tablespoons brown sugar or jaggery

Peel the carrots and cut into ¼-inch-thick rounds

Peel the turnips and quarter, lengthwise. Cut the quarters crosswise into ¼-inch-thick slices.

Put the mustard seeds into the container of a coffee grinder or other spice grinder. Grind coarsely.

Bring 3 cups of water to a boil in a 3-quart pot. Throw in the cut vegetables and bring to a boil again. Boil rapidly for 5 seconds. Drain thoroughly.

The vegetables need to be dried off a bit. Pat them with paper towels and then either leave in the sun for a couple of hours or place them in a 200° F oven for 45 minutes, all nicely spread out on a tray.

Make a paste of the ground mustard seeds, cayenne, salt, and ½ cup of the mustard oil in a bowl. Add the vegetables and mix. Spoon all the contents of the bowl into a quart jar or crock. Cover with a nonmetallic top and place the jar in a warm, sunny spot. For the next 4 to 5 days, make sure that the jar spends as many of the daylight hours as possible in a warm, sunny spot, indoors or outdoors. If it is put outdoors, it should be brought in at night. Shake the jar two or three times a day to ensure even pickling. After 4 to 5 days, the pickle will start to turn sour. Add the remaining ½ cup mustard oil and mix well. Continue to place

---

For information about ingredients and basic techniques that may be unfamiliar, see General Information, pages 418–36.

the jar in the sun for another 3 to 6 days or until the pickle has soured to your taste. (This process will take longer in the winter.) Now empty the contents of the jar into a bowl. Add 2 tablespoons of the sugar and mix. Taste for sweetness. Add more sugar, if you like. Put the pickle back in the jar. Cover. The pickle may now be refrigerated.

Sharad Nanavati's
SWEET-AND-SOUR LIME PICKLE
INDIA

I love to eat this pickle with Lentils with Spinach, rice, and yogurt. I also enjoy eating it with a cheese sandwich.

(makes about 5 cups)

6 limes
6 fresh hot green chilies
3 1-inch cubes of ginger, peeled
20 cloves of garlic, peeled
6 teaspoons salt
2 cups sugar
2 cups distilled white vinegar

Wipe off the limes and green chilies with a damp cloth. Leave to dry in an airy or sunny spot. Cut each lime, lengthwise, into six wedges. Cut the stems off the green chilies.

Cut the ginger into very thin slices and then cut the slices into very thin strips.

Quarter the cloves of garlic lengthwise.

Find a wide-mouthed jar or crock with a 5-cup capacity. Put in a layer of lime wedges at the bottom, with their cut sides facing upward. Sprinkle some of the garlic and ginger over the lime wedges. Lay a green chili over the garlic and ginger. Now sprinkle some salt over this first layer. (Make a guess about the number of layers your jar will hold. Mine takes six layers so I sprinkle 1 teaspoon of salt over each layer. You do not have to be too exact about all this.) Keep making such layers until the jar is full. Push down a bit, if necessary.

Heat the sugar and vinegar in a 7- to 8-inch-wide porcelain-lined or stainless-steel saucepan. When the syrup begins to boil, turn down the heat to keep up a fairly active simmer. Cook for 12 minutes or until you have a light syrup. Let this syrup turn lukewarm, then pour it over the layered limes in the jar. Cover with a nonmetallic lid.

This pickle must be put in a sunny area every day for at least a month. If it is taken outdoors, then it should be brought in in the evenings. If the top layer seems to float above the liquid, push it down every few days with a clean, stainless-steel spoon. After a month of sun, the pickle will still need another 2 to 4 weeks to mature. Taste it after 6 weeks and, if you like it, begin to eat it. Remember that this pickle, if any is left, will still be good enough to eat a year or more after you have made it. Long pickling makes the lime wedges turn almost gelatinous, and wonderfully tasty. It does not need refrigeration.

ATJAR KUNING
(Yellow Mixed Pickle)
INDONESIA

There are versions of this tasty pickle all through Indonesia. Basically, chopped-up or julienned vegetables are either blanched or quickly stir-fried in a little oil. They are then allowed to cook briefly in a "dressing" that contains, among other things, vinegar, lemon grass, ground almonds, garlic, ginger, and, of course, turmeric, which makes them all yellow. The result is a saladlike "pickle" that can be eaten as soon as it is made. It can also be refrigerated and eaten up to 5 to 6 days later. My pickle is only mildly hot. You can make it as hot as you like. As well as serving it with any kind of meal, I toss a little of it in with a green salad sometimes—it's very good.

(serves 4–6)

½ teaspoon sliced, dried lemon grass
1 teaspoon whole cumin seeds
¼ cup slivered, blanched almonds
½ teaspoon ground turmeric
½ teaspoon ground coriander seeds
¼ teaspoon cayenne pepper
2 cloves garlic, peeled and mashed
½ teaspoon peeled and very finely grated ginger
½ cup distilled white vinegar
3 tablespoons vegetable oil

¼ cup very finely slivered peeled shallots
½ cup peeled carrot cut into strips about 2 inches long and ¼-inch thick
½ cup green beans cut diagonally into 2-inch-long strips
⅓ cup strips green pepper, 2 inches long and ¼-inch wide
1½ cups cauliflower flowerets, 2 inches long, ¾-inch wide, and ⅓-inch thick
1¼ teaspoons salt, or to taste
¼ teaspoon sugar

Put the lemon grass and cumin seeds into the container of an electric coffee grinder reserved for spices. Grind to a powder. Add the almonds. Grind them along as well. Empty these ingredients into a small cup. Add the turmeric, coriander, and cayenne and keep the cup near the stove.

Mix the garlic and ginger and keep near the stove as well.

Mix the vinegar with ½ cup of water. Keep that nearby, too.

Put all your cut vegetables near the stove.

Heat the oil in a wok or heavy sauté pan over a medium flame. When hot, put in the shallots. Stir and fry for ½ minute. Put in the carrots, beans, green pepper, and cauliflower. Stir and fry for about ½ minute. Add all the spices in the cup as well as the garlic-ginger mixture. Stir for ½ minute. Add the vinegar-water mixture and stir once. Add the salt and sugar. Stir and bring to a simmer. Turn heat to low and simmer, stirring gently, for 2 to 3 minutes. The vegetables should stay crunchy.

For information about ingredients and basic techniques that may be unfamiliar, see General Information, pages 418–36.

ONIONS PICKLED IN VINEGAR
IRAN

(makes about 1 quart)

1 pound small, even-sized white boiling onions
15 cloves garlic, peeled
3 to 4 sprigs fresh mint
2 cups distilled white vinegar
3½ teaspoons salt

Peel the onions. Cut a deep cross into them, lengthwise, so that each onion is almost quartered but still stays attached at the bottom. Put the onions into the quart jar (you may have a couple left over).

Put the garlic cloves and mint into the container of a blender or food processor. Add ¼ cup of the vinegar (or a bit more, if you need it) and blend until you have a smooth paste. Pour in the remaining vinegar and salt and blend quickly to mix.

Pour this seasoned vinegar over the onions. Cover with a nonmetallic lid and set aside for 24 hours. The pickle is now ready. It may be refrigerated.

CAULIFLOWER PICKLED WITH DILL
IRAN

(makes 1½ cups)

6 ounces cauliflower
1 cup distilled white vinegar
1¾ teaspoons salt
12 whole black peppercorns
1 to 2 whole dried hot red peppers
¼ cup finely chopped fresh dill, or 1 teaspoon dried
2 cloves garlic, peeled and slivered

Cut the cauliflower into flowerets about 1½ to 2 inches long, ¾-inch wide, and ⅓-inch thick.

Mix the vinegar, salt, peppercorns, red pepper, dill, and garlic in a cup.

Bring 6 cups of water to a rolling boil. Put in the cauliflower and bring to a boil again. Immediately empty the pot into a colander set in the sink.

Put the flowerets in a jar that holds 1½ cups easily. Pour the seasoned vinegar over them. Cover with a nonmetallic top and set aside for 12 hours. The pickle is now ready. It may be refrigerated.

CABBAGE TSUKEMONO
(Salted Cabbage Pickle)
JAPAN

If you are using part of a Chinese cabbage, as I did here, cut it in half lengthwise, and core it before proceeding with the recipe. If half of the cabbage does not add up to 1¼ pounds, take some from the second half.

The Japanese usually make their pickles in large quantities. If you consume these pickles in vast amounts, you may easily double or quadruple the recipe. Just remember that the Japanese serve pickles in very tiny portions at each meal.

(makes about 2 cups)

1¼ pounds Chinese cabbage, cut in
  half lengthwise and cored
1 tablespoon plus 1 teaspoon salt

Wash the cabbage off and cut it crosswise into
2-inch-wide sections. Put in a glass or plastic bowl.
Add the salt and rub it well into the leaves. Find a
ceramic or glass plate that will not only sit on top
of the cabbage leaves inside the bowl, but will also
sink down with them as they reduce in bulk. Put
this plate on top of the cabbage and then put a
heavy jar, filled with water, on top of the plate.

The cabbage will soon begin to sweat profusely
and water will begin to accumulate. You may have
to adjust your jar as it might decide to tilt this way
or that. In about 3 to 4 days the pickle will probably have soured enough. If it has not, leave it
longer.

Put the pickle and its liquid into a jar and refrigerate.

To serve, remove as much pickle as you need.
Wash it off to rid it of extra saltiness, make a wad
of it, and then cut it crosswise into ½-inch-wide
sections. Each person should be served no more
than 1 cubic inch of pickle. Put this tiny portion
in the center of small individual plates or very
small individual bowls. It is traditional to dot one's
pickles with soy sauce before eating them.

KOMBU RELISH
JAPAN

Like most Japanese relishes, very little of this is
served with each meal, perhaps 4 to 5 slices on a
small plate that also holds other salty vegetable
preserves and pickles. The Japanese love to end
meals with plain rice, pickles, and tea.

(makes about ⅔ cup)

A piece of *kombu*
3 tablespoons rice vinegar
5 tablespoons soy sauce
3 tablespoons sugar
1 tablespoon *mirin*
1 tablespoon roasted sesame seeds

Use *kombu* that has previously been used to make
broth. Its original size when dry would have been
about 7 × 4 inches. Cut it into ½-inch squares. If
you wish to start out with a fresh piece of *kombu*,
just wipe a 7 × 4-inch section with a damp cloth,
drop it in boiling water for a minute, cut it into
½-inch squares, and proceed.

Combine the cut *kombu*, 4 cups water (you may
reuse some of the boiling water), and 1 tablespoon
of the vinegar in a small pot and bring to a boil.
Cover, lower heat, and simmer 2 hours or until
kombu is quite tender.

Add the other 2 tablespoons vinegar, the soy
sauce, sugar, and *mirin*. Boil, uncovered, until liquid is reduced to 1 to 2 tablespoons. Turn off heat.
Mix in the roasted sesame seeds. Put into a small
jar and let the relish cool. When it is cool, it can be
covered and refrigerated. It should last at least a
month.

*For information about ingredients and basic techniques that
may be unfamiliar, see General Information, pages 418–36.*

QUICK-SALTED WHITE RADISH PICKLE

JAPAN

(serves 6)

¾ pound white radish
2 teaspoons salt
2 teaspoons Japanese soy sauce
2 teaspoons rice vinegar
¼ teaspoon sugar
A dash of 7-spice seasoning

Peel the white radish and cut it into ¼-inch-thick slices. Depending upon the diameter of the radish, cut each slice crosswise into halves or quarters. A radish that is 2½ inches in diameter should be cut in quarters. A radish that is 1½ inches in diameter should be cut into halves. Smaller radishes should just be left in rounds. Put the radish slices in a bowl. Sprinkle the salt over the slices and mix well. Find a plate that will not only sit on top of the radish slices inside the bowl, but will also sink down with them as they wilt. Put this plate on top of the radish slices and then put a heavy jar, filled with water, on top of the plate. Set aside for 4 hours.

Drain the radish well. Add the soy sauce, vinegar, and sugar and mix well.

To serve, arrange 6 to 7 pieces for each person in small, individual saucers. Sprinkle with a little 7-spice seasoning.

SHOYU DAIKON
(White Radish Pickled in Soy Sauce)

JAPAN

(serves 6–9)

¾ pound white radish
½ cup Japanese soy sauce

Peel the radish and cut into ¼-inch-thick rounds. Depending upon the diameter of the radish, cut each slice crosswise into halves or quarters. A radish that is 2½ inches in diameter should be cut in quarters. A radish that is 1½ inches in diameter should be cut into halves. A radish that is smaller should be left in rounds.

Put the radish slices in a bowl. Pour the soy sauce over them. Mix well. Cover and refrigerate for 24 to 36 hours. Stir and mix every 4 hours during your waking periods in order to ensure even pickling and a uniformity in color.

To serve, lift the pickle out of the soy sauce and place 6 to 7 pieces each in small, individual saucers. The pickle should, if kept refrigerated, last 5 to 6 days. It goes well with most Japanese, Korean, and Chinese dishes.

GINGER QUICK-PICKLED IN SOY SAUCE

CHINA

It is best to make this dish with young ginger, the kind that has a pale golden, almost translucent skin which seems to turn to pink at the extremities. If you cannot find young ginger, use the regular kind.

(makes about ½ cup)

2   ounces young ginger (about 2 1-inch cubes)
¼   teaspoon salt
½   teaspoon sugar
6   tablespoons Chinese thin soy sauce

Peel the ginger (if the ginger is young, you should be able to just scrape off the skin) and then cut it into paper-thin slices. Add the salt and sugar, toss well, and set aside for 1 hour. Pour the soy sauce over the ginger and cover. Set aside for 24 hours. You may refrigerate the ginger, if you like.

To serve, put about 6 slices each in the center of small individual saucers or tiny individual bowls. Pass along some soy sauce. I have a very small "tea pot" for soy sauce that I bought in Japan that is just perfect for this purpose. It is customary to dot the cucumber pieces with soy sauce before eating them. The Japanese often end their meals with rice, pickles, and green tea.

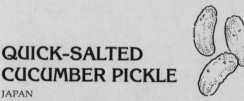

QUICK-SALTED CUCUMBER PICKLE

JAPAN

Make this dish only if you can find the smaller, pickling cucumbers. Japanese cucumbers, which are slim and delicate, are unavailable in America, as far as I know. If you grow them or can find them, do use them for this quickly made pickle.

(serves 4–6)

4   small pickling cucumbers (about ¾ pound)
1   teaspoon salt
Japanese soy sauce

Wash the cucumbers well but do not peel them. Trim the ends. Cut the cucumbers crosswise into ⅓-inch-thick rounds and put them in a bowl. Add the salt and mix well. Set aside for an hour. Drain thoroughly.

TOMATO, CUCUMBER, AND ONION RELISH

INDIA

(serves 4)

1   medium-sized, red-ripe tomato, peeled
1   smallish cucumber (pickling cucumber, if possible)
½   cup finely chopped onion
¼   teaspoon salt
¼   teaspoon ground roasted cumin
⅛   teaspoon cayenne pepper
1   tablespoon lemon juice

Cut the tomato in half, crosswise. Cup the halves, one at a time, in your hands—cut side down—and gently squeeze out and discard all the seeds. Now core the tomato shell and cut it into ¼-inch dice.

Peel the cucumber and cut it in half, lengthwise. Discard the seeds if they are big and hard. Cut the cucumber into ¼-inch dice.

In a small bowl, combine the tomato, cucumber, onion, salt, roasted cumin, cayenne, and lemon juice. Mix.

For information about ingredients and basic techniques that may be unfamiliar, see General Information, pages 418–36.

The Tawaraya Inn's
AOMIDAIKON
(Quick-Pickled Small White Radishes)
JAPAN

I had this pickle for the first time at the 300-year-old Tawaraya Inn in Kyoto. The radishes were small, about 2 inches long and ½ inch wide. While most of the larger leaves had been pulled off, the tender shoots had been left attached. *Aomidaikon* is a very popular accompaniment to *sake* and, indeed, compliments it very well, cutting through its silky potency with its own mellowed pungency.

If you cannot find white radishes of the required size, use slightly larger ones, halving or quartering them (lengthwise and crosswise, if necessary) to achieve the approximate size needed.

For this recipe, I bought 1 pound of white radishes—1 pound with all the leaves. Once I had trimmed the radishes, they weighed somewhat less than ¾ pound.

(serves 4–6)

1 pound small white radishes (see note above)
¾ teaspoon salt
½ cup slightly sweet yellow *miso*

Trim the radishes by pulling off all the large outer leaves—the tender inner leaves should be left attached—and by cutting off the taillike bottoms.

Peel or scrape the radishes. If they are too long or too thick, cut them up into pieces that are about 2 inches long, ½ to ¾ inch wide, and ½ inch thick. Put the radishes in a bowl and sprinkle the salt over them. Toss to distribute the salt and set aside for 4 hours.

Find a platter that will hold the radishes in a single layer. (You can do this in several layers, if you prefer.) Line the platter with a single layer of cheesecloth. Spread ¼ cup of the *miso* over the cheesecloth as if you were putting on a thin layer of peanut butter. Now cover the *miso* with another single layer of cheesecloth. Spread out the radishes on top of the cheesecloth. Do not let them overlap. Now cover the radishes with another layer of cheesecloth. Spread ¼ cup *miso* on this piece of cheesecloth and then cover the *miso* with a fresh layer of cheesecloth. Pat down the contents of the platter and then refrigerate for 1 to 4 days. If you like, you may cover the platter with another, upturned platter.

To serve, remove the cheesecloth. Rinse off the radishes lightly. Arrange them prettily in the center of a ceramic plate and serve with *sake* that has been warmed to just under the simmering point. (To warm *sake*, put it into a ceramic *sake* bottle and put the bottle into a pan of water. Heat the water. When the *sake* is hot, remove the ceramic bottle. *Sake* is served in small *sake* cups or small shallow *sake* bowls.) Or slice the radishes crosswise and serve with plain Japanese rice and tea at the conclusion of a Japanese meal.

WHITE RADISH PRESERVE
JAPAN

This is the very yellow-looking Japanese preserve that you might have seen in Japanese restaurants and grocery stores. The yellowness, unfortunately, comes from food coloring which I have eliminated in my recipe. As a result, the vegetable looks less appetizing, perhaps, but it is quite wonderful to eat. Like all Japanese pickles and preserves, this should be eaten in small quantities, either with a meal or at its conclusion with rice and tea.

(makes about 3 cups)

About 1½ pounds white radish (1 large or
  2 smaller)
1 cup sugar
3 tablespoons salt
4 tablespoons rice vinegar

Trim the ends of the white radish and peel it. Cut it in half lengthwise, and then slice crosswise into fine, ¹⁄₁₆-inch-thick pieces (a food processor can speed this up). Put white radish slices in a bowl.

Combine the sugar, salt, vinegar, and a cup of water in an enameled or stainless-steel pan. Bring to a boil. Stir the sugar so it dissolves. Pour the hot liquid over the radish slices and mix gently, pushing the radish into the liquid. Let cool. Put the radish slices and the liquid into a jar, cover, and refrigerate for 3 to 4 days. If kept in the refrigerator, this preserve will last indefinitely.

For information about ingredients and basic techniques that may be unfamiliar, see General Information, pages 418–36.

Kimchees

Just as a meal without wine is inconceivable for a Frenchman, a meal without *kimchee* is inconceivable for a Korean. *Kimchee* is not a liquor but a pickle—a hot, tart, often garlicky pickle that has an honored place at all Korean meals, from breakfast to dinner. *Kimchees* may be made out of several vegetables, like cucumbers and radishes, but the most popular *kimchee*—perhaps because it is the cheapest—is made with Chinese cabbage.

In the late fall, trucks piled high with the pale-green vegetable drive into towns and villages and the entire female population of the country succumbs to feverish bouts of pickle-making.

First the cabbage is washed and soaked in wooden tubs filled with salted water. It turns wan and pale under this initial treatment. Then the cabbage is smothered—or stuffed—with a mixture of ginger, garlic, scallions, salt, a little sugar, and lots of fiery red pepper freshly made from the new autumn crop. Now the cabbage is ready for a period of not-so-peaceful hibernation. It is packed into large, dark-brown clay vats—some waist high—loosely covered, and left to ferment. The fermenting takes its own time. It cannot be urged to hurry. The vats seethe and bubble. The cabbage eventually turns deliciously sour and is ready to be removed from the vats to be devoured.

In the severest winter months, *kimchee* vats are buried up to their necks in the earth and covered—first with a lid and then with hay. This keeps the pickle from freezing and helps provide necessary supplies until the coming of the spring.

Kimchees, full of vitamins and minerals, are not only eaten as a side dish, but also put into rice dishes, soups, and stews as a flavoring. A watery summer *kimchee* is an ingredient of *naeng myon*, one of Korea's spectacular noodle soups, while the regular cabbage *kimchee* is used to flavor everything from pancakes to country-style stews.

CABBAGE KIMCHEE
(Cabbage Pickle)
KOREA

(makes 2 quarts)

1   pound Chinese cabbage (about ½ a large head)
1   pound white radish
3   tablespoons salt
2   tablespoons finely minced fresh ginger
1½ tablespoons minced garlic
5   scallions, cut into fine rounds, including green
1   tablespoon cayenne or hot Korean red pepper
1   teaspoon sugar

If you are using a small, whole cabbage, cut it in half lengthwise, and then cut it across at 2-inch intervals. If you are using half of a large cabbage, cut it in half again lengthwise, and then crosswise at 2-inch intervals.

Peel the white radish, cut it in half lengthwise, and then cut it crosswise into ⅛-inch-thick slices. In a large bowl put 5 cups water and 2 tablespoons plus 2 teaspoons of the salt. Mix. Add the cabbage and radish to this water and dunk them in a few times, as they have a tendency to float. Leave the vegetables in the salty water. Cover loosely and set aside for 12 hours. Turn the vegetables over a few times.

Put the ginger, garlic, scallions, cayenne, sugar, and 1 teaspoon salt in another large bowl. Mix well.

Take the cabbage out of its soaking liquid with a slotted spoon (save the liquid) and put it in the bowl with the seasonings. Mix well.

Put this cabbage mixture into a 2-quart jar or crock. Pour enough of the salt water over it to cover the vegetables (about 2 cups). Leave 1 inch of empty space at the top of the jar. Cover loosely with a clean cloth and set aside for 3 to 7 days. In the summer, *kimchees* mature with much greater speed; in the winter, the process slows down unless the central heating is ferocious. Taste the pickle after 3 days to check on the sourness. When it is done to your liking, cover the jar and refrigerate.

To serve, remove just as much of the *kimchee* solids as you think you will need for a meal—a cupful is enough for 4 people—and put it in the center of a bowl. The *kimchee* liquid in this pickle is left behind in the jar and may be used to flavor stews and soups. Serve this cabbage *kimchee* with any Korean meal.

KAKDOOKI
(Pickle Made with Cubes of White Radish)
KOREA

(makes 1½ quarts)

1½ pounds white radish, peeled and cut into ¾-inch cubes
4   scallions, cut into fine rounds, including green
2   tablespoons minced garlic
2   teaspoons salt
2   teaspoons sugar
2   teaspoons cayenne or hot Korean red pepper

Put all the ingredients in a bowl and mix well. Cover and set aside for 6 to 8 hours.

Liquid will have accumulated at the bottom of the bowl. Pour this liquid and the seasonings in it into a 1½-quart jar. Now put in the cubes of radish, pushing them down so the liquid rises all the way to the top. Cover the jar loosely with a piece of cloth and set aside for 3 to 7 days. In the summer, *kimchees* mature with much greater speed; in the winter, the process slows down unless the central heating is ferocious. Taste the pickle after 3 days to check on the sourness. When it is done to your liking, cover the jar and refrigerate.

When serving, remove about 5 to 6 cubes for every person who is eating and put them in a glass or ceramic bowl. The liquid which is left behind in the jar may be used to flavor soups and stews when all the pickles have been consumed.

For information about ingredients and basic techniques that may be unfamiliar, see General Information, pages 418–36.

STUFFED CUCUMBER KIMCHEE

KOREA

(makes about 1½ quarts)

1½ pounds small pickling cucumbers (about 16)
3   tablespoons plus 2 teaspoons salt
¾ pound white radish
A 1-inch cube fresh ginger, peeled
2   tablespoons peeled and very finely minced
    garlic
6   scallions, cut into very fine rounds
1½ teaspoons sugar
2½ teaspoons cayenne or other ground hot red
    pepper

Scrub the cucumbers but do not peel them. Cut them across, slightly diagonally, at ½-inch intervals, letting the knife go only three-quarters of the way down. The cucumber "slices" should all remain attached at the bottom.

Make a solution of 5 cups water and 3 tablespoons salt in a bowl. Put in the cucumbers. As they will float, invert a plate, somewhat smaller in circumference than the top of the bowl, over them to keep them submerged. Set aside for 3 to 4 hours.

When the soaking period is almost over, prepare the stuffing. Peel the radish and cut it into very, very fine slices. You could use a potato slicer to do this. Now cut these slices crosswise into very, very fine julienne strips. The radish strips should not be longer than an inch. If necessary, cut them in half. Cut the ginger into paper-thin slices and then cut the slices across into very fine strips. Mix the radish, ginger, garlic, scallions, sugar, cayenne, and 2 teaspoons salt in a bowl.

Remove the cucumbers from their soaking liq-

uid and pat dry. (Save the liquid.) Put as much stuffing into the cucumber slits as they will hold easily, and put finished cucumbers in a bowl. Empty any remaining stuffing and stuffing juices over the cucumbers. Cover loosely and set aside for 8 hours.

Pack the cucumbers fairly tightly, but carefully, in a wide-mouthed, 1½-quart jar. Extra stuffing may be pushed in the spaces between cucumbers. All accumulated juices should be poured over the cucumbers. Push the cucumbers down slightly. Liquid should rise to the top. There should be ½ inch of liquid above the cucumbers. If you do not have enough liquid, pour in some of the salted water left over from soaking the cucumbers. Cover jar loosely with a plastic or ceramic top and set aside for 3 to 6 days or until the pickle has soured to your taste.

When you serve, the cucumber "slices" are neatly separated with a knife and arranged on a small plate.

DONG CHIMI
(White Radish Water Kimchee)
KOREA

Koreans serve water *kimchees* with nearly all their meals. Because of its cooling liquid, this pickle is particularly popular in the summer months. It is also used in the making of that delicious cold noodle soup, Naeng Myon (see page 294).

(makes about 5 cups)

½ pound white radish (without leaves)
½ pound turnips
2 scallions
1 clove garlic, peeled
A ¾-inch cube of ginger, peeled
½ to 1 fresh hot green chili
¼ teaspoon cayenne or other ground hot red pepper
4 teaspoons salt
½ teaspoon all-purpose white flour
½ teaspoon sugar

Peel the white radish and then cut it into rectangles that are roughly 1½ inches long, ½-inch wide, and ½-inch thick. Peel the turnips and cut them into similar rectangles.

Cut the scallions into 1½-inch sections and then cut the sections lengthwise into very thin strips.

Cut the garlic into very thin matchstick strips that are the length of the clove.

Cut the ginger into very fine slices and then cut the slices lengthwise into very thin strips.

Cut the green chili in half lengthwise and remove the seeds. Cut the halves into thin, 1½-inch-long strips.

Combine the radish, turnips, scallions, garlic, ginger, green chili, cayenne, and 2 teaspoons of the salt in a stainless-steel or nonmetallic bowl. Mix well. Cover loosely and set aside for 8 to 10 hours.

Put the flour in a small bowl. Slowly add 1 tablespoon of water to make a smooth paste. Add another 3 tablespoons of water and mix well. In a 1½-quart pot, combine 4 cups water, 2 teaspoons salt, and the sugar. Stir the flour mixture once and pour it into the pot. Stir again and bring to a boil. Turn heat to low and simmer very gently for 10 minutes. Turn off the heat and let the mixture cool completely.

Pour this cooled mixture into the radish bowl and mix. The *kimchee* may now be left in the bowl to sour or may be emptied into a wide-mouthed 1½-quart jar. Cover loosely with anything nonmetallic. The pickle should be ready in 1½ to 3 days in summer and 3 to 6 days in winter. Remove just a little bit of the liquid each day and taste it. When the liquid has soured to your satisfaction, the pickle is ready. It may now be covered more securely, again with something nonmetallic, and refrigerated.

For information about ingredients and basic techniques that may be unfamiliar, see General Information, pages 418–36.

SPICY TURNIP PICKLE

KOREA

(makes about 1 cup and serves 6–8)

2 small turnips (about 5 ounces without leaves)
1½ teaspoons salt
1 whole dried hot red pepper, coarsely crushed in
    a mortar
1 tablespoon minced scallions
3 cloves garlic, peeled and minced
¼ teaspoon sugar

Peel the turnips and cut them in half, lengthwise. Now cut them crosswise into ¹⁄₁₆-inch-thick, half-moon-shaped slices. Put turnip slices in a small bowl and sprinkle 1 teaspoon salt over them. Rub the salt in with your fingers. Set the bowl aside for 2½ to 3 hours, turning the slices over every half hour.

Drain the turnip slices and rinse under water. Drain again. Add the remaining ½ teaspoon salt as well as the red pepper, scallions, garlic, and sugar to the turnips and mix well.

Put the turnips in a small (12-ounce) glass jar. Pour enough water to cover the turnip slices. Cover the jar loosely with a small saucer and set aside, unrefrigerated, for 6 to 8 days. Once the pickle is sour enough for your taste, it can be lidded and refrigerated. Metal lids tend to corrode so it is a better idea to use plastic ones.

PICKLED GARLIC

KOREA

Most Asians believe that raw garlic is very good for all blood-circulation ailments. Pickled raw garlic exists in many versions and may be eaten with meals or cut up and put into salads. This Korean pickle is generally made with whole heads of green garlic. When served, the drained head is sliced crosswise into 3 rounds, exposing a very pretty cross-section of the cloves. All of the green garlic, including the skin, is edible. Since I could not find green garlic in New York, I have used whole peeled cloves instead.

(makes 1 cup)

1 cup large, peeled garlic cloves
½ cup Japanese soy sauce
½ cup rice vinegar
2 tablespoons sugar
½ teaspoon salt

Combine all ingredients in a glass jar or nonmetallic bowl. Cover, and set aside for 3 days.

Remove the cloves of garlic from the liquid and put them in a 1½-cup jar. Bring the liquid to a boil in a small pot. Turn heat to low and simmer, uncovered, until liquid has reduced to a little more than ½ cup (½ cup plus 1 tablespoon seems the right amount). Pour the liquid over the garlic cloves. Allow to cool. Cover and set aside for 3 to 4 weeks.

Desserts and Sweetmeats

Imagine a mound of shaved ice overflowing with a green-tea syrup and dotted with sweetened red beans. This ethereal summer dessert is served in one of Japan's most prestigious restaurants.

Asians are, on the whole, fairly familiar with European cakes, tarts, and jellies and serve them with the same easy familiarity that they show their own, more traditional desserts and sweetmeats. These traditional sweets are made with grains, such as rice, with beans, fruit, coconut, nuts, vegetables, and milk.

Halwas, of Middle Eastern origin, are now made in many parts of Asia. An enriching whole-wheat *halwa,* filled with nuts and raisins, is often made for new mothers, whereas carrot and gourd *halwas* are frequently made for banquets and feasts. If the idea of a vegetable *halwa* seems strange, you need think no further than a pumpkin pie or a carrot cake. The vegetables are grated and cooked slowly with milk until all the liquid evaporates. They are then sautéed in oil or butter, sweetened, and loaded with nuts. I have discovered that the humble zucchini makes a really delicious *halwa.*

In Japan, Korea, and China, the small red *azuki* bean is used to make a sweet paste that is very much like chocolate. Sweet "soups" are made with it, as well as stuffings for pastries and jellies. Rice creams and puddings are also very well liked, though as one travels further east, the use of glutinous rice becomes far more extensive. I like the sticky texture of glutinous rice. One of my favorite ways of eating it is with peeled slices of ripe mango, the way the Thais do it. In Thailand, glutinous rice is flavored with coconut milk, sugar, and salt and then served with some of the sweetest mangoes I have ever eaten. Extra coconut cream is offered on the side. The tastes and textures blend together most harmoniously.

The cassava root, or yucca, is a vegetable that resembles glutinous rice in its texture, especially when it is grated and cooked. The Filipinos add egg and coconut milk to this grated cassava and make a wonderfully sticky, chewy cake. Cassava can be found in most Spanish grocery stores. It is a shame that it is not better known.

You will find a recipe for the Middle Eastern baklava here, paper-thin pastry sheets layered with pistachios, walnuts, almonds, and sesame seeds; there is a Caucasian stew of dried fruit flavored with slices of fresh lemon; and you will also find a scrumptious sweet Chinese walnut soup that can be made fairly quickly in a blender. I have kept a whole section for Indian milk sweets because so many people in this country have been writing to me and asking for them.

Indian milk sweets are really a world unto themselves. The sweets that I have been asked about—such as *chumchum, rasgulla,* and *rasmalai*—are made with milk that is curdled, hung up briefly in a cheesecloth, and then kneaded until it is smooth. The resulting cheese is called *chhena* in Bengal, where these sweets originated. This *chhena* is then formed into different shapes—diamonds, hearts or balls—and boiled in syrup. The shapes, whatever they happen to be, puff up as they drink in the syrup, and become spongy. The sweets are then finished off as tradition dictates: *chumchums* are taken out of the syrup and "frosted" with freshly condensed milk; *rasgullas* are removed from the boiling syrup and put in a cleaner, lighter syrup where they bounce around until they are served; for *rasmalais*, the *chhena* balls are removed from the syrup and put into a large pot of thickened, cardamom-flavored milk to cook some more, after which time they are cooled in their milky sauce.

It might be said here that many of Asia's sweetmeats are eaten as snacks and that dinners and lunches often end with a bowl of fresh fruit.

BANANA FRITTERS IN TEMPURA BATTER

JAPAN

(serves 4–6)

4 to 5 bananas
About 1 cup flour for dredging
Vegetable oil for deep frying

FOR THE BATTER
Freshly made Tempura Batter Number II, (see page
    76), using 1¼ cups ice-cold water instead of
    1 cup
Confectioners' sugar

Cut the bananas crosswise into 1-inch chunks.
Dredge lightly in flour.

Heat the oil over a medium flame to about
375° F.

Dip the banana pieces a few at a time in the
batter and then fry in the oil until golden. Remove
with slotted spoon and drain on paper towels. Do
all bananas this way. This much can be done ahead
of time.

Just before you eat this sweet, heat the oil again
over a medium flame. When hot, fry the bananas
again. This will make them crisp.

Shake confectioners' sugar on the fritters and
serve immediately.

MANGOES WITH GLUTINOUS RICE

SOUTHEAST ASIA

For those who have a passion for sweet, ripe mangoes, glutinous rice, and coconut cream, this dish
is an ambrosial delight. Slices of peeled, ice-cold
mango are served with glutinous rice steeped in
sweetened coconut milk. Once you start eating it,
it is almost impossible to stop.

(serves 4)

2 cups freshly cooked glutinous rice (see page 121)
½ cup coconut cream
½ teaspoon salt
¼ cup sugar
2 chilled mangoes*

*NOTE: Mangoes are almost never fully ripe when bought in this
country. Ripen at home by wrapping each mango in several
layers of newspaper. Then lay the mangoes in a basket or box,
covering with another few layers of newspapers. Leave in a warm
place until ripe. Chill mangoes as you would champagne—drop
into a bucket of ice and water for a couple of hours.

Combine the hot, freshly cooked rice with the coconut cream, salt, and sugar. Set
aside until cool.

Peel the mangoes and cut
two wide slices off the
sides of each.

In each of four dessert
plates, arrange a slice of
mango and a mound of rice.

*For information about ingredients and basic techniques that
may be unfamiliar, see General Information, pages 418–36.*

STEWED DRIED FRUIT
CAUCASUS

I love to sip the liquid—the broth—that dried fruits produce. Which explains the abundance of it in this recipe. If you prefer, you could remove the fruits with a slotted spoon after they have been sweetened and reduce the liquid somewhat.

This stew may be served plain or with cream or yogurt.

(serves 4)

4 large dried prunes
½ cup small dried figs
1 cup dried apricots
4 slices lemon
1 cup sugar

Wash and drain the fruit. Put in a pot with 4 cups water. Add the lemon slices and bring to a boil. Cover, lower heat and simmer gently for ½ hour or until fruit is tender. Add the sugar and simmer another 5 minutes or until sugar has dissolved.
Serve warm or cold.

LECHE FLAN
(Coconut Custard)
PHILIPPINES

(serves 4)

1 cup canned, unsweetened coconut milk (stir before removing from can)
3 large eggs
1 cup sugar

Preheat oven to 350° F.

Heat the coconut milk on a lowish flame. When it starts bubbling, turn off the heat.

Beat the eggs. Add ½ cup of the sugar and beat again until the eggs are light and creamy. Add the hot coconut milk slowly, beating as you do so.

Put the remaining sugar in a small heavy pot over a low flame. Stir and let the sugar caramelize. As soon as it melts and turns a brownish color (do not let it burn) pour it out equally into four 8-ounce custard cups. Now strain the custard over the caramelized sugar, dividing it equally among the four cups.

Put the custard cups in a baking pan. Pour enough hot water around them so it comes halfway up the cups. Bake for 40 minutes.

When the custards have cooled slightly, run a knife around the edges of the bowls and invert onto plates. Chill.

FIRNEE
MIDDLE EAST/SOUTH ASIA

This is one of those light, aromatic creams that both children and adults find very soothing.
Firnee is generally set in very shallow bowls.

(serves 4)

5 teaspoons rice flour (also called rice powder)
3 tablespoons plus 2 cups milk
⅛ teaspoon cardamom seeds
¼ cup sugar, or to taste
1 tablespoon chopped pistachios

Put the rice flour in a bowl. Slowly add the 3 tablespoons milk and mix to a smooth paste.

For information about ingredients and basic techniques that may be unfamiliar, see General Information, pages 418–36.

Set the 2 cups milk to boil over a medium-low flame. Crush the cardamom seeds in a mortar and add them, as well as the sugar, to the milk. As soon as the milk begins to boil and rise, remove it from the fire. Stir the rice paste in the bowl once again. Slowly pour the hot milk into the bowl, mixing with a whisk as you do so. Now pour the contents of the bowl back into the pot and place over a low flame and bring to a simmer. Stir frequently with a whisk and simmer very gently for about 15 minutes. Pour into four shallow bowls and allow to cool and set slightly. Sprinkle the pistachios over the top and refrigerate. *Firnee* is always served cold.

PEANUT TAFFY

MOST OF ASIA

Almost every nation in Asia makes taffies and brittles. What varies is not so much the nuts and seeds that they contain, but the type of sugar that is used. For this recipe, I have used one of the oldest forms of raw cane sugar in the world— jaggery. Jaggery is available in Indian stores but you could use palm sugar, date sugar, or even brown sugar.

When my mother made this taffy for us, she always used freshly roasted peanuts—the kind that one has to shell. I remember all of us girls would sit around shelling the peanuts and then blowing their inner skins away. If you do not have access to such peanuts, you may use fried, unsalted peanuts instead.

I use a pie plate which is 7 inches in diameter at the bottom to set the taffy.

(makes a 7-inch disc that can then be cut up)

1 cup roasted, shelled, and skinned, unsalted peanuts
2 teaspoons vegetable oil
6 ounces jaggery

Break up the peanuts into halves.

Brush the pie plate with 1 teaspoon of the oil.

Put the jaggery, ½ cup water, and the remaining 1 teaspoon of oil in a small pot. Bring to a boil. Cover, turn heat to low, and simmer until the jaggery has melted completely. Remove the lid. Continue to cook the syrup on low heat, stirring now and then as you do so. The syrup should reduce considerably and get very thick. On a candy thermometer, it should register 250° F. Now take the pot off the flame. Mix the peanuts in and quickly pour the mixture into a 7-inch pie plate. Spread evenly and let it cool.

Cut into squares.

SESAME SEED TAFFY

MOST OF ASIA

Follow the directions for the preceding recipe, Peanut Taffy. Substitute 1 cup roasted sesame seeds (see General Information) for the peanuts. The seeds, of course, can be left whole.

(makes a 7-inch disc that can then be cut up)

SHAKKAR-PAARA
(Deep-Fried Cookies)
INDIA

Shakkar-paaras are sweet, diamond-shaped cookies that are deep-fried and flavored with cardamom, as many Indian sweetmeats are. You could substitute cinnamon as a flavoring, if you prefer. *Shakkar-paaras*, in some form or other, are found all over the India-Pakistan subcontinent.

(enough to fill a quart jar)

½ cup sugar
2 teaspoons cardamom seeds
1½ cups unbleached white flour
2 teaspoons *ghee* or softened unsalted butter
2 tablespoons vegetable shortening
Vegetable oil for deep frying

In a small pot, combine the sugar with ½ cup water. Turn heat to medium-low and allow the sugar to melt completely and form a syrup.

Meanwhile, crush the cardamom seeds fairly finely, either in a mortar or by placing the seeds between two sheets of waxed paper and pounding gently with the blunt end of a hammer. Add the crushed cardamom seeds to the sugar syrup. Turn off heat under syrup.

Sift the flour in a wide bowl. Add the *ghee* (or butter) and the shortening. Rub the *ghee* and shortening into the flour with your fingers until the mixture resembles coarse oatmeal. Now pour in the hot syrup (heat it if it has gone cold), mix, and gather the flour together so it holds and forms a ball. Knead lightly with the heal of your hand for a minute or two. Break dough into balls about 2 inches in diameter (4 balls).

Put oil to heat in a *karhai*, wok, or other utensil for deep frying over a medium flame. (You should have about 2 inches of oil.)

As the oil heats, roll out your cookies. You may roll and cut one batch at a time; while it fries you can roll and cut the next batch. Or, if you have the space, you can roll and cut out all the *shakkar-paaras* and fry them in several batches later. Dust your rolling pin and rolling surface *very lightly* with flour. Roll out a dough ball into a 6-inch round. Using a sharp knife, cut the round into 1¼-inch-wide strips going from north to south (as it were). Now cut diagonal strips, also 1¼ inches wide, going from northwest to southeast. You should thus end up with diamond shapes (see diagram). Scraps from the edges of the round that are not perfect diamonds can be collected to make another ball of dough. Make all *shakkar-paaras* this way.

The oil should be hot by now (about 350° F). Put as many *shakkar-paaras* into the oil as will fit in a single layer (a good-sized wok should hold all the cookies) and fry them about 2 to 3 minutes on each side or until they turn a golden honey color. Adjust your heat, if necessary. Remove with a slotted spoon, drain on paper towels, and allow to cool and harden. Fry all the *shakkar-paaras* this way, a batch at a time. Let each batch drain and cool.

Store the *shakkar-paaras* in an airtight tin or a wide-mouthed cookie jar; they should stay fresh for about a week.

For information about ingredients and basic techniques that may be unfamiliar, see General Information, pages 418–36.

ZUCCHINI HALWA

MIDDLE EAST/INDIA

Halwa is an Arabic word but the art of making it has spread all the way from the Mediterranean Sea to the Bay of Bengal. Among the most delicate of *halwas* are those made from vegetables. Here is one that I have adapted from the green bottle gourd. For all of you with overproductive zucchini patches, this is one more thing that you can do with that vegetable in the summer.

NOTE: Use a heavy pot with an even distribution of heat. I find cast-aluminum pots excellent.

(serves 4)

4　smallish zucchini (slightly over 1 pound)
2　cups milk
5　cardamom pods
2　tablespoons vegetable oil
6　tablespoons sugar, or to taste
1　tablespoon golden raisins
1　tablespoon pistachios, coarsely chopped

Scrub the zucchini and trim the ends. Grate coarsely by hand or in a food processor.

Combine the grated zucchini, milk, and cardamom pods in a heavy pot. Bring to a simmer over a medium flame. Turn the heat slightly lower and cook, stirring now and then, until almost all the milk has evaporated. Stir more frequently now and keep cooking until you cannot see any more liquid. Add the oil and sugar. Turn the heat down, if necessary, and keep frying for 10 minutes or until the *halwa* resembles mashed potatoes. Add the raisins and pistachios. Stir for another minute.

Serve at room temperature or cold.

WHOLE-WHEAT HALWA

MIDDLE EAST/INDIA

This simple, quick-cooking *halwa* is often prepared for new mothers who have recently given birth. It contains one of the most nourishing food combinations—whole grains (whole-wheat flour), nuts (pistachios, cashews, and almonds), dried fruit (raisins), and dairy products (butter and milk). It is also an excellent snack or dessert for growing children and active adults.

(serves 6)

1　stick (½ cup) unsalted butter
1　tablespoon blanched, slivered almonds
1　tablespoon pistachios, slivered
1　tablespoon coarsely chopped raw cashews
1　tablespoon golden raisins
1½　cups whole-wheat flour
6½　tablespoons sugar, or to taste
3　cups scalding hot milk

Take a square cake pan, about 8 × 8 × 1½ inches, and rub the inside lightly with the stick of butter. Set the pan aside.

Put the butter into an 8- to 10-inch, heavy-bottomed skillet and melt on medium-low heat. As soon as the butter melts, put in the almonds, pistachios, cashews, and raisins. Stir until the nuts turn a shade darker and the raisins swell. Do not let the butter burn. Add the whole-wheat flour and stir gently for about three minutes or until the flour is no longer raw and is lightly roasted. It will give off a wonderful smell of roasted wheat. Add the sugar and mix well. Add the scalding hot milk. Stir and mix. Cook, stirring, another minute or so.

Empty the contents of the skillet into the buttered cake pan. Spread the *halwa* and pat down evenly. Allow to cool. Cover with a plastic wrap until ready to eat.

Remove plastic wrap and cut *halwa* into 1½-inch cubes or diamond shapes. Serve at room temperature. This *halwa* may also be served warm, shortly after it is made.

BAKLAVA
(Filo Pastry Stuffed with Nuts)
MIDDLE EAST

Baklava is one of those sweets that looks as if it is very hard to make and is actually quite easy. The filo pastry itself may be bought from specialty, Middle Eastern, and Greek stores. Then, once you learn how to handle the sheets and keep them from drying out (for more details on filo pastry, see page 339), making baklava is really a breeze.

Just remember to be very generous with your butter and make sure that there is a layer of butter between every single sheet. And don't worry too much if you have a cake pan of a different size. (The cake pan I used was about 7 inches at the bottom and increased to about 7¾ inches at the top. *Officially*, it was 8 × 8 × 2.) Each pastry sheet is about 12 inches × 18 inches. How much of the sheet you will need to fold over to fit the cake pan can be easily adjusted.

(fills an 8-inch square cake pan)

FOR THE STUFFING
⅓ cup walnuts
⅓ cup pistachios
⅔ cup blanched almonds
¼ cup roasted sesame seeds
2 tablespoons sugar

FOR THE PASTRY
½ pound (2 sticks) unsalted butter, melted
11 sheets filo pastry (about ½ pound)

FOR THE SYRUP
2 cups sugar
3 tablespoons honey
1 stick cinnamon
5 whole cardamom pods (optional)

Chop the walnuts, pistachios, and almonds. (If each pistachio were chopped into 4 to 6 pieces, that would be a good indication of size.) In a bowl, combine the nuts, sesame seeds, and sugar.

Preheat the oven to 300° F.

Brush an 8-inch square cake pan generously with butter.

Keep all filo sheets that are not being used properly covered, first with a piece of kitchen parchment (or plastic sheet) and then with a damp towel. Remove one sheet at a time and work quickly.

Spread the first sheet in front of you on a clean, dry surface and brush generously with butter. Lay this sheet inside the cake pan. The sheet will overflow on two sides. Fold the short side over first.

For information about ingredients and basic techniques that may be unfamiliar, see General Information, pages 418–36.

Brush with butter. Then fold the long side over. Brush butter on the top. Repeat with two more sheets. After you have buttered the third sheet, sprinkle about 2½ tablespoons of the nut-seed mixture evenly over the top. Lay another buttered sheet over the nuts and seeds. Fold it as before and butter it. Put another layer of nuts and seeds. Alternate a sheet of pastry and a layer of nuts three more times. Top the final layer of nuts with 3 more buttered sheets. Butter the top generously. If there is any butter left, it may be poured over the top. (But do *not* pour the milky residue.) Using a sharp knife, cut the baklava to form five even rows. Cut again at a diagonal to form diamonds.

Bake at 300° F for ½ hour and at 350° F for another ½ hour.

Let the baklava cool.

Combine all the ingredients for the syrup with 1½ cups water. Bring to a simmer over a medium flame. Turn heat to very low and simmer, uncovered, for 8 to 10 minutes. Pour the hot syrup over the cool baklava, making sure it seeps through to the bottom of the pan.

BESAN BARFEE
(Chickpea Fudge)
INDIA/IRAN

(makes 144 little cubes)

1½ cups chickpea flour
1   cup vegetable oil
2   cups sugar
½ teaspoon ground cardamom seeds
2 to 3 tablespoons unsalted pistachios, lightly crushed
1 to 2 tablespoons coarsely chopped blanched almonds

Sift the chickpea flour. Heat the oil in a heavy, 10- to 12-inch skillet, wok, or sauté pan over a medium flame. Put in the sifted chickpea flour. Stir and fry 2 to 3 minutes or until flour turns a shade darker and is cooked (it should taste fried, not raw). Put the flour into a large bowl, stir once, and allow to cool.

Make a syrup with 1 cup water and the 2 cups sugar by bringing the water-sugar combination to a boil and then simmering very gently for about 20 minutes or until the syrup reaches a one-thread consistency. (To test this, dip in a wooden spoon and let coat slightly. Pinch some syrup off the back of the spoon with two fingers and then try separating the fingers. One sticky thread should form. This is the Indian method. If you have a better one, use it.)

Pour the hot syrup into the cooled chickpea-flour mixture. Add the ground cardamom seeds, the nuts, and mix well. Keep stirring until mixture begins to harden slightly. (It should still be pourable.) Pour into a 9-inch square cake pan, tilt pan so *barfee* mixture flows to the edges, and allow to cool. Cut into ¾-inch cubes.

Besan Barfee, if tightly wrapped in aluminum foil and then placed in plastic containers, freezes very well.

RAVA NA GHUGRA
(Sweet, Stuffed Pastry)

INDIA

Ghugras are small Gujarati turnovers that are stuffed with a sweetened, cardamom-flavored mixture of almonds, pistachios, raisins, and semolina. They are not baked, but deep fried. If packed in a tightly closed cookie tin, *ghugras* will last for several days.

(makes about 40 pastries)

1½ cups unbleached white flour
8   tablespoons *ghee*
¾ cup blanched almonds
½ cup shelled unsalted pistachios
¼ cup golden raisins
½ cup instant cream of wheat
1   tablespoon white poppy seeds
½ teaspoon ground cardamom seeds
¾ cup finely granulated sugar
Oil for deep frying

Make dough as for *samosa* pastry (see page 327), using the 1½ cups flour, 4 tablespoons of the *ghee*, and 5 tablespoons of water. Cover with plastic wrap and refrigerate.

Mince the almonds and pistachios very fine. Keep them separate. Set aside.

Heat the remaining 4 tablespoons of oil in a small, heavy-bottomed pot or in an 8-inch skillet over a medium flame. When hot, put in the raisins. Fry them for a few seconds, or until they swell. Remove them with a slotted spoon and put them with the minced pistachios. Add the cream of wheat, minced almonds, and poppy seeds to the *ghee* in the pot. Fry, stirring gently, until the cream of wheat, almonds, and poppy seeds turn a shade darker. Turn off heat. Add the pistachios, raisins, and crushed cardamom seeds to the pot. Mix well and allow to cool slightly. Mix in the sugar.

Take out the dough from the refrigerator and let it soften a bit. Break it into 40 balls. Keep balls covered with plastic wrap.

Flatten one ball at a time and roll it out into a 3½-inch round. Place about 1½ teaspoons of the nut mixture slightly off-center on the round of dough (see diagram). Wet the edge of half the round and fold it over to make a stuffed semicircle or a turnover. Press the seam so it closes and then flute it with a fork or with your fingers. Make all the pastry and keep in a single layer. Heat 1½ to 2 inches of oil in a utensil for deep frying over a medium flame. When the oil is hot (350° F) drop in as many turnovers as will fit easily and fry them until they are golden brown on both sides. Drain on paper towels. Do all *ghugras* this way. Allow to cool and then store in an airtight tin or cookie jar. This pastry will stay fresh for several days.

For information about ingredients and basic techniques that may be unfamiliar, see General Information, pages 418–36.

CARROT CAKE
WITH AN INDIAN FLAVOR
INDIAN STYLE

Over the years, as I ate American carrot cake, it occurred to me that it was so similar in taste to Indian carrot *halwa*. If one took away the cinnamon flavor and the walnuts, then added cardamom flavor and pistachios. . . . After experimenting for a while, I have come up with a carrot cake that tastes as if it came from the shop of an Indian *halvai* (sweetmaker).

(serves 6–8)

1½ teaspoons vegetable oil
1 cup unbleached white flour plus extra for dusting
1 teaspoon baking soda
¼ teaspoon salt
2 large eggs
¼ teaspoon ground cardamom seeds
1 cup granulated sugar
¼ cup softened *ghee*
1½ cups grated carrots, firmly packed
2 tablespoons chopped pistachios
2 tablespoons chopped blanched almonds
2 tablespoons raisins

I use a round, nonstick cake pan that is 9 inches in diameter and 1½ inches in height to make this cake. Rub it with the vegetable oil and then dust it very lightly with flour.

Preheat oven to 350° F.

Sift 1 cup flour with the baking soda and salt.

Beat the eggs well in a large bowl. Add the cardamom powder, sugar, and *ghee*. Keep beating until all ingredients are thoroughly mixed.

Add the sifted flour mixture to the ingredients in the large bowl and fold it in gently with a spatula. Add the carrots, pistachios, almonds, and raisins. Fold them in gently as well.

Empty the cake batter into the oiled and floured cake pan and bake in the preheated oven for 35 to 40 minutes or until a toothpick inserted inside comes out clean and the top is a golden-red color.

BIBINGKA KAMOTENG KAHOY
(Filipino-style Cassava Cake with Raisins)
PHILIPPINES

This coconut-flavored, raisin-studded cake has a delightfully glutinous texture. In the Philippines, thick individual pancakes are baked in earthen baking dishes lined with banana leaves to prevent sticking. I find that a nonstick cake pan makes a good substitute. Of course, I do end up with a larger cake, which then needs to be cut into wedges.

(serves 6)

2 cups freshly grated coconut
About 1½ pounds fresh cassava (yucca)
2 eggs
1 cup sugar
¼ teaspoon salt
¼ cup golden raisins

Put the grated coconut into the container of an electric blender or food processor and turn the machine on. Slowly add 1 cup hot water and let the machine run for a couple of minutes. Line a sieve with a triple thickness of cheesecloth and then balance the sieve in a bowl. Empty the contents of the blender or food processor into the sieve. Draw up the ends of the cheesecloth and squeeze out as much coconut milk as you can. Put this milk in a clear glass cup and set aside in a fairly warm place for 2 hours.

Preheat oven to 350° F.

Hold the cassava root under running water and peel it with a potato peeler. Grate the cassava coarsely, using a food processor if you have one.

Beat the eggs until they turn a pale yellow color. Add the sugar and salt. Keep beating until the mixture is smooth.

Thick coconut cream will have risen to the top of your coconut milk. You should be able to see it clearly through the glass. Remove 2 tablespoons of this cream and set it aside.

Combine the grated cassava, the egg mixture, raisins, and the remaining coconut milk in a bowl. Mix well.

Pour this batter into a round, nonstick, 9-inch cake pan and bake for 1 hour. Brush the top of the cake with the coconut cream and bake another 10 minutes. The top of the *bibingka* should be a nice golden-brown color. If it is not, place cake pan under broiler for a minute or so.

Let the cake cool and serve at room temperature.

CASSAVA SUMAN
(Small, Filipino-style Cassava Cakes)
PHILIPPINES

In the Philippines, these small cakes, containing grated cassava, coconut, and sugar, are wrapped in banana leaves and then steamed. They taste a bit like glutinous rice cakes, though they have a firmer texture. This *suman* is generally eaten at *merienda*—or afternoon snack-time, with some coconut sprinkled over it. What I do frequently is to offer it as an after-dinner dessert, along with neatly cut tropical fruit.

(makes 4 cakes)

About 1¼ pounds fresh cassava (yucca)
1¼ cups freshly grated coconut
¾ cup sugar

Hold the cassava root under running water and peel it with a potato peeler. Grate the cassava coarsely, using a food processor if you have one. You need 2 well-packed cups of grated cassava for this recipe.

In a bowl, mix the grated cassava, 1 cup of the coconut, and the sugar.

Spread out four pieces of aluminum foil, each about a foot square. Divide the cassava mixture into four parts and lay a portion onto the center of each of the pieces of foil. Pat each portion into a

For information about ingredients and basic techniques that may be unfamiliar, see General Information, pages 418–36.

cake that measures 3½ inches in length, 2 inches in width, and ¾ inch in height. Now wrap the foil neatly and tightly around each cake, making watertight bundles.

Arrange a utensil for steaming. If you are using a trivet that will be placed inside the water, make sure that the water level stays just below the top of the trivet. Bring the water to a boil. Put in the four bundles, cover, and steam on a medium-low flame for an hour.

The cakes are eaten at room temperature. Unwrap them when you are ready to serve them, sprinkling their tops with some freshly grated coconut. If you like, you could arrange individual dessert plates this way: Put half a cassava cake in the center, sprinkling it with some fresh coconut; around the cake, in a pretty ring, arrange a half slice of fresh pineapple, a slice of peeled, ripe mango, and 3 banana slices.

SWEET WALNUT SOUP—A CONTEMPORARY HONG KONG VERSION

HONG KONG

Served hot in the winter and cold in the summer, this delicious soup is really a dessert which is served at the end of meals. (I might add that my daughters like to eat it for breakfast and as a late-night snack.) Although it is made out of walnuts, it tastes, strangely enough, as if it had some grain in it as well.

The soup can be made easily and quickly, espe-

cially if you know what you are aiming for in each step. First the walnuts have to be blanched quickly in boiling salted water to remove a certain amount of scum. Then they have to be fried quickly in oil. The temperature of the oil is important as the walnuts must not burn or they will turn bitter. A good idea is to take the wok off the flame as soon as you have put the walnuts in. After that the walnuts are puréed in a blender. The purée, some water, sugar, and cornstarch for thickening are combined in a wok and the mixture cooked briefly. You could serve the soup just this way, but the addition of cream—and I suspect that the cream is British Hong Kong's contribution to this Chinese recipe—makes it exceedingly smooth and comforting.

It may be made ahead of time and reheated.

(serves 4)

2　teaspoons cornstarch
½　teaspoon salt
1　cup shelled walnut halves (a little over 3 ounces)
½　cup vegetable oil
3½ tablespoons sugar, or to taste
½　cup heavy cream

Mix the cornstarch with 2 tablespoons of water in a small cup and set aside.

Add salt to 5 cups of water and bring to a rolling boil. Drop in the walnuts and bring to a boil again. Boil for 10 seconds. The scum should rise to the top. Pour off half the water so the scum floats away and drain the walnuts in a strainer. Leave the walnuts in the strainer.

Heat the oil in a wok over a medium flame. When the oil is around 325° F (a medium heat—nowhere near smoking), put in the walnuts and take the wok off the fire. Stir and fry the walnuts for 5 seconds. Remove the walnuts with a slotted spoon and put them in a strainer placed over a bowl. Let them drain for a minute or two. Meanwhile wash and dry the wok.

Put the walnuts in the container of a blender and turn it on. Add 1 cup water, a little bit at a time. Blend until you have a fairly smooth mixture.

Empty the contents of the blender into the wok and set it to heat over a medium flame. Pour 1 cup water into the blender. Swish the water around so it picks up all remaining walnut paste and then pour this water into the wok. Add the sugar and mix. When the soup begins to simmer, stir the cornstarch mixture and add it to the contents of the wok. Stir and cook for 30 seconds. Put in the cream and bring to a simmer.

Ladle the soup into small Chinese soup bowls and serve as dessert or as a snack.

SWEET RED BEAN SOUP
CHINA

Like the preceding Walnut Soup, this is a dessert. In the winters, it is served hot. In the summers, it is served chilled with the addition of cream in more Westernized centers like Hong Kong. While this soup is generally eaten at the end of a meal, it may also be eaten as a snack.

(serves 6)

¾ cup *azuki* beans, picked over, washed, and
   drained
2 tablespoons long-grain or short-grain rice,
   washed and drained
6 to 8 tablespoons sugar
½ cup heavy cream (optional)

Put the beans, rice, and 6 cups water in a heavy pot and bring to a boil. Lower heat and simmer, uncovered, for 2 minutes. Turn off the heat and let the pot sit, uncovered, for 1 hour. Bring the beans and rice to a boil again. Cover in such a way as to leave the lid very slightly ajar. Turn heat to low and simmer very gently for 1 hour.

Pour the contents of the pot into an electric blender and blend until smooth.

Reheat the soup. Add the sugar and taste for sweetness. You may serve the soup this way. If you wish to serve the soup cold, add the cream and stir it in. Let the soup come to room temperature. Cover and refrigerate until chilled. Stir again before serving.

Pour into small soup bowls and serve at the end of a meal.

For information about ingredients and basic techniques that may be unfamiliar, see General Information, pages 418–36.

GREEN SNOW
(Green Tea Syrup and Sweet Beans on Shaved Ice)
JAPAN

I had this dish for the first time at the Kitcho restaurant on the outskirts of Kyoto. I was entranced by it. It was so light—and such a perfect way to finish off a summer meal. It consisted of a mound of shaved ice, overflowing with a green tea syrup and topped with sweet *azuki* beans. You may use one of two different types of powdered green tea for this dish. There is an instant green tea which is cheaper, and then there is the more expensive *matcha*, a fine powdered tea used in the elegant Japanese tea ceremony.

(serves 4)

FOR THE BEANS

¼ cup *azuki* beans

5 tablespoons sugar

FOR THE GREEN TEA SYRUP

½ cup sugar

4 teaspoons instant green tea or 1½ to 2 teaspoons *matcha*

4 cups shaved ice

Put the beans and 3 cups water in a small pot. Bring to a boil. Cover, turn heat to low and cook for 2 minutes. Turn off the flame. Let the pot sit, covered, for 1 hour. Bring to a boil again. Cover, turn heat to low and simmer 30 minutes. Add the 5 tablespoons sugar and simmer vigorously, uncovered, for another 10 to 12 minutes. Cool the beans in their liquid and then drain.

Combine the ½ cup sugar with ½ cup water in a small pot and bring to a boil. Turn heat to *very* low and simmer 3 to 4 minutes. Cool. Mix in the tea. (Taste as you go; add more or less tea, as you like.)

Pile a cup of shaved ice in the center of each of four ice-cream bowls. Divide the syrup over the ice. Divide the beans into four portions and scatter them over the top.

Audrey Chan's
CHINESE-STYLE JELLIED BEAN-CURD SWEETMEAT WITH A PEANUT TOPPING
SINGAPORE

The Chinese use agar-agar, a clear vegetable gelatin in the form of flat, noodlelike strips. As the packed wads generally weigh 1 ounce or less, it is a little difficult to tell you just how much you need in a recipe. The method that I have used for this book is to squeeze the ends of the strips together very tightly in my hand and to measure the diameter or thickness of the bundle just where I am squeezing it. Then I measure the length of the strips. This method is not too exact, but it does seem to work.

You need very soft bean curd for this dish. It needs to be mashed thoroughly. This can either be done by pushing it through a fine sieve and then beating it, or by whirring it in a food-processor or blender for a few seconds.

The main body of this sweetmeat is almond-flavored. For this, Audrey uses the bottled almond powder that is available in Chinese grocery stores.

(makes 16 2-inch squares)

Agar-agar strips, measuring 1½ inches in diameter
   when squeezed tightly, and 9 inches in length
½ cup sugar, or to taste
¼ cup almond powder
1 pound soft bean curd, mashed
½ cup roasted peanuts, crushed lightly

Bring 5 cups of water to a boil in a 2½- to 3-quart pot. Add the agar-agar and turn the heat to medium-low. Let the agar-agar melt completely. Add the sugar and let it dissolve. Blend the almond powder and mashed bean curd together with ⅓ cup water and stir into the agar-agar, mixing well.

Pour the contents of the pot into an 8-inch square cake pan. Allow it to cool slightly. When it has just begun to set, sprinkle the crushed peanuts over the surface. Let the sweetmeat set completely. Cut into 2-inch squares, cover, and refrigerate until ready to eat.

Chill for several hours before serving.

There is another way of serving this cooling dish as a dessert. Do *not* put the peanut topping on it. When it has cooled, cut it into rectangles that are 1 inch long and ½-inch wide. Put about 6 rectangles each into individual serving bowls. Add about 6 canned litchis and 6 canned loquats to each bowl, as well as a little of their syrup. Make sure that you have chilled the fruit thoroughly first.

Audrey Chan's
CHINESE-STYLE JELLIED WHOLE MUNG-BEAN SWEETMEAT
SINGAPORE

This is a simple and tasty sweetmeat, made with just whole mung beans, sugar, and agar-agar, the vegetable gelatin. See the note at the beginning of the recipe for Chinese-Style Jellied Bean-Curd Sweetmeat with a Peanut Topping, page 399, for directions on how to measure agar-agar.

(makes 36 1½-inch squares)

1 cup whole mung beans, picked over, washed,
   and drained
½ cup sugar
Agar-agar strips, 1½ inches in diameter when
   squeezed and 7 inches long

Combine the beans and 5 cups water in a heavy, 2½-quart pot and bring to a boil. Cover, turn heat to low and simmer very gently for 1 to 1½ hours or until beans are tender. Add the sugar. Mix. Put in the agar-agar. Cook, stirring occasionally, until the agar-agar has melted completely. Pour the contents of the pot into a 9-inch square cake pan. Allow to cool and set. Cut into 1½-inch squares.

For information about ingredients and basic techniques that may be unfamiliar, see General Information, pages 418–36.

JELLIED SWEET AZUKI-BEAN SQUARES

JAPAN

These small red beans (they are slightly larger than whole mung beans and are often labeled "red beans" in Oriental stores) are used in Japan and China to make sweetmeats of various sorts. A puréed and sweetened red bean paste looks very much like melted chocolate and is, in fact, used to make bars and cakes and sweet stuffings. Here is one of the simplest of these red bean sweetmeats—one that I was offered, along with green tea, in almost every Japanese home that I visited.

(makes about 64 squares)

½ cup whole red *azuki* beans, picked over, washed and drained
Agar-agar strips, 1½ inches in diameter when squeezed and 4 inches in length (see page 399)
1 cup sugar

Put the beans and 2½ cups water in a heavy, 1¾-quart pot and bring to a boil. Lower heat and simmer, uncovered, for 2 minutes. Turn off the heat and let the beans sit, uncovered, for 1 hour. Bring the beans to a boil again. Cover in such a way as to leave the lid very slightly ajar. Turn heat to low and simmer very gently (but the liquid should always have a few bubbles coming up) for 1 hour.

As the beans cook, cut up the agar-agar strips into ½-inch lengths with a pair of scissors and put them into a 1¾-quart pot. Add 1½ cups cold water and soak for 30 minutes. Now bring the contents of this pot to a simmer over a medium flame. Cover, turn heat to low and simmer very gently for 5 to 8 minutes or until all the agar-agar has melted. Turn off the heat. Leave the agar-agar covered in a warm spot.

When the beans have finished cooking, measure the amount you have. The beans and their liquid should add up to 1½ cups. If there is less water, add some hot water to make up the difference. Put the beans and their liquid into the container of an electric blender and blend until you have a smooth paste. Add the sugar. Blend again to mix. Pour this bean paste back into the pot in which you have been cooking the beans and bring to a simmer over a medium-low flame. Once it is bubbling, turn heat to low (there should still be some bubbles coming up) and cook, stirring all the time with a wooden spoon, for about 10 minutes. The mixture should now look like a very thick, chocolaty paste.

The agar-agar solution should still be hot and liquid. If not, put a low flame under it for a minute or two. Do not neglect the stirring of the bean paste, though, or it might burn. Pour the hot agar-agar solution into the bean paste. Stir and mix. Bring to a simmer over a medium-low flame. Now turn heat to low and cook, stirring all the time with a wooden spoon, for another 15 minutes or until the mixture resembles a thick chocolate sauce.

Pour this mixture through a strainer into an 8-inch square cake tin and allow to cool completely. It will set. Now cut the jellied paste with a knife into 1-inch squares.

HOW TO MAKE CHHENA
INDIA

Chhena is a fine-grained cheese that is used for making many Indian milk sweets. Its freshness is essential to the final quality of sweets. It does not keep well. Most sweets made with *chhena* should be eaten within forty-eight hours.

(makes about 1¼ cups)

2 quarts milk
¼ cup (approximately) lemon juice

Heat the milk in a large heavy pot. As soon as it comes to a boil, turn off the heat and slowly pour in the lemon juice, stirring constantly with a plastic or wooden spoon. *All* the milk should curdle, blobs of *chhena* separating from the thin, watery whey. (On rare occasions, all the milk will not curdle. You will see a few blobs of *chhena*, but most of the liquid will remain milky. In that case, bring to a second boil, add another tablespoon of lemon juice and repeat the process.) Leave the pot, covered, on a countertop for 10 minutes.

Line a sieve or colander with a man's handkerchief or a triple layer of cheesecloth.

(Put the sieve in a bowl if you wish to save the whey for cooking—use it instead of water.) Pour the curds and whey into the sieve. A lot of the whey will drain away. Lift the handkerchief by its four corners and tie the curd inside it into a loose bundle using a piece of twine. Suspend this bundle somewhere where it can drip for half an hour. (I hang the bundle on the faucet of my kitchen sink.) After about half an hour, the *chhena* should have dripped some more and be cool enough to handle. Squeeze out as much liquid with your hands as you can manage easily and empty the *chhena* onto a clean, smooth surface like a Formica countertop. Now knead the *chhena* by pressing it and spreading it out at the same time with the palm and heel of a flattened hand, gathering it up, and then repeating the process again and again. This technique is not unlike the "fraisage" used to incorporate butter into pastry dough, though it is much more thorough. Knead for 10 to 15 minutes or until the *chhena* is of a *very* fine, slightly grainy, spongy consistency, not unlike whipped cream cheese.

For information about ingredients and basic techniques that may be unfamiliar, see General Information, pages 418–36.

Snigdha Mukerji's
CHUMCHUM AND DILBAHAR
(Chhena Diamonds and Hearts)
INDIA

Made out of *chhena*, *chumchums* are diamond-shaped and often yellow in color whereas *dilbahars*, as their name indicates (*dil* means "heart," *bahar* means "spring"), are heart-shaped and may be white or yellow. Once the desired shapes have been formed out of the *chhena*, they are boiled in sugar syrup and then garnished with an "icing" of boiled-down milk—half-and-half in this case—as well as with cardamom-flavored crushed pistachios.

To make *chumchums* yellow, I use vegetable food coloring. You may omit the coloring, if you like. If you decide to make the sweets in two separate colors, boil the white batch in syrup first. Then do the yellow batch. If you do them together, the yellow color will bleed into the syrup and discolor the white sweets.

(makes about 16 pieces)

2 quarts milk
¼ cup (approximately) fresh lemon juice
2 cups half-and-half
2 cups sugar
4 whole cardamom pods
2 teaspoons fine-grained semolina
1 teaspoon yellow food coloring (optional)—use ½ teaspoon if coloring half the *chhena*
1 tablespoon shelled, unsalted pistachios, minced and mixed with ⅛ teaspoon ground cardamom powder

Make the *chhena* with the milk and lemon juice according to the recipe opposite, kneading it very thoroughly. Make a ball and set it aside.

Put the half-and-half into a heavy skillet or saucepan and bring to a boil. Turn heat to medium and cook, stirring frequently to prevent sticking, until it reduces to ¼ to ⅓ cup. Pour reduced half-and-half into a small cup and leave to cool.

In a large, 12- to 14-inch skillet or sauté pan (with lid, to be used later), combine the sugar, the cardamom pods, and 4 cups of water. Bring to a boil over medium heat. Once the sugar has dissolved completely, turn heat to low and let the syrup simmer for 2 minutes. Turn off the heat.

Flatten the ball of *chhena* and add the semolina to it. Knead again for 5 minutes, making sure that the semolina is well mixed in. If you are going to add the yellow food coloring to half or all of the *chhena*, do it now. Mix well and knead some more. Now make 16 firm, crack-free balls. Flatten the balls and make diamond and heart shapes. The diamonds should be no longer than 1½ inches, no wider than ¾ inch and no thicker than ¼ inch. The heart shapes may be 1¼ inches in length and width. If you have cookie cutters in these shapes, flatten all the *chhena* so it is ¼ inch in thickness and then cut out the diamond and heart forms. You will need to work the forms in your hands some more to make sure that they are tightly packed and crack-free. In order to make the sweets look more traditionally Bengali, round off all edges and points slightly.

Bring the syrup to a boil. Put in as many sweets as the skillet will hold easily in one layer, remembering that they will expand to 1½ times their size. Cover and boil on medium heat for 15 minutes. Every 4 minutes, lift the cover and pour 2 tablespoons of water into the syrup. Cover again and keep boiling. Remove the sweets with a slotted spoon and place on a platter. (If you need to do a second batch, add ½ cup water to the syrup and repeat the process.) The syrup may now be discarded.

Put about ½ teaspoon of reduced half-and-half on the center of each sweet. It will spread out a bit but should not cover the entire sweet. Nor should it dribble off it. Sprinkle the pistachio and cardamom mixture on top of the half-and-half "icing."

Like many Indian sweetmeats, *chumchums* and *dilbahars* are generally served at room temperature, either at tea-time—with tea or coffee—or after festive meals. But they may also be served cold. Arrange them in a single layer in a flat plastic container, cover, and refrigerate. You may keep them this way for 24 hours.

For information about ingredients and basic techniques that may be unfamiliar, see General Information, pages 418–36.

RASGULLAS
(Chhena Balls in Syrup)
INDIA

This is the sweet that you have probably seen in many Indian restaurants—white balls floating in syrup. When they were little, my children used to call them "squeaky balls" because the *rasgullas* squeaked a little as they bit into them. In India, *rasgullas*, perhaps Bengal's most popular sweet, are almost never made at home. They are made by professional *halvais*—sweetmakers—and sold in small, "take-out," terra-cotta pots. They are generally offered at tea-time, though they are sometimes served as dessert after a meal. But for me, *rasgullas* taste best if eaten just after someone near and dear has passed a final exam.

Let me explain. In Delhi, all final examinations for high school and college took place in the intense heat of April and May. That, of course, was bad enough. What was worse than sweating through the exams though, was sweating for the results, which never came privately in a sealed envelope as they do here. No, ours were boldly printed in a Delhi newspaper. If one managed to graduate at all from one's high school or college, all Delhi knew one's grades. So during the waiting period, students sweated and parents sweated as well.

When the results were finally announced, and if they were favorable, families did several things simultaneously—they hugged and kissed, made telephone calls to relatives who might have missed the news, and sent out for *rasgullas*. To pass an exam and *not* have *rasgullas* was quite unthinkable in our family. There would be a "tea-party" later with chilled mangoes and ice cream—and more *rasgullas*—but some *rasgullas* had to be bought immediately to "sweeten the mouths" of family members and friends who dropped by to offer their congratulations.

(makes 20 rasgullas)

2   quarts milk
¼ cup (approximately) lemon juice
5½ cups sugar
10 whole cardamom pods
1   teaspoon fine-grained semolina
3 to 4 drops rose essence

Make *chhena* with the milk and lemon juice according to directions on page 402, but *with this difference*. Hang up the milk curds for 2 hours instead of ½ hour. Knead the *chhena* thoroughly. Make a ball and set it aside.

You now need two batches of syrup—a thinner syrup for boiling the *chhena* balls and a slightly thicker one in which the balls can be immersed after they have cooked.

Put 3 cups of sugar, 6 cups of water, and 5 cardamom pods in a deep, 9½- to 10-inch skillet or sauté pan. Bring to a fast simmer over medium heat. Once the sugar has dissolved completely, turn heat to low and let the syrup simmer gently for 2 minutes. Turn off the heat. For purposes of clarity, I shall call this the first syrup.

Make the second syrup by combining the remaining 2½ cups sugar, 3½ cups water, and 5 cardamom pods in a medium-sized saucepan. Bring to a fast simmer over medium heat. Once the sugar has dissolved completely, turn heat to low and let the syrup simmer gently for 2 minutes. Turn off the heat. Put this syrup in a bowl (leave the cardamom pods in).

Flatten the ball of *chhena* and add the semolina as well as the rose essence to it. Knead again for 5 minutes, making sure that the semolina and the rose essence are well mixed in. Now make 20 crack-free balls, rolling each with just a little pressure between the palms of your two hands.

Bring the first syrup to a simmer over a medium flame. Drop the balls into the syrup. Bring to a simmer again. Adjust the heat so that the syrup simmers gently for 5 minutes. During this period, move the balls around and turn them over occasionally, using a *very* gentle touch. Make sure you do not damage the balls.

Turn the heat up and bring the syrup to what might be called a furious simmer. The syrup should look like a mass of tiny moving bubbles, but it should never boil over. Sprinkle the balls with 2 tablespoons of water, cover and cook for 10 minutes. During this period, the *rasgullas* should swell up.

Uncover, sprinkle another 2 tablespoons of water over the balls, cover and cook, simmering furiously for another 10 minutes. Turn off the heat. Using a slotted spoon, transfer the *rasgullas* to the second syrup in the bowl. (The first syrup can now be discarded.) Let the *rasgullas* cool. Cover and refrigerate for at least 4 hours or overnight. Serve at room temperature or cold.

Even though the syrup is essential for keeping the *rasgullas* moist, it is not eaten. If you put some *rasgullas* in a serving dish, offer a slotted serving spoon. This way, guests may take just the *rasgullas* and leave the syrup behind.

RASMALAI
(Chhena Balls in a Sweet Creamy Sauce)
INDIA

Rasmalai, a very close cousin of the *rasgulla*, is almost the same sweet, taken a step further. After the *rasgulla* is made, it is taken out of the syrup and soaked in half-and-half (rich milk is used in India). The half-and-half is then boiled down until it is creamier and it is further enriched with crushed pistachios and ground cardamom. *Rasmalai* may be made in a round patty form or in balls.

(makes 20 balls)

2 quarts milk
¼ cup (approximately) lemon juice
3 cups plus 1 tablespoon sugar
5 whole cardamom pods
1 teaspoon fine-grained semolina
3 to 4 drops rose essence
1 quart half-and-half
⅛ teaspoon cardamom seeds
1 tablespoon shelled, unsalted pistachios

Make the *chhena* with the milk and lemon juice according to directions on page 402 *with this difference*. Hang up the milk curds for 2 hours instead of ½ hour. Knead thoroughly. Make a ball and set it aside.

Put the 3 cups of sugar, 6 cups of water, and the cardamom pods in a deep 9½- to 10-inch skillet or sauté pan. Bring to a fast simmer over a medium flame. Once the sugar has dissolved completely, turn the heat to low and let the syrup simmer gently for 2 minutes. Turn off the heat.

Flatten the ball of *chhena* and add the semolina as well as the rose essence to it. Knead for 5 minutes, making sure that the semolina and rose essence are well mixed in. Now make 20 crack-free balls, rolling each with just a little pressure between the palms of your two hands.

Bring the syrup to a simmer over a medium flame. Drop the balls into the syrup. Bring to a simmer again. Adjust the heat so the syrup simmers gently for 5 minutes. During this period, move the balls around and turn them over occasionally, using a very gentle touch. Make sure you do not damage the balls.

Turn the heat up and bring the syrup to what might be described as a furious simmer. The syrup should look like a mass of tiny moving bubbles, but it should never boil over. Sprinkle the balls with 2 tablespoons of water, cover and cook for 10 minutes. During this period, the balls should swell up.

Uncover, sprinkle another 2 tablespoons of water over the balls, cover and cook, simmering furiously for another 10 minutes. Turn off the heat. Using a slotted spoon, transfer the balls to an empty bowl. (The syrup can now be discarded.) Pour the half-and-half over the balls and let them soak in it for 3 hours.

Take balls gently out of the half-and-half with a slotted spoon and put them in another bowl. Pour the half-and-half into a skillet or saucepan and boil it down until you have about 2 cups left. Turn off the heat. Crush the cardamom seeds finely in a mortar and mince the pistachios. Add the crushed cardamom, the minced pistachios, and the 1 tablespoon sugar to the reduced half-and-half. Pour this

---

For information about ingredients and basic techniques that may be unfamiliar, see General Information, pages 418–36.

half-and-half over the *chhena* balls. Allow to cool. Cover and refrigerate for at least 2 hours, and serve cold, as a dessert along with the creamy sauce.

Ismail's
SHEER KORMA
(An Indian Vermicelli Milk Dessert)
INDIA

My friend Ismail is a very good cook. He is more than that. He is a fast, relaxed cook. While other cooks labor and agonize in the kitchen, Ismail whips up exquisite meals with casual flicks of his hands. He never takes very long over anything. This *sheer korma* was cooked in less than 15 minutes, with Ismail talking, nonstop, about the Cannes Film Festival where he had just shown a film, about a holiday in Corfu, and about the latest Indian miniature painting that he had bought in London! Ismail takes all the seriousness out of cooking. This *sheer korma* is simplicity itself to make and it tastes wonderful.

Sheer korma is made with very, very fine *sev* — a kind of thin wheat vermicelli that is available only in Indian grocery stores. Ask for "Elephant" brand vermicelli marked "thinnest." The Indian stores also sell a vermicelli that has been browned. That is not what you want. You need the white vermicelli for this dish. To make *sheer korma*, you first brown the vermicelli in butter and then add milk, sugar, nuts, and saffron. You cook the *korma* until it thickens, which happens fairly quickly. That is all there is to the dish. You could, if you like, describe *sheer korma* as a glorious vermicelli pudding, which may be served hot, warm, or cold. If you want the pudding to be somewhat "flowing," use only 1 cup of *sev*; for a thicker dessert, use the 1¼ cups.

(serves 6–8)

¼ pound (1 stick) unsalted butter
1¼ well-packed cups Indian vermicelli, broken up into 2-inch pieces
1 quart milk
½ cup sugar
½ cup shelled, unsalted pistachios, minced
½ cup blanched, sliced almonds
¼ cup *charoli* nuts
10 threads saffron

Heat the butter in a 7- to 8-inch-wide, 2½- to 3-quart pot over a medium-low flame. Put in the vermicelli. Stir and sauté it until it turns an even golden color. Now add the milk. Turn the heat to medium and bring the milk to a boil. Lower heat again to let the milk simmer and add the sugar, nuts, and saffron. Cook, stirring frequently, for 3 to 5 minutes or until the *korma* has thickened.

Serve hot, warm or cold.

Sample Menus

The menus here should only serve as a guide to help you put together dishes of your choice. Even though I have indicated how different Asians eat their traditional foods, such information should only be used if it seems like fun.

TRADITIONAL KOREAN MENUS

In Korea, there is no great difference between breakfast, lunch, and dinner other than the number of dishes, which seem to increase as the day wears on. Most of the food, with the exception of the fruit, comes to the table at the same time. All food is

(THIS MENU IS IDEAL FOR THE SUMMER.)

Soy-Bean and Mung-Bean Sprouts Seasoned with Sesame Oil

Naeng Myon (Cold Noodle Soup)

Cabbage Kimchee

Cold Bori Cha (Cold Barley Tea)

Fruit

Oshitashi (Spinach with Roasted Sesame Seeds)

White Radish Soup

Carrots in Batter

Korean-Style Bean Curd in a Hot-Water Bath

Cabbage Kimchee

Honsik Bab (Rice with Barley)

Bori Cha (Barley tea)

Fruit

communal; only bowls of rice and glasses of barley tea are served individually. Each person is given a pair of thin, knitting-needlelike, metal chopsticks, long-handled spoons, and small, saucerlike plates. The chopsticks are for picking up solids, the spoon for liquids, and the plate for disposing of bones or for mixing individual combinations of foods. The fruit at the end of the meal always come peeled and sliced, with tiny forks, one for each person, embedded in them.

Bibimbab (Korean Rice with Egg and Vegetable Topping)
Cabbage Kimchee or Spicy Turnip Pickle
Bori Cha (Barley Tea)
Fruit

Korean-Style Cucumber Salad
Roasted Laver
Mushrooms Cooked in Aluminum Foil with Korean Dipping Sauce Number I
Noodles with Spinach and Mung-Bean Sprouts
Cabbage Kimchee
Bori Cha (Barley Tea)
Fruit

Carrot and White Radish Salad
Bindaetuk (Mung-Bean Pancakes) with Korean Dipping Sauce Number I
Chapchae (Cellophane Noodles with Vegetables)
Kakdooki (Pickle Made with Cubes of White Radish)
Bori Cha (Barley Tea)
Fruit

Sautéed Bean Curd with Korean Dipping Sauce Number 2
Rice with Bean Sprouts, Spinach, and Laver
Cabbage Kimchee
Bori Cha (Barley Tea)
Fruit

TRADITIONAL JAPANESE MENUS

Japanese food is eaten with chopsticks. Chinese-style soupspoons are used for custards such as *chawanmushi*. At formal meals, each person is served individually. Course follows course, with all the foods prearranged in attractive bowls and plates that do not, necessarily, belong to matching sets. Meals generally end with rice, pickles, and tea.

Carrots and Beans with a Bean-Curd Dressing

Chawanmushi with Scallions, Dried Shiitake Mushrooms, Water Chestnuts, and Snow Peas

Eggplant Slices with White Miso

Green Beans with Soy Sauce

Plain Japanese Rice with Cabbage Tsukemono (Salted Cabbage Pickle)

Ocha (Japanese Green Tea)

Japanese Cucumber Salad

Miso Soup with Bean Curd

Tempura (Vegetables in Batter)

Plain Japanese Rice

Kombu Relish and Cabbage Tsukemono (Salted Cabbage Pickle)

Ocha (Japanese Green Tea)

Oshitashi (Spinach with Roasted Sesame Seeds)

Miso Soup with Carrots and Mushrooms

Cabbage Cooked with Bean Curd

Plain Japanese Rice

Quick-Salted Cucumber Pickle

Ocha (Japanese Green Tea)

Cucumber and Dried Shiitake Mushroom Salad

Stew of Baked Wheat Gluten, Potato, Turnip, Carrot, and Cabbage Rolls

Plain Japanese Rice

Quick-Salted White Radish Pickle

Ocha (Green Japanese Tea)

Watercress Salad with Sesame Seeds

Mixed plate of Datémaki (Japanese Rolled Omelette), Hijiki with Shiitake Mushrooms, and Peas with Ginger

Udofu (Simmering Bean Curd with Seasonings)

Japanese Rice

Shoyu Daikon (White Radish Pickled in Soy Sauce)

Ocha (Japanese Green Tea)

Datémaki (Japanese Rolled Omelette) with Japanese Dipping Sauce

Thick Noodles in a Winter Stew

Cabbage Tsukemono (Salted Cabbage Pickle)

Ocha (Japanese Green Tea)

TRADITIONAL CHINESE MENUS

Formal Chinese meals start with cold dishes, go on from there to stir-fried foods, soups, simmered dishes, and spicy dishes to be eaten with rice. Tea comes at the very end. All dishes are placed in the center of the table and are communal. Each person has a plate, a pair of chopsticks, and a soupspoon. They reach out to the center for whatever they want.

Stir-fried Asparagus, Flavored with Sesame Oil
Sweet Corn and Egg Soup
Bean Curd with a Deliciously Spicy Sauce
Green Beans with Garlic and Red Pepper
Plain Boiled Rice
Any Chinese tea

Hot-and-Sour Soup
Crisp-Soft Noodles with a Broccoli, Mushroom, and Zucchini Topping
Peanuts with Long Green Beans
Plain Boiled Rice (if desired)
Any Chinese tea
Fruit

Chinese-Style Salad of Celery, Carrot, and Cucumber
Cold Noodles with Sesame Sauce
Bean Curd with Chinese Parsley
Zucchini Stir-fried with Garlic
Plain Boiled Rice
Any Chinese tea

Salad of Pressed Bean Curd, Mung-Bean Sprouts, and Agar-Agar
Cauliflower with Almonds and Lima Beans
Spicy Eggplant with Onion
Plain Boiled Rice
Any Chinese tea

Cold Chinese-Style Eggplant
Salad of Mung-Bean Sprouts and Egg Strands
Fried Wheat Gluten with Broccoli, Carrot, and Mushrooms
Plain Boiled Rice
Any Chinese tea

Clear Soup with Soft Bean Curd and Celery Cabbage
Three Aunties and Three Grandmothers (Three Kinds of Mushrooms and Three Kinds of Vegetables)
Plain Boiled Rice
Any Chinese tea
Fruit

TRADITIONAL INDIAN MENUS

Most Indians eat with their hands, though the more Westernized ones now and then do resort to knives, forks, and spoons. Generally speaking, all the food is placed in the center of the table at the same time. People help themselves to whatever they want, whenever they want it, putting it into their own plates before they eat it. In some parts of India, the food comes all prearranged in large, individual metal platters (*thalis*), with the more "wet" dishes ensconced in small bowls (*katoris*). These platters have everything from salty snacks, such as *samosas* (stuffed pastry cones) to sweets.

Chana Dal with Cucumber

Spiced Rice with Nuts and Raisins

Green Beans with Sesame Paste and Garlic

Cauliflower with Zucchini

Spiced, Heated Yogurt

Tomato, Cucumber, and Onion Relish

Very Spicy, Delicious Chickpeas

Sweet-and-Sour Eggplant

Potatoes with Whole Spices and Sesame Seeds

Yogurt with Cucumber and Mint

Bhaturas (Deep-Fried Leavened Breads)

Oily Toovar Dal with Green Beans and Tomatoes

Rice with Sautéed Onion and Mushrooms

Peas with Parsley and Coconut

Yogurt with Banana in the Gujarati Style

"Dry" Mung Dal

Khatte Baigan (Sour Eggplants)

Sauced Mushrooms with Sesame Seeds

Potatoes and Tomatoes Cooked with Fresh Coconut

Rotis or Pooris (Breads)

Sweet or Salty Lassi (Yogurt Drink)

South Indian Dosas (Rice and Urad Dal Pancakes)

Potatoes and Onions

Green Beans Cooked with Mustard Seeds and Red Pepper

Cabbage with Yogurt

Any Indian pickle

Sprouted Mung Beans with Spinach

Cabbage and Tomatoes Cooked in Mustard Oil

Vangi Bhat (Rice and Eggplant, Cooked in the Maharashtrian Style)

Yogurt with Chickpeas and Tomatoes

Any Indian pickle

MIDDLE EASTERN MENUS

The Middle East is, of course, a large region made up of many countries. As this area does not really have a history of vegetarianism but many fine vegetarian dishes, I have taken the liberty of putting these dishes together in a way that makes them quite compatible. (I might point out here that there are many religious figures in the Middle East who live on grains and yogurt.)

Pita Bread stuffed with
Falafel (Chickpea Patties)
Tahini Dipping Sauce (as well as some tomato and lettuce)
Yogurt with Garlic (on the side)

Stuffed Zucchini in a Hot Yogurt Sauce
Fresh Fava Beans (or frozen lima beans) with Thyme
Plain Baked Rice
Qahwah (Turkish Coffee)
Besan Barfee (Chickpea Fudge)

Persian-Style Cold Yogurt Soup
Rice with Fresh Herbs and Baby Lima Beans
Eggplant with Tomatoes
Fresh Melon
Tea

Lentils with Spinach
Plain Baked Rice II
Carrots with Raisins and Dates
Doogh (Yogurt Drink)
Fruit

Pilaf of Bulgar Wheat and Red Lentils
Yogurt with Spinach and Parsley
Okra with Tomatoes
Qahwah (Turkish Coffee)
Baklava

(THIS MENU IS IDEAL FOR THE SUMMER.)
Patlican (Fried Eggplant with a Yogurt Sauce)
Lentil Salad
Tabouleh (Bulgar Wheat and Parsley Salad)
Pita Bread
Stewed Dried Fruit

SUGGESTIONS FOR MIXED MENUS

LUNCH

Uppama (Semolina Pilaf)
Green Salad
Salty Lassi (Salty Yogurt Drink)

Kookoo with Zucchini, Dill, and Raisins (Egg Pie)
Green Salad
French bread, or Italian bread, or Naan
(Leavened Flat Bread)
Tea or Coffee

Bulgar Wheat with Chickpeas and Tomatoes
Green Beans Cooked with Mustard Seeds and Red Pepper
Fruit
Tea, Coffee, or a yogurt drink

Carrot and White Radish Salad
Cold Noodles with Sesame Sauce
Omelette with Bean Curd
and Japanese Dipping Sauce
Ocha (Japanese Green Tea)

Mongo (Mung Beans with Spinach and Tomatoes)
Rice with Garlic
Yogurt with Cucumber and Mint
Anise Tea

Soy-Bean Sprouts Sautéed with Fried Bean Curd
Kohlrabi with Chinese Black Mushrooms
Rice with Millet

Chickpea, Cabbage, and Dill Soup
Green Salad
French bread or Naan
Fruit

A COLD BUFFET

Cold Chinese-Style Eggplant
Chickpeas with Tahini
Artichoke Hearts and Potatoes, Cooked in Oil
and Lemon
Tabouleh
Yogurt with Zucchini
Dolma
Korean-Style Cucumber Salad
Chickpea and Green Bean Salad
Pita Bread, French bread or packaged
Scandinavian flat breads

DINNER

Lima Beans with Raisins
Baghara Baigan (Stuffed Eggplant)
Zarda Pullao (Sweet Saffron Rice)
Yogurt with Dill

Frozen Lima Beans Braised with Swiss Chard and Dill
Stuffed Zucchini in a Hot Yogurt Sauce
Gucchi Pullao (Morelle Pilaf)
Fruit

Stir-fried Asparagus Flavored with Sesame Oil
Chawanmushi with Shiitake Mushrooms, Water Chestnuts, and Snow Peas
Crisp-Soft Noodles with a Broccoli, Mushroom, and Zucchini Topping
Fruit
Ocha (Japanese Green Tea)

Persian-Style Cold Yogurt Soup
Zucchini "Meatballs"
Tomatoes Cooked in the Bengali Style
Fried Potatoes
Spiced Rice with Cashews

Chinese-Style Salad of Celery, Carrot, and Cucumber
Three Aunties and Three Grandmothers (Three Kinds of Mushrooms and Three Kinds of Vegetables)
Bean Curd with a Deliciously Spicy Sauce
Plain Boiled Rice
Any Chinese tea

Salad of Pressed Bean Curd, Mung-Bean Sprouts, and Agar-Agar
Inari-Zushi (Bags of Fried Bean Curd Stuffed with Sushi Rice)
Chapchae (Cellophane Noodles with Vegetables)
Green Beans with Garlic and Red Pepper
Bori Cha (Barley Tea)

Haak (Collard Greens)
Chickpea and Tomato Stew
Sweet-and-Sour Eggplant
Plain Basmati Rice
Doogh (yogurt drink)

GENERAL INFORMATION

Aburage See BEAN CURD, Fried.

Agar-Agar Unlike most other gelatins that are made from animal products, this vegetarian gelatin is made from a kind of red seaweed, available in Japanese, Korean, Chinese, and other East Asian grocery stores as powder, flakes, and sticks. Only the sticks, resembling clear, long, uneven noodles, are called for in this book. Cut off the required amount with a pair of scissors and store the rest in a tin or a plastic bag.

When soaked in cold water, agar-agar sticks turn pliable and bouncy but retain a nice crunch. They are excellent as is in salads and cold dishes, adding a new texture and picking up the flavors of the dressing. However, when agar-agar is cooked in hot water, it melts and may be used as gelatin for desserts and sweetmeats; it sets much faster than gelatin and does not require refrigeration. Desserts made with it may easily be cut into squares and diamonds without coming apart.

Age See BEAN CURD, Fried.

Ajwain This celery-seed-sized spice has a flavor that seems to combine anise and oregano with just a hint of black pepper. Used in Indian cooking and may be purchased from Indian stores.

Almond Powder Very finely ground almonds, used in Chinese desserts, available in Chinese grocery stores.

Aloo Bokhara Sour, dried plums (or prunes), available in Middle Eastern and Indian grocery stores.

Amazu Shoga Pink, pickled ginger, usually eaten with *sushi* dishes, available in Japanese grocery stores, packed in its briny pickling solution. Buy the paper-thin slices, otherwise you'll have to cut the chunks of pickled ginger into paper-thin slices yourself. Store unused portion in its brine in the refrigerator. An average serving with *sushi* is about a packed tablespoon of the slices, piled in a heap.

Amchoor Dried slices and powder, made from sour, unripe mangoes. *Amchoor* gives foods a slightly sweet sourness. My recipes call for only ground (i.e., powdered) *amchoor*, available in Indian grocery stores.

Anardana Dried seeds from sour pomegranates. Used in Indian cooking and available in Indian grocery stores.

Asafetida A brown, somewhat smelly resin used in small quantities in Indian cooking partly for its flavor and mostly for its digestive properties. Indian stores sell it both in its lump form and as a grainy powder. The lump is supposed to be purer. Break off a small chip with a hammer and then crush it between two sheets of paper to make your own powder.

Asakusa Nori See NORI.

Ata See CHAPPATI FLOUR.

Azuki Beans See BEANS, DRIED.

Baby Corn Tiny, delicate ears found only canned in Chinese grocery stores. Store unused portion covered with its own liquid in a jar in the refrigerator.

Bamboo Shoots Only canned bamboo shoots are, alas, available to us, sold whole, sliced, and diced. Once the can has been opened, store excess in a jar, well covered with fresh water, to be changed every day (they should last a week or more). If bamboo shoots taste very tinny, blanch them in rapidly boiling water for a minute and then drain them before using.

Basmati Rice See RICE.

Bean Curd White, milky, custardlike squares made out of soaked, mashed, and strained soy beans. It may be made at home (see page 164) or bought from health-food, Chinese, and Japanese grocery stores, either fresh or in cans. Fresh bean curd is generally available in three textures—soft, medium (or regular), and hard. It is best eaten the day it is made or bought, though the cakes may be put in a container with water to cover, changed daily, and refrigerated for 2 to 3 days. While there is a difference between Chinese and Japanese bean curds, for the purposes of this book just use whatever good, fresh bean curd you can get.

Fried bean curd Some types of fried bean curd may be made at home (see page 176). All fried bean curds may be bought from Chinese and Japanese grocery stores, either fresh or sometimes canned and frozen. Chinese fried bean curd, *udofu*, is usually sold in 1½-inch cubes, which may be kept, well covered, in the refrigerator for 4 to 5 days or else frozen. There are two major types of Japanese fried bean curd—**Age** and **Aburage** (or **Abura Age**). *Age* consists of thick, rectangular slabs of bean curd that have been fried so the outside is brown and crisp but the inside is still soft. *Aburage* consists of much thinner slabs of fried bean curd that can be opened up into pouches, with a brown and crisp outside; the inside, what there is of it, is spongy. Both *age* and *aburage* are sold in the refrigerated sections of Japanese stores. *Aburage* may also be bought canned and frozen. Most fried bean curd should be doused in boiling water to soften the exterior somewhat and to get rid of extra oil.

Fermented bean curd Sold as *"Fu-ju"* or *"Nam-yee"* in Chinese stores and as *"Tao-hoo-yee"* in Thai stores, it consists of ¾- to 1-inch cubes of bean curd sitting in a briny liquid in bottles and cans. The cubes taste like a soft, very salty and very strong cheese, which can be mashed and added as a flavoring to vegetables such as spinach or to sauces. I find some Thai sauces that cut the salty cheese with lime juice, ginger juice, and green chilies to be particularly delicious. There are many types of fermented bean curd. You can usually see them quite clearly when they are in bottles. Some look rather plain, others seem quite spicy, and yet another kind is packed in a red, winy broth (the latter, called **"red bean curd,"** is my favorite).

If stored in tightly closed bottles in the refrigerator, fermented bean curd can last indefinitely.

Pressed bean curd Sold as *"doufu kan"* in Chinese grocery stores, this bean curd has had much of the water pressed out of it. It is sold in about ½-inch-thick cakes. As the bean curd becomes quite hard, it may be cubed and julienned and then added to salads, almost as if it were, well, Swiss cheese. It may also be julienned and put into soups and stir-fried dishes. It should be stored in the refrigerator, covered with a salty solution—about 1 tablespoon salt to 1 quart of water. It could last for a couple of weeks this way.

Pressed seasoned bean curd Sold in Chinese grocery stores as *"pai doufu kan"* and very similar to the preceding bean curd, except that it has been cooked in star-anise-flavored soy sauce and therefore has a brownish color and a mild aniselike taste. It, too, may be julienned and added to salads, soups, and stir-fried dishes. Stored in the refrigerator covered with a solution that has about 1 teaspoon salt and ¼ cup Chinese dark soy sauce to 1 quart of water, it could last a couple of weeks.

Dried bean-curd skin This is really the skin that forms over soy milk when it is heated. It is sold by many different names according to size and shapes (sticks, small rectangular pieces, etc.) in Chinese stores. When I call for sheets of dried bean-curd skin, I mean the rectangular sheets 5 × 1½ × 1/32 inches labeled "Dried Bean Curd Skin, Sliced Type" to be found in small packages in Chinese grocery stores. The Japanese sell it as **yuba** in rolls, sheets, and rectangles. All kinds need to be soaked in water, the time varying according to the thickness of the skin—anywhere from 10 minutes to 1 hour. When reconstituted, bean-curd skin has a very rich, creamy taste. The dried skin does not need refrigeration, but should be used up quickly, as it can turn rancid in time.

Beans, Dried Legumes—dried beans and split peas—are rich sources of protein for Asians and are consumed, one way or another, at almost every single meal. All beans should be picked over and washed in several changes of water before cooking. Store in a dry, cool place in airtight containers. Remember that old beans will take much longer to cook than fresh ones.

Indian split peas, of which there are many varieties, are

called *dals*. Some *dals*, fried in small quantities, are also used as a flavoring, almost as if they were a spice.

Here are some of the more unusual Asian beans and split peas I have used:

Azuki bean Also called *aduki* bean. Small red beans sometimes cooked with rice, sometimes by themselves, and sometimes mashed into sweet pastes for desserts, available in Oriental, Indian, and health-food stores. Sometimes they are unlabeled, so you just have to learn to recognize them.

Chana dal The Indian version of yellow split peas, though somewhat smaller in size. *Chana dal* comes hulled and split and may be cooked by itself or with rice and vegetables. It has quite a nutty taste and is sometimes used as a spice in South India. Available both raw and roasted in Indian grocery stores. Roasted are used in Indian snack foods.

Fava beans Large beans sold with or without their seed coats in Middle Eastern and Chinese grocery stores. For more information, see page 89.

Masoor dal A hulled, salmon-colored split pea that is used both in Indian and Middle Eastern cooking. Available in some health-food stores and in all Indian and Middle Eastern stores. Called red lentils, *masoor dal*, and lentils respectively. This split pea loses its salmon color when cooked and turns yellowish.

Mung beans Small, green-skinned, slightly cylindrical beans sold in all Oriental, Indian, and health-food grocery stores. They may be cooked as beans or used for making the Oriental and Indian types of bean sprouts. (see pages 96–98).

Mung dal Split mung beans, available in Indian stores both hulled and unhulled. My recipes use only the hulled, all-yellow kind.

Soy beans Round, dull-yellow beans which may be boiled, fried, and also used to make soy milk, bean curd, and soy-bean sprouts. Available in all Oriental and health-food stores, sometimes in supermarkets. For soy-bean sprouts, see page 100.

Toovar dal Also called *"arhar dal"*, this hulled, dull-yellow split pea is somewhat larger than the American yellow split pea and has an earthy taste. Available in Indian grocery stores both plain and in its "oily" Western Indian form—rubbed with castor oil which acts as a preservative and also keeps off the bugs. The oil needs to be washed away in several changes of water. "Oily" *toovar* has a slightly different taste from the untreated, though they may be used interchangeably.

Urad dal The kind I've used is hulled and split and has a pale yellow color and a somewhat viscous texture. It is used by South Indians for savory cakes and pancakes, and sometimes as a spice. Available in Indian grocery stores.

Bean Sauce Available in cans in Chinese and other Oriental grocery stores, sometimes as a fine and other times as a coarse purée of fermented soy beans. It is salty, brown in color, and thickened with flour. After opening, it should be transferred to a glass jar and refrigerated. It lasts indefinitely.

Bitter Melon Zucchini-shaped and of the squash family, this green, crocodile-skinned vegetable can, indeed, be quite bitter. Asians decrease this bitterness somewhat by parboiling, salting, or soaking in salted water, but never eliminate it completely, as it is prized for cleansing the blood and for adding a new taste.

Bitter melons come in various sizes; I have only seen the larger variety in Chinese and Indian stores here. When cooking them, use only the skin. The pulp and the large seeds embedded in it should be scraped away.

Black Cumin Seeds See CUMIN SEEDS, BLACK.

Black Mustard Seeds See MUSTARD SEEDS, BLACK.

Black Salt See SALTS.

Bok Choy This Chinese vegetable of the cabbage family has thick, whitish stalks that turn into dark-green leaves. The entire vegetable may be cooked. Available in Chinese grocery stores and some supermarkets, where it is apt to be called Chinese cabbage. Study the drawing so you'll recognize it when you see it.

Bori Cha Roasted barley kernels used for making barley tea. Called *"bori cha"* in Korean stores and *"mugi cha"* in Japanese stores.

Bulgar Wheat The cracked kernels of boiled and dried wheat available in small, medium, and large sizes at Middle Eastern and health-food stores, as well as some supermarkets. For more information, see page 153.

Calpis A new, milky Japanese concentrate made out of nonfat dry milk and lactic acid, to be diluted with water to make hot and cold drinks. Available in Japanese and specialty stores.

Cardamom An aromatic spice, generally sold in its pod. The green-colored pods sold in Indian stores are more aromatic than the plump, bleached, whitish ones sold more generally in grocery stores. Some Indian stores sell the seeds separately, a great convenience when grinding spice combinations such as **garam masala**. If a recipe calls for ground or powdered cardamom seeds, just use a mortar and pestle as the quantities are usually quite small. Cardamom pods are often sucked in India as mouth fresheners.

Cardamom Pods, Large Black They look like black beetles and have an earthier, deeper flavor than green cardamoms. Sold in Indian grocery stores.

Cassava Also called yucca, manioc, and tapioca, this root of Brazilian origin resembles a large, brown, elongated sweet potato. It can be almost a foot long. It was introduced to tropical Asia by the Portuguese in the seventeenth century and has been used since in stews and desserts. In the southern Philippines it is grated and steamed and eaten as a staple instead of rice.

Cassava needs to be peeled under running water. It has a hard, white flesh which turns slightly glutinous when cooked. It is sold in Latin American stores as yucca. Some Filipino stores carry it, too, and call it cassava. Very few Indian stores have it but when they do, it is called tapioca.

Cayenne Pepper Use any powdered, hot red pepper. Korean and Indian supplies are usually fresher and brighter in color.

Celery Cabbage See CHINESE CABBAGE.

"Cellophane" Mung-Bean Noodles See NOODLES.

Chana Dal See BEANS.

Chappati Flour. Very finely ground whole-wheat flour generally made from a wheat that is low in gluten. It is also called *"ata"* and is used in making many kinds of Indian breads. Available in Indian grocery stores.

Charoli A small nut available shelled in Indian grocery stores. It is generally used in sweets and stuffings.

Chhena A very fine, fresh cheese made from curdled milk (see recipe, page 402). Used for making Indian milk sweets such as *rasgullas*.

Chickpea Flour Flour made out of chickpeas. Known as *farine de pois chiches* in specialty stores and as gram flour in some Indian stores. Used in India and the Middle East both as a thickener for sauces and stews and for making pancakes, dumplings, and sweetmeats. I store mine in the refrigerator to discourage bugs.

Chilies, Fresh Hot Green and Red Very rich sources of iron and vitamins A and C, chilies—or peppers—were introduced into Asia by the Portuguese in the sixteenth century. They were adopted with a vengeance. The chilies used for the recipes in this book are anywhere from 2 to 4 inches long and usually not more than ⅓ inch thick. They are available in Chinese, Indian, Mexican, Korean, Indonesian, and Thai grocery stores, as well as some Italian. As chilies vary in strength according to variety and strain, care should be exercised in using them. *Do not* substitute a whole jalapeño for a whole green chili in any of my recipes. One of my students tried it and nearly felled his guests. Just a section of the jalapeño would have sufficed. It is best to be cautious. Sometimes tasting a minute segment of a chili is quite a good idea as they can vary so much, even within the same batch. The top seeded section is usually much hotter than the tapering bottom. Handle cut chilies as little as possible. When you do, refrain from touching any part of your face, and wash your hands with soap and warm water right after. If fresh green chilies are unavailable, canned ones (usually not as hot) may be substituted; they are available mostly in Mexican grocery stores.

To store fresh green chilies, wrap them first in newspaper, then in plastic, and store in the refrigerator. They should last several weeks. Any that begin to rot should be discarded, as they tend to affect the whole batch.

Chili Paste with Soy Bean Also sold as **Chili Paste with Soy Bean and Garlic,** this paste has ground hot red chilies, fermented soy beans, and garlic in it. It is hot and quite delicious. Small amounts may be added to sauces that need perking up. Sold in jars in Chinese grocery stores. If kept well sealed and refrigerated, it should last indefinitely. If it starts to dry up, add a little sesame oil.

Chinese Black Mushrooms, Dried See MUSHROOMS.

Chinese Cabbage and Celery Cabbage Since there are many notions of what Chinese cabbage is, let me offer my own definition for the purposes of this book. Chinese cabbage is a slightly elongated but chunky, somewhat curly version of our regular cabbage, with fairly white and quite wide ribs. It is called *"hakusai"* in Japanese stores and is used to make *kimchee*, cabbage rolls, and assorted vegetable dishes. When a recipe calls for Chinese cabbage, do not substitute celery cabbage unless suggested.

There is a slimmer, much longer version of Chinese cabbage which does resemble celery but only in its length. This is celery cabbage and may be used in some of my soups and vegetable dishes. You can always substitute Chinese cabbage for celery cabbage, though not the other way around.

Look carefully at these illustrations and the drawings of *bok choy* (page 420) and *choy sum* (opposite).

Chinese cabbage is available in Chinese, Japanese, and Korean grocery stores.

Celery cabbage is sold more widely, even in some supermarkets.

Chinese Chives In Chinese markets where they are sold, Chinese chives resemble bunches of long grass with a mild onion-garlic flavor. Regular chives may be substituted. To store, refrigerate unwashed chives wrapped in newspaper and then in plastic.

Chinese Parsley Called *"cilantro"* in Latin American stores, fresh green coriander in Indian stores, and Chinese parsley in Oriental stores, this herb is used all the way from the Caucasus to Korea. Most countries use just the leaves. In India, the stalks are used to add flavor to beans and stocks. In Thailand, the roots are used in the making of various curry pastes.

Chinese parsley is the plant of the coriander seed and may be grown from the seed available in spice racks.

The best way to store Chinese parsley is to put the whole bunch, unwashed roots and all, in a container of water, as if it were a bunch of cut flowers. Cover the leaves and container with a plastic bag and refrigerate. Every other day, pick off the dead or rotted leaves. Your Chinese parsley should last several weeks this way.

Choy Sum This is yet another type of Chinese cabbage. It looks rather like **bok choy** except that it has slenderer, bright-green stems and leaves of almost the same color. Occasionally, there are some small, bright-yellow flowers as well. It is quite delicious. Stems and leaves are all eaten. Sold only in Chinese grocery stores.

Coconuts From the Philippines to Pakistan, coconuts are used in making dishes that include vegetables, beans, snacks, and desserts.

How to buy a coconut Look for a coconut that shows no sign of cracks and is free of mold. Pick it up and shake it. It should be heavy with water, which, in turn, ensures a moist interior. Always buy an extra coconut or two just in case one is rancid. Extra coconuts can always be grated and frozen.

How to break a coconut Take a heavy cleaver and, using the *un*sharpened side, hit the coconut all around its equator. You may rest the coconut on any hard, unbreakable surface or you may hold the coconut in one hand while hitting with the other. At the first sign of a crack, hold the coconut over a bowl to collect its water, which is generally not used in cooking, though in India it is highly recommended for "women's problems," whatever they be! The coconut should break into two halves. Most Asian coconut graters are designed to scrape meat off these two halves, but if you do not have such a gadget, break the coconut into smaller pieces with a hammer. Remove the tough outer shell by slipping a knife between it and the meat and then prying the meat off. Use a sharp paring knife or potato peeler to pare away the brown skin on the pieces of meat. Rinse off the coconut pieces.

There is yet another method of breaking open coconuts that has found much favor in the West. Preheat an oven to 400° F. Make two holes in the coconut, using an ice pick or a screwdriver. Drain the water and put the coconut in the oven for 15 minutes. Its shell should contract. Now hit the coconut with a hammer. The shell should come off. Even if it does not, you should be able to pry off the meat with greater ease. Peel the meat in the same way with a paring knife or with a potato peeler and then rinse off the coconut pieces.

Always taste a small piece of coconut just after you have broken it open. If it has turned rancid in the slightest, do not use it. Coconuts should be sweet and moist.

How to grate a coconut Excellent frozen grated coconut is available in many Mexican and Latin American stores in this country. My neighborhood Mexican store in New York City, Casa Moneo, carries a grated coconut from the Dominican Republic, packaged by Southland. It is frozen in flat rectangles and defrosts very fast. It may be used in all my recipes that call for grated fresh coconut. (It may also be used to make coconut milk.)

Also, there are some stores that will break open and grate coconuts for you. I know of one Filipino store in New York where I have taken 15 to 20 coconuts at a time for grating in large electric machines, so explore your own neighborhood for a similar Filipino, Thai, or Indonesian shop.

If none of the above options are open, grind the coconut yourself. Once you have opened and peeled the coconut, the grinding is simplicity itself, especially if you have a blender or food processor. The blender and food processor method: Cut the coconut into ¾- to 1-inch pieces. Throw them into a blender or a food processor *fitted with its metal blade*. Blend 3 to 5 minutes or until you have very fine particles. You may also grate coconut pieces by hand, using the finest holes in your grater.

Many stores sell dried coconut, both sweetened and unsweetened. The sweetened variety is rarely used in Asia and I do not call for it in any of my recipes. The unsweetened variety, however, is used but should not be substituted for the fresh kind unless that is indicated in the recipe.

How to make coconut milk and coconut cream To make 1 cup of coconut milk, put 1 cup (or 2 if you want a richer milk) of grated coconut into the container of a food processor or blender. Add 1 cup hot water and blend for 5 minutes. Let the mixture cool for about half an hour. Strain the mixture through a triple thickness of cheesecloth, making sure you get out as much liquid as possible. (This is sometimes called the first coconut milk. You can put the coconut grounds back into your food processor or blender, add another cup of hot water and repeat the process to get a second coconut milk.)

Put the strained coconut milk into a glass container and let it rest for half an hour or longer. The coconut cream will rise to the top. You should be able to see it through the glass and spoon it off with ease for recipes that require it. Otherwise just stir it into the milk and use it all as coconut milk.

Many Latin American and South Asian stores sell canned coconut milk as well as an unsweetened coconut cream packaged like butter. Use the canned milk whenever my recipes suggest it. It is much richer than what we can make with the coconuts available to us. Stir the contents of the can before removing the amount you need. If you wish to use the packaged coconut cream, you might want to thin it out with a little regular heavy or light cream. This combination is excellent as a topping for fruit and Southeast Asian desserts.

How to store coconuts, whole and grated Use coconuts as soon as possible. Store them in the refrigerator until that time. Grated coconuts freeze very well and defrost quite fast. It is a good idea to keep your freezer stocked with some freshly grated coconut.

Coriander Seeds These Chinese parsley seeds are used throughout much of the Middle East, South Asia, and East Asia, both whole and ground. If you wish to roast and grind coriander seeds, follow the general method given below for roasting and grinding cumin seeds. It is a good idea to sift the roasted and ground seeds with a fine sifter to get rid of some of the coarse shells. Indian stores sell both whole and ground seeds.

Cucumbers The Japanese and Korean cucumber is much slimmer, less seedy, and more flavorful than the American kind. Pickling Kirby cucumbers are the best substitute. If you cannot find them, use regular cucumbers with their seeds removed or else use the English-type cucumbers.

Cumin Seeds This spice is used a great deal in Middle Eastern and Indian cooking. Sometimes it is used whole, sometimes ground, and sometimes roasted and ground. It is fairly easy to find. Mexican stores call it *"comino."* Indian and Middle Eastern stores sell both the whole and the ground seeds.

To roast and grind cumin seeds, put about 4 tablespoons of the seeds into a small, heavy (preferably cast-iron) skillet and set it over a medium flame. Stir and roast the seeds until they turn a few shades darker and give out a wonderful "roasted" aroma. The seeds may now be ground in an electric coffee grinder or in a mortar. Store in a tightly closed jar in a cool, dark place. The flavor

will lessen with time but the seeds should still be good for a month or so. Ground roasted cumin seeds may be sprinkled into soups, salads, bean, and yogurt dishes.

Cumin Seeds, Black Also called *"siyah zeera"* and *"shah zeera."* The seeds are darker, finer, and more complex in flavor than ordinary cumin. They are also more expensive. Indian stores sell them in small packets.

Curry Leaves The highly aromatic fresh curry leaves, shaped rather like small bay leaves, are used a great deal in Indian cooking. Unfortunately, only the dried leaves are available in Indian grocery stores here. They have minimal aroma and flavor but may be used as a desperate measure.

Daikon See WHITE RADISH.

Dals See BEANS, DRIED.

Daun Salaam An aromatic leaf used fresh in Indonesian cooking. Only dried leaves with minimum flavor are available in Southeast Asian grocery stores.

Day-Lily Buds, Dried Also called "golden needles," these are, indeed, the dried buds of day lilies. Follow directions in recipes for soaking, draining, and cutting off the hard knots. Available in Chinese grocery stores.

Domsiah Rice See RICE.

Dried-Hair Seaweed Always used when cooking Buddha's Delight for Chinese New Year celebrations, this seaweed looks like a tangled mass of curly black hair. It needs to be soaked and pulled apart before cooking.

Dried Hot Red Peppers See RED PEPPERS.

Enok Mushrooms or Enokidake See MUSHROOMS.

Fava Beans, Dried See BEANS, DRIED.

Fava Beans, Fresh Very large beans occasionally sold fresh in specialty stores. The beans have to be shelled, just as if they were peas in pods.

Fennel Seeds These taste and look like anise seeds, only they are milder and plumper. Fennel seeds are used a great deal in Indian cooking and may be purchased from Indian grocery stores.

Roasted fennel seeds are often offered in India as an after-dinner mouth freshener and digestive. For roasting, follow general direction for cumin seeds. You can prepare a whole jar full, let it cool, and then put a tight lid on it.

Fenugreek Seeds Yellow, square, and flattish, these seeds are supposed to soothe the intestinal tract, even relax inflamed innards. (Fenugreek greens, though not sold in American grocery stores, are grown in parts of this country and used as green manure! Grab them when you can find them. They are excellent when cooked with carrots and new potatoes.) Fenugreek seeds are sold in Indian grocery stores.

Feta Cheese A crumbly goat's cheese found in many Greek and Middle Eastern grocery stores.

Filo Pastry Also called "phyllo" and "fila." Paper-thin sheets of pastry dough found in the refrigerators and freezers of most Middle Eastern and specialty grocery stores. The pastry has to be handled with care as it dries when left exposed. For more, see page 339.

Galanga Root Also called "*laos.*" A root of the ginger family, though somewhat larger in size. It is used in the cooking of much of Southeast Asia and is available in stores that sell Thai, Indonesian, and Malayan groceries. Unfortunately, it is only possible to get the dry root here. Both dried slices and powder are sold, though not always in the same places.

Garam Masala Every home in India and Pakistan probably has its own handed-down-from-grandmother recipe for **garam masala,** an aromatic mixture of spices such as cardamom, cloves, and cinnamon which are supposed to "heat" the body. My currently favorite **garam masala** recipe goes as follows: Put 1 tablespoon cardamom seeds, a 1-inch stick of cinnamon, 1 teaspoon whole black cumin seeds (use regular whole cumin as a substitute), 1 teaspoon whole cloves, 1 teaspoon black peppercorns, and about ⅓ of an average-sized nutmeg into the container of an electric coffee grinder. Grind until the spices are powdery. Yield: 3 tablespoons. There is another, slightly tarter **garam masala,** called "*multani garam masala,*" used in an area that is now northwestern Pakistan, that has sour pomegranate seeds in it. Here is that recipe: Put 1½ teaspoons whole black cumin seeds, 1½ teaspoons cardamom seeds, 1½ teaspoons black peppercorns, 2 teaspoons **anardana** (dried pomegranate seeds), a 1½-inch stick of cinnamon, and ½ teaspoon whole cloves into the container of an electric coffee grinder. Grind until the spices are powdery. Yield: 3½ tablespoons.

Any **garam masala** should be stored in a tightly lidded jar, away from heat and sunlight. As time goes on, the spice mixtures will inevitably lessen in aroma and potency. That is why they are made in small quantities. But do use them up.

Ghee This is butter that has been so well clarified that you can even deep-fry in it. Because it is totally free of all milk solids, it does not need refrigeration. **Ghee** has a very special, nutty taste. If you have access to Indian stores, my own advice would be that you buy ready-made **ghee.** The Netherlands, for example, exports an excellent quality which many Indian stores buy in bulk and then package in their own bottles. If you cannot buy ready-made **ghee,** here is how you go about making your own: Take a pound of the best quality unsalted butter that you can find. Put it in a heavy, smallish pot and let it melt over a low flame. Soon it will begin to simmer. Let it simmer on low heat for about 45 minutes (timing really depends upon the amount of water in the butter), or until the milky solids turn brownish and either cling to the sides of the pot or else fall to the bottom. Because you have to boil all the water away without letting the butter brown, you must watch it, especially toward the end of the cooking time. Now strain the **ghee** through a quadrupled layer of cheesecloth. Homemade *ghee* is best stored covered in the refrigerator. Like butter, it will not spoil.

Ginger, Dry Powdered The ground ginger available in most supermarkets and grocery stores.

Ginger, Fresh This is a knobby rhizome, known for its sharp, pungent, cleansing taste and its digestive properties. Its tan potatolike skin is usually peeled away, after which it is grated, sliced, or chopped. To make ginger paste in the food processor, it is best to start the machine first, with its metal blade in place. Then throw in coarsely chopped chunks of ginger through the feed tube. Add water last. If a recipe calls for "very finely grated ginger" or "ginger grated to a pulp," use one of the very efficient, fine-toothed ginger/horseradish graters sold in most Japanese grocery stores. The teeth in these graters catch the tough ginger fibers and all that you are left with is the pulp. If unavailable, use the finest part of a hand grater.

Always look for ginger with a smooth, unwrinkled skin. Wrinkles mean that the ginger has begun to dry out and will be quite hard and woody inside.

A quarter-sized slice of ginger just means a rough cross-section, about the size of a quarter.

Sometimes a very pale, pinkish, young ginger is available in Oriental and Indian markets. Because it is very tender, it is prized. It is therefore more expensive. Young ginger is ideal for pickling. If you find any, you could just scrape it, slice it, and then season it with lemon juice and salt. It will turn very pink—and make an excellent relish.

To store ginger, either wrap it up in newspaper and keep it in the vegetable bin of your refrigerator or else plant it in dryish soil and water it infrequently. If you plant it, the ginger might even sprout new shoots. If you use ginger quite a lot, as I do, just keep it in an airy basket, along with your onion and garlic.

Do not substitute dry ginger powder in any recipe that calls for fresh ginger.

Gingko Nuts Buy fresh gingko nuts, if you can get them. They can usually be found in the fall and winter in Oriental grocery stores. They must first be cracked open with a hammer to remove the hard shell. The inner skin can be removed by dropping them into boiling water for a couple of minutes and then peeling. Fresh gingko nuts turn a wonderful jade-green color when they are cooked. They can be stir-fried, skewered and grilled, and dipped in tempura batter and deep fried. If you cannot get fresh nuts, use the canned variety,

though their taste and texture hardly matches that of the fresh ones.

Fresh nuts may be stored in the refrigerator for a couple of months. Canned nuts should be kept in the refrigerator, covered with water that is changed every other day.

Ginseng The very prized Korean root considered to be a cure-all. The fresh root is used in Korea for salads and to flavor soups and stews. Only the dry kind is available here and may be used to make ginseng tea. For more, see page 344.

Gluten Flour A hard wheat flour with a very high gluten content (about 45%). It is very rich in protein and is used to make wheat-gluten balls (as well as breads and sauces). Generally available in health-food stores. If you cannot find it, write to El Molino Mills, P.O. Box 2250, City of Industry, California 91746.

Glutinous Rice See RICE.

Grape Leaves (vine leaves) Available already cleaned and packed in brine at all specialty as well as Greek and Middle Eastern stores. If you wish to use fresh leaves, see directions on page 341.

Green Mango Now that ripe mangoes have begun to make their way into American markets, perhaps unripe green mangoes will be next. It is these pectin-rich, sour green mangoes that are the basis for most Indian chutneys and pickles. They are also eaten raw in countries like the Philippines and Thailand. If you cannot find them, use the suggested substitutes.

Green Plantain Large green unripe plantains are used throughout South and Southeast Asia to make everything from chips to sweets. They can be found in most Latin-American grocery stores.

Gur See JAGGERY.

Hijiki A calcium-rich sea vegetable that resembles strands of black twine in its dried form. Sold in Japanese and most health-food stores.

Hoisin Sauce A slightly sweet, thick, smooth Chinese bean sauce with a light garlic flavor. It may be used in cooking or as a dip. Available widely in Chinese and specialty grocery stores. If canned, unused contents should be transferred to a lidded bottle and refrigerated. It lasts indefinitely.

Holy Basil Known as *"tulsi"* in India and *"bai ka-prow"* in Thailand, the fresh leaves are excellent for making a soothing tea and for flavoring soups, drinks, and vegetables. Available only in Southeast Asian grocery stores.

Jaggery A form of raw lump sugar, generally honey-brown in color. Available in Indian grocery stores. The best kind looks clean and is easily breakable, not brick hard. It should be stored in a tightly closed plastic container in the refrigerator.

Jujubes (Chinese Dates) They look like small, hard, red crinkly prunes and are available only in Chinese grocery stores. Jujubes need a good soaking before they can be used in cooking.

Kaffir Lime A dark-green knobby lime. Its peel, juice, and leaves are all used in Thai cooking. Only the dried leaves and dried peel are available in Thai and Southeast Asian grocery stores. The Thais call the fruit *magrut*.

Kala Namak (Black Salt) See SALTS.

Kalonji (Nigella) Little tear-shaped black seeds used in Iran and India when cooking breads and vegetables as well as for pickling. *Kalonji* is the name by which this spice is sold in Indian stores. Middle Eastern stores sell it as *"siyah-daneh"* or *"black seeds."* Sometimes it is also called *"onion seeds."* This spice has a wonderful flavor and, once you know it, you might want to sprinkle some on your breads before you bake them.

Kampyo Ribbon of dried gourd, available in Japanese stores. It has to be cooked (or soaked) in water or seasoned stock before it can be eaten.

Karhai See WOK.

Katori Small metal bowls made out of anything from gold and silver to the more common stainless steel, used for serving individual portions of food at Indian meals. Generally, several **katoris** are arranged just inside the rim of a matching **thali**, a large metal plate. There are usually as many **katoris** as there are dishes, though rice,

bread, and pickles are frequently placed directly on the **thali**.

Kim See NORI.

Kimchee Hot Korean pickle, generally made out of Chinese cabbage, white radish, or cucumber and sold in all Korean grocery stores as well as some Chinese and Japanese grocery stores. If you wish to make your own, see recipes on pages 379–82.

Ki-Soba See NOODLES.

Kochu Chang An absolutely delicious—and very hot—Korean paste made with fermented soy beans, hot red pepper, and, quite frequently, garlic as well. Available in Korean grocery stores. The best kind is sold from large barrels. If tightly covered and stored in a jar in the refrigerator, **kochu chang** can last indefinitely. Small quantities added to sauces, soups, and stews make a world of difference.

Kohlrabi A greatly neglected vegetable of the cabbage family. It consists of a solid green ball with stemmed leaves growing upward from its surface. It is the ball that is generally peeled and eaten, both raw and cooked. In India, we always cooked the tenderer leaves as well.

Kombu (or Konbu) Green, calcium-rich dried kelp, used in making stock *(dashi)* and preserves, available in Japanese and health-food stores. It resembles a large, long leaf and is sold either folded up or cut into smaller pieces. There is a light dusting of powdery stuff on *kombu* which should be wiped off with a damp cloth *very lightly* so as not to remove the flavor, which is very near the surface. Store leftover portions in an airtight container.

Kosher Salt See SALTS.

Laos See GALANGA ROOT.

Laver See NORI.

Litchi A delicious fruit, about the size of a small egg, grown in much of East and South Asia. The outside skin ranges in color from brown to red. Once peeled, the inside flesh is white and translucent, with an oval brown pit at its center. Sometimes available fresh at

Chinese and specialty grocery stores. Always available canned in syrup.

Lemon Grass A tall, hard, grayish-green grass used for its aroma and flavor in much of Southeast Asian cooking. Usually the lower 5 inches or so of the stalk are bruised and thrown into foods to release a lemon-peel-like taste. Fresh lemon grass is available in some Southeast Asian and Chinese grocery stores. If you cannot find it, use the sliced, dried kind. A stalk of lemon grass is equivalent to about 2 to 3 tablespoons of sliced dried.

Lo Mein See NOODLES.

Long Beans Also known as "asparagus beans," these fresh green beans can be about a foot long. Their flavor is somewhat stronger than ordinary green beans, though the latter may always be substituted. Available in Chinese and Indian grocery stores.

Loquat An egg-shaped, orange-colored, sweet-and-sour fruit from East and South Asia. Available fresh on rare occasions in Chinese and specialty stores. Always available canned in syrup in Chinese groceries.

Lotus Root Fresh lotus roots look a bit like plump sugar cane or link sausages from the outside. Inside, they are crisp, white, and filled with the most prettily arranged holes. The roots need to be peeled and cut into slices. Young roots may be eaten raw, perked up with a dressing of some sort. Maturer roots need to be cooked like potatoes. Even when the roots are cooked, they retain a nice crispness. They taste a bit like artichoke hearts, though there is an edge in there somewhere. Try throwing them into any stew that you are making. In India, they are invariably added to mixed pickles.

Lotus Seeds (Dried) Yellowish in color and about the size and shape of peanuts. Used in Chinese stews and desserts. In India, they are roasted to make a kind of popcorn. Available in Chinese grocery stores.

Mangoes My favorite fruit. Unfortunately, Florida growers have decided to develop a fibrous mango that travels well and has a long shelf life. Mexico, Haiti, and the Dominican Republic, on the whole, export a much better grade of eating mango. The best way to buy good mangoes is to taste one right in the shop. (I carry a penknife for the purpose.) If it is sweet and not too fibrous, buy as many as you need. They are probably hard and not fully ripe at this stage. Wrap each mango separately in newspaper and layer them close together in a cardboard carton or bowl. Cover with more newspapers and leave in a warm place several days if necessary until ripe. The mangoes should begin to smell like mangoes and be very slightly soft to the touch. They should not have black spots, though. You may now either refrigerate them or else chill them like champagne in a bucket of ice and water.

Marmite A dark-brown yeast extract, available in specialty and health-food stores. It may be used to flavor soups and sauces. The English eat it on toast. So do I.

Masoor Dal See BEANS, DRIED.

Matcha An excellent-quality powdered green tea generally whipped with hot water to make the ritual tea in a Japanese tea ceremony. Not cheap.

Mee See NOODLES.

Millet Tiny, hulled grains that look like birdseed. Available in Korean as well as health-food stores. May be cooked with rice or in place of rice. The Koreans also sell a hulled, glutinous millet.

Mirin A sweet, syrupy wine available in Japanese and Korean grocery stores. Used mainly for cooking.

Miso This term includes many pastes of different hues and textures that are made in Japan from fermented soy beans and grains. *Misos* are used to make soups, stews, sauces, and marinades. They are fairly salty and are sometimes used in Japan to pickle vegetables.

As there are just so many *misos* sold under different names in different parts of this country, I have basically identified them by color. "Red" *miso* is really reddish-brown; what is sold as "white" *miso* is sometimes yellow, and so on. You may use whichever *miso* you like for the soups. I think it is best to start with the "red." Each *miso* has a slightly different taste and a different proportion of salt and sugar. Lighter *misos* tend to be sweeter. You might want to mix two different *misos* in the same soup.

Misos are sold in Japanese, Korean, and most health-food stores. You should store them in a tightly closed container in the refrigerator. They last for several months and are wonderful for quick, nourishing soups.

Multani Garam Masala See GARAM MASALA.

Monukka Raisins Very large, brown raisins, available in health-food stores.

Morel Mushrooms See MUSHROOMS.

Mung Beans See BEANS, DRIED.

Mung-Bean Sprouts See BEANS, DRIED.

Mung-Bean Vermicelli See NOODLES.

Mung Dal See BEANS, DRIED.

Mushrooms

  Chinese dried black mushrooms are available in Chinese grocery stores. Soak in hot water for half an hour, then snip off their hard inedible stems.

Japanese Shiitake mushrooms are fairly similar to the Chinese black mushrooms, always available dried in Japanese and specialty stores. Some delicacy shops even sell them fresh. Dried need to be soaked for half an hour or longer until soft. Stems are coarse and must be cut off.

Enok mushrooms, or **Enokidake,** are slim, tiny mushrooms that are now sold fresh in packaged clusters at specialty shops. Be sure to cut off the lower parts of the stems. These mushrooms are great fun in salads and soups.

Morel mushrooms are the very expensive mushrooms that have elongated, black, spongy heads. They are sometimes available fresh. They can always be had dried from specialty stores. They should be washed well.

Straw mushrooms, when they are fresh, are among the world's tastiest mushrooms. They have very fleshy caps that seem to enclose the stems. I have only seen them canned in America. Chinese grocery stores as well as some specialty stores carry them.

Summer oyster mushrooms are large and meaty. They are only available canned in Chinese grocery stores.

Mustard Oil Rather like mustard seeds, mustard oil has a split personality. Raw, it smells hot and pungent. When it is heated, the pungency evaporates and the oil turns slightly sweet. Used a great deal in Bengali and Kashmiri cooking and throughout India for pickling. Experiment with it making salad dressings and sautéing vegetables. Mustard oil is sold in Indian grocery stores. It can get rancid, so store in a cool place.

Mustard Seeds, Black These tiny, round, blackish-reddish-brown seeds are used throughout India for pickling and for "seasoning" everything from yogurt to beans. "Seasoning" is a peculiar Indian-English translation of the word *"baghar,"* which means the quick popping of whole spices in very hot oil. Raw foods are then cooked in already "seasoned" oil or "seasoned" oil is poured over cooked foods just before they are served. When mustard seeds are used as "seasoning," they impart an earthy sweetness to all foods.

Quite another aspect of mustard seeds becomes evident when the seeds are ground or crushed for pickling and sauces. They turn nose-tinglingly pungent. I do my grinding in a coffee grinder. When a recipe calls for lightly ground mustard seeds, see that the seeds break up into halves or quarters and do not become powder.

Old mustard seeds tend to become bitter. This does not seem to matter much if you are using the seeds as "seasoning." However, if you are going to grind or crush them, it is best to have a fresh batch. Available in Indian grocery stores.

Nam Yee See BEAN CURD, Fermented.

Nigari I use natural *nigari* flakes, distilled from clean sea water, as a coagulant to curdle soy milk and make bean curd. These white flakes are sold in Japanese and health-food stores.

Noodles There must be hundreds of different types of noodles that are eaten in Asia, made from ingredients such as mung beans, buckwheat, wheat flour, chickpea flour, and rice. Here are the ones I have used in my recipes:

"Cellophane" mung-bean noodles, also called **Bean threads** and **Mung-bean vermicelli:** Very thin, brittle, opaque noodles made from mung beans and sold in all Oriental stores. When cooked, they are quite slippery.

Fresh Chinese egg noodles Ask for fresh *"lo mein"* noodles in Chinese grocery stores and for fresh *"larmen"* or *"ramen"* in Japanese grocery stores. Usually sold in 1-pound bags and found in the refrigerated sections. What you don't use either cover and refrigerate for 3 to 4 days or else freeze. Dry spaghettini may be used as a substitute in most dishes.

Ki-soba Thin, dried Japanese buckwheat noodles, available in Japanese stores. Spaghettini may be used as a substitute.

Korean buckwheat noodles Very thin dried noodles. Ask for Naeng Myon noodles in Korean grocery stores. Use Japanese *somen* or the very thin capellini as a substitute.

Mee Very thin, dried rice vermicelli sold in Thai grocery stores. If you cannot see what you want, ask for noodles to make Mee Krob. Use the thinnest possible Chinese rice sticks as a substitute.

Rice sticks A very thin, dried, crisp Chinese rice vermicelli, sold in Chinese grocery stores.

Sev Generally, this Indian word means crisp chickpea-flour noodles eaten as snack food. For recipe, see page 332.

Seviyan, sometimes also called *"sev."* Very, very thin wheat vermicelli from India, used mainly for desserts. Sold in Indian grocery stores.

Soba Japanese buckwheat noodles. I have used the dried kind, sold in Japanese and some health-food stores. Spaghetti may be used as a substitute.

Somen Very thin, dried wheat noodles, sold in Japanese grocery stores. Spaghettini or capellini may be used as a substitute.

Udon Thick, starchy Japanese wheat noodles, sold in Japanese stores. Spaghetti or linguini may be substituted.

Nori Although often called seaweed, even on the packages, this is really laver. There are many varieties and qualities, from dark green to purplish-black and from medium-priced to expensive. All *nori* is crisp and paper thin. I have used the sheets of *nori—asakusa nori*—for all the recipes in this book. In Korea, the same laver is called "*kim.*"

All *nori* needs to be toasted lightly before it is eaten (see page 324). It is rich in vitamin A and calcium and may be just nibbled as a toasted sheet or else it may be used to make sushi rolls. It may also be crumbled over rice and noodle dishes. Sold in Japanese, Korean, and health-food stores, it should be stored in an airtight container or frozen.

Ocha Japanese green leaf tea. Different qualities available at Japanese grocery stores and some specialty stores. The cheapest, *bancha*, generally has coarse leaves and even stems in it. It is brewed with boiling water in tea pots or in tall, handleless tea cups. *Sencha*, a higher grade of tea, is brewed in tea pots with very hot, not boiling water and then served, strained, in smaller cups than those used for *bancha*. *Gyokuru*, the best type of leaf tea, is brewed in small tea pots with water that is merely hot and then is sipped from tiny tea cups. The first time I was served this, I found the taste very strong; it does grow on one.

Oily Toovar Dal See BEANS, DRIED.

Oshi-Mugi See PRESSED BARLEY.

Palm Sugar Palm sugars are used throughout tropical Asia and come in different forms and colors. Each has its own very distinct flavor. The kind that is most easily available in Southeast Asian grocery stores here is sold in wide-mouthed jars and looks like smooth peanut butter.

Panchphoran (5-Spice Mixture) This very Bengali spice combination contains whole cumin seeds, whole black mustard seeds, whole fennel seeds, whole *kalonji*, and whole fenugreek seeds, mixed in equal proportions. You may put the mixture together yourself or else buy it already mixed from an Indian grocery store.

Paneer Indian-style fresh cheese. It has very little flavor of its own and is always cooked with other foods. Very rich in protein. For recipe, see page 237.

Papadum Also called "*papar.*" Indian wafers, generally made out of legumes, sold plain, with red pepper, with black pepper, and with garlic. The best varieties are, unfortunately, not sold in well-sealed tins but plastic packages, often clumsily stapled shut. The better quality specialty food stores generally carry the better packed but poorer quality *papadums*. It is best to buy them from an Indian grocery store. Keep what you do not use in a tightly sealed tin.

Peppers, Hot Green and Red See CHILIES.

Poha Indian puffing rice. What you buy are flattened rice grains that puff up when they are fried. There are usually two types of *poha* in Indian grocery stores: a small, dense kind and a flatter, flakier version. Buy the latter. If you have any doubts, ask for the *poha* to make *cheewra*.

Pomegranate Juice A sour concentrate, available in Middle Eastern grocery stores.

Poppy Seeds, White Used in both Indian and Japanese cooking. Available in Indian grocery stores. As it can get rancid, keep in a tightly lidded bottle and store in a cool place. You may even freeze poppy seeds.

Preserved Snow Cabbage Available canned in Chinese grocery stores. It is fairly salty and is used as a flavoring.

Pressed Barley I've had this only in Korea, though I am told that the Japanese eat it as well. It has the virtue of cooking faster than regular barley. Once it has been soaked for half an hour, it cooks in the same amount of time as rice, a grain with which it is often combined. The Korean stores in New York seem to sell it by its Japanese name, *oshi-mugi*.

Pressed Bean Curd See BEAN CURD.

Pressed Seasoned Bean Curd See BEAN CURD.

Quail Eggs Available fresh in specialty stores and in some Chinese poultry stores. Canned, boiled quail eggs are sold in most Chinese grocery stores but I can't say I like their taste or texture too much.

Red Bean Curd See BEAN CURD, Fermented.

Red Peppers, Dried Hot Also called dried hot red chilies. There are many varieties. The kind I have used are about 1½ inches long and ⅓-inch thick. They are quite commonly available. When used whole in a dish, it's a good idea to remove them before serving.

Rice Almost every region of Asia has its own favorite type of rice—very often a local rice, on which the inhabitants of the region have been nurtured since childhood. It could be smooth and firm, soft and fluffy, sticky and chewy, partially milled, long-grain, short-grain or whatever. Not every type of Asian rice is available in America and even if it were, you could not be expected to stock everything. Of the rices that one can get easily, I have chosen a few that seem to complement the major Asian cuisines. Of course, you are free to eat whichever rice you like best.

Basmati rice A fine-grained, aromatic rice from North India and Pakistan. It needs to be picked over and washed in several changes of water before it is used. Available in Indian and some specialty stores.

Brown rices, which are available both long-grain and short-grain in health-food stores, are unmilled—their hulls still on. I prefer the texture of the long-grain.

Carolina long-grain rice is an excellent-quality rice and is quite suitable for most Asian meals. This is the long-grain rice I have used throughout this book, unless otherwise stated, and because it is labeled "long grain" on the box, I have used that terminology.

Domsiah rice A fine-grained, expensive, Persian rice, sold in some Middle Eastern grocery stores. Needs to be picked over, washed, and soaked before cooking.

Japanese rice refers to the fat-grained rice sold in Japanese and Korean grocery stores. It has a somewhat sticky texture and needs to be washed before cooking. The most common brand seems to be Tanakaya Kokuho Rose.

Glutinous rice, sometimes called "sweet rice," has fat, opaque white grains. It is very sticky and is used in much of East Asia for desserts and snacks. This is sold in Chinese, Japanese, Korean, Thai, Filipino, and Indonesian groceries.

Texmati This is a new rice that Texas is experimenting with. It seems to be a cross between *basmati* and American long grain. It is not widely available at the moment but may soon be.

Rice Flour Also called "rice powder." Sold in all Indian and Oriental grocery stores.

Rice Vinegar See VINEGARS.

Rose Essence Used for flavoring sweets in the Middle East and India. The best kind is made from real roses, not chemicals. Read the label.

Saffron I have used only "leaf" saffron here—the whole, dried stigmas of the crocus. Find a good, reliable source for your saffron, as there is a great deal of adulteration. To bring out the flavor and color of saffron to its fullest, it is best to *dry-roast* it first. Put the required amount in a small, heavy skillet over a lowish flame. Stir it about until the threads turn a very dark reddish-brown color. Now crumble the threads into a small amount of hot milk (your recipe will say how much). Let the saffron soak for a few hours and then use this milk to tint and flavor rice or whatever else you want.

Sake A Japanese rice wine widely sold in most liquor stores. It is generally warmed in ceramic bottles and then served in tiny cups. It may be had before, during, and after meals. It is also used in Japanese cooking. Once a bottle has been opened, it should be used up fairly soon.

Salts Even though all my recipes call for regular salt, I generally prefer to cook with **kosher salt,** which is sold in large boxes at most supermarkets. It is very granular. A teaspoon of regular salt is equal to about 1¾ teaspoons of kosher salt.

Black salt or **Kala namak** is a dark, smelly salt that is used in some Indian foods for its digestive properties. It is available either ground or in a lump at Indian grocery stores. If you get the lump, store it in a tightly closed tin in a very dry place. Break off what you need and crush it in a mortar.

Salted Duck's Eggs These are raw eggs that have been kept in brine and are eaten almost as a condiment with congees and noodle dishes. The saltiness gets absorbed, all the way to the yolk. In Filipino stores, the eggs are sold already boiled. Their shells are always colored red. Chinese stores sell them raw so you have to boil them for about an hour. I like to change the water a few times to get rid of some of the saltiness.

Sambal This term is used in much of Southeast Asia and implies a chili-hot relish or else any dish that has been cooked with a paste of red hot chilies.

Sansho Pepper A fragrant Japanese pepper, available in Japanese grocery stores.

Semolina Granular durum wheat flour. Fine-grained semolina is sold in all Indian grocery stores. Sometimes regular cream of wheat may be used as a substitute; my recipes will indicate when.

Sesame Oil There is a refined, colorless sesame oil available in many American grocery stores. Do *not* use that for any of the recipes in this book. Buy the thick, brownish sesame oil available in Oriental grocery stores. It is very aromatic and smells gloriously of sesame seeds. It is used more as a flavoring than as a cooking oil. Store in a cool, dark place.

Sesame Seeds Extremely nutty and flavorful as well as a high source of protein and calcium, sesame seeds are used throughout Asia in dishes from main courses to salads and desserts. Three types of sesame seeds are available on the market: polished, hulled whitish seeds; unhulled buff-colored seeds; and unhulled black seeds. Here, sesame seeds refers to the unhulled buff-colored variety unless I specify otherwise.

Ideally, sesame seeds should be picked over before being used, especially if they don't look too clean. They should then be stored in a cool place, well enclosed in a tightly lidded jar.

To roast sesame seeds Heat a small, preferably cast-iron, skillet over a medium flame and put the required amount of sesame seeds into it. Stir and roast until they turn a few shades darker and begin to give out a slight

"roasted" smell. Sesame seeds have a tendency to fly out of the skillet as they are roasting; covering the skillet with a mesh spatter-shield or a strainer helps. If you roast sesame seeds a great deal, as I do, it is worth trying to find a Japanese *goma-iri* or sesame-seed roaster. The kind I have is quite cheap and looks like a very fine-meshed wire box with a handle. The box has a "door" at the top into which you feed the seeds. Then all you have to do is to hold the box over a flame and shake it.

(Many Indian recipes call for dropping sesame seeds into hot oil. This *quick-frying* brings out the nutty taste of the seeds the same way that roasting does. Again, the seeds tend to fly as they hit the hot oil. If this bothers you too much, use a spatter-shield.)

Roasted and ground roasted sesame seeds Roast the seeds as suggested above and then pulverize the seeds in one of the following ways: 1. Use an electric coffee grinder—stop the machine whenever it begins to slow down, dislodge the pastelike collection at the bottom of the machine, and start again; 2. use a Japanese *suri-bachi*; 3. use a mortar and pestle. Many recipes call for lightly ground or crushed seeds, which do not need to be totally pulverized. The Japanese now have a gadget that resembles a pepper grinder. It is kept permanently filled with roasted sesame seeds and can be adjusted to a coarse or a fine grind. You may also crush sesame seeds the way I have seen some Koreans do it—between two flat-bottomed ceramic plates.

Sesame paste Here is a simple paste that can enhance the taste of the simplest boiled or steamed vegetable: Roast and grind 3 tablespoons of sesame seeds. Slowly add 1 tablespoon of sesame oil, mixing it in as you do so. Yield: about 2 tablespoons. (Also see Tahini, page 359.)

Sev See NOODLES.

7-Spice Seasoning (Shichimi) Also sold as 7-Spice Red Pepper (Shichimi Togarashi). A hot Japanese spice mixture that can contain finely crushed red pepper flakes, coarsely ground **sansho** pepper, roasted sesame seeds, roasted white poppy or hemp seeds, tiny bits of orange peel, tiny bits of toasted **nori**, and white pepper, mixed in different proportions. It is available, already mixed, in Japanese grocery stores. You could also mix your own, if you like. It may be sprinkled on soups, salads, and noodle dishes.

Seviyan See NOODLES.

Shallots Small red onions used in abundance throughout tropical Asia.

Shaohsing Wine A Chinese cooking wine, available in some liquor stores. Dry sherry may be substituted.

Shichimi See 7-SPICE SEASONING.

Shiitake Mushrooms See MUSHROOMS.

Silver Ear Fungus Also called "white fungus" or "*pai mo-er*" in Chinese grocery stores. Resembles small pieces of whitish sponge or coral. Considered to be both medicinal and a delicacy. This fungus needs to be soaked in hot water for half an hour before being used. It expands considerably.

Snowpeas The flat, edible pods used in Oriental cooking. Snap off the stalk and pull backward to remove the coarse thread. The peas cook very fast.

Soba See NOODLES.

Somen See NOODLES.

Soy Beans, Fresh Small, hairy pods, available occasionally in Chinese markets. After boiling or steaming and peeling they make a nice snack.

Soy-Bean Sprouts See BEANS, DRIED.

Soy Milk The thick, milky liquid that is formed when dried soy beans are soaked, ground, and then strained. The recipe is on page 164.

Soy Sauce Every region of East and Southeast Asia has local soy sauces, going from light to dark to syrupy-sweet. To simplify matters, I have used just three soy sauces: **Japanese soy sauce,** which is the dark **Kikkoman** available almost everywhere in this country: **Chinese dark** (also called **"thick"**) **soy sauce** and **Chinese thin** (also called **"light"**) **soy sauce.** The last two are sold in Chinese and some specialty grocery stores. "Thin" soy sauces are lighter in color but also saltier.

Soy sauces are made from fermented soy beans and each type has its own flavor. You might want to experiment with many others that are in the market, including the **Japanese usukuchi shoyu,** a light soy sauce, and the **Indonesian ketjap manis,** which is sweet and syrupy.

Star Anise A star-shaped, anise-flavored spice used in Oriental cooking. Available in all Chinese grocery stores.

Sudare Mat A small bamboo mat that is very helpful in making Norimake-Zushi. Sold in Japanese stores.

Suribachi A bowl-like ceramic Japanese mortar with a wooden pestle to crush foods against its ridged interior. Sold in Japanese stores.

Szechuan Peppercorns Reddish-brown, highly aromatic pods, about the size of peppercorns. Store in a tightly closed jar. Available in Chinese grocery stores.

Tahini This is the ground paste made from hulled sesame seeds that is used in making a variety of Middle Eastern sauces and dips. Most Middle Eastern stores and health-food stores carry it. Erewhon makes an excellent *tahini* with mechanically, not chemically, hulled sesame seeds.

If you wish to make your own *tahini*, heat a 7-inch cast-iron skillet over a medium flame. When hot, put in a cup of hulled sesame seeds. Keep shaking the skillet until the seeds are roasted. Empty the seeds into a blender. Begin blending and adding cold water at the same time. Stop adding the water when you have a paste that is slightly thinner than peanut butter. You will probably need about 6 tablespoons of water. Excess may be refrigerated for a week or it may be frozen.

Tamarind These sour brown pods, rich in vitamins, get their name from the Arabic "*tamar-i-hind*" or "the dates of India." They are used in much of Asia as a souring agent, just as we use lemon. The pods may be sold whole, but generally they are peeled, seeded, and then packed into mounds or bricks—the cellophane-wrapped 1-pound bricks are what are most available in Indian stores in this country. Make sure that the brick you buy is slightly pliable. The harder it is, the longer it will take to release its pulp. To get the pulp—and this is the only part of the tamarind that is edible—break off as much tamarind as you need and soak it in water.

To make thick tamarind paste Break off half a pound from a brick of tamarind and tear into smaller pieces, if you can. Put in a stainless-steel or a nonmetallic bowl covered with 2 cups of very hot water, and set aside overnight or at least 5 hours. (In an emergency, you may simmer the tamarind for 10 minutes.) Set a sieve over a stainless-steel or nonmetallic bowl. Empty the soaked tamarind and its liquid into the sieve and push as much pulp through with your fingers or with the back of a wooden spoon as you can. Put whatever tamarind remains in the sieve back into the soaking bowl. Add ½ cup hot water to it and mash it a bit. Return it to the sieve and try to extract some more pulp. Do not forget to collect all the thick, strained paste clinging to the bottom of your sieve. Yield: about 1½ cups. (Whatever tamarind remains in your sieve may be used for polishing brass!) Tamarind paste freezes well and will also last a good 2 to 3 weeks in the refrigerator. As long as it has no mold on it, you may use it.

Tanaka A spouted, narrow-necked, long-handled pot for making Turkish coffee. Available in many sizes, including a 1-cup size, at Middle Eastern and specialty stores.

Tao-Hoo-Yee See BEAN CURD, Fermented.

Tempeh Flat "cakes" made with soy beans (as well as some other grains and seeds) that are allowed to develop a kind of edible mold. They are extremely rich in protein and the B-12 vitamin. For more on *tempeh*, see page 108. Available in the refrigerators of health-food stores.

Thali A platter-sized, round metal plate used in India for formal and informal dining. Although gold *thalis* are not entirely unknown, those made out of silver, stainless steel, and bell metal are more common. A *thali* set includes 3 to 6 matching *katoris* (bowls) and usually a metal tumbler for water as well. See drawing for details of arranging a *thali* meal. Each person is served a full, individual *thali*.

Tomatoes We can usually count on getting red-ripe tomatoes in the summer, and even during the winter months fairly good tomatoes have been known to appear from Mexico and Israel. You can improve the color and texture of even second-grade tomatoes by leaving them unrefrigerated until they turn a deep red color. When all else fails, use canned tomatoes.

To peel a tomato Drop the tomato into boiling water for 15 seconds. Remove with a slotted spoon and peel.

To seed a tomato Cut a peeled tomato in half. Cup one half in your hand, cut side down, and gently squeeze out the seeds into a bowl—or the sink. Repeat with the second half.

Toovar Dal See BEANS, DRIED.

Tree Ear Fungus Also called "cloud ears" and "mo-er mushrooms," looks like rounded pieces of charred paper. Sold in Chinese stores in two sizes, a larger, thicker kind and a smaller, thinner one. Buy the latter. Soak in hot water for about half an hour or less. It expands considerably.

Turmeric A rhizome of the ginger family. Fresh, it resembles fine, gingerlike fingers, bright yellow inside. Only the dried, ground turmeric is available here—also bright yellow. In India, it is considered a digestive. When used externally, it is an antiseptic. It is available widely but is probably freshest at Indian grocery stores.

Udon Noodles See NOODLES.

Umeboshi Preserved, very salty, very sour, pink plums that come in various sizes and are sold in Japanese and health-food stores. The Japanese eat them at breakfast because they believe they aid digestion and cleanse the system. They certainly wake one up! Can also be pitted, mashed, and used as a seasoning. Keep them refrigerated in a tightly closed jar.

Urad Dal See BEANS, DRIED.

Vinegars Each region in Asia produces its own vinegar—palm vinegars, cane vinegars, rice vinegars, and so on. The only two Asian vinegars I have used here are **Japanese**

rice vinegar, which is clear and light and sold quite widely, and **Chinese black vinegar,** also made from rice but very dark in color. The latter is sold only in Chinese grocery stores.

Wakame A dark, dried seaweed, rich in calcium and vitamins. It is sold in health-food and Japanese grocery stores. It needs a soaking, after which it turns green and fairly slippery.

Wasabi A strong, green Japanese horseradish, available here only prepared (powdered or paste). For more, see page 360. Sold in Japanese grocery stores.

Water Chestnuts Dark-skinned and chestnut-sized, they grow in the water and are sold fresh only in Chinese grocery stores. For more, see page 68. Canned water chestnuts do not compare with the fresh but may be used in an emergency.

Wheat Gluten Protein-rich gluten removed from gluten flour by washing away all the starch. Recipe for making wheat gluten and wheat-gluten balls is on page 183.

White Fungus See SILVER EAR FUNGUS.

White Poppy Seeds See POPPY SEEDS, WHITE.

White Radish These radishes vary in size from finger length to giants a foot long and 3 inches thick. It is the smaller, finger-sized ones that are used for Aomidaikon, the pickle on page 377. For all the other dishes, use whatever size you can find, and cut off what you need. White radishes are sold in Japanese grocery stores as *daikon*. Also available in Korean and Chinese grocery stores. The rad-

ishes that are about an inch in diameter are usually more tender and juicy than the very large ones.

Wok Also called *"karhai"* (in India). The wok is now very well known in America. It is excellent for stir-frying and very economical for deep frying. My only reason for mentioning it at all is that new woks have recently been designed that are not rounded off at the bottom so they sit firmly on electric ranges. If you have not bought a wok because you have an electric range, you might now wish to get one. Cast-iron and stainless-steel woks are the best; also the new Calphalon.

Yuba See BEAN CURD.

SOURCES

It is best to start in your own area. Look in the yellow pages under Indian, Japanese, Chinese, Korean, Middle Eastern, and Southeast Asian groceries. They might be all lumped under "Oriental groceries" or "specialty foods." Specialty stores, such as Balducci's and Dean & De Luca's in New York and The Oakville Grocery in San Francisco, do indeed carry many Asian ingredients, both fresh and dried. The foods of many Asian nations overlap—hence Middle Eastern stores may have some Indian foods, Korean stores may have Japanese ingredients, and Thai stores may have Indonesian and Chinese goods. Health-food stores carry many of the basics—sesame oil, ses-

ame seeds, soy sauce, nuts, bean curd, mung beans, azuki beans, and bulgar wheat.

What you cannot get easily in your area, you can send for. The Chinese Grocer in San Francisco, for example, will not only accept mail orders for cooking ingredients but for Oriental utensils as the rectangular skillet used in Japanese and Korean cooking.

Here is a list of stores that specialize in Asian groceries. Those that accept mail orders are marked with an asterik.*

Make sure that you request that all ingredients be labeled in English.

Indian Groceries

Bazaar of India
1131 University Ave.
Berkeley, CA 94702*

Bazaar of India
39112 State St.
Freemont, CA 94538*

Berjian Grocery
4725 Santa Monica Blvd.
Los Angeles, CA 90029*

Bharat Bazaar
3680 El Camino Real
Santa Clara, CA 95051

America Tea, Coffee
  and Spice Co.
1511 Champa St.
Denver, CO 80202*

India Health Foods
1161 State St.
Bridgeport, CT 06605*

Spices and Foods Unlimited
2018A Florida NW
Washington, DC 20009*

Raj Enterprises
881 Peachtree St.
Atlanta, GA 30309*

India Groceries
5022 North Sheridan Rd.
Chicago, IL 60640*

India Spice Co.
437 South Blvd.
Oak Park, IL 60302*

Central Grocery
923 Decatur St.
New Orleans, LA 70116*

Indian Super Bazaar
4707 Miller Ave.
Bethesda, MD 20014*

India Sub-Continental
  Stores
908 Philadelphia Ave.
Silver Springs, MD 20910*

Cambridge Coffee, Tea
  and Spice House
1765 Massachusetts Ave.
Cambridge, MA 02138

Vinod Shah
3 Prescott St.
North Woburn, MA 01801*

India Foods and Boutique
3729 Cass
Detroit, MI 48201*

India Food Center
15–43 McCausland Ave.
St. Louis, MO 63117*

Kumar Brothers
536 Bloomfield Ave.
Hoboken, NJ 07030

Annapurna
127 East 28 St.
New York, NY 10016*

Little India Store
128 East 28 St.
New York, NY 10016*

Antones
2606 Sheridan
Tulsa, OK 74129*

Porter's Foods Unlimited
125 West 11 Ave.
Eugene, OR 97401*

Bombay Emporium
3343 Forbes Ave.
Pittsburgh, PA 15213*

India Food Mart
808 South 47 St.
Philadelphia, PA 19143*

Indian Super Bazaar
4101 Walnut St.
Philadelphia, PA 19104*

Giant Foods of America
100 Oaks Shopping Center
Nashville, TN 37204

Antones Import Co.
4234 Harry Hines Blvd.
Dallas, TX 75219*

Antones Import Co.
South Boss Rd.
Houston, TX 77027*

House of Rice
4122 University Way NE
Seattle, WA 98105*

Indian Groceries and Spices
2527 West National Ave.
Milwaukee, WI 53208*

International House of Foods
440 West Gorham St.
Madison, WI 53703

Top Banana Ltd.
1526 Merivale Rd.
Ottawa, Ontario
Canada K2G 3JS

Korean Groceries

East–West Food Center
3300 West 8 St.
Los Angeles, CA 90005

Kal's Mart
606 South Beaumont Ave.
Los Angeles, CA 90005

Pacific Food Market
2147 Clement St.
San Francisco, CA 94121

Oriental Market
4700 Geary Blvd.
San Francisco, CA 94118

East–West Grocery Store
3810 West Lawrence
Chicago, IL 60625

Tong Yang Market
5131 North Western Ave.
Chicago, IL 60625

New Seoul
1555 Rockville Pike
Rockville, MD 20852

Sam Bok
3012–18 Edwin Ave.
Fort Lee, NJ 07024

Sammi Oriental Grocery
Store
444 Broad Ave.
Leonia, NJ 07605*

Sam Bok Grocery Store
127 West 43 St.
New York, NY 10036*

Daewoo Oriental Food
Market
42 West 36 St.
New York, NY 10018

Tong Dae Moon Grocery
Store
12 West 32 St.
New York, NY 10001

Korea Super Market
6427 Bissonet
Houston, TX 77074

Thai, Indonesian and Other Southeast Asian Groceries

Bangkok Market
4804–6 Melrose Ave.
Los Angeles, CA 90029*

Thai Food Market
5902–4 Hollywood Blvd.
Hollywood, CA 90028

Thai and Oriental Market
25795 East Highland Ave.
San Bernardino, CA 92404

Thai Grocery
1090 South Raritan St.
Denver, CO 80223

Krung Thai Grocery
10141 Montview Blvd.
Aurora, CO 80010

Merapi Inc.
139 White St.
Danbury, CT 06810*

Thai Market
3323–5 South Dale Mabry
Hwy.
Tampa, FL 33609

Thai Grocery
5014 North Broadway
Chicago, IL 60640*

Bangkok Grocery
412A Hunger Ford Dr.
Rockville, MD 20850

Asia Market
1101 East Charleston Blvd.
Las Vegas, NV 89104

Asian Food Market
5 Towne Center
Black Horse Pike
Turnerville, NJ 08012

Bangkok Market
106 Park St. (off Mott)
New York, NY 10013*

Siam Grocery
2754 Broadway
New York, NY 10025

Southeast Asia Trading Co.
68A Mott St.
New York, NY 10013

Mrs. De Wildt
R.D. #3
Bangor, PA 18013*
(Mail order by catalog only)

Thai Asian Market
2537 University Blvd.
Houston, TX 77005

Thailand Market
2216 West Granwyler
Plymouth Park Shopping
Irving, TX 75061

Thai House Groceries
1733 Wilson Blvd.
Arlington, VA 22209

Japanese and Other Oriental Groceries

K. Sakai Co.
1656 Post St.
San Francisco, CA 94115

International Market
2019 Fillmore St.
San Francisco, CA 94115

Asia Food Market
2000 Judah St.
San Francisco, CA 94122*

Dobashi Co.
240 East Jackson St.
San Jose, CA 95112

Oriental Grocery
3433 El Camino Real
Santa Clara, CA 95051

Orient Grocery
337 8 St.
Oakland, CA 94612

Ai Hoa Market
860 North Hill St.
Los Angeles, CA 90012*

Hughes–El Rancho Market
320 West Colorado Blvd.
Pasadena, CA 91105

Ann's Oriental Grocery
315 East Arvada St.
Colorado Springs,
CO 80906

Pacific Mercantile Grocery
1925 Lawrence St.
Denver, CO 80202*

East–West Trading Co.
68 Howe St.
New Haven, CT 06511

Kim's Oriental Shop
202 Park Rd.
West Hartford, CT 06119

Oriental Grocery
1705 Concord Pike
Wilmington, DE 19803*

Oriental Food and Gift
1531 South Dale Mabry Hwy.
Tampa, FL 33609

Asian Supermarket
2581 Piedmont Rd.
Atlanta, GA 30324*

Oriental Food and Gift
3656 Buena Vista Rd.
Columbus, GA 31907*

Far East Trading Co.
2837 North Western Ave.
Chicago, IL 60618*

Star Market
3349 North Clark St.
Chicago, IL 60657*

Jung's Oriental Food Store
913 East University Ave.
Des Moines, IA 50316*

Tokyo Foods
1005 Pierce St.
Sioux City, IA 51105*

Korea House
615 Orange St.
New Orleans, LA 70130*

Arirang House
7918 Georgia Ave.
Silver Springs, MD 20910

Yoshinoya
36 Prospect St.
Cambridge, MA 02139*

Sun Sun Co.
34 Oxford St.
Boston, MA 02111

Oriental Food Store
18919 West Seven Mile Rd.
Detroit, MI 48219

International House
of Foods
75 West Island Ave.
Minneapolis, MN 55401*

Kim's Mart
6692 Enright Ave.
St. Louis, MO 63114*

Oriental Market
611 North 27 St.
Lincoln, NB 68503

Oriental Food
953 East Sahara, E–31
Las Vegas, NV 89104

Aki Oriental Food Co.
1635 Lemoine Ave.
Fort Lee, NJ 07024

Asian Food Market
217 Summit Ave.
Jersey City, NJ 07306*

Katagiri Company
224 East 59 St.
New York, NY 10022*

Tanaka and Company
326 Amsterdam Ave.
New York, NY 10023*

Dayton Oriental Foods
812 Xenia Ave.
Dayton, OH 45410

Japan Imported Foods
808 N.W. 6 St.
Oklahoma City, OK 73106

Albertsons #505
5415 S.W.
   Beaverton–Hillsdale Hwy.
Portland, OR 97221

Asia Products Corp.
226 North 10 St.
Philadelphia, PA 19107

Persimmon Oriental Food
Market
University Heights Shopping
Plaza
Providence, RI 02904

Eastern Foods
8626½ Long Point
Houston, TX 77055

Kobawoo Oriental Market
5732 Cedar Springs Rd.
Dallas, TX 75235

Oriental House
7816 Richmond Hwy.
Alexandria, VA 22306

Albertsons #429
11656 68 Ave.
Seattle, WA 98178

Mikado
4709 Wisconsin Ave.
Washington, DC 20016

Mihamaya
392 Powell St.
Vancouver, Br. Columbia
Canada VGA 1G4*

Iwaki Japanese Food Store
2627 Yonge St.
Toronto, Ontario
Canada M4P 2J6

Chinese Groceries

The Chinese Grocer
209 Post St.
San Francisco, CA 94108*

Shing Chong and Co.
800 Grant Ave.
San Francisco, CA 94108

Kwa On Lung Co.
686 North Spring St.
Los Angeles, CA 90015*

Wing Chong Lung Co.
Grocery
922 South San Pedro St.
Los Angeles, CA 90015

South and Eastern Food
Supply
6732 N.E. 4 Ave.
Miami, FL 33138*

Asia Trading Co.
2581 Piedmont NE
Atlanta, GA 30324

A.B. Oriental Grocery
3707 Suit Shadeland Ave.
Indianapolis, IN 46226*

Asia House Grocery
2433 Saint Paul St.
Baltimore, MD 21218*

Wing Wing Imported
Groceries
79 Harrison Ave.
Boston, MA 02111

Legal Sea Foods Market
237 Hampshire St.
Cambridge, MA 02139

Joyce Chen Unlimited Inc.
172–174 Massachusetts Ave.
Arlington, MA 02134

Kwong Tung Noodle
Manufacturing Co.
326 Cedar Ave.
Minneapolis, MN 55404

King's Trading
3736 Broadway
Kansas City, MO 64111*

Lee's Oriental Gifts and
Foods
3053 Main St.
Buffalo, NY 14214*

Kam Man Food Products
200 Canal St.
New York, NY 10013*

Wing Woh Lung Co.
50 Mott St.
New York, NY 10013*

Wing Fat Co. Inc.
33–35 Mott St.
New York, NY 10013*

Delicacies Shop,
   Bloomingdale's
1000 Third Ave.
New York, NY 10022

Far East Co.
247 West McMillan St.
Cincinnati, OH 45219*

International House
   of Foods
712 Washington Ave. SE
Columbus, OH 43206

Harmony Oriental
247 Atwood St.
Pittsburgh, PA 15213*

Wing On
1005 Race St.
Philadelphia, PA 19107

Oriental Import–Export Co.
2009 Polk St.
Houston, TX 77003

Super Asian Market
2719 Wilson Blvd.
Arlington, VA 22201

Oriental House
4816 Richmond Hwy.
Alexandria, VA 22306

Wang's Co.
800 7 St. NW
Washington, DC 20001

Chinamart Trading Co.
210 Spadina Ave.
Toronto, Ontario
Canada

Middle Eastern Groceries

Bezjian Groceries
4725 Santa Monica Blvd.
Los Angeles, CA 90029*

G. B. Ratto and Co.
821 Washington St.
Oakland, CA 94607

Haig's Delicacies
441 Clement St.
San Francisco, CA 94118*

Dimyan's Market
116 Elm St.
Danbury, CT 06810*

Skenderis Greek Import
1612 20 St. NW
Washington, DC 20009*

Alex Bakery
878 S.W. 8 St.
Miami, FL 33130

Athens Imported Food
City Market 84–85
Indianapolis, IN 46204*

Central Grocery Store
923 Decatur St.
New Orleans, LA 70116

Model Food Importers
113–115 Middle St.
Portland, ME 04101*

Cardullo's Gourmet Shop
6 Brattle St.
Cambridge, MA 02138*

Syrian Grocery Import Co.
270 Shawmut Ave.
Boston, MA 02118*

Carnig Tashjian
380 Third Ave.
New York, NY 10016*

K. Kalustyan
123 Lexington Ave.
New York, NY 10016

Sahadi Importing Co.
187 Atlantic Ave.
Brooklyn, NY 11201

Stamoolis Brothers
   Company
2020 Pennsylvania Ave.
Pittsburgh, PA 15222

Near East Market
602 Reservoir Ave.
Cranston, RI 02907

Barzizza Brothers
3846 Delp St.
Memphis, TN 38118

Topping and Co.
1102 North Third St.
Milwaukee, WI 53203

Sayfy's Groceteria
265 Jean Talon East
Montreal, Quebec
Canada H2R 1S9

Index

A Note About the Author

Madhur Jaffrey was born in Delhi, India, and educated there.
For the past seven years she has traveled extensively in India,
Japan, Thailand, Indonesia, Korea, the Philippines, and many
parts of the world gathering vegetarian recipes and lore for this
book. Her first book, *An Invitation to Indian Cooking*, was
published by Knopf in 1973 and in paperback by Vintage in
1975, and she has contributed articles to *The New York Times*,
Gourmet, Travel and Leisure, Smithsonian, etc. She is a teacher
of Indian cooking and has completed a television series on the
subject for the BBC.

She has made New York City her home for the past twenty-two
years with her husband, Sanford Allen, the violinist, and their
three children.

A Note on the Type

The text of this book was set in a film version of Palatino, a type face designed by the noted German typographer Hermann Zapf. Named after Giovanbattista Palatino, a writing master of Renaissance Italy, Palatino was the first of Zapf's type faces to be introduced in America. The first designs for the face were made in 1948, and the fonts for the complete face were issued between 1950 and 1952. Like all Zapf-designed type faces, Palatino is beautifully balanced and exceedingly readable.

Composed by Superior Printing, Champaign, Illinois.
Printed and bound by Maple Press, York, Pennsylvania.
Typography by Margaret Wagner.
Calligraphy by Carole Lowenstein.
Binding design by Betty Anderson.